HANDBOOKS

D0061743

FLORIDA KEYS

LAURA MARTONE

FLORIDA KEYS

Big Cypress
National Preserve

Everglades
National Park

Gulf of Mexico

Big Torch
Key

Big Pine
Key

No Name
Key

Pigeon Key

Sugarloaf
Key

Saddlebunch
Keys

Little Torch
Key

Bahia Honda
State Park

Marquesas
Keys

Key West

Lower
Sugarloaf
Key

Straits of Florida

Fort Zachary Taylor
Historic State Park

Boca Chica
Key

© AVALON TRAVEL

Contents

Even those who have never ventured south of Disney World have probably heard of the Florida Keys. Stretching southwest from Miami between the Atlantic Ocean and the Gulf of Mexico, this diverse archipelago is, after all, legendary.

With its Mardi Gras vibe, much-publicized Hemingway connection, and ongoing "threat" to secede from the Union, Key West is surely the most well-known island in the region. This unique place nurtures a strange blend of hardy natives, eccentric artists, and wide-eyed tourists. But the Keys hold more than just the southernmost city.

If you're driving from Miami or the Everglades—both vibrant areas worth a look before heading south—you'll first encounter enticing Key Largo, the slowly burgeoning getaway for southern Floridians. It's the kind of place where locals can dock their boats just steps from laid-back waterfront eateries. With fascinating underwater coral reefs that extend along the eastern shore, it's also the self-proclaimed "diving capital of the world."

South of Key Largo, the remaining Upper Keys accessible by the Overseas Highway (U.S. 1) compose Islamorada, an area long celebrated for its bountiful sportfishing. After crossing a lengthy bridge, you'll be in the heart of the Middle Keys, a transitional space between the natural pleasures of the north and the unabashed revelry of the south. Centered around Marathon (which, like Islamorada, encompasses several keys), this region offers a number of wildlife-oriented activities, from bird-watching haunts to dolphin encounters.

For even more animal sightings, continue south to the Lower Keys, where wild creatures abound in the National Key Deer Refuge on and around Big Pine Key. Even farther down, you'll spy mammals of a different variety—the tourists and locals who descend upon the streets of Key West—especially from October to April, when the weather is usually sunny and mild and offers a respite from colder places.

Even those who are intimately familiar with the Florida Keys only know a small percentage of them. The Overseas Highway—the only drivable link to the mainland—connects less than 50 of the more than 800 islands of this unforgettable chain. Venture out by boat to explore the more elusive ones, a trip that promises mystery, adventure, and an experience like nowhere else. After all, that's what the Keys are all about.

Planning Your Trip

Where to Go

Miami and the Everglades

While some travelers head directly to Key West by boat or plane, most pass through the gateway areas of Miami and the Everglades before driving south to the Florida Keys. If you have time, consider exploring this diverse region, where you can stroll amid Miami Beach's colorful Art Deco District, soak up some sunshine on the Magic City's stunning beaches, snorkel above the coral reefs of Biscayne National Park, take a guided canoe trip among the cypress trees of Fakahatchee Strand Preserve State Park, and visit the critters at the Everglades Alligator Farm.

Key Largo

From the mainland, most motorists take U.S. 1, also called the Overseas Highway, to reach the Florida Keys. The first island encountered is Key Largo, the largest of this unique archipelago. Here you'll find several outdoor diversions, including Dolphin Cove and Dolphins Plus—sister facilities that offer a range of activities, from natural dolphin swims to trainer-for-a-day programs. Outdoors enthusiasts will especially enjoy John Pennekamp Coral Reef State Park, where you can swim alongside sandy beaches, kayak among mangrove trees, or dive amid offshore coral reefs.

Islamorada

Southwest of Key Largo are the islands that make up Islamorada, an upscale resort area favored by anglers and scuba divers. Outdoor attractions dominate here, where you can watch sea lion shows at Theater of the Sea, feed wild tarpon at Robbie's of Islamorada, and visit four different state parks, including Indian Key Historic State Park and Lignumvitae Key Botanical State Park, both of which are only accessible by boat. Sea lovers might also appreciate the History of Diving Museum, which houses a curious collection of diving paraphernalia.

Marathon and the Middle Keys

After experiencing Islamorada, you'll pass into the Middle Keys, the heart of which is the laid-back town of Marathon. Animal lovers can swim with dolphins at the Dolphin Research Center, observe pelicans and raptors at Curry Hammock State Park and Crane Point Museum and Nature Center, or visit recovering sea turtles at The Turtle Hospital. For a quieter experience, visitors can relax on the area's lovely beaches or head south to isolated Pigeon Key, a historic base camp accessible by ferry or the Old Seven Mile Bridge.

Big Pine and the Lower Keys

Once you've crossed the Seven Mile Bridge, you'll enter the Lower Keys, perhaps the most tranquil part of this legendary archipelago. Although Bahia Honda State Park lures numerous visitors to its beaches, campgrounds, hiking trails, and warm waters, which are ideal for both kayakers and snorkelers, you're likely to spy more wildlife in this region than fellow tourists. Among the plentiful offerings, recreationists will find wooded solitude in the National Key Deer Refuge on Big Pine Key, fishing charters on Summerland Key, and superb diving opportunities around Looe Key.

If You Have . . .

- **A WEEKEND:** Experience Key West.
- **FIVE DAYS:** Add Key Largo and Islamorada.
- **ONE WEEK:** Add Marathon and Big Pine Key.
- **TEN DAYS:** Add Miami and the Everglades.

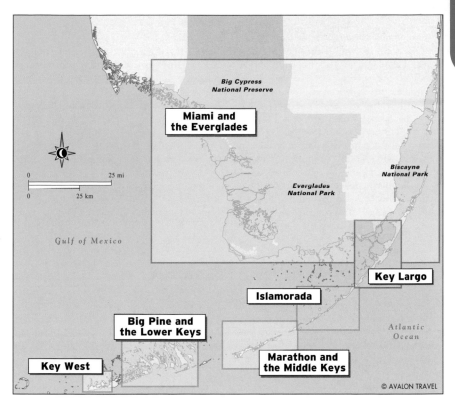

Big Cypress
National Preserve

Miami and
the Everglades

Biscayne
National Park

Everglades
National Park

Gulf of Mexico

Key Largo

Islamorada

Big Pine and
the Lower Keys

Atlantic
Ocean

Key West

Marathon and
the Middle Keys

© AVALON TRAVEL

Key West

Celebrated for its breezy hotels, sunset celebrations, and festive atmosphere, especially along Duval Street, the Southernmost City will certainly keep you busy for days on end. Here you can relax on numerous beaches, tour historical homes, visit engaging museums and nature centers, view the entire city from atop the Key West Lighthouse, or take a ferry to the Dry Tortugas. At night you'll find no shortage of lively bars, and throughout the year, you can participate in an array of festivals and events.

When to Go

You should allow at least a week for exploring southern Florida, where you could easily spend two days each in Miami, Key Largo, and Key West. Of course, where you go—and when you choose to come—will depend upon your interests.

Although southern Florida is a year-round destination, some businesses, namely restaurants in Key West, close during September.

In general, summer is the least crowded time to visit, perhaps because temperatures are fairly high from June to September, when the Atlantic hurricane season is at its peak.

Whereas spring and fall are comfortable in this subtropical region, winter is the high season in the Florida Keys, when the climate is much warmer than in the northern United States. In general, late December through

April is often the busiest period as snowbirds descend upon the Keys; lodging rates are usually higher during this peak tourist season as well as during major events and holiday weekends. Accommodations often cost less during the midseason, which typically ranges from May to July and from late October to mid-December. Hotels, inns, and resorts can be at their cheapest during the low season, which, save for holidays and festivals, is normally late summer and early fall, between August and mid-October. Although the accommodations listings in this guide reflect southern Florida's wide range in rates, be advised that every establishment has its own seasonal schedule and therefore its own pricing policy, so be sure to check each place in question before making travel plans.

Your activities can also determine the time of your trip. Swimmers and snorkelers might enjoy the slightly warmer waters of summer, but anglers must consider the varied fishing seasons before making plans. Blue marlins, for example, are prevalent from March to October while cobias are more common from November to April.

Events might sway your plans too. From December to February, several noteworthy art festivals are held in Miami and throughout the Keys. Then July lures visitors to Key West for Hemingway Days, and many flock to the Southernmost City for Fantasy Fest in late October.

Before You Go

Reservations might be necessary, especially for resorts and B&Bs during winter and spring. You should definitely call ahead if you're planning a trip in September, when many businesses close between seasons.

Transportation

Miami, the Everglades, and the Florida Keys constitute a fairly compact destination, especially given that one main highway (U.S. 1) links much of this region. Though most visitors come by car, motorcycle, or RV, it's possible to reach southern Florida using other forms of transportation. For instance, you can travel by train or bus to Miami, take a flight to Miami International Airport, or arrive in Key West by plane or cruise ship.

If you choose not to drive to southern Florida, your best bet would still be to rent a car and hit the road as soon as possible. After all, taxis can get expensive, and it's infinitely easier to travel the 110-mile Overseas Highway by car, as opposed to walking or biking. Just be prepared for the drive from Miami to Key West to take roughly 3.5-4 hours in the mid- and low seasons, and perhaps more than 5 hours during the high season. In the absence of traffic, it can take about an hour to drive from Miami to Key Largo, another half hour to reach Islamorada, roughly 45 minutes to hit the heart of Marathon, about a half hour to make it to Big Pine Key, and an additional 45 minutes to arrive in Key West—of course, the actual times depend on the actual distances, which can vary greatly in the Keys, depending upon your specific origin and destination.

The Best of the Florida Keys

First-time visitors to the Florida Keys should set aside at least a week to experience the best that these legendary islands—plus the gateway areas of Miami and the Everglades—have to offer.

Day 1

Since most travelers reach the Florida Keys by vehicle, you'll likely begin your trip in the Miami area. For a taste of the city's multicultural vibe, head to Little Havana, where you can sample authentic Cuban food and browse aromatic cigar shops. Then venture east to South Beach, where you can tour the colorful Art Deco District, view impressive art and artifact collections at the Jewish Museum of Florida–FIU or the World Erotic Art Museum, and relax at the popular Lummus Park Beach.

After lunch at one of South Beach's savory cafés, head southwest to Coconut Grove and Coral Gables, both of which boast a variety of historical structures and shopping options. Savor a fine meal and perhaps stay the

night at Coral Gables' 1920s-era Biltmore Hotel, where you can also play golf or enjoy a massage. If you'd rather experience Miami's nightlife, stay in one of the boutique hotels or world-class resorts in South Beach.

Day 2

Rise early and head to Bill Baggs Cape Florida State Park, where you can stroll along the beach, have breakfast at the Lighthouse Cafe, and take a guided tour of the 1825 Cape Florida Lighthouse, which provides panoramic views of Biscayne Bay. Afterward venture south to Biscayne National Park, where you can explore Boca Chita Key, Elliott Key, and other islands by kayak.

If you're an animal lover, stop by the Everglades Alligator Farm near Florida City, which features live alligator feedings and airboat rides in the Everglades. For a more intimate tour of this subtropical wilderness, take a canoe trip through Everglades National Park, Big Cypress National Preserve, or

the eager residents of Dolphins Plus in Key Largo

strolling along Duval Street in Key West's Old Town

Fort Zachary Taylor Historic State Park

Collier-Seminole State Park, all marvelous places to observe birds, alligators, and other native creatures.

To experience the region's heritage, head to the Miccosukee Indian Village on the Tamiami Trail or the Ah-Tah-Thi-Ki Museum on the Big Cypress Seminole Indian Reservation. After a day of sightseeing, unwind at the Miccosukee Resort & Gaming, where you'll find endless dining, entertainment, and lodging options.

Day 3

Venture south on U.S. 1 to the Florida Keys. In northern Key Largo, head to the tranquil Dagny Johnson Key Largo Hammock Botanical State Park, which lures hikers, bikers, and wildlife lovers daily. Farther south you'll encounter John Pennekamp Coral Reef State Park, where popular activities include kayaking, snorkeling, and scuba diving.

Afterward head to Dolphins Plus, where you can swim with dolphins and learn how to be a marine mammal trainer. Wildlife lovers will also appreciate the Florida Keys Wild Bird Center, home to rehabilitating brown pelicans, turkey vultures, and great horned owls.

Following a day of outdoor diversions, relax at one of Key Largo's many waterfront restaurants, most of which offer ideal spots to watch the sunset. Throughout Key Largo you'll find a variety of eateries, bars, and hotels, including those at the Key Largo Resorts Marina, which also features the historical *African Queen*.

Day 4

Continue southwest to the islands of Islamorada. Here art lovers can explore paintings, sculptures, and other unique creations at The Rain Barrel on Plantation Key while history buffs can learn about the ill-fated Overseas Railroad at Windley Key Fossil Reef Geological State Park. Farther southwest it's hard to miss the enormous sign for Theater of the Sea, which offers bottomless boat rides, entertaining marine mammal shows, and the chance to swim with the resident dolphins and sea lions. Meanwhile on Upper Matecumbe Key, you'll find the History of Diving Museum, which houses a curious collection of diving paraphernalia.

On Lower Matecumbe Key, Robbie's of Islamorada features boat rentals, fishing charters, and an open-air market. The marina

Sun and Sand

Fort Taylor Beach in Fort Zachary Taylor Historic State Park

The Florida Keys boast several picturesque beaches, which despite not being as famous as that of Miami's South Beach, can provide rest, relaxation, and people-watching year-round.

KEY LARGO

- **Cannon Beach:** This prized park offers two small artificially made beaches. It also provides easy access to a swimming area and the remnants of an old Spanish shipwreck. Offshore activities include snorkeling, fishing, and kayaking.

ISLAMORADA

- **Anne's Beach:** Dedicated to local environmentalist Anne Eaton, this tranquil beach on the ocean side of Lower Matecumbe Key features a shallow swimming area and boardwalk access to secluded stretches of sand.

MARATHON AND THE MIDDLE KEYS

- **Long Key State Park:** Situated between Layton and Marathon, Long Key State Park contains a narrow, grass-lined beach on the ocean side of U.S. 1. Only open to those staying in the state park campground, it tends to be more peaceful than the beaches farther south.

- **Curry Hammock State Park:** Little Crawl Key features a pleasant beach and playground area that is accessible by overnight campers and day-use visitors alike. Fishing, kayaking, picnicking, and beachcombing are popular activities here.

- **Sombrero Beach:** Located in the southern part of Marathon, this beautiful beach is one of the most favored in the Keys, particularly among locals. This curvy, palm-lined expanse of sand is also a preferred spot for nesting turtles from April to October.

BIG PINE AND THE LOWER KEYS

- **Sandspur Beach:** Arguably the most popular beach in the Florida Keys, this photogenic, sandy stretch includes breezy palm trees, turquoise waters, and white sand.

KEY WEST

- **Fort Zachary Taylor Historic State Park:** Praised by sunbathers, swimmers, snorkelers, and bird-watchers alike, the beach just south of Fort Zachary Taylor is surely the finest in Key West. The clear, deep waters nurture living coral and tropical fish.

- **Clarence S. Higgs Memorial Beach:** At the foot of White Street lies another popular beach, where sun worshippers can rent water-sports equipment or stroll amid pelicans and seagulls on the adjacent swimming pier.

- **Smathers Beach:** On warm sunny days, crowds flock to this lengthy beach alongside Roosevelt Boulevard, an ideal place to watch the sunrise.

- **Fort Jefferson Beach:** Only accessible via ferry or seaplane, this isolated beach is well worth the trip. Besides its proximity to historical Fort Jefferson, it provides a terrific locale for swimming, snorkeling, and overnight camping.

also provides boat tours of two remote islands: Indian Key Historic State Park, once the site of a lucrative cargo-salvaging business, and Lignumvitae Key Botanical State Park, where you can tour a virgin tropical forest. While all the islands of Islamorada are worth visiting, Upper Matecumbe Key boasts most of the area's shops, spas, bars, restaurants, and accommodations.

Day 5

Just past Layton in the Middle Keys, you'll come upon Long Key State Park, a tranquil place for canoeists, anglers, hikers, and snorkelers. Farther south, you can embrace other family-friendly diversions, such as hang gliding high above the islands and coral reefs via Conch Air, frolicking with dolphins at the Dolphin Research Center, exploring the wooded islands of Curry Hammock State Park, and relaxing on Sombrero Beach, popular with swimmers, picnickers, and volleyball enthusiasts.

If you have time, take a walking tour of The Turtle Hospital, a rescue facility on Vaca Key. Then stop by the Pigeon Key Gift Shop,

housed in a red train car, and purchase admission to Pigeon Key, an early 20th-century base camp for bridge workers. Admission includes a ferry ride to the island, which you can also access via the Old Seven Mile Bridge.

You'll find plenty of after-hours dining and lodging options in the Middle Keys. Though most lie on Vaca Key, Marathon's lengthiest island, you may prefer more isolated places, such as Hawks Cay Resort on Duck Key.

Day 6

After crossing the Seven Mile Bridge, you'll encounter the less populated Lower Keys, where Bahia Honda State Park lures kayakers, snorkelers, anglers, and bikers daily. On Big Pine Key, you might be able to spot a tiny Key deer in the National Key Deer Refuge or an alligator at the freshwater Blue Hole. While down here, take a snorkeling or diving trip to Looe Key Reef, where you'll spy large coral formations, spiny lobster, and the remains of a shipwreck.

Where you choose to spend your evening depends on your budget. If you can't afford the high dining and lodging prices at the exclusive Little Palm Island Resort & Spa,

The Conch Tour Train passes by the iconic Sloppy Joe's Bar in Key West.

consider some of the Lower Keys' more affordable options, from cottages on Big Pine Key to an RV park on Geiger Key.

Day 7

Head to Key West and survey its attractions aboard the Conch Tour Train. Then begin your self-guided tour on Duval Street in Old Town, where you can peruse art galleries, visit historical landmarks, and see colorful butterflies at The Key West Butterfly & Nature Conservatory. On nearby Whitehead Street, stroll among six-toed felines at the Ernest Hemingway Home and Museum, view the city from atop the Key West Lighthouse, and see John James Audubon's drawings at the Audubon House & Tropical Gardens.

Not far away, the impressive Mel Fisher Maritime Museum presents many of the treasures discovered in the famous *Atocha* shipwreck. Stroll to the nearby Custom House Museum, where you'll see portraits of famous Key West residents, and take a guided tour of the Harry S. Truman Little White House. If there's time, head to Fort Zachary Taylor Historic State Park, which offers guided tours of the 19th-century fort as well as the finest beach in town.

Be sure to experience the daily Sunset Celebration at Mallory Square, and enjoy the plethora of nearby shops, bars, and restaurants. While you'll find a variety of accommodations here, from low-key campgrounds to oceanfront resorts, consider staying in Old Town, which ensures easy access to Key West's most popular activities.

Romantic Key West Getaway

Luxury, history, and revelry combine on this whimsical island, a popular place for romantic getaways. Whether you fly or drive here, you and your sweetheart will surely have a memorable weekend in Key West. Here are a few suggestions for making the most of your time while visiting the Southernmost City.

Friday

When planning your romantic getaway, book a room at one of Key West's unique hotels, such as Eden House or the Marquesa Hotel, both of which offer deluxe accommodations and relaxing pool areas. For a stunning ocean view and access to a private beach, you might prefer a waterfront location like Southernmost on the Beach. No matter where you decide to stay, though, reservations are highly recommended, especially on weekends during the high season.

After checking into your hotel and freshening up, take a stroll to Mallory Square, where artists, musicians, acrobats, and tourists converge daily to pay homage to Key West's gorgeous sunsets. To avoid the crowds, head to The Westin Key West Resort & Marina, where you can watch the sunset while sipping cocktails on the Sunset Deck.

Once the sun goes down, head inland for an early dinner, perhaps at Michaels Restaurant or Café Solé, two of Key West's most intimate eateries. Afterward you can stroll along the quiet residential roads and make your way to Duval Street, a popular thoroughfare that's rife with lively, late-night bars—plus curious shops and art galleries, some of which feature enticing window displays.

For a sensual nightcap, stop by Better Than Sex on Simonton, a bordello-style lounge and restaurant that focuses exclusively on wine, beer, coffee, and decadent desserts. Often hosting live jazz, this romantic, dimly lighted gem is usually open until midnight.

Saturday

Start the day with breakfast at the Banana Cafe, a popular French-style eatery that specializes in delectable crepes. Afterward rent a pair of bicycles from Eaton Bikes on Margaret Street (or have them delivered to you) and tour Key West at your own pace. Be sure to ride up Whitehead Street, where you can visit such tranquil places as the Audubon House & Tropical Gardens and the Ernest Hemingway Home and Museum, both of which offer quiet

Get Out! Top Outdoor Adventures

A diver examines coral formations near the USS *Spiegel Grove* wreck.

The unique geography of the archipelago makes it an ideal destination for outdoors enthusiasts. Boating, sailing, waterskiing, kiteboarding, windsurfing, kneeboarding, parasailing, and stand-up paddleboarding are all popular. The most sought-after diversions in the Conch Republic include snorkeling, diving, fishing, kayaking, and to a lesser extent, biking.

BEST CORAL REEFS FOR FIRST-TIME SNORKELERS

Florida Keys National Marine Sanctuary features the world's third largest coral barrier reef system and more than 6,000 marine species. If you've never snorkeled before, though, head to Key Largo's **John Pennekamp Coral Reef State Park,** which provides all the necessary gear and offers guided tours to shallow offshore reefs. You'll likely spy kaleidoscopic parrotfish, brain coral, and spotted spiny lobsters.

BEST SHIPWRECK SITE

Besides living coral reefs, Florida Keys National Marine Sanctuary encompasses an assortment of curious shipwrecks, some of which were intentionally sunk as artificial reefs. Such was the case for the **USS *Spiegel Grove,*** a 510-foot Navy transport ship that was originally launched in 1955. It was towed to the waters east of Key Largo in 2002 to become an artificial reef. Today it allows experienced divers to see encrusted artifacts as well as various sponges, coral, tropical fish, and other marine creatures.

BEST SPORTFISHING

Anglers make a beeline for **Islamorada,** the self-proclaimed "sportfishing capital of the world." A plethora of full-service marinas, fishing charters, independent fishing guides, and boat rentals are available here. You're almost guaranteed to catch one of the region's many native species, from tarpon to red snapper.

BEST KAYAKING AMID THE MANGROVES

In the **Lower Keys,** from Bahia Honda Key to Key West, kayakers will find countless waterways, plenty of mangrove islands, and even opportunities for paddling in the open ocean.

BEST BIKING

Many hardy bikers have ventured from Key Largo to Key West, tackling U.S. 1 along the way. In addition, **Key West** offers several ways to rent a bicycle and take a tour. It's simply a lovely town to while away an afternoon and absorb the sights on your own timetable.

spots to relax and gaze at the lush foliage. If you have time, stop by the Key West Lighthouse, which lies opposite the Hemingway Home, and climb the spiral staircase for an incredible view of the verdant city below.

Pedal over to Duval Street and stroll through The Key West Butterfly & Nature Conservatory, which features a glass-enclosed habitat filled with colorful birds and butterflies. Roughly 10 blocks away lies Nancy Forrester's Secret Garden, yet another peaceful spot to relish nature. For lunch, head to the Schooner Wharf Bar, where you can enjoy fresh seafood on a breezy upper deck overlooking the yachts and sailboats in the adjacent Historic Seaport.

Following lunch, you can either continue your biking tour through Key West or head to Key West Eco Tours or Lazy Dog, both of which offer guided kayaking trips. Sharing a two-person kayak, you and your sweetheart can wind along mangrove creeks and get an up-close look at tropical fish, aquatic birds, and other marine wonders.

For another memorable adventure, spend the evening on a sunset cruise. Among those available, Sunset Watersports Key West offers a tropical buffet and a variety of libations during the excursion. Couples will especially enjoy watching the sunset together and dancing on the lighted dance floor.

After the cruise, head back to your hotel for some much-deserved relaxation. Of course, if you're not yet ready to call it a night, you'll find no shortage of distractions along Duval Street, from late-night dancing at the Aqua Nightclub to clothing-optional shenanigans at the rooftop Garden of Eden.

Sunday

If you have yet to return your bicycles to Eaton Bikes, a pickup can be arranged in the morning. After checking out of the hotel, stroll to Martin's Key West, a stylish German fusion restaurant on Duval, for brunch. Specialties include grilled bratwurst, seafood crepes, and eggs Benedict with lobster medallions. Following brunch, take a taxi or drive to Fort Zachary Taylor Historic State Park, where you can take some time to swim in the warm waters, snorkel amid colorful coral and parrotfish, and enjoy the best beach in town before heading back home.

waterfront dining in Key West's Mallory Square

Lush foliage surrounds the Key West Lighthouse.

Underwater Journey

The ocean waters along the eastern side of the Florida Keys constitute one of the finest—and most popular—underwater diving areas in the world. Stretching the length of the 220-mile archipelago, less than six miles offshore, the continental United States' only living coral barrier reef provides a thriving habitat for a wide array of fascinating marinelife, from sponges to kaleidoscopic fish, in waters ranging in depth from 5 to 70 feet.

Snorkelers and scuba divers—whether amateurs or aficionados—can easily spend five days exploring the historical shipwrecks, artificial reefs, and vibrant coral formations that are now protected within Florida Keys National Marine Sanctuary. If you plan to experience these underwater delights, there's no need to bring your own snorkeling gear and diving tanks; such equipment is available throughout the Keys.

Day 1

No matter when you plan to travel to the Florida Keys, you should reserve your accommodations in advance. For snorkelers and scuba divers, there are three ideal places: Amy Slate's Amoray Dive Resort in Key Largo, the Looe Key Reef Resort & Dive Center on Ramrod Key, and for an unparalleled experience, Jules' Undersea Lodge, which offers submerged quarters in Key Largo Undersea Park. Wherever you decide to stay, though, you'll be within relatively easy driving distance of the region's varied diving outfitters and operators.

Before checking into your hotel, make the most of the daylight hours and head to John Pennekamp Coral Reef State Park, America's first undersea park. Here you can take diving instruction, earn PADI Open Water certification, and participate in snorkeling or scuba-diving tours amid the offshore coral reefs east of Key Largo—such as Key Largo Dry Rocks, which contains the ever-popular Christ of the Abyss statue.

In addition to diving classes, other Key Largo-area operators, such as Horizon Divers, also offer diving trips to various reefs and wrecks. Such underwater sights include the Duane and the Bibb, two U.S. Coast Guard cutters used in World War II; the USS Spiegel Grove, a 510-foot Navy transport ship purposely sunk to create an artificial reef; and the sea caves of French Reef.

Day 2

Whether you're staying in the Upper or Lower Keys, you should focus the second day of your trip on the waters east of Islamorada, where you'll find an assortment of shipwrecks, wall formations, and shallow coral reefs. Through the Florida Keys Dive Center, based on the northern end of Plantation Key, you can take a diving class (if you haven't already) and see most of the nearby underwater attractions, including Conch Wall, home to a variety of conch, barrel sponges, and rare pillar coral. While down there, you might also spy green moray eels near Davis Reef, gorgonian coral along Crocker Wall, and the wrecked El Infante, a Spanish galleon that sank in a 1733 hurricane. You can also explore Alligator Reef, site of the shipwrecked USS Alligator, and the Eagle, a 287-foot freighter that became an artificial reef in the mid-1980s.

Day 3

On the third day, you should venture into the waters east of the Middle Keys. Tilden's Scuba Center, located in Marathon and open daily, provides classes, gear rentals, and Snuba diving, a patented, deepwater form of snorkeling. In addition, Tilden's offers a number of snorkeling and scuba-diving excursions, even night dives. On such tours, you're bound to see an assortment of underwater sites, including the spur-and-groove Sombrero Reef and the star, elkhorn, and brain coral of Delta Shoal. In this area, you can also survey two historical shipwrecks: the Adelaide Baker, essentially the remains of a three-masted iron-rigged ship, and the Thunderbolt, a 188-foot kayaking amid the mangroves of John Pennekamp Coral Reef State Park

vessel intentionally sunk in the mid-1980s and now home to coral, sponges, and angelfish.

Day 4

To explore the offshore reefs and wrecks of the Lower Keys, consult the Looe Key Reef Resort & Dive Center, which offers scuba classes as well as three-hour snorkeling and diving trips to the spectacular, 33-acre Looe Key Reef. Named for the HMS *Looe*, which ran aground in 1744, this spur-and-groove network now abounds with parrotfish, turtles, eagle rays, and whale sharks. Given its varying depths, the reef is ideal for both inexperienced snorkelers and advanced divers. Through the Dive Center, you can also survey the *Adolphus Busch*, an upright 213-foot freighter that was purposely sunk as an artificial reef and is now home to a wide array of marine creatures, from eels to jewfish.

Day 5

On the last day of your diving adventure, head south to Key West, where you'll find an array of vibrant coral reefs and engaging shipwrecks. While first-timers can easily snorkel in the waters near Fort Zachary Taylor Historic State Park, situated on the southern end of the island, or Dry Tortugas National Park, which lies roughly 68 miles to the west, most of the underwater attractions in this area are only accessible with the help of professional diving charters. One such local operator, Southpoint Divers, provides gear rentals, diving classes, and guided trips to two intriguing wrecks: the 187-foot *Cayman Salvage Master* and the 522-foot USNS *General Hoyt S. Vandenberg*, a former World War II troop transport ship and now the foundation for an artificial reef.

Several area operators also feature excursions to other wrecks, such as the weatherbeaten *Joe's Tug*, a deepwater vessel that's home to an assortment of coral formations and marine creatures. Some of these companies even provide trips to the spur-and-groove networks of Sand Key, Rock Key, and the Western Sambo Ecological Reserve. Other nearby sites include Kedge Ledge, a patch reef that features coral-encrusted anchors from 18th-century schooners, and the Ten-Fathom Ledge, a network of caves and outcroppings that attract lobster, grouper, and sharks, among other inhabitants.

Historic Architecture

the pool at the Ernest Hemingway Home and Museum

Look for these impressive cultural landmarks in the Miami and Key West region.

- The **Art Deco District** is a colorful area in Miami Beach that's listed on the National Register of Historic Places.

- Southwest of downtown Miami is the **Vizcaya Museum & Gardens** in Coconut Grove, once home to industrialist James Deering.

- In nearby Coral Gables, explore **The Biltmore Hotel,** a favorite spot for politicians and celebrities since its opening in the late 1920s, and the **Coral Gables Merrick House,** once home to city planner George Merrick and now an excellent example of 1920s-style architecture.

- Be sure to tour the 95-foot-tall **Cape Florida Lighthouse,** rebuilt in 1846 on Key Biscayne.

- South of Marathon, visit **Pigeon Key,** where you can stroll among the historical buildings that once served as the base camp for bridge workers in the early 20th century.

- In Key West, your first stop should be the **Ernest Hemingway Home and Museum,** built in 1851 by a marine architect and once the home of Key West's most famous resident.

- The **Key West Lighthouse,** erected in 1848, provides stunning views of the city.

- The **Audubon House & Tropical Gardens** is a gorgeous home built in the 1800s by Captain John H. Geiger, a harbor pilot and master wrecker.

- The **Harry S. Truman Little White House** is a breezy structure that once served as the command headquarters for the Key West Naval Station.

Animal Attractions

Given the varied landscapes and warm climate, it's probably no surprise that Miami, the Everglades, and the Keys contain their share of animal attractions.

MIAMI TO THE EVERGLADES

Zoo Miami is home to more than 1,000 different plant species and 500 different animal species, including endangered creatures like the tree kangaroo and Orinoco crocodile.

At **Miami Seaquarium** on Biscayne Bay, you can watch entertaining sea lions and killer whales, observe friendly manatees, and swim with dolphins.

Situated between downtown Miami and South Beach, **Jungle Island** is another fun stop for animal lovers. See parrot shows, watch tiger and primate presentations, interact with kangaroos, and wander among alligators in the Everglades habitat.

Venture into the Everglades, where roughly a dozen airboat operators guide visitors through the "river of grass" for an up-close look at alligators, turtles, birds, and other native inhabitants. Consider **Billie Swamp Safari, Everglades Safari Park, Gator Park,** and **Everglades Alligator Farm,** which is home to more than 2,000 alligators.

KEY LARGO TO ISLAMORADA

Venturing south onto Key Largo, **Dolphin Cove** and **Dolphins Plus** present an array of year-round activities, from structured dolphin swims to trainer-for-a-day programs.

The nonprofit **Florida Keys Wild Bird Center** hosts a slew of native species, including woodpeckers, brown pelicans, laughing gulls, and great white herons.

Islamorada boasts two curious animal attractions. At **Theater of the Sea,** you can swim with dolphins and sea lions and take a snorkeling cruise to an offshore coral reef. Several miles down U.S. 1, you can also feed visiting schools of tarpon at **Robbie's of Islamorada.**

MARATHON TO KEY WEST

At Hawks Cay Resort on Duck Key, **Dolphin**

an endangered sea turtle at The Turtle Hospital

Connection allows visitors to interact with dolphins from the dock or in the water. In Marathon, the **Dolphin Research Center** offers a variety of educational experiences, from brief dolphin dips to daylong research programs.

Other animal diversions include the **Crane Point Museum and Nature Center,** where birds congregate alongside Florida Bay, and **The Turtle Hospital,** where guests can take a guided tour of a sea turtle rehabilitation area.

On Big Pine Key, you can search for diminutive Key deer within the **National Key Deer Refuge** or look for turtles and alligators at the **Blue Hole.**

The **Key West Butterfly & Nature Conservatory** invites visitors into a vibrant, glass-enclosed habitat filled with colorful butterflies, birds, and flowering plants. In Mallory Square, the **Key West Aquarium** presents daily shark feedings, plus the chance to observe tarpon, parrotfish, and sea turtles.

The **Florida Keys Eco-Discovery Center** contains a 2,500-gallon reef tank filled with living coral and tropical fish.

MIAMI AND THE EVERGLADES

Unless you fly into the Marathon airport, arrive in Key West by plane or cruise ship, or have access to your own boat, you'll likely reach the Keys by car or bus. Given the geography of southern Florida, you'll have to pass through at least one of three gateway towns: Miami, Homestead, or Florida City. If you're not in a hurry, you should take some time to explore Miami's vibrant neighborhoods as well as the abundant foliage and serpentine waterways that define the Everglades.

While the Magic City's assortment of attractions, restaurants, and activities could consume you for a week or more, time and budget might dictate a shorter stay. If so, you should definitely visit the cultural microcosms of Little Havana and Little Haiti, take a self-guided walking tour of the pastel-hued Art Deco District, and soak in the ambience of infamous South Beach, a terrific place to shop for trendy apparel, dine alongside celebrities in sophisticated restaurants, and party the night away at one of numerous hip bars and dance clubs. Depending on your interests and the time of your visit, you might also catch a professional sporting event—this is, after all, the home of the Miami Dolphins, Miami Marlins, Miami Heat, and Florida Panthers. Of course, you're also not far from the coral reefs of Biscayne National Park, a favorite spot for snorkelers and scuba divers.

Although it would be impossible to cover all of the Everglades, you can definitely get a taste of this "river of grass" by visiting Everglades National Park—an International Biosphere Reserve, a World Heritage Site, and one of

HIGHLIGHTS

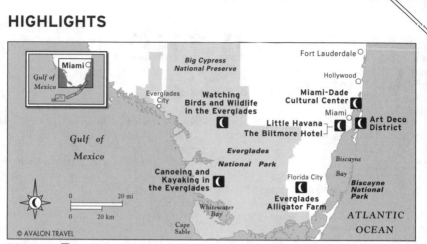

LOOK FOR **◖** TO FIND RECOMMENDED SIGHTS, ACTIVITIES, DINING, AND LODGING.

◖ Miami-Dade Cultural Center: Centered around a pleasant courtyard area, this downtown complex invites you to browse art exhibits at the Miami Art Museum, learn about the city's pioneers at HistoryMiami, and even peruse books about the state at the Main Library (page 32).

◖ Little Havana: Home to many Cuban exiles and Cuban Americans, this neighborhood offers a plethora of cigar shops, authentic markets and restaurants, live music venues, art galleries, and annual events like Calle Ocho, touted as the biggest Latino street party in the country (page 34).

◖ Art Deco District: This colorful part of the city's famous South Beach neighborhood features an incredible collection of art deco-style buildings, which you can experience through an assortment of guided and self-guided tours (page 35).

◖ The Biltmore Hotel: Since it opened in the 1920s, the historical, oft-photographed jewel of Coral Gables has welcomed countless politicians and celebrities. Even if you choose not to stay, dine, or play here, you have to see this architectural gem for yourself (page 42).

◖ Everglades Alligator Farm: What began as a mere airboat ride attraction in 1982 has since become southern Florida's oldest alligator farm. Take an airboat ride into the nearby Everglades, watch various animal shows, and stroll amid numerous alligators, crocodiles, caimans, and native snakes (page 73).

◖ Watching Birds and Wildlife in the Everglades: Whether you explore by airboat, hike along the many trails, or simply stroll along the Big Cypress Bend Boardwalk, you're bound to encounter wild animals, from wading great blue herons to lounging American alligators to the elusive Florida panther (page 78).

◖ Canoeing and Kayaking in the Everglades: Sawgrass marshes, cypress swamps, and mangrove forests are ideal spots to canoe or kayak, especially if you enjoy observing or photographing wild animals (page 80).

America's largest national parks. Here you can hike amid this fragile ecosystem, bike along the designated roads, or explore the marshy wonderland by kayak. Beyond the park's borders, you can even visit an alligator farm, join an airboat tour, or take a guided canoe trip through Fakahatchee Strand Preserve State Park, all experiences you'll surely never forget.

HISTORY

As evidenced by archaeological finds and the accounts of Spanish explorers in the early 1500s, the predominant tribes in this region were the Tequesta, who lived in the Biscayne Bay area near present-day Miami since at least the 1200s, and the Seminole, whose ancestors inhabited the Everglades for nearly 12,000 years. In 1513 Spanish explorer Juan Ponce de León was allegedly the first European to observe these native people, though there's no evidence that he actually interacted with them.

After Spain claimed the Florida territory as its own, European interactions with the native peoples increased. In 1565 when taking refuge from a storm, the Spanish explorers arrived in Biscayne Bay. Although the Tequesta initially welcomed them, Tequesta life soon changed drastically. A Spanish mission was established in the Miami area in 1567, and over the ensuing decades, many of the native people died from European diseases and various battles between the Spanish, French, and British. By the mid-1700s most of the Tequesta people had either moved elsewhere or been sold into slavery by the British. Those that remained were relocated to Cuba in 1763 when Spain transferred the Florida territory to Britain. Although the Seminole were also adversely affected by the Europeans' presence, they nonetheless managed to survive in the Everglades.

By the 1780s the United States had been formed, though Florida was once again under Spanish control. Given incidents like the First (1817-1818) and Second (1835-1842) Seminole Wars, it took some time for permanent settlements to take root, even after the Florida Territory had become part of the United States in 1821. In 1836 Fort Dallas was established in

the Miami area, where it served as a military base during the Second Seminole War.

Half a century later, however, the situation was quite different. Although some visitors felt that Miami held promise as a building site, it wasn't until Florida's Great Freeze of 1894, when all but Miami's crops were lost, that the settlement finally became a reality. Local citrus growers convinced Henry Flagler to extend his Florida East Coast Railway to Miami, and in July of 1896 it was officially incorporated as a city, with a population of only a few hundred. Soon afterward the city experienced a real estate boom and the population grew exponentially. Three decades later, Miami was thriving culturally and financially; it was during the 1920s, in fact, that it earned its nickname, the "Magic City." Tourism also began to expand in the Everglades largely because of the Seminole, who made their living from homemade crafts and alligator-wrestling spectacles. The 1928 opening of the Tamiami Trail between Tampa and Miami, the first official road across the Everglades, also helped the region prosper.

By the 1930s, however, the Great Depression had descended upon southern Florida. Miami was now experiencing an economic decline because of both the statewide real estate collapse and a devastating hurricane in the 1920s. World War II saved Miami from utter despair, especially given its location along the coast, an ideal spot in the battle against German submarines. By the 1950s tourism became the dominant industry throughout southern Florida, and a desire for natural conservation and cultural preservation was beginning to take hold. Everglades National Park was the first such success, established in 1947 to conserve this fragile ecosystem (which had been harmed by years of water drainage) and to prevent further degradation of its habitats, flora, and fauna. A decade later the Seminole Tribe of Florida was officially formed, and the Miccosukee Tribe of Indians of Florida, which separated from the Seminoles in the 1950s, was nationally recognized in 1962.

During the 1960s in the wake of Fidel Castro's rise to power, many Cubans emigrated to Miami, establishing their own community, known as Little Havana, and thereby increasing the city's multicultural population. In 1968 Biscayne National Monument was established north of Key Largo, eventually to become Biscayne National Park in 1980. Big Cypress National Preserve, which had long been home to the Seminole and Miccosukee Tribes, became one of the country's first federally protected preserves in 1974.

While tourism continued to grow in the Florida Keys during the 1980s and '90s, Miami was suffering from drug wars, hurricanes, increased crime, and scandals involving Cuban refugees. Although the refurbishment and gentrification of certain neighborhoods, such as the area south of Little Haiti, have helped to curb some of these problems, Miami is still one of the most dangerous cities in America. Nevertheless, certain industries continue to thrive here, including tourism, international trade, and international banking, and the greater metropolitan area supports roughly 5.6 million people of various ethnic and economic backgrounds.

PLANNING YOUR TIME

Given its wide assortment of museums, historical structures, art and architectural districts, trendy restaurants and nightclubs, inviting beaches, animal attractions, shopping enclaves, and annual events, Miami could easily entertain you for a week or more. Experiencing the various habitats and wildlife-watching opportunities that abound in the Everglades will undoubtedly add a few more days to your trip. Even if you've primarily come to southern Florida to explore the Keys archipelago, try to allow yourself a little time to hit the highlights of Miami and the Everglades.

Although public transportation, taxicabs, and shuttle services are available in Miami, and several tours are offered in the Everglades, it's best to explore this sprawling region by car. The plethora of major surface streets, state highways, and federal interstates makes it fairly easy to get around, though you should be prepared for traffic jams on weekdays and holiday

MIAMI AND THE EVERGLADES

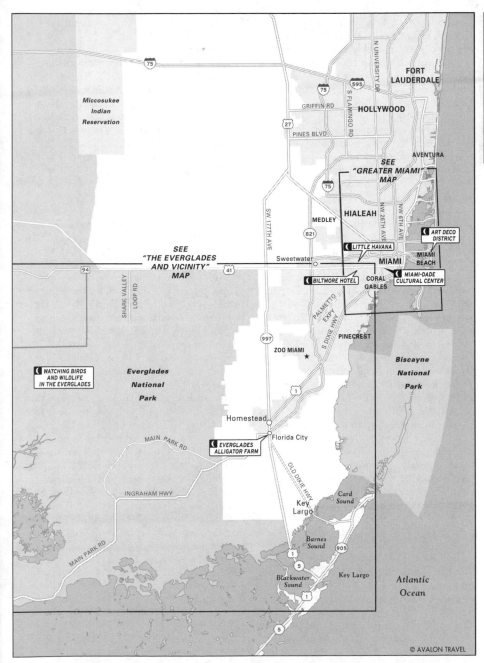

© AVALON TRAVEL

weekends. Of course, *when* you choose to pass through the gateway areas of Miami and the Everglades will probably depend on several factors, including annual events, intended activities, or your plans for the Florida Keys. Hotel reservations are encouraged, and be prepared for pricey accommodations in the safer neighborhoods.

It also helps to understand that, despite the weather being fairly warm and mild in Miami and the Everglades all year long, the peak tourist season typically extends from November to April. During the hot, humid summer months, you'll often find that certain activities and establishments aren't available (such as airplane tours in the Everglades), so always call ahead when in doubt. If you plan to visit the Everglades, it's also helpful to remember the difference between the wet season (May-Oct.) and the dry season (Nov.-Apr.). In Big Cypress National Preserve and Everglades National Park, for example, hikers, bird-watchers, and wildlife enthusiasts might prefer the dry season when there are fewer mosquitoes, more migratory birds, and an abundance of creatures in the ponds and canals; of course, there are also larger tourist crowds at this time, too. By contrast, the wet season tends to cause increased humidity, elevated temperatures, and higher water levels, which means you'll be less likely to spy alligators and wading birds, more likely to encounter mosquitoes, and yet able to enjoy the blooming flowers with fewer crowds.

As for safety, be aware that Miami can be a dangerous town, so always research an area or neighborhood before heading there. (Little Haiti, for example, is probably not a safe place for outsiders to explore at night.) Be aware of your surroundings at all times, especially when exploring non-touristy locations at night. If you want to experience the city's nightlife scene, consider heading to crowded, well-lit areas like South Beach, and keep an eye on your belongings at all times. While criminal activity is also a reality in the Everglades, the more pressing dangers involve the wildlife, so take care when exploring this vast wilderness and refrain from approaching any wild animals, no matter how docile those lounging alligators might appear to be.

For more information about this region, consult the **Greater Miami Convention & Visitors Bureau** (GMCVB, 701 Brickell Ave., Ste. 2700, Miami, 305/539-3000 or 800/933-8448, www.miamiandbeaches.com, 8:30am-6pm Mon.-Fri.) and the **Naples, Marco Island, Everglades Convention & Visitors Bureau** (2800 N. Horseshoe Dr., Naples, 239/225-1013 or 800/688-3600, www.paradisecoast.com, 9am-5pm Mon.-Fri.).

ORIENTATION

As big cities go, Miami isn't too hard to traverse by car or public transportation. Several major highways and interstates, such as U.S. 1, U.S. 27, U.S. 41, I-75, and I-95, link other Florida cities to Miami, and for the most part, all roads lead to the ocean. From downtown Miami, you can head north on I-95 or Biscayne Boulevard (U.S. 1) to reach North Miami, take U.S. 1 South or various surface streets to access Coconut Grove and Coral Gables, use I-195 or I-395 to cross Biscayne Bay toward Miami Beach, and hop on the Tamiami Trail (U.S. 41) to experience Little Havana and, farther west, the Everglades.

Of course, if you're planning to explore the Everglades, it's helpful to know how to reach the main towns. To reach Everglades City from Naples, for example, head east for 32 miles on U.S. 41, turn south on CR-29, and continue for roughly four miles. From downtown Miami, you can reach the same turnoff for Everglades City by taking I-95 North to SR-836 West (Dolphin Expy.), continuing west for about 10 miles, heading south on Florida's Turnpike (SR-821 S), merging onto the Tamiami Trail, and continuing west for roughly 65 miles. The gateway cities to the Florida Keys, Homestead and Florida City, are also easily accessible from the Miami area. Homestead lies about 26 miles southwest of downtown Miami via I-95 South and U.S. 1, and Florida City lies roughly 30 miles southwest of downtown Miami via I-95 South, U.S. 1, and Florida's Turnpike (SR-821 S). Tolls apply on certain portions of Florida's Turnpike.

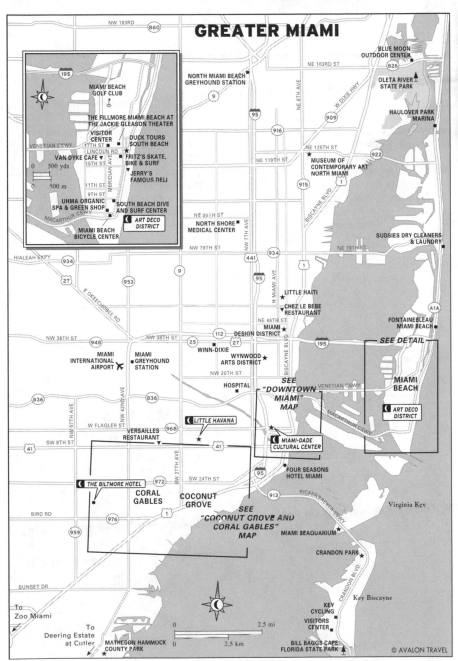

GREATER MIAMI

NW 183RD
860

BLUE MOON
OUTDOOR CENTER
826

NE 163RD ST

NORTH MIAMI BEACH
GREYHOUND STATION

OLETA RIVER
STATE PARK

195

MIAMI BEACH
GOLF CLUB

9

NE 6TH AVE

95

HAULOVER PARK
MARINA

THE FILLMORE MIAMI BEACH AT
THE JACKIE GLEASON THEATER

909

916

VISITOR
CENTER
17TH ST

LINCOLN RD

DUCK TOURS
SOUTH BEACH

NE 125TH ST

922

VENETIAN CSWY

NE 119TH ST

MUSEUM OF
CONTEMPORARY ART
NORTH MIAMI

VAN DYKE CAFE
15TH ST

FRITZ'S SKATE,
BIKE & SURF

MERIDIAN AVE

0   500 yds

JERRY'S
FAMOUS DELI

BISCAYNE BLVD

915

1

0   500 m

11TH ST

9TH ST

UHMA ORGANIC
SPA & GREEN SHOP

SOUTH BEACH DIVE
AND SURF CENTER

NE 95TH ST

A1A

MACARTHUR CSWY

ART DECO
DISTRICT

NORTH SHORE
MEDICAL CENTER

NW 7TH AVE

SUDSIES DRY CLEANERS
& LAUNDRY

MIAMI BEACH
BICYCLE CENTER

NW 79TH ST

934

1

NE 79TH ST

HIALEAH EXPY

934

441

934

FONTAINEBLEAU
MIAMI BEACH

27

E OKEECHOBEE RD

953

9

95

N MIAMI AVE

LITTLE HAITI

CHEZ LE BEBE
RESTAURANT

NE 46TH ST

A1A

NW 36TH ST

948

NW 36TH ST

112

25

27

MIAMI
DESIGN DISTRICT

195

SEE DETAIL

MIAMI
INTERNATIONAL
AIRPORT

MIAMI
GREYHOUND
STATION

WINN-DIXIE

WYNWOOD
ARTS DISTRICT

BISCAYNE BLVD

MIAMI
BEACH

NW 20TH ST

ART DECO
DISTRICT

836

NW 42ND AVE

836

HOSPITAL

SEE
"DOWNTOWN
MIAMI"
MAP

VENETIAN CSWY

MACARTHUR CSWY

NW 57TH AVE

W FLAGLER ST

VERSAILLES
RESTAURANT

968

LITTLE HAVANA

SW 8TH ST

41

SW 27TH AVE

41

MIAMI-DADE
CULTURAL CENTER

41

THE BILTMORE HOTEL

972

SW 24TH ST

95

FOUR SEASONS
HOTEL MIAMI

CORAL
GABLES

COCONUT
GROVE

913

RICKENBACKER CSWY

Virginia Key

BIRD RD

976

1

SEE
"COCONUT GROVE AND
CORAL GABLES"
MAP

MIAMI SEAQUARIUM

959

CRANDON PARK

SUNSET DR

CRANDON BLVD

Key Biscayne

To
Zoo Miami

0   2.5 mi

KEY
CYCLING

To
Deering Estate
at Cutler

MATHESON HAMMOCK
COUNTY PARK

0   2.5 km

VISITORS
CENTER

BILL BAGGS CAPE
FLORIDA STATE PARK

Sights

DOWNTOWN MIAMI
◖ Miami-Dade Cultural Center

Centered around a pleasant courtyard area, where people often relax, eat, and read, the **Miami-Dade Cultural Center** (101 W. Flagler St., Miami) is essentially a complex of separate buildings that feature engrossing exhibits. The **Miami Art Museum** (MAM, 305/375-3000, www.miamiartmuseum.org, 10am-5pm Tues.-Fri., noon-5pm Sat.-Sun., $8 adults, $4 seniors, free for children under 12 and students), for instance, houses more than 500 pieces of multicultural artwork from the 20th and 21st centuries. Founded in 1996, MAM presents the varied creations of contemporary artists like Cuban-born painter and sculptor Carlos Alfonzo, Dutch portrait photographer Rineke Dijkstra, and American sculptor and textile artist Ann Hamilton. In the museum lobby, you'll also find a curious gift shop (305/375-1729)

that features a wide selection of art books, unique jewelry, gorgeous stationery, visionary home and office furnishings, clever toys, and children's books.

This is just the tip of what awaits art lovers. By December 2013 the 200,000-square-foot Pérez Art Museum Miami (PAMM), part of a planned 29-acre Museum Park overlooking Biscayne Bay in downtown Miami, will heighten MAM's role as a "gateway between continents and cultures." This new park, which will replace the current Bicentennial Park, will also include public gardens, sculpture installations, and by 2015, the Patricia and Phillip Frost Museum of Science.

In addition to the current MAM, visitors to the Miami-Dade Cultural Center can peruse the various departments of the **Main Library** (305/375-2665, www.mdpls.org, 10am-6pm Mon.-Sat., free), featuring a specialized

the Miami Art Museum

DOWNTOWN MIAMI

Florida Department that contains an extensive collection of rare books, documents, and photographs about the Sunshine State, including Miami's history from pioneer days to the present. Nearby you can learn about the city's pioneers at **HistoryMiami** (305/375-1492, www.historymiami.org, 10am-5pm Tues.-Fri., noon-5pm Sat.-Sun., $8 adults, $7 seniors and students, $5 children 6-12, free for children under 6), which presents a permanent exhibit called *Tropical Dreams: A People's History of South Florida* as well as several temporary displays about the region's rich history that cover everything from infamous Prohibition-era gangsters to the drug wars of the 1980s to the multifaceted experiences of Miami adolescents since World War II.

Bayfront Park

About five blocks east of the Miami-Dade Cultural Center, alongside Biscayne Bay, lies the 32-acre **Bayfront Park** (301 N. Biscayne Blvd., Miami, 305/358-7550, www.bayfrontparkmiami.com, sunrise-sunset daily, no entrance fee though some activity and event fees apply), a well-landscaped municipal park that was created in the early 1920s and redesigned in the early 1980s by American sculptor Isamu Noguchi. Features include a sandy beach, a playground, a cascading fountain, a tropical rock garden and waterfall, and a variety of monuments and sculptures, including the Challenger Monument, a white, metal, 100-foot pipe tower that is dedicated to the memory of the Challenger astronauts. Containing two performance venues, the Klipsch Amphitheater and the Tina Hills Pavilion, Bayfront Park is host to numerous concerts, events, and other diversions, such as food trucks, trapeze lessons, and free yoga classes. The park offers both valet and self parking; in addition, several public parking lots are available in the area.

Wynwood Arts District

Given that Miami is home to a thriving community of artists, designers, and collectors, it's no surprise that you'll find several arts districts here. One of the largest is the **Wynwood Arts District** (www.wynwoodmiami.com), which is roughly bordered by 20th Street, 6th Avenue, 36th Street, and 2nd Avenue. The district has well over 70 galleries, studios, stores, bars, and restaurants all within walking distance. Highlights include **Gallery Diet** (174 NW 23rd St., Miami, 305/571-2288, www.gallerydiet.com, 11am-5pm Tues.-Sat.), representing a small group of emerging and midcareer artists, and **Miami Art Space** (MAS, 244 NW 35th St., Miami, 305/438-9002, www.miamiartspace.com, 10am-4pm Mon.-Fri.), which contains contemporary art exhibits inside and out.

◖ Little Havana

Home to many Cuban exiles and Cuban Americans since the 1960s, **Little Havana** (www.littlehavanaguide.com) lies just west of downtown Miami. A predominantly Latino neighborhood, *La Pequeña Habana* offers a plethora of cigar shops, quiet parks, authentic markets and restaurants, live music venues, art galleries, and annual events like Carnaval Miami, which takes place in March and features Calle Ocho, touted as the biggest Latino

a heated domino match in Little Havana

street party in the country. To experience the unique vibe of this ethnic enclave, you should simply stroll along the major streets, such as **Calle Ocho** (SW 8th St., Miami) and **Cuban Memorial Boulevard** (SW 13th Ave., Miami), taking note of various monuments, such as a memorial plaque of Cuba, the bust of Cuban poet and revolutionary José Martí, and the black obelisk dedicated to those who perished during the Bay of Pigs Invasion. In Little Havana, you'll also encounter places like **Maximo Gomez Park** (801 SW 15th Ave., Miami, 8am-8pm daily), named after a Cuban revolutionary who fought against Spanish oppression in the late 1800s. Affectionately known as Domino Park, this small meeting place is often filled with old-timers playing friendly, if competitive, rounds of chess or dominoes.

SOUTH BEACH
C Art Deco District

East of downtown Miami lies Miami Beach, an incorporated city and part of a barrier island that's linked to the mainland by four causeways: MacArthur (SR-A1A), Venetian, Julia Tuttle (I-195), and John F. Kennedy (SR-934). Surely the most famous portion of this island is the southern part, known as South Beach, where you'll encounter one of the most celebrated architectural districts in southern Florida. Officially listed as the Miami Beach Architectural District on the National Register of Historic Places, the colorful **Art Deco District** features an incredible collection of art deco-style buildings, roughly bounded by Alton Road, Dade Boulevard, the Atlantic Ocean, and 6th Street.

The best way to experience this historical neighborhood is with a walking, biking, or Segway tour, whether self-guided or otherwise. First-timers may especially appreciate the 90-minute **walking tour** (10:30am Fri.-Wed., 10:30am and 6:30pm Thurs., $20 adults, $15 seniors, students, and military veterans) that the **Miami Design Preservation League** (MDPL, Art Deco Welcome Center, 1001 Ocean Dr., 2nd Fl., Miami Beach,

305/672-2014, www.mdpl.org) offers daily. Departing from the Art Deco Gift Shop (1001 Ocean Dr., Miami Beach, 305/531-3484, 9:30am-7pm daily), this guided stroll explores hotels, restaurants, and other commercial structures, providing an introduction to the art deco, Mediterranean Revival, and Miami Modern (MiMo) styles found within this important district. Reservations are not required for this tour. As an alternative, the MDPL features a 90-minute **self-guided tour** ($15 pp) of the area. Using a rented iPod and an accompanying map, you can learn about the district's architectural history at your own pace. This tour (with commentary in English, Spanish, French, or German) is available from the Art Deco Gift Shop (9:30am-5pm daily).

No matter which tour you choose, you can easily reach South Beach by public bus or private vehicle. If you drive yourself, you'll find plenty of parking garages and metered street parking here ($1.25 hourly).

Museums and Memorials

Beyond its art deco splendor, South Beach contains several curious museums and memorials. Near the southern end of the island, you'll encounter the spacious **Jewish Museum of Florida–FIU** (301 Washington Ave., Miami Beach, 305/672-5044, www.jmof.fiu.edu, 10am-5pm Tues.-Sun., $12 families, $6 adults, $5 seniors and students, free for children under 6), including two former synagogues, one erected in 1929 and the other in 1936. Both synagogues are listed on the National Register of Historic Places, and together, they boast an extensive collection of photographs, documents, and artifacts that illustrate the Jewish experience in the Sunshine State. Three informative films are also available: *Synagogue to Museum,* which presents Florida's Jewish history as well as the museum's history; *Jewish Settlement in Florida,* which explores four diverse Jewish families; and *L'Chaim: To Life,* which depicts Jewish traditions, including holiday cycles. Admission is free for all visitors on Saturday, though the on-site Bessie's Bistro is closed that day in observance of Shabbat. The

LITTLE HAITI

© GREATER MIAMI CONVENTION & VISITORS BUREAU/WWW.GMCVB.COM

shopping options in Little Haiti

North of downtown Miami lies a curious place, the city's traditional center of Haitian Creole and Francophone culture—and the largest Haitian community outside of Haiti. Bordered by Little River to the north, Northeast 2nd Avenue to the east, Northeast 54th Street to the south, and North Miami Avenue to the west, this neighborhood has long been known as *La Petite Haïti*, or Little Haiti—and, traditionally, as Lemon City. Over the years, the people of Little Haiti have fluctuated between middle and lower class, and although crime does exist here today and the residents might look at you skeptically, this unique area is definitely worth visiting—if only in the daytime. Here you can gaze at multicolored facades, listen to snippets of Creole, visit fascinating art and voodoo shops, and of course, enjoy spicy authentic cuisine at eateries like the longstanding **Chez Le Bebe Restaurant** (114 NE 54th St., Miami, 305/751-7639, www.chezlebebe.com, 8am-midnight daily, $4-12), where you'll find inexpensive delicacies like *tasso* (fried goat), *griot* (fried pork),

and *mais* (grits). While eating, you might even learn a few Creole expressions, such as *souple* (please) and *mesi* (thank you), though the staff here isn't always so polite.

Not quite the ethnic enclave that Little Havana purports to be, Little Haiti has suffered culturally in recent years from the gentrification of the district itself as well as surrounding neighborhoods. Near the southern part of Little Haiti, for instance, lies the trendy **Miami Design District** (305/722-7100, www.miamidesigndistrict.net), an 18-block section featuring more than 120 art galleries, restaurants, bars, and showrooms filled with designer fashions, furnishings, lighting fixtures, kitchen and bathroom products, wall and floor materials, and fine rugs. Situated between Northeast 37th Street, Biscayne Boulevard, Northeast 42nd Street, and North Miami Avenue, the stylish design district, which has plans to expand, is certainly worthy of a daylong stroll, though it's obviously a world away from the heart of *La Petite Haïti*.

the Art Deco District in South Beach

entire museum complex is closed on Monday as well as on national and Jewish holidays.

The Wolfsonian-Florida International University (1001 Washington Ave., Miami Beach, 305/531-1001, www.wolfsonian.org, noon-6pm Thurs. and Sat.-Tues., noon-9pm Fri., $7 adults, $5 seniors, students, and children 6-12, free for children under 6), a wheelchair-accessible design museum in the heart of the Art Deco District, houses an intriguing collection of roughly 120,000 objects from the modern era (1885-1945), all of which demonstrate how art and design influence and reflect the human experience. Admission is free for the students, faculty, and staff of Florida's state universities—and for everyone after 6pm on Friday.

Another repository worth visiting is the **World Erotic Art Museum (WEAM)** (1205 Washington Ave., Miami Beach, 305/532-9336 or 866/969-9326, www.weam.com, 11am-10pm Mon.-Thurs., 11am-midnight Fri.-Sun., $15 adults, $14 seniors over 60, $13.50 students 18 and over), which is two blocks north of The Wolfsonian. Home to the continent's largest collection of erotic art, the 12,000-square-foot museum includes everything from Lady Godiva depictions to Indonesian and Caribbean artifacts, plus erotic chessboards, pin-up illustrations, gay photography, fetish artwork, and Picasso paintings, among other exhibits. Visitors to the WEAM will encounter 20 separate rooms, all part of a fascinating yet tasteful timeline of erotica, or the "art of love." The on-site gift shop contains an array of engaging erotic books, postcards, and posters. Not surprisingly, visitors must be 18 years or older to enter the museum.

Just south of Dade Boulevard, you'll encounter the **Holocaust Memorial of the Greater Miami Jewish Federation** (1933-1945 Meridian Ave., Miami Beach, 305/538-1663, www.holocaustmmb.org, 9am-sunset daily, free), erected to honor the six million Jews who perished during the infamous Holocaust. Constructed over a four-year period and dedicated in February 1990, the memorial features a reflecting pool; a black granite wall

MODERN ART

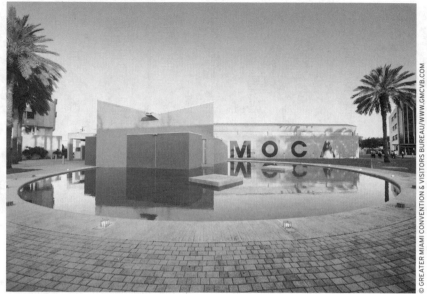

MOCA North Miami

After visiting the sights of South Beach, including the Art Deco District, art lovers should take a quick detour to North Miami, where you'll find the **Museum of Contemporary Art North Miami** (MOCA, Joan Lehman Bldg., 770 NE 125th St., 305/893-6211, www.mocanomi.org, 11am-5pm Tues. and Thurs.-Sat., 1pm-9pm Wed., noon-5pm Sun., $5 adults, $3 seniors and students, free for children under 12, military veterans, city employees, and North Miami residents). Known worldwide for its ability to establish new trends in contemporary art, MOCA houses a permanent collection of roughly 600 pieces of cutting-edge sculptures, paintings, photographs, videos, and multimedia creations from emerging and established artists, such as photographer Melanie Schiff and sculptor Dennis Oppenheim.

In addition to its impressive collection, MOCA, which has plans to expand its exhibition space threefold, also presents lectures, workshops, screenings, concerts, performances, and mind-bending temporary installations from the likes of Roy Lichtenstein, Keith Haring, and other innovators. If you're in town on the last Friday of the month, be sure to stop by for Jazz at MOCA from 7 to 10pm, and don't forget to visit the on-site gift shop, open during museum hours with one of the city's best selections of contemporary art books, imaginative jewelry, eye-popping designs, and other unique items. Just be advised that, given its currently limited space, MOCA must typically close during the installation of a new exhibition, so always call ahead before visiting.

presenting the history of the Holocaust (1933-1945) through text, pictures, and maps; and a narrow passage highlighting the most infamous death camps. From there visitors enter a large circular plaza paved in Jerusalem stone, surrounded by a high, black granite wall and featuring a 42-foot-high bronze sculpture composed of nearly 100 anguished figures. This engaging yet heart-wrenching tour culminates with the Memorial Wall, an ever-growing etched list of names, representing a multitude of fallen children, parents, and grandparents.

Not far away from the Holocaust Memorial lies yet another art repository, the **Bass Museum of Art** (2100 Collins Ave., Miami Beach, 305/673-7530, www.bassmuseum.org, noon-5pm Wed.-Sun., $8 adults, $6 seniors, students, and children 6-17, free for children under 6), which contains an enormous selection of European, Asian, North American, Latin American, and Caribbean paintings, sculptures, textiles, and photographs from the 15th through the 21st centuries, including the work of Peter Paul Rubens and Benjamin West. It has temporary art exhibits as well as a relatively new Egyptian gallery that includes an authentic mummy and sarcophagus. Free docent tours are available, and an on-site gift shop offers a curious selection of folk art, local jewelry, unique decorative items, educational toys, and art and photography books, plus a snack bar with free wireless Internet access.

Gardens and Beaches

Not far from the Holocaust Memorial on Meridian Avenue lies the **Miami Beach Botanical Garden** (2000 Convention Center Dr., Miami Beach, 305/673-7256, www.mbgarden.org, 9am-5pm Tues.-Sun., free), a 4.5-acre greenspace that invites visitors to relax amid vibrant orchids, tropical plants, and Japanese-style foliage. For a sandier landscape, consider visiting one of the many beaches that line the ocean side of this barrier island, including **Lummus Park Beach** (305/673-7730, sunrise-sunset daily, free), the main public beach

a lifeguard stand on Lummus Park Beach

parrots at Jungle Island

and penguins, watch tiger and primate presentations, feed various birds, and wander among the alligators in an Everglades habitat. Other activities include strolling through a lush greenhouse and relaxing on a private beach. With proper identification, all military personnel and veterans, firefighters, and law enforcement officers receive free admission year-round.

On the opposite side of the road, the wheelchair-accessible **Miami Children's Museum** (MCM, 980 MacArthur Cswy., Miami, 305/373-5437, www.miamichildrensmuseum. org, 10am-6pm daily, $16 adults and children, $12 Florida residents, free for children under 1 and military personnel) lures visitors with an array of interactive exhibits that allow children to operate a crane and navigate a cruise ship at Port of Miami, play in a world music studio, steer a fire truck, explore the Everglades, peer inside a 900-gallon marine tank, and learn how to take better care of themselves and their pets. Other exhibits feature the inner workings of a bank, a supermarket, and a television studio.

in South Beach. Lying just east of the Art Deco District, this white sandy stretch extends alongside Ocean Drive between 5th and 15th Streets. Favored among teenagers, families, tourists, and celebrities alike, this often-photographed beach is popular for swimming, sunbathing, and people watching. Amenities include public restrooms, volleyball courts, beach chair rentals ($10 daily), umbrella rentals ($12 daily), and of course, warm, clear ocean waters. If you're bringing the kids, though, keep in mind that topless sunbathing is common here.

Watson Island

En route from South Beach to downtown Miami via the MacArthur Causeway, you'll cross Watson Island in Biscayne Bay, which has two family-friendly attractions. On one side of the road lies **Jungle Island** (1111 Parrot Jungle Trl., Miami, 305/400-7000, www.jungleisland.com, 10am-5pm daily, $35 adults, $33 seniors 62 and over, $27 children 3-10, free for children under 3), where visitors can see parrot shows, view the antics of kangaroos

COCONUT GROVE

Situated southwest of downtown Miami, Coconut Grove is a favored shopping and dining destination that also boasts three winning attractions. From the downtown area, the first one you'll encounter is the **Miami Science Museum** (3280 S. Miami Ave., Miami, 305/646-4200, www.miamisci.org, 10am-6pm daily, $15 adults, $11 seniors 62 and over, students, and children 3-12, $13 Miami-Dade County adults, $9 Miami-Dade County seniors 62 and over, students, and children 3-12, free for children under 3), which features intriguing temporary exhibits, permanent interactive displays like the human yo-yo and the energy-capturing dance floor, and educational shows in the on-site wildlife center and planetarium.

Not far away lies the stunning **Vizcaya Museum & Gardens** (3251 S. Miami Ave., Miami, 305/250-9133, www.vizcayamuseum. org, 9:30am-4:30pm Wed.-Mon., $15 adults, $10 seniors 62 and over and students, $6 children 6-12, free for children under 6), an expansive property that served as the winter residence

© GREATER MIAMI CONVENTION & VISITORS BUREAU/WWW.GMCVB.COM

the Vizcaya Museum & Gardens, Coconut Grove

of American industrialist James Deering (vice president of an agricultural equipment company) from 1916 until his death in 1925. Construction on the Italian Renaissance-style mansion, which was intended to look like a 400-year-old estate that had been occupied and renovated by several familial generations, began in 1914 and continued until 1923. During this time, more than 1,000 European and Caribbean laborers and craftsmen worked on the 180-acre complex that included the house, the formal gardens, a farm, and several service facilities. Two hurricanes, one in 1926 and another in 1935, caused extensive damage to the house and surrounding grounds, and eventually most of the land was sold for development. In 1952, however, Deering's heirs sold the main house and formal gardens to the county and later donated the estate's substantial artwork and furnishings with the condition that Vizcaya be forever used as a public museum.

Today the house features 34 uniquely decorated rooms, with antique furnishings and art objects from the 15th through the 19th centuries. Although the architectural design once permitted the free flow of breezes through the open courtyard, the house now features a glass-enclosed courtyard and a system for climate and humidity control to better preserve the building and contents. The gardens, meanwhile, blend elements of French and Italian Renaissance designs, including fountains, statuary, and a central pool. Listed on the National Register of Historic Places since 1970, the museum welcomes visitors on narrated or self-guided tours of the opulent house, elaborate gardens, and impressive orchidarium. Audio tours ($5) are available, as are guidebooks ($3) in both English and Spanish. A café overlooks the historical swimming pool and serves sandwiches, salads, and desserts. A gift shop offers books, postcards, and jewelry, among other items. The facilities here are wheelchair-accessible, and the parking is free.

Farther south, alongside Biscayne Bay, **The Barnacle Historic State Park** (3485 Main Hwy., Coconut Grove, 305/442-6866, www.

floridastateparks.org/thebarnacle, 9am-5pm Fri.-Mon., $2 pp) preserves the former home and grounds of Ralph Middleton Munroe, a sailboat designer, civic activist, naturalist, author, and photographer who was also one of Coconut Grove's most influential trailblazers. Built in 1891, the colorful, Caribbean-style house was inspired, especially throughout the interior, by sturdy hurricane-resistant boat designs. With a lower porch and upper balcony, the building also takes advantage of the peaceful bayside views. Although you're free to stroll through the home as well as the surrounding tropical hardwood hammock and nearby boathouse, tours (10am, 11:30am, 1pm, and 2:30pm Fri.-Mon., $3 adults, $1 children 6-12, free for children under 6) are also available for an extra fee and are usually 45 minutes long. In addition, the park is open on Wednesday and Thursday for group tours if arranged in advance. No matter the season, this park is an excellent place for picnics and bird-watching opportunities. Just remember that entrance fees must be placed in the honor box, and correct change is required.

CORAL GABLES
◖ The Biltmore Hotel
Founded by George Merrick in the 1920s, the lovely community of Coral Gables is now home to the University of Miami and the historical **Biltmore Hotel** (1200 Anastasia Ave., Coral Gables, 855/454-0196, www.biltmore-hotel.com), designed in 1924 by renowned architect Leonard Schultze and developer S. Fullerton Weaver and now serves as a monument to Italian, Moorish, and Spanish architectural styles. After officially opening in January of 1926, the oft-photographed jewel of Coral Gables welcomed countless movie stars, politicians, and other celebrities in its early years, including Judy Garland, Bing Crosby, President Franklin D. Roosevelt, and Al Capone. World War II altered the property's fortunes, though, and from 1942 to 1968, The Biltmore served as a military hospital. After much lobbying by Coral Gables officials and city residents, The Biltmore was acquired by the city in 1973 and

remained vacant for a full decade until an extensive four-year restoration returned the resort to its former glory. Three years later, the hotel closed in the midst of the county's economic downturn, only to be bought and fully restored by a private corporation. In 1996 the federal government finally declared The Biltmore a National Historic Landmark, ensuring its well-deserved preservation. So even if you choose not to stay overnight, play golf or tennis here, dine in the Palme d'Or or Fontana restaurants, or enjoy a massage in the world-class spa—you simply must see this architectural gem for yourself. Free guided tours of The Biltmore are available on Sunday at 1:30pm, 2:30pm, and 3:30pm.

Other Attractions
Several blocks north of The Biltmore Hotel, you can visit the **Coral Gables Merrick House and Gardens** (907 Coral Way, Coral Gables, 305/460-5361, www.coralgables.com, 1pm-4pm Wed. and Sun., $5 adults, $3 seniors and students, $1 children 6-12, free for children under 6), which was once the home of city planner George Merrick and now listed in the National Register of Historic Places. Originally part of William and Sarah Gregory's 160-acre homestead, this property was acquired, sight unseen, by Reverend Solomon G. Merrick, who hoped to relocate his wife, Althea, and their children from the harsh climate of Massachusetts to the sunny Miami area. Solomon and his eldest son, George, preceded the rest of the family in order to cultivate the rocky, untamed land. By January 1900, Althea and the other children had arrived, and the immensely hard work continued. In fact, the Merrick men were forced to enlist the help of Bahamian workers from Coconut Grove in order to replace the pine palmetto with grapefruit trees.

By 1906, however, the groves had begun to flourish, and the family had successfully expanded their small wooden cottage into a spacious, New England-style home. Despite George's college education and career goals of becoming a lawyer, his father's death in 1911

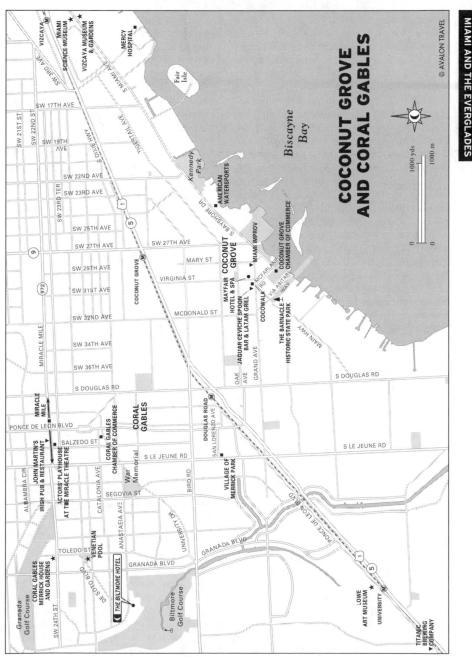

MIAMI AND THE EVERGLADES

© AVALON TRAVEL

COCONUT GROVE AND CORAL GABLES

Biscayne Bay

forced him to return to his family's Coral Gables Plantation, where, by the 1920s, he'd begun to envision a Mediterranean-style city with wide boulevards and lush landscaping. Eventually, George's vision became a reality when the City of Coral Gables was incorporated in 1925. Unfortunately, a 1926 hurricane stalled the city's momentum, and in an effort to save his new town, George lost all of his family's fortune except for the original house, where Althea continued to live with her daughter Ethel. In 1935 the house became an inn called Merrick Manor, and following Althea's death two years later, Ethel operated it until she passed away in 1961. By 1976 the City of Coral Gables purchased the house and restored it to its 1925 appearance. Today as part of the admission price, visitors can take a 45-minute **tour** (1pm, 2pm, and 3pm Wed. and Sun.) of the historical house, which contains much of the Merrick family's artwork, photographs, furniture, and personal treasures, offering an outstanding look at the early days of Coral Gables.

Naturally, on particularly hot days, many tourists venture to the nearby **Venetian Pool** (2701 De Soto Blvd., Coral Gables, 305/460-5306, www.coralgablesvenetianpool.com, 10am-4:30pm Tues.-Sun., $10.50 adults, $6 children 3-12, $3.75-4.75 Coral Gables residents), a tranquil coral rock lagoon designed by Coral Gables' founding father George Merrick, opened in 1923, and now listed on the National Register of Historic Places. Encircled by brilliant bougainvillea, coconut palms, and twin observation towers, the Venetian Pool is worth a photo stop, even if you don't take a dip. Unfortunately, children under the age of three are not allowed here. Operating hours can vary seasonally and the pool is closed on major holidays.

South of The Biltmore lies the University of Miami campus, where the **Lowe Art Museum** (1301 Stanford Dr., Coral Gables, 305/284-3535, www6.miami.edu/lowe, 10am-4pm Tues.-Sat., noon-4pm Sun., $10 adults, $5 seniors and students, free for children under 12 and University of Miami students, faculty, and staff) features a wide assortment of paintings, sculptures, and photography representing Greco-Roman, European, American, Asian, African, Pacific, and Latin American cultures. Founded in 1952, the museum also encompasses the relatively new Myrna and Sheldon Palley Pavilion for Contemporary Glass and Studio Arts, which, as the name indicates, presents an impressive collection of contemporary glasswork, ceramics, and fiber art. The museum is accessible via the University stop on the Metrorail and also has a metered parking lot.

The scenic **Matheson Hammock County Park** (9610 Old Cutler Rd., Miami, 305/665-5475, www.miamidade.gov, sunrise-sunset daily, $5-6 automobiles, $15 recreational vehicles, $12-15 boat trailers) lures visitors to Biscayne Bay, where they can enjoy an artificially constructed pool, a breezy beach, a full-service marina and restaurant, picnic pavilions, and nature trails. Another lovely oasis is the **Fairchild Tropical Botanic Garden** (10901 Old Cutler Rd., Coral Gables, 305/667-1651, www.fairchildgarden.org, 7:30am-4:30pm daily, $25 adults, $18 seniors 65 and over, $12 children 6-17, free for children under 6), an 83-acre property opened in 1938 that now nurtures an extensive collection of rare tropical plants, including palms, cycads, vines, succulents, and flowering trees.

KEY BISCAYNE

East of Coconut Grove and Coral Gables lies Key Biscayne, a barrier island in Biscayne Bay, accessible via the Rickenbacker Causeway. En route to Key Biscayne, you'll encounter Virginia Key, where the 38-acre **Miami Seaquarium** (4400 Rickenbacker Cswy., Key Biscayne, 305/361-5705 or 305/365-2501, www.miamiseaquarium.com, 9:30am-6pm daily, $40 adults, $30 children 3-9, free for children under 3, $8 parking) invites visitors to watch entertaining killer whales, dolphins, and sea lions, observe friendly manatees, and view shark feedings. There are several snack bars and gift shops throughout the park. For an extra fee, you can even experience an up-close animal encounter. Such programs include the **Dolphin Odyssey** ($199 participants, $45 observers 10 and over,

© GREATER MIAMI CONVENTION & VISITORS BUREAU/WWW.GMCVB.COM

a killer whale show at the Miami Seaquarium on Virginia Key

$36 observers 3-9, free for observers under 3), an intimate chance to touch, feed, train, and ride a dolphin; the **Dolphin Encounter** ($139 participants, $99 children 5-9, $45 adult observers, $36 observers 3-9, free for observers under 3), a shallow-water opportunity to touch, feed, and play with the dolphins; the **Sea Trek Reef Encounter** ($99 participants, $40 adult observers, $30 observers 3-9, free for observers under 3), a 20-minute underwater walking journey through a 300,000-gallon tropical reef; and the **Seal Swim** ($139 participants, $99 children 5-9, $40 adult observers, $30 observers 3-9, free for observers under 3), an occasion to swim alongside harbor seals in both shallow and deep water. Some programs have height and age restrictions.

On Key Biscayne, you'll encounter two lovely recreation areas. The first is **Crandon Park** (6747 Crandon Blvd., Key Biscayne, 305/361-5421, www.miamidade.gov, sunrise-sunset daily, $5-6 vehicles, activity fees apply), a former coconut plantation that now features

a golf course, a marina, tennis courts, nature trails, kayak and cabana rentals, guided tram tours, an amusement area, and the **Crandon Park Visitor and Nature Center** (8am-4pm daily). Visitors here can explore a variety of ecosystems, including coastal dunes, mangrove forests, tropical hardwood hammocks, and seagrass beds. Kayaking is an especially rewarding activity, as it affords you a leisurely, ecofriendly way to observe wading birds, raptors, sea turtles, and other marine creatures. Many visitors come for the gorgeous two-mile beach, which offers concession stands, picnic areas, several lifeguard towers, and plenty of parking. The beach, marina, tennis center, amusement area, nature center, gardens, and cabanas are all wheelchair-accessible.

At the southern end of Key Biscayne lies **Bill Baggs Cape Florida State Park** (1200 S. Crandon Blvd., Key Biscayne, 305/361-5811, www.floridastateparks.org/capeflorida, 8am-sunset daily, $8 vehicles with 2-8 passengers and day-use boaters, $4 motorcycles and single-occupant vehicles, $2 pedestrians, bikers, and extra passengers), home to the historical 95-foot-tall **Cape Florida Lighthouse,** a whitewashed conical tower built in 1825, reconstructed in 1846, and now considered the oldest standing structure in Miami-Dade County. The photogenic lighthouse grounds, which lie at the southern tip of Key Biscayne, are open from 9am to 5pm Thursday-Monday. You can watch a video presentation in the former cookhouse, view cultural displays about early island life in the lighthouse keeper's cottage, and visit the gift shop. Free guided tours of the lighthouse are offered at 10am and 1pm Thursday-Monday, though it's best to call the administrative offices (305/361-8779, 8:30am-4:30pm Mon.-Fri.) in advance, just in case a school group has reserved a tour. Be prepared to climb 109 steps in all, which can be a strenuous trek for some—though well worth the panoramic views, in spite of the cramped observation area. Unfortunately, and rather arbitrarily, children under 8 are not allowed to reach the top.

The park also features a 1.25-mile beach,

and popular activities here consist of biking, kayaking, sunbathing, swimming, shoreline fishing, and overnight boat camping. Other amenities include picnic pavilions ($100-150 daily), bicycle rentals ($3-15 per half hour, $5-25 hourly), beach chair rentals ($7), beach umbrella rentals ($10), kayak and hydro-bike rentals ($20-30 hourly), a primitive campground ($1-6 pp nightly), and two restaurants: the **Boater's Grill** (305/361-0080, www.lighthouserestaurants.com, 9am-sunset daily, $4-42) and the **Lighthouse Cafe** (305/361-8487, www.lighthouserestaurants.com, 9am-sunset daily, $2-38). Although leashed pets are allowed in the park, they are not permitted on the beach or playground, near the wetlands, within the lighthouse compound, or inside the restaurants.

SOUTHERN MIAMI

Even the southern suburbs contain a few interesting attractions. Beside Biscayne Bay, for instance, the 444-acre **Deering Estate at Cutler** (16701 SW 72nd Ave., Miami,

a white Bengal tiger lounging at Zoo Miami

305/235-1668, www.deeringestate.com, 10am-5pm daily, $12 adults, $7 children 4-14, free for children under 4) invites visitors to take daily nature tours of several protected habitats, including pine rocklands, tropical hardwood hammocks, salt marshes, and mangrove forests. In addition, the 1920s-era, Mediterranean Revival-style mansion, nicknamed the "Stone House," was once the home of Charles Deering—a wealthy Chicago industrialist, environmental preservationist, dedicated philanthropist, avid art collector, and amateur artist. It now boasts a fine collection of antique furniture, chandeliers, and other furnishings, plus several pieces of artwork, such as family portraits as well as paintings like *Ash Wednesday Procession in Barcelona,* one of several works that Deering commissioned from Spanish artist Ramon Casas in the early 1900s. During your tour of the house, which is listed on the National Register of Historic Places, you'll also spy some of Deering's original volumes, such as classic novels by Cervantes, Chaucer, Dickens, Kipling, and Melville, plus a two-volume 1800 edition of Henry Fielding's *The History of Tom Jones.*

For a completely different experience, head west to **Zoo Miami** (12400 SW 152nd St., Miami, 305/251-0400, www.miamimetrozoo.com, 9:30am-5:30pm daily, $16 adults, $12 seniors 65 and over and children 3-12, $8 military personnel, free for children under 3), home to more than 1,000 different plant species and 500 different animal species, including endangered creatures like the tree kangaroo and Orinoco crocodile. Here visitors can stroll through a children's zoo, learn about the links between birds and dinosaurs in the American Bankers Family Aviary, explore the relatively new, 27-acre *Amazon & Beyond* exhibit, and take a narrated **safari tram tour** (11am-4pm daily, $5 pp) through the Asian or African habitat. All trams and the zoo's monorail system ($3 pp) are wheelchair-accessible, and luckily, visitors can rent both strollers ($8-10) and wheelchairs ($8-30) here, with a required deposit.

BOAT TOURS

If you're a first-time visitor to the Miami area, consider taking a sightseeing boat tour of the city's coastline and lovely Biscayne Bay. One such option is **Island Queen Cruises** (401 Biscayne Blvd., Miami, 305/379-5119 or 800/910-5119, www.islandqueencruises.com, times vary daily, $17-69 adults, $12-25 children), based out of the Bayside Marketplace and offering a variety of excursions, including party fishing cruises, dance cruises, and speedboat cruises past "Millionaire's Row." Another option is **Duck Tours South Beach** (1661 James Ave., Miami Beach, 305/673-2217, www.ducktourssouthbeach.com, times vary daily, $32 adults, $26 seniors 65 and over, $18 children 4-12, $5 children under 4), featuring 90-minute narrated tours on amphibious vehicles that lead you past famous Miami landmarks before launching into Biscayne Bay. Duck Tours also has locations in downtown Miami and Fort Lauderdale.

Entertainment and Events

NIGHTLIFE

Miami is celebrated around the world for many reasons, not the least of which is its sultry nightlife. After all, this is a town that lures the young, wealthy, and beautiful, many of whom celebrate to excess at the city's numerous bars and dance clubs, where 24-hour liquor licenses are not unheard of. If you, too, hope to live it up in the Magic City, you surely won't run out of options any time soon.

In downtown Miami, for instance, you'll encounter **Tobacco Road** (626 S. Miami Ave., Miami, 305/374-1198, www.tobacco-road.com, 11:30am-5am daily, cover varies), which has been open since 1912 and once served as a speakeasy during Prohibition. These days the city's oldest bar and restaurant features live jazz and blues, plus a tasty menu.

For the quintessential Miami dance club experience, head north toward I-395 where **Club Space** (34 NE 11th St., Miami, 305/375-0001 or 786/357-6456, www.clubspace.com, 11pm-2pm Thurs.-Sat., cover varies), a multistory vintage warehouse, lures countless revelers nightly. Just be forewarned that drink prices and valet parking fees are high here, and you'll likely find it easier to breach the velvet ropes if you're attractive, well dressed, and female.

In nearby Coconut Grove, the **Miami Improv** (3390 Mary St., Miami, 305/441-8200, www.miamiimprov.com, show times and ticket prices vary) features an ever-evolving lineup of stand-up comedy routines. Meanwhile, at **John Martin's Irish Pub & Restaurant** (253 Miracle Mile, Coral Gables, 305/445-3777, www.johnmartins.com, 11:30am-midnight Sun.-Tues., 11:30am-2am Wed.-Sat., no cover), you can enjoy happy hour drink specials on weekdays (5pm-7pm Mon.-Fri.) and live entertainment on certain nights, as well as occasional events, such as an annual St. Patrick's Day celebration. This lively bar also offers full brunch, lunch, and dinner menus.

Of course, most night owls flock to neon-lit, gay-friendly South Beach, an area teeming with trendy bars, hot dance clubs, and outrageous cabaret shows. It's here that you'll find the biggest crowds, the longest lines, and the strictest door policies. In fact, if your hotel concierge can't add your name to the VIP list, your best bet is to arrive as early as possible. Some of the most exclusive, most popular South Beach clubs include—but are certainly not limited to—the **Mynt Lounge** (1921 Collins Ave., Miami Beach, 305/532-0727, www.myntlounge.com, 11:30am-5am Thurs.-Sat., cover varies), which has hosted the likes of Paris Hilton, Jennifer Lopez, and Jamie Foxx; **Dream** (1532 Washington Ave., Miami Beach, 305/674-8018 or 786/566-0393, www.dreammia.com, 10pm-5am daily, cover varies), a sexy, spacious nightclub that features themed gatherings, like Eye Candy Saturdays; **Cameo** (1445 Washington Ave., Miami Beach,

786/235-5800, www.cameomiami.com, 11pm-5am Thurs.-Tues., cover varies), an enormous dance club and celebrity magnet housed within a historical art deco-style movie theater; and **Jazid** (1342 Washington Ave., Miami Beach, 305/673-9372, www.jazid.net, 9pm-close daily, $10-20 cover), which, beyond killer drink specials, offers some of the best live funk, soul, jazz, reggae, and world music in the city.

If you're not ready to brave the nightclub crowds in South Beach, head first to the retro **Buck15** (437 Lincoln Rd., Miami Beach, 305/534-5488, 10pm-5am Fri.-Sat., no cover), an underground bar and lounge situated in a second-floor loft space, which promises affordable drinks, no velvet ropes, and plenty of spun music from reggae to rhythm and blues. For additional nightlife ideas, consult periodicals like *The Miami Herald* (www.miamiherald.com), *Miami New Times* (www.miaminewtimes.com), *Ocean Drive* (www.oceandrive.com), and *South Beach Magazine* (www.southbeach-usa.com).

THE ARTS

Cultural enthusiasts will find plenty of live performances in the Miami area. In the downtown performing arts district, for example, the **Adrienne Arsht Center for the Performing Arts of Miami-Dade County** (1300 Biscayne Blvd., Miami, 305/949-6722 or 786/468-2000, www.arshtcenter.org, show times and ticket prices vary) hosts an array of live entertainment, including intimate plays, Broadway musicals, one-act comedies and dramas, opera productions, contemporary dance performances, experimental multimedia shows, cabaret and comedy routines, family-friendly presentations, jazz and rock concerts, and even performances by the **Miami City Ballet** (305/929-7000, www.miamicityballet.org), **Florida Grand Opera** (305/854-1643, www.fgo.org), **New World Symphony** (305/673-3331, www.nws.edu), and **Miami Symphony Orchestra** (305/275-5666, www.themiso.org). To reach the center, you can use the Metrobus, Metrorail, or Metromover; if you plan to drive here, be prepared to pay for self-parking ($15

per vehicle) or valet parking ($25 per vehicle). Although you'll find several eateries in the downtown area, you can also enjoy a pre-show meal at Prelude, the center's on-site restaurant.

To the south, not far from Miami's Bayfront Park, is the **Olympia Theater at the Gusman Center for the Performing Arts** (174 E. Flagler St., Miami, 305/374-2444, www.gusmancenter.org, show times and ticket prices vary). Erected in 1926 as a silent movie theater, this magnificently restored venue is now home to live performances, various screenings, and community events, including shows hosted by the **Miami Lyric Opera** (www.miamilyricopera.org). Other unique venues include **The Fillmore Miami Beach at the Jackie Gleason Theater** (1700 Washington Ave., Miami Beach, 305/673-7300, www.fillmoremb.com, show times and ticket prices vary), which features live concerts, comedy routines, and dance performances, and the recently restored **Actors' Playhouse at the Miracle Theatre** (280 Miracle Mile, Coral Gables, 305/444-9293, www.actorsplayhouse.org, show times and ticket prices vary), presenting main stage performances as well as a children's theater series. To save some money, high school and college students between the ages of 13 and 22 can access various cultural events, festivals, and art exhibitions at affordable prices (typically $5 per ticket) by participating in **Culture Shock Miami** (305/375-1949, www.cultureshockmiami.com), a discounted ticketing program made possible through the **Miami-Dade County Department of Cultural Affairs** (111 NW 1st St., Ste. 625, Miami, 305/375-4634, www.miamidadearts.org).

FESTIVALS AND EVENTS
Art and Cultural Events

Like the Florida Keys, Miami honors its multifaceted culture with a wide array of annual festivals and events—too many, in fact, to list here. Given the city's passion for art, it's no wonder that many of Miami's most popular celebrations focus on architecture and other visual art disciplines. The annual **Art Deco Weekend** (www.artdecoweekend.com, activity fees vary),

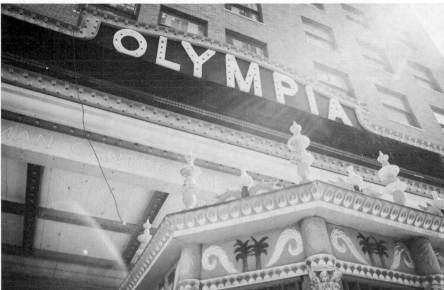

the Olympia Theater at the Gusman Center for the Performing Arts

for instance, lures more than 300,000 people to South Beach in mid-January. Begun in 1976 by the Miami Design Preservation League (305/672-2014, www.mdpl.org), this three-day event helps to cultivate an appreciation for the legendary Art Deco District with an assortment of guided tours, film and lecture series, art and antiques sales, classic automobiles, live music, a fashion show, and other activities.

Other area art festivals include the **Coconut Grove Arts Festival** (305/447-0401, www.cgaf.com, $5-10 pp daily), which attracts a multitude of painters, photographers, jewelry makers, and glass sculptors to the Coconut Grove area for a three-day weekend in mid-February, and the four-day **Art Basel Miami Beach** (www.artbasel.com, ticket prices vary), an extensive show in early December featuring an exclusive selection of more than 250 art galleries from North America, Latin America, Europe, Asia, and Africa. In addition, art lovers will appreciate the six-day **Art Miami** (305/515-8573, www.art-miami.com, one-day pass $25 adults, $10 seniors and students 12-18, free for children under 12), the city's longest-running contemporary and modern art fair, usually held in early December in the Midtown Miami Arts District.

Miami also hosts several cinematic, musical, theatrical, and literary events. Some of these much-anticipated happenings include the 10-day **Miami International Film Festival** (305/237-3456, www.miamifilmfestival.com, show times and ticket prices vary) in early March; the 10-day **Miami Gay and Lesbian Film Festival** (305/751-6305, www.mglff.com, show times and ticket prices vary) in late April or early May; the **Mainly Mozart Festival** (786/468-2251, www.mainlymozart.com, $20 per concert, $100 per series), a six-concert chamber music series in May and June; the three-week **International Ballet Fest of Miami** (305/549-7711, www.internationalballetfestival.org, show times and ticket prices vary) from late August to mid-September; and the eight-day **Miami Book Fair International** (305/237-3258, www.miamibookfair.com, ticket prices vary) in mid-November.

© GREATER MIAMI CONVENTION & VISITORS BUREAU/WWW.GMCVB.COM

a bird's-eye view of the Coconut Grove Arts Festival

Heritage Festivals

In addition, residents and visitors can experience the city's intriguing cultural mosaic through such unique festivals as the month-long **Carnaval Miami** (305/644-8888, www.carnavalmiami.com, entry fees vary), a celebration that takes place in Little Havana from early February to mid-March and features culinary and athletic competitions, live concerts, a domino tournament, and **Calle Ocho,** one of the largest Latino block parties in the country. Since 1976, the two-day **Miami/Bahamas Goombay Festival** (305/448-9501, prices vary), which usually takes place in early June, has honored the Bahamian roots of Coconut Grove with a plethora of authentic cuisine, live Caribbean and African music, and spirited festivities, including a vibrant parade of costumed dancers and musicians. Later in the year, typically on a Saturday in mid-November, thousands of spectators gather on Virginia Key for the free-to-watch **Miami International Dragon Boat Festival** (305/636-0902, www.miamidragon.

com, entry fees apply), an energetic boat race that features several colorfully decorated, Hong Kong-style dragon boats, combining a centuries-old Chinese tradition with modern-day teamwork and aiming to share this fast-growing, international sport with the greater Miami community.

Food and Sporting Events

Of course, the year wouldn't be complete without attending one of Miami's many culinary events or athletic competitions. For die-hard gourmands, it doesn't get much better than the **Food Network South Beach Wine & Food Festival** (877/762-3933, www.sobewineandfoodfest.com, event times and ticket prices vary), a star-studded, four-day event in late February that showcases the talents of the world's most renowned chefs, culinary personalities, and wine producers. Meanwhile, sports lovers and outdoors enthusiasts will appreciate such events as the five-day **Progressive Miami International Boat Show** (www.miamiboatshow.com, $20-35 daily, $85 for five-day pass, free for children under 16) in mid-February and the nine-day **Miccosukee Championship** (305/382-3930,

www.miccosukeechampionship.com), a mid-October golf tournament that usually benefits local charities.

Shopping

A mosaic of cultures and a hotbed of high fashion, the Miami area is indeed a shopper's paradise, offering a wide array of outdoor malls and shopping districts, even in suburbs like Aventura, Kendall, and other surrounding communities. Here are just some of the shopping areas available to residents and visitors.

DOWNTOWN MIAMI

Even Miami's downtown area offers a few intriguing options for shoppers, including the **Bayside Marketplace** (401 Biscayne Blvd., Miami, 305/577-3344, www.baysidemarketplace.com, 10am-10pm Mon.-Thurs.,

10am-11pm Fri.-Sat., 11am-9pm Sun.). Situated alongside lovely Biscayne Bay, this popular outdoor mall features daily live entertainment, varied restaurants, and numerous shops, ranging from Brookstone to Skechers— enough to fill a few hours, if not all day. Besides bicycle, Jet Ski, electric scooter, and wheelchair rentals, other helpful on-site amenities include ATM kiosks, taxi services, foreign currency exchange, sightseeing tours, and visitor information for local attractions.

In Miami's financial district to the south, you'll encounter another classy mall, **The Shops at Mary Brickell Village** (901 S. Miami

© GREATER MIAMI CONVENTION & VISITORS BUREAU/WWW.GMCVB.COM

Located beside Biscayne Bay, Bayside Marketplace features a wide assortment of shops and restaurants.

Ave., Miami, 305/381-6130, www.marybrick-ellvillage.com, 11am-9pm Mon.-Thurs., 11am-10pm Fri.-Sat., noon-6pm Sun.). Featuring three packed floors and an enormous parking structure, this neighborhood mall houses a plethora of curious boutiques, eateries, and other businesses, including wine and cigar shops, a fine seafood restaurant, an Irish pub, a day spa, an LA Fitness gym, even a Publix grocery store.

LITTLE HAVANA

Known as *La Pequeña Habana* in Spanish, Miami's **Little Havana** (www.littlehavana-guide.com), the culturally rich neighborhood west of the city's downtown area, is home to several cigar shops, fruit stands, art galleries, antiques shops, and clothing boutiques. If you only have time for a quick visit, be sure to stop by the **Little Havana Cigar Factory** (1501 SW 8th St., Miami, 305/541-1035, www.littleha-vanacigarfactory.com, 10am-6pm Sun.-Mon., 10am-8pm Tues.-Sat.), which offers a wide array of authentically fermented and matured cigars. Even if you're not a cigar aficionado, you're sure to appreciate the aroma.

SOUTH BEACH

The southern portion of Miami Beach, otherwise known as South Beach, is indeed a magnet for high fashion. In fact, you'll find an incredible array of upscale clothing emporiums, jewelry boutiques, art galleries, beauty salons, and specialty stores on or near **Lincoln Road** (www.lincolnroad.org), including such gems as the **9th Chakra** (1621 Alton Rd., Miami Beach, 305/538-0671, www.9thchakra.com, noon-8pm daily), which offers psychic readings as well as incense, massage oils, crystal jewelry, and other curious gifts, and **Kilwins** (612 Lincoln Rd., Miami Beach, 305/763-8991, www.kilwins.com, noon-2am daily), an outpost of the well-regarded confectioner. In addition, this thoroughfare is home to **The Lincoln Road Outdoor Antique & Collectible Market of Miami Beach** (www.antiquecollectiblemar-ket.com, free) on various Sundays throughout the year. Nearby **Collins Avenue** and **Ocean**

window-shopping along Lincoln Road in South Beach

Drive offer their own share of shopping wonders, such as the **Effusion Gallery** (1130 Ocean Dr., Miami Beach, 305/538-3558, www.effusiongallery.com, 10am-11pm daily), showcasing a curious array of colorful art, from mixed-media clocks and whimsical mirrors to three-dimensional glass paintings and surreal celebrity portraits.

For more information about shopping opportunities in South Beach, consult *South Beach Magazine* (www.southbeach-usa.com).

COCONUT GROVE

Situated southwest of downtown Miami, Coconut Grove is a family-friendly shopping enclave, ideal for a stroll in pleasant weather. One popular gathering place is **CocoWalk** (3015 Grand Ave., Coconut Grove, 305/444-0777, www.cocowalk.net, 10am-10pm Sun.-Thurs., 10am-11pm Fri.-Sat.), a Mediterranean-style, open-air complex that features several shops and restaurants, from Victoria's Secret to The Cheesecake Factory, plus late-night bars like Fat Tuesday, known for its New Orleans-style daiquiris. Other amenities include covered parking, secure bicycle racks, ATM kiosks, and 24-hour security.

CORAL GABLES

Northwest of Coconut Grove lies Coral Gables, an affluent, well-manicured village that features an array of sophisticated shopping options. One such option is the **Village of Merrick Park** (358 San Lorenzo Ave., Coral Gables, 305/529-0200, www.villageofmerrickpark.

com, 10am-9pm Mon.-Sat., noon-6pm Sun.), a cluster of fine shops and eateries centered around a lovely urban garden. Visitors here can peruse shoes at Cole Haan, jewelry at Tiffany & Co., cookware at Williams-Sonoma, and stylish apparel at department stores like Nordstrom and Neiman Marcus. In addition, you can visit **Equinox** (370 San Lorenzo Ave., 786/497-8200, www.equinox.com, 5:30am-11pm Mon.-Thurs., 5:30am-10pm Fri., 8am-8pm Sat.-Sun.) for a range of facials, body treatments, and massage therapies and afterward enjoy a casual meal at the **Yard House** (320 San Lorenzo Ave., 305/447-9273, www.yardhouse.com, 11am-12:30am Sun.-Thurs., 11am-1:30am Fri.-Sat.), which boasts an incredible selection of draft beer.

Not surprisingly, Coral Gables offers more than just a high-class mall experience. In the quaint downtown area, several boutiques, salons, art galleries, outdoor cafés, and convenient parking lots make up the **Miracle Mile** (www.shopcoralgables.com), a four-block stretch between Douglas and Le Jeune Roads as well as several surrounding streets. Of the many offerings here, you'll find classy lingerie at **Silvia's Corset Shoppe** (256 Giralda Ave., Coral Gables, 305/446-8484, www.silviascorsetshoppe.com, 10am-5:30pm Mon.-Sat.) and pricey hair-styling services, facials, and manicures at the **Avant-Garde Salon & Spa** (155 Miracle Mile, Coral Gables, 305/442-8136, www.avantgardesalonandspa.com, 10am-6pm Mon., 10am-7pm Tues. and Sat., 10am-8pm Wed.-Fri.).

Sports and Recreation

SPECTATOR SPORTS

Fans of spectator sports can't go wrong in Miami, where several professional teams are on display. From September to December, for instance, football fans can watch the **Miami Dolphins** (888/346-7849, www.miamidolphins.com, game times and ticket prices vary) take on other NFL teams at the **Sun Life Stadium** (347 Don Shula Dr., Miami Gardens, 305/943-8000, www.sunlifestadium.com), and from April to September, baseball lovers can flock to the brand-new **Marlins Park** (501 Marlins Way, Miami) to cheer on the **Miami Marlins** (305/480-1300 or 877/627-5467, http://miami.marlins.mlb.com, game times and ticket prices vary). From October to April basketball fans can catch the **Miami Heat** (786/777-4328, www.nba.com/heat, game times and ticket prices vary) at the

AmericanAirlines Arena (601 Biscayne Blvd., Miami, 786/777-1000, www.aaarena.com), and even hockey fans will be happy in the Magic City, where the **Florida Panthers** (954/835-7825, http://panthers.nhl.com, game times and ticket prices vary) typically play between October and April at the **BB&T Center** (1 Panther Pkwy., Sunrise, 954/835-7000, www.thebbtcenter.com).

GOLF

While the Florida Keys offer a few public golf courses, you'll find even more options in the Miami area, including the **Biltmore Golf Course** (1200 Anastasia Ave., Coral Gables, 305/460-5364, www.biltmorehotel.com, 7am-6pm daily in winter, 7:30am-7:30pm Mon.-Fri., 7am-7:30pm Sat.-Sun. in summer, $50-189 pp with cart), a well-landscaped 18-hole course that surrounds the legendary Biltmore Hotel and features a clubhouse, bar, and restaurant. Originally created in 1925 by Scottish designer Donald Ross and restored in 2007 by architect Brian Silva, this course has lured numerous movie stars, athletes, and dignitaries over the years.

Meanwhile, the **Miami Beach Golf Club** (2301 Alton Rd., Miami Beach, 305/532-3350, www.miamibeachgolfclub.com, 7am-sunset daily, $100-200 pp with cart) requires proper golf attire, offers rental shoes ($20 per pair) and clubs ($60 per set), and provides an on-site restaurant. Tee times can be reserved up to five days in advance. The **Miccosukee Golf & Country Club** (6401 Kendale Lakes Dr., Miami, 305/382-3930, www.miccosukee.com, 6:30am-10pm daily, $40-65 pp) is a picturesque course that features 27 challenging holes, a full-service golf shop, a sports bar, and an Olympic-size swimming pool.

HIKING

Although the Everglades offer more opportunities for long-distance hikers, the Miami area

Marlins Park, home to the Miami Marlins

MIAMI SPORTS ON SCREEN

Hot, sexy, and dangerous, Miami has long been a favorite backdrop for filmmakers and television producers. True, it's the criminal side that's most often on display—as evidenced by films like *Scarface* (1983), *The Mean Season* (1985), *Miami Blues* (1990), *Bad Boys* (1995), *Transporter 2* (2005), and *Miami Vice* (2006)—and though the city's vibrant nightlife scene and beautiful beach subculture also make their share of appearances, even shows on the small screen—including *Miami Vice* (1984-1990), *CSI: Miami* (2002-2012), *Dexter* (2006 present), *Burn Notice* (2007-present), and *Magic City* (2012-present)—seem to focus a lot of energy on Miami's notorious criminal activities, from murder to drug trafficking. Beyond beaches, clubs, and crime, however, the Magic City is also known for its vigorous professional sports teams—a fact that two memorable, if completely different, movies have explored.

In *Ace Ventura: Pet Detective* (1994), a zany comedy co-written by Jack Bernstein, director Tom Shadyac, and star Jim Carrey, the story focuses on an outrageous detective (Carrey) who specializes in animal-related cases—that is, reuniting owners with their lost or stolen pets. When he's hired to find the Miami Dol-

phins' misplaced mascot, a bottlenose dolphin named Snowflake, hilarity and wacky adventures ensue, and Ace soon finds himself tussling with a shark, facing down a transvestite, and trying to save quarterback Dan Marino from an untimely end.

Meanwhile, in *Any Given Sunday* (1999), a bold, energetic film co-written by John Logan and director Oliver Stone, the focus is again on football. Filmed at locations throughout Miami, including the now-demolished Orange Bowl stadium, this brash sports drama offers a behind-the-scenes look at the life-and-death struggles between an aging coach (Al Pacino), a quarterback legend (Dennis Quaid), an arrogant rookie (Jamie Foxx), and the young female owner (Cameron Diaz) of a fictitious Miami football team known as the Miami Sharks.

Appropriately, Dan Marino, perhaps the most famous athlete to be associated with the Magic City, has made his mark on both films. Besides co-starring in *Ace Ventura*, he also lends his spirit to *Any Given Sunday*, albeit in a not-so-obvious way. After all, the house where Jack "Cap" Rooney (Quaid's character) and his family live is actually Marino's real-life home.

---

definitely features a few choice spots. On Key Biscayne, for instance, you'll find several scenic nature trails on the west side of **Bill Baggs Cape Florida State Park** (1200 S. Crandon Blvd., Key Biscayne, 305/361-5811, www.floridastateparks.org/capeflorida, 8am-sunset daily, $8 vehicles with 2-8 passengers and day use boaters, $4 motorcycles and single-occupant vehicles, $2 pedestrians, bikers, and extra passengers). You can also utilize the hiking trails at **Oleta River State Park** (3400 NE 163rd St., North Miami, 305/919-1846, www.floridastateparks.org/oletariver, 8am-sunset daily, $6 vehicles with 2-8 passengers, $4 motorcycles and single-occupant vehicles, $2 pedestrians, bikers, and extra passengers), situated at the northern end of Biscayne Bay and considered Florida's largest urban park.

BIKING AND SKATING

If you favor biking, you'll find no shortage of opportunities in the Miami area, especially in places like **Oleta River State Park** (3400 NE 163rd St., North Miami, 305/919-1846, www.floridastateparks.org/oletariver, 8am-sunset daily, $6 vehicles with 2-8 passengers, $4 motorcycles and single-occupant vehicles, $2 pedestrians, bikers, and extra passengers) at the northern end of Biscayne Bay, with miles of off-road biking trails, ranging from novice to challenging. Luckily, bicycles can be rented from several different outfitters, including the **Miami Beach Bicycle Center** (601 5th St., Miami Beach, 305/674-0150, www.bikemiamibeach. com, 10am-7pm Mon.-Sat., 10am-5pm Sun., starting at $5 hourly, $14 daily, $60 weekly), which provides a variety of cruisers, hybrids, mountain bikes, tandems, and other bicycles, plus the use of a lock, helmet, and basket with each rental. Farther south, **Key Cycling** (328 Crandon Blvd., Ste. 121, Key Biscayne, 305/361-0061, www.keycycling.com, 10am-7pm Mon.-Fri., 10am-6pm Sat., 10am-3pm Sun., $24-50 daily, $80-200 weekly) features both mountain and hybrid options.

Beyond biking, a popular activity here is inline skating, especially in South Beach and along Biscayne Bay. If you haven't brought your own skates, stop by **Fritz's Skate, Bike & Surf** (1620 Washington Ave., Miami Beach, 305/532-1954, www.fritzsmiamibeach.com, 10am-9pm Mon.-Sat., 10am-8pm Sun.) that has offered the largest selection of inline skates, skateboards, and bicycles in South Beach since 1989. With a $100 refundable deposit, you can rent skates for $10 hourly, $24 daily, and $69 weekly. Protective gear is included with all skate rentals, and lessons are available. Bicycle rentals cost the same as skate rentals and include a lock and a helmet, though a $200 deposit is required.

FISHING AND BOATING

As with the rest of southern Florida, fishing and boating are both popular activities in the Miami area. If you're interested in deep-sea fishing, consider boarding the *Jumanji* (401 Biscayne Blvd., Miami, 786/486-7200, www.fishjumanji.com, rates vary), a 42-foot charter boat that offers year-round opportunities to snag a variety of fish, including kingfish, tuna, marlin, wahoo, swordfish, snapper, and grouper. Other available charter boats include the 41-foot *Old Hat* (305/773-0700, www.oldhat.com, rates vary) and the 57-foot *Spellbound* (305/785-0552, www.reeladventurecharters.com, $650-2,000 per half-day trip), both of which are located in the **Haulover Park Marina** (10800 Collins Ave., Miami Beach) and offer the chance to catch a variety of game fish, from amberjack to hammerhead shark.

If you'd rather bring your own boat to Miami, there's no shortage of boat ramps and marina slips. To rent a boat, head to Monty's Marina, where **American WaterSports** (2560 S. Bayshore Dr., Coconut Grove, 305/856-6559, www.americanwatersports.us, 10am-sunset daily) offers a range of powerboats ($140-180 hourly, $400-540 per half day, $600-900 daily).

CANOEING AND KAYAKING

Much like the Everglades and the Florida Keys, the Miami area is surrounded by water—specifically, Biscayne Bay and beyond that the Atlantic Ocean. So canoeists and kayakers will find no shortage of opportunities to explore these shimmering waters. **EcoAdventures** (305/365-3018, www.miamidade.gov/ecoadventures), for example, offers guided trips for paddling enthusiasts, including a leisurely canoe adventure ($33 pp) along the historical Coral Gables Waterway, a kayaking excursion ($40 pp) around Key Biscayne, and a canoe tour ($30 adults, $20 children 9-14) from the **Deering Estate at Cutler** (16701 SW 72nd Ave., Miami, 305/235-1668, www.deeringestate.com, 10am-5pm daily, $12 adults, $7 children 4-14, free for children under 4) to seven-acre Chicken Key.

If you'd rather venture out on your own, you can easily rent a vessel from several helpful outfitters, including the **Blue Moon Outdoor Center** (3400 NE 163rd St., North Miami Beach, 305/957-3040, www.bluemoonoutdoor.com, 9am-sunset Mon.-Fri., 8am-sunset Sat.-Sun.), which provides both kayaks ($22-32 for 90 min.) and canoes ($36 for 90 min.) in **Oleta River State Park.** Full-day rentals are also available.

DIVING AND SNORKELING

Although most diving enthusiasts head straight to Biscayne National Park or Florida Keys National Marine Sanctuary, Miami also offers helpful outfitters and operators. One such company is the **South Beach Dive and Surf Center** (850 Washington Ave., Miami Beach, 305/531-6110, www.southbeachdivers.com, 9am-7pm Mon.-Sat., 10am-6pm Sun.), a PADI 5 Star facility whose courses include an introduction class ($225 pp), a divemaster

© GREATER MIAMI CONVENTION & VISITORS BUREAU/WWW.GMCVB.COM

Paddlers favor the peaceful waterways of Oleta River State Park.

class ($695 pp), and a digital underwater photography class ($395 pp)—plus snorkeling ($65 pp) and diving trips ($85-120 pp) in the waters near Key Largo. Meanwhile, **Diver's Paradise** (4000 Crandon Blvd., Key Biscayne, 305/361-3483, www.keydivers.com, 10am-5pm Tues.-Fri., 8am-2pm Sat.-Sun.) has been assisting area divers since 1979 and features daily diving and snorkeling trips ($60 pp) to area wrecks and coral reefs as well as diving classes and equipment rentals.

SPAS AND YOGA

The Miami area features an array of rejuvenating spas, including those found at resorts like The Biltmore Hotel in Coral Gables. If you're not staying at such a resort, you'll find day spas in the vicinity, too. The **Uhma Organic Spa & Green Shop** (726 6th St., Miami Beach, 305/695-0996, www.uhmaspa.com, noon-7pm

Mon., 10am-7pm Tues.-Sat.), for instance, provides an ecofriendly urban sanctuary, where guests can enjoy an array of facials ($100-145 pp), body scrubs and wraps ($50-120 pp), massages ($65-185 pp), water therapies ($50-55 pp), yoga treatments ($170-225 pp), and other services.

The Miami area also boasts several opportunities for yoga enthusiasts. One curious option is the Tina Hills Pavilion in **Bayfront Park** (301 N. Biscayne Blvd., Miami, 305/358-7550, www.bayfrontparkmiami.com, sunrise-sunset daily, no entrance fee), where a certified yoga instructor offers free **yoga classes** (6pm Mon. and Wed., 9am Sat.) for beginners as well as advanced participants. All students must be at least 18 years old, and registration is based on a first-come, first-served basis, up to 40 participants. Everyone must bring his or her own yoga mat, water, and towel.

Accommodations

In general, staying overnight in the Miami area can be an expensive enterprise, especially if you'd prefer to stay in a safer, more tourist-friendly neighborhood like South Beach or Coral Gables. For more information about Miami's accommodations, consult **Miami Beach 411** (1521 Alton Rd., Ste. 233, Miami Beach, 305/754-2206 or 888/999-8931, www.miamibeach411.com).

DOWNTOWN MIAMI

While downtown Miami isn't known for the same swankiness that South Beach promises, a few premium options do exist in this part of the city. The **Four Seasons Hotel Miami** (1435 Brickell Ave., Miami, 305/358-3535, www.fourseasons.com/miami, rooms $290-650 d, suites $410-1,600) offers 221 stylish rooms and suites between the 20th and 29th floors of a 70-story tower made of glass and granite, overlooking beautiful Biscayne Bay. Besides a world-class spa and a magnificent pool, the hotel provides two amazing restaurants, a stylish lounge, and high-speed Internet access.

To the north, the **EPIC Hotel** (270 Biscayne Blvd., Miami, 305/424-5226 or 866/760-3742, www.epichotel.com, rooms $240-430 d, suites $400-770) guarantees an equally high-class experience. In addition to its 411 luxurious rooms and suites, in-house spa, amazing pools, and marina services, EPIC is also one of the few pet-friendly lodgings in downtown Miami.

SOUTH BEACH

If you're looking for a hip, youthful vibe, then South Beach is definitely the place for you. In this famous Miami Beach neighborhood, you'll find several classic options, including the **Z Ocean Hotel** (1437 Collins Ave., Miami Beach, 305/672-4554 or 866/418-1269, www.zoceanhotelsouthbeach.com, suites $290-500), which features 79 roomy suites, a private glass-bottom pool, rooftop hot tubs, and the Z Ocean Beach Club. **The Betsy Hotel** (1440

Ocean Dr., Miami Beach, 305/531-6100 or 866/792-3879, www.thebetsyhotel.com, rooms $350-650 d, suites $470-1,090), meanwhile, is a historical hotel featuring 63 rooms and suites. Located beside the beach, this intimate hotel also offers wireless Internet access, a full-range spa, two unique bars, and the BLT Steak, Laurent Tourondel's modern American steakhouse. Another winning option is the **Majestic Hotel South Beach** (660 Ocean Dr., Miami Beach, 305/455-3270 or 800/403-6274, www.majesticsouthbeach.com, $120-180 d), one of the most affordable lodgings in South Beach, despite being only steps away from this neighborhood's world-famous beach.

Farther north lies one of the most well-known hotels in Miami Beach—if not all of Miami. The **Fontainebleau Miami Beach** (4441 Collins Ave., Miami Beach, 305/538-2000 or 800/548-8886, www.fontainebleau.com, rooms $360-660 d, suites $560-4,265) has featured prominently in films like *The Bellboy* (1960) and *Goldfinger* (1964) and offers unparalleled luxury all year round. Following a $1 billion renovation and expansion, this enormous oceanfront resort now offers more than 1,500 airy, well-appointed rooms and suites, seven unique restaurants, three bars and nightclubs, a stylish pool area with private cabanas, a gym that overlooks the pool, and the 40,000-square-foot **Lapis Spa & Salon** (4441 Collins Ave., Miami Beach, 866/750-4772, www.fontainebleau.com, 9:30am-6:30pm Sun.-Fri., 9:30am-7:30pm Sat.).

COCONUT GROVE TO CORAL GABLES

Situated within an exclusive waterfront enclave of upscale restaurants, shopping, and nightlife, the stunning **Mayfair Hotel & Spa** (3000 Florida Ave., Coconut Grove, 305/441-0000 or 800/433-4555, www.mayfairhotelandspa.com, suites $180-260) contains a variety of luxurious suites, all of which have marble bathrooms,

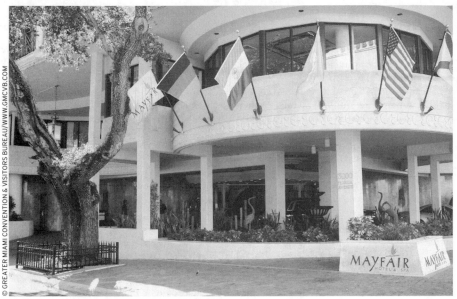

Coconut Grove's Mayfair Hotel & Spa

Japanese soaking tubs, flat-screen plasma TVs, and wireless Internet access. In addition to its convenient proximity to Miami's beaches and downtown area, the Mayfair features a 4,500-square-foot spa that provides guests with first-class massages and body treatments.

If you do plan to stay in the Miami area before heading to the Keys—even for a night—you simply must consider **(The Biltmore Hotel** (1200 Anastasia Ave., Coral Gables, 855/454-0196, www.biltmorehotel.com, rooms $310-460 d, suites $440-2,200), a historical 150-acre resort that features a vibrant, Mediterranean-style structure, topped by a magnificent tower and encompassing 275 sumptuous rooms and suites. Other on-site amenities include a championship golf course, an incredible spa and fitness center, 10 tennis courts, a world-famous pool area, and several celebrated restaurants.

CAMPING

Miami may not be known for its camping options, but that doesn't mean you won't find at least one here: **Bill Baggs Cape Florida State Park** (1200 S. Crandon Blvd., Key Biscayne, 305/361-5811, www.floridastateparks.org/cape-florida, 8am-sunset daily, $8 vehicles with 2-8 passengers and day-use boaters, $4 motorcycles and single-occupant vehicles, $2 pedestrians, bikers, and extra passengers). For a daily fee ($6 adults, $1 children), large groups can stay in a primitive campground that offers a restroom, showers, barbecue grills, picnic tables, benches, tent platforms, and accessible parking. Boaters can anchor overnight in No Name Harbor ($20 daily), where during operating hours they'll have access to restrooms, coin-operated laundry machines, a rinse shower, a picnic shelter, a free pump-out for all boats, and yummy meals at the Boater's Grill.

Food

Given the varied cultural influences in Miami, you'll find that the cuisine here ranges from Creole dishes in Miami's Little Haiti to *cubanos* (Cuban sandwiches) in Little Havana to fresh seafood and "Floribbean" cuisine throughout the city. For more information about available eateries in the Miami area, consult the **Miami DiningGuide** (www.miami.diningguide.com).

DOWNTOWN MIAMI

Just west of I-95 is an unassuming joint called **Peoples Bar-B-Que** (360 NW 8th St., Miami, 305/373-8080, 11:30am-midnight Mon.-Fri., 11:30am-1am Sat., 1pm-9pm Sun., $2-23), which as the name implies, serves excellent, affordable Southern-style barbecue. Since 1962 regulars have flocked to this casual, friendly place (even when it was in a different spot) for mouthwatering fried chicken, barbecue ribs, collard greens, cornbread, and other Southern staples. Unfortunately, it's not located in the safest part of town.

If you're looking for a fancier meal, you should head south to **Azul** (500 Brickell Key Dr., Miami, 305/913-8358, www.mandarinoriental.com, 7pm-11pm Tues.-Sat., $35-150) at the Mandarin Oriental hotel. Enhanced by gorgeous bay views and an incredible wine list, this elegant restaurant features Chef Jacob Anaya's diverse blend of New American, Asian, and European flavors, as evidenced in ever-revolving dishes like grilled Spanish octopus with tomato caviar and lobster pot pie with chanterelle mushrooms and foie gras. Even the desserts here are multicultural delights, including passion fruit *panna cotta* with raspberry sorbet and pumpkin butter cheesecake with bourbon ice cream. Reservations are highly recommended.

LITTLE HAVANA

In a neighborhood composed predominantly of Cuban Americans and Cuban exiles, you'll find plenty of authentic delicacies from *cafecito* (Cuban coffee without milk) and *cortadito*

(Cuban coffee with steamed milk) to *cubanos,* or flattened, grilled sandwiches made with sliced ham, slow-roasted pork, Swiss cheese, and pickles, popularized by Cuban immigrants who settled in Miami in the early 1900s.

For a romantic meal, head west from downtown via U.S. 41, toward **Casa Juancho** (2436 SW 8th St., Miami, 305/642-2452, www.casajuancho.com, noon-midnight Sun.-Thurs., noon-1am Fri.-Sat., $24-36), where the Spanish-style menu includes various steaks, paella dishes, and fish and shellfish entrées, such as *salmón con vieiras al albariño,* or fresh salmon and scallops in a reduced albariño wine and saffron sauce. Live music from La Tuna Universitaria de Oviedo (7:30 and 9:30pm daily) and accordionist Lino (8:30 and 10:30pm daily) enhances the romantic atmosphere. Unlike other eateries in Little Havana, Casa Juancho requires dressy casual or business attire; hats, shorts, and T-shirts are not allowed, and reservations are recommended.

Farther west along U.S. 41, the ◖**Versailles Restaurant** (3555 SW 8th St., Miami, 305/444-0240, www.versaillesrestaurant.com, 8am-1am Mon.-Thurs., 8am-2:30am Fri., 8am-3:30am Sat., 9am-1am Sun., $4-29) may sound—and even look—like a French restaurant, but it's actually been one of Miami's best Cuban-Caribbean restaurants since its opening in 1971. Given the frequent crowds here, it seems that the secret has long been out. Although its popularity makes parking at this restaurant rather difficult, it's a wonderful place to sample a traditional *cubano* or the fantastic garlic-roasted chicken. One tip is to take advantage of its late hours when parking is usually less of a hassle.

SOUTH BEACH

This trendy island neighborhood offers a plethora of unique eateries, including the ◖ **Van Dyke Cafe** (846 Lincoln Rd., Miami Beach, 305/534-3600, www.thevandykecafe.com,

Little Havana is an ideal place to sample Cuban coffee.

8am-2am daily, $8-30), which prepares inexpensive, diverse dishes like cheese blintzes and crêpes for breakfast, grilled mahimahi sandwiches for lunch, and fish and chips for dinner. After your meal, head upstairs to listen to some live jazz, blues, funk, Latin, or Afro-Caribbean music.

The fun, nostalgic **Jerry's Famous Deli** (1450 Collins Ave., Miami Beach, 305/532-8030, www.jerrysfamousdeli.com, 24 hours daily, $8-45) offers well over 600 items on its impressive menu, which might make it difficult for you to decide what to eat. First established as a chain in Southern California, this casual restaurant offers almost anything you'd like, anytime you want—whether you crave eggs Benedict for dinner or a Mexican pizza for breakfast.

Housed in an art deco-style dining car, the casual **11th Street Diner** (1065 Washington Ave., Miami Beach, 305/534-6373, www.eleventhstreetdiner.com, 24 hours daily, $4-19) serves traditional comfort food, from the Monte Cristo sandwich to Argentinian skirt steak—even in the wee hours. Farther south, **Joe's Stone Crab** (11 Washington Ave., Miami Beach, 305/673-0365, www.joesstonecrab.com, 5pm-10pm Sun.-Mon., 11:30am-2pm and 5pm-10pm Tues.-Thurs., 11:30am-2pm and 5pm-11pm Fri.-Sat. mid-Oct.-mid-May, shorter hours in summer, $6-40) may specialize in stone crabs and other locally caught seafood, but this popular eatery also features some amazing fried chicken—the dish most favored by former President Bill Clinton whenever he visits. Established in 1913, Joe's is actually one of the oldest restaurants in Miami.

COCONUT GROVE TO CORAL GABLES

For contemporary Latin American cuisine, head to the **Jaguar Ceviche Spoon Bar & Latam Grill** (3067 Grand Ave., Coconut Grove, 305/444-0216, www.jaguarspot.com, 11:30am-11pm Mon.-Fri., 11am-11:30pm Sat., 11am-11pm Sun., $9-33), a colorful eatery that offers a variety of ceviche, grilled meat, and

© GREATER MIAMI CONVENTION & VISITORS BUREAU/WWW.GMCVB.COM

the Van Dyke Cafe in South Beach

seafood dishes. If you appreciate finely crafted beer, then you simply must visit the **Titanic Brewing Company** (5813 Ponce de Leon Blvd., Coral Gables, 305/668-1742, www.titanicbrewery.com, 11:30am-1am Sun.-Thurs., 11:30am-2am Fri.-Sat., $8-20), where you can pair a wonderful sampler tray of microbrews with any number of tasty dishes, including steamed mussels, Florida Cobb salad, crawfish and andouille bisque, shrimp wraps, or 'Bama burgers. The nautical decor and scrumptious desserts, from rum cake to key lime pie, only add to the fun. The kitchen shuts down an hour before closing time.

Information and Services

INFORMATION
Tourism and Government Offices
For brochures, maps, and other information about Miami, stop by the **Greater Miami Convention & Visitors Bureau** (GMCVB, 701 Brickell Ave., Ste. 2700, Miami, 305/539-3000 or 800/933-8448, www.miamiandbeaches.com, 8:30am-6pm Mon.-Fri.). In addition, you'll find more localized tourism bureaus, such as the **Miami Beach Visitor and Convention Authority** (1701 Meridian Ave., Ste. 402A, Miami Beach, 305/673-7050, www.miamibeachvca.com, 9am-5pm Mon.-Fri.), the **Miami Beach Chamber of Commerce** (1920 Meridian Ave., Miami Beach, 305/674-1300, www.miamibeachchamber.com, 9am-6pm Mon.-Fri.), the **Miami Beach Latin Chamber of Commerce** (510 Lincoln Rd., Miami Beach, 305/674-1414, www.miamibeach.org, 9am-6pm Mon.-Fri.), the **Coconut Grove Chamber of Commerce** (2820 McFarlane Rd., Coconut Grove, 305/444-7270, www.coconutgrovechamber.com, 10am-4pm Mon. and Thurs.-Fri., 1pm-4pm Tues.), the **Coral Gables**

Chamber of Commerce (224 Catalonia Ave., Coral Gables, 305/446-1657, www.coralgableschamber.org, 8:30am-5pm Mon.-Thurs., 8:30am-4pm Fri.), and the **Key Biscayne Chamber of Commerce & Visitors Center** (88 W. McIntyre St., Ste. 100, Key Biscayne, 305/361-5207, www.keybiscaynechamber.org, chamber 9am-5pm Mon.-Fri., visitor center 24 hours daily). If you're interested in gay-related activities, accommodations, shops, bars, and restaurants, consult www.miamigaytravel.com or the **Miami-Dade Gay & Lesbian Chamber of Commerce** (1130 Washington Ave., 1st Fl., Miami Beach, 305/673-4440, www.gaybizmiami.com), which oversees the **LGBT Visitor Center** (305/397-8914, www.gogaymiami.com, 9am-6pm Mon.-Fri.) at the same address. For government-related issues, consult the comprehensive websites of **Miami-Dade County** (www.miamidade.gov), the **City of Miami** (www.miamigov.com), the **City of Miami Beach** (www.miamibeachfl.gov), and the **City of Coral Gables** (www.coralgables.com).

Media

Like any major U.S. city, Miami offers a number of helpful periodicals, including *The Miami Herald* (www.miamiherald.com) and the *Miami New Times* (www.miaminewtimes.com), which offer comprehensive listings of bars, restaurants, live music venues, art shows, current movies, and upcoming events. In addition, the monthly magazine *Ocean Drive* (www.oceandrive.com) offers a look at the latest trends in fashion, beauty, art, dining, travel, and entertainment.

In Miami, you'll also have access to several radio stations, including **Y100** (www.y100.com), which offers an assortment of popular music, from rock to hip-hop. Major television stations in town include **CBSMiami** (http://miami.cbslocal.com), **WSVN 7NEWS** (www.wsvn.com), and **NBC 6 South Florida** (www.nbcmiami.com).

SERVICES
Money

For banking needs, stop by the **First Bank of**

Miami (800/831-5763, www.firstbankmiami.com), which has five branches in the Miami area, including one in downtown Miami (235 SE 1st St., 305/579-4933) and another in Coral Gables (255 Aragon Ave., 305/444-4960).

Mail

For shipping, faxing, copying, and other business-related services, visit **The UPS Store** (www.theupsstore.com), with several locations in the Miami area, including one in downtown Miami (247 SW 8th St., 305/858-1221, 8:30am-7pm Mon.-Fri., 9:30am-3pm Sat.) and another in Coral Gables (1825 Ponce de Leon Blvd., 305/441-7161, 8:30am-7pm Mon.-Fri., 10am-5pm Sat.). **PostNet** (13550 SW 120th St., Ste. 406A, Miami, 786/293-9804, www.postnet.com, 9am-6pm Mon.-Fri.) offers similar services in the Miami area, but of course, you'll find more than four dozen **post offices** (800/275-8777, www.usps.com) in the greater metropolitan area, including one in Coconut Grove (3191 Grand Ave., 305/529-6700, 8:30am-5pm Mon.-Fri., 8:30am-2pm Sat.) and another in Coral Gables (251 Valencia Ave., 305/443-2532, 8:30am-6pm Mon.-Fri., 8:30am-2pm Sat.).

Groceries and Supplies

For groceries, fresh seafood, and other supplies, head to **Winn-Dixie** (3401 NW 18th Ave., Miami, 305/634-4492, www.winndixie.com, 7am-midnight daily), which houses an on-site pharmacy (305/634-1432, 8am-8pm Mon.-Fri., 9am-6pm Sat., 10am-5pm Sun.). For other pharmacy needs, stop by **Walgreens** (1 E. Flagler St., Miami, 305/371-5868, www.walgreens.com, 7am-7pm Mon.-Sat., 9am-5pm Sun.), which also offers photo processing, fresh coffee, and baked goods. Another option, **Publix** (800/242-1227, www.publix.com) provides plenty of grocery stores in the Miami area, including one near Little Haiti (4870 Biscayne Blvd., Miami, 305/573-8601, 7am-11pm daily).

Laundry

If you need to wash some clothes while you're

in town, laundry facilities include **Sudsies Dry Cleaners & Laundry** (6786 Collins Ave., Miami Beach, 305/864-3279 or 888/898-7837, www.sudsies.com, 7am-8pm Mon.-Fri., 8am-6pm Sat., 9am-3pm Sun.), which even offers pickup and delivery service (7am-7pm Mon.-Sat.).

Internet Access

If you need to access the Internet and your hotel doesn't offer such services, head to the **Planet Linux Caffe** (1430 Ponce de Leon Blvd., Coral Gables, 786/294-3947, www.planetlinuxcaffe. com, 10am-10pm Mon.-Fri., 9am-8pm Mon.-Sat.), a unique coffee shop and "hacker space" that offers high-speed Internet access, informative tech-centric workshops, and yes, scrumptious smoothies, sandwiches, and desserts.

Emergency Services

In case of an emergency that requires police, fire, or ambulance services, dial **911** from any cell or public phone. For medical assistance, you can also consult one of several hospitals in the greater metropolitan area, such as **Mercy Hospital** (3663 S. Miami Ave., Miami, 305/854-4400, www.mercymiami.com), the **University of Miami Hospital** (1400 NW 12th Ave., Miami, 305/689-5000, www.umiami-hospital.com), and the **North Shore Medical Center** (1100 NW 95th St., Miami, 305/835-6000, www.northshoremedical.com). For non-emergency assistance, contact the **Miami-Dade Police Department** (9105 NW 25th St., Doral, 305/476-5423, www.miamidade.gov/mdpd, 8am-5pm Mon.-Fri.), and for general county info, dial **311.**

Getting There and Around

GETTING THERE
By Air

To reach Miami by plane, you can fly directly into **Miami International Airport** (MIA, 2100 NW 42nd Ave., Miami, 305/876-7000, www.miami-airport.com), which is located about seven miles west of downtown Miami, or opt for **Fort Lauderdale-Hollywood International Airport** (FLL, 100 Terminal Dr., Fort Lauderdale, 866/435-9355, www.bro-ward.org/airport), which lies roughly 25 miles north of downtown Miami. Both accommodate major air carriers, including **American Airlines** (800/433-7300, www.aa.com), **Air Canada** (888/247-2262, www.aircanada.com), **Caribbean Airlines** (800/920-4225, www.ca-ribbean-airlines.com), and **Avianca** (800/284-2622, www.avianca.com). From either airport, you can rent a vehicle through such agencies as **Avis** (800/633-3469, www.avis.com), **Budget** (800/218-7992, www.budget.com), **Enterprise** (800/261-7331, www.enterprise.com), **Hertz** (800/654-3131, www.hertz.com), or **Thrifty** (800/847-4389, www.thrifty.com).

By Bus or Train

If you don't have a vehicle of your own and would prefer not to fly, you can certainly take a bus into the area. **Greyhound** (800/231-2222, www.greyhound.com) offers service to several different stations, including the **Fort Lauderdale Greyhound Station** (515 NE 3rd St., Fort Lauderdale, 954/764-6551, 5:30am-1:30am daily), the **North Miami Beach Greyhound Station** (16000 NW 7th Ave., North Miami, 305/688-7277, 5am-1am daily), the **Miami Greyhound Station** (4111 NW 27th St., Miami, 305/871-1810, 24 hours daily), and the **American Service Station** (10801 Caribbean Blvd., Cutler Bay, 305/296-9072, 8am-6pm daily).

As an alternative, you can choose to travel here by train. **Amtrak** (800/872-7245, www.amtrak.com) offers service via its Silver Service/Palmetto route. The three southernmost stations include **Fort Lauderdale** (FTL, 200 SW 21st Ter., Fort Lauderdale, 8:15am-6:15pm daily), **Hollywood** (HOL, 3001 Hollywood Blvd., Hollywood, 8am-6:20pm daily), and

Miami (MIA, 8303 NW 37th Ave., Miami, 6:30am-9pm daily).

Transport from Airports and Stations

If you arrive in the Miami-Fort Lauderdale area by plane, bus, or train, you can easily rent a car or hire a taxicab or shuttle service to reach your destination. From the lower arrival level at Miami International Airport (MIA), for instance, **SuperShuttle** (305/871-2000 or 954/764-1700, www.supershuttle.com) offers one-way trips to destinations like downtown Miami ($15-21 pp), Coconut Grove ($15-22 pp), Coral Gables ($12-27 pp), South Beach ($20-24 pp), and Key Biscayne ($25-27 pp). Each additional passenger (in the same group) will run about $5-25 extra, depending on the destination. Most taxicabs, which you can also hire from the lower arrival level at MIA, will run about $22 for a one-way trip to downtown Miami, Coconut Grove, and the University of Miami in Coral Gables. A trip to South Beach will cost roughly $32 or to Key Biscayne around $41.

From Fort Lauderdale-Hollywood International Airport (FLL), a taxicab ride to downtown Miami, South Beach, or Key Biscayne will run about $67-80. **GO Airport Shuttle** (954/561-8888 or 800/244-8252, www.go-airportshuttle.com) also offers shared ride service from FLL to destinations throughout Miami, including South Beach ($24 pp), downtown Miami ($30 pp), Coconut Grove ($34.50 pp), Coral Gables ($34.50 pp), and Key Biscayne ($34.50 pp). Cabs and shuttles are typically available 24 hours daily.

As an alternative, you can also use the **Tri-Rail** (954/783-6030 or 800/874-7245, www.tri-rail.com), a commuter train service operated by the **South Florida Regional Transportation Authority (SFRTA)** that links the Fort Lauderdale and Miami airports to several other communities in southern Florida, including Hollywood and West Palm Beach.

By Car

Miami is accessible via several major roads,

including I-75 from Tampa, Florida's Turnpike from Orlando, and I-95 from Jacksonville. No matter how you get here, though, be sure to call **511** for an up-to-the-minute traffic report.

By Boat

Given that **PortMiami** (1015 N. America Way, Miami, 305/347-5515, www.miamidade.gov/portmiami) is the "cruise capital of the world," you can certainly arrive here by boat if you so choose.

GETTING AROUND
By Car

The best way to travel through Miami is by car, truck, RV, or motorcycle—all of which offer easy access to the city's major thoroughfares. Given the sheer array of interstates, federal and state highways, county roads, and surface streets in the Miami area, traversing the city and its suburbs isn't too difficult a task, especially if you have a detailed map, such as the AAA Miami/Miami Beach foldout map, or access to an application like Google Maps on your cell phone. Although you can take surface streets pretty much everywhere, you'll probably save time by using major routes and highways. From downtown Miami, for instance, you can use I-95 or Biscayne Boulevard (U.S. 1) to reach North Miami, head south on the Dixie Highway (U.S. 1) to access Coconut Grove and Coral Gables, and take SR-913 to Key Biscayne. To reach Miami Beach, you can take I-195 East and head south on SR-A1A, and the Tamiami Trail (U.S. 41) offers relatively easy access to Little Havana and, farther west, the Everglades.

By Public Transit

Miami offers a convenient public transit system, including the **Metrobus** (305/891-3131, www.miamidade.gov/transit, $2-2.35 per ride, transfer fees may apply), which offers routes throughout southern Florida, even as far as Marathon in the Florida Keys. Each bus route has its own schedule, so some routes (such as #3 in downtown Miami) run 24 hours daily while others have very limited timetables.

As an alternative, you can travel through Miami using the light-rail system. The **Metrorail** (305/891-3131, www.miamidade. gov/transit, $2 per ride, $5 daily, $26 weekly, $100 monthly) features 23 stations, offering convenient access to stops such as the Civic Center and Coconut Grove. Yet another option is the **Metromover** (305/891-3131, www. miamidade.gov/transit), which provides free access to a number of stations in downtown Miami, including one near Bayfront Park and another near the Adrienne Arsht Center for the Performing Arts of Miami-Dade County. For both the Metrorail and the Metromover, trains typically operate between 5am and midnight every day.

For those who need to go a bit farther, the **South Florida Regional Transportation Authority (SFRTA)** offers the **Tri-Rail** (954/783-6030 or 800/874-7245, www.tri-rail. com), a commuter train service that links the Miami airport to Hollywood, Fort Lauderdale, West Palm Beach, and several spots in between. The southbound trains, which run from Mangonia Park to Miami International Airport, operate between 4am and 10:29pm on weekdays, and between 5:50am and 11pm on weekends and holidays. The northbound trains, meanwhile, operate between 4:18am and 11:35pm on weekdays, and between 5:20am and 11:45pm on weekends and holidays.

By Taxi

Taxicab companies like **Flamingo Taxis** (305/599-9999, $2.50 per pickup, $2.50 per mile) can help you get around Miami at any time of day or night.

By Bicycle or Boat

While you can certainly traverse Miami by bicycle, the sprawling nature of this region makes it challenging for novice riders. Still, it's a lovely, ecofriendly way to experience this subtropical city. Bicycles can be rented from

© GREATER MIAMI CONVENTION & VISITORS BUREAU/WWW.GMCVB.COM

The Metromover whizzes through downtown Miami.

several outfitters in the region. The **Miami Beach Bicycle Center** (601 5th St., Miami Beach, 305/674-0150, www.bikemiamibeach. com, 10am-7pm Mon.-Sat., 10am-5pm Sun., starting at $5 hourly, $14 daily, $60 weekly), for instance, offers a variety of cruisers, hybrids, mountain bikes, tandems, and other bicycles, in addition to accessories and repairs.

Of course, you can also experience the Miami coast by boat. Having your own vessel makes navigating these waters even easier, and you'll find no shortage of boat ramps and marina slips in Miami. If you'd rather rent a boat, head to Monty's Marina, where **American WaterSports** (2560 S. Bayshore Dr., Coconut Grove, 305/856-6559, www.americanwatersports.us, 10am-sunset daily) offers a range of powerboats ($140-180 hourly, $400-540 per half day, $600-900 daily).

The Everglades and Vicinity

West of Miami lies a vast, legendary region of subtropical wetlands known around the world as the Everglades. Part of southern Florida's massive watershed, this ever-evolving region has been shaped over the centuries by water, fire, storms, nonnative species, even human actions. Termed the "river of grass" by writer Marjory Stoneman Douglas in the late 1940s, the Everglades comprise a complex system of interdependent ecosystems, including sawgrass marshes, cypress swamps, mangrove forests, tropical hardwood hammocks, pine rocklands, coastal prairies, tidal mud flats, sloughs and estuaries, and the marine environment of Florida Bay. Despite prolonged damage caused by activities like water drainage, this mysterious landscape and its adjacent waters are preserved, in part, by two national parks, a national preserve, a wildlife refuge, and two state parks. As amazing as this region's natural resources are, though, there are cultural gems here, too, such as the Miccosukee Indian Village.

SIGHTS
Everglades National Park
Between Miami and Naples stretches **Everglades National Park** (40001 SR-9336, Homestead, 305/242-7700, www.nps.gov/ever, visitor center 9am-5pm daily, park 24 hours daily, $10 vehicles, $5 motorcycles, bikers, and pedestrians, free for children under 17), the largest subtropical wilderness in America and the third largest national park in the lower 48 states. Established in 1947 and since designated a World Heritage Site, an International Biosphere, and a Wetland of International Importance, this unique place protects more than 1.5 million acres and offers a plethora of outdoor diversions for recreationists, from hiking and canoeing trails to campgrounds and ample fishing opportunities. In addition, you can opt for ranger-led programs throughout the year, **narrated**

tram tours (305/221-8455, times and rates vary) in the Shark Valley area, and **boat tours** (239/695-2591, times and rates vary) through the Ten Thousand Islands region. No matter where you go, though, you're bound to see an array of wildlife, including white-tailed deer, alligators, crocodiles, turtles, snakes, herons, egrets, and unfortunately, mosquitoes. If you're lucky, you might even spy an endangered creature like the Florida panther or West Indian manatee.

This vast park has several helpful visitor centers, all of which offer educational displays and public restrooms, among other amenities. At the **Ernest Coe Visitor Center** (40001 SR-9336, Homestead, 305/242-7700, 9am-5pm daily), the main park entrance, you'll find an art exhibit, a bookstore, and nearby walking trails. Farther west, the **Shark Valley Visitor Center** (36000 SW 8th St., Miami, 305/221-8776, 9:15am-5:15pm daily) features walking trails, bicycle rentals, guided tram tours, and a nearby observation tower, and the **Gulf Coast Visitor Center** (815 Oyster Bar Ln., Everglades City, 239/695-3311, 8am-4:30pm daily mid-Nov.-mid-Apr., 9am-4:30pm daily mid-Apr.-mid-Nov.) provides boat tours and canoe rentals. Meanwhile, the **Flamingo Visitor Center** (239/695-2945, 9am-4:30pm daily) is the only visitor center situated deep within the park, roughly 38 miles south of the main park entrance. Here you can procure backcountry permits; rent canoes, kayaks, and bicycles; and access campground facilities, a marina store, a public boat ramp, and several hiking and canoeing trails.

Big Cypress National Preserve
North of Everglades National Park lies **Big Cypress National Preserve** (33100 E. Tamiami Trl., Ochopee, 239/695-2000, www.nps.gov/bicy, headquarters 8am-4:30pm Mon.-Fri., preserve 24 hours daily, free), a 720,000-acre region that protects the

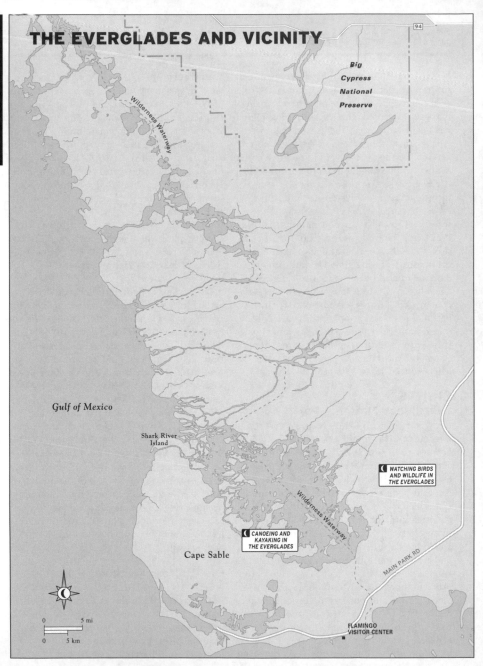

THE EVERGLADES AND VICINITY

Big Cypress National Preserve

94

Wilderness Waterway

Gulf of Mexico

Shark River Island

WATCHING BIRDS AND WILDLIFE IN THE EVERGLADES

Wilderness Waterway

CANOEING AND KAYAKING IN THE EVERGLADES

Cape Sable

MAIN PARK RD

FLAMINGO VISITOR CENTER

0   5 mi

0   5 km

© DANIEL MARTONE

Big Cypress Bend Boardwalk in the Everglades

freshwater ecosystem of Big Cypress Swamp, an area that helps to support the marine estuaries along Florida's southwestern coast. Home to tropical and temperate plant communities, Big Cypress nurtures a wide array of wildlife, including wild hogs, various birds, and the elusive Florida panther. Visitors here can hike along the Florida National Scenic Trail, hunt for deer and turkey in the backcountry (with the proper permits, of course), experience one of several paddling trails, or join a ranger-led nature walk (late Nov.-mid-Apr.). For reservations and other information, contact the **Big Cypress Swamp Welcome Center** (33000 E. Tamiami Trl., Ochopee, 239/695-4758, 9am-4:30pm daily) or the **Oasis Visitor Center** (52105 E. Tamiami Trl., Ochopee, 239/695-1201, 9am-4:30pm daily), each of which offers various exhibits, educational materials, an introductory film, a bookstore, and public restrooms. Note that although the park headquarters is closed on weekends, the preserve is actually open to the public every day of the year.

State Parks

While you'll find even more state parks in the Florida Keys, the vast Everglades region contains two that are worth a look. Often called "the Amazon of North America," the linear swamp forest known as **Fakahatchee Strand Preserve State Park** (137 Coastline Dr., Copeland, 239/695-4593, www.floridastateparks.org/fakahatcheestrand, 8am-sunset daily, free) beckons bird-watchers and wildlife lovers. Situated along the Tamiami Trail, this lush state park lies roughly 80 miles west of Miami and immediately west of Carnestown on SR-29. Here you can wander along 2,000-foot-long **Big Cypress Bend Boardwalk** or take guided swamp walks and canoe trips amid bald cypress trees, royal palm groves, and colorful orchids—home to alligators, varied birds and snakes, white-tailed deer, raccoons, endangered Florida panthers, and other engaging creatures.

Farther west along the Tamiami Trail, the 7,271-acre **Collier-Seminole State Park** (20200 E. Tamiami Trl., Naples, 239/394-3397, www.floridastateparks.org/colliersemi-nole, 8am-sunset daily, $5 vehicles with 2-8 passengers, $4 motorcycles and single-occupant vehicles, $2 pedestrians, bikers, and extra passengers) offers even more outdoor diversions. Visitors can canoe through mangrove swamps, hike or bike amid pine flatwoods, camp beneath majestic royal palm trees, fish in the Blackwater River, or simply take a stroll through the on-site nature center. Obviously, wildlife-watching opportunities abound in this bountiful park, which also offers picnic areas, playgrounds, a boat ramp, and guided tours along the nature trail and boardwalk. As a bonus, well-behaved pets on leashes are welcome here.

Biscayne National Park

Water enthusiasts should venture east of the Everglades to **Biscayne National Park** (9700 SW 328th St., Homestead, 305/230-1144, www.nps.gov/bisc, 7am-5:30pm daily, free), a stunning wonderland of aquamarine waters, peaceful islands, and living coral reefs, all within sight of downtown Miami. To explore

© DANIEL MARTONE

taking an airboat ride through the Everglades

this 172,000-acre park, **Biscayne National Underwater Park, Inc.** (305/230-1100, www.biscayneunderwater.com, 9am-5pm daily) offers canoe and kayak rentals as well as scuba-diving and snorkeling trips ($45-99 pp) in Biscayne Bay, around the islands inside the park, and to the fascinating underwater coral reefs. If you'd prefer a less active experience, you're welcome to board a glass-bottom boat tour ($45 pp) for a wonderful glimpse of the coral reefs as well as frolicking dolphins and other marine creatures. Tour tickets can be purchased in advance through **Zerve** (800/979-3370, www.zerve.com).

The islands are also worth exploring but can only be accessed with a canoe, kayak, or boat. Once a thriving community of wreckers, sponge makers, and pineapple farmers and now the park's largest island, **Elliott Key** offers ample picnicking, swimming, hiking, camping, fishing, and wildlife-viewing opportunities. Meanwhile, on **Boca Chita Key,** the park's most popular island, you can enjoy a relaxing picnic, stroll along a half-mile hiking trail, or

tour the 65-foot ornamental lighthouse, which is open intermittently and affords a fantastic view of nearby islands, Biscayne Bay, and the Miami skyline. One way to reach Boca Chita is by doing the **Boca Chita Lighthouse Adventure** (305/230-1100, www.biscayneunderwater.com, Oct.-mid-Mar., $35 pp), a three-hour boat ride and island tour offered through Biscayne National Underwater Park, Inc., from October to March. Although the water portion of Biscayne National Park is open 24 hours daily, the keys have different operating hours. Adams Key, for instance, is a day-use area only. Also keep in mind that there are no bridges or ferries to the islands and, consequently, no RV camping facilities on the islands themselves. For more information about tours and activities, consult the **Dante Fascell Visitor Center** (305/230-7275, 9am-5pm daily) near Convoy Point (9700 SW 328th St., Homestead) on the mainland.

Museums and Historic Sites

Despite serving as an outdoor paradise, the

Everglades aren't without their share of cultural diversions. The **Coral Castle Museum** (28655 S. Dixie Hwy., Homestead, 305/248-6345, www.coralcastle.com, 8am-6pm Sun.-Thurs., 8am-8pm Fri.-Sat., $15 adults, $12 seniors 62 and over, $7 children 7-12, free for children under 7), for instance, invites visitors to solve a long-standing mystery: How could a diminutive man like Edward Leedskalnin carve and sculpt 1,100 tons of coral all on his own? Erected secretly between 1923 and 1951, at a time when no modern construction conveniences existed, this strange sculpture garden has sparked countless debates over the years, and to this day, scientists and thinkers have yet to discern Edward's methods. While visiting this marvel, you can either take a guided tour or listen to a self-paced audio tour, available in English, Spanish, French, or German. Note, too, that the Coral Castle is part of the Historic Redland Tropical Trail, created to promote the agricultural heritage of the unique region between Miami and the Florida Keys.

To the west of Krome Avenue, on the south side of the Tamiami Trail in the Everglades, you'll encounter another cultural gem, the **Miccosukee Indian Village** (MM 70 U.S. 41, Miami, 305/552-8365, www.miccosukee.com, 9am-5pm daily, $8 adults, $5 children 6-11, free for children under 6). Here you can observe live alligator demonstrations, take an airboat ride into the Everglades, view historical artifacts and photographs at the Miccosukee Indian Museum, and taste authentic cuisine at the on-site restaurant. You're also welcome to observe Miccosukee people as they weave baskets, craft dolls, carve wood, and fashion colorful beadwork and patchwork, much of which you can purchase at the on-site gift shop. Two annual festivals here also highlight such handmade crafts: American Indian Day in late September and the Miccosukee Indian Arts Festival in late December.

For more Native American history, specifically about the Calusa people, as well as tales of southwestern Florida's pioneers, head farther west to the **Museum of the Everglades** (105 W. Broadway, Everglades City, 239/695-0008, www.evergladesmuseum.org, 9am-5pm Tues.-Fri., 9am-4pm Sat., free), which features both permanent and traveling displays of artifacts, sketches, photographs, and the like. In addition, the on-site Pauline Reeves Gallery presents monthly exhibits from local and regional painters, photographers, and artisans. One of five Collier County Museums (www.colliermuseums.com) in the region, the Museum of the Everglades is housed within an old laundry building that was built in 1927 by Barron Gift Collier, who had purchased the village in 1922 from the Storter family in order to create a company town that would serve as the new county seat and the engineering headquarters for the construction of Tamiami Trail. It's only appropriate then that this museum, the former laundry for Collier's company town, opened its doors on April 26, 1998, the 70th anniversary of the opening of the Tamiami Trail.

Faithfully restored to its 1920s-era appearance, the museum is listed on the National Register of Historic Places. During certain events, such as artists' receptions, you can take a guided walking tour (20 min.-1 hour) of the historical buildings near the museum, such as the landmark Everglades Rod and Gun Club, once known as the Allen House. Private tours can also be arranged. While admission and parking are free at this wheelchair-accessible museum, donations are gratefully accepted, even for the walking tours. Note, too, that no food, drink, or gum is allowed in the museum, and flash photography is prohibited in the galleries.

You can better understand the Seminole native people by visiting the **Ah-Tah-Thi-Ki Museum** (34725 W. Boundary Rd., Clewiston, 877/902-1113, www.ahtahthiki.com, 9am-5pm Wed.-Sun., $9 adults, $6 seniors, students, and military personnel, free for children under 5) on the Big Cypress Seminole Indian Reservation north of I-75. Featuring the country's largest display related to Florida Seminole culture, this spacious museum presents exhibits and artifacts

© DANIEL MARTONE

An American alligator lounges amid a sawgrass marsh.

that illustrate how the Seminole ancestors once lived in the Florida Everglades, from cooking customs to traditional Green Corn Ceremony dances. Besides perusing the exhibits, visitors can watch an orientation video, stroll along a one-mile boardwalk through a 60-acre cypress dome, experience a living village, and purchase authentic jewelry, carvings, beadwork, and patchwork clothing crafted by Seminole and Miccosukee tribes.

◖ Everglades Alligator Farm

Here in the Florida Everglades, you'll encounter a number of airboat tour operators, alligator exhibits, and live animal shows. Some places, like the **Everglades Alligator Farm** (40351 SW 192nd Ave., Homestead, 305/247-2628, www. everglades.com, 9am-6pm daily, $23 adults, $15.50 children 4-11, free for children under 4)—part of the Historic Redland Tropical Trail and situated about 40 miles southwest of Miami—offer all three. Beginning in 1982 as a mere airboat ride attraction, it's since become southern Florida's oldest alligator farm. Besides

taking a narrated airboat ride (roughly 30 minutes long) along curious canals in the nearby Everglades, today's visitors can witness riveting **alligator feedings** (noon and 3pm daily), **alligator shows** (11am, 2pm, and 5pm daily), and **snake shows** (10am, 1pm, and 4pm daily); observe and perhaps even hold a baby alligator or two; and stroll amid more than 2,000 alligators, caimans, native snakes, and specimens of three crocodile species: American, Nile, and Orinoco.

The on-site gift shop (9am-5:30pm daily) is also worth a quick visit, especially if you forgot to bring insect spray with you, which you'll need to deter mosquitoes for most of the year. The last airboat departs at 5:25pm each day. Wearing earplugs is strongly recommended, as airboats can be very loud. The basic admission price includes an airboat ride, a visit to the alligator farm, and access to all animal shows; if you're only interested in the farm and the shows, then you can opt for a lower ticket price ($15.50 adults, $10.50 children 4-11, free for children under 4).

Other Animal Attractions

Besides the Everglades Alligator Farm, you'll find another animal attraction on the Historic Redland Tropical Trail, created to promote the agricultural heritage of the unique region between Miami and the Florida Keys. Situated between Miami and Homestead, not far from Zoo Miami, lies the family-owned **Monkey Jungle** (14805 SW 216th St., Miami, 305/235-1611, www.monkeyjungle.com, 9:30am-5pm daily but ticket office closes at 4pm, $30 adults, $28 seniors 65 and over, $24 children 3-9, free for children under 3), where, as the facility's slogan indicates, "humans are caged and monkeys run wild!" Home to nearly 400 primates, this 30-acre reserve features the natural, unrehearsed antics of 30 different species, including gibbons, guenons, spider monkeys, howler monkeys, gorillas, orangutans, endangered golden lion tamarins, and descendants of the original Java monkeys that animal behaviorist Joseph DuMond released into a dense southern Florida hammock in 1933. There are no parking fees here.

Of course, monkeys aren't the only creatures you'll find in southern Florida. In addition to the Everglades Alligator Farm, several other airboat tour operators present engrossing alligator exhibits and shows. Along the Tamiami Trail, for instance, you'll spy **Gator Park** (24050 SW 8th St., Miami, 305/559-2255 or 800/559-2205, www.gatorpark.com, 9am-5pm daily, $23 adults, $12 children), where you can experience an **airboat ride** (roughly 40 minutes long) amid the birds, snakes, alligators, sawgrass, and hammocks of the nearby Everglades, and observe a fascinating wildlife show, during which staff members capture alligators using a barehanded technique favored by the Native Americans of southern Florida. Also on the premises is a souvenir shop, an **RV park** ($30 daily, $180 weekly, $420 monthly), and a restaurant that serves hamburgers, hot dogs, and regional delicacies like alligator sausage, catfish, and frog legs. The last wildlife show usually occurs at 4:30pm daily, and the last airboat ride starts at 5pm.

A little farther west, the **Everglades Safari Park** (26700 SW 8th St., Miami, 305/226-6923 or 305/223-3804, www.evergladessafaripark.com, 9am-5pm daily, $23 adults, $12 children 5-11, free for children under 5) offers an ecoadventure tour that includes a 30-minute narrated airboat ride; a show featuring alligators, crocodiles, turtles, and other wildlife; a stroll along the Jungle Trail boardwalk and elevated observation platform; a glimpse at a replica chickee (Seminole stilt house) village; and the chance to view more than 100 alligators on their very own island. The airboat tours here depart every half hour, and the last one leaves around 4pm. At both Gator Park and Everglades Safari Park, you'll even be able to hold a baby alligator, if you dare.

North of I-75, you'll find yet another intriguing animal attraction, albeit a bit more expensive. Situated on the 2,200-acre Big Cypress Seminole Indian Reservation, **Billie Swamp Safari** (30000 Gator Tail Trl., Clewiston, 863/983-6101 or 800/467-2327, www.billieswamp.com, 8am-6pm daily) invites visitors to experience the Everglades by **airboat** (10am-4:30pm daily, $25 pp) or **swamp buggy** (11am-5pm daily, $25 pp, free for children under 4), either of which offers you the chance to see native flora and fauna in an untamed landscape. The airboat ride is roughly 20 minutes long, and the swamp buggy tour takes an hour. While here, you can also visit **animal exhibits** (11am-4pm daily) and watch a show about native and nonnative swamp critters (1:15pm and 3:15pm daily), as well as an up-close presentation about venomous snakes, nonvenomous snakes, and of course, alligators (12:15pm and 2:15pm daily).

The park offers a day package ($50 adults, $46 seniors 62 and over, $36 children 4-12, free for children under 4) that includes all-day access to airboats, swamp buggies, and animal shows. Another option is the twilight swamp expedition that features campfire storytelling and a one-hour swamp buggy ecotour (7pm daily, $65 adults, $46 seniors 62 and over and children 4-12, free for children under 4). Some visitors may also opt for an overnight stay in a traditional Seminole chickee lodge ($40-60 daily). Both the twilight package and the overnight stay require advance reservations. Other combo packages are also available, and you'll find both a gift shop (8:30am-6pm daily) and a restaurant, the Swamp Water Café (7am-6pm daily, $4-21), on the premises. Children must be at least four years old to ride an airboat.

Fruit and Spice Park

If your interests lean more toward flora than fauna, you'll be pleased to know that the area near Homestead is home to a plethora of plant nurseries. One particularly curious stop is the **Fruit and Spice Park** (24801 SW 187th Ave., Homestead, 305/247-5727, www.fruitandspicepark.org, 9am-5pm daily, $8 adults, $2 children 6-11, free for children under 6), a 37-acre tropical botanical garden that hosts more than 500 varieties of plants, fruits, vegetables, spices, herbs, and nuts, including several varieties of mango, banana, and bamboo trees. Visitors can have a picnic on the premises or eat lunch at the on-site café. In addition, **guided tours** are conducted every day at 11am, 1:30pm, and 3pm, and various events regularly take place at the park, including the Redland International Orchid Show ($10 pp) in mid-May and the Redland Summer Fruit Festival ($8 pp, free for children under 12) in mid-June.

Marco Island

Along the coast of southwestern Florida lies a chain of islands and mangrove islets known as the Ten Thousand Islands region—despite the fact that the islands actually number in the hundreds, not the thousands. The largest, northernmost island in this chain, **Marco Island** (www.marco-island-florida.com) is a popular locale for outdoors enthusiasts, especially anglers, boaters, kayakers, bird-watchers, and beachcombers. In fact, Marco Island features two public beaches, **Tigertail Beach** (Spinnaker Dr. and Hernando Dr., 8am-sunset daily, $8 parking) and **South Marco Beach** (Collier Blvd. and Swallow Ave., 8am-sunset

daily, $8 parking). While South Marco offers no facilities, Tigertail features a concession stand, a playground, a butterfly garden, volleyball courts, public restrooms, and watersports rentals.

Besides outdoor diversions, Marco Island also boasts several specialty shops and waterfront restaurants, including those at **The Esplanade Shoppes, Residences and Marina** (760 N. Collier Blvd., Marco Island, 239/394-7772, www.theesplanade.com, hours vary daily), an Italian-style village on Smokehouse Bay. To reach Marco Island, head into the Everglades via the Tamiami Trail (U.S. 41), turn south onto Collier Boulevard, and continue until you reach the island.

ENTERTAINMENT AND EVENTS

While Miami offers a greater variety of entertainment options and annual events, the Everglades aren't without a dose of culture.

Nightlife

Unlike other parts of Florida, the area between Miami and the Everglades offers few choices for gamblers. One such place is the **Miccosukee Resort & Gaming** (500 SW 177th Ave., Miami, 305/222-4600, www.miccosukee.com, 24 hours daily), a casino resort that lies west of Miami and is operated by the Miccosukee Tribe of Indians of Florida, who separated from the native Seminole Indians in the 1950s and gained federal recognition in 1962. Here visitors can enjoy live entertainment, various dining options, cocktails in the Cypress Lounge and Martini Bar, and of course, an assortment of gaming options, including a high-stakes bingo hall, a 32-table poker room, and more than 1,900 video slot machines.

Festivals and Events

For about four decades, Everglades City has hosted the annual **Everglades Seafood Festival** (239/695-2277, www.evergladesseafoodfestival.org, free admission though fees apply for some activities), a family-friendly event that usually occurs during the first

© LAURA MARTONE

Miccosukee Resort & Gaming

weekend of February. Besides carnival rides, arts and crafts, and live music, attendees will be treated to plenty of delicious food, including standard American fare like hamburgers and corn on the cob. Of course, fresh seafood is the main event; highlights include fresh shrimp, catfish, lobster, stone crabs, and fish chowder.

Another curious event usually happens from late December to early January. Over the course of nine days, the **Miccosukee Indian Arts Festival** ($13 adults, $12 seniors, $9 children 7-12, free for children under 7) welcomes visitors to the Miccosukee Indian Village (MM 70 U.S. 41, Miami, 305/552-8365, www.miccosukee.com, 9am-5pm daily), where you can experience Native American dances and musical performances, marvel at traditional costumes, enjoy authentic foods, browse genuine arts and crafts from various Native American tribes, observe alligator demonstrations, and perhaps even take an airboat ride into the Everglades. As a bonus, proceeds from the festival help to fund educational programs for Native American youth.

SHOPPING

Though most folks don't venture into the Everglades on a shopping quest, several spots are worth visiting. Headed south of downtown Miami, toward Homestead, you'll encounter the nostalgic **Cauley Square Historic Village** (22400 Old Dixie Hwy., Miami, 305/258-3543 or 305/878-1410, www.cauleysquare.com, 11am-5pm Tues.-Sun.), part of the Historic Redland Tropical Trail, which was created to promote the agricultural heritage of the unique region between Miami and the Florida Keys. Here you can stroll along garden paths, enjoy tea and sandwiches at the on-site Victorian-style **Tea Room Restaurant** (305/258-0044, www.tearoombakery.com, 11am-4pm Tues.-Thurs., 11am-5pm Fri.-Sun.), and browse a variety of quaint cottages, housing a cornucopia of jewelry, candles, handmade crafts, antique furniture, and other specialty items. Also on the premises, you'll find **The Village Chalet** (305/258-8900 or 305/282-1391, www.villagechalet.com, 11am-9pm Tues.-Thurs. and Sun., 11am-10pm Fri.-Sat.), a cozy restaurant that features salads, sandwiches, steaks, seafood entrées, and pasta dishes, plus live rock and jazz on occasion.

Farther south you can shop for bargain name-brand clothes, shoes, jewelry, and perfume at the **Florida Keys Outlet Center** (250 E. Palm Dr., Florida City, 305/248-4727, www.premiumoutlets.com, 10am-9pm Mon.-Sat., 11am-6pm Sun.). Not far away, the **Schnebly Redland's Winery & Brewery** (30205 SW 217th Ave., Homestead, 305/242-1224 or 888/717-9463, www.schneblywinery.com, 10am-5pm Mon.-Thurs., 10am-11pm Fri.-Sat., noon-5pm Sun.), also part of the Historic Redland Tropical Trail, invites visitors to sample handcrafted wine and beer amid coral waterfalls.

The area in and around Homestead, especially along Krome Avenue (SR-997/SW 177th Ave.), is also known for its bountiful nurseries, including the **Santa Barbara Nursery** (20425 SW 177th Ave., Miami, 305/256-7577, www.santa-barbaranursery.com, 7:30am-5:30pm Mon.-Sat., 8am-5:30pm Sun.), which offers

MIAMI AND THE EVERGLADES

© GREATER MIAMI CONVENTION & VISITORS BUREAU/WWW.GMCVB.COM

sampling the wares of Schnebly Redland's Winery & Brewery

a wide assortment of trees, plants, and flowers. In addition, the Historic Redland Tropical Trail features three other agricultural delights, including **Miami Tropical Bonsai** (14775 SW 232nd St., Miami, 305/258-0865, www.miamitropicalbonsai.com, 9am-4:30pm Mon.-Sat.), selling an assortment of bonsai trees and supplies, and **R.F. Orchids** (28100 SW 182nd Ave., Homestead, 305/245-4570, www.rforchids.com, 9am-5pm Tues.-Sun.), which provides an array of vibrant orchids. Closer to Florida City is the third option, the **Robert Is Here Fruit Stand and Farm** (19200 SW 344th St., Homestead, 305/246-1592, www.robertishere.com, 8am-7pm daily Nov.-Aug.). Established in 1960, this store offers a range of seasonal produce and products, from oranges and mangoes to preserves and salsas.

Along the Tamiami Trail (U.S. 41), farther into the wetlands and hammocks of the Everglades, you'll spy the **Big Cypress Gallery** (52388 Tamiami Trl., Ochopee, 239/695-2428, www.clydebutcher.com, 10am-5pm daily) on the south side of the highway, roughly 37 miles

west of Krome Avenue and less than a mile east of Big Cypress National Preserve's Oasis Visitor Center. Featuring the black-and-white landscape photography of Clyde and Niki Butcher, this art gallery and studio also offers guided swamp walks (11am and 2pm Sat. early Oct.-Mar.,, $50 adults, $25 children under 18) behind the on-site cottage. Hats, long pants, old sneakers, insect repellent, snacks, and a waterproof camera are recommended for such tours.

RECREATION

Most visitors venture to the Everglades for recreational reasons, whether planning a long-distance hike, scheduling a canoe trip, or simply hoping to glimpse as many birds and alligators as possible.

Hiking and Biking

Given the wide array of habitats in the Everglades, hikers and bikers will encounter no shortage of fascinating opportunities. In **Everglades National Park** (40001 SR-9336, Homestead, 305/242-7700, www.nps.gov/ever, visitor center 9am-5pm daily, park 24 hours daily, $10 vehicles, $5 motorcycles, bikers, and pedestrians, free for children under 17), for instance, you'll find several hiking trails, some of which allow bicycles. These multipurpose trails include the 1.6-mile **Snake Bight Trail** and the 2.6-mile **Rowdy Bend Trail,** which if combined with the main park road, form a 12.6-mile, round-trip biking excursion from the Flamingo Visitor Center. Bicycle rentals ($8.50 hourly) are available in the park, courtesy of **Shark Valley Tram Tours** (305/221-8455, www.sharkvalleytramtours.com). Pets are not allowed on any park trails.

An even bigger challenge awaits in **Big Cypress National Preserve** (33100 E. Tamiami Trl., Ochopee, 239/695-2000, www.nps.gov/bicy, headquarters 8:30am-4:30pm Mon.-Fri., preserve 24 hours daily, free), where long-distance hikers can enjoy three different sections of the **Florida National Scenic Trail,** which incidentally connects with Gulf Islands National Seashore, a park that stretches alongside southern Mississippi and the Florida Panhandle. The longest section in Big Cypress extends for roughly 28 miles between the Oasis Visitor Center on U.S. 41 and the rest area at Mile Marker 63 on I-75 and along the way passes through a rugged, often overgrown habitat of pinelands, prairies, cypress swamps, and hardwood hammocks. Only experienced hikers should attempt this route. Make sure to bring enough drinking water with you, especially during the dry season (Nov.-Apr.).

Although you're welcome to use your own bicycle along the available trails in the Everglades, rentals are available. In the Everglades, for instance, the full-service **Glades Haven Marina** (801 S. Copeland Ave., Everglades City, 239/695-2628 or 239/695-2082, www.theeverglades florida.com, 6am-6pm Sun.-Thurs., 6am-9pm Fri.-Sat.) offers top-quality trail bicycles for rent ($15 hourly, $20 per half day, $25 daily). As an alternative, **Everglades Area Tours** (238 Mamie St., Chokoloskee Island, 239/695-3633 or 800/860-1472, www.ever gladesareatours.com) features guided three-hour Everglades bicycle tours ($99 pp) for

which reservations are required. All necessary equipment is included, though riders must be at least 12 years old.

◖ Bird-Watching and Wildlife-Viewing

The Everglades, which constitute one of the largest tracts of wilderness in the United States, boast a number of diverse habitats, from sawgrass marshes to tropical hardwood hammocks. Consequently, this massive region is home to hundreds of bird, fish, reptile, amphibian, and mammal species. In fact, whether you choose to explore the **East Everglades Expansion Area** by airboat, take a canoe trip through **Everglades National Park** (40001 SR-9336, Homestead, 305/242-7700, www.nps.gov/ever, visitor center 9am-5pm daily, park 24 hours daily, $10 vehicles, $5 motorcycles, bikers, and pedestrians, free for children under 17), or simply stroll along the 2,000-foot **Big Cypress Bend Boardwalk** in **Fakahatchee Strand Preserve State Park** (137 Coastline Dr., Copeland, 239/695-4593, www.floridastate parks.org/fakahatcheestrand, 8am-sunset daily, free), you're bound to encounter an array of curious birds and other wild animals, including great blue herons, American alligators, various snakes and turtles, and for the lucky few, the elusive Florida panther.

Although some conservationists worry about the presence of airboats in the Everglades, citing reasons like noise pollution and wildlife disturbance, most airboat operators are exceedingly passionate and knowledgeable about this fragile landscape. For those visitors who have little or no experience with activities like canoeing and kayaking, airboat tours provide a good opportunity to learn about this unique environment firsthand. Luckily, you'll find at least a dozen operators willing to guide you through this "river of grass" for an up-close look at birds, alligators, and other native inhabitants.

Along the Tamiami Trail, for instance, you'll encounter **The Original Coopertown Airboats** (22700 SW 8th St., Miami, 305/226-6048, www.coopertownairboats.com, 8am-6pm daily, $22 adults, $11 children 7-11, free for

© DANIEL MARTONE

Birding opportunities abound in the Everglades.

children under 7), which has been in operation since 1945 and now offers 40-minute narrated tours through a sawgrass marsh and an alligator hole.

Other options along the Tamiami Trail include **Gator Park** (24050 SW 8th St., Miami, 305/559-2255 or 800/559-2205, www.gatorpark.com, 9am-5pm daily, $23 adults, $12 children), which also presents an exciting wildlife show, and **Wooten's Everglades Airboat Tour** (32330 E. Tamiami Trl., Ochopee, 239/695-2781 or 800/282-2781, www.wootenseverglades.com, 9am-4:30pm daily, $15 adults, $10 children), which in addition to guiding airboat tours since 1953, also features 35-minute swamp buggy rides and an animal sanctuary. Several more operators are situated in Everglades City, including **Speedy's Airboat Tours** (621 Begonia St., Everglades City, 239/695-4448 or 800/998-4448, www.speedysairboattours.com, 9am-5pm daily, $40 adults, $25 children 3-10, free for children under 3); **Everglades City Airboat Tours** (907 Dupont St., Everglades City, 239/695-2400 or

877/222-6400, www.evergladescity-airboat-tours.com, 9am-5pm Mon.-Sat., $40 adults, $20 children 4-12), with one-hour rides; and **Jungle Erv's Airboat Tours** (804 Collier Ave., Everglades City, 877/695-2820, www.jungleervairboatworld.com, 9am-5pm daily, $27.50-80 adults, $17.50-50 children), featuring a variety of airboat tours.

From I-75 you can access airboat tours, too. **Billie Swamp Safari** (30000 Gator Tail Trl., Clewiston, 863/983-6101 or 800/467-2327, www.billieswamp.com, 8am-6pm daily), for instance, is located on the 2,200-acre Big Cypress Seminole Indian Reservation north of the interstate. Besides taking an **airboat tour** (10am-4:30pm daily, $25 pp) here, you'll also be able to spot wildlife on a swamp buggy ecotour through the wetlands or watch the on-site animal and reptile shows. The airboat ride is roughly 20 minutes long, and children must be at least four years old to ride one.

An even more unusual wildlife-watching opportunity awaits through **Everglades Area Tours** (238 Mamie St., Chokoloskee Island,

239/695-3633 or 800/860-1472, www.ever-gladesareatours.com, times vary Nov.-May), offering flights by an Alaskan bush plane from **Everglades Airpark** (650 E.C. Airpark Rd., Everglades City, 239/695-2778) and across various destinations, including Everglades National Park and Big Cypress National Preserve. Some of the flights include the 20-minute Everglades City Tour ($138 for up to three adults, free for children under 12), the 45-minute Marco Island Tour ($258 for up to three adults, free for children under 12), the hour-long Everglades National Park Tour ($336 for up to three adults, free for children under 12), the 90-minute Grand Tour ($504 for up to three adults, free for children under 12), and the one-day Key West Tour ($990 for up to three adults, free for children under 12). Each flight may be able to accommodate up to four passengers, depending on the overall weight.

Fishing and Boating

Since roughly one-third of **Everglades National Park** (40001 SR-9336, Homestead, 305/242-7700, www.nps.gov/ever, visitor center 9am-5pm daily, park 24 hours daily, $10 vehicles, $5 motorcycles, bikers, and pedestrians, free for children under 17) is covered by water, it's no wonder that fishing and boating have long been popular activities in this region. Anglers, in fact, will find both saltwater and freshwater fishing opportunities here, especially by boat, which allows access to a multitude of channels, shallow flats, and mangrove keys, not to mention Florida Bay. Depending on the time of year, you're likely to find snapper, redfish, bass, bluegill, and other varieties in these waters. Just be aware that saltwater and freshwater fishing require separate Florida fishing licenses, and remember that collecting plants and animals, such as orchids and conchs, is forbidden in protected waters.

Even if you don't like to fish, traversing the Everglades by boat can be a rewarding experience—though it's only advisable for skilled boaters. There are, after all, innumerable obstacles in the Everglades, from seagrass banks to oyster reefs. It helps to know the draft of your

vessel, be able to "read" the water for signs of shallow areas, and adhere to slow speed zones at all times. The same rules apply for boaters in **Biscayne National Park** (9700 SW 328th St., Homestead, 305/230-7275, www.nps.gov/bisc, water portion 24 hours daily, Convoy Point 7am-5pm daily, free admission though tour and rental rates apply), where it's also critical to understand the shifting tides.

Although having your own vessel might make boating in Everglades National Park and Biscayne National Park a bit more convenient, it's possible to rent one, too. In the Everglades, for instance, the full-service **Glades Haven Marina** (801 S. Copeland Ave., Everglades City, 239/695-2628 or 239/695-2082, www.theev-ergladesflorida.com, 6am-6pm Sun.-Thurs., 6am-9pm Fri.-Sat.), part of the Miller's World Resort, offers boat rentals ($50-75 hourly, $125-150 per half day, $150-175 daily, plus fuel charges), plus an easy-access boat ramp, plenty of docking space, a full-time mechanic, an on-site deli, and a bait and tackle shop that provides lures, bait, and fishing gear. As an alternative, **Chokoloskee Charters** (239/695-9107, www.chokoloskeecharters.com), helmed by Captain Charles Wright, provides guided, light-tackle fishing and fly-fishing trips into the Everglades backcountry. The rates depend on the trip length and the number of anglers. For two people, for example, a half-day trip costs $395, while a full-day trip costs $595. Six anglers, meanwhile, can expect a rate of $675 per half day and $900 daily. All charters include the necessary bait, tackle, gear, coolers, licenses, insurance, and safety equipment.

◖ Canoeing and Kayaking

The region between Miami and the Florida Keys offers a wealth of opportunities for canoeists and kayakers. With its sawgrass marshes, cypress swamps, and mangrove forests, the Everglades provide ideal spots for paddlers, especially those who enjoy observing or photographing wild animals in their element. In **Fakahatchee Strand Preserve State Park** (137 Coastline Dr., Copeland, 239/695-4593, www.floridastateparks.org/fakahatcheestrand,

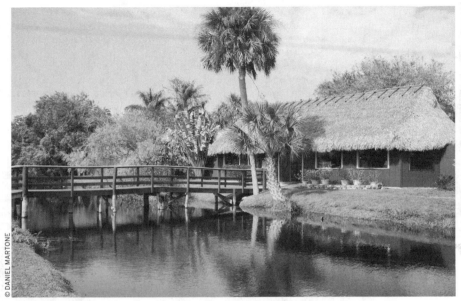

© DANIEL MARTONE

Fakahatchee Strand Preserve State Park is a canoeist's paradise.

8am-sunset daily, free), for instance, you can paddle amid a linear swamp forest while **Collier-Seminole State Park** (20200 E. Tamiami Trl., Naples, 239/394-3397, www.floridastateparks.org/collierseminole, 8am-sunset daily, $5 vehicles with 2-8 passengers, $4 motorcycles and single-occupant vehicles, $2 pedestrians, bikers, and extra passengers) offers a 13.6-mile canoe trail along the Blackwater River, lined by interlocked mangrove trees.

If you don't have a canoe or kayak of your own, don't worry. At Collier-Seminole State Park, for example, you can rent canoes by the hour ($5.30) or the day ($26.50), and from November to April, **Everglades Adventures** (107 Camellia St., Everglades City, 239/695-3299 or 877/567-0679, www.evergladesadventures.com) provides both canoe ($20-25 per half day, $28-35 daily) and kayak rentals ($28-35 per half day, $36-65 daily) as well as guided kayaking trips ($99-124 pp) through mangrove tunnels, cypress swamps, and sawgrass prairies. The full-service **Glades Haven Marina** (801 S. Copeland Ave., Everglades City,

239/695-2628 or 239/695-2082, www.theevergladesflorida.com, 6am-6pm Sun.-Thurs., 6am-9pm Fri.-Sat.), meanwhile, provides both canoe ($25 per half day, $35 daily) and kayak rentals ($35-50 per half day, $50-60 daily). In addition, **Everglades Area Tours** (238 Mamie St., Chokoloskee Island, 239/695-3633 or 800/860-1472, www.evergladesareatours.com) provides canoes ($45 per half day, $65 daily), recreational kayaks ($40-45 per half day, $60-65 daily), fishing kayaks ($45-55 per half day, $65-75 daily), and sea kayaks ($60-85 per half day, $75-105 daily).

You can even rent canoes ($16 for two hours, $22 per half day, $32 daily) and kayaks ($22.50-28.50 for two hours, $35-45 per half day, $45-55 daily) through **Everglades National Park** (40001 SR-9336, Homestead, 305/242-7700, www.nps.gov/ever, visitor center 9am-5pm daily, park 24 hours daily, $10 vehicles, $5 motorcycles, bikers, and pedestrians, free for children under 17), where well-equipped, well-prepared paddlers can explore a labyrinth of water and mangroves in the Ten Thousand Islands area. Of course, the Everglades don't have a monopoly on paddling adventures. **Biscayne National Underwater Park, Inc.** (305/230-1100, www.biscayneunderwater.com, rates vary) also offers canoe and kayak rentals for those hoping to explore the islands and coral-rich waters of **Biscayne National Park** (9700 SW 328th St., Homestead, 305/230-7275, www.nps.gov/bisc, water portion 24 hours daily, Convoy Point 7am-5pm daily, free).

Diving and Snorkeling

Despite all of the outdoor activities available in the Everglades, diving and snorkeling aren't common here. That's not the case, however, in **Biscayne National Park** (9700 SW 328th St., Homestead, 305/230-7275, www.nps.gov/bisc, water portion 24 hours daily, Convoy Point 7am-5pm daily, free), which is accessible by boat from the coast near Homestead. If you don't have a boat of your own, you can simply board a guided scuba-diving or snorkeling tour through **Biscayne National Underwater Park, Inc.** (305/230-1100, www.biscayneunderwater.com, $45-99 pp), which offers excursions around Biscayne Bay and trips to the offshore coral reefs that are part of the national park.

ACCOMMODATIONS

For the most part, the Everglades offers quiet inns, chain hotels, and campgrounds—ideal for those on a budget. Of course, even here, you'll find a few resort-style choices, too.

$100-200

Southwest of Miami, the communities of Homestead and Florida City offer several affordable lodging options—ideal for those hoping to explore Everglades National Park, Biscayne National Park, and the Florida Keys. Continuously operated since 1904, the historical **Hotel Redland** (5 S. Flagler Ave., Homestead, 305/246-1904 or 800/595-1904, www.hotelredland.com, $100-140 d), for instance, offers nicely decorated, nonsmoking rooms, free cable television, complimentary wireless Internet access, and an on-site eatery,

The Whistle Stop Restaurant & Bar, which specializes in old-fashioned comfort food. The closer your room is to the street, the noisier it may be.

If you're more comfortable with chain establishments, consider staying at the pet-friendly **Travelodge Florida City/Homestead** (409 SE 1st Ave., Florida City, 305/248-9777 or 800/758-0618, www.tlflcity.com or www.travelodge.com, $70-130 d), which offers ample parking, free high-speed Internet access, and a heated pool. Another familiar chain option is the **Holiday Inn Express Hotel & Suites Florida City/Gateway to the Keys** (35200 S. Dixie Hwy., Florida City, 305/247-3414 or 888/465-4329, www.hiexpress.com, $100-140 d), which provides guests with complimentary breakfast, high-speed Internet access, an outdoor pool, and an on-site fitness center.

The landmark **(Everglades Rod and Gun Club** (200 Riverside Dr., Everglades City, 239/695-2101, www.evergladesrodandgun.com, cottages $95-140), situated on the Barron River, borders Everglades National Park. Formerly known as the Allen House and converted to a private club in the 1920s, this historical building has hosted a number of famous guests over the years, including Ernest Hemingway, President Eisenhower, John Wayne, Jack Nicklaus, Mick Jagger, and Sean Connery. Inside, the hunting lodge-style decor includes dark, wood-paneled walls, old-fashioned furniture, and mounted tarpon, deer, and alligator trophies while outside, the airy screened porch entices guests to relax in the white wicker furniture and watch passing boats in the adjacent river. Overnight guests can choose from one of several private air-conditioned cottages—essentially cozy, raised, modern-looking structures with small porches, hardwood floors, comfortable beds, and convenient bathrooms. If you stay here, you can enjoy access to an on-site restaurant and lounge, a convenient marina, and an outdoor pool with a picturesque waterfall.

Over $200

At the intersection of Krome Avenue and

the Tamiami Trail, you'll be hard-pressed to miss the enormous **Miccosukee Resort & Gaming** (500 SW 177th Ave., Miami, 305/222-4600 or 877/242-6464, www.miccosukee.com, $390-680 d). Part of a complex that includes a 24-hour casino, a well-equipped fitness center, an indoor heated pool, a full-service European spa, a children's center, a teen arcade, a live entertainment venue, and five dining options, the hotel features 302 comfortable rooms and suites, all of which include wireless Internet access, premium cable television, 24-hour room service, and laundry services, among other amenities.

Farther west along the Tamiami Trail, **The Ivey House** (107 Camellia St., Everglades City, 239/695-3299 or 877/567-0679, www.iveyhouse.com, $89-269 d), a family-owned ecofriendly bed-and-breakfast, encompasses a variety of accommodations, including a lovely inn, historical lodge, and cozy cottage. Guests can also relax in a tropical pool, rent a canoe, join a guided kayaking trip, and enjoy free wireless Internet access in limited areas. The facilities here are nonsmoking, and pets are not allowed.

Camping

Between Miami and the Everglades, not far from the Monkey Jungle, lies the appropriately named **Miami Everglades Resort** (20675 SW 162nd Ave., Miami, 305/233-5300 or 800/917-4923, www.miamicamp.com). Here you'll find a slew of spacious RV and tent sites ($31-65 daily), some of which include patios and picnic tables, plus several different air-conditioned cabins and lodges ($49-179 daily) that can also be rented by the week or month. Campers will enjoy an array of recreational facilities, including a heated pool and hot tub, a large playground, a paved walking and jogging track, bicycle rentals, horseshoes, as well as volleyball, basketball, and shuffleboard courts. Other amenities include shady tiki huts, a recreation hall, a well-stocked camp store, a casual eatery, a propane filling station, modern restrooms, laundry facilities, wireless Internet access, and free U-pick avocados and mangoes.

For a more unusual experience, consider camping on the islands of **Biscayne National Park** (9700 SW 328th St., Homestead, 305/230-7275, www.nps.gov/bisc, water portion 24 hours daily, Convoy Point 7am-5pm daily, free admission though tour and rental rates apply), which lies between Key Biscayne and Key Largo. Tent camping ($15 daily) is available on popular **Boca Chita Key,** featuring a grassy waterside camping area with picnic tables, grills, and toilets, and spacious **Elliott Key,** offering waterside and forested camping areas, picnic tables, grills, drinking water, and restrooms with cold showers. Group camping ($30 daily) is also available, and boaters are welcome to stay in either of the two harbors for a fee ($20 daily). RV camping isn't possible in the park, and any vessel still in the harbor after 5pm is presumed to be staying overnight and will be charged as such. The islands are only accessible by boat; if you don't have your own, you can easily arrange transportation through **Biscayne National Underwater Park, Inc.** (305/230-1100, www.biscayneunderwater.com, rates vary).

Along the Tamiami Trail (U.S. 41), you'll find a slew of camping options, including the eight campgrounds available within **Big Cypress National Preserve** (33100 E. Tamiami Trl., Ochopee, 239/695-2000, www.nps.gov/bicy, headquarters 8am-4:30pm Mon.-Fri., preserve 24 hours daily, free), two of which are seasonal and six of which are open all year. While most of these are primitive campgrounds with no available drinking water, the year-round **Midway Campground** features a dump station, restrooms, drinking water, a day-use area, 10 tent sites ($16 daily), and 26 RV sites ($19 daily) with electric hookups. All campgrounds are available on a first-come, first-served basis. For more information about campground availability and potential closures, contact the **Oasis Visitor Center** (52105 E. Tamiami Trl., Ochopee, 239/695-1201, 9am-4:30pm daily).

Farther west, alongside the Barron River, you'll find relative luxury at **Everglades Isle** (803 Collier Ave., Everglades City,

239/695-2600, www.evergladesisle.com, $79-99 daily), an exclusive motorhome retreat offering 61 landscaped and paved sites. Each site includes a social membership in the Lighthouse Club and the option of having your own wet slip at the on-site marina. Other amenities include a pool and hot tub, a movie theater, a fitness center, a restaurant and lounge, a boat launch, spa treatment salons, golf cart rentals, satellite television, and wireless Internet access.

Along U.S. 41 lies **Collier-Seminole State Park** (20200 E. Tamiami Trl., Naples, 239/394-3397, www.floridastateparks.org/collierseminole, 8am-sunset daily, $5 vehicles with 2-8 passengers, $4 motorcycles and single-occupant vehicles, $2 pedestrians, bikers, and extra passengers), which offers a 120-site, pet-friendly campground ($22 daily) and primitive camping for hikers and canoeists. Nestled amid gumbo limbo trees and royal palms, the official campground can accommodate tents as well as motorhomes. Every site offers water and electric service and other amenities include an activity building as well as restrooms with showers. For reservations, contact **ReserveAmerica** (800/326-3521, www.reserveamerica.com).

Naturally, **Everglades National Park** (40001 SR-9336, Homestead, 305/242-7700, www.nps.gov/ever, visitor center 9am-5pm daily, park 24 hours daily, $10 vehicles, $5 motorcycles, bikers, and pedestrians, free for children under 17) offers several camping options as well, including two frontcountry campgrounds (518/885-3639 or 877/444-6777): the **Long Pine Key Campground** ($16 daily), which provides 108 tent and RV sites on a first-come, first-served basis, plus restrooms, a dump station, a picnic area, and a fishing pond, and the **Flamingo Campground,** where reservations are strongly recommended for the 276 available tent and RV sites ($16-30 daily), 41 of which have electrical hookups. At the Flamingo Campground, which is situated alongside Florida Bay, campers can utilize cold showers, two dump stations, picnic tables, an amphitheater, and several nearby hiking and canoe trails. Everglades National Park also allows backcountry camping (free May-mid-Nov., $10

per permit, plus $2 pp daily mid-Nov.-Apr.), though a permit must be secured less than 24 hours in advance.

If you'd prefer to stay closer to I-75, you can always opt for the year-round **((Big Cypress RV Resort** (30290 Josie Billie Hwy., Clewiston, 863/983-1330 or 800/437-4102, www.bigcypressrvresort.com), which lies 18 miles north of the interstate on SR-833. Situated on the Big Cypress Seminole Indian Reservation, this campground offers easy access to Billie Swamp Safari and the Ah-Tah-Thi-Ki Museum. Facilities here include tent sites ($30 daily), RV sites ($35-45 daily, $210-280 weekly, $575-700 monthly), and air-conditioned cabins ($75-140 daily)—all of which typically require reservations. All tent sites include water and electric service, and RV sites feature water and electric service, plus sewer access. Other amenities include a heated pool and hot tub, a general store, a clubhouse, an exercise room, a playground, a miniature golf course, basketball courts, a propane/dump station, and laundry facilities.

FOOD

Although you'll find a greater variety of restaurants in Miami and the Florida Keys, the Everglades do indeed offer a share of dining options, including the popular chain restaurant **Sonny's Real Pit Bar-B-Q** (33505 S. Dixie Hwy., Florida City, 305/245-8585, www.sonnysbbq.com, 11am-10pm daily, $12-22), which should satisfy your craving for barbecue beef, pork, and chicken, not to mention Southern-style sweet tea. On the adjacent street, **Richard Accursio's Capri Restaurant** (935 N. Krome Ave., Florida City, 305/247-1542, www.dine-capri.com, 11am-9:30pm Mon.-Thurs., 11am-10:30pm Fri., 4pm-10:30pm Sat., 4pm-9pm Sun., $9-27), a family-owned operation since 1958, serves fine Italian cuisine, from traditional dishes like chicken marsala to unique concoctions such as Shrimp Casino, which features sautéed shrimp, onions, peppers, bacon, and garlic butter served over angel hair pasta.

From Florida City, head north to the Tamiami Trail and drive west into the

© LAURA MARTONE

Visitors often stop at the Coopertown Restaurant before joining an airboat tour.

Everglades, where you'll find the **Coopertown Restaurant** (22700 SW 8th St., Miami, 305/226-6048, www.coopertownairboats. com, 8am-6pm daily, $8-14), a convenient stop before taking a Coopertown airboat ride. Offering an authentic taste of the Everglades, this no-frills, country-style eatery serves standard fare as well as frog legs, catfish, and alligator tail.

Everglades City features several options, including the **Island Cafe** (305 Collier Ave., Everglades City, 239/695-0003, 6am-3pm daily, $5-14), which prepares decent breakfast dishes, plus inexpensive sandwiches, burgers, and seafood. Just down the street, the Spanish-style **Everglades Seafood Depot** (102 Collier Ave., Everglades City, 239/695-0075, www. evergladesseafooddepot.com, 10:30am-9pm daily, $7-50) offers similar cuisine in a waterfront setting beside Lake Placid. If you're really hungry, try "The Depot Special" ($50 pp), which includes gator and lobster tails, fried fish and shrimp, and frog legs. From mid-October to mid-May, you can also opt for the impressive

all-you-can-eat seafood buffet (Thurs.-Sat., $39 pp), featuring everything from oysters and scallops to stone crab claws and caviar.

INFORMATION AND SERVICES
Tourism and Government Offices

For maps, brochures, and information about the Everglades, consult the **Naples, Marco Island, Everglades Convention & Visitors Bureau** (2800 N. Horseshoe Dr., Naples, 239/225-1013 or 800/688-3600, www.paradisecoast. com, 9am-5pm Mon.-Fri.), the **Everglades Area Chamber of Commerce Welcome Center** (32016 E. Tamiami Trl., Everglades City, 239/695-3941, www.evergladeschamber.net, 9am-4pm daily), **Everglades National Park** (40001 SR-9336, Homestead, 305/242-7700, www.nps.gov/ever, 9am-5pm daily), and the **Greater Homestead/Florida City Chamber of Commerce** (455 N. Flagler Ave., Homestead, 305/247-2332, www.chamberinaction.com, 9am-5pm Mon.-Fri.).

The nonprofit **Tropical Everglades Visitor**

Association (TEVA) (160 U.S. 1, Florida City, 305/245-9180, www.tropicaleverglades.com, 8am-5pm Mon.-Sat., 10am-2pm Sun.), which is part of the Historic Redland Tropical Trail, is a helpful resource, too. *The Mullet Rapper* (www.evergladesmulletrapper.com), a local newspaper available at establishments throughout Everglades City and Chokoloskee, as well as websites like www.florida-everglades.com may prove useful.

For government-related issues, you'll have to first figure out which county you need to contact. The Everglades, after all, constitute a large area—so large in fact that it extends across three different counties: **Miami-Dade County** (www.miamidade.gov), **Monroe County** (www.monroecounty.gov), and **Collier County** (www.colliergov.net). You can also call the local governments directly, such as the **City of Homestead** (www.cityofhomestead.com).

Mail

If you need to purchase stamps or send packages while you're in the Everglades, you'll find a handful of **post offices** (800/275-8777, www.usps.com) in the area, including one in Everglades City (601 Collier Ave., 239/695-2174, 10am-noon and 1pm-3pm Mon.-Fri.).

Groceries and Supplies

Though the Everglades may seem to be filled with flyspeck towns and undeveloped hinterlands, there are several groceries and other helpful stores here. **Publix** (www.publix.com), for instance, offers several branches in Homestead, including one within the **Homestead Towne Square** (891 N. Homestead Blvd., 305/242-1500, 7am-11pm Mon.-Sat., 7am-10pm Sun.). Even isolated Marco Island has a **Winn-Dixie** (625 N. Collier Blvd., 239/642-9126, www.winndixie.com, 7am-11pm daily), with a deli, a bakery, fresh seafood, ATMs, and an on-site pharmacy (239/393-0843, 8am-8pm Mon.-Fri., 9am-6pm Sat., 10am-5pm Sun.).

Emergency Services

In case of an emergency that requires police, fire, or ambulance services, dial **911** from any cell or public phone. For nonemergency assistance, contact the **Miami-Dade Police Department** (9105 NW 25th St., Doral, 305/476-5423, www.miamidade.gov/mdpd, 8am-5pm Mon.-Fri.) or the **Collier County Sheriff's Office** (3319 E. Tamiami Trl., Bldg. J, Naples, 239/774-4434, www.colliersheriff. org, 8am-5pm Mon.-Fri.). If you're seeking medical assistance, simply consult one of several hospitals in southern Florida, including **Mercy Hospital** (3663 S. Miami Ave., Miami, 305/854-4400, www.mercymiami.com) or the **NCH Downtown Naples Hospital** (350 N. 7th St., Naples, 239/624-5000, www.nchmd.org).

GETTING THERE
By Air

To reach the Everglades by plane, you can either fly major carriers into **Miami International Airport (MIA)** (2100 NW 42nd Ave., Miami, 305/876-7000, www.miami-airport.com) or commuter flights into **Naples Municipal Airport (APF)** (160 N. Aviation Dr., Naples, 239/643-0733, www.flynaples.com). From either one, you can rent a vehicle through such agencies as **Avis** (800/633-3469, www.avis.com), **Enterprise** (800/261-7331, www.enterprise.com), **Hertz** (800/654-3131, www.hertz.com), or **Thrifty** (800/847-4389, www.thrifty.com).

By Bus or Train

If you don't have a vehicle of your own and would prefer not to fly, you can simply take a bus or train to southern Florida and then rent a vehicle to reach the Everglades. **Greyhound** (800/231-2222, www.greyhound.com), for instance, offers service to several different stations, including the **Miami Greyhound Station** (4111 NW 27th St., Miami, 305/871-1810, 24 hours daily) and the **Central Park Bus Terminal** (2669 Davis Blvd., Ste. 1, Naples, 239/774-5660, 8:15am-10:30am and 1:30pm-5pm Mon.-Sat.).

Amtrak (800/872-7245, www.amtrak.com), meanwhile, offers service via its Silver Service/Palmetto route. The three southernmost stations include **Fort Lauderdale (FTL)** (200 SW 21st Ter., Fort Lauderdale, 8:15am-6:15pm daily), **Hollywood (HOL)** (3001 Hollywood Blvd., Hollywood, 8am-6:20pm daily), and **Miami (MIA)** (8303 NW 37th Ave., Miami, 6:30am-9pm daily).

By Car

The Everglades region is accessible via several major roads, including I-75 from Tampa, U.S. 41 from Miami, and U.S. 1 from the Florida Keys. No matter how you get here, though, be sure to call **511** for an up-to-the-minute traffic report.

GETTING AROUND
By Car

In lieu of a kayak or airboat, the most efficient way to travel through the Florida Everglades is by car, truck, RV, or motorcycle—all of which offer easy access to major highways as well as detours to places like Marco Island. Essentially,

you can traverse the Everglades via two main routes, both of which offer access to Big Cypress National Preserve: I-75, also known as Alligator Alley or the Everglades Parkway, runs from Tampa to Fort Lauderdale, and U.S. 41, more commonly called the Tamiami Trail, connects Naples to Miami.

By Boat

Of course, you can also experience the Everglades by canoe, kayak, or airboat. Although having your own vessel makes navigating these waters even easier, you can simply rent one from several different outfitters, including **Everglades Adventures** (107 Camellia St., Everglades City, 239/695-3299 or 877/567-0679, www.evergladesadventures.com), which provides both canoe ($20-25 per half day, $28-35 daily) and kayak rentals ($28-35 per half day, $36-65 daily) from November to April.

MIAMI AND THE EVERGLADES

KEY LARGO

Nestled between the Everglades and the continental United States' only living coral reefs, Key Largo is the northernmost community in the Florida Keys and the largest island in this one-of-a-kind archipelago. It also includes part of the community of Tavernier (the rest of which lies on Plantation Key), and although Key Largo has become a getaway town for southern Floridians and northern snowbirds alike—and as a result, has suffered a bit from overcrowding and overdevelopment—it's still a quieter, more laid back destination than Miami or even Key West, the infamously eccentric city at the southern end of the Overseas Highway.

Here locals can dock their boats just steps from their favorite waterfront eateries or tiki bars, and visitors can stay at any number of intimate inns and posh resorts, some of which are linked to well-equipped marinas. But, of course, the area's biggest claim to fame is its wealth of outdoor diversions, including sportfishing, paddling, snorkeling, and scuba diving. In fact, thanks to the fascinating underwater coral reefs, shipwrecks, and landmarks, such as the *Christ of the Abyss* statue, that extend along the Atlantic shoreline—part of Florida Keys National Marine Sanctuary, established in 1990—Key Largo is also the self-proclaimed "diving capital of the world."

No first-time visitor should skip John Pennekamp Coral Reef State Park, America's first undersea park and one of the jewels of Florida's state park system. Beyond informative marine exhibits in the visitor center, the park offers daily glass-bottom boat tours, snorkeling trips, and scuba-diving excursions. In addition,

© DANIEL MARTONE

HIGHLIGHTS

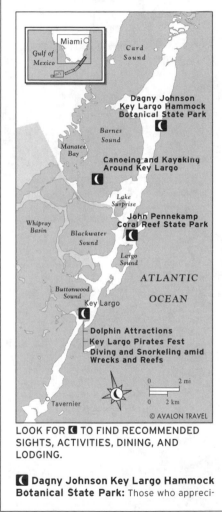

© AVALON TRAVEL

LOOK FOR ◖ TO FIND RECOMMENDED SIGHTS, ACTIVITIES, DINING, AND LODGING.

◖ **Dagny Johnson Key Largo Hammock Botanical State Park:** Those who appreci-

ate solitude and serenity will relish wandering these backcountry trails, which offer a chance to spy threatened or endangered species like the Key Largo woodrat and American crocodile (page 92).

◖ **John Pennekamp Coral Reef State Park:** The most popular state park in the Keys lures a wide array of outdoors enthusiasts with its pleasant beaches, reasonable canoe and kayak rentals, snorkeling and diving excursions, and glass-bottom boat tours of fascinating offshore coral reefs (page 93).

◖ **Dolphin Attractions:** Two incredible dolphin facilities in Key Largo, Dolphin Cove and Dolphins Plus, feature a variety of interactive programs, including structured swims with the resident dolphins (page 95).

◖ **Key Largo Pirates Fest:** While Fantasy Fest is happening down in Key West, revelers in Key Largo celebrate the region's curious past with this four-day event, featuring zany activities like pirate costume contests, a pirate bazaar and thieves' market, and an underwater treasure hunt (page 99).

◖ **Canoeing and Kayaking Around Key Largo:** The islands, patch reefs, tidal flats, and mangrove creeks of the Upper Keys are ideal places to observe wild dolphins, birds, and for the lucky ones, a gentle manatee or two (page 103).

◖ **Diving and Snorkeling amid Wrecks and Reefs:** The self-proclaimed "diving capital of the world" offers a variety of snorkeling and scuba-diving operators to assist visitors in exploring the underwater coral reefs of the Florida Keys National Marine Sanctuary (page 104).

visitors can opt to rent a canoe or kayak for a bird-watching adventure in the park's winding mangrove creeks.

Other enticing attractions in Key Largo include interactive dolphin programs, a wild bird center, a wooded state park at the northern end of the island, not to mention the weathered old boat used famously in the Bogart-Hepburn film *The African Queen*. Of course, if you desire a taste of the zaniness that you'll encounter farther south, you might want to plan your vacation around the annual Key Largo Pirates

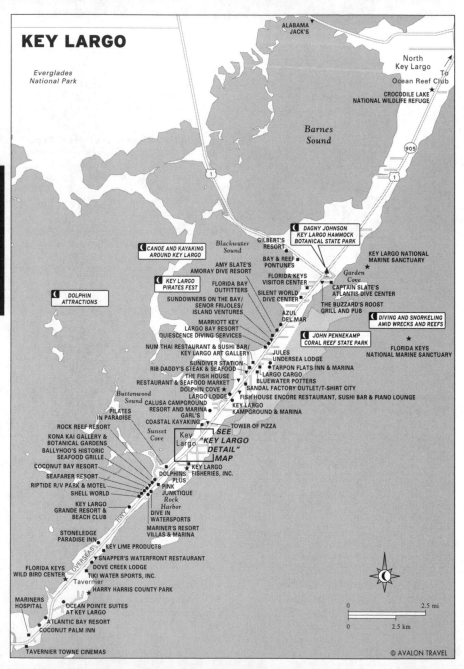

KEY LARGO

*Everglades
National Park*

North
Key Largo
To
Ocean Reef Club

CROCODILE LAKE
NATIONAL WILDLIFE REFUGE

ALABAMA
JACK'S

*Barnes
Sound*

905

1

DAGNY JOHNSON
KEY LARGO HAMMOCK
BOTANICAL STATE PARK

*Blackwater
Sound*

GILBERT'S
RESORT

CANOE AND KAYAKING
AROUND KEY LARGO

BAY & REEF
PONTUNES

KEY LARGO NATIONAL
MARINE SANCTUARY

AMY SLATE'S
AMORAY DIVE RESORT

FLORIDA KEYS
VISITOR CENTER

*Garden
Cove*

KEY LARGO
PIRATES FEST

FLORIDA BAY
OUTFITTERS

SILENT WORLD
DIVE CENTER

CAPTAIN SLATE'S
ATLANTIS DIVE CENTER

DOLPHIN
ATTRACTIONS

SUNDOWNERS ON THE BAY/
SENOR FRIJOLES/
ISLAND VENTURES

THE BUZZARD'S ROOST
GRILL AND PUB

AZUL
DEL MAR

MARRIOTT KEY
LARGO BAY RESORT

DIVING AND SNORKELING
AMID WRECKS AND REEFS

QUIESCENCE DIVING SERVICES

JOHN PENNEKAMP
CORAL REEF STATE PARK

NUM THAI RESTAURANT & SUSHI BAR/
KEY LARGO ART GALLERY

JULES
UNDERSEA LODGE

FLORIDA KEYS
NATIONAL MARINE SANCTUARY

RIB DADDY'S STEAK & SEAFOOD

SUNDIVER STATION

TARPON FLATS INN & MARINA

THE FISH HOUSE
RESTAURANT & SEAFOOD MARKET

LARGO CARGO

BLUEWATER POTTERS

DOLPHIN COVE

SANDAL FACTORY OUTLET/T-SHIRT CITY

LARGO LODGE

FISH HOUSE ENCORE RESTAURANT, SUSHI BAR & PIANO LOUNGE

*Buttonwood
Sound*

CALUSA CAMPGROUND
RESORT AND MARINA

KEY LARGO
KAMPGROUND & MARINA

PILATES
IN PARADISE

GARL'S

COASTAL KAYAKING

TOWER OF PIZZA

ROCK REEF RESORT

*Sunset
Cove*

*Key
Largo*

SEE
"KEY LARGO
DETAIL"
MAP

KONA KAI GALLERY &
BOTANICAL GARDENS

BALLYHOO'S HISTORIC
SEAFOOD GRILLE

COCONUT BAY RESORT

KEY LARGO
FISHERIES, INC.

SEAFARER RESORT

DOLPHINS
PLUS

RIPTIDE R/V PARK & MOTEL

PINK

SHELL WORLD

Junktique

KEY LARGO
GRANDE RESORT &
BEACH CLUB

*Rock
Harbor*

DIVE IN
WATERSPORTS

STONELEDGE
PARADISE INN

MARINER'S RESORT
VILLAS & MARINA

KEY LIME PRODUCTS

SNAPPER'S WATERFRONT RESTAURANT

FLORIDA KEYS
WILD BIRD CENTER

DOVE CREEK LODGE

TIKI WATER SPORTS, INC.

Tavernier

HARRY HARRIS COUNTY PARK

MARINERS
HOSPITAL

OCEAN POINTE SUITES
AT KEY LARGO

ATLANTIC BAY RESORT

COCONUT PALM INN

TAVERNIER TOWNE CINEMAS

OVERSEAS HWY

0   2.5 mi

0   2.5 km

© AVALON TRAVEL

KEY LARGO

Fest, a lively October event with pirate costume contests, a pirate bazaar and thieves market, and an underwater treasure hunt.

HISTORY

As with the rest of the Florida Keys, local historians believe that the earliest residents of Key Largo were the Calusa Indians and other Native American tribes common to southern Florida. Most of these native inhabitants eventually moved or died out by the 1820s, about the time the U.S. Navy managed to scare away most of the marauding pirates that once roamed these waters. Permanent settlers soon followed, many of whom farmed the land, producing key lime groves, tamarind groves, and pineapple fields, among other produce. It was 16th-century Spanish explorers, however, who gave this lengthy island its name—Cayo Largo, which essentially means "long islet" in Spanish—even though there's no real evidence that they ever came ashore.

With little record of its early years, though, it's difficult to pinpoint the exact history of Key Largo prior to the mid-19th century when various passengers aboard passing ships noted the presence of a small community on the island. But it seems that the prevalence of mosquitoes and the reality of hurricanes slowed the expansion of tiny settlements like Planter, Rock Harbor, Basin Hills, and High Mangroves. For instance, the 1870 census revealed a population of merely 60 individuals, which only rose to 230 by 1885. During this time, no centralized community existed, as evidenced by the repeated relocation of a communal post office, from Rock Harbor to Planter—the southern part of Key Largo, which is today known as Tavernier.

In 1908 scheduled daily train service via the Florida East Coast Railway helped to bring a few more settlers to the area—but, ultimately, the presence of the railroad merely shifted the primary mode of distribution and transportation from ships to trains. At that time there were four stations: Jewfish Creek, Key Largo, Rock Harbor, and Tavernier. By the 1920s the community of Key Largo was well established,

and the population continued to grow, even after the destruction of the Overseas Railroad in the Labor Day Hurricane of 1935.

Over the next few decades, tourism became an increasingly important factor in the growth of Key Largo, and even Hollywood took notice, highlighting this unique locale in the Bogart-Bacall film *Key Largo* (1948). Of course, it was the offshore coral reef system that really set Key Largo apart from other vacation destinations in America. With the establishment of John Pennekamp Coral Reef State Park (America's first undersea park) in 1960, Key Largo National Marine Sanctuary in 1975, and Florida Keys National Marine Sanctuary in 1990, the island found its niche as a world-class underwater diving destination—a designation that has endured into the 21st century.

Today as a self-reliant community filled with as many family-owned businesses as corporate chains, Key Largo has an estimated population of 10,430 (plus about 1,240 in North Key Largo and 2,140 in Tavernier). Although the number of year-round residents has decreased over the last decade, the town is still considered a desirable bedroom community for those escaping Miami's urban sprawl—not to mention a thriving tourist center. For more information about Key Largo's past, consult the **Historical Preservation Society of the Upper Keys** (www.keyshistory.org).

PLANNING YOUR TIME

Despite being the largest island in the Florida Keys, Key Largo has fewer overall diversions than, for instance, Key West—and not much in the way of museums, historical districts, or cultural attractions. Still, the interactive dolphin programs, diverse state parks, sightseeing boat tours, and underwater coral reefs can keep you busy for at least three days. If you choose to pursue other outdoor activities like full-day fishing charters, kayaking excursions, and scuba-diving trips, you'll need to stay two or three days more.

With access to a vehicle, this is an easy island to navigate—in spite of its large size and the spread-out nature of its attractions and lodgings. Stretching from Mile Marker 110 to Mile Marker 91, Key Largo is easily traversed via the Overseas Highway (U.S. 1). Just be aware that much of the thoroughfare is divided by a wide median here, often making it necessary to use the center access roads to reach destinations on the opposite side of U.S. 1.

Given how popular Key Largo can be in winter and early spring, traffic congestion is often an issue from December to April, so be sure to give yourself plenty of time to get around, especially if you have tour reservations. During this peak season, you're also sure to encounter higher lodging rates and more crowded attractions. When planning a trip to Key Largo, you might also want to consider factors like annual events and fishing seasons. The weather is an equally important consideration. Although usually comfortable, the climate can be a little too chilly for sunbathing in January and rather hot and humid from June to September—an ideal time for water-related activities like snorkeling.

As for safety, while Key Largo is relatively crime-free, certain outdoor activities—such as kayaking or scuba diving—can be dangerous without proper instruction. It also helps to have a full understanding of any necessary guidelines or regulations before venturing out, especially if you're a first-timer.

For more information about Key Largo, consult the **Monroe County Tourist Development Council** (1201 White St., Ste. 102, Key West, 305/296-1552 or 800/352-5397, www.fla-keys. com, 9am-5pm Mon.-Fri.) and the **Key Largo Chamber of Commerce and Florida Keys Visitor Center** (106000 Overseas Hwy., Key Largo, 305/451-4747 or 800/822-1088, www. keylargo.org or www.keylargochamber.org, 9am-6pm daily).

Sights

◖ DAGNY JOHNSON KEY LARGO HAMMOCK BOTANICAL STATE PARK

If you're driving to Key Largo, as most people do, your first stop should be in the northern part of the island, north of the U.S. 1 turn-off and not far from Crocodile Lake National Wildlife Refuge, which is closed to the public. Here on the ocean side of the county road lies the tranquil **Dagny Johnson Key Largo Hammock Botanical State Park** (CR-905, www.floridastateparks.org/keylargohammock, 8am-sunset daily, $2.50 pp). Spared from becoming a condominium development in the early 1980s and named after a local environmental activist, this 2,421-acre preserve now protects 84 plant and animal species, plus one of the country's largest tracts of West Indian tropical hardwood hammock.

With a backcountry permit, hikers, bikers, bird-watchers, photographers, and other wildlife lovers can explore the park's more than six miles of backcountry trails, where you might spot mahogany mistletoe, semaphore cactus, Key Largo woodrats, varied butterflies, migratory birds, or an American crocodile. If you have the time, consider bringing a picnic lunch and relaxing at one of the designated tables near the butterfly garden—and of course, don't forget to pack out any and all trash.

Unlike other state parks in the Florida Keys, you'll find no on-duty park ranger near the front gate, so you're expected to use the honor box to pay the requisite park fee. Remember that motorized vehicles are prohibited in the park, as is the collection of any plants or animals. Moreover, you should keep to the paved roadways and designated trail unless you have a backcountry permit, which is available through the John Pennekamp Coral Reef State Park office (305/451-1202). Leashed, well-behaved pets are welcome in the picnic areas and on the self-guided nature trail; of course, service animals are welcome throughout the park. In addition, the park's main, half-mile trail can accommodate bicycles and wheelchairs.

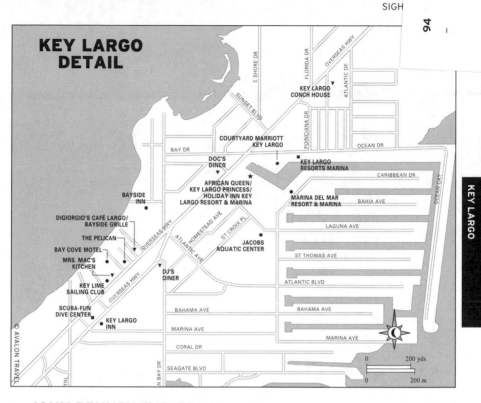

KEY LARGO
DETAIL

KEY LARGO
CONCH HOUSE

COURTYARD MARRIOTT
KEY LARGO

BAY DR

DOC'S
DINER

KEY LARGO
RESORTS MARINA

AFRICAN QUEEN/
KEY LARGO PRINCESS/
HOLIDAY INN KEY
LARGO RESORT & MARINA

BAYSIDE
INN

MARINA DEL MAR
RESORT & MARINA

DIGIORGIO'S CAFÉ LARGO/
BAYSIDE GRILLE

THE PELICAN

BAY COVE MOTEL

JACOBS
AQUATIC CENTER

MRS. MAC'S
KITCHEN

KEY LIME
SAILING CLUB

DJ'S
DINER

SCUBA-FUN
DIVE CENTER

KEY LARGO
INN

© AVALON TRAVEL

KEY LARGO

JOHN PENNEKAMP CORAL REEF STATE PARK

For nature lovers, one of the primary stops in Key Largo should be the incredible **John Pennekamp Coral Reef State Park** (102601 Overseas Hwy., 305/451-1202 or 305/451-6300, www.floridastateparks.org/pennekamp or www.pennekamppark.com, 8am-sunset daily, $8 vehicles with 2-8 passengers plus $0.50 pp, $4.50 motorcycles and single-occupant vehicles, $2.50 pedestrians, bikers, and extra passengers), America's first undersea park—and the perfect spot for a wide range of outdoor activities, from sunbathing to bird-watching to sportfishing. Established in 1960 and situated on the ocean side of U.S. 1, this well-regarded park offers several picnic areas, pavilion rentals ($32-54 daily), a small campground (with modern restrooms), a souvenir and gift shop, a boat ramp ($10 per vessel),

and convenient access to two sandy beaches, including Cannon Beach, which features the remnants of an old Spanish shipwreck.

Visitors enjoy swimming in the relatively warm waters here, plus paddling through the mangrove swamps. Luckily, you can even rent canoes and kayaks on-site (8am-3:45pm daily, $12-20 hourly). Also available are diving tours ($55 pp) and glass-bottom boat tours ($24 adults, $17 children under 12) on the flagship *Spirit of Pennekamp*. In addition, visitors can opt for 2.5-hour snorkeling tours ($30 adults, $25 children under 18) or 4.5-hour snorkeling tours ($39 pp) amid the vibrant shallow-water coral reefs of Florida Keys National Marine Sanctuary—part of the only living coral reef system in the continental United States and a real treat for underwater explorers. Here you'll likely spot parrotfish, yellow cherubfish, brain and staghorn coral, spotted spiny lobster, sea

AN EYE ON MAILBOXES

© LAURA MARTONE

clever mailboxes throughout the Florida Keys

Given the varied landscapes, creatures, activities, and architectural styles that abound in the Florida Keys, it's no wonder that plenty of creative people have found their way here, including artists like John James Audubon, widely known for his bird paintings, and Robert Wyland, a marine conservationist celebrated around the world for his impressive Whaling Walls. While art galleries, filled with the work of local and regional visionaries, extend from Key Largo to Key West, one of the most wonderful aspects of this unique region is that art often exists where you least expect to find it—and life is certainly never dull in southern Florida. Everywhere you turn, for example, you're liable to spy a clever, colorful mailbox inspired by this diverse place. From lighthouses and manatees on the Overseas Highway to fishing lures and mini bungalows on the side streets, these photo-worthy mailboxes are a common sight. So keep a sharp lookout for them as you venture through the Florida Keys. If you decide you'd like a memorable mailbox of your own, simply contact an online company like **BudgetMailboxes.com** (866/505-6245, www.budgetmailboxes.com), which features everything from dolphins to brown pelicans—or better yet, ask the locals where they got theirs.

hermit crabs, and other amazing sealife, all of which are even more vibrant on a sunny cloudless day.

For nominal fees, the park also offers all necessary rental gear for snorkelers, including masks, snorkels, fins, and wetsuits, so there's typically no need to bring more than a swimsuit and a towel. While first-time snorkelers are common here, scuba divers must be certified to participate in the park's reef adventures. Fortunately, the park offers scuba instruction (305/451-6322 or 877/727-5348). All anglers must have a saltwater fishing license. Although this is definitely the spot for active visitors, individuals with disabilities are welcome aboard the glass-bottom boat tours and snorkeling

trips, provided that they are able to get in and out of the water on their own or with the assistance of accompanying helpers.

For those who prefer a less up-close-and-personal underwater encounter, the park's visitor center (8am-5pm daily) features several natural history exhibits as well as a 30,000-gallon saltwater aquarium, housing many of the tropical fish, sea creatures, and other organisms you might see in the ocean. Do yourself a favor, though: Don't leave this park without venturing into the sometimes choppy waters of Florida Keys National Marine Sanctuary. The sight of all those kaleidoscopic fish—and perhaps a sand shark or two—is an experience you'll never forget.

WHO IS JOHN PENNEKAMP?

Established in 1960, **John Pennekamp Coral Reef State Park** (102601 Overseas Hwy., 305/451-1202 or 305/451-6300, www.floridastateparks.org/pennekamp or www.pennekamppark.com) lures a plethora of visitors every year. If you're one of them, you've probably come to snorkel amid the vibrant offshore coral reefs, peer at them from a glass-bottom boat, or kayak through seagrass beds and mangrove swamps. While doing so, you might, if ever so briefly, wonder about the name of the park.

Ultimately, this one-of-a-kind locale serves as a tribute to the late John D. Pennekamp, a longtime journalist, *Miami Herald* editor, and regional environmentalist who was instrumental in preserving the land that would eventually become Everglades National Park. Born in 1897, Pennekamp worked for 14 years at *The Cincinnati Post* before heading to southern Florida, where he joined the *Miami Herald* staff in 1925. First serving as a city editor and later as the associate editor, Pennekamp stayed with the *Herald* until his retirement in 1976.

Beyond his editorial duties, though, Pennekamp had a passion for the environment—and a desire to help preserve it for future generations. So subsequent to his efforts to establish Everglades National Park, he became a member of the Everglades National Park Commission from 1945 to 1947. He also served as chairman of the Florida Board of Parks and Historic Memorials, the precursor to the Division of Recreation and Parks, from 1953 to 1976. During the 1960s, Governor LeRoy Collins honored the journalist's unwavering dedication to conservation by naming America's first undersea park after him. When Pennekamp died in 1978 at the age of 81, only two years after retiring from the *Herald*, he left behind a legacy of appreciation for the natural world, a legacy that endures today through the more than one million visitors who venture inside the park annually.

KEY LARGO

◖ DOLPHIN ATTRACTIONS

Together the sister facilities **Dolphin Cove** (MM 101.9 BS U.S. 1, 305/451-4060 or 877/365-2683, www.dolphinscove.com, 8am-6pm daily, nonparticipating admission $10 adults, $5 children 7-17, free for children under 7) and **Dolphins Plus** (31 Corrine Pl., 305/451-1993 or 866/860-7946, www.dolphinsplus.com, 8am-6pm daily, nonparticipating admission $10 adults, $5 children 7-17, free for children under 7) pursue marine mammal research, promote environmental awareness, and present year-round educational opportunities to the visiting public. At Dolphin Cove, visitors can touch bottlenose dolphins through **shallow-water encounters** (10am and 1pm daily, $155 pp), experience dorsal tows and belly rubs in **structured swims** (10am, 1pm, and 3pm daily, $195 pp), or snorkel alongside dolphins in **natural swims** (8:30am daily, $150 pp).

Other activities include **painting with dolphins** ($125 pp) and the **trainer-for-a-day program** (8:30am-3:30pm daily, $670 pp) for participants 12 years of age or older, which offers a behind-the-scenes look at this fascinating marine mammal facility, including the basics of animal training, dolphin behavior, and food preparation, plus participation in various dolphin swims. Combo packages are also available, though age, height, and physical restrictions may apply. Reservations are highly recommended for all programs.

A little farther south, Dolphins Plus is accessible via Ocean Bay Drive on the ocean side of U.S. 1, just south of Mile Marker 100. Here visitors can also participate in **structured swims** (9:15am, 1pm, and 3pm daily, $195 pp) and **natural swims** (8:30am and 2pm daily, $150 pp) with bottlenose dolphins, plus an engrossing **trainer-for-a-day program** (9am-4pm daily, $670 pp). Animal lovers can opt for dolphin **body-language workshops** (8am-noon daily, $395 pp), a **combination structured and natural swim** ($280 pp), or an educational,

KEY LARGO

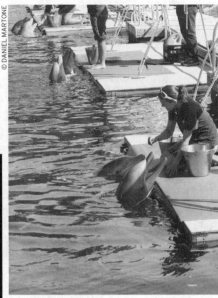
© DANIEL MARTONE

interacting with the dolphins of Dolphins Plus

one-on-one swim (11:30am and 3pm daily, $140 pp) with a frisky California sea lion named Wono that is preceded by a 30-minute briefing about sea lion habitats, feeding habits, reproductive biology, and conservation, among other topics.

Truly passionate souls can also sign up for the full-day **marine biologist program** (9am-4pm daily, $600 pp) during which they'll learn about dolphin behavior and sampling techniques, participate in a study about mother-calf interactions, help to prepare fish and vitamin regimens for the on-site marine mammals, and engage in a private natural swim. Participants in this program must be at least 14 years of age, and anyone under the age of 18 must have a signed release form from a parent or legal guardian. Age and height restrictions may also apply with other activities, and reservations are highly recommended, especially for the full-day programs.

Both of these facilities are top-notch, staffed with passionate, helpful individuals who are all committed to the conservation and protection

of marine mammals around the world. They both offer some truly inspirational and educational programs that for most visitors become once-in-a-lifetime experiences, so it's not necessary to visit both during your trip to Key Largo—unless, of course, you simply can't get enough of these loving, playful creatures.

FLORIDA KEYS WILD BIRD CENTER

While Key Largo is mainly known for its wide assortment of water-related activities, you should also consider taking a walk through the **Laura Quinn Wild Bird Sanctuary** (93600 Overseas Hwy., Tavernier, 305/852-4486, www.fkwbc.org, sunrise-sunset daily, $5 pp donation requested), part of the nonprofit **Florida Keys Wild Bird Center,** founded in 1984 when veterinarian Bob Foley asked retired teacher Laura Quinn to assist with the rehabilitation of several wild birds that he had treated. Mainly operated by volunteers and comprising natural habitats as well as open-air enclosures, the 5.5-acre sanctuary allows visitors to stroll along a narrow shaded boardwalk, where they can observe a variety of caged species, from cormorants to laughing gulls to great horned owls—most of whom have been injured as a result of human activities, such as mercury poisoning and fishing tackle entanglements, and are currently undergoing rehabilitation.

In the adjacent black and red mangrove wetlands and along the Florida Bay shoreline, you'll spot a slew of native birds, including brown pelicans, common egrets, and great white herons, most of whom are usually waiting for the afternoon feeding. Almost more curious, though, is the innumerable mass of makeshift, wooden sponsor plaques affixed to the cages and boardwalk railing—a testament to all of the individuals and organizations who have helped to support the sanctuary and the separate hospital space (93997 Overseas Hwy., Tavernier) over the years.

After visiting the bird center, consider heading south to Mile Marker 92.6, where you can cross the highway via Burton Drive. From here continue on Burton to 1st Street, and take

© DANIEL MARTONE

Birds flock to the open habitats of the Florida Keys Wild Bird Center.

East Beach Road to **Harry Harris County Park** (305/852-7161, 7:30am-sunset daily, $5 non-county residents 16 or older Sat.-Sun. and holidays, free for children under 16 and Monroe County residents), a popular place on the weekends and the perfect spot to watch one of the Keys' sensational sunsets. Other amenities here include a sandy beach, a swimming area, a boat ramp, playground equipment, two baseball fields, numerous picnic tables and pavilions, barbecue grills, and public restrooms. Fortunately, pets are allowed in the park, though not along the beach.

BOAT TOURS

Every day the **Coral Reef Park Company, Inc.** (305/451-6300) operates three separate 2.5-hour glass-bottom boat tours ($24 adults, $17 children under 12) out of **John Pennekamp Coral Reef State Park** (102601 Overseas Hwy., 305/451-1202, www.floridastateparks. org/pennekamp or www.pennekamppark. com, 8am-sunset daily, $8 vehicles with 2-8

passengers plus $0.50 pp, $4.50 motorcycles and single-occupant vehicles, $2.50 pedestrians, bikers, and extra passengers). Such excursions are offered on the flagship *Spirit of Pennekamp,* a 65-foot, high-speed catamaran that's capable of whisking up to 130 passengers toward the coral formations and vibrant sealife of Florida Keys National Marine Sanctuary in the ocean waters east of Key Largo. Tours run at 9:15am, 12:15pm, and 3:15pm, and all tours require a minimum number of passengers to leave the marina; limited wheelchair accessibility is available on board.

Farther south you'll find other glass-bottom boat tours, such as the **Key Largo Princess** (305/451-4655 or 877/648-8129, www.keylargoprincess.com, $30 adults, $17 children, free for children under 2), a luxurious 70-foot, 129-passenger yacht that operates three daily two-hour excursions (10am, 1pm, and 4pm). Docked at the Holiday Inn Key Largo Resort & Marina (99701 Overseas Hwy., 305/451-2121, www.holidayinnkeylargo.com), the *Key Largo Princess* also offers private cocktail cruises (complete with underwater lights). If you choose one of the daytime excursions, try to get a seat on the sun deck, which affords you a panoramic offshore view of the Florida Keys and the multicolored ocean waters around you. Once you reach the living coral reef, you'll be able to observe varied coral specimens and kaleidoscopic fish through a 280-square-foot viewing window below your feet. Advance tickets can be purchased through **Zerve** (800/979-3370, www.zerve.com).

Before heading out on the *Princess,* take note of the small weathered boat docked beside her. Built in 1912 for service in Africa, the **African Queen** was used until 1968 by the British East Africa Railway to ferry cargo passengers across Lake Albert. During that time, the *Queen* was featured in the eponymous 1951 John Huston film that also starred Humphrey Bogart and Katharine Hepburn. Feel free to take photographs of this famous vessel or step into Bogie's shoes and reserve an unforgettable ride (305/451-4655) aboard the *Queen* herself.

KEY LARGO

A little farther south, **Caribbean Watersports** (Hilton Key Largo Resort, 97000 Overseas Hwy., 305/852-4707, www.caribbeanwatersports.com, 9am-6:30pm daily) offers two-hour champagne sunset cruises ($60 pp) and "Enviro-Tours" ($60 adults, $45 children) across Florida Bay and into the Everglades. These personalized two-hour excursions, which can accommodate up to six passengers at a time, provide an intimate glimpse at the diverse ecosystems of southern Florida, from mangrove forests to shallow creeks and bays. Along the way, you may also encounter any number of wild creatures, including bottlenose dolphins, laughing gulls, bald eagles, and endangered manatees.

Entertainment and Events

NIGHTLIFE

Key Largo isn't exactly a hotbed of nighttime activity—certainly not like Miami to the north or Key West to the south. Still, you will find several after-hours diversions here, mostly in the form of live entertainment—or at the very least, curious people-watching and sunset-gazing opportunities—at area bars and restaurants. The **Caribbean Club** (MM 104 BS U.S. 1, 305/451-4466, www.caribbeanclubkl.com, 7am-4am daily), which has been locally owned and operated since 1963, is one such joint. Although it may look like a typical Keys-style bar, you'll soon notice that it's filled with locals. Don't let the motorcycles parked outside dissuade you; this is an amiable, dog-friendly place, noted for its cheap drinks and vittles, daily happy hour (4pm-6pm), and live music Thursday-Sunday nights. Besides, the bikers weren't the first tough guys to frequent the Caribbean Club. It was here, after all, that Humphrey Bogart and Lauren Bacall filmed their famous 1948 movie *Key Largo,* memorabilia from which now fills this famous watering hole. Just as in the days of Bogie, the club allows smoking inside, though the doors stay open to let in some fresh Florida air. So order a burger and a cocktail, and enjoy the laid-back atmosphere.

Several miles south, at Mile Marker 94.5, **Snapper's Waterfront Restaurant** (139 Seaside Ave., 305/852-5956, www.snapperskeylargo.com, 11am-10pm Mon.-Thurs., 11am-11pm Fri.-Sat., 10am-10pm Sun.) is another winning spot for nightly entertainment, from magic acts to blues, jazz, reggae, and classic rock performances. In addition, on the last Sunday of every month, Snapper's hosts a "Turtle Club Party," a thematic daylong event featuring live music, games, giveaways, and specials, plus free food for all Turtle Club members. Past parties have revolved around everything from crawfish boils to Mardi Gras.

In Key Largo—and really throughout the Florida Keys—most bars and some restaurants offer regular happy hours, complete with appetizer and drink specials. For more information about such watering holes, consult **Happy Hour Keys** (www.happyhourkeys.com). If in doubt about the accuracy of information on this third-party website, contact the bar or restaurant directly.

THE ARTS

Key West certainly boasts the lion's share of live music, dance performances, and theatrical venues in the Florida Keys, but that doesn't mean that Key Largo is without cultural diversions. Since 1978, **The Key Players** (305/453-0997, www.thekeyplayers.org, show times and ticket prices vary) has presented live theater in the Upper Keys. Typically, this nonprofit community troupe produces four shows each year, ranging from Broadway musicals to lesser-known comedies and dramas, in assorted venues.

The **Florida Keys Community Concert Band** (305/451-4530, www.keyscommunityconcertband.org) was founded in 1992 by a small group of dedicated musicians and usually performs free family concerts at Islamorada's Founders Park (Nov.-Apr.). On occasion, it offers an extra concert in Key Largo's Murray E. Nelson Government and Cultural Center at Mile Marker 102. Check the band's online schedule for specific dates, and consult the **Florida Keys Council of the Arts** (1100 Simonton St., Key West, 305/295-4369, www.keysarts.com) for information about other cultural events in the Upper Keys.

If you enjoy arts of a more cinematic bent, you can always head to the **Tavernier Cinema 5** (91298 Overseas Hwy., Tavernier, 305/853-7003, show times and ticket prices vary), at the southern end of Key Largo. Although this isn't the fanciest movie theater you'll ever encounter, you'll certainly be able to catch the latest flicks here, and it's rarely crowded.

FESTIVALS AND EVENTS
◖ Key Largo Pirates Fest
For four fun-filled days in late October, the annual **Key Largo Pirates Fest** (305/394-3736, www.keylargopiratesfest.com, activity prices vary) invites visitors to celebrate the pirating lifestyle—in particular, the legend of the notorious African pirate Black Caesar, who allegedly prowled Florida's coastal waters in the 1700s. Before heading south to Key West for the annual Fantasy Fest extravaganza, which also takes place in late October, consider getting a taste of the island mayhem with this lively event. Festival activities include a pirate parade, pirate costume contests, a pirate bazaar and thieves market, an underwater treasure hunt, choreographed pirate shows, and various celebrations at area restaurants.

Other Area Festivals
Besides holiday gatherings like the St. Patrick's Day Parade and New Year's Eve fireworks display, Key Largo hosts several other annual events, including fishing tournaments and food festivals. In mid-January, for instance, the 10-day **Uncorked... the Key Largo & Islamorada Food & Wine Festival** (305/394-3736, www.

delicious samples at the annual Key Largo Stone Crab & Seafood Festival fkrm.com/uncorked, activity prices vary) lures gourmands with wine tastings, wine classes, cooking demonstrations, and progressive wine dinners. Then during the last weekend of the month, the **Key Largo Stone Crab & Seafood Festival** (305/451-4502, www.keylargoseafoodfestival.com, $5 adults, free for children under 12) features an array of fresh seafood, cooking demonstrations, fishing workshops, eating contests, arts-and-crafts vendors, live entertainment, and other distractions.

In late April, the eight-day **Key Largo Conch Republic Days** (305/394-3736, www.keylargoconchrepublicdays.com, activity prices vary) honors the 1982 ceremonial secession of the Florida Keys from the United States with a lineup of zany activities at area restaurants, such as a Jimmy Buffett songwriting contest, a conch-fritter eating contest, a key lime dessert cookoff, a co-ed stiletto strut, and an attempt at the world record for conch-shell blowing.

Of course, if you're here in early or mid-December, consider watching the **Holiday Boat Parade** (305/451-4502, www.keylargoboatparade.com, dates vary) on Blackwater Sound, near Mile Marker 104 on the bay side of U.S. 1. With a different theme each year, this magical lighted boat parade, which typically occurs on a Saturday evening, is a festive, family-friendly way to kick off the holiday season—whether you decide to participate in the parade, view from your boat, or observe the proceedings from shore. Each year, cash prizes are awarded in various categories, including best use of the selected theme.

Shopping

In general, travelers flock to Key Largo for its bountiful outdoor diversions, not its shopping opportunities. That's probably because beyond the Tradewinds Shopping Center and several diving emporiums, shoppers won't find as many options in this part of the Florida Keys as in, for instance, Key West. Nevertheless, several area stores are worth mentioning.

ART GALLERIES
Although art aficionados will find more selections in Islamorada and Key West, they'll still appreciate the **Key Largo Art Gallery** (103200 Overseas Hwy., Ste. 10, 305/451-0052, www.keylargoartgallery.com, 10am-5pm Tues.-Sat., 10am-1pm Sun.), with its occasional jewelry classes and a wide array of kaleidoscopic paintings from new artists as well as veterans like Jackie Campa and Teresa Kelley.

Bluewater Potters (102991 Overseas Hwy., Ste. A, 305/453-1920, www.bluewaterpotters.com, 11am-5pm daily) features on-site pottery production and kiln firing, the beach-inspired pottery of owners Kim and Corky Wagner, plus items from other local, regional, and national artists. Recently, the Wagners opened a second location near Mile Marker 81.5 in Islamorada.

Stephen Frink Photographic (102600 Overseas Hwy., 305/451-3737 or 800/451-3737, www.stephenfrink.com or www.stephenfrinkphoto.com, 10am-5pm Mon., 8am-5pm Tues.-Sat.) displays the stunning images of one of the world's most widely published underwater photographers.

You'll find the tastefully displayed paintings of several world-renowned artists at **The Gallery at Kona Kai** (97802 Overseas Hwy., 305/852-7200, www.g-k-k.com, 9am-7pm daily or by appointment), an elegant gallery situated amid the lush foliage of the Kona Kai Resort. For more information about these and other art galleries, consult the **Florida Keys Council of the Arts** (1100 Simonton St., Key West, 305/295-4369, www.keysarts.com).

GIFT AND SOUVENIR SHOPS
For gifts and souvenirs, you'll spot a handful of curious shops, including the **Florida Keys Gift Company** (102421 Overseas Hwy., 305/453-9229, www.keysmermaid.com,

9am-7pm Mon.-Sat., 9am-6pm Sun.), a repository of tropical jewelry, clothing, and decor, plus regional products like the aromatic roasts of Baby's Coffee, a store in the Lower Keys. Nearby, **Largo Cargo** (103101 Overseas Hwy., 305/451-4242 or 800/795-8889, www.largocargo.com, 8:30am-8:30pm daily), which has been in operation since 1985, offers an assortment of tropical apparel, Panama Jack hats, Future Beach kayaks, island music, maps and books, and collectable coins, fragrances, and glassware.

You can pick up any number of seashells, seasonal outfits, and other souvenirs at the 20,000-square-foot **Shell World** (97600 Overseas Hwy., 305/852-8245, www.shellworldflkeys.com, 9am-8pm daily), situated on the median of U.S. 1 as well as an alternate location on the northern end of Key Largo (106040 Overseas Hwy., 305/451-9797, 9am-5pm daily). Then if you're short on beach staples like towels, sunglasses, hats, sandals, and other apparel—not to mention souvenirs—stop by the touristy **Sandal Factory Outlet/T-Shirt City** (102411 Overseas Hwy., 305/453-9644, 9am-8pm Mon.-Sat., 9am-6pm Sun.), which also has locations in Islamorada and Marathon.

FOOD AND CIGAR EMPORIUMS

If you have a hankering for regional treats, head to **Key Lime Products** (95200 Overseas Hwy., 305/853-0378 or 800/870-1780, www.keylimeproducts.com, 8am-5pm Mon.-Sat.), offering a wide assortment of tangy delights, from key lime iced tea to key lime thimble cookies to key lime shampoo. If you're staying in a room, suite, or cottage equipped with kitchen facilities, you might also want to partake of the fresh fish, crab, lobster, shrimp, and conch as well as the key lime pie and other delectables that **Key Largo Fisheries, Inc.** (1313 Ocean Bay Dr., 305/451-3782 or 800/432-4358, www.keylargofisheries.com, 7am-5:30pm Mon.-Sat.) has been serving since 1972.

Even cigar lovers will find shopping bliss in

© LAURA MARTONE

Tourists can find a wealth of souvenirs at Shell World.

Key Largo. The **Island Smoke Shop** (103400 Overseas Hwy., 305/453-4014 or 800/680-9701, www.islandsmokeshop.com, 10am-6pm daily) offers pipes, ashtrays, humidors, lighters, and over 1,200 brands and sizes of handmade premium cigars, including El Original maduros. Besides its vast inventory, it also boasts the largest walk-in humidor in southern Florida.

Sports and Recreation

GOLF

At the exclusive **Ocean Reef Club** (35 Ocean Reef Dr., 305/367-5912 or 800/741-7333, www.oceanreef.com) on the northern end of Key Largo, guests staying in on-site vacation rentals or at the 144-room inn have access to two championship 18-hole courses. Both the Hammock Course, partially situated within a mangrove and tropical hardwood hammock, and the Dolphin Course, with fairways that wind past mahogany trees and coconut palms, feature incredible vistas and challenging holes. Instructional sessions are also available. Unfortunately, you must be a social member of the Ocean Reef Club or a member's guest in order to access the golf courses, lodgings, and other areas of this private community. Guests of the Ocean Reef Club may reserve tee times by contacting the Membership Office (305/367-5921, rates vary seasonally).

HIKING AND BIKING

Although Key Largo is primarily a water lover's playground, there are certainly some favored activities among landlubbers. Hikers, for instance, can experience the winding self-guided nature trail through **Dagny Johnson Key Largo Hammock Botanical State Park** (CR-905, www.floridastateparks.org/keylargohammock, 8am-sunset daily, $2.50 pp). Of course, to really experience the woods of this serene 2,421-acre preserve, which protects more than 80 different plant and animal species, you should explore the six miles of backcountry trails, for which you'll need a backcountry permit, available through **John Pennekamp Coral Reef State Park** (102601 Overseas Hwy., 305/451-1202, www.floridastateparks.org/pennekamp or www.pennekamppark.com,

8am-sunset daily, $8 vehicles with 2-8 passengers plus $0.50 pp, $4.50 motorcycles and single-occupant vehicles, $2.50 pedestrians, bikers, and extra passengers). If you're a birding enthusiast, you'll especially appreciate Dagny Johnson State Park, where you're likely to spot a variety of species, from white-crowned pigeons to red-bellied woodpeckers to great blue herons. Rare sightings might include mangrove cuckoos, masked boobies, black vultures, and great horned owls. With its two beaches and three nature trails, nearby John Pennekamp also offers a treasure trove of species for avid bird-watchers.

Bikers, too, will enjoy the backcountry trails of Dagny Johnson State Park (provided you secure a permit). In addition, a 15.5-mile biking path, part of the **Florida Keys Overseas Heritage Trail,** runs past numerous businesses and parks in Key Largo between Mile Marker 106.5 and Mile Marker 91. Bicycles can be rented from the **Key Largo Bike Shop** (100109 Overseas Hwy., 305/393-2453, www.keylargobike.com, 8am-5pm daily, $18-60 daily), offering road bikes as well as hybrids. Weekly rates are also available, and helmets and locks are included with all rentals.

FISHING AND BOATING

While anglers and boaters will find even more options down south in Islamorada (the self-proclaimed "sportfishing capital of the world"), Key Largo certainly features a wide array of fishing charters and boat rentals. Probably the best place to start your search for a fishing charter is the **Key Largo Resorts Marina** (MM 100 OS U.S. 1, 305/453-7171, www.keylargo-marina.com), hard to miss beside the Holiday Inn. Of the numerous options available, you'll find **Beaver Charters** (305/394-0679, www. sportfishinginthekeys.com), which offers half-day charters ($600 per trip), full-day charters ($900 per trip), evening tarpon trips ($350 per trip), and swordfishing excursions ($900 per trip). All charters include bait, tackle, ice, and temporary fishing licenses.

In the same marina, you'll encounter the **Sailors Choice** party fishing boat (305/451-1802, www.sailorschoicefishingboat.com), a 65-foot vessel offering two daily trips (9am-1pm and 1:30pm-5:30pm, $40 pp) as well as special night trips (7:30pm-midnight) on Friday and Saturday, all of which you can book through **Zerve** (800/979-3370, www. zerve.com). Passengers will likely catch snapper, grouper, wahoo, and other offshore fish, though every experience is unique. Also here is **Key Largo Fishing Adventures** (305/923-9293, www.keyssportfishing.com), featuring the 38-foot *Fin Razer* ($735 per half day, $1,050 daily), ideal for reef and offshore fishing, plus swordfishing ($1,350 per trip) night or day.

Operating out of the Dove Creek Lodge, which is situated on the ocean side of U.S. 1 near Mile Marker 94.5, **Blackfoot Charters** (305/481-0111, www.blackfootfishing.com, $400 per night or half day, $550-600 daily) offers backcountry, flats, and canoe fishing in the Upper Keys, the Everglades, and Biscayne National Park. Captain Mike Makowski, a native of southern Florida, invites novice and veteran anglers alike to seek out bonefish, tarpon, permit, snook, redfish, and other seasonal species—while listening to his colorful tales of local history. Other area charters include **Reel Chaos Charters** (305/587-1150, www.reel-chaoscharters.com, $400 per half day, $600 daily), which specializes in backcountry and flats fishing for redfish, tarpon, snook, and other species; **Rodeo Charters** (305/852-3829 or 305/522-2638, www.rodeocharters.com, rates vary), which has featured offshore, reef, wreck, and backcountry fishing since 1973; and **Tails Up Fishing Charters** (305/394-1383, www.tailsupfishing.com, $400-450 per half day, $600-700 daily), which targets redfish,

bonefish, snook, and tarpon in the backcountry and flats.

If you'd prefer a private fishing trip, consider renting a boat from **PonTunes Boat Rentals & Marina** (107690 Overseas Hwy., 305/453-5007, www.pontunes.com, rates vary), which offers an assortment of vessels, from fishing boats to luxury pontoon boats ideal for snorkelers. If you'd rather purchase a vessel while you're in the Keys, consult **Tiki Water Sports, Inc.** (94381 Overseas Hwy., 305/852-9298 or 800/726-2102, www.tikiwatersports.net, 8am-6pm Mon.-Thurs., 8am-4:30pm Fri., 11am-3pm Sat.-Sun.), a one-stop shop that sells sailboats, kayaks, pedal boats, and stand-up paddleboarding (SUP) boards; offers a wide array of marine supplies; and provides boat maintenance, repairs, and dry boat storage. You can also rent kayaks ($50-75 daily, $250-400 weekly) as well as sailboats ($100-300 daily, $300-1,000 weekly) during store hours.

◖ CANOEING AND KAYAKING

With access to mangrove swamps, the Atlantic Ocean, Florida Bay, and of course, the wildlife-rich waterways of the Everglades, Key Largo provides an ideal landscape for canoeists and kayakers alike. Many first-timers head initially to **John Pennekamp Coral Reef State Park** (102601 Overseas Hwy., 305/451-1202, www. floridastateparks.org/pennekamp or www.pennekamppark.com, 8am-sunset daily, $8 vehicles with 2-8 passengers plus $0.50 pp, $4.50 motorcycles and single-occupant vehicles, $2.50 pedestrians, bikers, and extra passengers) in the northern part of Key Largo, where the **Coral Reef Park Company, Inc.** (305/451-6300) offers enough canoe ($20 hourly) and kayak rentals ($12-17 hourly) to accommodate several individuals, couples, and families at any given time. No matter when you visit, it seems that you'll always spot a brightly colored kayak winding its way through the mangrove trees—the ideal mode of transport for those hoping to get an up-close, yet unobtrusive, look at area birds and other critters.

Of course, the Coral Reef Park Company isn't the only game in town. **Caribbean**

KEY LARGO

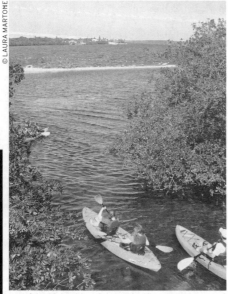

© LAURA MARTONE

a guided kayaking trip amid the mangroves of the Upper Keys

Watersports (Hilton Key Largo Resort, 97000 Overseas Hwy., 305/852-4707, www.caribbeanwatersports.com, 9am-6:30pm daily) offers both kayak ($12-30 hourly, $20-45 for two hours) and paddleboat rentals ($30-40 hourly, $45-55 for two hours). Additionally, **Florida Bay Outfitters** (104050 Overseas Hwy., 305/451-3018, www.kayakfloridakeys.com, 8:30am-6pm daily) and **Garl's Coastal Kayaking** (305/393-3223, www.coastal-kayaking.com, trip times vary) both provide guided kayaking trips throughout the Upper Keys and the Everglades—and both typically offer pickup service to the launch point.

In fact, Florida Bay Outfitters features a wide array of trips, ranging from three-hour tours to Dusenberry Creek ($60 pp), where dolphin and manatee spottings are probable, to three-day kayak sailing excursions amid the islands of Florida Bay ($495 pp, including meals and camping gear). Free pickups and drop-offs at participating resorts are offered for most trips, and reservations are necessary

for all of them. In addition to guided tours, Florida Bay Outfitters—one of Florida's largest paddle-sports retailers—also offers rental canoes, sea kayaks, pedal and sail kayaks, sit-on-tops, and rec boats ($30-100 per half day, $40-125 daily), plus three-hour instructional sessions ($75 pp with rental gear) focused on specific topics like kayaking basics, advanced skills, or rescue techniques.

Meanwhile, Garl's half-day Florida Bay trips ($75 pp) allow you to explore the mangrove islands near Key Largo; besides kayaking in a glass-bottom boat, you'll also have the opportunity to snorkel amid a variety of marine creatures, from starfish to horseshoe crabs. For the Everglades trips ($95-125 per half day, $125-150 daily), Garl can transport passengers (when there's room in his jeep) from Key Largo to Flamingo. Depending on the weather conditions and the type of trip, Garl guides paddlers on a combination of hikes to alligator holes, freshwater kayaking excursions amid mangroves and crocodiles, and saltwater kayaking tours at sunset. No matter which trip you choose, Garl encourages you to wear your swimsuit and bring your camera. Single and double kayaks are available, and reservations are required for all trips.

◖ DIVING AND SNORKELING

In the ocean waters east of Key Largo lies Florida Keys National Marine Sanctuary, a 220-mile-long coral reef ecosystem that stretches from the southern end of Key Biscayne to the Dry Tortugas—incidentally, the only living coral reef system in the continental United States and the third largest coral reef system in the world. If you're new to snorkeling and scuba diving, head first to **John Pennekamp Coral Reef State Park** (102601 Overseas Hwy., 305/451-1202, www.floridastateparks.org/pennekamp or www.pennekamppark.com, 8am-sunset daily, $8 vehicles with 2-8 passengers plus $0.50 pp, $4.50 motorcycles and single-occupant vehicles, $2.50 pedestrians, bikers, and extra passengers). Through the **Coral Reef Park Company, Inc.** (305/451-6300, 305/451-6322, or 877/727-5348), you can take diving

© STEPHEN FRINK/FLORIDA KEYS NEWS BUREAU

snorkeling above the famous *Christ of the Abyss* statue

KEY LARGO

Company isn't the only diving outfitter in Key Largo. For instance, **Amy Slate's Amoray Dive Resort** (104250 Overseas Hwy., 305/451-3595 or 800/426-6729, www.amoray.com) offers an array of diving classes, from a two-hour beginner's class ($75 pp) to a three-day PADI rescue diver class ($450 pp), plus twice-daily snorkeling excursions (8:30am and 1pm, $45-50 pp) and two-location diving trips (8:30am and 1pm daily, $85 pp with gear). In addition to diving classes, diving trips (and, in most cases, snorkeling excursions) to the reefs and wrecks that compose Florida Keys National Marine Sanctuary are offered by operators such as the well-regarded **Silent World Dive Center** (105952 Overseas Hwy., 305/451-3252, www.silentworld.com, 7:30am-6pm daily, trips 8:30am and 12:30pm daily, $80-100 pp), **Island Ventures** (103900 Overseas Hwy., 305/451-4957 or 866/293-5006, www.islandventure.com, trips 8am and 12:30pm daily, $75-85 pp), the **Key Largo Dive Center** (100670 Overseas Hwy., 305/451-5844, www.keylargodivecenter.com, 7:45am-6pm daily, trips 8:30am and 1:30pm daily, $84 pp, $420 per charter), and the **Sea Dwellers Dive Center** (99850 Overseas Hwy., 305/451-3640 or 800/451-3640, www.seadwellers.com, 8am-5pm daily, trips 8:30am and 1pm daily, $65-80 pp with gear). Underwater sights include the *Duane* and the *Bibb,* two U.S. Coast Guard cutters used in World War II, and the **USS Spiegel Grove,** a 510-foot Navy transport ship originally launched in November 1955, prematurely sunk in May 2002 to create an artificial reef, and shifted into an upright position by Hurricane Dennis in 2005. In this region, you might also see star coral, elkhorn coral, and other formations on **Molasses Reef,** the **Benwood** shipwreck south of **Dixie Shoals,** the sea caves of **French Reef,** and the *City of Washington* shipwreck near **Elbow Reef.**

You'll also find a number of diving operators in the nearby **Key Largo Resorts Marina** (MM 100 OS U.S. 1, 305/453-7171, www.keylargomarina.com). Such options include **BlueWater Divers of Key Largo** (99701 Overseas Hwy., 305/453-9600, www.bluewaterdiver.net,

instruction ($185-385 pp), earn PADI Open Water certification ($485 pp), and participate in 2.5-hour snorkeling trips ($30 adults, $25 children under 18, plus gear rentals), 4.5-hour snorkeling trips ($39 pp, plus gear rentals), or scuba-diving tours ($55 pp, plus $29 for gear rental) amid the vibrant coral reefs a few miles offshore.

Out here, you'll encounter amazing sealife like parrotfish, yellow cherubfish, brain and staghorn coral, spotted spiny lobster, and sea hermit crabs, plus formations such as **Grecian Rocks** and **Key Largo Dry Rocks,** which contains elkhorn coral and the ever-popular, often-photographed *Christ of the Abyss* statue (also known as *Christ of the Deep*). Before heading out on a snorkeling or diving trip, consider stopping by the park's visitor center (8am-5pm daily) to see several saltwater aquariums housing many of the kaleidoscopic tropical fish, coral formations, and other sea creatures you might see while exploring the ocean.

As with kayaking, the Coral Reef Park

PROTECTING FLORIDA'S CORAL REEFS

While visiting **John Pennekamp Coral Reef State Park** (102601 Overseas Hwy., 305/451-1202 or 305/451-6300, www.floridastateparks.org/pennekamp or www.pennekamppark.com), take a moment to stop by the on-site visitor center. The center aims to protect the fragile coral reef system that extends for 220 miles along the eastern side of the Florida Keys—the 2,900-square-mile Florida Keys National Marine Sanctuary. The following boating and diving regulations are strictly enforced by state park officials:

- Always consult weather conditions ahead of time, as it's best not to go out in rough seas. Poor visibility, strong winds, and increased waves can hinder safe interaction with coral reefs.

- Be sure to maintain all equipment to avoid inadvertent discharges of oil and other toxic substances.

- Do not discharge any raw sewage into offshore waters; instead, use official pump-out facilities, available throughout the Keys.

- Do not litter in the ocean or abandon structures on the seabed, especially near the reefs; if you see such debris, please retrieve it and properly dispose of it on land.

- Use nautical and tidal charts to practice safe navigation, know your boat's draft, and be aware of the variations in surface water color: Deepwater areas, for instance, are typically blue; shallower areas are often green; brown usually indicates shallow coral reefs and seagrass beds; and white signifies sandbars and rubble areas.

- Stay in marked channels, and do not approach lighthouses, reef light towers, shoal markers, or yellow buoys, which usually indicate shallow reef and seagrass areas.

- Slow down to an idle speed in dive areas, and stay at least 100 feet from a red-and-white, diver-down flag.

- Be careful while navigating a boat around coral reefs and seagrass beds, and do not drop anchors on or near living coral; instead, use the white-and-blue mooring buoys or anchor in the sandy patches adjacent to the reef.

- Do not damage or remove markers and mooring buoys.

- If you run aground, immediately turn the engine off and, if possible, tilt the motor

8:30am and 1pm daily, $75-80 pp), **Horizon Divers** (100 Ocean Dr., 305/453-3535 or 800/984-3483, www.horizondivers.com, 8am-6pm daily, $80-90 pp), the **Keys Diver & Snorkel Center** (99696 Overseas Hwy., 305/451-1177 or 888/289-2402, www.keysdiver.com, 8am-5pm daily, trips 7:15am and 11:30am daily, $70-80 pp), and **Ocean Divers** (522 Caribbean Dr., 305/451-1113 or 800/451-1113, www.oceandivers.com, 7:30am-5pm daily, trips 8am and 1pm daily, $85-90 pp). Other area operators that feature diving classes as well as diving excursions include **Captain Slate's Atlantis Dive Center** (51 Garden Cove Dr., 305/451-3020 or 800/331-3483, www.captainslate.com, 7:30am-5pm daily, $70-110 pp), which hosts an annual Underwater Easter Egg Hunt; **Quiescence Diving Services** (103680 Overseas Hwy., 305/451-2440, www.keylargo-diving.com, 8am-6pm daily, $75-85 pp with gear); and the **Scuba-Fun Dive Center** (99222 Overseas Hwy., 305/394-5046 or 877/977-3483, www.scuba-fun.com, 8am-5pm daily, $80-149 pp), which is hard to miss due to the stunning Wyland Wall on its exterior.

Of course, many of these operators also offer snorkeling as an option. You can also enjoy snorkeling excursions to the reefs within John Pennekamp Coral Reef State Park by boarding the *Sundiver III,* operated by the **Sundiver Station Snorkel Shop** (102840 Overseas Hwy., 305/451-2220 or 800/654-7369, www.snorkelingisfun.com, trips 9am, noon, and 3pm daily, $33 adults, $27 children under upward; wait until high tide to remove the vessel by walking or poling, and if necessary, call the **Florida Fish and Wildlife Conservation Commission (FWC)** (888/404-3922) for assistance. Be prepared to incur towing fees as well as fines for damaging the seagrass habitat.

- To avoid standing on the coral, use inflatable vests (if snorkeling) and practice proper buoyancy control (if diving).

- Avoid touching, kicking, defacing, or sitting on living coral formations.

- Do not collect historical resources (such as parts of shipwrecks), plantlife, living coral, seashells, tropical fish, queen conch, sea stars, or other marine creatures near the reef.

- Do not engage in spearfishing or release exotic species near the reef.

- Don't feed fish, seabirds, or marine mammals. Avoid any wildlife disturbance.

You can assist in the welfare of such coral reefs even when you're not in the water. Choose seafood from fisheries that have the least negative impact on the ocean, and minimize your use of chemically enhanced pesticides and fertilizers, which may end up in offshore waters. Avoid purchasing coral jewelry and souvenirs, unless you know for certain that such decorative objects were not illegally harvested.

Be sure to report all damage to coral reefs to dive operators or conservation groups that monitor coral reef health, such as the tri-agency **Coral Reef Conservation Program** (866/770-7335). For more information about area coral reefs, consult **Florida Keys National Marine Sanctuary** (305/852-7717 or 305/809-4700, www.floridakeys.noaa.gov). To learn how to protect these beautiful, complex, and surprisingly fragile formations, contact the **Project AWARE Foundation** (949/858-7657, www.projectaware.org) or the **Reef Relief Environmental Center & Headquarters** (631 Greene St., Key West, 305/294-3100, www.reefrelief.org), two non-profit organizations dedicated to preserving the living coral reef ecosystems around the world.

KEY LARGO

13 and passengers, plus gear rentals), as well as the **Reef Roamer** (99751 Overseas Hwy., 877/453-0110, www.reefroamersnorkel.com, trips 8:30am, 11:30am, and 4:30pm daily, $26-35 pp) and the **Morning Star** (Key Largo Fisheries, 1313 Ocean Bay Dr., 305/451-7057, www.morningstarcharters.com, trip 9am-1pm daily, $75 pp with gear).

For more information about snorkeling and diving sites around Key Largo, consult the **Upper Keys Artificial Reef Foundation** (106000 Overseas Hwy., 305/451-1414 or 800/822-1088, www.keylargowrecks.com), which offers information about both shipwrecks and coral reefs in the surrounding waters. Another helpful resource is the local office of **Florida Keys National Marine Sanctuary** (95230 Overseas Hwy., 305/852-7717, www.floridakeys.noaa.gov).

OTHER OUTDOOR ACTIVITIES

As an alternative to activities like fishing or snorkeling, consider taking flight. **Key Largo Parasail** (877/904-8865, www.keylargoparasail.com, 10am-4pm daily, $39-59 pp, $10 observers), weather permitting, welcomes people of all ages to fly 500 to 1,000 feet above the ocean. Boat trips leave from Sundowners at Mile Marker 104, on the bay side of U.S. 1. Single and tandem rides are available on a first-come, first-served basis. Farther south, **Caribbean Watersports** (97000 Overseas Hwy., 305/852-4707, www.caribbeanwatersports.com, 9am-6:30pm daily), based out of the Hilton Key Largo Resort, has offered parasailing flights ($70 per flyer, $130 per tandem) for more than two decades. Caribbean Watersports also provides WaveRunner rentals ($75 per half hour, $120 hourly), for which certain riders (ages 14-21) must have Florida-approved boater certification, as well as stand-up paddleboard rentals ($30 hourly, $45 for two hours).

Another option for stand-up paddleboarding (SUP), a sport that's growing in popularity, is **PADDLE! the Florida Keys** (94401 Overseas Hwy., Tavernier, 305/434-5930, www.paddle-thefloridakeys.com, 9am-5pm daily). In addition to renting paddleboards ($30-50 daily, $100-200 weekly) and kayaks ($30-45 daily, $100-175 weekly), it also offers two-hour ($99 per couple, $40 for each extra person) and three-hour ($149 per couple, $55 for each extra person) lessons and ecotours via paddleboard or kayak. Of course, PADDLE! also sells a wide array of paddleboards, kayaks, skateboards, clothing, and accessories.

Located in Key Largo Community Park at Mile Marker 99.6, on the ocean side of U.S. 1, the **Jacobs Aquatic Center (JAC)** (320 Laguna Ave., 305/453-7946, www. jacobsaquaticcenter.org, 10am-6pm daily Oct.-Apr., 10am-7pm daily May-Sept., day passes $21-25 families, $8-10 adults, $6-8 children 11-17, and $5-6 children 3-10) offers three different swimming pools, each of which has separate temperature controls. One pool, ideal for children, features a "spray" gym and a pirate ship with water slides. Other amenities here include a multipurpose activity room, bathrooms with showers and lockers, and a wide array of activities and classes, including water aerobics, water polo, swimming lessons, pilates, and scuba certification. Multiple pass and long-term rates are also available.

You might find an even greater release at **Pilates in Paradise** (LivingFit Wellness Center, 103400 Overseas Hwy., Ste. 255, 305/453-0801, www.pilatesinparadise.net or www.livingfitwellnesscenter.net, 7am-8pm Mon.-Sat., prices vary), where depending on how long you'll be in the area, you can experience just one class or a series of them. Several options are available here, from a mat session that teaches breathing, stretching, and strengthening exercises to a Nia program that fosters a unified body-mind-spirit fitness and lifestyle practice.

Accommodations

$100-200

Initially built as a fishing camp in 1903, **Gilbert's Resort** (107900 Overseas Hwy., 305/451-1133, www.gilbertsresort.com, rooms $100-140 d, suites $140-150) presents a laid-back atmosphere that's especially apparent in the on-site tiki bar, which offers live music and a full menu. The standard rooms provide two double beds, air conditioners, small refrigerators, and cable television. Also available are bayside rooms, with waterfront patios, and spacious family suites. Unlike at many establishments in the Upper Keys, pets are allowed here, though for an extra charge.

Situated beside Florida Bay, ◖ **Amy Slate's Amoray Dive Resort** (104250 Overseas Hwy., 305/451-3595 or 800/426-6729, www.amoray. com, rooms $79-289 d, apartments $109-269) caters to the diving or snorkeling enthusiast. Peppered with palm trees, this breezy property offers a wide variety of airy accommodations, with ceiling fans, tropical decor, free wireless Internet access, and in some cases, full kitchens. Even better, you can take a variety of scuba-diving classes on the premises, and while staying here, you'll be just steps away from the resort's two on-site boats: the 45-foot *Amoray Diver* and the 26-foot *Just-In-Time,* both of which deliver guests to the reefs and wrecks of John Pennekamp Coral Reef State Park and Florida Keys National Marine Sanctuary.

For a blend of Victorian charm and

Caribbean flair, reserve a room at the year-round **(Tarpon Flats Inn & Marina** (29 Shoreland Dr., 305/453-1313 or 866/546-0000, www.tarponflats.com, $170-220 d). This well-appointed bed-and-breakfast offers lovely rooms and suites, with British Colonial-style furnishings and intimate verandas that open onto stunning Largo Sound. Besides amenities like satellite television and kitchenettes, the inn's major claim to fame is its proximity to an assortment of natural pleasures and outdoor diversions. You'll find swimming, sailing, and kayaking opportunities right at your doorstep, and you'll be within walking distance of several tiki bars and waterfront restaurants. You're also not far from the wonders of John Pennekamp Coral Reef State Park—not to mention the Everglades, which are just a 30-minute boat ride away.

If you're traveling with your cat or dog, the **Marina Del Mar Resort & Marina** (527 Caribbean Dr., 305/451-4107, www.marinadelmarkeylargo.com, rooms $130-200 d, studios $170-220) offers 76 pet-friendly rooms, studios, and apartments. Queen-size or king-size beds are provided, as well as cable television and free wireless Internet access. Other amenities include a heated pool, tennis courts, and a free continental breakfast. The 56-unit pet-friendly **Bayside Inn** (99490 Overseas Hwy., 305/451-4450 or 800/242-5229, www.baysidekeylargo.com, rooms $130-225 d, suites $275-400), meanwhile, includes one-bedroom waterfront suites, bay-view rooms, and island-view rooms. Each contains a small refrigerator and a large flat-screen television, and the suites also have full kitchens. In addition, the property features a relaxing pool.

In the heart of Key Largo, on Florida Bay, the **Bay Cove Motel** (99446 Overseas Hwy., 305/451-1686, www.baycovemotel.com, $100-325 d) provides accommodations to suit every kind of traveler. The single and double cottages, efficiencies with kitchens, and spacious house (which accommodates up to eight people) are all within walking distance of many restaurants and shops. Guests can utilize the boat ramp and large dock, and after a long day

of boating or fishing, you can relax under a palm tree on the private beach.

Not far away, **The Pelican** (99340 Overseas Hwy., 305/451-3576 or 877/451-3576, www.hungrypelican.com, rooms $60-160 d, suites $195-220, cottages $85-95) offers 23 rooms, suites, and cottages, all of which are equipped with cable television, refrigerators, and air conditioners. The hotel also provides free wireless Internet access to help you keep in touch with friends back home or plan your next Key Largo adventure. While staying here, take advantage of the bayfront beach, where gorgeous sunsets are common, or feel free to rest on one of the available hammocks. Anglers and boaters will also appreciate the on-site boat ramp and docks.

Just a little farther south lies one of the few smoke-free hotels in Key Largo, the weathered **Key Largo Inn** (99202 Overseas Hwy., 305/451-2478 or 866/488-3020, www.keylargoinn.com, $74-119 d), which features a two-story Caribbean-style building surrounded by a pool and a tropical courtyard. The rooms are clean but simple and contain extra-long queen-size beds; additional amenities include a complimentary breakfast and free wireless Internet access. The staff members here are usually amiable, helpful, and more than willing to offer solid recommendations for local restaurants and activities.

The **(Rock Reef Resort** (97850 Overseas Hwy., 305/852-2401 or 800/477-2343, www.rockreefresort.com, $77-175 d) is a year-round oasis beside Florida Bay that was once part of an old key lime grove. Operated since 1989 by on-site owners Linda and David Adams, this low-key resort offers a wide range of comfortable accommodations. Beyond the main hotel, a white two-story building that contains standard and deluxe rooms as well as efficiencies, lie the lush, spacious grounds, where amid shady palm trees and vibrant bougainvillea are more intimate lodgings, from well-furnished apartments ($125-260 daily) to beachside cottages ($160-250 daily). With several hammocks among the trees, numerous lounge chairs on the beach, a fishing pier with docking facilities

© LAURA MARTONE

the lush setting of the Rock Reef Resort

($15 daily), a hot tub in the garden, a waterfront tiki hut, and a communal picnic and barbecue area, it's no wonder that the 21-unit resort is a popular option for wedding parties and family reunions. Other amenities include cable television, laundry services, wireless Internet access, and on-site parking. Those seeking romance and relaxation will also appreciate the no-pet and no-fireworks policies.

Offering suites, cottages, villas, and efficiencies—all with full kitchens—the lush, 2.5-acre **Coconut Bay Resort** (97702 Overseas Hwy., 305/852-5695 or 800/385-0986, www.coconutbaykeylargo.com, rooms $75-185 d, cottages $145-235, suites $230-310, villas $195-445) can accommodate any type of Upper Keys vacation. Every room has cable television, barbecue grills, and shady huts. A phone-free and smoke-free environment, the resort also provides free wireless Internet access in selected areas.

Perfect for divers, anglers, and snorkelers, the **Seafarer Resort** (97684 Overseas Hwy., 305/852-5349, www.seafarerresort.com,

$65-175 d) features a private beach ideal for relaxing, watching a romantic sunset, or embarking upon a variety of water-related adventures. Here you can choose to snorkel in the turquoise waters nearby, arrange a fishing trip with one of the many local guides, or enlist the help of the on-site dive center. With studio and standard rooms, as well as cottages ($105-190 daily), a family apartment ($105-180 daily), and a beach house ($110-190 daily), the resort can even accommodate large groups.

Farther south, the low-key **Stoneledge Paradise Inn** (95320 Overseas Hwy., 305/852-8114, www.stoneledgeparadiseinn.com, $78-118 d) offers basic lodgings alongside Florida Bay. As with most places in the Keys, the rooms range in size, with some providing full kitchens, and for families, there's even a two-bedroom house ($185-250 daily) with an extra queen-size sofabed. Situated on Florida Bay, the **Atlantic Bay Resort** (160 Sterling Rd., Tavernier, 305/852-5248 or 866/937-5650, www.atlanticbayresort.com, rooms $89-175 d, suites $129-350, cottages $175-219) features

500 feet of relaxing waterfront, plus 20 efficiencies, cottages, and suites, all of which have full kitchens. In addition, guests can utilize the boat ramp and dock.

OVER $200

Among the pricier lodging options that Key Largo offers is the **Azul del Mar** (104300 Overseas Hwy., 305/451-0337, www.azulkeylargo.com, suites $149-349), a small, quiet, adults-only boutique hotel that features six suites with ocean or garden views, various water sports and ecoadventures, and a rejuvenating beach beside Florida Bay. Each room here provides a king-size bed, a kitchenette, a large television, and wireless Internet access.

The **Marriott Key Largo Bay Resort** (103800 Overseas Hwy., 305/453-0000 or 888/731-9056, www.marriottkeylargo.com, rooms $179-309 d, suites $599-699), meanwhile, offers a complete resort experience with full water-sports facilities, a full-service day spa, and access to the Keysgate championship 18-hole golf course only 25 minutes away. In addition, the property houses three separate eateries: the open-air Breezer's Bar and Grill, ideal for sunset watching; Flipper's Poolside Tiki Bar (11am-sunset daily); and Gus' Grille (7am-11pm daily), featuring award-winning Floribbean cuisine. The rooms here range from standard accommodations with two double beds to a two-bedroom suite, and all include cable television, small refrigerators, and wireless Internet access.

Formerly an underwater research habitat, **Jules' Undersea Lodge** (51 Shoreland Dr., 305/451-2353, www.jul.com, $675 per individual, $800 per couple) is now open to the public for a unique lodging experience. To enter the lodge, you must dive 21 feet beneath the sea, making this the perfect base camp for diving enthusiasts. The lodge consists of the same creature comforts you would expect above the sea: hot showers, a well-stocked kitchen, a common room for winding down after a long day of scuba diving, and two bedrooms with 42-inch windows, offering a fascinating glimpse of the ocean floor. If you decide to come with friends, you're in luck; group economy packages are also available.

Near some of the best fishing and diving waters, the **Largo Lodge** (101740 Overseas Hwy., 305/451-0424, www.largolodge.com, rooms $150-265 d, suite $195-265, bungalows $175-235) lies only a mile from John Pennekamp Coral Reef State Park. Located on three acres alongside Florida Bay, the waterfront suite, two bungalows, and three units here offer free wireless Internet access and cable television, plus kitchenettes or full kitchens—making them especially economical for families.

Relish some quiet time near the poolside tiki bar at the **Courtyard Marriott Key Largo** (99751 Overseas Hwy., 305/451-3939 or 888/731-9092, www.marriott.com, rooms $180-270 d, suites $270-290), perhaps after returning from a dive or fishing adventure provided by one of the many guides in the adjacent marina. Every room features comfortable king-size or queen-size beds, cable television, and free wireless Internet access. The king Jacuzzi suites also include wraparound balconies with spectacular views of the marina.

The 130 rooms at the **Holiday Inn Key Largo Resort & Marina** (99701 Overseas Hwy., 305/451-2121 or 888/465-4329, www.holidayinnkeylargo.com, $150-260 d) are all tropically themed, some with private balconies overlooking the oceanside marina and the onsite Bogie's Café. The rooms offer queen-size or king-size beds, plus cable television and free wireless Internet access. Besides the immediately available water sports, the hotel features two freshwater pools as well as a poolside tiki bar.

If you're an experienced sailor who's come to the Keys without a boat of your own, the **Key Lime Sailing Club** (99306 Overseas Hwy., 305/451-3438, www.keylimesailingclub.com, cottages $140-350) has one at your disposal. For a smaller vessel, try one of the available kayaks, canoes, paddleboats, or rowboats. With a variety of cottages on-site, this hideaway has something for every occasion. Be aware, though, that each cottage charges a one-time cleaning fee ($50-100), the specific one of several suites at the Kona Kai Resort, Gallery & Botanic Gardens

amount of which depends upon the size of the cottage.

Barely visible from the highway, the **Kona Kai Resort, Gallery & Botanic Gardens** (97802 Overseas Hwy., 305/852-7200 or 800/365-7829, www.konakairesort.com, rooms $199-419 d, suites $259-1,038) provides a lush, intimate setting with 11 guest rooms and suites. The grounds have been transformed into a beautiful botanic garden, offering a serene setting to relax and replenish. Guests can pamper themselves by tanning on one of the largest private beaches in Key Largo, swimming in the beachside pool, or napping in one of the shaded hammocks. The property also features an elegant art gallery.

To take advantage of the self-proclaimed "diving capital of the world," head to the **Mariner's Resort Villas & Marina** (97501 Overseas Hwy., 305/853-1111 or 305/853-5000, www.keyscaribbean.com, villas $154-349), which features direct access to a beautiful marina. Luxury town homes and villas offer a

quiet escape in this gated resort. The grounds also promise plenty of adventure, with two freshwater pools—one of which is supposedly the largest pool in the Keys.

Perhaps one of the Hilton chain's prettiest properties is the **Hilton Key Largo Resort** (97000 Overseas Hwy., 305/852-5553 or 888/871-3437, www.keylargoresort.com, rooms $159-289 d, suites $169-359), hidden away on 13 acres of lush forestland. Boasting all of the expected amenities of any complete resort, the Hilton Key Largo equally suits family vacations, with its impressive lineup of water sports, as well as romantic getaways, given the solitude offered by its sumptuous grounds. The rooms and suites all feature queen-size or king-size beds, cable television, free wireless Internet access, and private balconies with either bayside or forest views. Other on-site amenities include a beachside watering hole, a swimming pool and adjacent bar, and the newly renovated Treetops Bar & Grill (7am-10pm Sun.-Thurs., 7am-11pm Fri.-Sat.), which offers panoramic views of Florida Bay.

For an intimate island-style boutique hotel, try the **Dove Creek Lodge** (147 Seaside Ave., 305/852-6200 or 800/401-0057, www.dovecreeklodge.com, rooms $169-329 d, suites $229-699), where you'll find 21 comfortable choices, including one-bedroom and two-bedroom suites, with small refrigerators, cable television, free wireless Internet access, and lockers to store your fishing, boating, or diving equipment. The two-bedroom luxury suites, Keylime and Mango, each have a well-equipped gourmet kitchen, two full bathrooms, and a private screened patio. In addition to comfortable accommodations at the **Ocean Pointe Suites at Key Largo** (500 Burton Dr., Tavernier, 305/853-3000 or 800/882-9464, www.providentresorts.com, suites $159-279) the resort specializes in arranging snorkeling, fishing, and ecotours as package deals. Spend the day at the private beach or the freshwater pool, and then grab a bite to eat at the on-site café and lounge.

As one of the Keys' most unique hotels, the pet-friendly **Coconut Palm Inn** (198

Harborview Dr., Tavernier, 305/852-3017 or 800/765-5397, www.coconutpalminn.com, rooms $139-259 d, suites $249-439) offers 20 rooms and suites, varying between standard rooms with garden views, patio rooms with bay views and screened porches, and suites with separate living areas, bay views, and balconies or decks. Here you'll also enjoy a sandy beach hidden among a grove of coconut trees, some of which have hammocks hanging between them.

CAMPING

Key Largo offers several budget-friendly campgrounds, ideal for families and outdoors enthusiasts. Near the northern end of Key Largo, **John Pennekamp Coral Reef State Park** (102601 Overseas Hwy., 305/451-1202, www.floridastateparks.org/pennekamp or www.pennekamppark.com, 8am-sunset daily, $8 vehicles with 2-8 passengers plus $0.50 pp, $4.50 motorcycles and single-occupant vehicles, $2.50 pedestrians, bikers, and extra passengers) offers a full-facility 47-site campground for both RVs and tents ($36 daily) with access to a dump station, wheelchair-accessible restrooms, and hot showers. Besides full hookups, each site features a picnic table and a grill. While this pet-friendly campground might not be as stunning as other state park campgrounds in the Florida Keys, it's a terrific home base for park activities, from sunbathing to snorkeling, and recent renovations have certainly improved its facilities. For reservations, contact **ReserveAmerica** (800/326-3521, www.reserveamerica.com) up to 11 months in advance.

Located on 40 acres alongside the Atlantic Ocean, the **Key Largo Kampground & Marina** (101551 Overseas Hwy., 305/451-1431 or 800/526-7688, www.keylargokampground.com, $35-75 daily, $220-470 weekly) presents a variety of campsites, from tent sites with no hookups to waterfront full-hookup sites ideal for RVs. Amenities here include laundry facilities, a general store for limited grocery needs, and a dock that offers boat owners easy access to the Atlantic Ocean.

Not far away, the gated **Calusa Campground Resort and Marina** (325 Calusa St., 305/451-0232, www.calusacampground.com, $65-105 daily, $405-654 weekly, $1,560-2,520 monthly) features a relaxing pool, direct access to the marina, and three types of full-hookup RV sites: inland, canal, and bayfront. Other amenities include shady palm trees, picnic tables, and a small playground. Meanwhile, the **Riptide Carefree RV Resort** (97680 Overseas Hwy., 305/852-8481, www.carefreervresorts.com, starting at $53 daily, $378 weekly, $919 monthly) offers 39 palm-shaded sites with oceanfront views, cement patios, full hookups, and free cable TV and Wi-Fi access. Additional amenities include a dump station, laundry facilities, a bayside picnic pavilion, a private beach, a shuffleboard area, a small motel, and various communal activities, from bingo games and karaoke nights to barbecues and ice cream socials. Tents are welcome.

Food

SEAFOOD

Considering Key Largo's allure for anglers and other water lovers, it surely comes as no surprise that seafood restaurants abound on this island. One such place is **Alabama Jack's** (58000 Card Sound Rd., 305/248-8741, 11am-7pm daily, $8-24), a family-owned eatery since 1947—its motto of "anything goes" could apply to the food as well as the country-western dancing on the weekends. Given the waterfront access, you can dock your boat and be eating in no time at all, and while the place doesn't have a complex menu, what the cooks do, they do well. The conch fritters, for instance, have been voted among the best in the Keys. It's no wonder, then, that locals flock to this beloved roadhouse on a regular basis.

Just past the junction of U.S. 1 and CR-905,

The Buzzard's Roost Grill and Pub (21 Garden Cove Dr., 305/453-3746, www.buzzardsroostkeylargo.com, 11am-9pm Mon.-Thurs., 11am-10pm Fri.-Sat., 10:30am-9pm Sun., $9-34) offers an extensive menu, including many hook-and-cook options. Provided you catch a fish at its legal size and in its proper season, then clean and fillet it yourself, the staff will prepare it for you, whether you prefer your fish fried, grilled, blackened, or jerked. Not far from Buzzard's, you'll spot the **Shipwrecks Bar & Grill** (45 Garden Cove Dr., 305/453-3153, www.shipwrecksklfl.com, 11am-10pm daily, $5-15), a friendly, casual joint that was opened in 2008 by Captain Mark Hutchings and has earned rave reviews ever since. Locals especially favor this hidden gem, which offers a daily happy hour (4pm-6pm), not to mention a wide array of draft and bottled beers, plus a menu that boasts everything from homemade coconut onion rings and pork sandwiches to seafood baskets and mahimahi tacos.

Farther south on U.S. 1 lies **Sundowners** (103900 Overseas Hwy., 305/451-4502, www.sundownerskeylargo.com, 11am-10pm daily, $9-40), one of the finest places to watch a sunset in the Upper Keys. Specializing in sandwiches, steaks, and of course, seafood, Sundowners features many local favorites, including conch chowder, Florida lobster tails, key lime pie, and lightly blackened snapper with mango salsa. Not surprisingly, the Friday night fish fry ($18 pp) is a popular draw.

Both a restaurant and a seafood market for more than 25 years, **The Fish House** (102401 Overseas Hwy., 305/451-4665, www.fishhouse.com, 11:30am-10pm daily, $9-40) presents a relaxed atmosphere and specializes in yellowtail snapper, mahimahi, and other fresh local seafood. After sampling the smoked fish or homemade chowders at The Fish House for lunch, consider planning your dinner at **The Fish House Encore** (102341 Overseas Hwy., 305/451-0650, www.fishhouse.com, 5pm-10pm daily, $12-33), a fine-dining eatery that features seafood, steaks, pasta dishes, a raw bar, plus expertly prepared sushi—and, as with most Florida Keys restaurants, tangy key lime pie. Beyond the main dining room, Encore also serves dinner in the outdoor patio or the piano lounge. Not surprisingly, reservations are recommended.

Whether it's for breakfast, lunch, or dinner, the airy, pet-friendly **❰ Key Largo Conch House** (100211 Overseas Hwy., 305/453-4844, www.keylargocoffeehouse.com, 8am-10pm daily, $9-30) offers an amazing menu in a lovely wooded setting. Try the cracked conch Benedict for breakfast, the fish tacos for lunch, or the mahi key lime almandine for dinner. Additional specialties include the conch chowder, conch fritters, and the lobster and conch ceviche. If the weather is pleasant, dine on the porch or relax in the courtyard, which is surprisingly pleasurable despite the eatery's proximity to busy U.S. 1. Feel free to take advantage of the free wireless Internet access while you eat.

If you appreciate a lovely view, head south to the **Bayside Grille** (99530 Overseas Hwy., 305/451-3380, www.keylargo-baysidegrill.com, 11:30am-10pm daily, $8-32), a friendly,

© DANIEL MARTONE

the pet-friendly Key Largo Conch House

family-owned eatery situated beside Florida Bay, directly behind DiGiorgio's Café Largo. Both restaurants are, in fact, owned by the same family, though the Bayside Grille is a better spot to watch drifting sailboats, swaying palm trees, and incredible sunsets. The cuisine, meanwhile, is often delicious. Lunchtime offerings include blackened mahimahi, coconut shrimp baskets, fried oyster baskets, and nonseafood dishes like maple-glazed meatloaf. The dinner menu is a bit more extensive, with everything from conch fritters to seafood enchiladas to filet mignon. The place prides itself on more than just fresh seafood, though—everything here is made on the premises daily, from the tuna salad to the grilled pineapple salsa. To enhance your experience, order a refreshing cocktail like Martha's Bayside Blue Margarita or Jim's Orange Blossom Mojito and watch the sun sink into the bay.

Established in 1976, **[Mrs. Mac's Kitchen** (99336 Overseas Hwy., 305/451-3722, www.mrsmacskitchen.com, 7am-9:30pm Mon.-Sat.,

$6-27) is an extremely popular and often crowded joint, filled with as many locals as tourists. If you're looking for a meal like Mom used to make—especially if Mom was a gourmet chef—then look no farther than this casual eatery. Featuring plenty of Keys favorites, the extensive menu includes everything from "Konk" chowder to relleno-style hogfish. The decor is a winner, too. Making use of the entire space, inside and out, Mrs. Mac's feels like a kid's clubhouse, with beer bottles along the rafters, license plates all over the walls and ceiling, overhead lamps cleverly fashioned from similar license plates, and small aluminum-can planes hanging everywhere. Recently, a second restaurant, the aptly named **Mrs. Mac's Kitchen II** (99020 Overseas Hwy., 305/451-6227), opened up on the nearby median.

Nestled on the median, **Ballyhoo's Historic Seafood Grille** (97860 Overseas Hwy., 305/852-0822, www.ballyhoosrestaurant.com, 11am-10pm daily, $8-36) sits in a lovingly preserved Conch-style structure that started as a

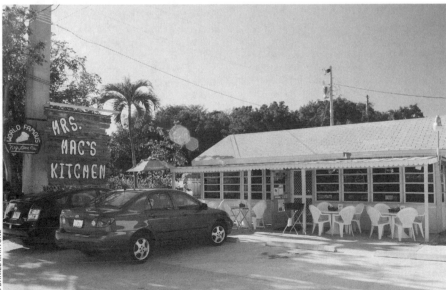

© DANIEL MARTONE

Mrs. Mac's Kitchen, a local favorite

fishing camp and now serves an array of seafood, steaks, and sandwiches. Try the Bimini stuffed shrimp, the Caribbean pan-fried scallops, fresh fish prepared in any number of interesting ways, and when in season, all-you-can-eat stone crabs.

Following its opening in 1989, **Snapper's Waterfront Restaurant** (139 Seaside Ave., 305/852-5956, www.snapperskeylargo.com, 11am-10pm Mon.-Sat., 10am-10pm Sun., $9-28) quickly became one of Key Largo's busiest eateries—not to mention a hot spot for live nighttime entertainment. For a truly unique dish, try the key lime lobster or the Thai seared tuna.

AMERICAN AND EUROPEAN

The **Tower of Pizza** (100600 Overseas Hwy., 305/451-1461, 11am-11pm daily, $10-19) has never closed down, not even for a hurricane. In addition to excellent pizza, this eat-in, take-out, and delivery joint offers other Italian fare, from minestrone to veal parmesan. Of course, if you don't feel like dining out, simply have a large pepperoni pizza and, to appease the diet, a Caesar salad delivered to your hotel.

Bogie's Café (99701 Overseas Hwy., 305/451-2121, www.holidayinnkeylargo.com, 7am-9pm daily, $8-16) is part of the Holiday Inn complex and just steps from the historical *African Queen*. You can enjoy the American and continental-style dishes inside or in the garden patio, and the entire menu is also available at the hotel's tiki bar (11am-close daily).

The family-run **Doc's Diner** (99696 Overseas Hwy., 305/451-2895, www.docsdinerkeylargo.com, 6am-2pm daily, $5-9) is a local favorite for breakfast and lunch. If you're here with your family, try Doc's Feast, which offers a huge assortment of the joint's most popular breakfast foods, including ham steak, pancakes and French toast, creamy grits, warm biscuits, a dozen scrambled eggs, and more. For an equally casual meal, stop by the 1950s-style **DJ's Diner** (99411 Overseas Hwy., 305/451-2999, http://djsdinerkeylargo.com, 7am-9pm Mon.-Fri., 7am-3pm Sat.-Sun., $5-14). Sample a breakfast burrito, a burger, or the meatloaf dinner while gazing at celebrity photos on the walls.

For a taste of Europe, stop by **DiGiorgio's Café Largo** (99530 Overseas Hwy., 305/451-4885, www.keylargo-cafelargo.com, 4:30pm-11pm daily, $8-30), which serves a fantastic assortment of Italian dishes, from traditional fare like littleneck clams and linguini to Conch-style items such as the yellowtail snapper. This family-run restaurant, established in 1992, also offers basic pizzas and subs for those in a hurry. The DiGiorgio family also owns the Bayside Grille, which lies between Café Largo and Florida Bay.

ASIAN AND LATIN AMERICAN

Two cuisines are better than one at the **Num Thai Restaurant & Sushi Bar** (103200 Overseas Hwy., 305/451-5955, 11am-9pm daily, $8-16), where you can sample a spicy tuna roll or some excellent pad thai all in the

---

THE BOGIE CONNECTION

Several famous people, from novelists to singers to presidents, are inextricably linked to the Florida Keys. One such celebrity is Humphrey Bogart, whose 1948 film *Key Largo* was actually filmed on the northernmost island. Of course, this well-regarded crime drama, directed by John Huston, is not the only reminder of Bogart's connection to Key Largo. Over the years, Bogart has been such a legendary presence here that you'll even find pets named after him, such as Bogie, the beloved yellow-naped Amazon parrot at the Rock Reef Resort near Mile Marker 98. Even better, you can view the one-and-only *African Queen,* the actual vessel featured in the eponymous 1951 film starring Bogart and Katharine Hepburn. When not reserved for private rides, the small, weathered vessel is typically docked beside the aptly named **Bogie's Café,** a casual eatery at the Holiday Inn Key Largo Resort & Marina near Mile Marker 100.

same night. Of course, if you're in the mood for some killer Mexican food, head north to **Señor Frijoles** (103900 Overseas Hwy., 305/451-1592, www.senorfrijolesrestaurant.com, 11am-10pm daily, $12-22), which has been serving delicious south-of-the-border dishes and fantastic margaritas since 1981. One local favorite is the steak fajita burrito, filled with marinated beef tenderloin and served with citrus pico de gallo, frijoles, and a tasty chipotle sour cream—all wrapped in a large tortilla, topped with ranchero sauce, and covered with Monterey jack cheese.

Of course, some restaurants are harder to classify. At the award-winning **C Tasters Grille & Market** (91252 Overseas Hwy., Tavernier, 305/853-1177, www.tastersgrille. com, 5pm-9pm Sun.-Mon. and Wed., 5pm-10pm Thurs.-Sat., $10-29), for instance, since the restaurant opened in 2009 Chef George Adam Patti has been preparing an eclectic, fusion-style cuisine that infuses local Caribbean food with Asian, Low Country, and Mediterranean flavors. Depending on the day, dishes might include the Bahamian conch chowder, Peruvian ceviche, Cantonese baby back ribs, Asian duck pizza, and pan-seared local black grouper with fennel, shiitake mushrooms, red watercress, and a purée made of spinach, ginger, and toasted pecans. Take advantage of the beer, wine, and dinner specials, and save room for the lauded desserts.

Information and Services

INFORMATION
For brochures, maps, and other information about Key Largo, stop by the **Key Largo Chamber of Commerce and Florida Keys Visitor Center** (106000 Overseas Hwy., 305/451-4747 or 800/822-1088, www.keylargo.org or www.keylargochamber.org, 9am-6pm daily), a two-story yellow building on the bay side of U.S. 1, near Mile Marker 106, and inside you'll spy an 18th-century British cannon, one of several found in an offshore patch reef. You can also consult the **Monroe County Tourist Development Council** (1201 White St., Ste. 102, Key West, 305/296-1552 or 800/352-5397, www.fla-keys.com, 9am-5pm Mon.-Fri.) for questions about Key Largo and the rest of the Florida Keys. For government-related issues, contact the **Monroe County offices** (1100 Simonton St., Key West, 305/294-4641, www.monroecounty-fl.gov, 8am-5pm Mon.-Fri.).

For local news, consult *The Reporter* (www. keysnet.com), **The Weekly Newspapers** (www. keysweekly.com), and **KeysNews.com.** In addition, the daily *Miami Herald* (www.miamiherald.com), the daily *The Key West Citizen* (www.keysnews.com), and the biweekly *Florida Keys Keynoter* (www.keysnet.com) are available throughout the Keys.

In Key Largo, you'll also have access to several radio stations, including **Thunder Country** (WCTH-FM 100.3, www.thundercountry.com) and, for classic rock, the **SUN** (WFKZ-FM 103.1, www.sun103.com).

SERVICES
Money
For banking needs, stop by **Capital Bank** (103330 Overseas Hwy., 305/451-2000 or 800/639-5111, www.capitalbank-us.com, 9am-4pm Mon.-Thurs., 9am-6pm Fri., 9am-1pm Sat., extended drive-through hours) or the **First State Bank of the Florida Keys** (97670 Overseas Hwy., 305/852-2070 or 866/298-1858, www.keysbank.com, 9am-4pm Mon.-Thurs., 9am-6pm Fri., extended drive-through hours).

Mail
For shipping, faxing, copying, and other business-related services, visit **The UPS Store** (101425 Overseas Hwy., 305/453-4877, www. theupsstore.com, 8am-6pm Mon.-Fri., 9am-5pm Sat.). You'll also find two **post offices** (800/275-8777, www.usps.com) in the area:

Stop by the Key Largo visitor center for maps and brochures.

one in Key Largo (100100 Overseas Hwy., 305/451-3155, 8:30am-4:30pm Mon.-Fri., 10am-1pm Sat.) and one in Tavernier (91220 Overseas Hwy., 305/853-1052, 9am-4:30pm Mon.-Fri.).

Groceries and Supplies

If you require groceries and other supplies, head to **Winn-Dixie** (105300 Overseas Hwy., 305/451-0328, www.winndixie.com, 7am-10pm daily), which houses an on-site pharmacy (305/451-3591, 8am-8pm Mon.-Fri., 9am-6pm Sat., 10am-5pm Sun.). In the Tradewinds Shopping Center, you'll spot a **Publix** (101437 Overseas Hwy., 305/451-0808, www.publix.com, 7am-10pm daily), which, in addition to groceries and other services, includes an on-site pharmacy (305/451-5338, 9am-9pm Mon.-Fri., 9am-7pm Sat., 10am-5pm Sun.). In addition, **Walgreens** (99501 Overseas Hwy., 305/451-4385, www.walgreens.com, 7am-10pm daily) offers a pharmacy drive-through (9am-5pm daily) as well as a full liquor department.

Laundry

If you need to clean some clothes during your trip, you'll find several coin-operated laundromats in the area, including the **Waldorf Plaza Coin Laundry** (99607 Overseas Hwy., 305/451-4575, 7:30am-9pm Sun.-Fri., 7:30am-8pm Sat.).

Internet Access

For Internet access, head to the **Key Largo Conch House** (100211 Overseas Hwy., 305/453-4844, www.keylargocoffeehouse.com, 8am-10pm daily), which offers free wireless Internet access with the purchase of a meal. **Snapper's Waterfront Restaurant** (139 Seaside Ave., 305/852-5956, www.snapperskeylargo.com, 11am-10pm Mon.-Thurs., 11am-11pm Fri.-Sat., 10am-10pm Sun.) provides free wireless Internet access throughout the entire property. You can also access free Wi-Fi at the **Key Largo Branch Library** (101485 Overseas Hwy., 305/451-2396, www.keyslibraries.org, 9:30am-6pm Mon.-Tues. and Thurs.-Fri., 9:30am-8pm Wed., 10am-6pm Sat.) in the Tradewinds Shopping Center.

Emergency Services

In case of an emergency that requires police, fire, or ambulance services, dial **911** from any cell or public phone. Even in less critical situations, you can consult the **Key Largo Fire Rescue Department** (305/451-2700 or 305/451-2701, www.keylargofire.com), which operates two fire stations: one at 220 Reef Drive and the other at 1 East Drive. For non-emergency assistance, contact the **Monroe County Sheriff's Office** (Roth Bldg., 50 High Point Rd., Ste. 100, Tavernier, 305/853-3211, www.keysso.net, 8am-5pm Mon.-Fri.).

For medical assistance, consult the **Mariners Hospital** (91500 Overseas Hwy., Tavernier, 305/434-3000, www.baptisthealth.net). Foreign visitors seeking help with directions, medical concerns, business issues, law enforcement needs, or other problems can receive **multilingual tourist assistance** (800/771-5397) 24 hours daily.

Getting There and Around

GETTING THERE
By Air

Despite the presence of a private airport at the **Ocean Reef Club** (35 Ocean Reef Dr., 305/367-2611, www.oceanreef.com), Key Largo has no major airport of its own. To travel here by plane, you'll need to fly into **Fort Lauderdale-Hollywood International Airport** (FLL, 100 Terminal Dr., Fort Lauderdale, 866/435-9355, www.broward.org/airport), **Miami International Airport** (MIA, 2100 NW 42nd Ave., Miami, 305/876-7000, www.miami-airport.com), **Key West International Airport** (EYW, 3491 S. Roosevelt Blvd., Key West, 305/296-5439 or 305/296-7223, www.keywestinternationalairport.com), or **Florida Keys Marathon Airport** (MTH, 9400 Overseas Hwy., Marathon, 305/289-6060). From there you can rent a vehicle from agencies like **Avis** (800/633-3469, www.avis.com), **Budget** (800/218-7992, www.budget.com), or **Enterprise** (800/261-7331, www.enterprise.com) to reach Key Largo.

By Bus or Train

The **Miami-Dade County Metrobus** (305/891-3131, www.miamidade.gov/transit) operates the **301 Dade-Monroe Express** between Florida City and Marathon (5:15am-10:40pm daily, $2.35 per one-way trip), with stops in Key Largo and Tavernier until 9:25pm and 9:40pm, respectively. In addition, **Greyhound** (800/231-2222, www.greyhound.com) offers limited bus service to Key Largo. **Amtrak** (800/872-7245, www.amtrak.com), however, provides train service only as far south as Miami. Of course, you can always rent a car or hop a shuttle to reach the Florida Keys.

Transport from Airports and Stations

If you arrive in the Fort Lauderdale-Miami area via plane, bus, or train—or Key West via plane or bus—you can either rent a car or hire a shuttle service to reach Key Largo. Some of these companies include **Keys Shuttle** (305/289-9997 or 888/765-9997, www.keysshuttle.com, $60-70 pp for shared ride, $275-325 for exclusive service) and **Keys Tropical Transportation** (305/852-3595, www.keystropicaltransportation.com, starting at $130 or $165 per ride, depending on the airport of origin), both of which provide service from the Miami and Fort Lauderdale airports; **SuperShuttle** (305/871-2000 or 954/764-1700, www.supershuttle.com, $189 for up to 10 passengers), which provides nonstop van service for Key Largo visitors flying into Miami; and **TO'n'FRO** (305/393-0955, www.tonfro.com, $55-65 pp for shared van ride, $170-190 per luxury sedan ride), a personalized van and car service that offers transportation between the Miami and Fort Lauderdale airports and any destination in the Keys.

By Car

To reach Key Largo from Miami, simply head south on U.S. 1 (Overseas Hwy.) and continue through Key Largo to your destination. If you're headed from the Everglades via I-75 (Everglades Pkwy.), drive south on U.S. 27, veer right onto SR-997 (Krome Ave.), and follow the signs to U.S. 1. From U.S. 41 (Tamiami Trl.) in the Everglades, head south on SR-997 and continue toward U.S. 1. If you arrive during the high season (Dec.-Apr.), be sure to call **511** for an up-to-the-minute traffic report.

GETTING AROUND
By Car

The best way to travel through Key Largo is by car, truck, RV, or motorcycle—all of which offer easy access to U.S. 1 and other roads, such as CR-905, which traverses the northern part of Key Largo, where you'll find Dagny Johnson Key Largo Hammock Botanical State Park and the exclusive Ocean Reef Club.

KEY LARGO

By Van Service

While staying in Key Largo, if you have a sudden desire to head to Key West for the evening—and would rather leave your vehicle at the hotel, resort, or campground where you're staying—consider boarding **Sea the Keys** (305/896-7013, www.keywestdaytrip.com, rates vary), a passenger van service that will pick you up from your hotel in the Upper Keys and drop you off in Key West around 11am. While down there, you'll be free to explore any number of restaurants, bars, museums, and other attractions, before making the return trip around 7 or 8pm.

By Taxi

Taxicab companies such as **Key Largo Cabs** (305/451-9700, $7 per pickup, $2.50 per mile) and **Mom's Taxi** (305/852-6000, $7 per pickup, $2.50 per mile) can help you get around Key Largo and Tavernier.

By Bicycle or Boat

While you can certainly traverse Key Largo via bicycle, the sprawling nature of this region makes it challenging for novice riders. Nevertheless, it's a lovely, ecofriendly way to experience the northernmost island, and there's even a 15.5-mile biking path that runs past numerous businesses and parks between Mile Marker 106.5 and Mile Marker 91. Bicycles can be rented from places like the **Key Largo Bike Shop** (100109 Overseas Hwy., 305/393-2453, www.keylargobike.com, 8am-5pm daily, $18-60 daily), which offers road bikes as well as hybrids. Weekly rates are also available, and helmets and locks are included with all rentals.

Of course, you can also experience Key Largo via boat. Having your own vessel might make navigating these waters a bit easier, and you'll find no shortage of boat ramps and marina slips in Key Largo. If you'd rather rent a boat, contact **PonTunes Boat Rentals & Marina** (107690 Overseas Hwy., 305/453-5007, www.pontunes.com, rates vary), which offers an assortment of vessels, from fishing boats to luxury pontoon boats.

ISLAMORADA

South of Key Largo, most of the remaining Upper Keys have become part of Islamorada (pronounced eye-lah-more-AH-dah), an incorporated town long celebrated for its bountiful sportfishing opportunities. Its name—derived from the Spanish phrase *islas moradas* (purple islands) by European explorers centuries ago—might refer, depending on the resident you ask, to the region's incredible violet-tinted sunsets or the brilliant flowers that blossom here or even the purplish snail shells that once peppered the shores of these islands.

Regardless of its origin, however, this "Village of Islands," allegedly the first inhabited place in the Florida Keys, includes several keys that are accessible via the Overseas Highway—namely, Plantation Key (which includes part of the Tavernier community),

Windley Key, Upper Matecumbe Key, and Lower Matecumbe Key—plus a pair of state-park islands only reachable by boat. If you have the time, in fact, you should definitely venture to these two remote locales: Indian Key Historic State Park, site of a former 19th-century settlement, and Lignumvitae Key Botanical State Park, home to a virgin tropical hardwood hammock.

Islamorada, one of the wealthier areas in the Florida Keys, boasts several high-end art galleries, boutiques, and full-service spas as well as sophisticated restaurants and resorts, but it's the sportfishing that lures most people. The clear warm waters around Islamorada— the self-proclaimed "sportfishing capital of the world"—teem with tarpon, trout, redfish, snapper, sailfish, and other worthy species. It's

ISLAMORADA

HIGHLIGHTS

Spas and Yoga in Islamorada
Islamorada, Village of Islands
Theater of the Sea
History of Diving Museum
Kayaking Around Islamorada
Fishing and Boating near Islamorada
Lignumvitae Key Botanical State Park
Indian Key Historic State Park

Miami
Gulf of Mexico
Florida Bay
Shell Key
Lignumvitae Key
Upper Matecumbe Key
Lower Matecumbe Key
Craig Key
ATLANTIC OCEAN

0   2 mi
0   2 km

© AVALON TRAVEL

LOOK FOR ◖ TO FIND RECOMMENDED SIGHTS, ACTIVITIES, DINING, AND LODGING.

◖ **Theater of the Sea:** Established in 1946, the world's second oldest marine mammal facility invites visitors to swim with dolphins and sea lions, watch them frolic and paint, enjoy a bottomless boat ride, and even take a snorkeling cruise to an offshore coral reef (page 126).

◖ **History of Diving Museum:** This curious collection of diving paraphernalia includes fantastic diving machines, old-fashioned scuba tanks, and diving helmets from around the world, plus treasures recovered from the ocean (page 127).

◖ **Indian Key Historic State Park:** Only accessible via canoe, kayak, or boat, this lovely offshore island lures hikers, swimmers, sunbathers, bird-watchers, snorkelers, scuba divers, and anglers alike (page 128).

◖ **Lignumvitae Key Botanical State Park:** Only accessible via boat, canoe, or kayak, this offshore island features the kind of virgin tropical hardwood hammock that once thrived

in the Upper Keys (page 129).

◖ **Fishing and Boating near Islamorada:** The self-proclaimed "sportfishing capital of the world" boasts several full-service marinas and an enormity of fishing charters, independent fishing guides, and boat rentals, ideal for those who hope to search the bountiful backcountry and offshore waters of the Upper Keys (page 135).

◖ **Kayaking Around Islamorada:** Islamorada also offers a wealth of opportunities for kayakers, who can either rent kayaks or opt for a guided kayaking excursion amid backcountry waters and offshore islands (page 137).

◖ **Spas and Yoga in Islamorada:** Filled with upscale accommodations, the Village of Islands also provides several rejuvenating spas where you can enjoy refreshing facials, body treatments, massages, and, sometimes, beachside yoga (page 141).

a snap to rent a boat, hire a fishing guide, or charter a full crew, if you so desire.

If fishing is not your preference, you'll find several other distractions in the area, including a geological state park on Windley Key that

was once linked to Henry Flagler's ill-fated Overseas Railroad. In addition, you can watch entertaining dolphins and sea lions at a year-round marine-mammal center; peruse one of the world's largest collections of diving helmets

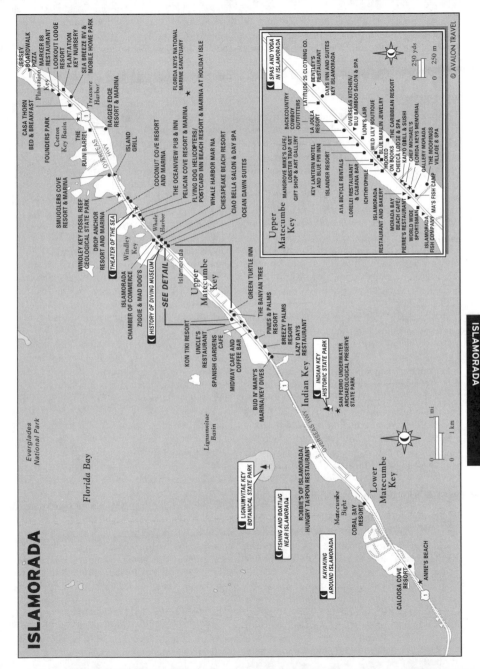

ISLAMORADA

© AVALON TRAVEL

ISLAMORADA

Everglades National Park

Florida Bay

Lignumvitae Basin

JERSEY BOARDWALK PIZZA
MARKER 88 RESTAURANT
LOOKOUT LODGE RESORT
PLANTATION KEY NURSERY
SEA BREEZE RV & MOBILE HOME PARK

Plantation Key

CASA THORN BED & BREAKFAST

FOUNDERS PARK

Cotton Key Basin

THE RAIN BARREL

Treasure Harbor

RAGGED EDGE RESORT & MARINA

ISLAND GRILL

FLORIDA KEYS NATIONAL MARINE SANCTUARY

COCONUT COVE RESORT AND MARINA

THE OCEANVIEW PUB & INN

PELICAN COVE RESORT & MARINA

FLYING DOG HELICOPTERS/ POSTCARD INN BEACH RESORT & MARINA AT HOLIDAY ISLE

WHALE HARBOR MAR NA

CHESAPEAKE BEACH RESORT

CIAO BELLA SALON & DAY SPA

OCEAN DAWN SUITES

SMUGGLERS COVE RESORT & MARINA

WINDLEY KEY FOSSIL REEF GEOLOGICAL STATE PARK

DROP ANCHOR RESORT AND MARINA

Windley Key

Whale Harbor

ℂ THEATER OF THE SEA

ISLAMORADA CHAMBER OF COMMERCE

ZIGGIE & MAD DOG'S

ℂ HISTORY OF DIVING MUSEUM

Islamorada

SEE DETAIL

GREEN TURTLE INN

THE BANYAN TREE

PINES & PALMS RESORT

BREEZY PALMS RESORT

LAZY DAYS RESTAURANT

Upper Matecumbe Key

KON TIKI RESORT

UNCLE'S RESTAURANT

SPANISH GARDENS CAFE

MIDWAY CAFE AND COFFEE BAR

BUD N' MARY'S MARINA/KEY DIVES

ℂ INDIAN KEY HISTORIC STATE PARK

Indian Key

SAN PEDRO UNDERWATER ARCHAEOLOGICAL PRESERVE STATE PARK

ℂ LIGNUMVITAE KEY BOTANICAL STATE PARK

ℂ FISHING AND BOATING NEAR ISLAMORADA

ROBBIE'S OF ISLAMORADA/ HUNGRY TARPON RESTAURANT

ℂ KAYAKING AROUND ISLAMORADA

Matecumbe Bight

Lower Matecumbe Key

CORAL BAY RESORT

ANNE'S BEACH

CALOOSA COVE RESORT

OVERSEAS HWY

1

0   mi
0   1 km

Detail:

Upper Matecumbe Key

MANGROVE MIKE'S CAFE/ LOBSTER TRAP ART GIFT SHOP & ART GALLERY

BACKCOUNTRY COWBOY OUTFITTERS

LATITUDE 25 CLOTHING CO.

BENTLEY'S RESTAURANT

DAYS INN AND SUITES KEY ISLAMORADA

LA JOLLA RESORT

OVERSEAS KITCHEN/ BLU BAMBOO SALON & SPA

KEY LANTERN MOTEL AND BLUE FIN INN

ISLANDER RESORT

WILD LILY BOUTIQUE

LION'S LAIR

A1A BICYCLE RENTALS

BLUE MARLIN JEWELRY

LORELEI RESTAURANT & CABANA BAR

HOOKED

ON BOOKS

ICHTHYOPHILE

ISLAMORADA RESTAURANT AND BAKERY

MORADA BAY BEACH CAFE/ PIERRE'S RESTAURANT

CHEECA LODGE & SPA

KAIYO GRILL & SUSHI

CHEF MICHAEL'S

WORLD WIDE SPORTSMAN

FLORIDA KEYS MEMORIAL

GALLERY MORADA

THE MOORINGS VILLAGE & SPA

ISLAMORADA FISH COMPANY

MAS FISH CAMP

THE CARIBBEAN RESORT

ℂ SPAS AND YOGA IN ISLAMORADA

0   250 yds
0   250 m

ISLAMORADA

and artifacts; feed wild tarpon at Robbie's of Islamorada; and explore an underwater archaeological state park, which preserves the wreck of a Spanish treasure-fleet ship that sank here nearly three centuries ago.

HISTORY

Despite the commonly heard claim that Islamorada is the longest inhabited place in the Florida Keys, it's difficult to know the exact origin of the community that now thrives here. As with the rest of the Florida Keys, the four livable islands, two remote state parks, and one private key that compose this "Village of Islands"—Plantation Key, Windley Key, Upper Matecumbe Key, Lower Matecumbe Key, Indian Key, Lignumvitae Key, and Teatable Key—were likely frequented by the Calusa and Tequesta native peoples, as well as other Native American tribes, long before Europeans, Floridians, and other Americans encountered them.

Nevertheless, local historians believe that the earliest community in the Upper Keys existed on Indian Key—which the Spanish originally called *Cayuelo de Matanza* (Small Slaughter Key) during the salvaging operations of the *San Pedro,* a Spanish ship that wrecked during a 1733 hurricane and now forms the basis of an archaeological state park. In 1836 Indian Key became the first county seat of Dade County. At that time, this diminutive island, which lies on the ocean side of the Overseas Highway, was also the site of John Jacob Housman's lucrative cargo-salvaging business—that is, until 1840 during the Second Seminole War when the Seminole native people invaded the island, plundered the buildings, and allegedly killed several settlers, despite the presence of Fort Paulding on nearby Teatable Key. Today Indian Key is a historical state park, and Teatable has become a private residence.

The other islands that compose Islamorada have equally curious histories. Once the site of a large American Indian mound, Plantation Key has had many names over the years, from Bull Island to Long Island to Vermont Key, and in 1935 it was home to a large coral rock quarry

operated by World War I veterans. Windley Key, to the south, was also once the site of a rock quarry enterprise. Formerly two islands, known as the Umbrella Keys, Windley Key became one island in the early 20th century when workers for Henry Flagler's ill-fated Overseas Railroad filled in the space between the two keys. At the time, three separate quarries were in operation on Windley Key, and they provided the fossilized coral used to build the railroad. Today the former quarry complex has become a geological state park, one that explores the island's critical role in the Overseas Railroad, which was effectively destroyed by the Labor Day Hurricane of 1935.

According to historical documents, Upper Matecumbe Key and Lower Matecumbe Key were both settled in the late 1800s. It wasn't until 1907, however, that the name "Islamorada" reemerged. Although it's actually a Spanish term, meaning "purple islands" and attributed to early explorers, William Krome was the first to use it in an official capacity, when he planned a subdivision on Upper Matecumbe Key called the "Townsite of Islamorada." Soon the moniker spread, inspiring the name of the railroad depot and in 1908 the Islamorada Post Office. Islamorada was eventually incorporated on December 31, 1997, as "Islamorada, Village of Islands." Today with a population of more than 6,180, it includes all of the aforementioned keys—even Lignumvitae Key, the wooded offshore island on the bay side of U.S. 1. Once known as Jenkinson Island, Lignumvitae (which means "tree of life") has been home to various individuals since at least the 1830s, including William J. Matheson, a wealthy Miami chemist who bought the island in 1919 and whose former hideaway is now the visitor center within a botanical state park. For more information about Islamorada's past, consult the **Historical Preservation Society of the Upper Keys** (www.keyshistory.org).

PLANNING YOUR TIME

Though Islamorada comprises several islands between Mile Marker 91 and Mile Marker 72, with attractions and resorts stretching from

Plantation Key to Lower Matecumbe Key, it's fairly simple to navigate this area by car, via the Overseas Highway (as with the rest of the Florida Keys). In fact, the only main attractions that will require a boat ride are the underwater coral reefs and shipwrecks as well as the two island state parks: Indian Key and Lignumvitae Key.

In Islamorada, you'll find a wide range of diversions, from marine mammal shows to day spas to a diving museum, so you could indeed spend a full weekend here—conceivably a whole week if you also plan to hire a fishing charter or visit the offshore state parks. As with other parts of the Keys, you may encounter traffic congestion, crowded restaurants and attractions, and higher lodging rates during the peak tourist season—from December to April—so plan accordingly.

When scheduling a trip to Islamorada, you might also want to consider factors like annual events, fishing seasons, and climate. For instance, while the hot, humid summer months can be less popular among tourists, those who favor snorkeling and scuba diving might appreciate the warmer waters. No matter when you visit, however, it's important to understand the risks of outdoor activities like kayaking and scuba diving, which can be dangerous without proper instruction and preparation.

For more information about Islamorada, consult the **Monroe County Tourist Development Council** (1201 White St., Ste. 102, Key West, 305/296-1552 or 800/352-5397, www.fla-keys.com, 9am-5pm Mon.-Fri.) and the **Islamorada Chamber of Commerce** (P.O. Box 915, Islamorada, 305/664-4503 or 800/322-5397, www.islamoradachamber.com, 9am-5pm Mon.-Fri., 9am-4pm Sat., 9am-3pm Sun.).

Sights

PLANTATION KEY

If you're driving to Islamorada from Key Largo, you'll first encounter **Plantation Key,** just west of Mile Marker 91, across Tavernier Creek. Primarily a residential area that includes part of Tavernier, Plantation Key contains a handful of curious diversions, including several art galleries, the Tavernier Creek Marina, and **Founders Park** (87000 Overseas Hwy., Plantation Key, 305/853-1685, www.islamorada.fl.us, 8am-6pm daily, $8 adults, $5 seniors 65 and over and children 3-17, free for children under 3 and residents), a 42-acre public park on the bay side of U.S. 1. Its many features include a large heated Olympic-style swimming pool and children's water park, a playground and skateboard park, an open-air amphitheater, a sandy beach, a dog park, and access to the Plantation Yacht Harbor Marina, which also offers a boat ramp (8am-6pm daily). In addition to family-friendly diversions like water-sports rentals, fitness and walking trails, tennis and basketball courts, and multiuse fields, Founders Park

hosts events throughout the year, from the "Pops in the Park" concert series (Nov.-Apr.) to an annual Easter egg hunt. For a current schedule of events, contact the park directly. There's a fee for use of the pool and skate park (hours vary daily, $3 adults, $2 seniors 65 and over and children 3-17, free for children under 3).

WINDLEY KEY
Windley Key Fossil Reef Geological State Park

Once two separate islands, known as the Umbrella Keys, Windley Key is one of the highest islands in the Florida Keys archipelago—which was formed from Key Largo limestone (fossilized coral) over 125,000 years ago. In the mid-1800s, the Russell family homesteaded the easterly Umbrella Key until it was sold to the Florida East Coast Railway in 1908. Soon afterward railroad workers filled in the gap between the two Umbrella Keys forming the Windley Key of today. From 1908 until the completion of Henry Flagler's Overseas id in 1912, the three coral rock quarries on the eastern end of Windley Key were used to supply thousands of tons of limestone for the railbed and bridges that eventually stretched all the way to Key West. Today the **Windley Key Fossil Reef Geological State Park** (MM 84.9 BS U.S. 1, Windley Key, 305/664-2540, www.floridastateparks.org/windleykey, 8am-5pm Thurs.-Mon., education center 9am-5pm Fri.-Sun., $2.50 pp, free for children under 6) invites visitors to walk along self-guided trails through the former quarries: the Windley Quarry, the Flagler Quarry, and the Russell Quarry. Here you can view old mining equipment and walk along eight-foot-high quarry walls to see cross sections of the ancient coral. In addition, the Alison Fahrer Environmental Education Center features informative exhibits about the connection between the quarry complex and the ill-fated railroad, which came to an end with the Labor Day Hurricane of 1935. One-hour guided tours ($3 pp, free for children under 6) are available Friday-Sunday at 10am and 2pm, though reservations are suggested. Given the small size and limited nature of this park, it's best to visit when you can take full advantage of the education center and guided tours.

Theater of the Sea

Around Mile Marker 84.5 on Windley Key, you'll be hard-pressed to miss the enormous sign for **Theater of the Sea** (84721 Overseas Hwy., Windley Key, 305/664-2431, www.theaterofthesea.com, 9:30am-5pm daily, $30 adults, $21 children 3-10, free for children under 3), the second oldest marine mammal facility in the world. Established in 1946, this lush 17-acre marine animal park features entertaining dolphin, sea lion, and parrot shows every day of the year. Such shows integrate lessons about anatomy, physiology, husbandry, natural history, and conservation into an informative, interactive, and often hilarious presentation. In addition to watching the varied shows, you can stroll amid habitats containing enormous sea turtles, alligators, tropical birds, reptiles, and other marine creatures—and

perhaps catch a glimpse of a free-roaming iguana.

Some visitors choose to take a guided bottomless boat ride or board a four-hour adventure and snorkeling cruise (8:30am and 1pm daily), which includes visits to an offshore coral reef, two island state parks, and Robbie's of Islamorada. Of course, many visitors come to Theater of the Sea to interact with the animals themselves. Here you can watch dolphins and sea lions paint colorful abstract pictures, learn the hand signals for natural behaviors like waving and kissing, and even swim with the resident dolphins, sea lions, and stingrays in the on-site lagoon.

The cost of admission includes access to the lagoon-side beach, the guided marinelife tour, the bottomless boat ride, snorkel gear, and the dolphin, sea lion, and parrot shows. Additional charges apply for special programs, such as swimming with the rays ($65 pp), meeting a sea lion or dolphin ($85 pp), swimming with a sea lion ($145 pp), wading with a dolphin ($175 pp), swimming with a dolphin ($185 pp), and the adventure cruise ($69 adults, $45 children 5-12). Reservations may be required for certain programs, and restrictions such as age and physical fitness may apply, so be sure to call ahead. Be aware, too, that the shows run continuously, so you can simply join the one in progress as soon as you arrive. Allow roughly three hours to experience everything except the adventure cruise and other special programs.

Flying Dog Helicopters

Based on the lower end of Windley Key at the Postcard Inn Beach Resort & Marina, **Flying Dog Helicopters** (84001 Overseas Hwy., Windley Key, 305/564-6690 or 866/435-4743, www.flyingdoghelicopters.com, flight times vary) enables visitors to get a bird's-eye view of the islands, beaches, coral reefs, and bountiful waters that the Upper Keys comprise. Truly an incredible experience, such tours promise animal lovers a chance to spot dolphins, sharks, stingrays, turtles, and other sea creatures from far above the Atlantic Ocean. Specific tours include the Sand Bar Loop ($70 pp); Alligator

A talented sea lion paints for the public at Theater of the Sea.

Reef Lighthouse ($100 pp); Shark Hunt ($100 pp); Lighthouse and Shark Hunt ($130 pp); Sandbar, Lighthouse, and Shark Hunt ($155 pp); Molasses Reef ($155 pp); 50 Mile Trip (rate varies); and 100 Mile Trip (rate varies).

UPPER MATECUMBE KEY
History of Diving Museum

On the bay side of Mile Marker 83 on Upper Matecumbe Key, sea lovers will enjoy the interactive, educational **History of Diving Museum** (82990 Overseas Hwy., Upper Matecumbe Key, 305/664-9737, www.divingmuseum.org, 10am-5pm daily, $12 adults, $11 seniors and veterans, $6 children 5-11, free for children under 5 and military personnel). Even nondivers might appreciate this well-designed attraction, which packs a lot of information and artifacts into a deceptively small space.

Following an orientation video, you'll be able to stroll amid a curious collection of diving paraphernalia, including improbable diving machines, rare diving helmets, armored diving suits, vintage U.S. Navy diving gear, underwater photographs, old-fashioned scuba tanks, recovered coins, and other treasures relating to sea exploration. Here you'll even be able to test your ability to hold your breath, sit inside Halley's enormous diving bell, crank several hand-operated air pumps, view a reef aquarium from inside a diving helmet, and check out Captain Nemo's submarine and diving helmet from the Disney film *20,000 Leagues Under the Sea* (1954).

Founded by Dr. Joseph A. Bauer Jr. and his wife, Dr. Sally E. Bauer, whose extensive personal collection forms the basis of these engrossing exhibits, the museum is intended to demonstrate "man's quest to explore under the sea" over the course of 4,000 years, from the ancient times of Gilgamesh to the modern days of recreational diving. Ask the museum staff about free monthly programs, with a range of topics from the 1733 Spanish galleon treasure fleet to life as a female Navy diver.

Florida Keys Memorial

While traveling across Upper Matecumbe

© LAURA MARTONE

Curiosities abound at the History of Diving Museum.

Key, most people whiz right past the **Florida Keys Memorial** at Mile Marker 81.6 on the ocean side of U.S. 1. It's easy to do, after all. The memorial itself is fairly simple and nondescript, but still, if you have a moment, you ought to stop and take a look; it's even free to do so. Dedicated in 1937 and now listed on the National Register of Historic Places, the memorial commemorates the fateful Labor Day Hurricane that took many lives, caused much property damage, and effectively destroyed Henry Flagler's Overseas Railroad. As the bronze plaque says, the memorial is "dedicated to the memory of the civilians and war veterans whose lives were lost in the hurricane of September Second, 1935"—a sobering reminder of nature's power over humanity.

LOWER MATECUMBE KEY
Robbie's of Islamorada
At the northern end of Lower Matecumbe Key, on the bay side of U.S. 1 near Mile Marker 77.5, you'll find **Robbie's of Islamorada**

(77522 Overseas Hwy., Lower Matecumbe Key, 305/664-8070 or 877/664-8498, www.robbies.com, 7am–sunset daily), a full-service family-friendly marina that has been offering outdoor distractions since 1976. Here you can rent boats, board an offshore sportfishing charter, opt for a snorkeling excursion, peruse crafts and souvenirs in an open-air market, and grab a bite in the Hungry Tarpon restaurant (305/664-0535). You can also feed visiting schools of tarpon from the dock ($1 pp, $3 per bucket of fish) or take advantage of the marina's status as the official tour operator (800/979-3370, www.zerve.com) for two remote islands: **Indian Key Historic State Park** and **Lignumvitae Key Botanical State Park.** The marina is typically open from sunrise to sunset year-round, which means you can expect later hours during the spring, summer, and fall months, following the daylight saving time change in mid-March.

Anne's Beach
On the ocean side of Lower Matecumbe Key lies **Anne's Beach** (MM 73.5 OS U.S. 1, Lower Matecumbe Key, sunrise–sunset daily, free), a peaceful place to watch the sunrise or sunset, swim in the Atlantic Ocean, give kiteboarding a try, or spend some quiet time with your friends and loved ones. Dedicated to local environmentalist Anne Eaton, this pet-friendly beach features several covered picnic tables, plus a half-mile boardwalk that allows access to more secluded stretches of sand. Public restrooms and ample parking are also available.

OFFSHORE STATE PARKS
◖ Indian Key Historic State Park
Evidently the earliest Upper Keys community existed on this 11-acre island, which in 1830 became the site of John Jacob Housman's lucrative cargo-salvaging business. In 1836 it was designated the first county seat of Dade County, and in 1840 during the Second Seminole War, the Seminole invaded the island, plundered the buildings, and allegedly killed several settlers, despite the presence of Fort Paulding on nearby Teatable Key. From

feeding the tarpon at Robbie's of Islamorada

children under 6) aboard the *Happy Cat* snorkeling catamaran. Just remember that pets are not allowed on the island, though service animals are permitted. Also, if you head to the island via your own vessel and plan to dive or snorkel in the offshore waters, you must use a red-and-white diver-down flag. For more information, contact **Windley Key Fossil Reef Geological State Park** (MM 84.9 BS U.S. 1, Windley Key, 305/664-2540, www. floridastateparks.org/windleykey, 8am-5pm Thurs.-Mon.).

San Pedro Underwater Archaeological Preserve State Park

South of Indian Key lies **San Pedro Underwater Archaeological Preserve State Park** (www.floridastateparks.org/sanpedro, 8am-sunset daily, free), site of the *San Pedro,* a 287-ton Spanish ship that wrecked here during a hurricane on July 13, 1733. Discovered in 1960, the wreck site underwent major salvaging efforts over the subsequent decade, so today all that remains is a large pile of ballast stones. Later enhanced with seven replica cannons and an anchor, the site (which usually lies in 18 feet of water) now forms an artificial reef, home to many tropical fish and, therefore, popular among snorkelers and scuba divers. Swimmers, kayakers, and boaters also favor this site. Listed on the National Register of Historic Places, San Pedro Underwater Archaeological Preserve State Park is also officially part of the Florida Keys National Marine Sanctuary Shipwreck Trail. For more information, contact **Windley Key Fossil Reef Geological State Park** (MM 84.9 BS U.S. 1, Windley Key, 305/664-2540, www.floridastateparks.org/windleykey, 8am-5pm Thurs.-Mon.).

the early 1900s until it became a state park, Indian Key was uninhabited.

Today the lovely **Indian Key Historic State Park** (MM 78.5 OS U.S. 1, Indian Key, www. floridastateparks.org/indiankey, 8am-sunset daily, free), which lies on the ocean side of the Overseas Highway, is only accessible by canoe, kayak, or boat and lures hikers, swimmers, sunbathers, bird-watchers, and anglers alike. In addition, the park offers an interpretive trail through a re-created street system and also features one of the few close-to-shore areas where snorkelers and scuba divers can explore living coral. Although visitors have access to an observation tower and a boat dock, there are no restrooms or picnic facilities on-site, and most facilities are not wheelchair-accessible. To reach the island, you can rent a kayak or powerboat from **Robbie's of Islamorada** (77522 Overseas Hwy., Lower Matecumbe Key, 305/664-8070 or 877/664-8498, www.robbies.com, 7am-sunset daily) or opt for a three-hour island heritage tour (800/979-3370, www.zerve.com, 9am daily, $35 adults, $20 children 6-12, free for

◖ Lignumvitae Key Botanical State Park

Situated on the bay side of the Overseas Highway and only accessible by boat, canoe, or kayak, the wooded **Lignumvitae Key Botanical State Park** (MM 78.5 BS U.S. 1, www.floridastateparks.org/lignumvitaekey,

© BOB KRIST/FLORIDA KEYS NEWS BUREAU

LIGNUMVITAE KEY CHRISTMAS

Although the wooded **Lignumvitae Key Botanical State Park** (MM 78.5 BS U.S. 1, www.floridastateparks.org/lignumvitaekey) is fun to explore all year long, visiting this historical island at Christmastime can be even more magical. On the first Saturday of December, the Lignumvitae Key Christmas is presented by the park staff and the Friends of the Islamorada Area State Parks for the benefit of the park and invites visitors to step back in time and experience the holiday traditions of the early 20th century. As part of this annual event, dulcimer players welcome arriving visitors, who can then take ranger-guided walking tours of the historical Matheson House, typically decorated for the holidays with tropical greenery, handmade ornaments, and other Keys-inspired decorations. Visitors can also take a guided tour of the nearby virgin hardwood hammock, enjoy free key limeade and homemade cookies, and paint holiday themes on sea beans, oyster shells, and sea grape leaves to create souvenir ornaments.

During the event, which usually runs from 9am to 3pm, guests can board the 43-foot *Happy Cat* catamaran at **Robbie's of Islamorada** (77522 Overseas Hwy., Lower Matecumbe Key, 305/664-8070 or 800/979-3370, www.robbies.com) to reach the island. Though it normally costs $2.50 per person to visit the park, the fee is slightly higher during this Christmas event—usually around $5 per adult, but it's free for children under 12. For more information, contact the **Windley Key Fossil Reef Geological State Park** (MM 84.9 BS U.S. 1, Windley Key, 305/664-2540, www.floridastateparks.org/windleykey, 8am-5pm Thurs.-Mon., education center 9am-5pm Fri.-Sun.).

9am-5pm Thurs.-Mon., $2.50 pp) features the kind of virgin tropical hardwood hammock that once thrived in the Upper Keys. Formerly known as Jenkinson Island, Lignumvitae (pronounced lig-num-VIE-tee and meaning "tree of life") has been home to various individuals since at least the 1830s—including William J. Matheson, a wealthy Miami chemist who bought the island in 1919 and soon afterward built a caretaker's home, with a cistern for rainwater and a windmill for electricity. Today Matheson's former hideaway is now the park's visitor center.

Here you can take a one-hour, ranger-guided tour ($2 adults, $1.50 children, free for children under 6) amid the peaceful foliage or inside the Matheson house. The tours, which are offered twice daily (10am and 2pm) from Friday to Sunday, enable you to access trails through the preserve that would normally be off limits to visitors. To reach the island, you can rent a kayak or powerboat from **Robbie's of Islamorada** (77522 Overseas Hwy., Lower Matecumbe Key, 305/664-8070 or 877/664-8498, www.robbies.com, 7am-sunset daily) or opt for a three-hour island heritage tour (800/979-3370, www.zerve.com, 9am daily, $35 adults, $20 children 6-12, free for children under 6) aboard the *Happy Cat* snorkeling catamaran, which when available, includes transportation to and from Lignumvitae Key as well as Indian Key. Just remember that pets are not allowed in this remote park, though service animals are permitted. The boat is wheelchair-accessible, but arrangements must be made in advance; unfortunately, accessibility is limited on the island itself. For more information, contact **Windley Key Fossil Reef Geological State Park** (MM 84.9 BS U.S. 1, Windley Key, 305/664-2540, www.floridastateparks.org/windleykey, 8am-5pm Thurs.-Mon.).

Entertainment and Events

NIGHTLIFE

As with much of the Florida Keys region, most of the nightlife options in Islamorada consist of bars and restaurants that offer live entertainment or a chance to watch televised sports with like-minded folks. The **Island Grill** (85501 Overseas Hwy., Plantation Key, 305/664-8400, www.keysislandgrill.com, 7am-10pm Sun.-Thurs., 7am-11pm Fri.-Sat.), for instance, features nightly performers, from local funk and blues singers to magicians and rock 'n' roll bands. Just down the road, **The Oceanview Pub & Inn** (MM 84.5 BS U.S. 1, Windley Key, 305/664-8052, www.theocean-view.com, 7am-2am daily) has the distinction of securing the first liquor license in the Florida Keys. For well over a decade, this longstanding watering hole has been co-owned by former NFL players Gary Dunn and Dennis Harrah, who despite extensive renovations, have maintained the casual vibe that residents and local anglers have adored for years. Stop by for some cold beer and your favorite televised sporting event; if need be, you can always stay the night at the adjacent inn or enjoy a dip in the on-site pool.

The **Postcard Inn Beach Resort & Marina at Holiday Isle** (84001 Overseas Hwy., Windley Key, 305/664-2321, www.holidayisle.com) boasts several different bars, including the **Holiday Isle Tiki Bar** (noon-close Mon.-Fri., 11am-close Sat.-Sun.), with live rock and pop bands perform on the weekends (8pm-1am Fri.-Sat.). Apparently, it's also home of the first-ever rum runner cocktail. Another option is the multilevel thatched-roof **Rum Runner's Island Bar** (10am-midnight daily), where locals and tourists alike can enjoy balmy breezes, frozen drinks, as well as live pop, rock, folk, and country music. Other on-site bars include **The Cantina,** the **Wreck Bar,** and **Jaw's Raw Bar,** all of which feature tropical drinks and stunning views.

At the **Lorelei Restaurant & Cabana Bar** (81924 Overseas Hwy., Upper Matecumbe Key,

305/664-2692, www.loreleicabanabar.com, 7am-midnight daily), you can enjoy happy-hour specials every day (4pm-6pm) and live pop, rock, country, folk, or rhythm-and-blues every night (5pm-9pm)—not to mention waterfront dining, free wireless Internet access, and an ideal spot to watch a classic bayside sunset. A little farther south, the **Morada Bay Beach Café** (81600 Overseas Hwy., Upper Matecumbe Key, 305/664-0604, www.moradabay-restaurant.com, 11:30am-close daily) presents an array of activities, from happy hours to open jam sessions around a bonfire. Of course, the most popular event at Morada Bay is surely the well-publicized Full Moon Party (dates vary, $20-30 cover) each month. Essentially a large beach bash, this lively event consists of multiple bonfires, specialty drinks at the indoor and outdoor bars, a fireworks display, and a menagerie of live performers, including flamenco and jazz guitarists, electric reggae bands, stilt walkers, balloon artists, acrobats, and fire blowers.

THE ARTS

While cultural enthusiasts will definitely find more live music, dance performances, and theatrical venues in Key West, Islamorada still offers a few options for those seeking an alternative to outdoor activities. Since 1978 **The Key Players** (305/453-0997, www.thekeyplayers.org, show times and ticket prices vary) has presented live comedies, dramas, and Broadway musicals in venues throughout the Upper Keys, such as the **Murray E. Nelson Government and Cultural Center** (MM 102 U.S. 1) and the **Lions Club** (MM 99.6 U.S. 1), both of which are located in Key Largo. The nonprofit community theater troupe typically produces four shows every year.

From November to April, the **Florida Keys Community Concert Band** (305/451-4530, www.keyscommunityconcertband.org), founded in 1992 by a small group of dedicated musicians, features "Pops in the Park," a free monthly concert series at the open-air Capital Bank Amphitheater in Founders Park, near Mile Marker 87 on Plantation Key. The performances are held on a Saturday afternoon (4pm-5pm) each month during the concert season, and attendees are welcome to bring chairs and blankets, as there are no seats on the lawn. Check the band's online schedule for specific dates.

In addition, **Islamorada Community Entertainment** (ICE, 305/395-6344, www.keysice.com, show times and ticket prices vary) helps to bring plays, operas, concerts, and film festivals to the Capital Bank Amphitheater in Founders Park and the Coral Shores High School Performing Arts Center (89901 Old Hwy., Tavernier) on Plantation Key. For information about other cultural events in the Upper Keys, consult the **Florida Keys Council of the Arts** (1100 Simonton St., Key West, 305/295-4369, www.keysarts.com).

If you're craving a bit of cinematic entertainment, simply head east of Plantation Key on what's technically the southern end of Key Largo, where you'll find the **Tavernier Cinema 5** (91298 Overseas Hwy., Tavernier, 305/853-7003, show times and ticket prices vary). While this might not be the fanciest movie theater in southern Florida, you'll at least be able to catch the latest flicks here.

FESTIVALS AND EVENTS

Besides numerous annual fishing competitions—such as the four-day **Islamorada Sailfish Tournament** (305/852-2102, www.islamoradasailfishtournament.com), which takes place in late November or early December—Islamorada hosts several popular events throughout the year. In mid-January, for instance, art lovers are invited to spend the Saturday prior to Martin Luther King Jr. Day perusing the arts and crafts at **Art Under the Oaks** (305/360-8556, www.artundertheoaks.com, free admission), a longstanding community event that's taken place at the San Pedro Catholic Church (MM 89.5 BS U.S. 1, Tavernier, 305/852-5372, www.sanpedroparish.org) on Plantation Key for more than three

decades. Beyond fine art and original crafts, you'll be treated to local musicians, specialty food booths, a raffle, and a self-guided nature walk. Parking is available on-site ($5 donation requested) or at the nearby Coral Shores High School (89901 Old Hwy., Tavernier, free parking and shuttle service), also situated on Plantation Key.

In late February, locals flock to Founders Park (87000 Overseas Hwy., Plantation Key) for the two-day **Gigantic Nautical Flea Market** (305/712-1818, www.giganticnauticalfleamarket.org, $5 donation suggested), a popular event hosted by the Upper Keys Rotary Club. Here you'll find hundreds of vendors offering bargains on new and used boats, anchors and motors, other marine and dock equipment, diving and fishing gear, clothing, electronics, antiques, jewelry, sunglasses, and nautical arts and crafts. In addition, each morning begins with a $5 all-you-can-eat pancake breakfast. Free parking as well as free shuttle service are available at Coral Shores High School on Plantation Key. While there's technically no admission fee to attend the flea market, the Rotary Club encourages all adults to donate $5 to the event, which ultimately raises money to fund college scholarships for area youth.

Islamorada Community Entertainment (ICE, 305/395-6344, www.keysice.com, show dates and ticket prices vary) hosts several events throughout the year, including the annual **Bay Jam,** a premier one-day outdoor music festival that typically occurs in Founders Park in the spring, some time between mid-March and early April. If you're here in early December, consider attending the full-day **Florida Keys Holiday Festival,** which takes place every year in Founders Park (87000 Overseas Hwy., Plantation Key) and features a holiday parade, an arts-and-crafts bazaar, and carolers singing around an enormous holiday tree. For more information about the holiday festival and other area events, contact the **Islamorada Chamber of Commerce** (MM 83.2 BS U.S. 1, Upper Matecumbe Key, 305/664-4503 or 800/322-5397, www.islamoradachamber.com, 9am-5pm Mon.-Fri., 9am-4pm Sat., 9am-3pm Sun.).

Shopping

Although many avid shoppers head straight to Key West, Islamorada lures quite a few eager spenders with its assortment of art galleries, clothing boutiques, gift shops, and other unique emporiums.

ART GALLERIES

You'll find it hard to miss Betsy, the giant 30-foot-tall lobster sculpture that welcomes art lovers to **The Rain Barrel** (86700 Overseas Hwy., Plantation Key, www.keysdirectory.com/rainbarrel, 9am-5pm daily), a working village of artists situated in a lush, rustic setting on the bay side of U.S. 1. A popular stop for locals and tourists alike, this unusual complex features several eye-popping galleries, including the **Main Gallery** (305/852-3084), the barnlike structure marking the entrance, and the **Rain Barrel Sculpture Gallery** (305/852-8935,

The Rain Barrel encompasses several different art galleries.

© LAURA MARTONE

www.rainbarrelsculpture.com), situated at the rear of the property and offering bronze statues and stoneware items fashioned by gallery owners Dwayne and Cindy King. Among other options here, you'll encounter **King's Treasure** (305/852-9797), which features Dwayne King's nautical-themed jewelry creations; the **Spectrum Studio of Glass Design** (800/488-7780), which presents Micheal Robinson's delicate glass sculptures of tropical fish and other marinelife prevalent in the Florida Keys; and the **Stacie Krupa Gallery** (305/942-0614, www.staciekrupa.com), which showcases Krupa's expressionistic visions of animals.

Farther south, on Upper Matecumbe Key, Krupa operates another gallery, the **Stacie Krupa Studio Gallery of Art** (82935 Overseas Hwy., Upper Matecumbe Key, 305/517-2631, www.staciekrupa.com, 10am-6pm daily) while the unique **Lobster Trap Art Gift Shop & Art Gallery** (82200 Overseas Hwy., Upper Matecumbe Key, 305/664-0001, www.lobstertrapart.com, 8am-6pm daily) features the vivid sea-inspired paintings of Nadine and Glenn Lahti as well as other local artists. Interestingly, all the wooden frames in this gallery have been crafted from old lobster traps that were once used throughout the Florida Keys; since 2003, the gallery has produced more than 10,000 of these handmade, customized frames.

As the name indicates, **Ichthyophile** (81904 Overseas Hwy., Upper Matecumbe Key, 305/664-8960, www.ichthyophile.com, 10am-5pm daily) is an ideal gallery for fish lovers, as every painting, antique print, wall fixture, lamp, hanging mobile, cookbook, novel, and piece of jewelry or pottery in the store focuses on fish or fishing enthusiasts. The **Gallery Morada** (81611 Old Hwy., Upper Matecumbe Key, 305/664-3650, www.gallerymorada.com, 10am-6pm daily), meanwhile, represents the imaginative jewelry, dishware, lamps, clocks, glass sculptures, and other creations of more than 200 artisans. Farther south, **Pasta's**

ISLAMORADA

Signature Gallery (81599 Old Hwy., Upper Matecumbe Key, 954/290-4262, www.art-bypasta.com, 10am-5pm daily) is home to the colorful paintings and wooden sculptures of marinelife artist Pasta Pantaleo. For more information about these and other art galleries, consult the **Florida Keys Council of the Arts** (1100 Simonton St., Key West, 305/295-4369, www.keysarts.com).

CLOTHING BOUTIQUES

Whether you're a serious clotheshorse or just in need of a casual outfit, you'll find a handful of clothing boutiques in Islamorada, including the **Latitude 25 Clothing Co.** (82748 Overseas Hwy., Upper Matecumbe Key, 305/664-4421 or 866/664-4421, www.floridakeysstore.net, 9:30am-5:30pm daily), which offers a wide array of women's and men's apparel, from Body Glove bikinis to Tommy Bahama shirts, plus shoes, accessories, sunscreen, pet toys, and tropical gifts. The **Lion's Lair** (82185 Overseas Hwy., Upper Matecumbe Key, 305/664-9921 or 800/220-1691, www.lionslairdesigns.com,

9:30am-7pm daily), meanwhile, features an assortment of ladies' swimwear and lingerie, and the one-of-a-kind **Wild Lily Boutique** (81933 Overseas Hwy., Upper Matecumbe Key, 305/517-9222, www.wildlilyboutique.com, 10am-6pm Mon.-Fri., 10am-5pm Sat., 11am-5pm Sun.) lures shoppers with its ever-changing collection of youthful apparel, creative jewelry, and island-style accessories.

GIFT AND BOOK SHOPS

For those who hope to bring a special souvenir home with them, Islamorada doesn't disappoint. You'll find a wide array of emporiums in the Village of Islands, all of which commemorate a particular aspect of this unique region. The **Plantation Key Nursery** (MM 88 OS U.S. 1, Plantation Key, 305/852-9190, www.plantationkeynursery.com, 9am-5pm daily), for instance, offers native plants and colorful accessories for garden lovers while **Blue Marlin Jewelry** (81915 Overseas Hwy., Upper Matecumbe Key, 305/664-8004 or 888/826-4424, www.bluemarlinjewelry.com,

Hooked on Books offers plenty of local guidebooks.

9:30am-5:30pm Mon.-Sat., 11am-5pm Sun.) features nautical-inspired jewelry, from swordfish pendants to earrings made of salvaged treasure coins.

Hooked on Books (81909 Overseas Hwy., Upper Matecumbe Key, 305/517-2602, www.hookedonbooksfloridakeys.com, 10am-5:30pm daily), provides a wealth of Florida-related selections, including regional travel guides, novels by Florida-based writers, and books about Florida Keys history, cuisine, activities, and wildlife.

On the bay side of the highway, the two-story **World Wide Sportsman** (81576 Overseas Hwy., Upper Matecumbe Key, 305/664-4615, www.basspro.com, 9am-8:30pm Sun.-Thurs., 9am-9pm Fri.-Sat.) looms large in a sprawling complex that includes the Bayside Marina and the Islamorada Fish Company. Inside this vast well-designed store, you'll find casual clothes and shoes, inshore and offshore fishing gear, as well as souvenirs. In addition, you can peruse the displayed memorabilia, mounted fish, and engrossing aquariums; visit an elegant art gallery; step aboard the *Pilar,* the sister ship to Ernest Hemingway's famous fishing boat; and relax on the balcony of the Zane Grey Long Key Lounge. For something a bit more intimate, head to **The Banyan Tree** (81197 Overseas Hwy., Upper Matecumbe Key, 305/664-3433, www.banyantreegarden.com, 10am-5pm Mon.-Thurs. and Sat., 10am-9pm Fri., noon-4pm Sun.), which features a plethora of antiques, linens, housewares, ceramics, home furnishings, garden fixtures, and exotic plants and flowers.

Sports and Recreation

HIKING AND BIKING

While Islamorada doesn't offer much for long-distance hikers, you can certainly enjoy a pleasant stroll through places like **Indian Key Historic State Park** (MM 78.5 OS U.S. 1, www.floridastateparks.org/indiankey, 8am-sunset daily, free), which has an interpretive trail, and **Lignumvitae Key Botanical State Park** (MM 78.5 BS U.S. 1, www.floridastateparks.org/lignumvitaekey, 9am-5pm Thurs.-Mon., $2.50 pp), featuring guided ranger walks. Both islands are only accessible by boat, and neither has a direct phone number. For more information about either island, contact **Windley Key Fossil Reef Geological State Park** (MM 84.9 BS U.S. 1, Windley Key, 305/664-2540, www.floridastateparks.org/windleykey, 8am-5pm Thurs.-Mon.).

Given Islamorada's sprawling nature and numerous bridges, bikers will undoubtedly appreciate the region even more—though care should always be taken on the Overseas Highway, and a proper helmet should be worn at all times. Between Mile Marker 91 and Mile Marker 71, you'll even find 10 miles of actual biking paths, part of the **Florida Keys Overseas Heritage Trail.** Bicycles can be rented from **A1A Bicycle Rentals** (81984 Overseas Hwy., Upper Matecumbe Key, 305/664-4535, www.keyswatersports.com, 9am-5pm daily, rates vary), which offers daily, weekly, and monthly rates and even provides delivery service. **Backcountry Cowboy Outfitters** (82240 Overseas Hwy., Upper Matecumbe Key, 305/517-4177, www.backcountrycowboy.com, 10am-6pm Mon.-Sat., 10am-5pm Sun., $15-20 per half day, $20-25 daily, $35-100 for multiple days, $95-115 weekly) offers both one-speed and three-speed bicycle rentals—plus helmets, combination locks, and copies of the state's bicycle laws. Local delivery is also available.

❰ FISHING AND BOATING

Anglers and boaters will find a treasure trove of options in the Islamorada area. Boasting one of the largest fishing fleets in Florida, it might just be, as residents claim, the "sportfishing capital of the world." Just consider all of the resorts that offer access to fishing charters and boat

ISLAMORADA

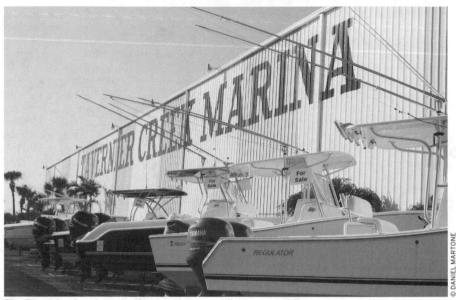

©DANIEL MARTONE

The Tavernier Creek Marina is home to several fishing and diving operators.

rentals, such as the **Ragged Edge Resort & Marina** (243 Treasure Harbor Rd., Plantation Key, 305/852-5389, www.ragged-edge.com) and **Smugglers Cove Resort & Marina** (85500 Overseas Hwy., Windley Key, 305/664-5564, www.smugglerscoveislamorada.com). In fact, besides Smugglers Cove, Windley Key offers a slew of such fishing-friendly resorts, including the **Drop Anchor Resort and Marina** (MM 85 OS U.S. 1, Windley Key, 305/664-4863, www.dropanchorresort.com), **Coconut Cove Resort and Marina** (84801 Overseas Hwy., Windley Key, 305/664-0123, www.coconutcove.net), **Pelican Cove Resort & Marina** (84457 Overseas Hwy., Windley Key, 305/664-4435, www.pcove.com), and **Postcard Inn Beach Resort & Marina at Holiday Isle** (84001 Overseas Hwy., Windley Key, 305/664-2321, www.holidayisle.com).

Farther south, on Upper Matecumbe Key, lies **Bud N' Mary's Marina** (79851 Overseas Hwy., Upper Matecumbe Key, 305/664-2461, www.budnmarys.com), which has been around since 1944 and now features more than 40 fishing captains and guides, making it the oldest and largest fishing fleet in the Florida Keys. Here anglers can find backcountry fishing expeditions ($400-425 per half day, $575 daily), offshore fishing charters (rates vary), and a 65-foot party fishing boat ($65 pp), the *Miss Islamorada,* plus a tackle and bait shop, boat storage, diving excursions, and an outdoor eatery. Of the many boats docked here, you'll encounter the 44-foot *Redfish* (305/664-8497, www.redfishsportfishing.com, hours and rates vary), operated by veteran Captain Merv Finch and featuring offshore trips in search of (depending on the season) mahimahi, sailfish, wahoo, snapper, grouper, marlin, tuna, permit, tilefish, amberjack, swordfish, and king mackerel.

Another option is to visit one of the non-resort marinas in the area, such as the **Tavernier Creek Marina** (90800 Overseas Hwy., Tavernier, 305/852-5854, www.taverniercreek-marina.com), which lies on the bay side of Plantation Key and boasts the largest dry storage facility in the Florida Keys. Here

JUST THE FACTS ABOUT DOLPHINS

The Atlantic bottlenose dolphin *(Tursiops truncatus)* inhabits temperate coastal waters throughout the world. Here are some curious facts about these playful creatures:

- Active predators who feed on small, schooling fish, bottlenose dolphins can live into their 40s, grow to 10 feet in length, weigh up to 600 pounds, and reach sexual maturity between ages 5 and 12.

- Calves, born after a year-long gestation period, can be three feet long and 30 pounds at birth, will typically nurse for two to four years, and begin to eat fish at a few months of age.

- The bottlenose, or rostrum, is used for touching and pushing while the small, cone-shaped teeth (dolphins typically have 88) are used for grasping and tearing food, not chewing.

- The blowhole on the top of each dolphin's head serves as a nostril, through which the dolphin typically breathes twice per minute.

- Dolphins can conveniently breathe and eat at the same time, and they can hold their breath for eight minutes if necessary.

- The blowhole, not the throat, produces their vocalizations, which they can manipulate to mimic other sounds, such as human laughter.

- The pectoral fins, containing all the bones of a land animal's forelimbs and located on the dolphin's sides, are used for steering, while the dorsal fin, made entirely of cartilage and located on the dolphin's back, is used for balance.

- The peduncle is the muscular area that powers the flukes, or two halves of the tail, allowing dolphins to swim up to 17 miles per hour.

- Dolphins can only swim forward, not backward, and they can shut down half of their brains while resting and still manage to swim, hunt, and communicate.

- Although Atlantic bottlenose dolphins have no sense of smell, they have excellent eyesight above and below the water, and they can also hear well, especially below the water, where they navigate, detect prey, and locate other objects by utilizing echolocation—a sonar-like system whereby high-pitched sounds are emitted, reflected off other surfaces, and interpreted by sensory receptors, typically the jowls.

- Dolphins appreciate eye contact, which is why they tend to be more motivated when you look at and speak to them directly.

ISLAMORADA

you can hire such charters as **Blue Water Blues** (305/731-9612, www.bluewaterblues.com, hours and rates vary), operated by Captain George Coffey who offers reef trips for grouper, snapper, and kingfish, plus evening excursions for tarpon and shark. Farther south, on Upper Matecumbe Key, lie two more impressive fleets: one at the **Whale Harbor Marina** (83413 Overseas Hwy., Upper Matecumbe Key, 305/664-4959, ext. 201, www.whaleharborinn.com, trips and rates vary) and the other at the **World Wide Sportsman Bayside Marina** (81576 Overseas Hwy., Upper Matecumbe Key, 305/394-7484, www.islamoradafishingguidesandcharters.com, trips and rates vary). Of course, many anglers head even farther south to **Robbie's of Islamorada** (77522 Overseas

Hwy., Lower Matecumbe Key, 305/664-8070 or 877/664-8498, www.robbies.com, 7am-sunset daily), which offers an array of backcountry, patch-reef, and offshore fishing opportunities (trips and rates vary). In addition, Robbie's provides boat rentals, including 18-foot Wagner skiffs ($150 per half day, $200 daily), 18-foot Wagner powerboats ($135 per half day, $185 daily), and 23-foot deck boats ($185 per half day, $235 daily).

◖ KAYAKING

While sportfishing is indeed the most popular activity in Islamorada, kayakers also appreciate the bountiful waters surrounding this Village of Islands. After all, some attractions—such as Indian Key Historic State Park, San Pedro

JUST THE FACTS ABOUT SEA LIONS

The California sea lion *(Zalophus californianus)*, is considered a pinniped, along with seals, walruses, and four other types of sea lions. Typically California sea lions inhabit the temperate coastline and islands of the western Americas, from British Columbia to Ecuador, spending much time at sea and coming ashore frequently to sleep or bask in the sun. Although related to seals, sea lions are markedly different in that they tend to have external ear flaps, possess much larger fore flippers, and move about on land by walking on all fours, as opposed to seals' customary wriggling. In addition, while sea lions move their fore flippers in an up-and-down motion to propel themselves through the water, seals move their hind flippers in a side-to-side motion. Here are some other facts about California sea lions:

- Agile, active predators who feed on squid, octopus, and fish, California sea lions maneuver well both on land and in water, and they can live for roughly 25 years.

- Male sea lions usually have a darker fur coat than females and weigh up to 900 pounds, three times the weight of female sea lions.

- Breeding season typically occurs between May and August, and pups are born after a year-long gestation period; weighing roughly 13 pounds at birth, these pups can nurse for up to a year.

- Sea lions have 34 to 38 teeth that are designed for grasping and tearing food, not chewing (as with dolphins).

- Although they usually stay submerged for 3 minutes or less, they can hold their breath for up to 15 minutes.

- Sea lions are tactile, social creatures that communicate with one another through vocalizations and postural displays. They have 25 whiskers, which they use to explore objects on land and in water.

- The fore flippers contain all the bones of a land animal's forelimbs but are modified to allow for swimming at speeds of up to 23 miles per hour.

- The hind flippers, meanwhile, are used for steering and can be rotated underneath the body, enabling them to walk on all fours.

- Three nails on the hind flippers are used in grooming, and a small, flattened tail can be found between the flippers.

- California sea lions see well on land and in water, and their large eyes are very light-sensitive; although they have a poor sense of taste, their hearing and sense of smell are both keen.

Underwater Archaeological Preserve State Park, and Lignumvitae Key Botanical State Park—are only accessible via kayak, canoe, or boat.

Even if you haven't lugged your own kayak with you, you're in luck. There are several kayaking outfitters in the region, including **Founders Park Watersports** (87000 Overseas Hwy., Plantation Key, 305/434-8984, www.foundersparkwatersports.com, 11am-5pm Mon.-Fri., 11am-6pm Sat.-Sun., $15-35 hourly), operating from the beach in Founders Park and offering kayak, pedal boat, and Hobie Wave rentals.

You can also rent a single or double kayak from **Backcountry Cowboy Outfitters** (82240 Overseas Hwy., Upper Matecumbe Key,

305/517-4177, www.backcountrycowboy.com, 10am-6pm Mon.-Sat., 10am-5pm Sun.) for a half day ($45-60), a full day ($60-80), multiple days ($85-165), or an entire week ($165-195). Backcountry Cowboy also offers three different two-hour guided kayaking excursions: the backcountry nature tour ($45 adults, $22.50 children under 13), the sunset tour ($45 pp), and the historical Indian Key tour ($45 pp).

Based out of the local Days Inn, **A1A Watersports** (82749 Overseas Hwy., Upper Matecumbe Key, 305/664-8182, www.keyswatersports.com, 7am-9pm daily, rates vary) offers single and double kayaks for half-day, full-day, multiday, weekly, and monthly rentals, all of which include instruction, seat backs, paddles, life jackets, and a navigational chart. Local delivery and pickup is possible for multiday rentals. A1A has several other locations in the Florida Keys, including the Keys Motel (90611 Overseas Hwy., Tavernier, 305/664-8182) and the Fiesta Key Recreation Destination (70001 Overseas Hwy., Fiesta Key, 305/664-9192).

Located at Robbie's of Islamorada, **Florida Keys Kayak** (77522 Overseas Hwy., Lower Matecumbe Key, 305/664-4878, www.kayak-thefloridakeys.com, 9am-sunset daily) provides single and double kayaks ($40-55 per half day, $50-65 daily), stand up paddleboards ($50 per half day), single and double Hobie pedal kayaks ($50-65 per half day, $60-75 daily), and canoes ($60 per half day). Free delivery is available to local resorts and residences, and earlier hours (such as sunrise) are possible with 24-hour notice. Florida Keys Kayak features three two-hour guided excursions: the backcountry tour ($45 pp), the sunset tour ($45 pp), and the Indian Key snorkeling tour ($45 pp).

DIVING AND SNORKELING

Whether you're a novice or an experienced underwater explorer, you should definitely reserve part of your trip for the waters east of Islamorada, an area filled with shallow coral reefs, curious wall formations, and shipwrecks. Through the **Conch Republic Divers** (Tavernier Creek Marina, 90800 Overseas Hwy., Tavernier, 305/852-1655 or 800/274-3483, www.conchrepublicdivers.com) or the **Florida Keys Dive Center** (90451 Old Hwy., Tavernier, 305/852-4599 or 800/433-8946, www.floridakeysdivectr.com), both of which are based on the northern end of Plantation Key, you can take various diving classes, rent scuba-diving gear, and join twice-daily diving excursions (8:30am and 1pm, $80 pp) to explore many of the nearby underwater attractions.

Some of the sights you might encounter include the **Conch Wall,** noted for barrel sponges, rare pillar coral, and of course, conch; the **Davis Reef,** an ideal spot to observe green moray eels; the **Crocker Wall,** home to gorgonian coral and eagle rays; **Hens and Chickens,**

an area that offers mounds of star and plate coral; and **Little Conch Reef,** adjacent to the wrecked *El Infante,* a Spanish galleon that sank in the 1733 hurricane. In these waters, you'll also find the **Alligator Reef,** site of the shipwrecked **USS *Alligator,*** and the *Eagle,* a 287-foot freighter donated by the Eagle Tire Company as an artificial reef in 1985 and now teeming with countless fish.

Besides Conch Republic Divers and the Florida Keys Dive Center, several other diving operators are found in the area. Such alternative options, all of which provide instructional scuba-diving programs, include the **Holiday Isle Dive Shop** (84001 Overseas Hwy., Windley Key, 305/664-3483, www.diveholidayisle.com, 8am-6pm daily, $75 pp), based out of the tropical-style Holiday Isle Resort & Marina, and **Key Dives** (79851 Overseas Hwy., Upper Matecumbe Key, 305/664-2211 or 800/344-7352, www.keydives.com, 8am and 12:30pm daily, $85-110 pp), offering professional underwater tour guides for small groups of up to six divers. All four of the aforementioned dive operators also offer affordable daily snorkeling excursions ($30-40 adults, $25-40 children).

In addition, you can opt for a private two-hour snorkeling trip through the **Bay and Reef Company** (81801 Overseas Hwy., Upper Matecumbe Key, 305/393-1779 or 305/393-0994, www.bayandreef.com, $250 per group, $75 hourly beyond the initial two hours), which is based out of the Cheeca Lodge & Spa, or board the *Happy Cat* at **Robbie's of Islamorada** (77522 Overseas Hwy., Lower Matecumbe Key, 800/979-3370, www.robbies.com, 9am, noon, 3pm, and 6pm daily, $35 adults, $20 children).

Snorkelers and scuba divers can also rent a kayak or boat from **Robbie's of Islamorada** (77522 Overseas Hwy., Lower Matecumbe Key, 305/664-8070 or 305/664-9814, www.robbies.com, 7am-sunset daily, rates vary) and head toward the **San Pedro Underwater Archaeological Preserve State Park** (305/664-2540, www.floridastateparks.org/sanpedro, 8am-sunset daily, free), south of

UNDERWATER SAFETY TIPS

Thousands of snorkelers and scuba divers flock to the Florida Keys every year. All underwater enthusiasts should take several precautions:

- Check weather conditions before venturing out as strong winds and rough seas can create unsafe conditions.

- If operating your own vessel, make sure you stay at least 300 feet from diver-down flags in open water and at least 100 feet from flags in rivers and inlets; if you cannot maintain such distance, slow down to an idle speed when passing other divers.

- Make sure you've had proper snorkeling and/or scuba-diving instruction.

- When in doubt about your abilities, don't hesitate to join a professional guide or tour.

- Always tell someone on land where you're planning to go and when you intend to return.

- If you plan to be in the water for a while, apply ample waterproof sunscreen or wear a shirt to avoid sunburn.

- Make sure your mask and flippers fit properly, and check that you have all necessary equipment, such as inflatable vests for snorkelers and weights and tanks for scuba divers.

- If you find it difficult to walk on the boat while wearing flippers, carry them into the water before putting them on.

- Never snorkel or dive without displaying a proper red-and-white, diver-down flag on your vessel, and always remove said flag when all divers have returned to the boat.

- Always snorkel or dive with a buddy, and try to stay together.

- Plan your entry and exit points before jumping into the water.

- Swim into the current upon entering the water, and then ride the current back to your exit point.

- Don't touch any tempting sea creatures, as they may sting you.

- Look above the water every now and again to ensure that you haven't drifted too far away from the boat; try to stay within 300 feet of the diver-down flag when in open water and within 100 feet when in a river or inlet.

- If you have a diving emergency, dial 911 from your cell phone, or use a VHF radio to signal a "MAYDAY."

A helpful saying to remember is "Snorkel aware, dive with care!" For scuba divers, another helpful saying is "Dive ALIVE," with the letters in "ALIVE" standing for these tips:

- **Air:** Monitor your air supply, always surface with at least 500 PSI, and practice out-of-air procedures.

- **Lead Weights:** Wear only enough lead to achieve proper buoyancy, and know how to release your and your buddy's weight systems.

- **Inspection:** Inspect your gear before every dive trip, replace missing or worn gear, replace batteries in any electronics, and have regulators serviced annually.

- **Verification:** Verify your dive skills, and review your dive plan, signals, and lost-buddy procedures with your diving buddy.

- **Escape:** Always dive with surface-signaling devices. If you become entangled, remain calm and do what you can to free yourself. If you're lost on the surface, inflate your buoyancy compensation device (BCD), remain calm, maintain your position if possible, and try to attract others' attention.

For more safety tips, consult area diving operators or **Florida Keys National Marine Sanctuary** (305/852-7717 or 305/809-4700, www.floridakeys.noaa.gov).

Indian Key. Here underwater explorers will find the remains of the *San Pedro*, a 287-ton Spanish ship that wrecked in this location during a 1733 hurricane. Since its discovery in 1960, it's undergone several salvaging attempts and now forms an artificial reef, home to plenty of tropical fish.

◖ SPAS AND YOGA

Save for Key West, Islamorada is surely the best locale in the Florida Keys to seek pampering rejuvenation for the body, mind, and soul. The **Cheeca Lodge & Spa** (81801 Overseas Hwy., Upper Matecumbe Key, 800/327-2888, www.cheeca.com, spa 9am-8pm daily, fitness center 6am-midnight daily, rates vary) features a 5,700-square-foot "oasis of relaxation and rejuvenation." Here resort guests (age 18 or older) can choose from an array of fitness classes, steam rooms, salt scrubs, skin and body treatments, refreshing facials, and massage therapies—in private treatment rooms, poolside cabanas, or an oceanside tiki hut.

Unlike the Cheeca Lodge, **The Moorings Village & Spa** (123 Beach Rd., Upper Matecumbe Key, 305/664-4708, www.themooringsvillage.com) allows nonguests to partake of the facials, massages, and beachside yoga lessons provided at the on-site **Island Body & Sol Spa** (305/664-3264, www.islandbodyandsolspa.com, by appointment daily, $50-190 per treatment).

Beyond such resort-type facilities, you'll find several day spas in the area, including the appointment-only **Kiki's Spa** (89240 Overseas Hwy., Ste. 2, Tavernier, 305/852-0011, www.tavernierspa.com, 10am-6pm Tues.-Sat.) on Plantation Key, where you can opt for manicures ($15-35 pp), pedicures ($25-45 pp), facials ($45-200 pp), massages ($15-125 pp), waxing treatments ($12-70 pp), tanning services ($45-70 pp), and other options. On Upper Matecumbe Key, the European-style **Ciao Bella Salon & Day Spa** (82913 Overseas Hwy., 305/664-4558, www.theislamoradaspa.com, 9am-6pm Tues.-Sat.) specializes in hair care

© LAURA MARTONE

ISLAMORADA

Rejuvenation awaits at The Moorings Village & Spa.

(rates vary), natural manicures and pedicures ($20-50 pp), clean waxing treatments (rates vary), clinical facials ($85-125 pp), and healing massages for both men and women ($45-250 pp). Appointments are recommended, and a 24-hour cancellation notice is required.

Just down the road, the **Blu Bamboo Salon & Spa** (82205 Overseas Hwy., Upper Matecumbe Key, 305/664-9342, www.blubamboo.com, 9am-6pm Tues.-Sat.) encourages you to "indulge your senses and soothe your soul" with an array of facials ($15-135 pp), waxing services ($10-65 pp), hand treatments ($5-50 pp), foot treatments ($5-80 pp), and massages ($80-90 pp). Appointments are advisable, and the spa requires 24-hour notice to cancel.

Accommodations

UNDER $100

As Islamorada's only B&B, the pet-friendly **Casa Thorn Bed & Breakfast** (114 Palm Ln., Plantation Key, 305/852-3996, www.casathorn.com, $79-239 d) houses five comfortable rooms, ranging from the moderate Secret Garden Room, equipped with a small refrigerator, to the Moroccan Room, with its king-size four-poster bed and a tub made for two. Other on-site amenities include a lovely tropical garden and a refreshing swimming pool.

Situated on a large grassy property alongside the Atlantic Ocean, the **Ragged Edge Resort & Marina** (243 Treasure Harbor Dr., Plantation Key, 305/852-5389, www.ragged-edge.com, $69-259 d) offers standard motel rooms with small refrigerators, efficiencies with kitchenettes, large studios with full kitchens and balconies or screened porches, plus a deluxe two-bedroom suite with two bathrooms, a full kitchen, a balcony, and a large family room. Anglers will especially like this resort, which offers access to a full-service marina and a fishing pier. Clang the cowbell when you arrive and the manager will be with you shortly.

The **Coconut Cove Resort and Marina** (84801 Overseas Hwy., Windley Key, 305/664-0123, www.coconutcove.net, $75-195 d) presents three types of accommodations: the Captain's Cottages, each of which includes a single bed, a queen-size bed, and a kitchen; the General Quarters, which also boast luxurious hot tubs; and the Admiral's Accommodations, each containing two queen-size beds, a queen-size sleeper sofa, and a kitchen. In addition, the resort's friendly staff can help you arrange any kind of fishing excursion in the area.

The **La Jolla Resort** (82216 Overseas Hwy., Upper Matecumbe Key, 305/664-9213 or 888/664-9213, www.lajollaresort.com, $79-329 d) provides both garden-facing rooms and bayfront rooms. Some offer only basic amenities while others sport well-equipped kitchens and porches with hammocks and barbecue grills. Free wireless Internet access is available throughout the property.

If you're looking for basic lodgings at an affordable price, consider the **Sunset Inn** (82200 Overseas Hwy., Upper Matecumbe Key, 305/664-3454, www.sunsetinnkeys.com, $75-85 d), which offers rooms with either one king-size bed or two double beds, plus efficiencies with full kitchens. Every room has cable television and small refrigerators. When not exploring Islamorada, take a dip in the on-site freshwater pool. For an even better deal, stay at the **Key Lantern Motel and Blue Fin Inn** (82150 Overseas Hwy., Upper Matecumbe Key, 305/664-4572, www.keylantern.com, $39-68 d), perhaps the cheapest place in the entire Florida Keys archipelago. Here you'll find basic rooms with kitchenettes and free wireless Internet access.

More difficult to categorize—at least where cost is concerned—the **Pines & Palms Resort** (80401 Overseas Hwy., Upper Matecumbe Key, 305/664-4343, www.pinesandpalms.com, rooms and suites $89-239 d, cottages $139-299, houses and villas $359-579) encompasses a variety of accommodations, from a budget-priced efficiency with a queen-size bed to an enormous three-bedroom villa, featuring two king-size beds and a sofa bed. All rentals come with well-equipped kitchens and free wireless Internet access. The property also includes an oceanfront freshwater pool, a free boat ramp, and dockage at no extra charge.

$100-200

If you hope to visit upscale Islamorada without blowing your entire vacation budget, consider moderately priced lodgings like the pet-friendly **Lookout Lodge Resort** (87770 Overseas Hwy., Plantation Key, 305/852-9915 or 800/870-1772, www.lookoutlodge. com, $100-399 d), which has one-bedroom and two-bedroom suites with bay views, mini suites with bay or garden views, and two-bedroom garden suites, all equipped with kitchenettes. The resort also features a relaxing private beach area with swimming access, as well as assistance in arranging diving, snorkeling, or fishing excursions.

On Windley Key, the peaceful **Smugglers Cove Resort & Marina** (MM 85.5 BS U.S. 1, Windley Key, 305/664-5564, www.smugscove.com, $119-139 d) offers convenient access to both the Atlantic Ocean and the Gulf of Mexico. At Smugglers Cove, you'll find not only 11 clean, comfortable rooms and one spacious suite, but also a 30-slip, deepwater marina, a fully stocked bait and tackle shop, a gas station for boats, a waterfront bar and restaurant, plus several dependable fishing charters. Other amenities include air-conditioning, wireless Internet access, cable television, and stunning views.

Also on Windley Key, the **Drop Anchor Resort and Marina** (84959 Overseas Hwy., 305/664-4863 or 888/664-4863, Windley Key, www.dropanchorresort.com, $125-219 d) has 18 individualized rooms, ranging from basic lodgings with a mini fridge and a coffeemaker to a two-bedroom suite with a full kitchen, living room, and dining area. This oceanfront hideaway also offers a nice private beach, a heated freshwater pool, a boat launch, and bulkhead docking.

The **Pelican Cove Resort & Marina** (84457 Overseas Hwy., Windley Key, 305/664-4435 or 800/445-4690, www.pcove.com, $169-279 d) offers standard hotel rooms with mini refrigerators and private balconies, as well as efficiencies with full kitchens, plus a luxury suite ($369-389 daily). Despite mixed reviews about the management and a need to update the furnishings, a bonus for many travelers is that certain rooms are pet friendly (though there is a fee per pet), which is not always the case in the Florida Keys. The entire resort features free wireless Internet access, and other amenities include a tennis court, an oceanfront hot tub, a freshwater pool, water-sports equipment, and an on-site restaurant called the Cabana Club.

The spacious **Postcard Inn Beach Resort & Marina at Holiday Isle** (84001 Overseas Hwy., Windley Key, 305/664-2321 or 800/327-7070, www.holidayisle.com, $149-229 d) features a range of accommodations, from standard rooms with queen-size beds to oceanfront suites with kitchenettes. In this laid-back palm-studded setting, guests can easily while away their vacation, relaxing by the pool or sunning themselves on the beach. Of course, if you have a little more energy, be sure to take advantage of the available personal watercraft rentals, sportfishing charters, scuba-diving trips, and snorkeling excursions. Pets up to 45 pounds are allowed, provided that you're willing to part with a small, nonrefundable deposit. In addition, although you'll find several fine restaurants in Islamorada, you'll surely appreciate the presence of the on-site Sportfish Grill, not to mention six tropical bars, including the multilevel Rumrunners, reminiscent of the Swiss Family Robinson's island home.

The pet-friendly **Days Inn and Suites Key Islamorada** (82749 Overseas Hwy., Upper Matecumbe Key, 305/664-3681, www.daysinnflakeys.com, rooms $109-209 d, suites $169-339) houses an array of accommodations, from courtyard efficiencies with two double beds and a kitchenette to a two-bedroom 2,000-square-foot oceanfront suite ($368-508 daily) with two bathrooms and a full kitchen. The property also features a boat ramp, boat dockage up to 21 feet, personal watercraft and boat rentals, and an oceanside tiki bar.

The first thing you'll notice as you arrive at the **Kon Tiki Resort** (81200 Overseas Hwy., Upper Matecumbe Key, 305/664-4702, www.kontiki-resort.com, rooms $129-285 d, villas and houses $298-427) is the lush tropical landscape, featuring tempting hammocks, a barbecue grill and picnic area, and a heated freshwater pool alongside a private lagoon. Here guests can dock and launch their boats on-site, and the 27 uniquely decorated rooms and villas provide enough options and amenities (from cable television to screened porches) to suit any vacationer.

Avid anglers can certainly plan a memorable fishing trip at **Bud N' Mary's Fishing Marina** (79851 Overseas Hwy., Upper Matecumbe Key, 305/664-2461 or 800/742-7945, www.budnmarys.com, $120 d), where in addition to lodgings, you'll find a spacious marina, housing a fleet of more than 40 fishing boats, plus a tackle shop and outdoor eatery. Beyond comfortable, standard rooms, the complex offers a penthouse with a full kitchen ($300 daily) and a two-bedroom beach house ($400 daily) with a full kitchen, a backyard, and access to a dock. In addition, Bud N' Mary's provides a houseboat rental with a queen-size bed and a small kitchenette.

The family-friendly **Breezy Palms Resort** (80015 Overseas Hwy., Upper Matecumbe Key, 305/664-2361 or 877/412-7339, www.breezypalms.com, $100-269 d) is a terrific home base for your Florida Keys adventures. Offering boat rentals and dockage, the resort can easily assist you in arranging your next fishing excursion. Meanwhile, the accommodations range from a standard motel room, with one bedroom, one bath, and a small refrigerator, to a two-bedroom suite, with king-size and queen-size beds, a sofa sleeper, a full kitchen, and a dining room.

Lined by hibiscus and bougainvillea, the **Coral Bay Resort** (75690 Overseas Hwy., Lower Matecumbe Key, 305/664-5568, www.coralbayresort.com, rooms $119-179 d, one-bedroom apartments $139-199, two-bedroom apartments $189-305, cottages $210-305) features everything from a standard bedroom with a small refrigerator to a comfortable cottage with four double beds, two bathrooms, and a well-equipped kitchen. Each unit includes cable television, as well as a cozy patio or covered porch.

Situated on a 10-acre estate, the **Caloosa Cove Resort** (73801 Overseas Hwy., Lower Matecumbe Key, 888/297-3208, www.caloosacove.com, $195-275 d) houses 30 rooms, including luxury efficiencies and one-bedroom suites, all with kitchen areas and private balconies. In addition, the resort features a full-service marina, a bait and tackle shop, boat rentals, tennis courts, a heated freshwater pool, and a large sandy beach.

OVER $200

Islamorada presents some of the most upscale, exclusive resorts in the entire Florida Keys archipelago. One such option is the tranquil **Chesapeake Beach Resort** (83409 Overseas Hwy., Upper Matecumbe Key, 305/664-4662 or 800/338-3395, www.chesapeake-resort.com, rooms $210-340 d, villas $225-450) on Upper Matecumbe Key. Providing a quiet place to relax and replenish, this luxurious, well-landscaped property features a variety of accommodations, from tastefully furnished hotel rooms with garden views to premium ocean villa suites. In addition to the 6.5-acre tropical garden, the resort offers two heated oceanfront pools, a hot-water spa, tennis and shuffleboard courts, and a tiki-style observation deck, plus the ubiquitous kayaks, lounge chairs, and hammocks.

Ocean Dawn Suites (82885 Overseas Hwy., Upper Matecumbe Key, 305/664-4844 or 866/540-5520, www.oceandawnsuites.com, $200-275 d) presents eight Caribbean-style luxury suites alongside the Atlantic Ocean. Possible amenities include giant plasma televisions, full kitchens, or private balconies. While staying here, feel free to cook the day's catch on a communal barbecue grill, relax beneath an oceanside tiki hut, or watch the sunset from the resort's private beach.

Situated on 25 lush acres, the **Islander**

Resort (82100 Overseas Hwy., Upper Matecumbe Key, 305/664-2031, www.island-erfloridakeys.com, $235-285 d) provides full kitchens, screened lanais, free Internet access, and free continental breakfasts daily. Three lodging types are available here: courtyard rooms with a lanai and one double bed, ocean-view rooms with two double beds, and pool-side rooms with a lanai and two double beds. The resort also features a lanai courtyard room where pets are allowed with a nonrefundable fee. Other amenities here include two heated pools, a hot tub, the Bluewater Tiki Bar, and 1,300 feet of sandy beach, with a shallow snorkeling area.

If you're looking for all the comforts of a well-appointed oceanfront home, look no farther than **The Caribbean Resort** (117 S. Carroll St., Upper Matecumbe Key, 305/664-2235 or 800/799-9175, www.thecaribbeanresort.com, one-bedroom homes $350-400 d, two-bedroom homes $400-500, three-bedroom homes $1,500), situated far enough from U.S. 1 that it's easy to forget about the traffic for a while, especially during the peak winter months. This sumptuous property contains an array of spacious homes, each with its own unique style. On-site amenities include lush gardens filled with tropical flowers and banana trees; a gorgeous pool and spa oasis, graced with waterfalls and arching coconut palms; as well as private sun decks, gazebos, tables, and lounge chairs scattered throughout the grounds.

Established in 1946, the lavish 【 **Cheeca Lodge & Spa** (81801 Overseas Hwy., Upper Matecumbe Key, 305/664-4651 or 800/327-2888, www.cheeca.com, rooms $209-490 d, suites $259-899, two-bedroom suites $559-998, bungalows $319-597) has lured an array of U.S. presidents and movie stars since its opening. Today the recently renovated resort provides guests with a relaxing, pampering, tropical playground, where you can play tennis or golf, fish from the 525-foot pier, relax on the private beach, or seek rejuvenation in the incredible on-site spa. You may just feel like royalty in the spacious Caribbean-style rooms, suites, and adults-only bungalows, which include 42-inch

televisions, wet bars, luxurious furniture, and marvelous views of the ocean, beach, lagoon, and resort. In fact, it's the varied views, as well as the shifting seasons, that determine the wide range in lodging rates. Besides the lovely surroundings, the amenities here include two fine restaurants, Atlantic's Edge and Nikai Sushi, and an adults-only pool.

Perhaps the best example of Islamorada's luxury and seclusion is 【 **The Moorings Village & Spa** (123 Beach Rd., Upper Matecumbe Key, 305/664-4708, www.themooringsvillage.com, one-bedroom inland homes $250-750 daily, two-bedroom oceanfront bungalow $3,150-4,550 weekly, two-bedroom inland homes $3,850-5,600 weekly, one-bedroom oceanfront home $4,200-5,775 weekly, two-bedroom oceanfront homes $6,650-9,100 weekly), a serene, splendidly lush property on the ocean side of U.S. 1, near Mile Marker 81.6. Once part of a coconut plantation in the 1930s, the verdant 18-acre resort offers 18 private homes and cottages (which greatly range in price depending on the season), from small, brightly painted Caribbean bungalows tucked amid the foliage to a three-bedroom French Colonial plantation house ($7,700-10,500 weekly) directly beside the ocean. These self-sufficient residences, many of which lure the same travelers year after year, contain televisions, telephones, well-equipped kitchens, luxurious beds, and sometimes, washers and dryers. All lodgings require a two-night or one-week minimum stay, and all are only a short stroll from a private Polynesian-style beach—complete with swaying palm trees, cushioned lounge chairs, relaxing hammocks, and complimentary kayaks. It's no wonder, then, that the beach is often used as a backdrop in movies and catalog photo shoots.

Other on-site amenities include tennis courts, a stunning pool area, and the **Island Body & Sol Spa** (305/664-3264, www.island-bodyandsolspa.com, $50-190 per treatment), which offers a selection of rejuvenating facials and massages. The family-owned resort also boasts two of the finest eateries in the Keys—the Morada Bay Beach Café, ideal for light lunches beside the beach, and Pierre's

ISLAMORADA

© DANIEL MARTONE

The Moorings Village & Spa has a wide array of well-appointed cottages and vacation homes.

Restaurant, perfect for a romantic dinner. Both restaurants lie on the bay side of the Overseas Highway, only a short drive from the Moorings.

CAMPING

Despite its plethora of accommodations, Islamorada has few options for campers, especially those hoping to stay awhile. The **Sea Breeze RV & Mobile Home Park** (87425 Old Hwy., Plantation Key, 305/852-3358, www.seabreezervlots.com), situated on the ocean side of U.S. 1, is one such option. Essentially a residential mobile home park, Seabreeze offers several full-hookup RV lots, including some with oceanfront views, on a month-to-month basis (starting from $650 May-Oct., $900 Nov.-Apr.). The park is conveniently located across the street from Islamorada's Founders Park and only a few miles northeast of attractions like Windley Key Fossil Reef Geological State Park and Theater of the Sea. Other amenities include on-site laundry facilities, a boat ramp, a fish-cleaning station, cable television, phone service, boat dockage ($135 monthly), and dry-dock storage ($80 monthly).

Food

SEAFOOD

Given Islamorada's focus on fishing and boating, the prevalence of seafood restaurants should be less than surprising. Seafood lovers should head first to the **Island Grill** (85501 Overseas Hwy., Plantation Key, 305/664-8400, www.keysislandgrill.com, 7am-10pm Sun.-Thurs., 7am-11pm Fri.-Sat., $11-33), which features a fried seafood platter for two, complete with shrimp, scallops, mahimahi, crab clusters, and crab cakes—more than enough to satisfy a pair of seafood gourmands. Come for dinner, and you'll be treated to live music from one of the local bands that perform here nightly.

In the **Whale Harbor Restaurants and Marina** complex (83413 Overseas Hwy., Upper Matecumbe Key, www.whaleharborinn.com) on Upper Matecumbe Key, you'll find three unique restaurants, anchored by the **Whale**

© DANIEL MARTONE

The Whale Harbor Restaurant boasts a popular seafood buffet.

Harbor Restaurant (305/664-4959, ext. 205, www.whaleharborrestaurant.com, 4pm-9pm Mon.-Thurs., 4pm-10pm Fri., 2pm-10pm Sat., noon-9pm Sun., $29 adults, $14.50 children), which offers one of the Florida Keys' most popular seafood buffets, with everything from snow crab to whole fried yellowtail snapper. Also on the premises are **Wahoo's Bar & Grill** (305/664-9888, www.wahoosbarandgrill.com, 11am-10pm Sun.-Thurs., 11am-11pm Fri.-Sat., $12-26), an ideal spot to enjoy fresh seafood and waterfront views, and the **Braza Leña Brazilian Steakhouse** (305/664-4940, www.brazalena.com, 5pm-9:30pm Tues.-Sun., $42 adults, $20 children 6-12, free for children under 6), which features a fixed-price dinner menu that includes an extensive salad bar plus an assortment of meat selections, from pork ribs to lamb chops to filet mignon. Of course, seafood lovers will be happy to hear that Braza also offers à la carte specialties like tiger prawns, a 16-ounce lobster tail, and a fresh local catch.

With its New Orleans cuisine and Bahamian-style cooking, it's easy to see why **Bentley's Restaurant** (82779 Overseas Hwy., Upper Matecumbe Key, 305/664-9094, www.bentleysrestaurant.net, 11am-9pm daily, $9-29) is considered one of the top seafood restaurants in the Upper Keys. For a real treat, order the Louisiana spicy shrimp à la carte or over a bed of linguini.

Mangrove Mike's Cafe (82200 Overseas Hwy., Upper Matecumbe Key, 305/664-8022, www.mangrovemikes.com, 6am-2pm daily, $6-22), meanwhile, offers more than just a meal. With breakfast and lunch, you might also receive a history lesson about the Conchs. Still, the food is paramount here. Many locals believe Mike's has one of the best breakfast menus in the Keys. Among favored dishes is the Mangrove Oscar, a toasted English muffin with sautéed spinach, poached eggs, and your choice of blue crab, grilled shrimp, or grilled mahimahi, covered in a béarnaise sauce.

ISLAMORADA

A bit farther south, you'll encounter a relatively new addition to Islamorada's dining scene. Situated in the building that once housed the well-regarded Chanticleer South, **❰ Chef Michael's** (81671 Overseas Hwy., Upper Matecumbe Key, 305/664-0640, www.foodtotalkabout.com, 5pm-10pm Mon.-Sat., 10am-2pm and 5pm-10pm Sun., $7-40) has quickly developed a reputation for fresh top-quality seafood. In fact, the catch-of-the-day selection here changes daily and may include hogfish, tuna, mahimahi, mangrove snapper, and swordfish, just to name a handful of the varieties available in the Florida Keys. Appropriately, the walls here are decorated with colorful, fish-focused art, and whether you choose to eat in the dining room or sit on the shaded patio, you'll be treated to cloth napkins and white linen tablecloths, offering a small touch of class in this airy island-style restaurant. Beyond its signature seafood dishes, such as broiled

Situated beside Florida Bay, Pierre's Restaurant offers fine dining in a plantation-style mansion.

twin lobster tails in a coconut curry sauce, the menu here also offers options for meat lovers, such as grilled filet mignon with crispy fried spinach, thai barbecue sauce, and crazy taters. If possible, save room for dessert, which at times, has ranged from six-layer carrot cake to key lime pie.

While they may share the same beach, the **❰ Morada Bay Beach Café** (81600 Overseas Hwy., Upper Matecumbe Key, 305/664-0604, www.moradabay-restaurant. com, 11:30am-10pm Sun.-Thurs., 11:30am-11pm Fri.-Sat., $11-33) and **❰ Pierre's Restaurant** (81600 Overseas Hwy., Upper Matecumbe Key, 305/664-3225, www. pierres-restaurant.com, 5pm-10pm Sun.-Thurs., 5pm-11pm Fri.-Sat., $34-40) offer far different dining experiences. With several colorful tables set upon the sand—in addition to its indoor and patio seating, of course—Morada Bay takes full advantage of its laid-back beachside setting. Although this breezy eatery does many dishes well, from the island-style conch chowder to fresh salads and sandwiches, a definite highlight is the seared jumbo scallops in a coconut pad thai sauce. If you're not hungry enough for an entrée, try the tapas menu, which includes dishes like *Fritto Mediterraneo* with calamari, shrimp, zucchini, and chipotle aioli in a tangy marinara sauce. The bar is open later than the dining areas, and if you're here at the right time, be sure to stick around for Morada Bay's Friday night jam sessions and monthly Full Moon Parties.

Housed within a picturesque French Colonial-style mansion (which, incidentally, is identical to the plantation house on offer at the affiliated Moorings Village across the highway) Pierre's provides one of the best fine-dining experiences in the Keys. With an interior that blends sailing motifs with an exotic Moroccan-themed decor, which even pervades the restrooms, the first-floor lounge and second-floor dining area are, at once, comfortable and elegant. Your meal will be especially memorable on the candlelit balcony that overlooks Florida Bay and the beach below, which is often lined with alluring tiki torches. Pierre's features a small but eclectic menu, the star of which is the tempura lobster tail over hearts of palm hash—truly a heavenly dish that's been popular ever since it was initially offered. Reservations are recommended here, though the dress code is decidedly casual. The wine list is on the pricey side.

For a no-frills seafood dining experience, head to **Ma's Fish Camp** (105 Palm Ave., Upper Matecumbe Key, 305/517-9611, 11am-9pm daily, $6-16), which offers simple, yet tasty, meals for an affordable price. Favored for its excellent service, this popular eatery promises a laid-back atmosphere for dining on delectable dishes like coconut curry shrimp, grilled fish tacos, and key lime pie.

The World Wide Sportsman complex (now part of the Bass Pro Shops chain) features the waterfront **Islamorada Fish Company** (81532 Overseas Hwy., Upper Matecumbe Key, 305/664-9271, www.fishcompany.com, 11am-11pm daily, $9-21). With 175 outdoor seats overlooking the beach, this exceptional eatery provides the perfect spot to watch the sunset or host a party. Serving classic Florida Keys cuisine, the Fish Company excels with its fried baskets and grilled platters. For lighter fare, consider venturing to the adjacent World Wide Sportsman, which features the **Zane Grey Long Key Lounge** (81576 Overseas Hwy., Upper Matecumbe Key, 305/517-2190, www.basspro.com, 11am-10pm daily, $10-16) on the upper level. After returning from a long day of fishing, you can relax here on the open-air balcony that overlooks the marina, have a cocktail, and sample seafood treats like coconut shrimp and lobster salad.

Serving both classic and contemporary cuisine, the **Green Turtle Inn** (81219 Overseas Hwy., Upper Matecumbe Key, 305/664-2006, www.greenturtlekeys.com, 6am-10pm Tues.-Sun., $10-35) serves breakfast, lunch, and dinner in a historical, recently renovated building. For breakfast, try the Keys Benedict, featuring two poached eggs, crab cakes, tomatoes, and hollandaise sauce, and then later, return for dinnertime delicacies like the herb-seared

tuna served over hearts of palm hash. The **Lazy Days Restaurant** (79867 Overseas Hwy., Upper Matecumbe Key, 305/664-5256, www.lazydaysrestaurant.com, 11am-9:30pm Sun.-Thurs., 11am-10pm Fri.-Sat., $6-25), as the name suggests, provides a relaxing oceanfront dining experience, where you can relish a fried oyster sandwich for lunch or jumbo stuffed shrimp for dinner.

Although open for both breakfast and lunch, the **Hungry Tarpon Restaurant** (77522 Overseas Hwy., Lower Matecumbe Key, 305/664-0535, www.hungrytarpon.com, 6:30am-close daily, $12-27) lures even more diners, especially locals, for the dinner menu. Based at Robbie's of Islamorada, the Tarpon serves favorites like the Purple Island Mahi-Mahi, topped with a brandy lobster sauce, or the Filet à la Annie, with a mushroom, shallot, and red wine demi-glace. Come down for Robbie's famous tarpon feedings and stay to feed yourself.

AMERICAN

Overlooking Florida Bay, the **Marker 88 Restaurant** (88000 Overseas Hwy., Plantation Key, 305/852-9315, www.marker88.info, 11am-11pm daily, $11-36) is a wonderful place to relax for a while and relish dishes like cheeseburgers and poached Florida lobster. Dine indoors or sit outside to enjoy a beautiful view of the ocean. Just across the road, you'll encounter the **M.E.A.T. Eatery & Tap Room** (88005 Overseas Hwy., Plantation Key, 305/852-3833, www.meateatery.com, 11am-9pm Sun.-Thurs., 11am-10pm Fri.-Sat.,), a casual, friendly joint that serves all-American burgers, hot dogs, sausages, pulled pork sandwiches, and other treats, such as lobster "mac-n-cheese," truffled bistro fries, homemade pork rinds, and Wisconsin beer cheese soup. The Tap Room also offers microbrewed sodas, organic wines, and specialty beers. Another fun-loving spot is the **Hog Heaven Sports Bar & Grill** (85361 Overseas Hwy., Windley Key, 305/664-9669, www.hogheavensportsbar.com, 11am-3:30am daily, $7-19). Situated just opposite Windley

ZANE GREY: AUTHOR AND ANGLER

While Ernest Hemingway is undoubtedly the most famous novelist ever to be linked to the Florida Keys, he is most certainly not the only one. As evidenced by places like the **Zane Grey Long Key Lounge** (81532 Overseas Hwy., Upper Matecumbe Key, 305/664-9271, www.basspro.com) in Islamorada's World Wide Sportsman, it's apparent that American novelist Zane Grey was also part of this archipelago's colorful history.

After discovering the Florida Keys in the early 1900s, Grey began fishing the local waters of Long Key, Duck Key, and Grassy Key. In 1910 he first stayed at the Long Key Fishing Camp, a luxurious fishing resort built in 1906 by Henry Flagler's East Coast Hotel Company on the ocean side of Long Key. Featuring a large wooden lodge, a store, a post office, a railroad station, roughly 30 small cottages, and a tunnel beneath the roadbed connecting the camp with the bayside docks, the resort attracted famous, wealthy sportfishing enthusiasts such as Andrew Mellon, William Hearst, Herbert Hoover, Franklin D. Roosevelt, and of course, Zane Grey, who became the Long Key Fishing Club's first president in 1917.

Born Pearl Zane Grey in 1872 in Zanesville, Ohio, Grey wrote his first novel in 1903. By the 1920s, he was earning half a million dollars per year from his writing career, and he owned several homes in California, fishing camps in Oregon and New Zealand, and a hunting lodge in Arizona. Although he traveled throughout the world, from Catalina Island to Mexico to Tahiti, he always returned to Long Key, where he favored not only the marvelous fishing but also the quietude, which allowed him to write such Western classics as *Wild Horse Mesa* (1928) and *Code of the West* (1934).

Though Grey was best known for his novels about the American West, some fans still prefer his real-life fishing adventures, including *Tales of Fishes* (1919), in which he wrote about light-tackle fishing for sailfish and kingfish near Long Key and the surrounding islands, and *The Bonefish Brigade* (1922), in which he described his companions at the Long Key Fishing Camp and their obsessive quest for the elusive bonefish. In fact, such pioneering accounts helped to lure more wealthy sportfishing fans to the region at a time when most local residents were using spears and harpoons to snag their supper from the passes between the keys.

To reach the Long Key Fishing Camp, Grey and his fellow anglers would travel on the Key West Extension of the Florida East Coast Railway. While staying at the camp, he would dine on such delicacies as stone crab, grouper chowder, conch fritters, broiled king mackerel, coconut pudding, and key lime pie—cuisine that's still popular today. In fact, Grey loved the camp so much that after the terrible Labor Day Hurricane of 1935 destroyed the lodge, the buildings, and roughly 30 miles of Henry Flagler's railroad tracks, he honored the vacation spot in the foreword of a saltwater fishing book. "It is sad to think that Long Key, doomed by a hurricane, is gone forever," he wrote. "But the memory of that long white winding lonely shore of coral sand, and the green reef, and the blue Gulf Stream will live in memory, and in such fine books as this."

Four years after the storm that destroyed the Long Key Fishing Camp, Grey passed away in Altadena, California, having sold more than 27 million copies of his novels and nonfiction books. Since then that number has risen dramatically, and more than 110 movies have been made from his stories, including a silent D. W. Griffith short called *Fighting Blood* (1911) as well as the most recent version of *Riders of the Purple Sage* (1996), which stars Ed Harris and Amy Madigan. Although Grey's beloved Long Key Fishing Camp was eventually replaced by a state park, sportfishing is still popular in the Upper and Middle Keys—for the rich and the not-so-rich alike.

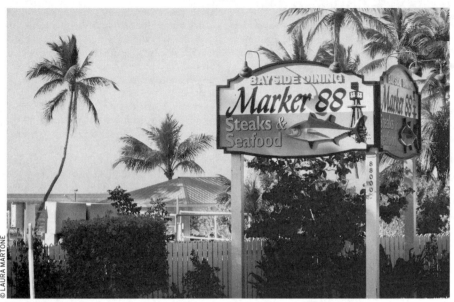

The Marker 88 Restaurant offers casual waterfront dining next to Florida Bay.

Key Fossil Reef Geological State Park, this late-night joint features happy-hour specials, beachfront dining, and a range of vittles, from tuna melts to barbecue rib platters.

Farther south, **Ziggie & Mad Dog's** (83000 Overseas Hwy., Upper Matecumbe Key, 305/664-3391, www.ziggieandmaddogs.com, 11:30am-10pm Sun.-Thurs., 11:30am-11pm Fri.-Sat., $16-42) serves a variety of soups, salads, seafood dishes, steaks, and chops. One of several favorite dishes is the key lime chipotle chicken with sausage and cornbread stuffing. For tasty, inexpensive breakfast, lunch, or dinner, try the **Lorelei Restaurant & Cabana Bar** (81924 Overseas Hwy., Upper Matecumbe Key, 305/664-2692, www.loreleicabanabar.com, 7am-10pm daily, $4-23). Between three-egg omelets, spinach salads, cracked conch sandwiches, and baby back ribs, there's surely something for everyone.

If you're staying at the exclusive Cheeca Lodge & Spa or looking for a fine-dining alternative, consider **Atlantic's Edge** (81801 Overseas Hwy., Upper Matecumbe Key, 305/517-2000, www.cheeca.com, 7am-10pm daily, $23-52). With indoor and outdoor seating—most of which offers remarkable ocean views—it can be a pleasant place for the discerning gourmand, especially if you don't mind the slightly elevated prices on both the menu and the wine list. Specialties include the dry aged bone-in ribeye steak and the Florida Keys barrel fish.

Open for breakfast and lunch, the **Islamorada Restaurant and Bakery** (81620 Overseas Hwy., Upper Matecumbe Key, 305/664 8363, www.bobsbunz.com, 6am-2pm daily, $2-8) is one of those places that locals would prefer to keep a secret. Although the popular eatery offers a hundred different breakfast and lunch items, most people come for Bob's Bunz. Taste one, and you too will be hooked. Meanwhile, excellent coffee, breakfast selections, and vegetarian dishes make a trip to the **Midway Café and Coffee Bar** (80499 Overseas Hwy., Upper Matecumbe Key, 305/664-2622, 6am-9pm daily, $5-14) equally worthwhile.

EUROPEAN AND ASIAN

For fine Italian dining, visit the **Old Tavernier Restaurant** (90311 Overseas Hwy., Tavernier, 305/852-6012, www.oldtavernier.com, 4pm-11pm daily, $12-46) on Plantation Key, which provides both indoor and outdoor seating. Although the portions here aren't enormous, the quality is top notch, especially if you enjoy sampling inspired dishes like scallops de Provence. If you have a hankering for more basic Italian cuisine, try **Jersey Boardwalk Pizza** (20 High Point Rd., Plantation Key, 305/853-3800, www.jerseyboardwalkpizza. com, 11am-9pm Mon.-Fri., 11am-10pm Sat.-Sun., $4-17) for tasty pizzas, subs, salads, and pasta. If you'd prefer to stay in your hotel, remember that Boardwalk will deliver to any location in Islamorada.

While in the land of fresh seafood, if you get a sudden craving for some excellent Greek cuisine, stop by the **Overseas Kitchen** (82205 Overseas Hwy., Upper Matecumbe Key, 305/664-0848, www.overseaskitchenislamorada.com, 11am-10pm Mon.-Fri., 11am-6pm Sat., $4-17), where you'll be treated to inexpensive Mediterranean salads, hummus wraps, pita sandwiches, and heftier dishes such as the Greek-style rack of lamb. For those in a hurry, the café also offers carry-out service and free delivery between Mile Marker 74 and Mile Marker 90.

The **Kaiyo Grill & Sushi** (81701 Overseas Hwy., Upper Matecumbe Key, 305/664-5556, www.kaiyokeys.com, 11am-11pm daily, $13-36) considers itself a Florida-inspired Asian cuisine restaurant. Besides sushi, Kaiyo offers a lunch buffet that features a variety of alternating dishes, plus dinner entrées like the macadamia yellowtail with Jean's famous mango sauce. You can continue with the macadamia theme by trying the white chocolate macadamia pie for dessert.

Several countries over—at least in spirit—the year-round **Uncle's Restaurant** (80939 Overseas Hwy., Upper Matecumbe Key, 305/664-4402, www.unclesrestaurant.com, 5pm-10:30pm Tues.-Sun., $12-26) specializes in ample portions of fresh seafood and classic Italian cuisine. With its soft lighting, laid-back patio, and fishing snapshots galore, this casual, friendly eatery might remind you of eating at your uncle's house, that is, if your uncle were a longtime fishing guide turned award-winning restaurateur who boasts his own herb garden and has over 40 nieces and nephews. Although it's difficult to choose just one entrée, you can't go wrong with authentic dishes like bouillabaisse, pasta primavera, veal marsala, rack of lamb with port wine demi-glace, or chargrilled teriyaki tuna with wasabi aioli.

The **Spanish Gardens Cafe** (80925 Overseas Hwy., Upper Matecumbe Key, 305/664-3999, www.spanishgardenscafe.com, 11am-9pm daily, $6-22) serves sandwiches and salads for lunch, plus a dinner menu that includes a variety of tapas, ranging from mussels marinara to bison *empanadillas* (small empanadas). The seafood paella comes in various sizes—depending on how many of you will be sharing it.

Information and Services

INFORMATION

For brochures, maps, and other information about Islamorada, stop by the **Islamorada Chamber of Commerce and Visitors Center** (MM 83.2 BS U.S. 1, Upper Matecumbe Key, 305/664-4503 or 800/322-5397, www. islamoradachamber.com, 9am-5pm Mon.-Fri., 9am-4pm Sat., 9am-3pm Sun.) or consult the **Monroe County Tourist Development Council** (1201 White St., Ste. 102, Key West, 305/296-1552 or 800/352-5397, www.fla-keys.com, 9am-5pm Mon.-Fri.). For government-related issues, contact the **Islamorada Village Administration Center & Public Safety Headquarters** (86800 Overseas Hwy., Plantation Key, 305/664-6400, www.

islamorada.fl.us, 8am-5pm Mon.-Fri.) or the **Monroe County offices** (1100 Simonton St., Key West, 305/294-4641 or 305/852-1469, www.monroecounty-fl.gov, 8am-5pm Mon.-Fri.).

For local news, consult *The Reporter* (www.keysnet.com), the Upper Keys *Free Press* (www.keysnews.com), and **The Weekly Newspapers** (www.keysweekly.com). The daily *Miami Herald* (www.miamiherald.com), the daily *The Key West Citizen* (www.keysnews.com), and the biweekly *Florida Keys Keynoter* (www.keysnet.com) are available throughout the Keys.

In Islamorada, you'll also have access to several radio stations, including the **SUN** (WAIL-FM 99.5, www.wail995.com), which offers a classic rock format. For other stations, visit www.keysradio.com.

SERVICES

Money

For banking needs, stop by the **Capital Bank** (80900 Overseas Hwy., Upper Matecumbe Key, 305/664-4483 or 800/639-5111, www.capitalbank-us.com, 9am-4pm Mon.-Thurs., 9am-6pm Fri., extended drive-through hours) or the **First State Bank of the Florida Keys** (81621 Overseas Hwy., Upper Matecumbe Key, 305/664-9070, www.keysbank.com, 9am-4pm Mon.-Thurs., 9am-6pm Fri., extended drive-through hours).

Mail

For shipping, faxing, copying, and other business-related services, visit **PostNet** (88005 Overseas Hwy., Plantation Key, 305/853 1101, www.postnet.com, 9am-5pm Mon.-Fri., 10am-1pm Sat.). You can also package and ship items at the local **post office** (82801 Overseas Hwy., Upper Matecumbe Key, 305/664-4738 or 800/275-8777, www.usps.com, 8am-4:30pm Mon.-Fri., 9am-noon Sat.).

Groceries and Supplies

For groceries, baked goods, and other supplies, head to the nearest **Winn-Dixie** (92100 Overseas Hwy., Tavernier, 305/852-5904, www.winndixie.com, 7am-11pm daily), which houses an on-site pharmacy (305/852-5069, 8am-8pm Mon.-Fri., 9am-6pm Sat., 10am-5pm Sun.). A **CVS/pharmacy** (82894 Overseas Hwy., Upper Matecumbe Key, 305/664-2576, www.cvs.com, 8am-10pm daily) offers limited supplies as well as an on-site pharmacy (8am-8pm Mon.-Fri., 8am-7pm Sat., 9am-6pm Sun.).

Laundry

If you need to clean some clothes during your trip, you'll find several coin-operated laundries in the area, including the **Coral Shores Coin Laundry** (90071 Old Hwy., Tavernier, 305/852-5497, 8am-7pm Mon.-Fri., 8am-5pm Sat., 9am-4pm Sun.) on Plantation Key.

Internet Access

For wireless Internet access, consult your hotel or resort, as many offer free access nowadays. You'll also find useful services at the **Islamorada Branch Library** (81830 Overseas Hwy., Upper Matecumbe Key, 305/664-4645, www.keyslibraries.org, 9:30am-8pm Tues., 9:30am-6pm Wed.-Fri., 10am-6pm Sat.).

Emergency Services

In case of an emergency that requires police, fire, or ambulance services, dial **911** from any cell or public phone. For nonemergency assistance, contact the **Monroe County Sheriff's Office** (87000 Overseas Hwy., Plantation Key, 305/853-7021, www.keysso.net, 8am-5pm Mon.-Fri.). For medical assistance, consult the **Mariners Hospital** (91500 Overseas Hwy., Tavernier, 305/434-3000, www.baptisthealth.net). Foreign visitors seeking help with directions, medical concerns, business issues, law enforcement needs, or other problems can receive **multilingual tourist assistance** (800/771-5397) 24 hours daily.

ISLAMORADA

Getting There and Around

GETTING THERE
By Air
Despite the presence of a private airstrip at **TavernAero Airport Park** (MM 90 BS U.S. 1, www.tavernaero.com) on Plantation Key, Islamorada has no major airport of its own. To travel here by plane, you'll need to fly into **Fort Lauderdale-Hollywood International Airport (FLL)** (100 Terminal Dr., Fort Lauderdale, 866/435-9355, www.broward.org/airport), **Miami International Airport (MIA)** (2100 NW 42nd Ave., Miami, 305/876-7000 or 800/825-5642, www.miami-airport.com), **Key West International Airport (EYW)** (3491 S. Roosevelt Blvd., Key West, 305/809-5200 or 305/296-5439, www.keywestinternationalairport.com), or **Florida Keys Marathon Airport (MTH)** (9400 Overseas Hwy., Marathon, 305/289-6060). From there you can rent a vehicle from agencies like **Avis** (800/331-1212, www.avis.com), **Budget** (800/527-0700, www.budget.com), **Enterprise** (800/325-8007, www.enterprise.com), **Hertz** (800/654-3131, www.hertz.com), or **Thrifty** (800/367-2277, www.thrifty.com) to reach Islamorada.

By Bus or Train
The **Miami-Dade County Metrobus** (305/891-3131, www.miamidade.gov/transit) operates the **301 Dade-Monroe Express** between Florida City and Marathon (5:15am-8:40pm daily, $2.35 per one-way trip), regularly stopping in Islamorada. In addition, **Greyhound** (800/231-2222, www.greyhound.com) offers bus service to the Burger King in Islamorada (82201 Overseas Hwy., Upper Matecumbe Key). **Amtrak** (800/872-7245, www.amtrak.com), however, only provides train service as far south as Miami. Of course, you can always rent a car or hop a shuttle to reach the Florida Keys.

Transport from Airports and Stations
If you arrive in the Fort Lauderdale-Miami area via plane, bus, or train—or Key West via plane or bus—you can either rent a car or hire a shuttle service to reach Islamorada. Some of these companies include **Keys Shuttle** (305/289-9997 or 888/765-9997, www.keys-shuttle.com, $70-80 per shared ride, $300-350 for exclusive service) and **Keys Tropical Transportation** (305/852-3595, www.keys-tropicaltransportation.com, starting at $130 or $165 per ride, depending on the airport of origin), both of which provide service from the Miami and Fort Lauderdale airports. Another option is **SuperShuttle** (305/871-2000 or 954/764-1700, www.supershuttle.com, $235 for up to 10 passengers), which only serves visitors flying into Miami. In addition, you can rely on **TO'n'FRO** (305/393-0955, www.tonfro.com, $55-65 per shared van ride, $170-190 per luxury sedan ride), a personalized van and car service that offers transportation between the Miami and Fort Lauderdale airports and any destination in the Keys.

By Car
To reach Islamorada from Miami, simply head south on U.S. 1 (Overseas Hwy.) and continue through Key Largo, toward your destination on the islands of Islamorada. If you're headed from the Everglades via I-75 (Everglades Pkwy.), drive south on U.S. 27, veer right onto S.R. 997 (Krome Ave.), and follow the signs to U.S. 1. From U.S. 41 (Tamiami Trl.) in the Everglades, head south on S.R. 997 and continue toward U.S. 1. If you arrive during the peak season (Dec.-Apr.), be sure to call **511** for an up-to-the-minute traffic report.

GETTING AROUND
By Car
The best way to travel through Islamorada is by car, truck, RV, or motorcycle—all of which offer easy access to U.S. 1 as well as the side roads.

By Van Service or Tour Bus

While staying in Islamorada, if you have a sudden desire to head to Key West for the evening—and would rather leave your vehicle at the hotel, B&B, resort, or campground where you're staying—consider boarding **Sea the Keys** (305/896-7013, www.keywestdaytrip. com, rates vary), a passenger van service that will pick you up from your hotel in the Upper Keys and drop you off in Key West around 11am. While down there, you'll be free to explore any number of restaurants, bars, museums, and other attractions before making the return trip around 9pm.

By Taxi

Taxicab companies such as **Mom's Taxi** (305/852-6000, $7 per pickup, $2.50 per mile), **Islamorada Taxi** (305/664-4100, $7 per pickup, $2.50 per mile), and **Spring's Island Taxi** (305/664-4331, www.springsislandtaxi. com, $7 per pickup, $3 per mile after initial two miles) can help you get around Islamorada.

By Bicycle or Boat

While you can certainly traverse Islamorada via bicycle, the region's sprawling nature and numerous bridges make it challenging for novice riders. Nevertheless, it's a lovely, ecofriendly way to experience the Upper Keys. Between Mile Marker 91 and Mile Marker 71, you'll even find 10 miles of actual biking paths.

Bicycles can be rented from **A1A Bicycle & Scooter Rentals** (81984 Overseas Hwy.,

Upper Matecumbe Key, 305/664-4535, www.keyswatersports.com, 9am-5pm daily, rates vary), which offers daily, weekly, and monthly rates and even provides delivery service. **Backcountry Cowboy Outfitters** (82240 Overseas Hwy., Upper Matecumbe Key, 305/517-4177, www.backcountrycowboy.com, 10am-6pm Mon.-Sat., 10am-5pm Sun., $15-20 per half day, $20-25 daily, $35-100 for multiple days, $95-115 weekly) offers both one speed and three-speed bicycle rentals—plus helmets, combination locks, and copies of the state's bicycle laws.

Of course, you can also experience the islands of Islamorada by boat. In fact, certain locales, such as Indian Key Historic State Park, are only accessible by boat, canoe, or kayak. Having your own vessel might make navigating these waters a bit easier, and you'll find no shortage of boat ramps and marina slips in Islamorada. If you'd rather rent a boat, just head to **Robbie's of Islamorada** (77522 Overseas Hwy., Lower Matecumbe Key, 305/664-8070 or 877/664-8498, www. robbies.com, 7am-sunset daily), which offers an array of vessels ($135-185 per half day, $185-235 daily), ranging from 18 to 23 feet in length. As an alternative, you can rent a kayak from **Backcountry Cowboy Outfitters** (82240 Overseas Hwy., Upper Matecumbe Key, 305/517-4177, www.backcountrycowboy. com, 10am-6pm Mon.-Sat., 10am-5pm Sun., $45-60 per half day, $60-80 daily, or $165-195 weekly).

ISLAMORADA

MARATHON AND THE MIDDLE KEYS

For those seeking some peace and quiet, the Middle Keys definitely have their appeal. Beyond the bridges south of Islamorada and the minuscule community of Layton, the first major stop—Long Key State Park (often claimed by the Upper Keys) is an idyllic place to escape the crowds of other islands. Hiking, canoeing, kayaking, snorkeling, and picnicking are favored pastimes here, and unlike other public beaches in the region, the narrow stretch of sand at Long Key is only available to overnight campers, making it decidedly more tranquil than the beaches of Key West.

After crossing the Long Key Viaduct, you'll be in the "Heart of the Keys," a transitional middle-of-the-road space between the outdoor pleasures of Key Largo and the unabashed revelry of Key West. Family-friendly activities seem to reign supreme in the Middle Keys, from up-close dolphin encounters on Duck Key to the playground and picnic areas of Sombrero Beach, popular among swimmers and windsurfers alike and the site of a spirited dragon boat festival each year. Past Duck Key you'll encounter the town of Marathon, an unassuming 13-mile-long community that stretches from Grassy Key to Knight's Key.

Besides casual seafood eateries and motel hideaways, this sleepy region offers several wildlife-oriented activities, from dolphin swims to bird-watching haunts. On Grassy Key, you'll find a nonprofit dolphin and sea lion center that offers tours and interactive programs, and farther south lie the islands that make up a 260-acre state park especially favored among kayakers, who frequently spot

© LAURA MARTONE

HIGHLIGHTS

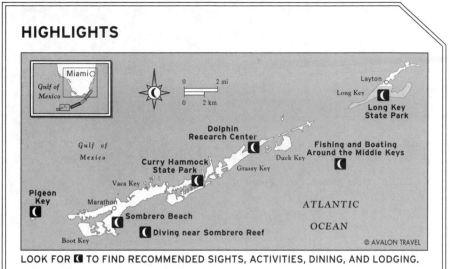

© AVALON TRAVEL

LOOK FOR ◖ TO FIND RECOMMENDED SIGHTS, ACTIVITIES, DINING, AND LODGING.

◖ **Long Key State Park:** This tranquil park, once the site of a posh fishing resort, offers easy ocean access for swimmers, snorkelers, and anglers (page 160).

◖ **Dolphin Research Center:** Once home to the frisky dolphins that starred in the 1963 film *Flipper,* this nonprofit marine mammal facility on Grassy Key offers a variety of educational experiences, including dolphin encounters (page 162).

◖ **Curry Hammock State Park:** This family-friendly park features a campground, a 1.5-mile nature trail through a preserved hardwood hammock, and a pleasant beach and playground area (page 162).

◖ **Sombrero Beach:** This curvy, palm-lined expanse of sand is a preferred spot among swimmers, beachcombers, and from April to

October, nesting turtles (page 164).

◖ **Pigeon Key:** Accessible by ferry or the defunct Old Seven Mile Bridge, this tiny coral island invites history buffs to stroll amid several picturesque buildings that served as the base camp for railroad workers in the early 20th century (page 165).

◖ **Fishing and Boating Around the Middle Keys:** Full-service marinas, fishing charters, and boat rentals help anglers in search of permit, bonefish, and tarpon (page 172).

◖ **Diving near Sombrero Reef:** Learn the ropes of scuba diving before venturing out to explore the elkhorn coral and tropical fish of this spur-and-groove reef formation, designated by a 142-foot tower (page 175).

manatees, raptors, herons, egrets, and other birds in the area.

Marathon also has relaxing spas, a public golf course, several campgrounds, a commuter airport, and numerous adventure outfitters and operators that assist visiting bikers, anglers, boaters, and scuba divers. A popular attraction

among children is the Crane Point Museum and Nature Center, which encompasses a natural history museum, a bird center, a nature trail, and one of the oldest houses in the Florida Keys.

En route to the Lower Keys, you'll cross the Seven Mile Bridge—a long stretch across open

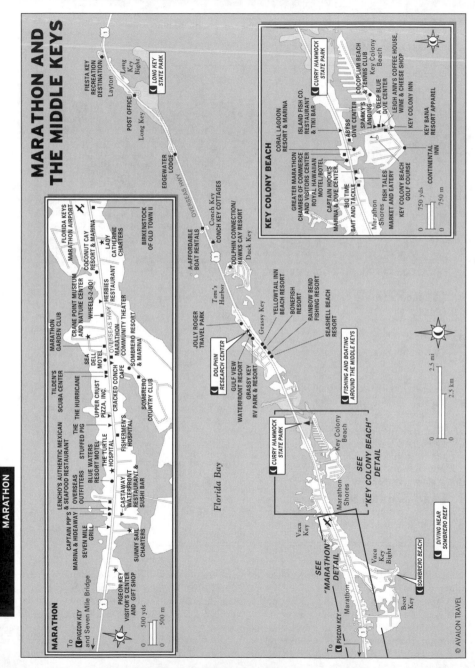

MARATHON AND THE MIDDLE KEYS

MARATHON

To PIGEON KEY and Seven Mile Bridge

PIGEON KEY VISITOR'S CENTER AND GIFT SHOP

CAPTAIN PIP'S MARINA & HIDEAWAY
SEVEN MILE GRILL
LENCHO'S AUTHENTIC MEXICAN & SEAFOOD RESTAURANT
OVERSEAS OUTFITTERS
BLUE WATERS RESORT MOTEL
THE TURTLE HOSPITAL
FISHERMEN'S HOSPITAL
CASTAWAY WATERFRONT RESTAURANT & SUSHI BAR
SUNNY SAIL CHARTERS

TILDEN'S SCUBA CENTER
THE HURRICANE
THE STUFFED PIG
UPPER CRUST PIZZA, INC.
CRACKED CONCH CAFE
MARATHON GARDEN CLUB
SEA DELL MOTEL
SOMBRERO RESORT & MARINA
MARATHON COMMUNITY THEATER
SOMBRERO COUNTRY CLUB

CRANE POINT MUSEUM AND NATURE CENTER
WHEELS-2-GO!
HERBIES RESTAURANT
COCONUT CAY RESORT & MARINA
FLORIDA KEYS MARATHON AIRPORT
LADY CATHERINE CHARTERS
BIRKENSTOCK OF OLD TOWN II

500 yds
500 m

OVERSEAS HWY

Florida Bay

CURRY HAMMOCK STATE PARK
Marathon Shores
SEE "KEY COLONY BEACH" DETAIL
Key Colony Beach
Vaca Key
SEE "MARATHON" DETAIL
Vaca Key Bight
SOMBRERO BEACH
DIVING NEAR SOMBRERO REEF
Boot Key
To PIGEON KEY
Marathon

JOLLY ROGER TRAVEL PARK
DOLPHIN RESEARCH CENTER
GULF VIEW WATERFRONT RESORT
GRASSY KEY RV PARK & RESORT
Tom's Harbor
Grassy Key
YELLOWTAIL INN BEACH RESORT
BONEFISH RESORT
RAINBOW BEND FISHING RESORT
SEASHELL BEACH RESORT
FISHING AND BOATING AROUND THE MIDDLE KEYS

A-AFFORDABLE BOAT RENTALS
Conch Key
CONCH KEY COTTAGES
DOLPHIN CONNECTION/ HAWKS CAY RESORT
Duck Key

2.5 mi
2.5 km

FIESTA KEY RECREATION DESTINATION
Long Key Bight
Layton
LONG KEY STATE PARK
Long Key
POST OFFICE
EDGEWATER LODGE

1

KEY COLONY BEACH

CORAL LAGOON RESORT & MARINA
ISLAND FISH CO. RESTAURANT & TIKI BAR
CURRY HAMMOCK STATE PARK
GREATER MARATHON CHAMBER OF COMMERCE AND VISITORS CENTER
ROYAL HAWAIIAN MOTEL/MOTEL
CAPTAIN HOOK'S MARINA & DIVE CENTER
BIG TIME BAIT AND TACKLE
Marathon Shores
FISH TALES MARKET AND EATERY
KEY COLONY BEACH GOLF COURSE
ABYSS DIVE CENTER
DIVE CENTER
SPARKY'S LANDING
A DEEP BLUE DIVE CENTER
COCOPLUM BEACH & TENNIS CLUB
LEIGH ANN'S COFFEE HOUSE, WINE & CHEESE SHOP
KEY COLONY INN
Key Colony Beach
KEY BANA RESORT APPAREL
CONTINENTAL INN

750 yds
750 m

© AVALON TRAVEL

MARATHON

water that's unnerving for some. Along the way, you'll pass tiny Pigeon Key, a historical early 20th-century work camp situated beside the Old Seven Mile Bridge, an engineering marvel that was once considered the Eighth Wonder of the World.

HISTORY

The original inhabitants of the islands that now constitute the Middle Keys were Native American tribes (as with the rest of the Florida Keys) who probably came to the region as early as 2000 BC. Primarily hunters and gatherers, these groups relied on food from the ocean, including manatees, which at that time were more plentiful in these waters. Given that manatees are also known as "sea cows" and that the Spanish word for "cow" is *vaca,* it's no wonder that the earliest known name for Marathon's biggest island was Key Vaca.

According to many historical accounts, New England fishermen ventured to Key Vaca in the early 1800s. Here they spent the winter months fishing the surrounding waters in order to sell their catches in Cuba. It's believed that, eventually, these fishermen relocated to Key West because it offered a much better harbor.

The next settlers to arrive on Key Vaca were undoubtedly former Bahamian nationals who moved here to fish, farm, and salvage wrecks. By 1840 the settlement known as Conch Town encompassed 50 homes and a school, but the community's existence was short-lived. In August of that year when the Seminole raided Indian Key to the north, the Conch Town inhabitants fled south to Key West.

Once the threat of Native American attacks had subsided, roughly 20 families returned to Key Vaca in the late 1840s, but by 1870 the island was once more deserted. Over three decades later, a group of black Bahamians settled at what is now Crane Point Hammock. The settlement, known as Adderley Town, was named after the group's leader, George Adderley, and its remnants now constitute the oldest house in the Keys outside of Key West.

In 1904 construction of Henry Flagler's Overseas Railroad commenced on Key Vaca.

Here the Florida East Coast Railway erected construction headquarters, central supply facilities, shops, a church and a school, a hospital and a hotel, as well as living quarters for hundreds of railroad workers. According to legend, Flagler was pushing his workers so hard to complete the railroad that one worker exclaimed, "Building this railroad has become a regular marathon!" Soon afterward the town's name changed from Key Vaca to Marathon—though it's interesting to note that the largest island in the Middle Keys is still known as Vaca Key.

Following the 1912 completion of the railroad, the population of Marathon quickly declined. By World War II, Marathon experienced a resurgence largely caused by additions like electricity, a water pipeline, an airport, and the overseas highway. Attracted to the region by its pleasant climate and excellent fishing opportunities, new residents sparked the area's growth in the 1950s, and today the population of Marathon (which consists of the islands between Grassy Key and Knight's Key) now exceeds 8,380.

PLANNING YOUR TIME

Like Islamorada and the Lower Keys, Marathon and the rest of the Middle Keys are made up of numerous islands, most of which are easily accessible by car, via the Overseas Highway. Given the sheer variety of attractions, extending from Long Key at Mile Marker 67 to Pigeon Key near Mile Marker 45, a proper visit may take at least three days—perhaps even a week if you plan to add activities like fishing, kayaking, camping, windsurfing, and golf to your itinerary.

Just be prepared, as with other parts of the Florida Keys, to deal with traffic congestion, crowded restaurants and attractions, and higher lodging rates during late winter and early spring. When planning a trip to the Middle Keys, you should also consider factors like climate, fishing seasons, and annual events. If you're a novice to certain activities, such as scuba diving, you might also want to allow for proper instruction time.

Where you decide to stay, however, is entirely

MARATHON

и. With a car, it's easy enough to navi-gate the entire region, so whether you choose a resort near Mile Marker 69 or a campground near Mile Marker 47, you should be able to reach everything you hope to see and experience in the Middle Keys.

For more information about Marathon and the Middle Keys, consult the **Monroe County**

Tourist Development Council (1201 White St., Ste. 102, Key West, 305/296-1552 or 800/352-5397, www.fla-keys.com, 9am-5pm Mon.-Fri.) and the **Greater Marathon Chamber of Commerce and Marathon Visitors Center** (12222 Overseas Hwy., Marathon, 305/743-5417 or 800/262-7284, www.floridakeysmarathon.com, 9am-5pm daily).

Sights

❰ LONG KEY STATE PARK

Between the flyspeck community of Layton and the lengthy town of Marathon lies Long Key, a strangely shaped island that appears to resemble the open jaws of a vicious snake. Perhaps that's why Spanish explorers originally called this island *Cayo Vivora*, which means "Rattlesnake Key." In the early 20th century, it was the site of a luxurious fishing resort that was favored by the author Zane Grey and other saltwater anglers. Eventually, the resort was wiped out by the Labor Day Hurricane of 1935, the same terrible tempest that destroyed Henry Flagler's Overseas Railroad. Nowadays Long Key often appears on maps of the Upper Keys, but given that it's not technically part of Islamorada and that its upscale past has now been usurped by a quiet, nature-oriented vibe, it seems more suited for the Middle Keys. Just bear in mind that not everyone will agree with such a sentiment.

Today Long Key is home to the aptly titled **Long Key State Park** (67400 Overseas Hwy., Long Key, 305/664-4815, www.floridastateparks.org/longkey, 8am-sunset daily, $5 vehicles with 2-8 passengers plus $0.50 pp, $4.50 motorcycles and single-occupant vehicles, $2.50 pedestrians, bikers, and extra passengers), a popular place among anglers, swimmers, snorkelers, picnickers, and campers since it was established in 1969. Encompassing roughly 1,000 acres, this pleasant preserve features a variety of foliage, including mangrove forests, lush vegetation, and

scrubby grass, vibrant wildflowers, and dense inland trees like poisonwood, gumbo limbo, and coconut palm. Given such greenery, hikers may appreciate the two on-site nature trails—the **Golden Orb Trail,** named after a native spider and offering a 1.2-mile stroll through various plant communities, and the **Layton Trail,** a 0.3-mile walk on the bay side of the park—while bird-watchers will relish spying a wide array of vibrant species, from wading egrets to red-bellied woodpeckers, which are particularly prevalent during the winter months.

Canoeists especially favor this tranquil place, which features the leisurely **Long Key Lakes Canoe Trail** through a shallow lagoon. Canoe rentals ($5 hourly, $10 daily) and a self-guided brochure make this a relatively easy diversion for novices, too. For some visitors, another highlight is the narrow, rocky, grass-lined beach on the ocean side of the park, not far from picnic pavilions, public showers, and a canoe/kayak launching area. Only open to those staying in the state park campground, it tends to be more peaceful than the beaches farther south, though it can also be rather muddy at times. Guided, two-hour trail walks (10am Wed., free) and interpretive programs (10am Thurs., free), from bird-watching talks to snorkeling excursions, are periodically available, and be aware that leashed, well-behaved pets are ostensibly permitted here, but they are not allowed on the beaches, in the picnic shelters, or in the restrooms. Fireworks and hunting are also prohibited.

© DANIEL MARTONE

caring for the residents of the Dolphin Research Center

DOLPHIN ATTRACTIONS
Dolphin Connection

If you're driving west from Long Key, you'll cross the Long Key Channel and pass through the Conch Keys before encountering the secluded, 60-acre island known as Duck Key on the ocean side of the highway. Situated here is the luxurious **Hawks Cay Resort** (61 Hawks Cay Blvd., Duck Key, 305/743-7000, www.hawkscay.com), which offers a slew of diversions, from water sports and spa services to the **Dolphin Connection** (305/289-9975 or 888/251-3674, www.dolphinconnection.com, 9am-5pm daily), which was established in 1990 as a marine mammal education, breeding, and research facility. Like the other interactive dolphin facilities in the Florida Keys, the Dolphin Connection allows visitors to mingle with these friendly marine mammals from the dock or within the on-site saltwater lagoon.

Three basic programs are available here. The 30-minute **Dockside Dolphins program** ($60 pp) allows you to feed, play with, and interact with the dolphins without ever getting in the water, though splashing may still be involved; while all ages are welcome, children under 6 must be accompanied by a paid adult. Meanwhile, the 45-minute **Dolphin Discovery program** ($175 pp) offers you the chance to touch, kiss, hug, splash, and swim with the dolphins; although there are no age restrictions, participants must be at least 4.5 feet tall. Lastly, the engrossing **Trainer for a Day program** ($325 pp) offers participants (who must be at least 10 years of age and 4.5 feet tall) a three-hour behind-the-scenes look at the daily activities of the training team; Dockside Dolphins and Dolphin Discovery are both included with this program. Advance reservations (operators available 8am-9pm Mon.-Fri., 9am-7pm Sat.-Sun.) are required for all programs, all of which are preceded by a proper orientation, and short-style wetsuits are provided free of charge to those entering the water. Unlike other dolphin facilities in the Florida Keys, the Dolphin Connection does not charge for merely observing the programs.

MARATHON

▮ Dolphin Research Center

On the bay side of Grassy Key, you'll spot the hard-to-miss sign for the **Dolphin Research Center** (DRC, 58901 Overseas Hwy., Grassy Key, 305/289-1121 or 305/289-0002, www. dolphins.org, 9am-4:30pm daily, $20 adults, $17 military personnel and veterans, $15 children 4-12, free for children under 4), a nonprofit education, research, and rescue facility that "promises peaceful coexistence, cooperation, and communication between marine mammals, humans, and the environment." Adhering to this mission statement, DRC features a wide array of programs—from brief dolphin dips to daylong research programs—that could easily be classified as "edutainment."

Founded in 1984, the facility that is now DRC has a much longer history, in fact. Despite a shift in ownership over the years, this site has been continuously operated as a marine mammal facility since 1956, when fisherman Milton Santini captured several bottlenose dolphins, including one he called "Mitzi," and formed Santini's Porpoise School. In 1963 Mitzi starred in the original *Flipper* movie, along with five other resident dolphins. When Mitzi passed away in 1972, Santini sold the property to an entertainment conglomerate that operated the site as Flipper's Sea School. It wasn't until 1977, however, that the facility began to shift its purpose to the one upheld today—among other things, cultivating environmental ambassadors among the visiting public.

Today visitors can watch a variety of educational shows and demonstrations, during which dolphins get a chance to display their learned behaviors, while trainers can offer a bit of insight into caretaking aspects that are rarely seen by the public, such as administering medicine to a sick dolphin. In addition, guests can opt to meet a dolphin from the dock ($25 pp), toss toys to the dolphins ($60 pp), paint with a dolphin ($65 pp), play learning games with the dolphins ($75 pp), splash with a sea lion ($80 pp), experience a group dip with the dolphins ($119 adults, $50 children under 5), or have a shallow-water or deepwater dolphin encounter ($199 adults, $50 children under 5). Truly immersive activities include the trainer-for-a-day ($675 pp) and researcher-for-a-day ($525 pp) programs, both of which provide an intensive all-day look into the folks that operate DRC. Age restrictions may apply for some of these programs, and almost all require advance reservations. DRC welcomes guests with disabilities, and staff members will do their best to accommodate them.

▮ CURRY HAMMOCK STATE PARK

West of Grassy Key is the largest uninhabited parcel of land between Key Largo and Big Pine Key. True, it's composed of several wooded islands, with names like Crawl Key, Little Crawl Key, Long Point Key, Deer Key, and Fat Deer Key, but nonetheless, **Curry Hammock State Park** (56200 Overseas Hwy., Marathon, 305/289-2690, www.floridastateparks.org/curryhammock, 8am-sunset daily, $5 vehicles with 2-8 passengers plus $0.50 pp, $4.50 motorcycles and single-occupant vehicles, $2.50 pedestrians, bikers, and extra passengers) constitutes an impressive, nearly development-free place in the heart of a fairly populated region. Encompassing more than 1,000 acres, Curry Hammock protects sizable seagrass beds, mangrove swamps, and rockland hammocks, including one of the country's largest populations of thatch palms.

Established in 1991 and named after Lamar Louise Curry—a respected Miami teacher whose father, Thomas, purchased large tracts of land in the Upper and Middle Keys—this popular park offers a full-facility campground, picnic tables and pavilions, and easy access to swimming, windsurfing, canoeing, and kayaking opportunities. Visitors can even rent single and double kayaks on-site ($17.20-21.50 for two hours). In addition, hikers can stroll along a 1.5-mile **nature trail** through a preserved hardwood hammock on Fat Deer Key. Little Crawl Key features a pleasant beach and playground area, which is accessible by overnight campers and day-use visitors alike.

© LAURA MARTONE

Kayaking is a popular diversion at Curry Hammock State Park.

Fishing and beachcombing are popular activities here, and bird-watchers will also appreciate this park, which lies on a critical bird migration route and hosts the annual Florida Keys Birding and Wildlife Festival. The beaches, hammock, and grass flats are home to a wide array of herons, egrets, plovers, sanderlings, white-crowned pigeons, pelicans, osprey, and bald eagles. Wildlife lovers might also spot Key Vaca raccoons, nurse sharks, spotted rays, dolphins, and manatees.

Bikers are welcome to ride along the park roads as well as a two-mile stretch of the **Florida Keys Overseas Heritage Trail,** which leads to and from Marathon. Just remember to wear a helmet at all times, and be advised that biking is not permitted on the boardwalks, foot paths, or nature trail inside the park. You should be aware, too, that while leashed, well-behaved pets are ostensibly permitted here, they are not allowed along the shoreline, in the water, or in the picnic area and restrooms. Fireworks and hunting are also prohibited.

CRANE POINT MUSEUM AND NATURE CENTER

Near Mile Marker 50, on the bay side of U.S. 1 in the heart of Marathon, lies the **Crane Point Museum and Nature Center** (5550 Overseas Hwy., Marathon, 305/743-9100, www.cranepoint.net, 9am-5pm Mon.-Sat., noon-5pm Sun., $12.50 adults, $11 seniors 65 and over, $8.50 children 5-13, free for children under 5), a sprawling 63-acre preserve that families with young children especially favor. Your first stop is typically the **Museum of Natural History,** where you can learn about the human history of the Florida Keys, including facts about the Calusa native people that once inhabited these islands, the Spanish and British explorers that later discovered them, and the Bahamian pioneers that eventually called them home. Here you'll also discover stories about various shipwrecks and the ill-fated Overseas Railroad. Other dioramas and exhibits explore the flora, fauna, and geology that define this diverse region, including mangroves, butterflies, sea turtles, and coral reefs.

MARATHON

om the museum, most visitors venture outside, where you can view a 10-minute orientation video, watch daily fish feedings in the saltwater lagoon, and interact with marine creatures like conch and starfish in the on-site touch tanks. Afterward you can explore ever-changing creature exhibits in a Cracker-style bungalow, venture across a butterfly meadow peppered with aromatic flowers, and stroll amid thatch palm trees and mangroves. Additionally, nature trails lead to three curious destinations, including the historical **Adderley House,** an open, weathered, Bahamian-style structure built in the early 1900s by Bahamian immigrant George Adderley. Formed from Tabby, a concrete-like material made of burned conch and other shells, the Adderley House is the oldest house in the Florida Keys north of Key West and now invites visitors to wander amid old-fashioned beds, chests, and other furnishings, reminiscent of those used by George and Olivia Adderley when they lived here between 1902 and 1949.

Other accessible stops along the way include the **Marathon Wild Bird Center,** which aims to rescue, rehabilitate, and release injured gulls, osprey, and other native birds, and the art deco-style **Crane House,** constructed in the 1950s and once home to Francis and Mary Crane, a Massachusetts couple who purchased the land here in 1949. Both passionate conservationists and horticulturists, the Cranes worked hard to preserve and enhance the preserve with flowering trees and shrubs. The family retained the property until the late 1970s, and by 1989, it was purchased by the Florida Keys Land and Sea Trust in order to spare it from impending development. Eventually, this preserve of palm and hardwood hammocks, mangrove forests, tidal lagoons, and wetland ponds was named for Francis and Mary Crane, whose former home isn't far from **Crane Point** itself, where you can observe pelicans, raptors, and other native bird species along the shore of Florida Bay. If possible, try to visit the nature preserve on a sunny day, when the foliage looks infinitely better than on an overcast one.

(SOMBRERO BEACH

Located at the end of Sombrero Beach Road, near Mile Marker 50 in Marathon, **Sombrero Beach** (305/743-0033, free) is definitely one of the more popular beaches in the Florida Keys. Part of a public park that offers picnic pavilions, volleyball courts, public restrooms, and a small playground, this curving, palm-lined expanse of sand is also a preferred spot for nesting turtles from April to October. Favored among swimmers, snorkelers, picnickers, windsurfers, and volleyball enthusiasts, Sombrero Beach is also home to the **Battle in the Bay,** an annual dragon boat race that usually takes place in May. Although there are no concessions, equipment rentals, or camping facilities on-site, families, couples, and active individuals simply adore this place, especially on a sunny, cloudless day—and unlike many beaches in the Keys, Sombrero allows pets, provided they're well behaved.

THE TURTLE HOSPITAL

Situated on the western end of Vaca Key and dedicated to ensuring the survival of sea turtles, **The Turtle Hospital** (2396 Overseas Hwy., Marathon, 305/743-2552, www.turtlehospital.org, 9am-6pm daily, $15 adults, $7.50 children 4-12, free for children under 4) is the only state-certified veterinary hospital of its kind in the world. Featuring up-to-date medical equipment, the nonprofit facility strives to rescue and rehabilitate injured sea turtles, with the goal of releasing them back into the wild. The turtle species typically found in the Florida Keys include the threatened loggerhead turtles as well as the endangered green, hawksbill, leatherback, and Kemps Ridley turtles. In recent years, threats to such turtles have come from fishing line and net entanglements; boat strikes; oil spills; coastal development, which damages nesting sites; and intestinal impaction due to the ingestion of floating debris. The hospital can receive as many as 70 turtles yearly—even more during particularly cold winters when hundreds of stunned sea turtles have been found floating in the ocean. To

Sombrero Beach, home to the Battle in the Bay

date, this working hospital has successfully released more than 1,000 sea turtles.

As part of its educational outreach component, The Turtle Hospital features an education center (plus gift shop) and invites guests to take a guided 1.5-hour tour of the facility. Seven such tours are offered daily (10am, 11am, noon, 1pm, 2pm, 3pm, and 4pm) and consist of a slide show presentation, a behind-the-scenes look at the hospital facilities, a visit to the outdoor turtle rehabilitation area, and an opportunity to feed the permanent residents. Bear in mind that this tour will require a minimal amount of walking; limited wheelchair access is available. Reservations for these tours are highly recommended, given the space limitations. Poor weather and turtle emergencies may supersede any scheduled tour. All minors under the age of 18 must be accompanied by an adult.

◖ PIGEON KEY

To reach the Lower Keys from Marathon, simply head west across the **Seven Mile Bridge.** Along the way, you'll spy an isolated, palm-dotted island tucked beside the **Old Seven Mile Bridge,** once considered an engineering marvel and, by some historians, the Eighth Wonder of the World. This tiny coral island, known as **Pigeon Key,** has been lovingly preserved by the Pigeon Key Foundation (305/289-0025, www.pigeonkey.net) to capture the atmosphere of the early 1900s when it served as a base camp for railroad workers. Here you can take a self-guided walking tour of the grounds, which includes educational facilities, a small museum, and of course, the historical buildings that once housed more than 400 workers, who labored 14 hours a day, six days a week to construct Henry Flagler's ill-fated Overseas Railroad. Besides the history lesson, you might also enjoy picnicking on this lovely little island. Snorkeling is also a possibility; you can either bring your own snorkel and mask or borrow the gear that's available on Pigeon Key.

You can purchase tickets to Pigeon Key at the **Pigeon Key Visitor's Center and Gift Shop** (1 Knight's Key Blvd., Knight's Key, 305/743-5999, 9:30am-4pm daily, $12 adults,

MARATHON

© ANDY NEWMAN/FLORIDA KEYS NEWS BUREAU

The Old Seven Mile Bridge crosses the former railroad workers' camp on Pigeon Key.

$9 Monroe County residents and children 5-13, free for children under 5), housed in a red train car near Mile Marker 47. The admission price grants you access to Pigeon Key all day and includes a guided ferry ride from Knight's Key to the island (10am, noon, and 2pm daily) and back again (10:30am, 12:30pm, 2:30pm, and 4pm daily). Reservations for the ferry are definitely advised, especially on holidays and weekends. You can also access this historical site by walking or biking down a 2.2-mile segment of the Old Seven Mile Bridge from Knight's Key; you can also reach the island via private boat. If you opt not to use the ferry service and choose to come by foot, bicycle, or private vessel, the admission fees and docking charges will still apply, so be sure to stop by the gift shop to make advance arrangements for your visit.

BOAT AND AIR TOURS

For a relaxing tour of the surrounding waters, consider heading to the Seascape Resort &

Marina (1275 E. 76th St. Ocean, Marathon), where you can hire **Lady Catherine Charters** (305/743-5544 or 305/240-4030, www.dive-andfishmarathon.com, hours vary daily, $200 per cruise) for a private, two-hour sunset cruise. Such cruises can be customized, whether you'd like to toast the occasion with champagne or, as other guests have done, even renew your marital vows in the midst of a glorious Florida Keys sunset. The boat can accommodate up to 22 passengers, so bring your friends and loved ones along for the ride. As an alternative, you can board a 43-foot sailing ketch through **Sunny Sail Charters** (Marathon Marina & Boatyard, 1021 11th St. Ocean, Marathon, 305/394-4319, www.sunnysailcharters.com), a seasonal touring company that offers couples or small groups (up to six passengers) the chance to journey across ocean waters for two-hour sunset sails (times vary daily depending on the sunset, $190 couples, $50 additional couples), four-hour luncheon sails (times vary daily, $300 couples, $75 additional couples), four-hour sunset dinner cruises (times vary daily depending on the sunset, $350 couples, $100 additional couples), or customized trips. Reservations are a must for both companies.

In Layton, near Mile Marker 65.5 on U.S. 1, **Conch Air** (305/395-1117, www.conchair.com), which formerly offered bi-plane rides, now provides exhilarating, hang gliding experiences high above the Florida Keys and the shimmering waters of Florida Bay and the Atlantic Ocean. Instructional flights can take you to varying heights, from 1,500 feet ($99-119 pp) to 2,500 feet ($159 pp) to 3,500 feet ($199 pp) above the region. Farther south, between Key Colony Beach and the Crane Point Museum, you'll surely spot Florida Keys Marathon Airport, where **Island Hoppers Aerial Adventures** (9850 Overseas Hwy., Marathon, 305/619-9603, www.ravenair.net) offers helicopter adventures high above the beaches, coral reefs, and aquamarine waters of the Middle and Lower Keys. Some of these excursions include the 10-minute Keys Discovery Tour ($59 pp) above Marathon and Pigeon Key, the 14-minute Duck Key/Hawks Cay Tour

($79 pp), the 18-minute Sunshine Key Tour ($99 pp), the 25-minute Bahia Honda/Seven Mile Bridge Tour ($139 pp), and the hour-long Key West Adventure ($299 pp). There must be a minimum of two passengers, and all tours are limited to three passengers, with a maximum combined weight of 580 pounds.

For a completely different experience, board one of the three vintage World War II airplanes operated by **History Flight** (5409 Overseas Hwy., Marathon, 888/743-3311, www.

historyflight.com, times and rates vary). Under the guidance of a certified flight instructor, you can fly the flagship *Mitchell,* a North American B-25 bomber; the *Texan,* a North American AT-6 trainer; or the *Stearman,* a Boeing N2S biplane. While you're learning to fly, know that you're helping a worthy cause because all flight proceeds fund the nonprofit organization's ongoing research efforts and recovery expeditions dedicated to bringing missing-in-action servicepeople home.

Entertainment and Events

NIGHTLIFE
If you're looking for a plethora of dance clubs and late-night bars, heading south to Key West might be your best bet. That doesn't mean, however, that you won't find nighttime diversions in the Middle Keys. As in the Upper and Lower Keys, several area bars and restaurants feature live music throughout the week.

At **The Hurricane** (4650 Overseas Hwy., Marathon, 305/743-2220, www.hurricaneblues.com, 11am-midnight daily), for instance, patrons can watch televised sports and enjoy nightly entertainment, from blues bands to country rock performers.

Farther down the road, Barbara and Johnny Maddox invite nighttime revelers to their ever-popular **Porky's Bayside BBQ Restaurant** (1410 Overseas Hwy., Marathon, 305/289-2065, www.porkysbaysidebbq.com, 11am-10pm daily), which offers a daily happy hour (4pm-7pm) and live bluegrass, country, or rock 'n' roll nightly (6:30pm-9:30pm) in a classic, laid-back Keys atmosphere.

In Key Colony Beach, near Mile Marker 53.5, you'll find two winning spots to while away the evening. Owned and operated by Matt and Carolyn Anthony, the rustic **Sparky's Landing** (400 Sadowski Cswy., Key Colony Beach, 305/289-7445, www.sparkyslanding.com, 11am-10pm daily) provides locals and tourists a quintessential Florida Keys experience, featuring a daily happy hour (4pm-6pm)

as well as live folk, rock, country, and reggae music Wednesday-Saturday. Not far away, the family-owned **Key Colony Inn Restaurant and Lounge** (700 W. Ocean Dr., Key Colony Beach, 305/743-0100, www.kcinn.com, 11am-9:30pm daily) has been a favorite among residents and visitors for well over 15 years—not just for the delicious cuisine, but also for the live piano music in the on-site lounge every night.

THE ARTS
Though cultural enthusiasts will definitely find more concerts, dance performances, and theatrical venues in Key West, the Middle Keys still offer a few options for those seeking an alternative to outdoor activities. The **Marathon Garden Club** (5270 Overseas Hwy., Marathon, 305/743-4971, www.marathongardenclub.org), for example, has been known to host live performances, such as productions by the Island Opera Theatre (show times and ticket prices vary). The club also features exhibits, workshops, educational programs, flower shows, and home and garden tours, not to mention an on-site garden and gift shop (10am-2pm Mon.-Fri.).

The **Marathon Community Theater** (5101 Overseas Hwy., Marathon, 305/743-0994, www.marathontheater.org) has presented live theater and other entertainment to the Middle Keys since 1944. In addition to offering dance classes, readings, and screenings, such as classic movies every Wednesday at 2pm (305/743-0288 for schedule), the theater features live performances (show times vary, $18 for plays, $24 for musicals), including modern farces, comedies, thrillers, and dramas, plus Broadway musicals. Recent productions have included the musical *Guys and Dolls* and the comedy-thriller *Deathtrap*. Performances are usually held Thursday-Saturday in the winter months, but events occur throughout the year. Student tickets ($9 pp) are available for nonmusical performances, and patrons can purchase season passes ($54-70 pp) every year.

Near Mile Marker 49, the **Marathon Community Park** (200 36th St. Ocean, Marathon, 305/743-6598, www.ci.marathon.fl.us, 7am-10pm daily) contains an amphitheater for live performances, among other facilities. Call the park for current events. In addition, the **Florida Keys Concert Association** (305/289-1110, www.floridakeysconcerts.com) has been hosting live musical performances, from piano concerts to string quartets, for more than four decades. Seasons usually run from January to March, and most performances take place at the San Pablo Catholic Church (550 122nd St. Ocean, Marathon, 305/289-0636, www.sanpablo1.hypermart.net) near Mile Marker 53.5. For information about other cultural events in the Middle Keys, consult the **Florida Keys Council of the Arts** (1100 Simonton St., Key West, 305/295-4369, www.keysarts.com).

FESTIVALS AND EVENTS

Although Key West offers the lion's share of annual festivals and events—some of which even lure visitors during the hottest parts of the year—you'll certainly encounter a few curious celebrations in the Middle Keys.

Pigeon Key Art Show

For over 15 years, art lovers have ventured to Marathon for the **Pigeon Key Art Show** ($7 adults, $3 students, free for children under 13), hosted annually by the Pigeon Key Foundation (1 Knight's Key Blvd., Knight's Key, 305/743-5999, www.pigeonkey.net). Established by a gathering of local artists in 1995, this popular art show spent the first decade of its existence on Pigeon Key, the small, isolated island that sits beside the Old Seven Mile Bridge west of Marathon. For logistical reasons, the well-attended art festival, which typically takes place during the first weekend of February, shifted venues in 2005 to Marathon Community Park on the ocean side of U.S. 1, near Mile Marker 49, where the attendance has continued to rise, even without the ambience of Pigeon Key.

Presented by volunteers, this annual event features live music, art raffles, and the artwork of roughly 85 artists from around the country—artwork that usually includes photography, jewelry, sculpture, glassware, fine crafts, and graphic arts, as well as watercolor, acrylic, and oil paintings. Food and beverages are often available, and the admission price includes a ferry ride to historical Pigeon Key—an excellent deal, considering ferry tickets usually cost $12 for adults and $9 for children. Pets, except for service animals, are not allowed during the festival.

Battle in the Bay

Each May, visitors flock to Marathon's Sombrero Beach, an oceanside stretch of sand accessible via Sombrero Beach Road near Mile Marker 50, to watch the **Battle in the Bay Dragon Boat Festival** (www.battleinthebay.org), an annual race of festively decorated dragon boats. Launched directly from the beach, the colorful boats constitute more than just a heated competition on the water. Every year, the dragon boat teams are encouraged to gather pledges for the charities of their choice.

In addition, race organizers typically donate part of the proceeds from this event to local nonprofit organizations, such as Reef Relief. Although it costs a considerable amount to register a team for the race, it's absolutely free to watch the festivities—good news for locals and visitors alike. Parking ($3) is available at Marathon High School, located on Sombrero Beach Road about a mile from the

DUANWU FESTIVAL

Though Marathon's **Battle in the Bay Dragon Boat Festival** (www.battleinthebay. org) epitomizes the spirited vibe of the Florida Keys, dragon boat festivals are certainly not unique to this part of the world. In fact, dragon boat racing is an ancient Chinese tradition. For more than 5,000 years, dragon boats have been used for ceremonial purposes in China, but it wasn't until the death of the beloved scholar, statesman, and poet Qu Yuan roughly 2,300 years ago that the Duanwu Festival was born.

As the story goes, Qu Yuan, a loyal minister to the King of Chu, was favored by the Chinese people, but his erudite ways greatly unnerved the other court officials, so much so that he was framed for conspiracy and exiled from his home. During the exile, he wrote numerous poems to express his ire and despair over his king, his country, and his people. Then in the year 278 BC, at the age of 37, he tried to drown himself in a nearby river. Because he was still considered a righteous man by the people, several individuals leaped into their boats and searched the waters for him, but their efforts were futile. Since then the Dragon Boat Festival has commemorated this ill-fated attempt to rescue Qu Yuan.

Celebrated annually in various Asian countries, including Taiwan, Singapore, and Malaysia, the festival typically occurs on the fifth day of the fifth month of the lunar calendar and, among other activities, always features dragon boat racing. In the 1970s, Hong Kong was instrumental in the development of dragon boat racing as a modern sport. Today the Duanwu Festival is an official national holiday in China, and the sport, which is governed by the **International Dragon Boat Federation** (www.idbf.org), enthralls more than 50 million people worldwide. So be sure to visit Marathon during its one-day version of this centuries-old celebration, which usually takes place in early or mid-May.

race site. Typically, the one-day event occurs on a Saturday in early or mid-May, and area bars usually host fun-filled parties before and after the race.

Recently, though, there was a major shake-up behind the scenes of this beloved event. Following problematic negotiations with the City of Marathon, Battle in the Bay was shifted temporarily to Key West, before being cancelled there (because of a conflict with the U.S. Navy's harbor regulations) and after a public outcry relocated to Sombrero Beach. So check the website for updates before making travel plans.

Florida Keys Birding and Wildlife Festival

In late September, animal lovers head to the Middle Keys for the **Florida Keys Birding and Wildlife Festival** (305/872-0774, www.keysbirdingfest.org). Typically based out of **Curry Hammock State Park** (56200 Overseas Hwy.,

Marathon, 305/289-2690, www.floridastateparks.org/curryhammock, 8am-sunset daily, entrance fees apply), the five-day festival, which began in 1999, usually features an environmental fair and a series of field trips. Such educational excursions—some of which are free and several of which range in price—may include a biking tour of the Florida Keys Overseas Heritage Trail, a self-guided stroll through the Florida Keys Wild Bird Center, a snorkeling trip to Looe Key Reef, or an all-day bird-watching journey to Dry Tortugas National Park.

Other Annual Events

Besides community events like the annual **Key Colony Beach Boat Parade** (305/743-7214)—a nighttime procession that usually takes place in mid-December and features lighted, decorated vessels amid the canals and cuts of Key Colony Beach—the Middle Keys host numerous fishing tournaments throughout the year. In early March, for instance,

MARATHON

© DANIEL MARTONE

the marina beside Sparky's Landing, site of the Leon Shell Memorial Sailfish Tournament

anglers can participate in the three-day **Leon Shell Memorial Sailfish Tournament** (www.leonshelltournament.com), which honors the late Captain Leon Shell (who died of brain cancer in 1997 while under the care of hospice workers) by benefiting the Hospice of the Florida Keys and Visiting Nurse Association (www.hospicevna.com). Champions of the Leon Shell tournament are usually awarded a variety of trophies, prizes, and cash purses at Sparky's Landing in the Key Colony Beach Marina. Other popular fishing events include the three-day **Marathon International Tarpon Tournament** (305/289-2248) in early May, the three-day **Burdines Waterfront Dolphin & Blackfin Tuna Tournament** (305/743-5317, www.burdineswaterfront.com) in late June, and the four-day **Marathon International Bonefish Tournament** (305/304-8682) in mid-September.

Shopping

Truly dedicated shoppers will surely make a beeline for Key West, a town that abounds in art galleries, clothing shops, and other unique emporiums. Here in the Middle Keys, outdoor diversions, family-friendly attractions, and practical chain stores are definitely more prevalent than unique shopping opportunities. In fact, for the most part, you'll find little more than souvenir stores in the Marathon area.

On Vaca Key, for instance, you'll find a slew of gifts and souvenirs at the **Tropical Island Outlet** (305/289-0250, 10am-6pm daily) and **Marooned in Marathon** (305/743-3809, 10am-6pm daily), which share the same building (11528 Overseas Hwy., Marathon) and, together, offer T-shirts, beach towels, puzzles and games, tropical art and ornaments, and fine cigars. Also on Vaca Key, you can shop for Birkenstocks, Teva sandals, Crocs, and other footwear at **Birkenstock of Old Town II** (8915 Overseas Hwy., Marathon, 305/289-9999, 9:30am-5pm Mon.-Sat.) and stock up on hats, sunglasses, sandals, beach towels, souvenirs, and other island necessities at the **Sandal Factory Outlet/T-Shirt City** (5195 Overseas Hwy., Marathon, 305/743-5778, 9am-8pm Mon.-Sat., 9am-6pm Sun.), which also has locations in Key Largo and Islamorada.

Even Key Colony Beach, which you can access via the Sadowski Causeway at Mile Marker 53.5, features a worthwhile boutique near the intersection of Key Colony Beach Causeway and West Ocean Drive. For more than 25 years, locals and tourists have frequented **Key Bana Resort Apparel** (MM 53.5 OS, Key Colony Beach Causeway, Key Colony Beach, 305/289-1161, www.keybana.com, 9:30am-5:30pm Mon.-Sat.) for women's and men's tropical-style clothes and other accessories, which nowadays might include Beer Can Island shorts, Tommy Bahama swimwear, designer suits, shoes, sunglasses, and more.

Sports and Recreation

GOLF

Established in the 1950s, the **Sombrero Country Club (SCC)** (4000 Sombrero Blvd., Marathon, 305/743-2551, www.sombrerocc.com) allows its members, many of whom don't even live in the Keys year-round, access to lighted tennis courts, an 18-hole golf course, and an active clubhouse. In lieu of purchasing a membership to SCC, which can require a $10,000 initiation fee, you can simply stop by the **Key Colony Beach Golf Course** (8th St., Key Colony Beach, www.keycolonybeach.net/recreation.html, 7:30am-sunset daily, $11), which offers a nine-hole par-three golf course, plus tennis courts that are free for the public to use. Golf memberships ($265-385 yearly) are available, as are club rentals ($3) and pull carts ($2).

HIKING AND BIKING

Like much of the Florida Keys, the greater Marathon area doesn't typically appeal to long-distance hikers. Nevertheless, you can certainly enjoy a pleasant stroll through places like **Long Key State Park** (67400 Overseas Hwy., Long Key, 305/664-4815, www.floridastateparks.org/longkey, 8am-sunset daily, $5 vehicles with 2-8 passengers plus $0.50 pp, $4.50 motorcycles and single-occupant vehicles, $2.50 pedestrians, bikers, and extra passengers), which features two nature trails: the 1.2-mile Golden Orb Trail, named after a native spider, and the shorter 0.3-mile Layton Trail, located on the bay side of the park.

Curry Hammock State Park (56200 Overseas Hwy., Marathon, 305/289-2690, www.floridastateparks.org/curryhammock, 8am-sunset daily, $5 vehicles with 2-8 passengers plus $0.50 pp, $4.50 motorcycles and single-occupant vehicles, $2.50 pedestrians, bikers, and extra passengers) contains a 1.5-mile nature trail that winds through the hardwood hammock preserved by the park. In the heart of Vaca Key, the **Crane Point Museum and Nature Center** (5550 Overseas Hwy., Marathon, 305/743-9100, www.cranepoint.net, 9am-5pm Mon.-Sat., noon-5pm Sun., $12 adults, $10 seniors over 65, $8 children 6-12, free for children under 6) even features a 1.5-mile nature trail through palm trees and mangroves, alongside historical structures, and not far from Florida Bay.

Given the Middle Keys' numerous bridges and sprawling nature, bikers will undoubtedly relish the region even more—though care should always be taken on the Overseas Highway, and a proper helmet should be worn at all times. Between Mile Marker 58 and Mile Marker 40, you'll find an 11-mile biking path, part of the **Florida Keys Overseas Heritage Trail,** plus a wide shoulder along the **Seven Mile Bridge.** Bicycles can be rented from **Bike**

MARATHON

Marathon Bike Rental (305/743-3204, www. bikemarathonbikerentals.com, 8am-6pm daily, $35 weekly, $99 monthly), Marathon's first and oldest bicycle rental company, which also offers free delivery and free pickup service in Marathon and Key Colony Beach. Each rental includes a free basket and lock.

You can also rent bicycles from **Wheels-2-Go!** (5994 Overseas Hwy., Marathon, 305/289-4279, www.wheels-2-go.com, 10am-6pm daily, $10-15 daily, $65 weekly), which also supplies free helmets, locks, baskets, and car racks if needed. The family-owned **Overseas Outfitters** (1700 Overseas Hwy., Marathon, 305/289-1670, www.overseasoutfitters.com, 9am-6pm Mon.-Fri., 9am-3pm Sat., $10 daily, $60 weekly) features a wide array of bicycle rentals and sales, plus repair service. In addition, the vast inventory includes sandals, sunglasses, athletic clothing and shoes, and plenty of other sporting goods, from volleyballs and tennis rackets to pool cues and snorkel masks. Free bicycle delivery is available.

◖ FISHING AND BOATING

While perhaps not as abundant as in Islamorada, fishing charters and boat rentals are available throughout the Middle Keys. If you're new to the area, your best bet would be to stop by one of the many marinas down here. Several area resorts, for instance, feature on-site marinas, where guests and nonguests can book offshore and backcountry fishing charters. Some of these include **Hawks Cay Resort** (61 Hawks Cay Blvd., Duck Key, 305/743-7000, www.hawkscay.com), **Coral Lagoon Resort & Marina** (12399 Overseas Hwy., Marathon, 866/904-1234, www.corallagoonresort.com), and **Captain Pip's Marina & Hideaway** (1410 Overseas Hwy., Marathon, 305/743-4403 or 800/707-1692, www.captainpips.com).

Another option is **Burdine's Waterfront Marina** (1200 Oceanview St., Marathon, 305/743-5317, www.burdineswaterfront.com, 6:30am-6pm daily), which not only assists with fishing charters, but also offers a bait and tackle shop, fishing and boating equipment, picnic supplies, and boat dockage that includes bathrooms, showers, water and electric service, cable television, and laundry facilities. As a bonus, you can relax at the **ChikiTiki Bar & Grille** (11:30am-9pm daily) and choose from cheeseburgers, fresh sandwiches, key lime pie, and cold beer. Return after your fishing trip, and the restaurant will cook your fresh, cleaned catch any way you like it.

The Middle Keys has entirely too many fishing charters to name them all, but there are at least two stand-outs. **Sweet E'Nuf Fishing Charters** (1406 Ocean View Ave., Marathon, 305/610-4778, www.sweetenufcharters.com, $450 per half day, $550 per six hours, $650-850 daily, $100 per additional hour, fuel charges apply) offers both sportfishing and reef-fishing trips while **Flat Out Sportfishing** (941 E. 75th St. Ocean, Marathon, 305/743-7317 or 305/395-1228, www.floridakeysflats.com, trips and rates vary daily) enables anglers to fish for permit, bonefish, tarpon, and shark in the backcountry.

Lady Catherine Charters (305/743-5544, www.diveandfishmarathon.com, daily, $550 per half day, $850 daily), situated at the Seascape Motel and Marina (1275 E. 76th St. OS, Marathon), offers diving excursions and sunset cruises in addition to offshore, reef, and bay fishing, and the *Marathon Lady* (MM 53 OS U.S. 1, Marathon, 305/743-5580, www.marathonlady.net, 8:30am, 12:30pm, 1:30pm, and 5:30pm daily, $45 pp, $5 per rod and reel) provides a party boat fishing experience that's ideal for families on a budget. For all fishing charters, reservations are highly recommended—and, oftentimes, absolutely necessary. Also take note that while the cost for most charters includes a fishing license fee, you should always confirm such details when booking your trip.

If, however, you'd rather venture out on your own, you can simply rent a boat from **Fish 'n Fun Boat & Watersports Rentals** (4590 Overseas Hwy., Marathon, 305/743-2275 or 800/471-3440, www.fishnfunrentals.com, 8am-6pm daily), which offers vessels from 19 feet ($140 per half day, $190 daily, $965 weekly) to 26 feet in length ($235 per half

© DANIEL MARTONE

Fishing from old bridges is a popular activity in the Keys.

day, $285 daily, $1,565 weekly). You can also try **A-Affordable Boat Rentals** (3 N. Conch Ave., Conch Key, 305/304-8733, www.a-affordableboatrentals.com, 10am-5pm daily), which is based near Mile Marker 63 and has three different vessel types ($85-150 daily plus gas), in addition to reef-fishing charters (starting at $325 per four-hour trip). Depth finders, swimming ladders, diver-down flags, VHF radios, maps, anchors, and bimini tops are included with every rental. Other options include **Tropical Boat Rentals** (91 Ave. A, Marathon, 305/481-7006, www.tropicalboatrentals.com, 8am-8pm daily, rates vary daily and weekly) and **Boat Rentals in Paradise** (Captain Hook's Marina & Dive Center, 11833 Overseas Hwy., Marathon, 305/743-2444 or 800/278-4665, www.boatrentalsmarathon.com, 6am-7pm daily, $125-200 per half day, $165-375 daily, $794-1,804 weekly), both of which offer a wide array of vessels, plus delivery service. For live, fresh, or frozen bait, plus fuel, apparel, rod and reel rentals, and other supplies, stop by **Big Time Bait and Tackle** (11499 Overseas Hwy.,

Marathon, 305/289-0199, www.bigtimetackle.com, 6:30am-6pm daily) on Vaca Key before heading out on your fishing trip.

CANOEING AND KAYAKING

As with the rest of the Florida Keys, paddling enthusiasts won't be disappointed in the greater Marathon area. There are not only plenty of nooks and crannies for you to explore by kayak, but also several operators and guides to help you navigate these bountiful waters. At **Long Key State Park** (67400 Overseas Hwy., Long Key, 305/664-4815, www.floridastateparks.org/longkey, 8am-sunset daily, $5 vehicles with 2-8 passengers plus $0.50 pp, $4.50 motorcycles and single-occupant vehicles, $2.50 pedestrians, bikers, and extra passengers), for instance, canoeists can enjoy a leisurely trip along the **Long Key Lakes Canoe Trail** through a shallow lagoon. Canoe rentals ($5 hourly, $10 daily) and a self-guided brochure make this a relatively easy diversion even for novices. Meanwhile, at Hawks Cay Resort, **Sundance Watersports** (61 Hawks Cay Blvd.,

MARATHON

FROM CAPTIVITY TO THE WILD: DOLPHINS IN THE KEYS

The primary mission of **The Turtle Hospital** (2396 Overseas Hwy., Vaca Key, 305/743-2552, www.turtlehospital.org), a nonprofit facility in southern Marathon, is to rescue, rehabilitate, and reintroduce injured sea turtles into the wild. While this particular organization has successfully released more than 1,000 sea turtles into the waters surrounding the Florida Keys, not all captive animals, such as the dolphins that reside at **Dolphin Connection** (61 Hawks Cay Blvd., Duck Key, 305/289-9975 or 888/251-3674, www.dolphinconnection.com) and the **Dolphin Research Center (DRC)** (58901 Overseas Hwy., Grassy Key, 305/289-1121 or 305/289-0002, www.dolphins.org), can or should be released into the wild.

For one thing, reintroducing an animal must be done in a manner that protects wild populations as well as the individual being released. Though the marine mammal community returns hundreds of stranded animals to the wild each year, it can be dangerous to reintroduce one that's been in long-term human care. Such dangers include disease transmission, unwanted genetic exchange, the inability for the released animal to nourish and defend itself, and perhaps most notably, the fact that said animal has lost its natural fear of humans.

Typically, wild animals keep their distance from people, but a marine mammal accustomed to interacting with and being fed by humans can become vulnerable to a variety of problems. Such animals may, for instance, take on some of the following behaviors:

- Spend a lot of time near boats, where they can be struck by hulls and cut by propellers

- Learn to steal fish from fishing lines, thereby ingesting monofilament line and hooks

- Eat inappropriate food, such as spoiled fish, beer, ice cream, or nonedible items

- Get pushy and aggressive when they don't get the handouts they've come to expect

- Encounter people who view them as nuisances, which can get them shot or otherwise injured

In the gulf and ocean waters surrounding the Florida Keys, you'll find plenty of opportunities to see wild dolphins, whether from shore or by boat. Although watching them in their natural habitat can be an amazing experience, it's important that you practice responsible viewing. Approaching such creatures too closely, moving too quickly, or making too much noise can increase the risk of harassment and possibly disrupt natural behaviors like migration, sheltering, breeding, nursing, feeding, and breathing—which is actually against federal law. For more information about the responsible viewing of wild dolphins in Florida Keys National Marine Sanctuary, consult **Dolphin SMART** (www.dolphinsmart.org), a program that promotes these helpful tips:

- **S**taying at least 50 yards from dolphins
- **M**oving away cautiously if dolphins show signs of disturbance
- **A**lways putting your engine in neutral when dolphins are near
- **R**efraining from feeding, touching, or swimming with wild dolphins
- **T**eaching others to be Dolphin SMART

Duck Key, 305/743-0145, www.sundancewatersports.net, 8am-5pm daily) provides single and double kayak rentals by the hour ($20-25), half-day ($40-45), and full day ($65-69). You can also rent single and double kayaks ($17.20-21.50 per two hours) from the ranger station at **Curry Hammock State Park** (56200 Overseas Hwy., Marathon, 305/289-2690, www.

floridastateparks.org/curryhammock, 8am-sunset daily, $5 vehicles with 2-8 passengers plus $0.50 pp, $4.50 motorcycles and single-occupant vehicles, $2.50 pedestrians, bikers, and extra passengers), a wonderful place to paddle in the shallow waters that surround several wooded islands.

On Vaca Key, **Wheels-2-Go!** (5994 Overseas

Hwy., Marathon, 305/289-4279, www.wheels-2-go.com, 10am-6pm daily) offers free delivery for all single and double kayaks, which you can rent by the hour ($10-15), day ($29-55), or week ($129-195). Besides paddleboard rentals ($15 hourly), Wheels-2-Go! also provides three-hour guided kayak tours ($49 pp) through the mangrove islands and backcountry waters. Near Mile Marker 49.5, **Fish 'n Fun Boat & Watersports Rentals** (4590 Overseas Hwy., Marathon, 305/743-2275 or 800/471-3440, www.fishnfunrentals.com, 8am-6pm daily) offers a range of vessels, including single kayaks ($30 per half day, $45 daily) and tandem kayaks ($45 per half day, $60 daily), plus pedal boats and Hobie Cat sailboats. Anchors and diver-down flags are provided with all rentals.

◖ DIVING AND SNORKELING

Whether you're a first-time snorkeler or an experienced scuba diver, you should take some time to explore the waters east of the Middle Keys. Situated in the heart of Vaca Key, **Tilden's Scuba Center** (4650 Overseas Hwy., Marathon, 305/743-7255 or 888/728-2235, www.tildensscubacenter.com, 8am-6pm daily), a full-service diving facility and retail store, provides equipment rentals and Snuba diving ($100-190 pp), a patented deepwater form of snorkeling. In addition, you can take scuba-diving classes through Tilden's, including an introduction course ($126 pp), a first-aid course ($151 pp), an advanced certification course ($350 pp), a rescue diver course ($451 pp), an open-water certification course ($400-600 pp), and several other specialty options; some classes have age restrictions. Through Tilden's, you can also participate in snorkeling ($36-46 pp) and scuba-diving adventures ($61-116 pp), even wreck ($86 pp) and night dives ($81-91 pp).

Other area operators include **Dive Duck Key** (Hawks Cay Resort, 61 Hawks Cay Blvd., Duck Key, 305/289-4931 or 877/386-3483, www.diveduckkey.com, 8am-6pm daily), **A Deep Blue Dive Center** (400 Sadowski Cswy., Key Colony Beach, 800/978-3483, www.adeepbluedive.com, 8am-5pm daily), the **Abyss**

Dive Center (12565 Overseas Hwy., Marathon, 305/743-2126 or 800/457-0134, www.abyssdive.com, 8am-5pm daily), and **Captain Hook's Marina & Dive Center** (11833 Overseas Hwy., Marathon, 305/743-2444 or 800/278-4665, www.captainhooks.com, 6am-7pm daily)—all offer lessons, equipment rentals, and daily snorkeling and diving trips to area reefs. For snorkel-only excursions, consider boarding catamarans like the *Spirit* (MM 47.5 BS U.S. 1, Marathon, 305/289-0614, www.spiritsnorkeling.net) or *Starfish* (MM 47.5 BS U.S. 1, Marathon, 305/481-0407, www.starfishsnorkeling.com); each offers two trips daily (9am and 1pm, $30 pp) as well as seasonal sunset cruises (times vary depending on sunset, $35 pp) and specialty trips.

Of the more than 25 underwater sites that you might see on such diving and snorkeling tours, two of the most popular ones include the **Delta Shoals,** a network of coral canyons that nurture star, elkhorn, and brain coral heads, and **Sombrero Reef,** a spur-and-groove reef formation featuring elkhorn coral and designated by a 142-foot tower. Also in these waters lie two curious shipwrecks: the *Adelaide Baker,* the remains of a three-masted, iron-rigged ship now lying in 25 feet of water, and the *Thunderbolt,* a 188-foot ship sunk in 1986 and now encrusted with coral and sponges, which lure deepwater fish like jacks and angelfish.

A helpful resource for divers is *Teall's Guide: Marathon Key West,* a detailed nautical map prepared by Keys Charts, Inc. that indicates water depths throughout the Middle Keys as well as official dive sites—from East Turtle Shoal to Sombrero Reef.

OTHER OUTDOOR ACTIVITIES

If you're hoping to travel the waters of the Middle Keys on something faster than a kayak, you're in luck. Several area companies provide personal watercraft rentals, which can be ideal transportation for both swimming and snorkeling jaunts. At Hawks Cay Resort, **Sundance Watersports** (61 Hawks Cay Blvd., Duck Key, 305/743-0145, www.sundancewatersports.net) provides Jet Ski rentals (9am-5pm daily,

MANATEE RESCUE

a manatee and her calf

While visiting the Florida Keys, you might be fortunate enough to spy an endangered **West Indian manatee,** also known as a "sea cow," in the warm coastal waters surrounding this archipelago—especially during the winter months, when ocean temperatures drop. A giant yet gentle creature and the state's of-ficial marine mammal, the manatee inhabits shallow estuaries and saltwater bays, feeds on aquatic vegetation, and has sadly been di-minished by boat collisions, propeller injuries, rope and fishing line entanglements, vandal at-tacks, poachers, habitat destruction, oil spills, and cold stress.

© PATRICK M. ROSE/SAVE THE MANATEE CLUB/WWW.SAVETHEMANATEE.ORG

$149 pp) for all ages, though solo riders must be at least 22 years old or alternatively 18-21 years old with a safe boaters card. Sundance Watersports also offers wakeboard experiences (8:30am-5pm daily, $89 per half hour, $129 per 45 minutes, $149 hourly, $199 per 90 minutes, $259 per two hours, $359 per three hours) for riders that are at least 8 years old, plus parasail-ing adventures (9am-5pm daily) for single fliers ($79) or tandem trips ($139). Farther west, you can also try **Fish 'n Fun Boat & Watersports**

Rentals (4590 Overseas Hwy., Marathon, 305/743-2275 or 800/471-3440, www.fishn-funrentals.com, 8am-6pm daily), which pro-vides anchors and diver-down flags with every Yamaha WaveRunner rental ($85 hourly, $275 per half day, or $500 daily).

Those hoping to experience a little less activity, or simply relax after a long day in the sun, should consider making an appoint-ment at the **Calm Waters Spa** (61 Hawks Cay Blvd., Duck Key, 305/289-4810, www.

Although protected from harassment, hunting, capture, or killing by the Marine Mammal Protection Act of 1972 and the Endangered Species Act of 1973, the manatee continues to suffer from human actions—despite the fact that anyone convicted of violating such federal laws may face a fine of up to $100,000 and/or a year in prison. In fact, it's believed by many experts that there are less than 3,300 of these precious mammals left in the wild. Luckily, nonprofit organizations like the **Save the Manatee Club** (SMC, 500 N. Maitland Ave., Maitland, 407/539-0990 or 800/432-5646, www.savethemanatee.org), begun in 1981 by singer-songwriter Jimmy Buffett and former Florida governor and U.S. senator Bob Graham, are doing what they can to protect these endangered creatures and their habitat for future generations.

The **Dolphin Research Center** (DRC, 58901 Overseas Hwy., Grassy Key, 305/289-1121 or 305/289-0002, www.dolphins.org) is actively involved in manatee conservation efforts. The DRC even has a manatee rescue team, nicknamed the Gray Cross, but naturally, the efforts of the SMC and DRC are greatly enhanced by assistance from the public. Here are just a few ways that you can protect endangered manatees and aid in conservation efforts:

- Stay in marked, deepwater channels, where manatees are less likely to be.

- Obey all signage and speed laws when boating in coastal waters.

- Drive slowly and designate a lookout person, who will watch for wildlife, swimmers, boaters, and obstructions.

- Do not enter designated manatee sanctuaries.

- Wear polarized glasses to make it easier to spot the surface swirls that indicate a manatee is near.

- If you see wild manatees, please observe them from the water's surface and at a distance of at least 50 feet.

- Avoid excessive noise and splashing if a manatee appears in your swimming area, and use snorkel gear, in lieu of noisier scuba gear, when observing the manatees.

- Do not touch, chase, feed, or give water to wild manatees, as such actions can put them on the defensive, alter their natural behavior, and ultimately cause them to vacate warmer areas for fear of being harassed.

- Never isolate an individual or separate a mother and her calf.

- If you spot an injured, entangled, tagged, orphaned, or deceased manatee, call the **Florida Fish and Wildlife Conservation Commission** (FWC, 888/404-3922) or use VHF Channel 16 on your marine radio.

- Do not approach or try to assist such a manatee. This can put you at risk and potentially scare away the injured animal.

- Report any criminal activities involving these marine mammals.

MARATHON

hawkscay.com/spa, 9am-7pm daily) at Hawks Cay Resort. Featuring an array of island-inspired manicures and pedicures ($30-140 pp), facials ($70-200 pp), massages ($110-280 pp), body exfoliation treatments ($70-180 pp), and other services, the Calm Waters Spa also offers daily exclusives, such as Sea Stone Saturday when patrons can receive complimentary aromatherapy with every sea stone massage or a complimentary eye treatment with every Sun N' Sea facial. Appointments are highly recommended, and cancellations must be made at least four hours prior to your scheduled treatment time.

HOW ARTIFICIAL REEFS WORK

The 2,900-square-mile Florida Keys National Marine Sanctuary encompasses more than just living coral reefs. This incredible preserve also contains several artificial reefs—essentially, artificially constructed underwater structures that have been utilized around the world for a variety of purposes. Centuries ago, ancient Persians and Romans used such reefs to defend waterways or trap enemy ships. In more recent times, the reefs have been employed to improve fishing, control beach erosion, enhance hydrodynamics for surfing, or as is typically the case in the Florida Keys, promote marine life in areas of featureless bottom.

While artificial reefs can be erected using various materials, including rubble, tires, concrete, and construction debris, those that you'll find in the Florida Keys are usually one of two varieties: actual shipwrecks or vessels intentionally sunk. Once preserved on the sea floor, these structures lure algae, barnacles, oysters, sponges, coral formations, and other invertebrates. The gradual natural accumulation of such diverse marinelife then provides an intricate structure as well as sustenance for a variety of tropical fish, game fish, and other marine creatures.

Naturally, such lively artificial reefs lure both anglers and scuba divers to the Florida Keys. Near Key Largo, for instance, you'll encounter the **USS Spiegel Grove,** a 510-foot Navy transport ship originally launched in November 1955 and prematurely sunk in May 2002 to create an artificial reef. Closer to Key West lies the 522-foot **USNS General Hoyt S. Vandenberg,** a former troop transport ship used during World War II, intentionally sunk in May 2009, and now a marinelife habitat that offers a fascinating look at the developing stages of coral growth. The Marathon area has its share of enticing artificial reefs, including the **Thunderbolt,** a 188-foot steel ship built in 1942, purposely sunk in 1986 four miles south of Key Colony Beach, and now encrusted with coral and sponges, which attract deepwater fish like jacks and angelfish.

It's important to remember that artificial reefs provide a necessary service for the ocean environment, offering a home to countless fish and marine creatures. Though the public is welcome to explore and enjoy them, conservation is still a top priority. To that end, scuba divers should avoid defacing or damaging these reefs and refrain from collecting any natural or historical resources found there. Likewise, anglers should avoid anchoring too close to such reefs and, whenever possible, practice catch-and-release fishing in these areas, which helps to protect fisheries from excessive harvest. If you're not familiar with catch-and-release fishing, follow these simple guidelines:

· Use artificial lures, barbless hooks, and fishing line that's strong enough to bring in the fish quickly.

· Wet your hands before handling the fish, and minimize the time that it's out of the water.

· Be gentle and keep your fingers away from the gills and eyes.

· Measure and photograph the fish while it's in the water.

· Use long-nosed pliers to back the hook out of its entrance hole, and if possible, remove the hook quickly and gently while keeping the fish in the water.

· Cut the line near the hook if the fish is hooked deeply.

· Move the fish back and forth until it is revived and swims from your hands.

For more information about catch-and-release fishing, consult the Marine Fisheries Management Division of the **Florida Fish and Wildlife Conservation Commission** (FWC, 850/487-0554, www.myfwc.com), and for more information about artificial reefs in this region, consult **Florida Keys National Marine Sanctuary** (305/852-7717 or 305/809-4700, www.floridakeys.noaa.gov).

Accommodations

UNDER $100

The **Edgewater Lodge** (65656 Overseas Hwy., Long Key, 305/664-2662, www.edgewaterlodge.com, $89-110 d) offers standard motel rooms, plus efficiencies and two-bedroom cottages with full kitchens. On site amenities include large sun decks, a freshwater pool, a fishing pier, and a boat ramp. In Key Colony Beach, meanwhile, the **Continental Inn** (1121 West Ocean Dr., Key Colony Beach, 305/289-0101 or 800/443-7352, www.marathonresort.com, $95-152 d) invites you to a secluded retreat on the Atlantic Ocean. The one-bedroom and two-bedroom apartments all have full kitchens and cable television. In addition, the inn offers free boat dockage, access to a par-three golf course, and assistance in satisfying all of your water-sports needs.

On Vaca Key, the **Coconut Cay Resort & Marina** (7196 Overseas Hwy., Marathon, 305/289-7672 or 877/354-7356, www.coconutcay.com, $69-179 d) possesses all the charms of a Bahamian resort. The accommodations vary from standard rooms, with one or two double beds and a small refrigerator, to the Coral Cove rental, with three bedrooms and a full kitchen. Pleasantly lined with palm trees, the lovely property features a swimming pool with a 4,000-square-foot sunning deck. Kayak and boat rentals are also available.

On U.S. 1, the clean, affordable units at the **Sea Dell Motel** (5000 Overseas Hwy., Marathon, 305/743-5161 or 800/648-3854, www.seadellmotel.com, $89-159 d) include refrigerators and a variety of bed sizes. The pet-friendly, "waterview" efficiency features two double beds and a full kitchen and is also available for weekly rentals. Situated amid palm trees and lush foliage, this family-friendly motel also offers a heated freshwater pool, picnic and barbecue areas, and high-speed Internet access.

Just east of the Seven Mile Bridge, the **Blue Waters Resort Motel** (2222 Overseas Hwy., Marathon, 800/222-4832, www.bluewatersresortmotel.com, $89-159 d) provides deepwater access to Florida Bay, the Atlantic Ocean, and the only living coral reef in U.S. waters. In addition, the property features efficiencies with full kitchens, a freshwater pool, protected boat dockage, and access to area fishing and water sports.

$100-200

Nestled amid palm trees and flowering plants on the bay side of Long Key, the intimate **Lime Tree Bay Resort** (MM 68.5 BS U.S. 1, Layton, 305/664-4740, www.limetreebayresort.com, rooms $89-129 d, studios $129-184, mini suites $129-194, suites $189-304, townhouses $200-365) features 44 different units, ranging from standard rooms to townhouses. Certain lodgings are pet friendly, for a daily fee of $15 per pet. In addition, guests have free use of the sunning beach, swimming pool and heated spa, boat dockage, wireless Internet access, kayaks, hammocks, and barbecue grills.

The secluded **Conch Key Cottages** (62250 Overseas Hwy., Walker's Island, 305/289-1377 or 800/330-1577, www.conchkeycottages.com, $159-399 d) is a small, tranquil boutique resort far enough from highway to make you feel as though you're on your own private island. Each unit has its own unique ambience, from the stilted two-bedroom cottages to the beachfront bungalows, and each features a well-equipped kitchen and amenities like plush robes, cable television, and free continental breakfasts. Guests are welcome to relax in the gated swimming pool or launch complimentary two-seater kayaks from the private beach for a bird-watching excursion among the mangroves. For a fee, you can also launch and dock your own boat during your stay. In addition, the beach and lounging tiki area are ideal places to watch a gorgeous sunrise or sunset.

On Grassy Key, the **Gulf View Waterfront Resort** (58743 Overseas Hwy., Marathon,

MARATHON

Conch Key Cottages

© LAURA MARTONE

305/289-1414 or 877/289-0111, www.gulfviewwaterfrontresort.com, $110-214 d) features 11 units, ranging from guest rooms with refrigerators to two-bedroom apartments with full kitchens. This pet-friendly resort also has one of the largest freshwater pools in the Florida Keys plus complimentary canoes, kayaks, and pedal boats. If you just want to relax, feel free to take advantage of one of the on-site hammocks or tiki huts. For a no-frills place at a reasonable price, check out the **Yellowtail Inn Beach Resort** (58162 Overseas Hwy., Marathon, 305/743-8400 or 800/605-7475, www.yellowtailinn.com, $100-220 d), also on Grassy Key. The traditional guest rooms have one queen-size bed or two double beds, a small refrigerator, and a microwave oven. The efficiencies and cottages, meanwhile, feature full kitchens, and some even boast private balconies or porches. Other on-site amenities include a small swimming pool, a private beach, and a fishing pier.

Farther west on Grassy Key, the quiet **Rainbow Bend Fishing Resort** (57784 Overseas Hwy., Marathon, 305/289-1505 or 800/929-1505, www.rainbowbend.com, $150-270 d) houses one-bedroom and two-bedroom oceanfront suites and one-bedroom patio efficiencies with full kitchens. As a bonus, a full complimentary American breakfast is served at the Hideaway Café each morning. Given that it's a fishing resort, it's probably no surprise that Rainbow Bend also offers free use of the on-site motorboats. In addition, the staff can easily arrange a fishing charter for you.

As the only "botel" in this part of the Florida Keys, the **Royal Hawaiian Motel/Botel** (12020 Overseas Hwy., Marathon, 305/743-7500, www.royalhawaiianmotelbotel.com, $109-200 d) promises easy access to the Gulf of Mexico and Atlantic Ocean through the Vaca Cut. Each standard room contains two double beds and a small refrigerator while each kitchenette comes with two double beds and a full kitchen. In addition, guests are entitled to free boat dockage during their stay.

If you're looking for a one-stop vacation shop, consider the **Sombrero Resort & Marina**

(19 Sombrero Blvd., Marathon, 800/433-8660, www.sombreroresortmarina.com, $159-299 d), which offers standard rooms and efficiencies. While here, you can satisfy all of your watersports needs at slip #53, where you can rent a canoe, kayak, or fishing boat. After playing a few sets on the lighted tennis courts, take a dip in the heated pool, then sip a piña colada while relaxing at the poolside tiki-hut bar. If you get hungry, you're in luck: The on-site Marathon Pizza & Pasta serves an array of salads, pizzas, and pasta dishes. In addition, the cooking staff will prepare your day's catch any way you like it.

OVER $200

Located on 60-acre Duck Key, █ **Hawks Cay Resort** (61 Hawks Cay Blvd., 305/743-7000 or 888/313-5749, www.hawkscay.com, $225-450 d) almost lulls you into believing you're on a luxurious Caribbean island. With gorgeous rooms and villas, five unique eateries (including Tom's Harbor House), five different swimming pools, a world-class spa, a slew of water-related activities, and its own interactive dolphin facility, Hawks Cay promises a unique all-encompassing experience in the Florida Keys. Beyond well-appointed West Indies-style hotel rooms and suites, the resort offers luxury villas in four separate areas: Sunset Village, Marina Village, Harbor Village, and Sanctuary Village.

Situated on Grassy Key, the **Bonefish Resort** (58070 Overseas Hwy., Marathon, 305/743-7107 or 800/274-9949, www.bonefishresort.com, $299-399 d) offers an assortment of accommodations to suit a variety of vacation needs. Beyond standard guest rooms, efficiencies, and deluxe efficiencies, you'll find deluxe oceanfront efficiencies that offer full kitchens, queen-size beds, and spacious living areas. Anglers will especially appreciate the chance to fish right from the property.

For a taste of Old Florida, head to the **Seashell Beach Resort** (57612 Overseas Hwy., Marathon, 305/289-0265, www.seashellbeachresort.com, $299-399 d), a Grassy Key property that attempts to transport you to the simple, hospitable days of the 1950s. The on-site efficiencies and suites all have full kitchens, and guests will surely enjoy the private beach, the 100-foot and 300-foot fishing docks, and the complimentary kayaks.

A bit off the beaten path lies the stunning **CocoPlum Beach & Tennis Club** (109 Coco Plum Dr., Marathon, 305/743-0240 or 800/228-1587, www.cocoplum.com, $107-425 d), which features 20 separate two-bedroom villas. Each elevated unit consists of three stories: The ground floor has a washer and dryer, plus storage units; the first floor contains the kitchen and dining room, as well as a large screened porch; and the second floor features two bedrooms, two bathrooms, and a living room. Other on-site amenities include a beachfront swimming pool featuring a zero-edge concept plus a nine-slip docking area designed for boats up to 40 feet in length.

The **Coral Lagoon Resort & Marina** (12399 Overseas Hwy., Marathon, 866/904-1234, www.corallagoonresort.com, $299-399 d) presents Conch-style villas and detached marina homes. All of the two-bedroom villas, three-bedroom villas, and single family homes feature 2.5 bathrooms, full kitchens, lower and upper porches, and excellent views, in addition to cable television and free wireless Internet access. The on-site water-sports program offers everything you'll need to fish, snorkel, dive, or simply enjoy the water.

Given that most of its guest rooms are named after fish, it's no wonder that █ **Captain Pip's Marina & Hideaway** (1410 Overseas Hwy., Marathon, 305/743-4403 or 800/707-1692, www.captainpips.com, $225-450 d) specializes in arranging the ultimate fishing vacation. This low-key resort near the western end of Vaca Key even offers a few boats that are free for guests to enjoy, and the adjacent marina features a variety of boat rentals, plus fishing guides that can show you the best spots in the bay, ocean, or reefs. Lodgings range from waterfront guest rooms to comfortable efficiencies to spacious apartments. Other on-site amenities include the popular Porky's Bayside BBQ Restaurant.

MARATHON

CAMPING

Campers will find plenty of options in the Middle Keys. Just south of Islamorada is the **Fiesta Key Recreation Destination** (70001 Overseas Hwy., Fiesta Key, 305/664-4922, www.morganrvresorts.com, $40-100 daily), which offers tent sites, RV sites with water and electricity, and full-hookup RV sites on a day-to-day basis. The 28-acre property also features an Olympic-size freshwater pool and a complete marina with available slip rentals.

Long Key State Park (67400 Overseas Hwy., Long Key, 305/664-4815, www.floridastateparks.org/longkey, 8am-sunset daily, $5 vehicles with 2-8 passengers plus $0.50 pp, $4.50 motorcycles and single-occupant vehicles, $2.50 pedestrians, bikers, and extra passengers) presents 60 campsites ($36 daily), each with water and electricity, overlooking the Atlantic Ocean. The park also offers a canoe trail and two land-based nature trails. As a bonus to campers, the beach is only open to those staying in the campground, so you'll surely find this to be one of the more private beaches in the Keys. Reservations can be made up to 11 months in advance through **ReserveAmerica** (800/326-3521, www.reserveamerica.com).

On Grassy Key, the **Jolly Roger Travel Park** (59275 Overseas Hwy., Marathon, 800/995-1525, www.jrtp.com, $50-75 daily) has full-hookup RV sites, van sites with optional water and electric service, and tent spaces. The park offers daily, weekly, and monthly rates. On-site amenities include high-speed wireless Internet access, cable television hookups, snorkeling and swimming areas, a boat dock with slip rentals, and a free boat ramp for guests.

The **Grassy Key RV Park & Resort** (58671 Overseas Hwy., Marathon, 305/289-1606, www.grassykeyrvpark.com, $50-110 daily, $300-715 weekly, $720-2,310 monthly) accepts RVs of all sizes, including the "big rig" motor coaches. The waterfront, premium, and standard sites are all equipped with water, sewer access, 30/50-amp electricity, and cable television. Other on-site amenities include a freshwater pool, a lounging beach, a clubhouse, laundry facilities, and new boat dockage ($1.25 per foot daily, $6 per foot weekly, $10 per foot monthly) that allows access to both the Gulf of Mexico and the Atlantic Ocean. Pets are welcome here with some restrictions. Please be aware that camping rates can vary greatly depending on the specific site and season; also note that rates for stays longer than a month are also available.

Another state park option is **Curry Hammock State Park** (56200 Overseas Hwy., Marathon, 305/289-2690, www.floridastateparks.org/curryhammock, 8am-sunset daily, $5 vehicles with 2-8 passengers plus $0.50 pp, $4.50 motorcycles and single-occupant vehicles, $2.50 pedestrians, bikers, and extra passengers), which has a 28-site campground ($36-39 daily) equipped with picnic tables, charcoal grills, water service, and 20/30/50-amp electricity. A dump station is available at the park. No motorized vessels can be launched here—only kayaks and canoes. Leashed pets are allowed in the campground, but not on the beach. Although bikers, anglers, swimmers, paddlers, and picnickers favor this park, Curry Hammock is especially popular with birding enthusiasts, who will often spot herons, egrets, ibises, plovers, and sanderlings along the shore. Reservations can be made up to 11 months in advance through **ReserveAmerica** (800/326-3521, www.reserveamerica.com).

On the western end of Marathon, beside the Seven Mile Bridge, you'll spot the **Knights Key RV Resort & Marina** (1 Knight's Key Blvd., Knight's Key, 305/743-4343 or 800/348-2267, www.keysdirectory.com/knightskeycampground, $46-93 daily), which has provided affordable accommodations here since 1962. Offering spacious RV sites with lovely ocean views, this breezy campground also provides tent sites ($35-45 daily), boat dockage, a private beach, and easy access to the Pigeon Key ferry.

Food

SEAFOOD

It's probably no surprise that the Middle Keys offer a wealth of seafood options. The laid-back **Island Fish Co. Restaurant & Tiki Bar** (12648 Overseas Hwy., Marathon, 305/743-4191, www.islandfishco.com, 11:30am-close daily, $8-32), for instance, features one of the largest menus in the Keys, including burgers, sandwiches, fried island platters, and fried key lime pie, among other items. The house specialties feature some winning choices, among them a particularly tasty Caribbean dish of sea-soned pan-seared grouper served with island rice, black beans, and pineapple salsa. If you favor alcoholic drinks, be sure to try the key lime pie martini, in a glass that's cleverly ringed with graham cracker crumbs. The spacious is-land-style restaurant offers rustic indoor seating as well as outdoor seating alongside the water.

© DANIEL MARTONE

the delectable display case at Fish Tales Market and Eatery

If you return from a long day of fishing empty-handed, never fear. Less than a mile west of the Island Fish Co., the family-owned **Fish Tales Market and Eatery** (11711 Overseas Hwy., Marathon, 305/743-9196 or 888/662-4822, www.floridalobster.com, 10am-6pm Mon.-Sat., $4-10) offers plenty of fresh, locally caught seafood, from fish and lobster to shrimp and stone crabs. In addition, the market offers hand-cut steaks, plus a whole slew of spices, spreads, rubs, and hot sauces, not to mention suggested recipes. Before or after making your purchases, be sure to stay for a meal in the cozy, inexpensive eatery; if you're a seafood lover, you surely won't regret sampling everything from the red conch chowder to steamed shrimp to a grilled yellowfin tuna sandwich.

If you have a hankering for conch—in-deed a popular item in southern Florida—there's probably no place in the Keys that boasts as many conch dishes than the aptly named **Cracked Conch Cafe** (4999 Overseas Hwy., Marathon, 305/743-2233, www.con-chcafe.com, 9:30am-10:30pm Mon.-Thurs., 7am-10:30pm Fri.-Sun., $16-28), just west of the Crane Point nature preserve. Popular with locals for more than three decades, this casual eatery offers delicious conch fritters, both cream-based and tomato-based conch chowders, and several conch specialties, in-cluding "conch in the weeds," a conch dish that features spinach and mushrooms. With a relaxing outdoor patio and a simple interior that sports an "old Florida" vibe, the Cracked Conch even relies on ceiling fans—in lieu of an air conditioner—to keep the joint cool dur-ing the warm months.

Another popular seafood eatery is the **Keys Fisheries Market & Marina** (3502 Gulfview Ave., Marathon, 305/743-4353 or 866/743-4353, www.keysfisheries.com, 11am-9pm daily, $9-29), which lies roughly half a mile west of the Cracked Conch and features picnic tables overlooking the marina. Try the famous lobster scrumptious blue cheese chips at Sparky's Landing

© LAURA MARTONE

Reuben, the key lime scallops over linguini, or the whiskey peppercorn snapper.

For a more eclectic menu, head to the spacious **《Castaway Waterfront Restaurant & Sushi Bar** (1406 Oceanview Ave., Marathon, 305/743-6247, www.jonesn4sushi.com, 11am-10pm daily, $14-40). Prior to a massive renovation that dramatically expanded and modernized the space, it was the oldest intact building on the island. Owned for the past decade by ever-present husband-and-wife duo John and Arlene, Castaway can get fairly crowded with tourists and locals (including other area restaurant owners) during the high season, despite its hidden location on a side street in western Marathon. The menu boasts such tasty dishes as the hogfish stuffed with shrimp and scallops, premium queen conch lightly egg-battered and fried, and sautéed alligator tail smothered in mushrooms and scallions—not to mention a full lineup of top-notch sushi. Beyond the incredible food and outdoor seating alongside the adjacent marina, Castaway even offers a casual outer bar where

you can listen to live music before or after your meal.

AMERICAN

South of Mile Marker 53.5, you'll spot **《Sparky's Landing** (400 Sadowski Cswy., Key Colony Beach, 305/289-7445, www. sparkyslanding.com, 11am-10pm daily, $7-29), a popular local hangout situated beside the Key Colony Beach Marina. This rustic, unassuming eatery offers an extremely eclectic menu, with everything from standard burgers to bacon-wrapped scallops. Even the appetizers are varied, ranging from shrimp pot stickers to blue cheese chips, essentially homemade potato chips covered in blue cheese and drizzled with an herb vinaigrette. The shrimp and bacon pizza, fish tacos, and key lime pie are also worth a try. Like several other restaurants in the Florida Keys, Sparky's promises to cook whatever you catch. As a bonus, the low-key eatery features live music Wednesday-Saturday and hosts the annual Leon Shell Memorial Sailfish Tournament.

©DANIEL MARTONE

Willie B. Bacon oversees the tiki-covered patio of the popular Stuffed Pig.

Not far away, you'll encounter **Leigh Ann's Coffee House, Wine & Cheese Shop** (301 Sadowski Cswy., Key Colony Beach, 305/743-2001, www.leighannscoffeehouse.com, 7am-5pm Mon.-Fri., 7am-3pm Sat., 8am-noon Sun., $4-12), which recently relocated from its longstanding spot on the Overseas Highway. Operated by Leigh Ann and her daughters and highlighting the recipes of Leigh Ann's mother, this quaint, ecofriendly eatery serves freshly baked pastries for breakfast and scrumptious salads, like the chicken and tuna with mango slaw, for lunch. If you have a chance, be sure to sample the Italian-style spinach pie during your visit.

While the decor at **Herbies Restaurant** (6350 Overseas Hwy., Marathon, 305/743-6373, 11am-11pm Tues.-Sat., $9-22) may not win any Vaca Key eatery awards anytime soon, it's the delicious food that ensures return customers. Among the offerings is one of the best conch chowders in the Florida Keys, plus popular dishes like sautéed fish

and a burger with onion rings. Herbies only accepts cash.

Farther west, **The Hurricane** (4650 Overseas Hwy., Marathon, 305/743-2220, www.hurricaneblues.com, 11am-midnight daily, $7-19) serves salads, sandwiches, and entrées like the Hurricane Chicken, topped with shrimp and crabmeat stuffing. In addition, you can enjoy live music here Tuesday-Saturday.

Even farther west, you can relish a dynamite breakfast at ◖**The Stuffed Pig** (3520 Overseas Hwy., Marathon, 305/743-4059, www.thestuffedpig.com, 5am-2pm Mon.-Sat., 6am-noon Sun., $6-18), which offers lunch, too. Locals especially favor this casual joint, where you dine indoors, on the side patio, or beneath the enormous tiki hut. Winning items include the blueberry pancakes, the popular Pig's Breakfast, and the seafood Benedict, which is served with two poached eggs, crab, shrimp, and scallops.

Although traditional Florida Keys-style dishes are available at **Porky's Bayside BBQ Restaurant** (1410 Overseas Hwy., Marathon, 305/289-2065, www.porkysbaysidebbq.com, 11am-10pm daily, $9-18), it's the exceptional barbecue, as the name indicates, that separates this popular eatery from other area restaurants. While here, try the Citrus Mojo Marinade Cuban Pork or, if you've come with a friend, the BBQ Dinner for Two, which includes chicken, spareribs, and pork or beef, plus your choice of four sides.

If you're planning an afternoon trip to Pigeon Key or the Lower Keys, you might want to head to the well-favored **Seven Mile Grill** (1240 Overseas Hwy., Marathon, 305/743-4481, www.7-mile-grill.com, 7am-9pm daily, $4-11), located just east of the bridge that inspired its name. The friendly staff here will make you feel like a regular, and the food is prepared and served with little delay. For more than 45 years, the Seven Mile Grill has offered large portions at reasonable prices. The extensive menu features everything from three-egg omelets to deluxe cheeseburgers to seafood baskets—ideal for breakfast, lunch, or dinner. Consider trying

MARATHON

the excellent conch chowder before heading out on your next adventure.

LATIN AND MEXICAN

Hawks Cay Resort boasts several dining options, including the Latin-inspired **Alma** (61 Hawks Cay Blvd., Duck Key, 305/743-7000, www.hawkscay.com, 6pm-close daily, $24-41), a festive upscale restaurant featuring the culinary creations of Executive Chef Juan Natal, whose Puerto Rican roots have certainly shaped the menu. Dishes evolve daily depending on the availability of fresh seafood and other ingredients, but typical options may range from the savory seafood paella to the grilled churrasco with boniato mash, cilantro aioli, and a tomato and avocado salad. The restaurant also boasts an extensive selection of wine and rum. Although friends and colleagues often congregate here, Alma is also an ideal place for a romantic meal, particularly if enjoyed in an intimate banquette or on the candlelit veranda.

Lencho's Authentic Mexican & Seafood Restaurant (1622 Overseas Hwy., Marathon, 305/743-4500, www.lenchorestaurant.com, 11am-10pm daily, $9-19) is considered by many locals to be the best Mexican eatery in the Keys. With dine-in and take-out options, this popular joint features such winners as chimichangas, enchiladas, and unique entrées like the El Oaxaqueno, a flame-grilled New York steak served with two flautas covered in mole sauce.

EUROPEAN

A wonderful place for a romantic meal, the **Hideaway Café** (57784 Overseas Hwy.,

Marathon, 305/289-1554, www.hideawaycafe.com, 7am-5pm Mon.-Fri., 7am-3pm Sat., 8am-noon Sun., $7-19), located at the Rainbow Bend Fishing Resort on Grassy Key, offers both a unique menu and a relaxing atmosphere. Try the escargot appetizer and the Hideaway seafood special: the day's catch sautéed with shrimp and scallops in a scampi sauce. As an alternative, try the filet medallions à la "beurre noir," essentially slices of filet mignon flambéed with cognac, garlic, and shrimp. Enjoy your meal while gazing out at the palm-lined ocean from this true island "hideaway."

Head to Key Colony Beach for a tasty espresso martini at the **Key Colony Inn** (700 W. Ocean Dr., 305/743-0100, www.kcinn.com, 11am-9:30pm daily, $12-29), where you'll find plenty of seafood, often merged with French and Italian cuisine. The New Brunswick baked sea scallops dish, for instance, features bacon in a light cream sauce with a hint of rosemary, and the baked lasagna seafood contains layers of noodles, local snapper, scallops, shrimp, cheese, and sauce.

PIZZA

Even in the seafood capital of the world, you might sometimes have a craving for pizza. Luckily, **Upper Crust Pizza, Inc.** (3740 Overseas Hwy., Marathon, 305/743-7100, www.uppercrustpizzainc.com, 11am-11pm daily, $8-20) can satisfy any such craving. Situated on Vaca Key, this roomy, super casual joint serves traditional Italian dishes in addition to pizza, and if you'd rather not eat out, you're in luck. Upper Crust happily offers both take-out and delivery service.

Information and Services

INFORMATION

For brochures, maps, and other information about Marathon and the Middle Keys, stop by the **Greater Marathon Chamber of Commerce and Visitors Center** (12222 Overseas Hwy., Marathon, 305/743-5417 or 800/262-7284, www.floridakeysmarathon.com, 9am-5pm daily), near Mile Marker 53 on the bay side, or consult the **Monroe County Tourist Development Council** (1201 White St., Ste. 102, Key West, 305/296-1552 or 800/352-5397, www.fla-keys.com, 9am-5pm Mon.-Fri.). For government-related issues, contact the **City of Marathon** (9805 Overseas Hwy., Marathon, 305/743-0033, www.ci.marathon.fl.us, 8am-5pm Mon.-Fri.) or the **Monroe County offices** (1100 Simonton St., Key West, 305/294-4641 or 305/743-0079, www.monroecounty-fl.gov, 8am-5pm Mon.-Fri.).

For local news, consult the *Marathon & Big Pine Free Press* (www.keysnews.com) and **The Weekly Newspapers** (www.keysweekly.com). The daily *Miami Herald* (www.miamiherald.com), the daily *The Key West Citizen* (www.keysnews.com), and the biweekly *Florida Keys Keynoter* (www.keysnet.com) are also available throughout the Keys.

In Marathon, you'll also have access to several radio stations, including **WGMX** (94.3 FM) and **WAVK** (97.7 FM), which offer an adult contemporary format, as well as **WFFG** (1300 AM), which provides news and talk radio.

SERVICES

Money

For banking needs, stop by one of the two local branches of **Capital Bank** (800/639-5111, www.capitalbank-us.com). There's one in Marathon Shores (11401 Overseas Hwy., 305/743-7845, 9am-4pm Mon.-Thurs., 9am-6pm Fri., extended drive-through hours) and one in Marathon (2348 Overseas Hwy., 305/743-0072, 9am-4pm Mon.-Thurs., 9am-6pm Fri., extended drive-through hours). You can also visit the **First State Bank of the Florida Keys** (6900 Overseas Hwy., Marathon, 305/289-4393, www.keysbank.com, 9am-4pm Mon.-Thurs., 9am-6pm Fri., extended drive-through hours).

Mail

For shipping, faxing, copying, and other business-related services, visit **The UPS Store** (5409 Overseas Hwy., Marathon, 305/743-2005, www.theupsstore.com, 8am-6pm Mon.-Fri., 9am-5pm Sat.). You can also package and ship items at the four area **post offices** (800/275-8777, www.usps.com). There's one on Long Key (68340 Overseas Hwy., 305/664-4112, 8am-4:30pm Mon.-Fri.), another in Marathon Shores (11400 Overseas Hwy., Ste. 120, 305/743-6050, 9:30am-12:30pm Mon.-Fri.), one in Key Colony Beach (600 W. Ocean Dr., 305/743-2249, 11am-1pm and 2pm-4pm Mon.-Fri.), and another in Marathon (5171 Overseas Hwy., 305/743-5238, 8:30am-5pm Mon.-Fri., 9am-noon Sat.).

Groceries and Supplies

For groceries, baked goods, and other supplies, head to the nearest **Winn-Dixie** (5585 Overseas Hwy., Marathon, 305/743-3636, www.winndixie.com, 7am-10pm daily), not far from the local **Publix** (5407 Overseas Hwy., Marathon, 305/289-2920, www.publix.com, 7am-10pm Mon.-Sat., 7am-9pm Sun.), which includes an on-site pharmacy (305/289-3192, 9am-9pm Mon.-Fri., 9am-7pm Sat., 10am-5pm Sun.). The area also features a **CVS/pharmacy** (5575 Overseas Hwy., Marathon, 305/743-9484, www.cvs.com, 8am-10pm daily), which offers limited supplies as well as an on-site pharmacy (8am-8pm Mon.-Fri., 8am-7pm Sat., 9am-6pm Sun.).

Laundry

If you need to clean some clothes during your trip, you'll find coin-operated machines at **Coyne's Laundry** (11201 Overseas Hwy.,

MARATHON

Marathon, 305/743-3244, 9am-7pm Mon.-Sat., 9am-4pm Sun.).

Internet Access

For wireless Internet access, consult your hotel or resort, as many offer free access nowadays, or you can typically use the Internet at the **Marathon Branch Library** (3251 Overseas Hwy., Marathon, 305/743-5156, www.keyslibraries.org, 9:30am-6pm Tues. and Thurs.-Fri., 9:30am-8pm Wed., 10am-6pm Sat.).

Emergency Services

In case of an emergency that requires police, fire, or ambulance services, dial **911** from any cell or public phone. For nonemergency assistance, contact the **Monroe County Sheriff's Office** (Marathon Substation, 3103 Overseas Hwy., Marathon, 305/289-2430, www.keysso.net, 8am-5pm Mon.-Fri.). For medical assistance, consult the **Fishermen's Hospital** (3301 Overseas Hwy., Marathon, 305/743-5533, www.fishermenshospital.com). Foreign visitors seeking help with directions, medical concerns, business issues, law enforcement needs, or other problems can receive **multilingual tourist assistance** (800/771-5397) 24 hours daily.

Getting There and Around

GETTING THERE
By Air

Although you can fly small planes directly into **Florida Keys Marathon Airport (MTH)** (9400 Overseas Hwy., Marathon, 305/289-6060), most travelers reach the Middle Keys by first flying into one of the other area airports, including **Fort Lauderdale-Hollywood International Airport (FLL)** (100 Terminal Dr., Fort Lauderdale, 866/435-9355, www.broward.org/airport), **Miami International Airport (MIA)** (2100 NW 42nd Ave., Miami, 305/876-7000 or 800/825-5642, www.miami-airport.com), or **Key West International Airport (EYW)** (3491 S. Roosevelt Blvd., Key West, 305/809-5200 or 305/296-5439, www.keywestinternationalairport.com). From there you can rent a vehicle from agencies like **Avis** (800/331-1212, www.avis.com), **Budget** (800/527-0700, www.budget.com), **Enterprise** (800/325-8007, www.enterprise.com), **Hertz** (800/654-3131, www.hertz.com), or **Thrifty** (800/367-2277, www.thrifty.com) to reach the Marathon area.

By Bus or Train

The **Miami-Dade County Metrobus** (305/891-3131, www.miamidade.gov/transit) operates the **301 Dade-Monroe Express** between Florida City and Marathon (5:15am-8:40pm daily, $2.35 per one-way trip), with several stops in between. In addition, the **Key West Department of Transportation (KWDoT)** (305/600-1455, www.kwtransit.com, $3 per ride, $16 weekly, $50 monthly) provides bus service from Key West to Marathon between 5am and 11pm daily. Reduced fares may apply for students under 22 years old, senior citizens over 59 years old, military personnel, and disabled individuals.

In addition, **Greyhound** (800/231-2222, www.greyhound.com) offers bus service to Marathon (12222 Overseas Hwy., 305/296-9073). **Amtrak** (800/872-7245, www.amtrak.com), however, only provides train service as far south as Miami. Of course, you can always rent a car or hop a shuttle to reach the Florida Keys.

Transport from Airports and Stations

If you arrive in the Fort Lauderdale-Miami area by plane, bus, or train—or Key West by plane or bus—you can either rent a car or hire a shuttle service to reach the Marathon area. Some of these companies include **Keys Shuttle** (305/289-9997 or 888/765-9997, www.keysshuttle.com, $70-80 per shared ride, $300-350 for exclusive service) and **Keys Tropical**

MARATHON

Transportation (305/852-3595, www.keystropicaltransportation.com, starting at $130 or $165 per ride, depending on the airport of origin), both of which provide service from the Miami and Fort Lauderdale airports. Another option is **SuperShuttle** (305/871-2000 or 954/764-1700, www.supershuttle.com, $255 per ride for up to 10 passengers), which only serves visitors flying into Miami. In addition, you can rely on **TO'n'FRO** (305/393-0955, www.tonfro.com, $55-65 per shared van ride, $190-200 per luxury sedan ride), a personalized van and car service that offers transportation between the Miami and Fort Lauderdale airports and any destination in the Keys.

By Car
To reach the Middle Keys from Miami, simply head south on U.S. 1 (Overseas Hwy.), drive through Key Largo and Islamorada, and continue toward your destination. If you're headed from the Everglades via I-75 (Everglades Pkwy.), drive south on U.S. 27, veer right onto S.R. 997 (Krome Ave.), and follow the signs to U.S. 1. From U.S. 41 (Tamiami Trl.) in the Everglades, head south on S.R. 997 and continue toward U.S. 1. If you arrive during the peak season (Dec.-Apr.), be sure to call **511** for an up-to-the-minute traffic report.

GETTING AROUND
By Car
The best way to travel through the Middle Keys is by car, truck, RV, or motorcycle—all of which offer easy access to U.S. 1 as well as the side roads, such as Sombrero Beach Road.

By Taxi
Taxicab companies such as **On Time Taxi** (305/289-5656, $4 per pickup, $1 per mile

after initial two miles) can help you get around the Middle Keys.

By Bicycle or Boat
While you can certainly traverse the Middle Keys by bicycle, the region's sprawling nature and numerous bridges make it challenging for novice riders. Nevertheless, it's a lovely, eco-friendly way to experience the Middle Keys. Between Mile Marker 58 and Mile Marker 40, you'll even find an 11-mile biking path, plus a wide shoulder along the Seven Mile Bridge. Bicycles can be rented from **Bike Marathon Bike Rental** (305/743-3204, www.bikemarathonbikerentals.com, 8am-6pm daily, $35 weekly, $99 monthly), Marathon's first and oldest bicycle rental company, which also offers free delivery and free pickup service in Marathon and Key Colony Beach.

Of course, you can also experience the Middle Keys by boat. Having your own vessel makes navigating these waters even easier, and you'll find no shortage of boat ramps and marina slips in the Marathon area, a region popular among boating enthusiasts. If you'd rather rent a boat or kayak for the day, stop by **Fish 'n Fun Boat & Watersports Rentals** (4590 Overseas Hwy., Marathon, 305/743-2275 or 800/471-3440, www.fishnfunrentals.com, 8am-6pm daily), near Mile Marker 49.5, which offers a range of vessels, including single and tandem kayaks ($30-45 per half day, $45-60 daily), personal watercraft ($85 hourly, $275 per half day, $500 daily), 19-foot fishing boats ($140 per half day, $190 daily, $965 weekly), and 26-foot fishing boats ($235 per half day, $285 daily, $1,565 weekly). While Fish 'n Fun provides kayak and personal watercraft rentals for up to a full day, you can rent six varieties of fishing boats on a day-to-day or weekly basis.

MARATHON

BIG PINE AND THE LOWER KEYS

Stretching from Little Duck Key to Boca Chica Key, the Lower Keys (which for most residents don't include Key West and the Dry Tortugas) are the largest and least developed part of the Florida Keys archipelago. Composed of numerous keys and island clusters, the Lower Keys possess a far more sedate vibe than that of Key West to the south. In this region, beaches, campgrounds, and a host of animals—including birds, snakes, alligators, rabbits, and raccoons—take precedence over tourists and museums, making the Lower Keys the ideal place to escape from the world for a while, even in the winter months, when snowbirds help to increase the population.

West of the Seven Mile Bridge, the first major stop, Bahia Honda State Park, is one of the most popular parks in the Keys. Its three sandy beaches, with access to the Atlantic Ocean and the Gulf of Mexico, are routinely voted some of the best in the state and are favored among photographers. Soft, white sand and calm, shallow waters make this the perfect place for swimmers, snorkelers, and kayakers, though seaweed is often an issue. Fishing, boating, biking, and hiking are also preferred pastimes here.

Among the remaining islands, Big Pine Key boasts the lion's share of diversions. From here visitors can take biking and diving trips, glass-bottom boat tours, deep-sea fishing charters, full-day kayaking adventures, and island excursions. Also on Big Pine lies part of the 84,351-acre National Key Deer Refuge, established in the late 1950s to preserve the

HIGHLIGHTS

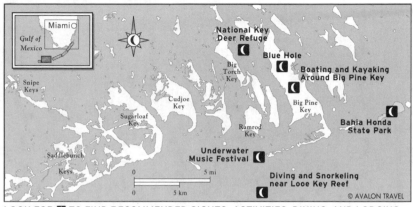

© AVALON TRAVEL

LOOK FOR ◖ TO FIND RECOMMENDED SIGHTS, ACTIVITIES, DINING, AND LODGING.

◖ **Bahia Honda State Park:** This recreational treasure, which encompasses all of Bahia Honda Key, offers ideal waters for recreation and also boasts some of the most photographed beaches in the Florida Keys (page 194).

◖ **National Key Deer Refuge:** Established in 1957, this 84,351-acre sanctuary provides critical habitat for hundreds of native and migratory species, including the diminutive Key deer (page 196).

◖ **Blue Hole:** Once an active limestone quarry, this tranquil, well-visited body of water nurtures an array of creatures, from green herons to turtles and alligators (page 197).

◖ **Underwater Music Festival:** For three decades, this whimsical event has welcomed hundreds of divers and snorkelers to an underwater concert while promoting the preservation of the coral reef ecosystem (page 200).

◖ **Boating and Kayaking Around Big Pine Key:** Experience the backcountry islands, bountiful waters, and amazing creatures of the Lower Keys by kayak, skiff, powerboat, or glass-bottom catamaran (page 202).

◖ **Diving and Snorkeling near Looe Key Reef:** This classic spur-and-groove formation is home to parrotfish, barracuda, moray eels, varied sharks, and other marinelife (page 204).

dwindling population of the petite Key deer. Nowadays this amazing refuge protects several other threatened plants and animals as well, many of which you might spot at the Blue Hole, the largest freshwater source in the Keys.

While adjacent Little Torch Key offers access to the exclusive Little Palm Island Resort & Spa, it's still a laid-back locale and a terrific jumping-off point for scuba divers and snorkelers. Part of Florida Keys National Marine Sanctuary, the incredible Looe Key

Reef—named after a long-ago shipwreck—sits amid several historical wreck sites and is home to the fascinating Underwater Music Festival every July. Other keys—such as Ramrod, Summerland, Cudjoe, and Sugarloaf—offer their own share of diversions, from fishing charters to kayaking excursions. Besides, even though outdoor diversions are paramount here, you're not so far away from Key West that you can't make a day trip to the bars, museums, and people-watching hot spots that await.

BIG PINE AND THE LOWER KEYS

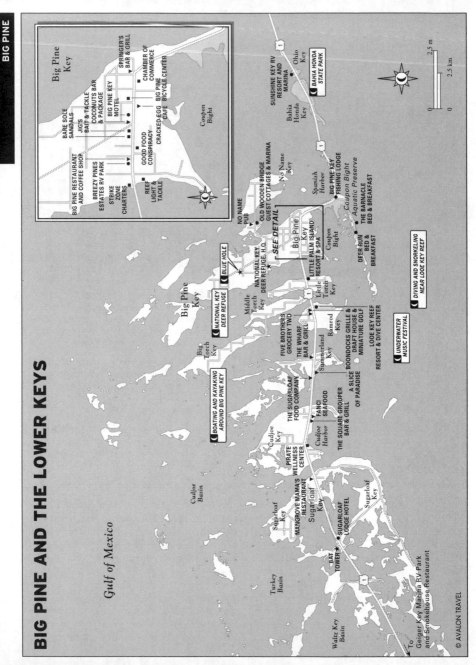

© AVALON TRAVEL

HISTORY

As with other parts of the Florida Keys, it's believed that American Indians, specifically tribes like the Calusa and Tequesta, were the original inhabitants of the Lower Keys. The memoirs of a shipwrecked Spaniard, dated in the mid-1500s, have revealed the presence of such tribes, who evidently subsisted on fish, lobster, turtles, snails, raccoons, and manatees.

Unfortunately, little is known about the Lower Keys until the 1800s, long after many of the tribes had either moved or died out. Only the remnants of shipwrecks, such as the HMS *Looe*, which crashed against the eponymously named Looe Key Reef in February 1744, sheds some light on the 18th century. After all, the lack of bridges, the presence of mosquitoes, and the inability to make a living in the untamed Lower Keys made it difficult to settle here.

During the second half of the 19th century, however, settlements began to expand on places like No Name Key—filled both with wealthy part-time residents of Key West, who would travel by boat to their country homes in the Lower Keys, and with hardy full-time inhabitants, who managed to eke out a living by farming, fishing, collecting sponges, and producing charcoal. For instance, Sugarloaf Key—once called Glenn Key and later Perkey—became a grower and supplier of sugarloaf pineapples.

With the fulfillment of Henry Flagler's lifelong dream to construct an Overseas Railroad, linking the Florida Keys to the mainland, the Lower Keys finally began to flourish. Between 1905 and 1912, during construction of the railroad, buildings were being erected in the Lower Keys to serve as train stations, residences for station agents, and homes for settlers. The railroad took seven years, much of Flagler's fortune, and hundreds of workers to build. It operated from 1912 until it was destroyed by the terrible Labor Day Hurricane of 1935. Soon afterward, what remained of the railroad was sold to the State of Florida. During its operation, though, islands like Bahia Honda Key became legitimate settlements.

In the years that followed the destruction of the Overseas Railroad, developments such as the state-funded Overseas Highway (which was initially an arduous combination of roads and ferries), the 1957 establishment of the National Key Deer Refuge, and the 1981 designation of Looe Key National Marine Sanctuary helped to bring attention to the Lower Keys. Still, in many areas this part of the Florida Keys is even less developed and less populated than it was in the early 20th century.

PLANNING YOUR TIME

Although many travelers simply pass through this region on their way to Key West, the Lower Keys are definitely worth a look. You might not find museums or historical districts here, but you'll certainly encounter a wealth of outdoor sights and activities, from underwater coral reefs to fishing charters to kayaking excursions. While the attractions and lodgings are spread across numerous islands, it's not terribly difficult to traverse this region by car, especially since the Overseas Highway links several of the main islands, such as Bahia Honda Key, Big Pine Key, and Sugarloaf Key. Still, some places, like the No Name Pub, can be a bit challenging to find.

Most people only need a day or two to hit the highlights of this region, such as Bahia Honda State Park and the Blue Hole. The length of your stay, however, depends upon your chosen activities. Fishing, kayaking, snorkeling, and diving—all popular activities here—could easily extend your trip to a full week. Such activities might also determine when you choose to visit.

Luckily, you won't often face crowds and congestion in the Lower Keys, unless you head to a Bahia Honda beach on a particularly warm, sunny day—or hope to reach Key West in a timely manner during a popular event. Also, if you're a novice to certain activities, such as scuba diving, you might want to allow for proper instruction time. Regarding other safety issues, crime isn't a major problem in the Lower Keys, but you should still stay alert in the more isolated areas.

For more information about Big Pine Key and the Lower Keys, consult the **Monroe**

County Tourist Development Council (1201 White St., Ste. 102, Key West, 305/296-1552 or 800/352-5397, www.fla-keys.com, 9am-5pm Mon.-Fri.) and the **Lower Keys Chamber of Commerce** (P.O. Box 430511, Big Pine Key, 305/872-2411 or 800/872-3722, www.lower-keyschamber.com, 9am-5pm Mon.-Fri., 9am-3pm Sat.).

Sights

LITTLE DUCK KEY

Just past the western end of Seven Mile Bridge lies **Little Duck Key** (www.littleduckkey.com), a small island that features **Veterans Memorial Park** (MM 40 BS/OS U.S. 1, Little Duck Key, 305/292-4431, 24 hours daily, free), formerly known as Little Duck Key County Park. Although most people bypass this key for the well-visited Bahia Honda State Park farther down the Overseas Highway, it's a pleasant stop for those who appreciate a quiet beach, with access to the Gulf of Mexico and the Atlantic Ocean. Amenities here include picnic pavilions, grills, restrooms, a small parking lot, and a paved boat ramp. Just remember that dogs must be leashed at all times, and no overnight parking is allowed.

◖ BAHIA HONDA STATE PARK

From the Seven Mile Bridge, you'll cross three tiny islands—Little Duck Key, Missouri Key, and Ohio Key—before encountering one of southern Florida's recreational jewels. Encompassing all of Bahia Honda Key, the 524-acre **Bahia Honda State Park** (36850 Overseas Hwy., Bahia Honda Key, 305/872-2353 or 305/872-3210, www.floridastateparks.org/bahiahonda or www.bahiahondapark.com, 8am-sunset daily, $8 vehicles with 2-8 passengers plus $0.50 pp, $4.50 motorcycles and single-occupant vehicles, $2.50 pedestrians, bikers, and extra passengers) features three breezy, coconut palm-studded beaches that together offer access to the Atlantic Ocean as well as the Gulf of Mexico. The smallest beach, Calusa, provides several small picnic pavilions and shares a bathhouse and outdoor freshwater showers with Loggerhead

Beach, considered the shallowest of the three. Sandspur, the largest and most popular beach, has three picnic pavilions, plus restrooms with outdoor showers. It's a perfect place to relax, enjoy the warm waters, and watch one of the Keys' famous sunsets.

Ideal for swimmers, the park also provides kayak and snorkel gear rentals, a concession building, three campgrounds, vacation cabins, and two-hour **snorkeling excursions** (305/872-3954, 9:30am and 1:30pm daily, $30 adults, $25 children under 18, plus gear rentals) to the offshore **Looe Key Reef**. In addition, bikers can utilize the paved 3.5-mile road that runs the length of the island, while anglers can fish from shore or launch their own boats at the on-site boat ramps ($10 per launch). Nature lovers might also appreciate the small on-site **Sand and Sea Nature Center** (305/872-9807, 9am-5pm Thurs.-Mon., free), which offers exhibits about offshore coral formations and the island's native plants and animals, from mangroves to iguanas.

Of course, the park's three nature trails offer bird-watchers and wildlife lovers the opportunity to see real specimens in action. One trail, called the Silver Palm Trail, is situated near the Sandspur area and offers a look at mangrove trees, sand dunes, and a tropical hardwood hammock while another winds through the Wings and Waves Butterfly Garden, planted in 1998 beside the Loggerhead parking lot and now frequented by vibrant butterflies, including the zebra longwing butterfly and the endangered Miami blue butterfly. The third trail, situated beside the Calusa beach, leads to the top of the Old Bahia Honda Bridge, a seemingly unfinished concrete-and-steel structure that once spanned the Bahia Honda Channel

KEYS NAMED AFTER WRECKS

Two islands in the Lower Keys—**Ramrod Key** and the submerged **Looe Key Reef**—were named after a pair of sunken ships. Originally known as Roberts Island, Ramrod Key derives its modern moniker from a Spanish vessel that wrecked on an offshore coral reef in the early 19th century. Little is generally known about the ship itself or the circumstances of its demise.

Such is not the case, however, for the HMS *Looe*, the 44-gun British frigate that inspired the name of Looe Key Reef. According to Bob "Frogfoot" Weller—the author of such books as *Famous Shipwrecks of the Florida Keys* (1990) and *Galleon Alley: The 1733 Spanish Treasure Fleet* (2001)—the HMS *Looe* was outfitted in Longreach, England, with 190 crewmen and spent the first years of her service patrolling the English Channel and searching for Barbary pirates. After her crew captured four Spanish vessels in Vigo Bay, Spain began attacking Fort Frederick in Georgia and harassing British settlers along America's East Coast. When the governor of South Carolina petitioned to have a warship protect the coastline, Captain Ashby Utting took the *Looe* on its final voyage.

After the ship reached Charleston, a storm damaged the *Looe*. With orders to seek out and destroy enemy ships near Florida, the *Looe* headed to Jamaica for repairs. By December 1743, the ship was again ready to sail, and on February 4, 1744, she was in the Bahama Channel when an enemy ship was sighted. The *Looe* wasted little time in capturing the *Snow*, which upon closer examination, turned out to be a British ship, the *Billander Betty*, which had been taken by the Spanish. The captain decided to escort the ship back to Charleston. Before retiring for the night, he ordered that the lead line be thrown every 30 minutes to sound for depth.

Around 1am, the on-duty crewmen tossed the lead line and found no bottom at 300 feet.

Not 15 minutes later, however, the officer of the watch was alarmed to spot breakers directly ahead. A crosswind caught the sails and the stern collided with the reef, and the *Looe* began to fill with water. Utting ordered that his men save as much of the bread and gunpowder as possible. Meanwhile, the *Snow* met a similar fate against a nearby reef.

By morning, Utting and his men found themselves on a small, sandy key, which they rightly assumed would soon be underwater. When they sighted a sloop offshore, Utting armed his small boats and sent them in pursuit. The next morning, the boats returned with the sloop in tow, and by February 8, the entire crews of the two fallen ships—274 men in all—were rescued. Before leaving, Utting set fire to the *Looe*, which exploded into several pieces.

Although Utting and his crew arrived in Jamaica on February 13, 1744, the wreck wasn't discovered until 1951, when Art McKee, Mendel Peterson, Dr. Barney Crile, and his wife dove down to the wreck site and managed to recover one of the cannons on the *Looe*, plus a number of artifacts. The next year, the group returned and recovered additional artifacts from the *Looe*, including cannonballs, coins, buttons, and a pewter teapot. While down there, they supposedly located one of the anchors from the *Snow* (although there's still some debate as to whether the *Looe* was even towing the *Snow* at the time of its demise). In the early 1970s, Art Hartman and Bobby Jordan explored the site and recovered even more artifacts, from utensils to pewter mugs to silver candlestick holders.

Nowadays, the wreck site—including any remaining artifacts—and living coral reef are protected features of Florida Keys National Marine Sanctuary. As Bob "Frogfoot" Weller has written, "Salvaging artifacts is illegal, but sightseeing is encouraged."

© LAURA MARTONE

remnants of the Overseas Railroad at Bahia Honda State Park

as part of Henry Flagler's Overseas Railroad. Built in the early 1900s, the bridge was partially destroyed in the infamous Labor Day Hurricane of 1935, and today it affords a panoramic view of the entire island as well as the surrounding waters. From here you may spot fish, eagle rays, sea turtles, bottlenose dolphins, West Indian manatees, and an array of wading birds, shorebirds, and raptors, including great white herons, spotted sandpipers, laughing gulls, mourning doves, mangrove cuckoos, red-bellied woodpeckers, brown pelicans, turkey vultures, and bald eagles.

Other activities here include ranger-led beach walks, various nature and history programs, and in late January, a reenactment of the first train ride on Flagler's former railroad. Reservations are recommended for campgrounds, cabin rentals, boat slips, and snorkeling excursions. Unlike at many places in the Florida Keys, pets are welcome at Bahia Honda, though their access is limited, and they must be well behaved and kept on six-foot handheld leashes at all times.

BIG PINE KEY

As the largest island in the Lower Keys, **Big Pine Key** anchors a region defined by its numerous island clusters and bountiful natural resources—a region that remains the last undeveloped holdout of the Florida Keys. While Big Pine Key, the second largest island in the entire archipelago, contains the lion's share of attractions, shops, services, and the like, it still represents the laid-back vibe prevalent throughout the Lower Keys, a place where people come to escape the more commercialized—and often more crowded—communities of Key West and Islamorada.

【 National Key Deer Refuge

Founded in 1957, this 84,351-acre sanctuary encompasses mangrove and pine forests, freshwater and salt-marsh wetlands, and tropical hardwood hammocks on 25 islands in the Lower Keys. The primary purpose of the refuge is to provide critical habitat for hundreds of native and migratory species, including the docile Key deer, a miniature version of the

© DANIEL MARTONE

a peaceful afternoon at the Blue Hole on Big Pine Key

The wheelchair-accessible **visitor center** (179 Key Deer Blvd., Big Pine Key, 305/872-0774, 9am-4:30pm Mon.-Fri.) is in the Big Pine Shopping Center near the intersection of U.S. 1 and Key Deer Boulevard. Here you'll also find information about other refuges in the so-called Florida Keys Complex, including **Great White Heron National Wildlife Refuge** (www.fws.gov/nationalkeydeer/greatwhiteheron) and **Key West National Wildlife Refuge** (www.fws.gov/nationalkeydeer/keywest), two protected areas that encompass numerous backcountry islands in Florida Bay and the Gulf of Mexico, set aside by the federal government to maintain a preserve and breeding ground for native birds. Unlike the National Key Deer Refuge, these two are only accessible by boat.

◖ BLUE HOLE

Once an active limestone quarry—utilized during the construction of Henry Flagler's ill-fated Overseas Railroad in the early 20th century—**Blue Hole** is a tranquil, much-visited body of water that nurtures an array of creatures, from green herons to turtles to alligators. Situated within the National Key Deer Refuge on Big Pine Key and free to visit, it lures bird-watchers, wildlife lovers, and photographers alike. The observation platform offers an unobstructed view of the water, where if you're lucky, you might spot a Key deer stopping for a refreshing drink. To reach the Blue Hole, take U.S. 1 to Mile Marker 30, turn northwest onto Key Deer Boulevard, continue past Watson Boulevard, and look for the sign on the left, near Big Pine Street.

white-tailed deer, which only grow to 24-32 inches tall and whose diminishing population originally inspired the creation of the **National Key Deer Refuge** (28950 Watson Blvd., Big Pine Key, 305/872-2239, www.fws.gov/nationalkeydeer, free).

Visitors are welcome 24 hours daily in at least part of the refuge, most notably within designated areas of Big Pine Key and No Name Key. Here you'll find the wheelchair-accessible **Fred C. Manillo Wildlife Trail** (0.1 mile) and the **Jack C. Watson Wildlife Trail** (0.7 mile), both of which offer photographers and nature lovers the opportunity to observe many different species of birds, reptiles, and mammals, including great white herons, brown pelicans, various raptors and songbirds, lizards, turtles, alligators, and Key deer, which though said to swim easily between the islands, mainly dwell on Big Pine. Early morning and late afternoon are typically the best times to spot a Key deer, especially at the northern end of Key Deer Boulevard.

SUGARLOAF KEY

En route to Key West, you'll encounter several quiet residential areas on islands like Little Torch Key and Big Coppitt Key, all the way to the Key West Naval Air Station on Boca Chica Key. Along this route lies **Sugarloaf Key,** a charming residential island that contains its share of friendly eateries, laid-back campgrounds, and curious attractions—plus a small airport of its own.

RULES OF THE REFUGE

Created in 1957 to protect endangered Key deer and other precious wildlife resources, the **National Key Deer Refuge** (28950 Watson Blvd., Big Pine Key, 305/872-0774 or 305/872-2239, www.fws.gov/nationalkeydeer) now preserves roughly 84,351 acres of land and water in the Lower Keys. Unlike in some national wildlife refuges, however, visitors (and leashed pets) are allowed within its boundaries. Though public access is prohibited in much of the refuge—in order to protect wildlife and critical habitat, as well as visitors—you'll find walking and hiking trails, a visitor center, and opportunities for fishing, biking, wildlife watching, and noncommercial photography on Big Pine Key and No Name Key. Surprisingly, you can even drive in parts of the refuge.

Of course, despite such accessibility, certain activities are prohibited, including the following:

- Bringing weapons onto refuge lands, unless they are unloaded, cased, and secured in vehicles or boats
- Using metal detectors to search for antiquities or treasure
- Bringing horses onto refuge lands, as their manure might carry the seeds of invasive plants
- Camping on refuge lands since there are no sanitary facilities for campers

- Using poles or pipes, such as beach umbrellas, which might penetrate turtle nests
- Igniting campfires, which can start destructive wildfires
- Storing equipment or property on refuge lands
- Feeding wildlife, which can cause animals to become less wary of humans and potentially increase their exposure to poachers, diseases, parasites, and vehicle collisions
- Injuring or harassing wildlife
- Removing wildlife, plants, or natural items from refuge lands
- Introducing exotic plants or wildlife, which can cause competition with existing native species

In addition, you're expected to drive carefully throughout the refuge—even on the Overseas Highway, which crosses several of the 25 islands contained within the preserve. You must stay alert for Key deer at all times, but especially at sunrise and sunset, when they're more likely to emerge. The speed limit, which is 35 miles per hour at night, is strictly enforced, and tickets can be costly. Vehicle collisions are one of the leading threats to these endangered animals, and of course, killing one on purpose can result in steep fines and possible imprisonment.

Bat Tower

At Mile Marker 17, those headed to the Sugarloaf Key Airport must turn northwest onto Bat Tower Road. En route to the airport, you should stop for an up-close look at the weather-beaten **Bat Tower,** erected in 1929 by entrepreneur Richter Clyde Perky as part of a pesticide-free plan to eliminate mosquitoes from his tourist attractions in the Lower Keys. Based on the theory that bats have a notoriously ravenous appetite for mosquitoes and other insects, the 30-foot-tall pine tower was intended to house a colony of imported bats which would, in turn, solve Perky's pest problem. Despite his creative thinking, however, the bats didn't stay, and the plan subsequently failed. Today the defunct tower, which is listed on the National Register of Historic Places and costs nothing to view, serves as a monument to one man's inability to control nature.

Entertainment and Shopping

NIGHTLIFE

If you need a place to unwind, the Lower Keys can certainly satisfy you. For more than 30 years, **Coconuts Bar & Package** (30535 Overseas Hwy., Big Pine Key, 305/872-3795, www.thefloridakeysbar.com, 7am-4am daily) has lured night owls with beer, liquor, darts, pool tables, and arcade games—and the fact that it's air-conditioned is a big plus in the summertime. It doesn't hurt either that this casual, late-night lounge now offers wireless Internet access.

The **Looe Key Tiki Bar & Restaurant** (27340 Overseas Hwy., Ramrod Key, 305/872-2215 or 877/816-3483, www.looekeytikibar.com or www.diveflakeys.com, 7:30am-11pm daily) features a daily happy hour (4pm-7pm) and live entertainment nightly (usually 6pm-10pm Wed.-Thurs. and 7pm-11pm Fri.-Sat.),

from acoustic guitarists to funk bands to karaoke. Across the highway, **Boondocks Grille & Draft House & Miniature Golf** (27205 Overseas Hwy., Ramrod Key, 305/872-4094, www.boondocksus.com, 11am-close daily) provides an open-air tiki bar where you can enjoy happy hour (4pm-6pm) on weekdays as well as bingo tournaments, trivia contests, and live folk, country, and rock music throughout the week.

Meanwhile, **Mangrove Mama's Restaurant** (19991 Overseas Hwy., Sugarloaf Key, 305/745-3030, www.mangrovemamasrestaurant.com, 8am-10pm daily) offers a daily happy hour (4pm-6pm) plus live blues from local and national musicians on certain nights (5:30pm-9:30pm Wed.-Thurs., 6:30pm-10:30pm Fri.-Sat.). Closer to Key West, the **Geiger Key Marina RV Park** (5 Geiger Rd., Geiger Key,

© DANIEL MARTONE

Boondocks Grille & Draft House features live music.

305/296-3553, www.geigerkeymarina.com) also features live music—typically laid-back tunes from the 1970s, '80s, and '90s—on Friday, Saturday, and Sunday nights at the on-site **Smokehouse Restaurant** (305/294-1230, 8am-10pm daily).

FESTIVALS AND EVENTS
◖ Underwater Music Festival

For roughly three decades, the Lower Keys have promoted the preservation of the spectacular Looe Key Reef with a unique summertime event, the whimsical daylong **Underwater Music Festival,** which usually takes place in mid-July. This annual underwater concert features an array of seaworthy tunes, from humpback whale songs to ditties by Jimmy Buffett, the Beatles, and other legendary musicians. Every year, hundreds of snorkelers and scuba divers flock to the area for this one-of-a-kind celebration—an ideal time for you to explore this vibrant coral reef, home to a wide variety of tropical fish, while you listen to a four-hour

© BILL KEOGH/FLORIDA KEYS NEWS BUREAU/HO

A diver blows a "trombone fish" during the annual Underwater Music Festival.

uninterrupted underwater musical broadcast, presented by a local radio station. For more information, contact the Lower Keys Chamber of Commerce (31020 Overseas Hwy., Big Pine Key, 305/872-2411 or 800/872-3722, www. lowerkeyschamber.com).

Big Pine & the Lower Keys Island Art Festival

Typically held in early to mid-December, the **Big Pine & the Lower Keys Island Art Festival** features a full day of arts, crafts, exhibits, raffle drawings, and live music on the grounds of the Lower Keys Chamber of Commerce (31020 Overseas Hwy., Big Pine Key, 305/872-2411 or 800/872-3722, www. lowerkeyschamber.com) near Mile Marker 31, on the ocean side of the Overseas Highway. Food and beverages are available on-site, and admission and parking are free. For more information, contact the chamber of commerce or the Florida Keys Council of the Arts (1100 Simonton St., Key West, 305/295-4369, www. keysarts.com).

Other Annual Events

The Lower Keys host a wide array of other annual events, including the **Big Pine & Lower Keys Nautical Flea Market,** typically held in mid- to late January at the Lower Keys Chamber of Commerce (31020 Overseas Hwy., Big Pine Key, 305/872-2411 or 800/872-3722, www.lowerkeyschamber.com, free admission and parking) and featuring an emporium of boats, motors, and other nautical items, plus live music, food, and beverages. Anglers might also enjoy area fishing tournaments like the three-day **Big Pine & Lower Keys Dolphin Tournament** (305/872-2411 or 800/872-3722, www.lowerkeyschamber.com, entry fees apply) in mid-May, which has taken place for two decades and typically offers over $35,000 in prizes.

SHOPPING

Although avid shoppers will find a slew of options farther south in Key West, the pickings are much slimmer in this part of the Lower

Keys. Still, there are at least a few shops worth mentioning.

Near Mile Marker 30.4, on the gulf side of Big Pine Key, the **Big Pine Shopping Center** (www.bigpineshopping.com) houses several choices, including clothing boutiques and specialty shops like the **Key West Key Lime Pie Co.** (271 Key Deer Blvd., Big Pine Key, 305/872-7400 or 877/882-7437, www.keywestkeylimepieco.com, 10am-6pm Mon.-Sat., noon-5pm Sun.), which sells award-winning key lime pies in addition to gourmet jellies, marinades, cookies, candies, spices, cookbooks, and other treats. Here you'll also spot the **Artists in Paradise Gallery** (221 Key Deer Blvd., Big Pine Key, 305/872-1828, www.artistsinparadise.com, 10am-2pm Sun.-Mon., 10am-6pm Tues.-Sat.), a co-op gallery that spotlights the jewelry, photography, sculptures, stained glass, mixed media, watercolor paintings, and other artwork of over 30 local artists. Created in 1994, the gallery also provides framing services and hosts periodic demonstrations, workshops, auctions, and other events—such as an annual Judge Show.

For last-minute shoe needs, head to nearby **Bare Sole Sandals** (30313 Overseas Hwy., Big Pine Key, 305/872-1882, www.baresolesandalsstore.com, 9am-5:30pm Mon.-Fri., 9am-5pm Sat., 11am-4pm Sun.), where you can peruse a large selection of sandals, clogs, flip-flops, and water shoes for men, women, and children, plus jewelry, handbags, hats, and other accessories. Not far away lies the **Good Food Conspiracy** (MM 30.2 OS U.S. 1, Big Pine Key, 305/872-3945 or 305/872-9119, www.goodfoodconspiracy.com, 9:30am-7pm Mon.-Sat., 11am-5pm Sun.), which sells natural foods, vitamins, herbs, and oils in addition to offering a juice bar, deli, and holistic health center.

Depending on the season, the wholesale and retail fish market known as **Fanci Seafood** (22290 Overseas Hwy., Cudjoe Key, 305/745-3887, www.fanciseafood.com, 8am-6pm daily) can provide seafood lovers with fresh fish, shrimp, lobster, and stone crab. Near Mile Marker 15 on the ocean side of U.S. 1, you can choose from a range of roasts at the highly touted **Baby's Coffee** (3178 Overseas Hwy., Saddlebunch Keys, 305/744-9866 or 800/523-2326, www.babyscoffee.com, 6:30am-6pm Mon.-Fri., 7am-5pm Sat., 8am-5pm Sun.), which serves many restaurants and hotels in Key West. Choices include the nutty Baby's Wrecker's Roast, the full-bodied Hemingway's Hair of the Dog, the chicory-free Voodoo Queen, and other cleverly named concoctions. In addition to gourmet coffee, Baby's offers a wide selection of beer, wine, sodas, fruit juices, chocolate, pastries, and gourmet sandwiches—everything you might need for a picnic by the sea.

Sports and Recreation

BIKING

In the Lower Keys, biking enthusiasts can explore a variety of different biking paths on Big Pine Key, No Name Key, the Saddlebunch Keys, and Big Coppitt Key. Many of these short paths connect to county roads, allowing for longer rides and terrific opportunities to view wildlife, from herons to Key deer. Eventually, the **Florida Keys Overseas Heritage Trail** (www.floridastateparks.org/floridakeys) will make it much easier for bikers to traverse the Lower Keys, from the Seven Mile Bridge to Stock Island. For now, you must venture along the shoulder of the Overseas Highway, which can be dangerous at times. No matter where you travel, though, always wear a helmet.

If you didn't bring a bicycle of your own, don't fret. The **Big Pine Bicycle Center** (31 County Rd., Big Pine Key, 305/872-0130, www.bigpinebikes.com, 9am-5pm Mon.-Fri., 9am-3pm Sat., $8 per half day, $10 daily, $40 weekly) offers beach cruiser rentals, in addition

WILD ANIMAL ENCOUNTERS

Lizards, iguanas, roosters, and feral cats roam freely in the Florida Keys. You'll see them everywhere—in parking lots, on porches, even amid the foliage. Because such creatures are so accustomed to people, it's sometimes easy to forget how to handle an encounter with truly wild animals.

Whether you spot a lounging alligator, a tiny Key deer, or something else entirely, you should always adhere to the following rules:

- Observe wildlife from a distance; do not follow or approach the animals.

- Never feed wildlife; feeding wild animals can damage their health, alter their natural behavior, and expose them to predators.

- Never taunt or disturb wildlife.

- Protect wildlife by storing your food and trash securely.

- Control pets at all times, or leave them at home.

- Avoid wildlife during sensitive phases, such as mating or nesting.

For more information about respecting wildlife, consult the recreation and parks division of the **Florida Department of Environmental Protection** (850/245-3029 or 850/245-2157, www.dep.state.fl.us or www.floridastateparks. org) or contact the Colorado-based **Leave No Trace Center for Outdoor Ethics** (303/442-8222 or 800/332-4100, www.lnt.org).

to repairs, parts, and accessories. All bicycle rentals include helmets, baskets, and locks.

FISHING

While anglers tend to favor the bountiful waters of Islamorada, the Lower Keys certainly offer their share of fishing opportunities. **Strike Zone Charters** (29675 Overseas Hwy., Big Pine Key, 305/872-9863, www.strikezonecharter.com, 8am-5pm daily, rates vary) provides deep-sea fishing trips for up to six people, as well as other excursions. Half-day and full-day trips are available, as are backcountry fishing outings. Reservations are highly recommended.

Some area fishing guides have no specific port, but can still be reached to arrange a variety of charters. Two such companies include **Key Flat Charters** (305/304-3152, www.lowerkeysflatsfishing.com, $400-550 per trip), operated by Captain Luke Kelly and covering the flats and backcountry inshore waters, and **Last Cast Charters** (305/744-9796, www.lastcastcharters.net, $400-1,100 per trip), operated by Captain Andrew Tipler and featuring flats, inshore, reef, gulf, and offshore fishing, plus swordfish excursions. Also in the area, you'll find **Sea Boots Charters** (305/745-1530 or 800/238-1746, www.seaboots.com, $700-1,100

per trip), operated from Summerland Key by Captain Jim Sharpe and featuring big game fishing, from wahoo to sharks.

There are also several bait shops in the Lower Keys, including **Jig's Bait & Tackle/Guns and Ammo** (30321 Overseas Hwy., Big Pine Key, 305/872-1040, www.jigsbaitandtackle.com, 7am-7pm Mon.-Sat., 7am-6pm Sun.), a one-stop shop for fishing equipment, bait, tackle, firearms, and charts, and **Reef Light & Tackle** (29770 Overseas Hwy., Big Pine Key, 305/872-7679, www.reeflighttackle.com, 6am-6pm daily), which offers fishing reels and rods in addition to bait. Another option is **Fanci Seafood** (22290 Overseas Hwy., Cudjoe Key, 305/745-3887, www.fanciseafood.com, 8am-6pm daily), a wholesale and retail fish market that provides anglers with bait, chum, and ice throughout the day, not to mention fresh seafood for retail customers beginning at 10am each morning.

◖ BOATING AND KAYAKING

Given the topography of the Lower Keys, with plenty of open water, curious islands, and backcountry channels, this is truly a water lover's playground and an ideal place for boating and kayaking. To help you explore the region, **Strike Zone Charters** (29675 Overseas Hwy.,

© LAURA MARTONE

Kayaking is a popular activity at Bahia Honda State Park.

Big Pine Key, 305/872-9863, www.strike-zonecharter.com, 8am-5pm daily, $59 pp) offers all-inclusive island excursions on glass-bottom catamarans. Such five-hour trips combine a breezy boat ride with history and ecology lessons, bird-watching, light-tackle fishing, a fish cookout, and a snorkeling experience amid the offshore coral reefs, part of Florida Keys National Marine Sanctuary. Reservations are recommended.

Boat owners who would prefer to explore this region on their own will find several marinas and public boat ramps at their disposal. Of course, if you didn't bring a boat with you, you can easily rent one from **Big Pine Key Boat Rentals** (33000 Overseas Hwy., Big Pine Key, and 24500 Overseas Hwy., Summerland Key, 305/745-1505 or 305/849-0130, www.bigpineboatrentals.com, 8am-5pm daily, $190-350 daily) and go cruising, fishing, and snorkeling at your own pace. Reservations are a must; typically, the hours of operation are flexible, and help is only available if the staff knows you're coming.

For kayak rentals, guided kayaking nature tours, skiff ecotours, and backcountry catamaran cruises, consult **Big Pine Kayak Adventures** (305/872-7474, www.keyskayaktours.com, 8am-5pm daily, rentals $20 for two hours, $5 for each additional hour, guided tours start at $50 pp), based out of the Old Wooden Bridge Marina (1791 Bogie Dr., Big Pine Key, 305/872-2241) and operated by Captain Bill Keogh, a well-respected naturalist, educator, photographer, and author who has lived in the Lower Keys for more than two decades. In addition, the **Coral Reef Park Company, Inc.** (305/872-3210) offers kayak rentals at **Bahia Honda State Park** (36850 Overseas Hwy., Bahia Honda Key, 305/872-2353, www.floridastateparks.org/bahiahonda or www.bahiahondapark.com, 8am-sunset daily, $8 vehicles with 2-8 passengers plus $0.50 pp, $4.50 motorcycles and single-occupant vehicles, $2.50 pedestrians, bikers, and extra passengers), including single kayaks ($10 hourly, $30 per half day) and those meant for two passengers ($18 hourly, $54 per half day).

NO SNORKELING FOR FIDO

In general, it's rather difficult to travel with your pets in the Florida Keys, including the islands that compose the Lower Keys. Only a handful of Big Pine-area hotels–such as the **Sugarloaf Lodge Hotel** (17001 Overseas Hwy., Sugarloaf Key, 305/745-3211 or 800/553-6097, www.sugarloaflodge.net) and the **Old Wooden Bridge Guest Cottages & Marina** (1791 Bogie Dr., Big Pine Key, 305/872-2241, www.oldwoodenbridge.com)–are pet friendly, so it's always best to call ahead if you're considering bringing your cat or dog with you.

Although it's often easier for pet owners to stay in a campground, such as those available at **Bahia Honda State Park** (36850 Overseas Hwy., Big Pine Key, 305/872-2353 or 305/872-3210, www.floridastateparks.org/bahiahonda or www.bahiahondapark.com), certain restrictions still do apply. While service and guide dogs, with proper identification, are welcome in all areas of the park, pets are typically not allowed in cabins, bathhouses, pavilions, or the concession building. They're also not allowed on the beaches or in the water, which unfortunately means that you won't be able to swim or snorkel with your pet.

In the limited areas where pets are permitted–such as the campgrounds–they must be well behaved and kept on a six-foot handheld leash at all times. Perhaps it goes without saying, but owners must always pick up and properly dispose of their pets' waste–no matter where they leave it.

◖ DIVING AND SNORKELING

Roughly five nautical miles south of Big Pine Key lies one of the finest and most diverse coral reefs in the Florida Keys. Established in 1981, **Looe Key National Marine Sanctuary,** now part of Florida Keys National Marine Sanctuary, features a 33-acre spur-and-groove network of coral fingers, sand channels, and turtle grass that abounds with over 150 species of fish, including parrotfish, angelfish, yellowtail, barracuda, grouper, turtles, eagle rays, whale sharks, and moray eels. Named long ago after the HMS *Looe* (which supposedly ran aground here in February 1744), the U-shaped reef comprises patch reefs as well as outside reefs and has depths that vary from 8 to 40 feet, making it ideal for first-time snorkelers as well as advanced scuba divers. Either way, visitors will get an up-close look at a variety of coral, including elkhorn, staghorn, star, fire, and brain. For most of the year, the water clarity is excellent, and the sea conditions are moderate; January is often the only month during which visibility can be less than ideal. No matter when you visit, however, certain activities are absolutely prohibited, including spearfishing and the collecting of shells and tropical fish.

Several area operators provide tours to this one-of-a-kind reef, including the **Looe Key Reef Resort & Dive Center** (27340 Overseas Hwy., Ramrod Key, 305/872-2215 or 877/816-3483, www.diveflakeys.com, 7:30am-8pm Sun.-Thurs., 7:30am-9pm Fri.-Sat.), which has offered scuba-diving instruction and half-day diving and snorkeling trips (7:30am and 12:15pm daily, $69 divers, $39 snorkelers, $25 passengers) to Looe Key Reef since 1978. Through the dive center, you're also able to experience the *Adolphus Busch,* a 210-foot freighter that was intentionally sunk in 1998 to create an artificial reef. Upright in roughly 110 feet of water, the intact shipwreck has become a haven for a wide variety of marine invertebrates and fish, from moray eels to 250-pound goliath grouper often seen in the wheelhouse or cargo holds. Typically, the dive center offers a wreck trip on Wednesday and every other Sunday; the trip includes a dive on the *Adolphus Busch,* plus one dive on Looe Key Reef ($79 divers, $25 passengers). All trip prices include tanks, weights, masks, snorkels, and fins; gas fills, equipment rentals, and repair services are also available on-site.

Additionally, **Strike Zone Charters** (29675 Overseas Hwy., Big Pine Key, 305/872-9863, www.strikezonecharter.com, 8am-5pm daily, reservation required) offers both PADI instruction ($175-395 pp) and daily half-day snorkeling and diving trips ($38-48 pp, plus gear rental) to Looe Key Reef on roomy glass-bottom catamarans. **Coral Reef Park Company, Inc.** (36850 Overseas Hwy., Bahia Honda Key, 305/872-3210, www.bahiahondapark.com, 8am-5pm daily), meanwhile, provides twice-daily, 1.5-hour snorkeling trips (9:30am and 1:30pm, $30 adults, $25 children under 18, $4 snorkel, $2 mask, $2 fins) from Bahia Honda State Park (where park entrance fees apply) to Looe Key Reef. Even in the waters near Bahia Honda, though, you're bound to see curious marine creatures, including queen conch, red rock urchin, spiny lobster, sea cucumbers, seahorses, horseshoe crabs, cushion sea stars, tube sponges, moon jellies, and nurse sharks. Luckily, snorkel gear rentals ($6 wetsuit, $6 diver-down flag, $5 snorkel, $5 safety vest, $4-5 mask, $4 fins) are available daily in the park.

For more information about snorkeling and diving sites in the Lower Keys, consult the Key West office of **Florida Keys National Marine Sanctuary** (Nancy Foster Florida Keys Environmental Complex, 33 E. Quay Rd., Key West, 305/809-4700, www.floridakeys.noaa.gov).

OTHER OUTDOOR ACTIVITIES

If you're looking for a land-based diversion in this watery playground, stop by **Boondocks Grille & Draft House & Miniature Golf** (27205 Overseas Hwy., Ramrod Key, 305/872-4094,

www.boondocksus.com, 10am-10pm daily), where you can play an 18-hole round of golf ($10 adults, $7 children) amid the caves and waterfalls of this tropical setting, then enjoy some snacks and libations at the 19th Hole Party Zone. It's an ideal activity for travelers with children.

For a more exhilarating experience, head to the Sugarloaf Key Airport at Mile Marker 17 on Sugarloaf Key, where **Sky Dive Key West** (305/745-4386, www.skydivekeywest.com, by appointment daily, $245-265 pp) offers tandem jumps for an aerial view of the Lower Keys from two miles above the earth. Skydivers must be at least 18 years old, and certain weight restrictions could apply. Reservations are necessary for all jumps; note that cash transactions will save you $20 per person.

SPAS AND YOGA

Although outdoor activities are paramount in the Lower Keys, you'll also find more relaxing pursuits like yoga and massage. The **Good Food Conspiracy** (MM 30.2 OS U.S. 1, Big Pine Key, 305/872-9119, www.goodfoodconspiracy.com, 9:30am-7pm Mon.-Sat., 11am-5pm Sun., rates vary), for instance, offers massage, reflexology, facials, as well as light and raindrop therapies. The **Pirate Wellness Center** (21460 Overseas Hwy., Cudjoe Key, 305/744-3348, www.piratewellnesscenter.com, 7:30am-8pm Mon.-Thurs., 7:30am-4pm Fri., 7:30am-noon Sat., rates vary), which offers short-term memberships, provides a range of holistic treatments, including Swedish massage, deep tissue massage, shiatsu massage, acupressure, and reflexology, plus various yoga, tai chi, and pilates classes.

© DANIEL MARTONE

the course at Boondocks Grille & Draft House & Miniature Golf

Accommodations

While places like Islamorada and Key West boast a wider range of lodging choices, including chain hotels, the Lower Keys still have their share of options—from intimate bed-and-breakfasts to affordable campgrounds—almost all of which are privately owned. Just remember that, as with most of the Florida Keys, accommodations are far less expensive in the off-season, which is typically May-November, though it depends on the establishment.

UNDER $100

Just as fishing enthusiasts have several suitable choices in the Lower Keys, snorkelers and scuba divers can pursue their passion at the spacious **【 Looe Key Reef Resort & Dive Center** (27340 Overseas Hwy., Ramrod Key, 305/872-2215 or 877/816-3483, www.diveflakeys. com, $65-99 d). In addition to comfortable air-conditioned rooms—equipped with cable

television, telephone service, and free wireless Internet access—the resort offers a dive shop, a swimming pool, an on-site restaurant and tiki bar, varied scuba-diving courses, plus snorkeling and diving excursions to nearby coral reefs and shipwrecks.

$100-200

In general, vacations can be expensive in the Florida Keys, but luckily, you'll find a handful of bargain-friendly lodgings in the Lower Keys, including the **【 Big Pine Key Fishing Lodge** (33000 Overseas Hwy., Big Pine Key, 305/872-2351, $109-149 d), a laid-back waterfront establishment on Spanish Harbor that's been family owned and operated since 1972. Besides efficiencies, lodge and loft rooms, and mobile homes, amenities here include a heated pool, a recreation room, a convenience store and gift shop, laundry facilities, wireless Internet access, diving equipment, camping and fishing supplies, a marina with boat dockage and rentals, plus fishing charters and diving excursions. The no-frills **Big Pine Key Motel** (30725 Overseas Hwy., Big Pine Key, 305/872-9090 or 888/872-9191, www.bigpinekeymotel.com, $69-139 d) offers 32 units, including efficiencies and apartments, with cable television, air-conditioning, and access to a swimming pool. Visitors might also appreciate the spacious boat parking area and the motel's proximity to the Cracked Egg Cafe. North of the highway lies the **Old Wooden Bridge Guest Cottages & Marina** (1791 Bogie Dr., Big Pine Key, 305/872-2241, www.oldwoodenbridge. com, cottages $95-200), a resort and marina facility on five waterfront acres. Situated at the intersection of Watson Boulevard and Bogie Drive, just west of the No Name Key Bridge, this peaceful resort provides 14 efficiency cottages, a boat ramp, a swimming pool, laundry facilities, cable television, and on-site kayak rentals and tours. For the cottages, weekly rates ($600-1,257) are also available.

On adjacent Little Torch Key, near Mile Marker 28.5, you'll find two more laid-back waterfront choices: the pet-friendly **Dolphin Marina and Cottages** (28530 Overseas Hwy., Little Torch Key, 305/872-2685 or 800/553-0308, www.dolphinmarina.net, $99-229 d) on the ocean side and **Parmer's Resort** (565 Barry Ave., Little Torch Key, 305/872-2157, www.parmersresort.com, rooms $99-239 d, suites $139-299, cottage $248-459) on the gulf side, both of which are ideally situated for people hoping to explore the National Key Deer Refuge and Looe Key Reef. While Dolphin Marina offers a boat ramp, a marina store, boat rentals, and well-landscaped, air-conditioned cottages with cable television, screened porches, and in some cases, full kitchens, Parmer's provides a complimentary breakfast, tiki-style picnic pavilions, hammocks and barbecue grills, a private boat dock, a swimming pool, and a variety of comfortable accommodations.

The pet-friendly **Sugarloaf Lodge Hotel** (17001 Overseas Hwy., Sugarloaf Key, 305/745-3211 or 800/553-6097, www.sugarloaflodge.

net, $120-165 d) houses 31 waterfront rooms, which are somewhat outdated but equipped with air-conditioning and cable television. Other amenities include tennis and shuffleboard courts, a miniature golf course, a heated swimming pool, an on-site tiki bar, a recently renovated restaurant, a fully equipped marina, and a nearby airstrip.

OVER $200

Although Key West features many more high-priced hotels, inns, and resorts than the rest of the Lower Keys, you'll encounter at least three expensive options in this region. South of the Big Pine Key Fishing Lodge, for instance, a long, scenic route winds past mangrove trees and beachfront hideaways, such as **The Barnacle Bed & Breakfast** (1557 Long Beach Dr., Big Pine Key, 305/872-3298 or 800/465-9100, www.thebarnacle.net, $165-285 d). This lush inn offers two relaxing air-conditioned rooms as well as the private Blue Heron Cottage, and all accommodations have satellite TV, wireless Internet access, beach towels, Bahama fans, king-size beds, and private bathrooms. All lodgings come with a full breakfast, and other amenities include a hot tub, a relaxing hammock, a tiki hut, complimentary kayaks, and a private, sandy beach that inspires guests to swim, snorkel, or simply relax. Just remember: All rooms are smoke-free, and pets and children under 16 are not allowed here.

Along the same route lies the remote, eco-friendly **Deer Run Bed & Breakfast** (1997 Long Beach Dr., Big Pine Key, 305/872-2015, www.deerrunfloridabb.com, $255-375 d), a serene oasis beside the Atlantic Ocean. The four rooms—with names like Atlantis, Utopia, Heaven, and Eden—are each decorated in a unique way, but all include organic linens, private baths, screened porches, original artwork, and a hot vegetarian breakfast. Other amenities include a sandy beach, a pool and hot tub, and on-site massage therapy. Guests may also enjoy biking and kayaking during their visit. Take note, however, that as with The Barnacle, pets, children, and smoking aren't permitted here.

Of course, the pinnacle of luxury can be

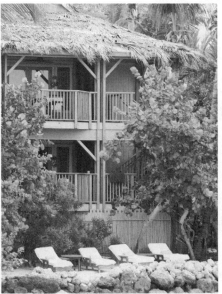

The Little Palm Island Resort & Spa offers seclusion and luxury amid a tropical oasis.

found at the secluded 🟢 **Little Palm Island Resort & Spa** (28500 Overseas Hwy., Little Torch Key, 305/872-2524 or 305/515-4004, www.littlepalmisland.com, bungalows $595-990, suites $1,140-2,810), once the site of a family-owned fishing village and now an award-winning, private, five-acre island getaway south of Little Torch Key, only accessible by private yacht, ferry, or seaplane. Filled with swaying Jamaican palm trees, surrounded by aquamarine waters, and favored by presidents, movie stars, famous athletes, and countless other celebrities, Little Palm Island is probably the most gorgeous and certainly one of the most unique locales in the entire Florida Keys archipelago.

Here you'll encounter white sandy beaches, a stunning outdoor pool, cushioned lounge chairs, two grand suites, and 28 thatched-roof oceanfront bungalows—many of which have Polynesian-style furnishings, lawn furniture, and hammocks, as well as private showers, hot tubs, and verandas. Besides the remote

location, incredible views, and opportunity to spot Key deer frolicking on the lawn, other amenities include free wireless Internet access, complimentary valet parking on Little Torch Key, a boutique and gift shop, a romantic on-site spa (SpaTerre) that provides exotic, spirit-revitalizing massages and treatments, and an on-site restaurant that features gourmet "Floribbean" cuisine in a candlelit dining room, on the breezy terrace, or if you're truly daring, directly on a sandbar. Activities range from yoga classes and kayaking to sailing, fishing, and scuba-diving excursions. What you won't find here are phones, televisions, vehicles, and folks under 21. No wonder it's a popular place for weddings.

CAMPING

The Lower Keys contain several laid-back campgrounds, including the 🟢 **Sunshine Key RV Resort and Marina** (38801 Overseas Hwy., Ohio Key, 800/852-0348, www.rvonthego.com/Sunshine-Key-RV-Resort.html, $65-110 daily, $392-749 weekly, $885-2,679 monthly), situated on the gulf side of Ohio Key, southwest of the Seven Mile Bridge. A private 75-acre island resort, Sunshine Key offers a wide array of full-hookup campsites with 30/50-amp electric service and cable television. Picnic tables, waterfront views, and pull-through sites are available. Other amenities include a 172-slip marina, a fishing pier and boat ramp, a heated 24-hour outdoor pool, sandy volleyball courts, a shuffleboard area, tennis and basketball courts, ping-pong tables, an on-site restaurant and a poolside café, a convenience store and gas station, a fitness center, a coin-op laundry, barbecue and kennel facilities, high-speed Internet access, watercraft rentals, a video game center, a dump station, restrooms, rental cottages, sightseeing tours, and on-site activities, such as weekly potlucks and dances. Leashed pets are welcome, though some restrictions may apply.

A couple miles west, the year-round 🟢 **Bahia Honda State Park** (36850 Overseas Hwy., Bahia Honda Key, 305/872-2353 or 305/872-3210, www.floridastateparks.org/

the campground and marina at the Big Pine Key Fishing Lodge

bahiahonda or www.bahiahondapark.com, 8am-sunset daily, $8 vehicles with 2-8 passengers plus $0.50 pp, $4.50 motorcycles and single-occupant vehicles, $2.50 pedestrians, bikers, and extra passengers) offers three budget-friendly campgrounds—Buttonwood, Sandspur, and Bayside—which collectively contain 80 campsites ($36 daily) for tent and RV campers. Buttonwood has gravel sites, each with electric and water service, a picnic table, and access to a dump station, restrooms, and hot showers. Some of the sites are situated beside the water, and all can accommodate a variety of setups, from small tents to 40-foot RVs. Sandspur, located in a hardwood hammock, has much smaller sites, with lower clearance—ideal for tents and RVs less than 14 feet in length. Some of the sites have electricity and waterfront views, and all have a picnic table, a grill, and water service. Bayside is the smallest campground, with eight sites and a tiny restroom, but all campers are allowed to use the dump station and restrooms in Buttonwood.

To reach Bayside, your vehicle must be able to travel under the new Bahia Honda Bridge, which has a height restriction of six feet, eight inches. Also available for rent near the Bayside campground are three stilted duplex cabins ($120-160 daily) that overlook the bay. Each of the six cabins has a full bath, a kitchen/dining room, a living room with a sofa bed, one or two bedrooms, and central heating and cooling; five of the cabins accommodate up to six people, and one is wheelchair-accessible. Although pets are prohibited in the cabins, they're permitted in the campgrounds, provided that they're confined, leashed, or otherwise kept under control. In addition to campgrounds and cabins, Bahia Honda provides 19 boat slips for overnight rental ($2 per foot, $30 minimum), which includes water, electricity, and the use of park facilities such as restrooms, showers, and trash disposal. For reservations, contact **ReserveAmerica** (800/326-3521, www.reserveamerica.com).

Near Mile Marker 33 on the ocean side of U.S. 1, the family-owned, year-round **Big Pine Key Fishing Lodge** (33000 Overseas Hwy., Big Pine Key, 305/872-2351, $39-57 daily, $246-360 weekly, $936-1,370 monthly) offers a spacious RV campground in addition to its cabins and motel-style rooms. Rustic, full-hookup, pull-through, and shaded sites are available. Amenities include 30-amp electric service, cable television, phone access, propane gas, a heated swimming pool, a recreation room, a convenience store and gift shop, laundry facilities, a marina, boat dockage, boat rentals, and restrooms with showers. Anglers and scuba divers will especially appreciate the easy access to the ocean, as well as the availability of fishing charters and diving excursions to the nearby Looe Key Reef. With its helpful staff and neighborly atmosphere, the campground is popular among families and long-term RVers, many of whom are repeat visitors. Tents are welcome here, but dogs are not allowed.

The recently renovated **Breezy Pines Estates RV Park** (29859 Overseas Hwy., Big Pine Key, 305/872-9041, www.breezypinesrv.com, $33-50 daily, $250-350 weekly,

$650-1,000 monthly) is on the gulf side of U.S. 1, not far from the National Key Deer Refuge. In fact, Key deer are often spotted at Breezy Pines—which despite its name is filled with palm trees, not pines. An ideal base for fishing, kayaking, diving, and snorkeling, this park offers full-hookup, gravel sites, equipped with 30/50-amp electric service, wireless Internet access, cable television, and phone service. Other amenities here include a laundry and an outdoor pool. As with other RV parks in this region, leashed pets are allowed here, and many of the lots are for sale.

Near Mile Marker 20, the beachfront **Sugarloaf Key/Key West KOA** (251 SR-939, Sugarloaf Key, 305/745-3549 or 800/562-7731, www.keywestkoa.com, $58-92 daily) contains both RV and tent spaces, some of which offer 30/50-amp electric service, cable television, waterfront views, or pull-through access. This tropical resort provides easy access to a private sandy beach, where visitors can savor gorgeous sunsets and warm ocean breezes, as well as snorkeling, fishing, and ecotour excursions. Other amenities include a heated swimming pool and hot tub, air-conditioned trailer rentals ($172-192 daily), clean restrooms and hot showers, wireless Internet access, propane gas, a pet playground, beach volleyball, a snack bar, an open-air pavilion with a pub and a restaurant, a full-service marina with boat rentals, ramps, and slips, a floating water trampoline and banana bicycle rentals, seasonal activities, and shuttle service to Key West.

On the ocean side of Sugarloaf Key, near Mile Marker 19.8, is the picturesque 28-acre **Lazy Lakes RV Resort** (311 Johnson Rd., Sugarloaf Key, 305/745-1079 or 866/965-2537, www.lazylakeskeyscamping.com, $40-115 daily, $240-700 weekly, $800-2,200 monthly), which offers 99 RV/tent spaces, some of which have full hookups with water, sewer access, 30/50-amp electric service, cable television, and wireless Internet access. Lakefront sites are also available. Other amenities include seasonal trailer rentals ($100 daily, $750 weekly, $2,500 monthly Apr.-Nov.), a clubhouse, a camp store, a heated pool, laundry facilities and

clean restrooms, paddle boats, and complimentary kayaks. In addition, visitors can swim, fish, and snorkel in the seven-acre saltwater lake and participate in on-site activities like bingo, darts, horseshoes, game and movie nights, potluck dinners, and ice cream socials. A limited number of sites are available for ownership. Both of the Sugarloaf campgrounds allow leashed pets, although Lazy Lakes does not permit pets in the trailer rentals.

Closer to Key West, near Mile Marker 14.5, you'll encounter the **Bluewater Key RV Resort** (2950 Overseas Hwy., Saddlebunch Keys, 305/745-2494 or 800/237-2266, www.bluewaterkey.com, $76-155 daily, $513-648 weekly), which offers spacious, individually owned lots for rent. Divided into waterfront, poolside, and canal sites, all are landscaped with shady, tropical foliage and equipped with tiki huts, picnic tables, cable television, wireless Internet access, water, sewage access, and 30/50-amp electric service. Fishing, snorkeling, and sunbathing are popular pastimes here, and amenities include a swimming pool, clubhouse, bathhouse, laundry, and boat dock.

For those who want to be as close to Key West as possible, without surrendering the unhurried vibe of the Lower Keys, the pet-friendly **◖ Geiger Key Marina & RV Park** (5 Geiger Rd., Geiger Key, 305/294-1230, www.geigerkeymarina.com, $80-112 daily, $480-672 weekly, $1,440-2,100 monthly) offers the best of both worlds. Founded over five decades ago by two fishermen, Geiger Key still has the vibe of old Florida. An off-the-beaten-path oasis and a terrific base for snorkeling, scuba diving, and deep-sea fishing, Geiger Key is the sort of place where locals arrive by boat, just to enjoy a relaxing breakfast, lunch, or dinner at the onsite Smokehouse Restaurant and Tiki Bar. Amenities here include waterfront spaces, full-hookup sites, laundry and shower facilities, live music on the weekends, and convenient boat slips ($28 daily, $85 weekly, $170 monthly) for vessels up to 20 feet in length; of course, longer boats will be charged more. Luckily, though, if you really enjoy your stay, it's possible to become a permanent resident here.

Food

SEAFOOD

Like the rest of the Florida Keys, the Lower Keys boast several seafood options. On the Overseas Highway, the **Looe Key Tiki Bar & Restaurant** (27340 Overseas Hwy., Ramrod Key, 305/872-2215 or 877/816-3483, www.looekeytikibar.com or www.diveflakeys.com, 7:30am-11pm daily, $4-21) is part of a resort and dive center on the ocean side of U.S. 1. In addition to a daily happy hour (4pm-7pm) and live entertainment, the restaurant features breakfast dishes, soups, salads, sandwiches, burgers, and seafood baskets, plus a cook-your-catch option for $10 per person. Meanwhile, it's hard to miss the thatched tiki-style structures of the **Boondocks Grille & Draft House & Miniature Golf** (27205 Overseas Hwy., Ramrod Key, 305/872-4094, www.boondocksus.com, 11am-11pm, $8-23), which offers an open-air, fully-stocked bar, plus burgers, sandwiches, soups, salads, seafood baskets, and entrées like broiled lobster tail. You can also enjoy a weekday happy hour (4pm-6pm) as well as random contests and live musical performances.

On the gulf side of U.S. 1, near Mile Marker 25.5, **The Wharf Bar & Grill** (25163 Overseas Hwy., Summerland Key, 305/745-3322, www.wharfbarandgrill.com, 11am-10pm daily, $10-18) houses a marina, a fish market, and a seafood restaurant, serving fresh fish, seafood sandwiches and baskets, and Sunday brunch 10am-2pm. Anglers can also purchase bait, ice, beer, and additional supplies on the premises. The restaurant is often understaffed and the food more spicy than you might expect. For innovative cuisine in a contemporary setting, look no farther than ◖ **The Square Grouper**

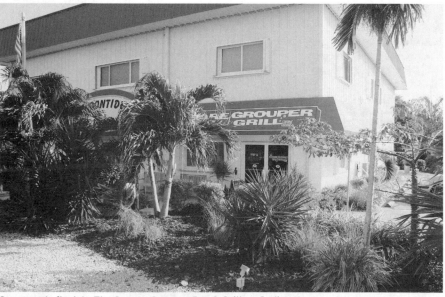

© DANIEL MARTONE

Gourmands flock to The Square Grouper Bar & Grill on Cudjoe Key.

Bar & Grill (22658 Overseas Hwy., Cudjoc Key, 305/745-8880, www.squaregrouperbarandgrill.com, 11am-2:30pm and 5pm-10pm Tues.-Sat., $10-32), a favorite among residents and tourists alike. Housed in an inconspicuous two-story building beside the highway and jokingly named for the compressed bales of marijuana that used to wash ashore in the Lower Keys, this curious eatery spotlights Floribbean dishes like toasted almond-encrusted grouper with warm Caribbean-style pineapple relish; be sure to save room for the chocolate or turtle fondue.

Besides a daily happy hour (4pm-6pm) and live music on the weekends, **Mangrove Mama's Restaurant** (19991 Overseas Hwy., Sugarloaf Key, 305/745-3030, www.mangrovemamasrestaurant.com, 8am-10pm daily, $8-30) offers a wide array of options, including omelets, salads, sandwiches, steaks, seafood dishes, and of course, classic key lime pie.

AMERICAN

Besides several seafood restaurants, the Lower Keys present an array of casual all-American eateries, such as **Springer's Bar & Grill** (31251 Ave. A, Big Pine Key, 305/872-3022, 11am-close daily, $9-16). Essentially a spacious sports bar, featuring pool tables, dartboards, and several televisions tuned to a variety of spectator sports, Springer's offers a full menu of steaks, pizzas, sandwiches, burgers, and local seafood. Adjacent to the Big Pine Key Motel, the **Cracked Egg Cafe** (30739 Overseas Hwy., Big Pine Key, 305/872-7030, 6am-7pm Fri.-Mon., 6am-3pm Tues.-Thurs., $4-10) is popular with the breakfast crowd, who especially favor the pancakes, omelets, and hot coffee; in addition, you'll find soups, sandwiches, beer, wine, and daily specials, including an all-you-can-eat fish fry every Friday. Though the food is usually tasty, the service here is rather unpredictable; on some days, you might encounter lukewarm dishes and abrupt servers.

Vegetarians will appreciate the low-key **((Good Food Conspiracy** (MM 30.2 OS U.S. 1, Big Pine Key, 305/872-3945 or 305/872-9119, www.goodfoodconspiracy.com, 9:30am-7pm Mon.-Sat., 11am-5pm Sun., $4-12), a health food store and juice bar that serves smoothies, fresh juices, homemade soups, raw desserts, vegetarian sandwiches, organic salads, and other healthy treats. Of course, if you have a hankering for something a little less diet conscious, the nearby **Big Pine Restaurant and Coffee Shop** (29943 Overseas Hwy., Big Pine Key, 305/872-2790, 6am-9pm Tues.-Sat., 6am-2pm Sun., $4-24) offers a wide array of homey dishes, from omelets to fried chicken to barbecue pork ribs.

Another favored neighborhood place is the **((No Name Pub** (30813 N. Watson Blvd., Big Pine Key, 305/872-9115, www.nonamepub.com, 11am-11pm daily, $8-15), a friendly, out-of-the-way joint that's been luring locals and tourists alike since 1936. Considered the oldest bar on Big Pine Key, this former bait-and-tackle shop certainly has a rough-hewn appeal, with its gravel parking lot, shady patio area, private garden, and no-frills interior, the walls and ceiling of which are plastered with autographed dollar bills (what the owner calls "early and late American clutter")—a common feature in similarly casual hangouts throughout the Keys. Besides beer and other libations, you'll find basic vittles like pizza, meatballs, smoked fish dip, and seafood baskets—not to mention some interesting local characters. To reach this long-standing haunt, take U.S. 1 to Mile Marker 30 on the gulf side, turn northwest on Key Deer Boulevard, turn right onto Watson Boulevard, and veer to the north, toward (but not past) the No Name Key Bridge.

You'll find even cheaper vittles at the **Five Brothers Grocery Two** (27023 Overseas Hwy., Ramrod Key, 305/872-0702, 6am-6:30pm Mon.-Sat., 7am-2pm Sun., $2-7), which sells breakfast dishes, daily soups, and various sandwiches, including a traditional *cubano*. Meanwhile, **The Sugarloaf Food Company** (24171 Overseas Hwy., Summerland Key, 305/744-0631, www.sugarloaffood.com, 7am-3pm Mon.-Fri., 7am-noon Sat., $5-10) prepares salads, sandwiches, and baked goods for breakfast or lunch. Both joints are popular among locals and tourists alike.

© DANIEL MARTONE

No Name Pub, the oldest bar on Big Pine Key

Another local favorite is the █ **Geiger Key Marina Smokehouse Restaurant and Tiki Bar** (5 Geiger Rd., Geiger Key, 305/294-1230, www.geigerkeymarina.com, 8am-10pm daily, $5-22), a family-friendly eatery well off the beaten path. Serving breakfast, lunch, and dinner, this popular joint features Southern favorites like fried green tomatoes, fish tacos, shrimp po'boys, and crab cakes. On the weekends, you'll be treated to live music and a Sunday barbecue—a 20-year tradition that includes barbecue chicken, smoked ribs, grilled shrimp, jalapeño cornbread, cole slaw, wild rice, and baked beans ($17 pp).

PIZZA

If you have a sudden craving for casual Italian cuisine, you'll encounter at least two options in the Lower Keys. Situated in the Big Pine Shopping Center, **Pizzaworks** (229 Key Deer Blvd., Big Pine Key, 305/872-1119, www.big-pinepizzaworks.com, 11am-9pm Mon.-Thurs., 11am-10pm Fri.-Sat., noon-9pm Sun., $8-19) can deliver salads, pizzas, subs, pasta dishes,

and key lime pie right to your hotel, and **A Slice of Paradise** (24458 Overseas Hwy., Summerland Key, 305/744-9718, 11am-9pm Mon.-Fri., 11am-11pm Sat.-Sun., $6-23) offers salads, hot and cold subs, and specialty pizzas. Both of these low-key joints are popular among locals.

EUROPEAN

For an exceptionally exquisite meal, take a boat ride from Little Torch Key to the exclusive █ **Little Palm Island Resort & Spa** (28500 Overseas Hwy., Little Torch Key, 305/872-2551, www.littlepalmisland.com, 8am-10:30am, 11:30am-2:30pm, and 6pm-10pm daily, prices vary depending on the menu), which welcomes the public to its on-site waterfront restaurant for breakfast, lunch, and dinner daily as well as Sunday brunch (11am-2:30pm). Although the French-Latin fusion cuisine is ever evolving, sample dishes might range from shrimp and yellowtail snapper ceviche to coriander-crusted elk with dried fruit compote, toasted asparagus, and port wine

© DANIEL MARTONE

outdoor dining at the Little Palm Island Resort & Spa

sauce—not to mention the cashew-crusted key lime pie.

The only snag for some Keys vacationers, though, might be that proper "country club" attire is required—that is, men should wear polo shirts with nice shorts for lunch and collared shirts with long pants for dinner while women would be okay with a nice sundress at lunch and elegant pants and a blouse at dinner. Also, children under 16 aren't allowed, making it a poor choice for families with kids—but an ideal spot for a romantic meal for two. You can make it even more memorable by requesting the discreet Chef's Table in the kitchen, where Executive Chef Luis Pous will attend to you personally, preparing and presenting a multicourse tasting menu paired with the perfect wine selection. You can also dine outside on the sandbar, an especially exotic choice for dinner when the romantic atmosphere is enhanced by cool night breezes and flaming tiki torches. Of course, no matter how you choose to enjoy this one-of-a-kind dining experience, advance reservations are required, and while the prices vary from day to day, a couple can expect to pay at least $250 for a multicourse dinner, excluding alcohol.

CUBAN

While you won't find many Latin American options in the Lower Keys, those who favor Cuban cuisine might appreciate the long-standing, extremely no-frills **Coco's Kitchen** (283 Key Deer Blvd., Big Pine Key, 305/872-4495, www.cocoskitchen.com, 7am-2pm and 4:30pm-7pm Tues.-Sat., $3-18), one of several businesses in the Big Pine Shopping Center on Big Pine Key. Though the food here is served on disposable plates, hungry visitors will likely care more about the menu options, which range from *huevos rancheros* for breakfast and Cuban mix sandwiches for lunch to nightly dinner specials like Tuesday's *ropa vieja* (shredded beef in tomato sauce), followed by flan for dessert. Of course, diners will also find plenty of American dishes, such as cheeseburgers, fried shrimp, and barbecue spare ribs. Happily, Coco's is a non-smoking joint that conveniently accepts both cash and credit cards.

Information and Services

INFORMATION

For brochures, maps, and other information about Big Pine Key and the Lower Keys, consult the **Lower Keys Chamber of Commerce** (31020 Overseas Hwy., Big Pine Key, 305/872-2411 or 800/872-3722, www.lowerkeyschamber.com, 9am-5pm Mon.-Fri., 9am-3pm Sat.) near Mile Marker 31 or the **Monroe County Tourist Development Council** (1201 White St., Ste. 102, Key West, 305/296-1552 or 800/352-5397, www.fla-keys.com, 9am-5pm Mon.-Fri.). For government-related issues, contact the **Monroe County offices** (1100 Simonton St., Key West, 305/294-4641, www.monroecounty-fl.gov, 8am-5pm Mon.-Fri.).

For local news, consult *The Key West Citizen* (www.keysnews.com), **The Weekly Newspapers** (www.keysweekly.com), the *News-Barometer* (www.newsbarometer.com), and www.bigpinekey.com. *The Miami Herald* (www.miamiherald.com) and the *Florida Keys Keynoter* (www.keysnet.com) are also available throughout the Keys.

SERVICES

Money

Although the Lower Keys have fewer businesses than the rest of the Keys, you'll still find helpful resources in—or near—the region. For banking needs, stop by **Capital Bank** (30480 Overseas Hwy., Big Pine Key, 305/872-0295 or 800/639-5111, www.capitalbank-us.com, 8am-4pm Mon.-Thurs., 8am-6pm Fri.) or the **First State Bank of the Florida Keys** (30515 Overseas Hwy., Big Pine Key, 305/872-4778, www.keysbank.com, 9am-5pm Mon.-Thurs., 9am-6pm Fri.).

Mail

For shipping, faxing, copying, and Internet needs, visit **Big Pine Shipping** (30342 Overseas Hwy., Big Pine Key, 305/600-1390, www.bigpineshipping.com, 8am-6pm Mon.-Fri., 10am-2pm Sat.). You'll also find two **post offices**

(800/275-8777, www.usps.com) in the area: one on Big Pine Key (29959 Overseas Hwy., 305/872-2531, 8:30am-4:30pm Mon.-Fri., 9am-noon Sat.) and one on Summerland Key (24700 Overseas Hwy., 305/745-3391, www.usps.com, 9:30am-4:30pm Mon.-Fri., 9am-noon Sat.).

Groceries and Supplies

For groceries, head to the **Winn-Dixie** (251 Key Deer Blvd., Big Pine Key, 305/872-4124, www.winndixie.com, 7am-11pm daily) in the **Big Pine Shopping Center** (MM 30.4 BS U.S. 1, Big Pine Key, www.bigpineshopping.com), a complex that offers a number of useful services, including hair salons, a laundromat, and a public library (213 Key Deer Blvd., Big Pine Key, 305/872-0992, www.keyslibraries.org, 9:30am-6pm Mon. and Wed.-Fri., 9:30am-8pm Tues., 10am-6pm Sat.). In addition, the Winn-Dixie features an on-site pharmacy (305/872-4850, 8am-8pm Mon.-Fri., 9am-6pm Sat., 10am-5pm Sun.).

Emergency Services

In case of an emergency that requires police, fire, or ambulance services, dial **911** from any cell or public phone. For nonemergency assistance, contact the **Monroe County Sheriff's Office** (Freeman Substation, 20950 Overseas Hwy., Cudjoe Key, 305/745-3184, www.keysso.net, 8am-5pm Mon.-Fri.). For medical assistance, consult the **Fishermen's Community Hospital** (3301 Overseas Hwy., Marathon, 305/743-5533, www.fishermenshospital.com) or the **Lower Keys Medical Center** (5900 College Rd., Key West, 305/294-5531, www.lkmc.com). Foreign visitors seeking help with directions, medical concerns, business issues, law enforcement needs, or other problems can receive **multilingual tourist assistance** (800/771-5397) 24 hours daily.

Getting There and Around

GETTING THERE
By Air

Despite the presence of small airports like the **Sugarloaf Key Airport** (MM 17 BS U.S. 1, Sugarloaf Key), the Lower Keys have no major airport of their own. To travel here by plane, you'll need to fly into **Fort Lauderdale-Hollywood International Airport** (FLL, 100 Terminal Dr., Fort Lauderdale, 866/435-9355, www.broward.org/airport), **Miami International Airport** (MIA, 2100 NW 42nd Ave., Miami, 305/876-7000, www.miami-airport.com), **Key West International Airport** (EYW, 3491 S. Roosevelt Blvd., Key West, 305/296-5439 or 305/296-7223, www.keywestinternationalairport.com), or **Florida Keys Marathon Airport** (MTH, 9400 Overseas Hwy., Marathon, 305/289-6060) and then rent a vehicle from agencies like **Avis** (800/633-3469, www.avis.com), **Budget** (800/218-7992, www.budget.com), **Enterprise** (800/261-7331, www.enterprise.com), **Hertz** (800/654-3131, www.hertz.com), or **Thrifty** (800/847-4389, www.thrifty.com) to reach the Lower Keys.

By Bus or Train

To reach the Lower Keys using the regional bus system, you can take the **Miami-Dade County Metrobus** (305/891-3131, www.miamidade. gov/transit), which operates the **301 Dade-Monroe Express** between Florida City and Marathon (5:15am-10:40pm daily, $2.35 per one-way trip). From Marathon, you can then use the **Lower Keys Shuttle** (either the LIME or PINK route, $4 per ride), operated by the **Key West Department of Transportation** (KWDoT, 305/600-1455 or 305/809-3910, www.kwtransit.com), to complete the rest of your journey. The shuttle runs from Marathon to Key West between 5:30am and 11:15pm daily, and from Key West to Marathon between 5am and 11pm daily. Other stops include Sunshine Key, Bahia Honda State Park, Big Pine Key, Little Torch Key, Ramrod Key,

Sugarloaf Key, and several other Lower Keys. Reduced fares may apply for students under 22 years old, senior citizens over 59 years old, military personnel, and disabled individuals.

In addition, **Greyhound** (305/296-9072 or 800/231-2222, www.greyhound.com) offers bus service to the Lower Keys by making regular bus stops at the Big Pine Key Motel (30725 Overseas Hwy., Big Pine Key). **Amtrak** (800/872-7245, www.amtrak.com), however, only provides train service as far south as Miami. Of course, you can always rent a car or hop a shuttle to reach the Lower Florida Keys.

Transport from Airports and Stations

If you arrive in the Fort Lauderdale/Miami area by plane, bus, or train—or Key West by plane or bus—you can either rent a car or, in some cases, hire a shuttle service to reach the Lower Keys. Some of these companies include **Keys Shuttle** (305/289-9997 or 888/765-9997, www.keysshuttle.com, $80-100 per shared ride, $350-450 for exclusive service) and **Keys Tropical Transportation** (305/852-3595, www. keystropicaltransportation.com, starting at $130 or $165 per ride, depending on the airport of origin), both of which provide service from the Miami and Fort Lauderdale airports. Another option is **TO'n'FRO** (305/393-0955, www.tonfro.com, $300-400 per luxury sedan ride), a personalized van and car service that offers transportation between the Miami and Fort Lauderdale airports and any destination in the Keys.

By Car

To reach the Lower Keys from Miami, simply head south on U.S. 1 (Overseas Hwy.), continue through Key Largo, Islamorada, and Marathon, and cross the Seven Mile Bridge. If you're headed from the Everglades via I-75 (Everglades Pkwy.), drive south on U.S. 27, veer right onto SR-997 (Krome Ave.), and follow the signs to U.S. 1. From U.S. 41 (Tamiami Trl.) in the Everglades, head south on SR-997 and continue toward U.S. 1.

If you arrive during the high season (Dec.-Apr.), be sure to call **511** for an up-to-the-minute traffic report.

GETTING AROUND
By Car

The best way to travel through the Lower Keys is by car, truck, RV, or motorcycle—all of which offer easy access to U.S. 1 and the smaller roads, such as Key Deer Boulevard on Big Pine Key, Watson Boulevard on No Name Key, and Sugarloaf Boulevard on Sugarloaf Key.

By Taxi

Taxicab companies such as **Big Pine Taxi** (305/872-2662, $2 per mile, flat rates available) can help you get around the Lower Keys.

By Bicycle or Boat

While you can certainly traverse the Lower Keys by bicycle, the sprawling nature of this region makes it challenging for novice riders.

Nevertheless, it's a lovely, ecofriendly way to experience the major islands, and even if you didn't bring your own bicycle, you're in luck. The **Big Pine Bicycle Center** (31 County Rd., Big Pine Key, 305/872-0130, www.big-pinebikes.com, 9am-5pm Mon.-Fri., 9am-3pm Sat., $8 per half day, $10 daily, $40 weekly), near Mile Marker 30.9 on the gulf side, offers beach cruiser rentals as well as repairs.

Of course, biking will only get you so far. Most of the islands down here stand alone, and without the benefit of roads or bridges, you can only reach them by boat. Having your own boat makes navigating these islands, especially those in the backcountry, even easier, and you'll find no shortage of boat ramps and marina slips in the Lower Keys. It's also possible to explore this marvelous region by kayak. If that piques your interest, contact **Big Pine Kayak Adventures** (305/872-7474, www.keyskayaktours.com, 8am-5pm daily, $20 for two hours, $5 for each additional hour), which is based out of the Old Wooden Bridge Marina (1791 Bogie Dr., Big Pine Key, 305/872-2241) and even offers kayak rentals for multiple days.

KEY WEST

At the end of the Overseas Highway lies the southernmost point in the continental United States—on a quirky little island known as Key West, where biking and walking are the preferred modes of transportation. Residents here are proud to call themselves "conchs"—a remnant of the past, when Bahamian immigrants called this unique place home. To many, the Conch Republic (a term that mainly refers to Key West, though some people also apply it to the entire Florida Keys archipelago) is more than just an excuse for souvenirs; it's a symbol of the island's distinctive vibe. No wonder famous visionaries like Ernest Hemingway, Tennessee Williams, Robert Frost, and John James Audubon had such an affinity for this town.

These days Key West is home to a blend of varied folks, including vacationing families, retired couples, eccentric artists, newlyweds, adventurers, corporate escapees, and hardy natives who can withstand the humidity, isolation, and hurricane season. The island also has a sizable gay population—as evidenced by male-only resorts, gay-themed tours, and events like Fantasy Fest.

Those who have heard of Key West but never seen it for themselves often liken it to a 24-hour Mardi Gras celebration in the New Orleans French Quarter, but the Southernmost City is not so easy to characterize. In fact, it's as diverse as the rest of the Keys. While there's indeed a party vibe in some of the Old Town bars and restaurants—such as Sloppy Joe's, home to the famous Hemingway Look-Alike Contest during the city's annual Hemingway Days—that's not all that Key West has to offer.

© LAURA MARTONE

HIGHLIGHTS

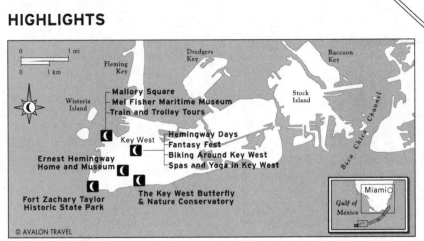

© AVALON TRAVEL

LOOK FOR 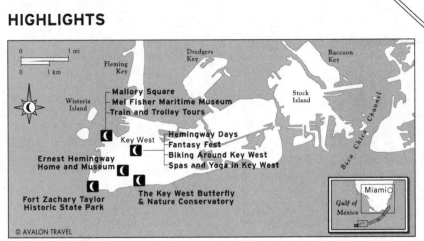 TO FIND RECOMMENDED SIGHTS, ACTIVITIES, DINING, AND LODGING.

◖ Mallory Square: Situated in Key West's Old Town, this waterfront plaza presents several eateries, shops, monuments, and attractions, including the daily Sunset Celebration (page 227).

◖ Mel Fisher Maritime Museum: Besides educating visitors about marine archaeology, this impressive repository highlights many of the treasures that Mel Fisher's crew discovered in the famous *Atocha* shipwreck (page 229).

◖ Ernest Hemingway Home and Museum: Surrounded by lush gardens, this 19th-century mansion was once home to novelist Ernest "Papa" Hemingway, who wrote *To Have and Have Not* in the backyard studio (page 233).

◖ The Key West Butterfly & Nature Conservatory: Stroll amid hundreds of vibrant flowers, birds, and butterflies in a glass-enclosed habitat (page 234).

◖ Fort Zachary Taylor Historic State Park: Centered around an intriguing Civil War fort, Florida's southernmost state park features nature trails, a popular beach, and access to incredible snorkeling opportunities (page 236).

◖ Train and Trolley Tours: A 90-minute narrated tour aboard either the Conch Tour Train or the Old Town Trolley provides an overview of the city's major sights and diversions (page 240).

◖ Hemingway Days: In honor of Key West's most famous former resident, this annual summertime event offers an array of activities, from a marlin tournament to a Hemingway Look-Alike Contest (page 249).

◖ Fantasy Fest: Prior to Halloween, this zany 10-day event provides a quintessential look at Key West culture, complete with outrageous costumes, colorful parades, brazen drag queens, wet T-shirt contests, and toga parties (page 250).

◖ Biking Around Key West: Residents and visitors alike enjoy touring this one-of-a-kind town by bicycle. Experience its historical homes, lovely gardens, and scenic beaches (page 260).

◖ Spas and Yoga in Key West: Befitting this tropical paradise, several resorts and day spas provide rest and rejuvenation with a variety of massages, body treatments, and sometimes, yoga lessons (page 266).

KEY WEST AND STOCK ISLAND

OVERSEAS HWY

ANDY GRIFFITHS CHARTERS

MEAN GREEN CHARTERS

BOYD'S KEY WEST CAMPGROUND

EL MAR RV RESORT

AMAZING GRACE

LOWER KEYS MEDICAL CENTER

KEY WEST GOLF CLUB

Stock Island

SAFE HARBOUR MARINA

TENNESSEE WILLIAMS THEATRE

HURRICANE HOLE RESTAURANT & MARINA

LEO'S CAMPGROUND

STOCK ISLAND

OLD ISLAND HARBOR

SUNSET MARINA

ALMOST THERE SPORTFISHING CHARTERS

Key West Tropical Forest and Botanical Garden

KEY WEST MARRIOTT BEACHSIDE HOTEL

S ROOSEVELT BLVD

KEY WEST INTERNATIONAL AIRPORT

FORT EAST MARTELLO

KEY WEST GREYHOUND STATION

Sigsbee Park

DIVE KEY WEST

KENNEDY DR

FLAGLER AVE

KEY WEST LAUNDERETTE

SOLAR SPA OF KEY WEST

HABANA PLAZA COIN LAUNDRY

S ROOSEVELT BLVD

Smathers Beach

SEE "KEY WEST" MAP

KEY WEST

THE KEY WEST BUTTERFLY & NATURE CONSERVATORY

ERNEST HEMINGWAY HOME AND MUSEUM

WHITEHEAD ST

EATON ST

To Dry Tortugas National Park

TRAIN AND TROLLEY TOURS

MALLORY SQUARE

MEL FISHER MARITIME MUSEUM

FORT ZACHARY TAYLOR HISTORIC STATE PARK

© AVALON TRAVEL

1 mi
1 km
0
0

Old Town contains a number of Victorian inns, tropical gardens, and luxurious spas—not to mention a plethora of reliable restaurants, offering everything from fresh seafood to Caribbean cuisine to tangy key lime pie. Historical attractions abound here, too—from the Ernest Hemingway Home and Museum to the Audubon House & Tropical Gardens. Other curious diversions, like trolley tours, maritime museums, sunset celebrations at Mallory Square, and The Key West Butterfly & Nature Conservatory, can keep history buffs, relentless revelers, and nature lovers busy for days on end.

Shoppers will also find an array of enticing boutiques and emporiums. Cultural enthusiasts will be delighted by the variety of concerts and plays available. Recreationists can play golf, rent a kayak, embark on a fishing excursion, snorkel in the surrounding waters, or venture to the Dry Tortugas, and if that's not enough, Key West also hosts an assortment of festivals and events throughout the year, from the Conch Republic Independence Celebration to the Lighted Boat Parade during the winter holiday season.

Still, while Key West isn't as easy to characterize as some may believe, it is indeed a laid-back locale, where the island time seems to move at a pace all its own. As if to accentuate this easygoing persona, the tunes of Jimmy Buffett—the quintessential mascot for Key West and the Florida Keys—seem to feature prominently in every bar, restaurant, and local performer's repertoire, no matter the time of day or night.

HISTORY

During pre-Columbian times, the Calusa native people inhabited the island now known as Key West. Although Spanish explorer Juan Ponce de León was probably the first European to visit the island during his second expedition to Florida in 1521, it wasn't until Florida became a Spanish colony that a fishing and cargo-salvaging village was established here.

When initially settled by the Spanish, the island was apparently littered with bones, a fact that sparked its name: *Cayo Hueso* (Bone Island). In 1763 the British took control of Florida and relocated the community of Spaniards and Native Americans to Havana. Even after Florida returned to Spanish control in the 1780s, the island was only informally used by Cuban and Bahamian fishermen.

Key West then passed through several different hands before U.S. businessman John W. Simonton—who had been informed of the deep harbor and strategic location by his friend John Whitehead—was able to gain title to the "Gibraltar of the West." In 1822 Matthew C. Perry, who reported on piracy problems in the Caribbean, planted the U.S. flag on the island, symbolically claiming the Florida Keys for America. Although Perry tried renaming it Thompson's Island for Secretary of the Navy Smith Thompson, the name never stuck.

Soon after his purchase, Simonton subdivided the island into plots and sold some of the land to John Whitehead, John Fleming, and two men who quickly resold their share to Pardon C. Greene. Today all four of these early developers have been immortalized on the city grid in the form of street names. Other early residents of Key West include black Bahamian immigrants, known as "Conchs," who came in even larger numbers after 1830 and claimed an area west of Old Town now known as Bahama Village.

In the early 1800s, major industries in Key West included fishing, salt production, and cargo salvaging. By 1860 Key West had become the largest and richest city in Florida mainly because most of the inhabitants were salvaging high-priced cargo from shipwrecks on nearby reefs.

The latter half of the 19th century was an active period for Key West. During the American Civil War, the island remained in Union hands because of the naval base there, even though the rest of Florida joined the Confederate States of America. Fort Zachary Taylor, which was erected and fortified near Key West between 1845 and 1866, became a significant outpost during the Civil War. Meanwhile, Fort Jefferson, which was constructed in

KEY WEST

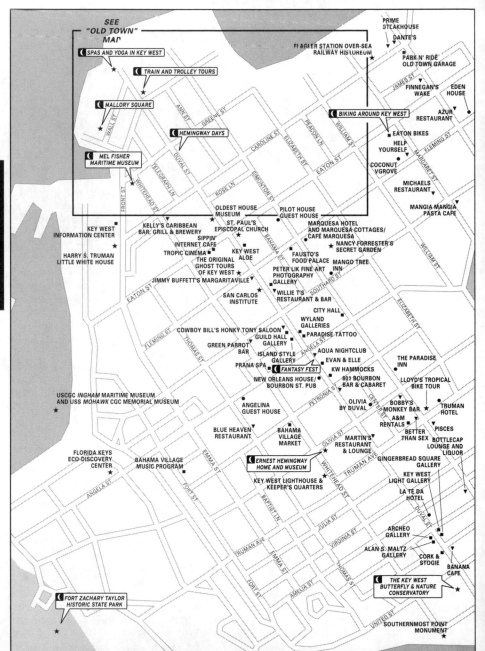

SEE "OLD TOWN" MAP

SPAS AND YOGA IN KEY WEST

TRAIN AND TROLLEY TOURS

MALLORY SQUARE

HEMINGWAY DAYS

MEL FISHER MARITIME MUSEUM

PRIME STEAKHOUSE

DANTE'S

FLAGLER STATION OVER-SEA RAILWAY HISTOREUM

PARK N' RIDE OLD TOWN GARAGE

FINNEGAN'S WAKE

EDEN HOUSE

BIKING AROUND KEY WEST

AZUR RESTAURANT

EATON BIKES

HELP YOURSELF

COCONUT VGROVE

MICHAELS RESTAURANT

MANGIA MANGIA PASTA CAFE

KEY WEST INFORMATION CENTER

HARRY S. TRUMAN LITTLE WHITE HOUSE

OLDEST HOUSE MUSEUM

PILOT HOUSE GUEST HOUSE

MARQUESA HOTEL AND MARQUESA COTTAGES/ CAFÉ MARQUESA

KELLY'S CARIBBEAN BAR, GRILL & BREWERY

ST. PAUL'S EPISCOPAL CHURCH

SIPPIN' INTERNET CAFE

TROPIC CINEMA

KEY WEST ALOE

FAUSTO'S FOOD PALACE

NANCY FORRESTER'S SECRET GARDEN

THE ORIGINAL GHOST TOURS OF KEY WEST

MANGO TREE INN

PETER LIK FINE ART PHOTOGRAPHY GALLERY

JIMMY BUFFETT'S MARGARITAVILLE

SAN CARLOS INSTITUTE

WILLIE T'S RESTAURANT & BAR

CITY HALL

WYLAND GALLERIES

COWBOY BILL'S HONKY TONY SALOON

PARADISE TATTOO

GUILD HALL GALLERY

GREEN PARROT BAR

AQUA NIGHTCLUB

ISLAND STYLE GALLERY

EVAN & ELLE

THE PARADISE INN

PRANA SPA

FANTASY FEST

KW HAMMOCKS

NEW ORLEANS HOUSE/ BOURBON ST. PUB

801 BOURBON BAR & CABARET

LLOYD'S TROPICAL BIKE TOUR

USCGC INGHAM MARITIME MUSEUM AND USS MOHAWK CGC MEMORIAL MUSEUM

OLIVIA BY DUVAL

BOBBY'S MONKEY BAR

TRUMAN HOTEL

ANGELINA GUEST HOUSE

A&M RENTALS

PISCES

BLUE HEAVEN RESTAURANT

BAHAMA VILLAGE MARKET

MARTIN'S RESTAURANT & LOUNGE

BETTER THAN SEX

BOTTLECAP LOUNGE AND LIQUOR

GINGERBREAD SQUARE GALLERY

FLORIDA KEYS ECO-DISCOVERY CENTER

BAHAMA VILLAGE MUSIC PROGRAM

ERNEST HEMINGWAY HOME AND MUSEUM

KEY WEST LIGHTHOUSE & KEEPER'S QUARTERS

KEY WEST LIGHT GALLERY

LA TE DA HOTEL

ARCHEO GALLERY

ALAN S. MALTZ GALLERY

CORK & STOGIE

BANANA CAFE

FORT ZACHARY TAYLOR HISTORIC STATE PARK

THE KEY WEST BUTTERFLY & NATURE CONSERVATORY

SOUTHERNMOST POINT MONUMENT

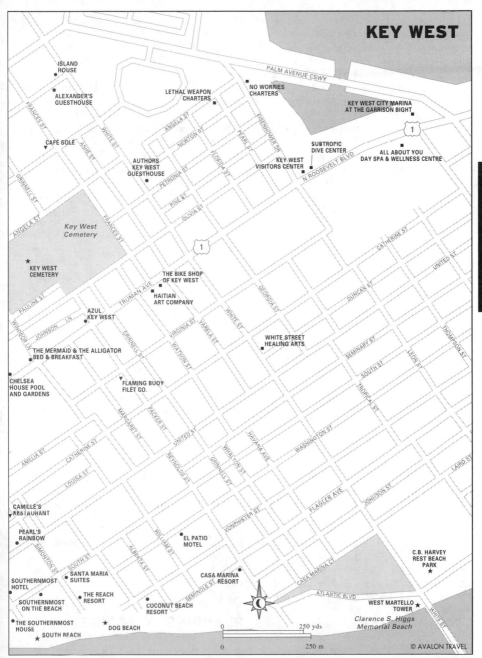

KEY WEST

ISLAND HOUSE

ALEXANDER'S GUESTHOUSE

LETHAL WEAPON CHARTERS

NO WORRIES CHARTERS

PALM AVENUE CSWY

KEY WEST CITY MARINA AT THE GARRISON BIGHT

CAFÉ SOLÉ

AUTHORS KEY WEST GUESTHOUSE

KEY WEST VISITORS CENTER

SUBTROPIC DIVE CENTER

ALL ABOUT YOU DAY SPA & WELLNESS CENTRE

KEY WEST

Key West Cemetery

KEY WEST CEMETERY

THE BIKE SHOP OF KEY WEST

HAITIAN ART COMPANY

AZUL KEY WEST

WHITE STREET HEALING ARTS

THE MERMAID & THE ALLIGATOR BED & BREAKFAST

CHELSEA HOUSE POOL AND GARDENS

FLAMING BUOY FILET CO.

CAMILLE'S RESTAURANT

PEARL'S RAINBOW

EL PATIO MOTEL

C.B. HARVEY REST BEACH PARK

SOUTHERNMOST HOTEL

SANTA MARIA SUITES

CASA MARINA RESORT

SOUTHERNMOST ON THE BEACH

THE REACH RESORT

WEST MARTELLO TOWER

THE SOUTHERNMOST HOUSE

COCONUT BEACH RESORT

Clarence S. Higgs Memorial Beach

SOUTH BEACH

DOG BEACH

ATLANTIC BLVD

0   250 yds

0   250 m

© AVALON TRAVEL

the Dry Tortugas about 68 miles west of the Southernmost City, became a military prison during and after the war. The 1860s and 1870s witnessed a rise in Cuban refugees, who were responsible for pioneering Key West's cigar-making industry, which eventually upstaged the flagging cargo-salvaging and salt-producing industries in the late 1800s.

In spite of such prosperity, the city of Key West suffered a setback in the mid-1880s. During the early morning hours of April 1, 1886, a fire began in the San Carlos Hall on Duval Street. Because of high winds and inadequate firefighting equipment, the fire quickly spread through the downtown area, ultimately killing four people and destroying more than six wharves and 50 buildings, including St. Paul's Episcopal Church. Following the Great Fire of 1886, the area now known as Old Town underwent several years of restoration, resulting in such architectural gems as the red-brick Custom House on Front Street.

Despite being the largest and wealthiest city in Florida in the 1890s, Key West remained fairly isolated until it was linked to the Florida mainland via the Overseas Railroad in 1912. Although the Labor Day Hurricane of 1935 essentially destroyed the railroad and killed hundreds of residents, Key West did not remain isolated for long. By 1938 the U.S. government had completed the Overseas Highway, an extension of U.S. 1. It was also in the 1930s, and later in the 1940s, that Key West began to see an influx of celebrities, from President Harry S. Truman to writer Tennessee Williams.

Key West's most famous resident, Ernest Hemingway, spent a lot of time on the island in the late 1920s and actually lived here during the 1930s, in a lovely two-story home on Whitehead Street, which is now a tourist attraction. It was during this time, in fact, that Hemingway published several of his most famous novels, including *A Farewell to Arms* (1929), *To Have and Have Not* (1937), and *For Whom the Bell Tolls* (1940).

Despite its widespread appeal, Key West suffered a financial slump in the 1930s, which was remedied by the expansion of the naval base.

By World War II, the U.S. Navy had increased its presence from 50 to 3,000 acres, which included the Naval Air Station on Boca Chica Key and the Fort Taylor Annex—later renamed the Truman Annex, after President Harry S. Truman, who used the commandant's house as his wintertime White House. It was also in the 1940s that the island literally doubled in size, with a landfill now known as New Town.

By the late 1960s, tourism was beginning to take hold in Key West. The 1970s saw an increase in cruise ships, hotels, and other tourism-related establishments. The area also saw a rise in drug trafficking during this decade, and as a result, the growing tourism industry was hit hard in the early 1980s when a U.S. Border Patrol blockade near Florida City caused an enormous traffic jam for those leaving the Florida Keys via U.S. 1. In response to this disruptive search for illegal aliens and possible drug runners, Key West and the rest of the Florida Keys briefly declared their secession from the Union in 1982, subsequently forming the Conch Republic. This incident successfully ended the Border Patrol blockade, and today is celebrated with an annual Conch Republic Independence Celebration in Key West and a similar event in Key Largo.

Nowadays tourism is still the lifeblood of Key West, whose population of about 24,650 is the largest in the Florida Keys. Nearby Stock Island and faraway Dry Tortugas National Park also benefit from tourists' dollars. Once favored among marauding pirates, the small island of Key West is today divided into two distinct halves. On the western side lies Old Town, a historical district that includes most of the city's major tourist destinations, such as Mallory Square, Fort Zachary Taylor, Duval and Whitehead Streets, and the oceanside beaches. Meanwhile, the eastern side of the island, known as New Town, comprises shopping centers, residential areas, schools, and Key West International Airport.

PLANNING YOUR TIME

With its plethora of beaches, museums, nature centers, cultural events, train and trolley tours, sunset cruises, and other outdoor activities, Key West is definitely the most active town in the Florida Keys. In fact, it's no surprise that many travelers bypass the other islands to make Key West their primary destination.

Ironically, despite its diversions, it's also the most compact region in the Florida Keys. Including adjacent Stock Island, the area stretches from Mile Marker 5 to Mile Marker 0 on the Overseas Highway, which makes this an incredibly easy town to navigate. You can walk, bike, or drive around at your own pace. In addition, taxicabs and pedicabs are available day and night—which means you can stay wherever you want, from an Old Town bed-and-breakfast to a coastal resort.

Given all that there is to see and do, you could conceivably stay a long weekend in the Southernmost City—a week if you plan an extra trip to Dry Tortugas National Park. Deciding when to visit Key West will depend on several factors, not the least of which is whether or not you hope to catch annual events like Hemingway Days, which usually takes place in mid-July, or Fantasy Fest, which typically occurs in late October. Since Key West is popular at such times, as well as during the winter months, you should be prepared for higher lodging rates, crowded restaurants and bars, and the need for reservations.

Although crime is not a huge problem in the Florida Keys, bear in mind that Key West is a city, where anything is possible. As with many other tourist havens, muggings do occur from time to time, so it's advisable to stay alert and avoid walking on desolate, poorly lit streets at night.

For more information about Key West, consult the **Monroe County Tourist Development Council** (1201 White St., Ste. 102, Key West, 305/296-1552 or 800/352-5397, www.fla-keys.com, 9am-5pm Mon.-Fri.) and the **Key West Chamber of Commerce** (510 Greene St., 1st Fl., Key West, 305/294-2587, www.keywest-chamber.org, 8am-6:30pm daily).

Sights

Of all the inhabited Florida Keys, Key West has, by far, the most museums, cultural attractions, and sightseeing tours, many of which are suitable for the entire family. Although New Town and Stock Island have a few curious locales between them, most of the tourist-friendly spots can be found in Old Town, Key West's original settlement.

OLD TOWN

Just a self-guided stroll through Old Town, part of which is a National Historic District, is a worthy attraction in itself, especially for architecture lovers. Along the way, you'll spot historical buildings like the majestic **Old City Hall** (510 Greene St.), constructed in 1891; the red-brick **Custom House** (281 Front St.), also erected in 1891 and once the workplace of Thomas Edison; and innumerable Conch-style homes, ornate Victorian mansions, and unusual eyebrow houses. While wandering the streets of Key West, you're sure to find a myriad of worthy attractions to entice you off the side-walk—at least for a little while.

Flagler Station Over-Sea Railway Historeum

Although technically not part of Old Town, the **Historic Seaport at Key West Bight** (www.keywestseaport.com), which lies along the edge of this historical district, lures many a visitor onto the picturesque harbor walk—especially on sunny days, when it's pleasant just to amble along the waterfront, taking in the sights of majestic schooners, private yachts, and other boats in the harbor. Before completing this stroll, which stretches from Grinnell Street to Simonton, take a short detour inland to the corner of Caroline and Margaret Streets, where you'll spot the **Flagler Station**

KEY WEST

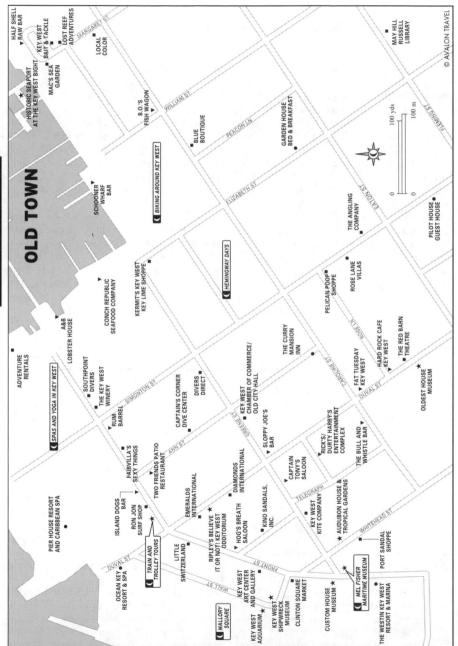

OLD TOWN

- HALF SHELL RAW BAR
- KEY WEST BAIT & TACKLE
- LOST REEF ADVENTURES
- LOCAL COLOR
- MAY HILL RUSSELL LIBRARY
- HISTORIC SEAPORT AT THE KEY WEST BIGHT
- MAC'S SEA GARDEN
- B.O.'S FISH WAGON
- SCHOONER WHARF BAR
- BLUE BOUTIQUE
- GARDEN HOUSE BED & BREAKFAST
- ⚑ BIKING AROUND KEY WEST
- THE ANGLING COMPANY
- CONCH REPUBLIC SEAFOOD COMPANY
- KERMIT'S KEY WEST KEY LIME SHOPPE
- ⚑ HEMINGWAY DAYS
- PILOT HOUSE GUEST HOUSE
- A&B LOBSTER HOUSE
- ROSE LANE VILLAS
- PELICAN POOP SHOPPE
- ADVENTURE RENTALS
- ⚑ SPAS AND YOGA IN KEY WEST
- SOUTHPOINT DIVERS
- THE KEY WEST WINERY
- THE CURRY MANSION INN
- FAT TUESDAY KEY WEST
- HARD ROCK CAFE KEY WEST
- THE RED BARN THEATRE
- RUM BARREL
- CAPTAIN'S CORNER DIVE CENTER
- DIVERS DIRECT
- KEY WEST CHAMBER OF COMMERCE/ OLD CITY HALL
- ★ OLDEST HOUSE MUSEUM
- FAIRVILLA'S SEXY THINGS
- TWO FRIENDS PATIO RESTAURANT
- SLOPPY JOE'S BAR
- RICK'S/ DURTY HARRY'S ENTERTAINMENT COMPLEX
- THE BULL AND WHISTLE BAR
- PIER HOUSE RESORT AND CARIBBEAN SPA
- ISLAND DOGS BAR
- RON JON SURF SHOP
- EMERALDS INTERNATIONAL
- DIAMONDS INTERNATIONAL
- CAPTAIN TONY'S SALOON
- KEY WEST KITE COMPANY
- AUDUBON HOUSE & TROPICAL GARDENS
- PORT SANDAL SHOPPE
- OCEAN KEY RESORT & SPA
- ⚑ TRAIN AND TROLLEY TOURS
- LITTLE SWITZERLAND
- RIPLEY'S BELIEVE IT OR NOT! KEY WEST ODDITORIUM
- HOG'S BREATH SALOON
- KINO SANDALS, INC.
- ★ MEL FISHER MARITIME MUSEUM
- ⚑ MALLORY SQUARE
- KEY WEST AQUARIUM
- KEY WEST ART CENTER AND GALLERY
- ★ KEY WEST SHIPWRECK MUSEUM
- CLINTON SQUARE MARKET
- CUSTOM HOUSE MUSEUM
- THE WESTIN KEY WEST RESORT & MARINA

MARGARET ST
WILLIAM ST
PEACON LN
ELIZABETH ST
EATON ST
FLEMING ST
ROSE LN
CAROLINE ST
DUVAL ST
SIMONTON ST
GREENE ST
ANN ST
TELEGRAPH
WHITEHEAD ST
FRONT ST
DUVAL ST
WALL ST

100 yds
100 m

© AVALON TRAVEL

Over-Sea Railway Historeum (901 Caroline St., 305/293-8716, www.flaglerstation.net, 9am-5pm daily, $5 adults, $2.50 children). Completed in January of 1912, the station now serves as a tribute to Henry Flagler's determination to construct a 130-mile extension of the Florida East Coast Railway all the way to Key West.

In spite of his many critics, Flagler achieved his dream, with the help of hundreds of tireless workers. Although the Labor Day Hurricane of 1935 effectively destroyed the Overseas Railroad, this historical feat is still worthy of exploration, and at the Flagler Station that's exactly what visitors can do. Here you'll encounter an assortment of intriguing artifacts, photographs, memorabilia, and eyewitness accounts. After passing through a reconstruction of the original station and a themed mercantile store, you'll step inside an actual railroad car, listen to informative storytellers, and watch various film presentations—including one about the construction of "Flagler's Folly" and another about the celebrations that took place on the day that Flagler and his wife arrived in Key West after riding the train all the way from New York.

Key West Turtle Museum

At the northern end of Margaret Street, between the Flagler Station Over-Sea Railway Historeum and the Historic Seaport at Key West Bight, lies one of the city's newest attractions: the enlightening **Key West Turtle Museum** (200 Margaret St., 305/294-0209, www.keywestturtlemuseum.org, 10am-5pm Tues.-Sat., donation suggested). Housed in a former turtle cannery and overseen by the lauded Mel Fisher Maritime Museum, this small attraction educates visitors about the long history of sea turtles in the Florida Keys. Sea turtles were a main source of sustenance for the Native American tribes that once inhabited these islands, and even the famous explorer Juan Ponce de León noted an abundance of loggerhead turtles in the surrounding waters. In fact, he was so impressed that he named the islands Tortugas, which means "turtles" in

Spanish. Unfortunately, turtl decimated the local sea turtle the early 1900s. Since the 1950s, h servation and rescue efforts have h endangered creatures by protecting t tats, tagging them for research purposes, and promoting public awareness of their plight. Besides featuring exhibits that explore Key West's maritime history, including its negative impact on area sea turtles and the subsequent efforts by conservationists like Archie Carr to save them, the museum also presents free lectures and other family-friendly programs, such as educational summer camps.

Ripley's Believe It or Not! Key West Odditorium

Half a block southeast of Front and Duval Streets, you'll encounter the two-story 8,000-square-foot **Ripley's Believe It or Not! Key West Odditorium** (108 Duval St., 305/293-9939, www.ripleys.com/keywest, 9:30am-11pm daily, $15 adults, $9 children 5-12, free for children under 5) on Duval. While not the most unique place in town, Ripley's is still very popular among visitors, especially children. Boasting over 500 unusual exhibits in 13 themed galleries, this bizarre attraction features everything from a stuffed rare white buffalo to a portrait fashioned from butterfly wings. Also on display are some of Ernest Hemingway's former belongings, including a typewriter and a shrunken torso.

◖ Mallory Square

Nestled alongside the Gulf of Mexico between Duval and Front Streets lies **Mallory Square** (1 Whitehead St., www.mallorysquare.com), a popular destination for residents and tourists alike. Stretching from the Ocean Key Resort to the cruise ship pier, this open-air district features several eateries and shops, such as those enclosed within the air-conditioned **Clinton Square Market.** You'll also find several attractions, including the **Key West Historic Memorial Sculpture Garden** (www.keywestsculpturegarden.org), which features 36 bronze busts of the town's pioneers, and the

© LAURA MAR

KEY WEST

strolling by the Key West Shipwreck Museum

Key West-Florida Keys Historic Military Memorial, which honors the city's involvement in America's major wars.

Also located here is the **Key West Shipwreck Museum** (1 Whitehead St., 305/292-8990, www.shipwreckhistoreum.com, 9:40am-5pm daily, $15 adults, $6.50 children 4-12, free for children under 4), where live performers, films, and actual artifacts let visitors experience a 19th-century wrecker's warehouse and learn about the 1856 *Isaac Allerton* shipwreck and subsequent salvage. You can also discover how Key West once became the richest city in America and even pretend to spot wrecks from the 65-foot lookout tower atop the museum, the last of 20 such towers in Key West. Just steps from the Shipwreck Museum, the **Key West Aquarium** (1 Whitehead St., 305/296-2051 or 888/544-5927, www.keywestaquarium.com, 10am-6pm daily, $15 adults, $7.50 children 4-12, free for children under 4) presents daily shark and turtle feedings as well as hands-on touch tanks featuring starfish, queen conch, and other regional marinelife. Opened

in 1934, the aquarium also offers visitors the chance to observe moray eels, barracuda, grouper, tarpon, parrotfish, sea turtles, alligators, and other sea creatures in a 50,000-gallon tank that represents a typical mangrove ecosystem in the Florida Keys.

At least once during your visit to Key West, stroll to Mallory Square in the late afternoon, when artists, musicians, acrobats, and tourists converge to pay homage to Key West's gorgeous sunsets during the daily **Sunset Celebration.** To avoid the crowds along the shore, head to The Westin Key West Resort & Marina at 245 Front Street, where you can watch the sunset while sipping cocktails on the aptly named **Sunset Deck.**

Custom House Museum

Beside the Clinton Square Market in Mallory Square stands the Custom House, a gorgeous red-brick structure erected in 1891 and once home to a post office, a courthouse, and a government center during a time when salvaging cargo from nearby shipwrecks had made Key West the wealthiest city per capita in the United States. By the 1930s, the city had gone bankrupt, and the Custom House was eventually abandoned. Following a nine-year, $9-million restoration project, the Key West Art & Historical Society opened the historical building to the public in 1999 as the Key West Museum of Art and History at the Custom House, now simply known as the **Custom House Museum** (281 Front St., 305/295-6616, www.kwahs.org, 9:30am-4:30pm daily, $7 adults, $6 seniors 62 and over and Key West residents, $5 children and students, free for children under 6) and listed in the National Register of Historic Places. Among the fascinating exhibits here you'll see Paul Collins's portraits of famous Key West residents, from Henry Flagler to Ernest Hemingway; Mario Sanchez's brightly colored wood paintings of life in Key West during the early 1900s; and various artifacts from Ernest Hemingway's adventurous life before and during his time on the island. You'll also learn about the pirates that once prowled the waters of the Florida Keys and how the U.S. Navy eventually expunged these looters and marauders from the region.

◀ Mel Fisher Maritime Museum

Not far from the hard-to-miss Custom House on Front Street stands the massive **Mel Fisher Maritime Museum** (200 Greene St., 305/294-2633, www.melfisher.org, 8:30am-5pm Mon.-Fri., 9:30am-5pm Sat.-Sun., $12.50 adults, $10.50 students, $6 children), one of the most impressive treasure collections and marine archaeology museums in the world. After passing through the gift shop just beyond the front entrance, you'll encounter an array of fascinating exhibits, the first of which explains Mel Fisher's 16-year search for the *Nuestra Señora de Atocha* and the *Santa Margarita,* two Spanish galleons that shipwrecked off the coast of the Florida Keys in 1622. Both vessels were part of a treasure fleet bound for Spain. Loaded with gold, silver, copper, tobacco, indigo, gems, and other valuables, the ships encountered a severe hurricane in early September of 1622, driving them

onto the coral reefs near the Dry Tortugas and drowning many of those on board. Although Spain managed to recover some of the cargo from the *Santa Margarita,* salvagers were never able to locate the *Atocha,* which had apparently sunk in more than 50 feet of water. The shipwreck attained legendary status when Fisher's determination finally prevailed.

Subsequent museum displays feature a mere fraction of the multimillion-dollar treasures that Fisher and his crew uncovered and preserved after the 1985 discovery. Here you'll see practical items such as daggers, corroded skillets, olive jars, shackles, thimbles, even an enormous anchor. In the adjacent chamber, you'll find it hard not to be awed by the varied treasures, from gold chains and silver coins to copper chunks and tobacco leaves. Especially intriguing is the 78-carat emerald that seems to glow like plutonium.

Following an exhibit about Mel Fisher's life, you'll head upstairs for the *La Plata del Mar* exhibit, highlighting the diverse collection of silver artifacts that were carried aboard the 1622 Spanish fleet. With holy music playing in the background, you'll stroll past enormous silver bars and varied display cases filled with silver reales, goblets, mirror frames, and other intriguing items. In the adjacent rooms, you'll learn about other sunken vessels, including the 1715 Plate Fleet and the *Henrietta Marie* slave ship. After your comprehensive tour, if your yen for treasure hunting has yet to be sated, consider stopping by Mel Fisher's Treasures, a separate jewelry store in the rear of the museum. And if that's not enough, you can opt to be an investor in the ongoing salvaging efforts of the *Atocha,* which is still yielding interesting, and often incredibly valuable, finds.

Audubon House & Tropical Gardens

Directly opposite the Mel Fisher museum on Greene Street—and, oddly enough, a gigantic water tank—you'll spot the **Audubon House & Tropical Gardens** (205 Whitehead St., 305/294-2116 or 877/294-2470, www.audubonhouse.com, 9:30am-5pm daily, $12 adults,

the impressive Mel Fisher Maritime Museum

$7.50 students, $5 children 6-12, free for children under 6), one of several tranquil, historical properties in Key West. Built in 1847 by Captain John H. Geiger, a shipwreck salvager and the city's first harbormaster, this gorgeous three-story home is a quintessential example of 19th-century architecture, with a symmetrical tropical-style design that features first-floor porches, second-level balconies, white walls and columns, and dark wooden shutters. Interestingly, John James Audubon never lived here, although the celebrated naturalist presumably visited the property in 1832 during a research trip to the Florida Keys and Dry Tortugas.

Inside the lovely mansion, you'll see plenty of antiques and period furniture, though the most interesting items are the numerous original renditions and reprints of Audubon's ornithological paintings throughout the second and third floors. Among the regional species on display are roseate spoonbills, Florida cormorants, booby gannets, brown pelicans, mangrove cuckoos, blue-headed pigeons, noddy terns, reddish egrets, and mango hummingbirds.

Following your tour of the house, feel free to meander along the brick pathways through the ecofriendly tropical gardens, shaded by palm trees and bursting with vibrant orchids and bromeliads. On your way out, take a moment to peruse the **Audubon House Gallery of Natural History,** a small art gallery near the entrance.

Harry S. Truman Little White House

Just south of Caroline and Front Streets, the Truman Annex features the **Harry S. Truman Little White House** (111 Front St., 305/294-9911, www.trumanlittlewhitehouse.com, 9am-5pm daily, $16 adults, $14 seniors, $5 children 5-12, free for children under 5 and Key West residents), another remarkable example of Key West architecture and a fascinating piece of the town's history. This breezy white structure, which was constructed in 1890 and once served as the command headquarters for the Key West Naval Station, became Truman's wintertime White House from 1946 to 1952 and later a retreat for five other U.S. presidents.

Now serving as Florida's only presidential museum and listed on the National Register of Historic Places, this restored home invites visitors to amble amid original furnishings and learn about President Truman's personal and professional life, the politics of the Cold War, the naval history of Key West, and the origin of the Department of Defense. **Guided tours** are offered every 20 minutes, between 9am and 4:30pm daily, and usually last between 45 and 55 minutes; scripts are available for the hearing-impaired. Guests can also take free self-guided tours of the adjacent **botanical gardens,** usually between 7am and 6pm daily, and the gift shop is open 9am-5pm daily. The museum offers wheelchair-accessible restrooms and allows service animals to accompany their owners onto the premises. Incidentally, parking is only available at Mallory Square or the Westin parking garage.

© LAURA MARTONE

the Audubon House & Tropical Gardens

KEY WEST

© ANDY NEWMAN/FLORIDA KEYS NEWS BUREAU

the shady grounds of the Harry S. Truman Little White House

Oldest House Museum

Currently operated by the **Old Island Restoration Foundation** (OIRF, www.oirf. org), the **Oldest House Museum** (322 Duval St., 305/294-9501, 10am-4pm Mon.-Tues. and Thurs.-Sat., free) is literally the oldest house in southern Florida. Supposedly erected in 1829 by Richard Cussans, a Bahamian builder and merchant, and moved to its current location in the mid-1830s, this white one-story country-style structure was the longtime home of Captain Frances Watlington, a sea captain, shipwreck salvager, and one-time state senator. The historic home remained in the Watlington family until 1972 when it was purchased by an individual and soon afterward deeded to the Historic Key West Preservation Board.

Over the decades, the stalwart house has survived fires, hurricanes, financial hardships, even the occupation of Union troops. Though docents and staff members are available to provide historical information about the property, visitors are free to roam through the tranquil rear garden as well as the house itself, which features many family portraits, original furnishings, plus other period pieces, ship models, and documents that relate to wrecking activities.

St. Paul's Episcopal Church

No matter how you choose to explore Duval, Old Town's main drag, you'll find it hard to miss the imposing white structure on the southeastern corner of Duval and Eaton Streets. Founded in 1831, **St. Paul's Episcopal Church** (401 Duval St., 305/296-5142, www. stpaulskeywest.org, 9am-5:30pm daily, free) is the oldest church community south of St. Augustine, though the building itself is far younger. Originally constructed in 1839, the first church, made of coral rock, was leveled in an 1846 hurricane. Rebuilt in 1848, the second church, a wooden structure, was destroyed by the city's Great Fire of 1886. The third church, also made of wood, was completed in 1887 and taken by a hurricane in 1909.

The fourth incarnation of the church, the concrete structure that exists today, was designed in 1911, completed in 1919, and heavily renovated in 1993. With a striking frame, gorgeous stained-glass windows, and a traditional tin roof, St. Paul's is truly a magnificent building and the widely accepted centerpiece of downtown Key West. No wonder it's often photographed by both residents and out-of-towners. Music lovers will especially appreciate this historical sanctuary, where the organist offers free lunchtime concerts, and musical events are featured throughout the year.

San Carlos Institute

Just over a block southeast of the prominent St. Paul's Episcopal Church, you'll spot another fine example of Floridian architecture. Founded in 1871 by Cuban exiles and featuring an ornate Spanish-style facade, the **San Carlos Institute** (516 Duval St., 305/294-3887, www.institutosancarlos.org, noon-6pm Fri.-Sun., free) is one of the state's most historic landmarks. Dubbed *"La Casa Cuba"* by Cuban poet José Martí, the San Carlos was the site of Martí's 1892 attempt to unite the politically divided Cuban exile community in a bid for Cuba's independence. Today this venerable institution serves as a nonprofit multipurpose facility, featuring a museum, a library, a school, an art gallery, and a 360-seat theater that often hosts seminars and live concerts. Of particular interest to most visitors are the permanent exhibits relating to the history of Cuba and Florida's Cuban-American community, such as the photographs of poet José Martí and the portraits of Cuba's constitutional presidents.

Nancy Forrester's Secret Garden

Two blocks east of Duval Street lies a private tropical oasis that has been open to the public for years. Also known as Key West's Exotic Tropical Botanical Garden, **Nancy Forrester's Secret Garden** (1 Free School Ln., 305/294-0015, www.nancyforrester.com, 10am-5pm daily, $10 adults, $5 children 5-11) is widely celebrated for its gorgeous landscape of ferns, aroids, shade palms, edible fruits, medicinal plants, and other rare foliage—an ideal home for the macaws who live here. In the center of this enticing sanctuary stands a small cottage that has often served as an inspiring artist's studio—and can even be rented by those hoping to escape amid nature for a while.

Created by local artist and environmental educator Nancy Forrester, this lush garden is more than just a tourist attraction. It's also meant to represent the artist's wish for humanity to restore balance to the natural world. Unfortunately, this lovely spot—the last undeveloped wooded acre in the heart of Old Town—needs the public's help to remain open, so if you relish this peaceful place, consider contributing to the capital campaign on your next visit.

Key West Cemetery

On the eastern side of Old Town, you'll find the intriguing palm-lined **Key West Cemetery** (701 Passover Ln., 305/292-8177, www.keywestcity.com, 7am-7pm daily in summer, 7am-6pm daily in winter, free). Established in 1847, following a disastrous 1846 hurricane that unearthed the original cemetery, this fenced 19-acre property now contains beautiful statuary, historical gravestones, amusing epitaphs, and the remains of more than 80,000 Bahamian mariners, Cuban cigar makers, Spanish-American War veterans, soldiers and civilians, millionaires and paupers, whites and blacks, Catholics, Protestants, and Jews, and other unique individuals, illustrating Key West's incredibly diverse heritage.

Bordered by Windsor Lane and Angela, Frances, and Olivia Streets, the front entrance actually lies near the intersection of Angela and Margaret, where you can pick up a free comprehensive self-guided tour map from the office (8:30am-3:30pm Mon.-Fri.). Guided one-hour tours (9:30am Tues. and Thurs., $15 pp donation suggested) are also available through the **Historic Florida Keys Foundation** (Old City Hall, 510 Greene St., 305/292-6718, www.historicfloridakeys.org), though reservations are required. Whether you come alone or as part of a tour group, remember that the cemetery is still an active place of reflection, so be respectful of mourners when visiting.

© DANIEL MARTONE

Visitors can take a tour of the Key West Cemetery.

restoration by the Key West Art & Historical Society two decades later—the same year that it was featured in a pivotal scene in *Licence to Kill* (1989)—it became the tourist attraction it is today.

Now visitors can climb the dizzying 88-step spiral staircase to a wraparound observation deck—just beneath the active 175-watt metal halide light—for an incredible 360-degree view of the verdant city. Helpful cards indicate important locales throughout Key West, including the Casa Marina resort in the distance and the grounds of the Ernest Hemingway Home down below. Also on the well-manicured grounds lies a small gift shop, plus the former keeper's quarters, constructed in 1887 to replace the original keeper's dwelling. Today the faithfully restored quarters serve as a museum, offering a look at turn-of-the-20th-century life with historical furniture, period furnishings, and old photographs. In addition, you'll find a collection of lighthouse artifacts, instruments, maps, and photographs within various exhibits that shed some light on the maritime history of the Florida Keys.

Key West Lighthouse & Keeper's Quarters

Near the intersection of Truman Avenue and Whitehead Street, it's difficult to ignore the stately white lighthouse towering above the trees. Here at the **Key West Lighthouse & Keeper's Quarters** (938 Whitehead St., 305/294-0012, www.kwahs.org, 9:30am-4:30pm daily, $10 adults, $9 seniors 62 and over and Key West residents, $5 students and children, free for children under 6), you'll learn about yet another facet of the coastal town's riveting history.

Erected in 1847 on a spot 14 feet above sea level, the 66-foot-tall brick lighthouse effectively replaced the original 46-foot wooden tower on Whitehead Point, which had been built in 1825 to aid ships navigating the dangerous offshore reefs and was unfortunately destroyed in 1846 by a hurricane. In 1894 the city added a 20-foot extension to the second lighthouse, which was decommissioned by the U.S. Coast Guard in 1969. After an expensive

◖ Ernest Hemingway Home and Museum

Directly across the street from the Key West Lighthouse lies the **Ernest Hemingway Home and Museum** (907 Whitehead St., 305/294-1136, www.hemingwayhome.com, 9am-5pm daily, $13 adults, $6 children, free for children under 5), one of the most popular attractions in all of Key West. Built in 1851 by Asa Tift, a marine architect and salvage wrecker, the airy two-story structure features white walls and olive-green shutters, wraparound porches on both the lower and upper levels, and arched windows and doors on all sides, which invite a lot of natural light. Curiously, this island-style domicile once housed the city's most famous resident, Papa Hemingway himself, and has since become a registered National Historic Landmark. Situated amid picturesque palm trees and blooming foliage, the home invites visitors to retrace the footsteps of Ernest Hemingway, an American novelist and

KEY WEST

the Ernest Hemingway Home and Museum, one of Key West's most famous landmarks

short-story writer known all around the world as a big-game hunter, sport fisherman, war veteran, and unabashed adventurer.

Inside the mansion, you'll see a cornucopia of memorabilia, including period furnishings, family photographs, original artwork, and war medals. The lovingly preserved home looks much as it did during the 1930s, when Hemingway and his wife Pauline lived here. Some of the docents, while happy to share stories about Hemingway, joke that they wish Hemingway's wife hadn't replaced all of the original ceiling fans with chandeliers—a decision that seems regrettable on the hottest days, when box fans can be found throughout the house.

If you're a first-time visitor to the Hemingway Home, you should definitely opt for a 30-minute **guided tour,** available throughout the day, before exploring the grounds on your own. Beyond the house, you'll encounter a lovely pool, quiet garden nooks, a bookstore and gift shop (305/294-1575), and the

Nobel Prize winner's well-preserved studio, where he spent his most productive years. It was here, after all, that he wrote and published some of his most enduring novels, nonfiction books, and short-story collections, including *A Farewell to Arms* (1929), *Death in the Afternoon* (1932), *Green Hills of Africa* (1935), and *To Have and Have Not* (1937). While here, you'll also see a plethora of six-toed felines, the descendants of Hemingway's legendary, polydactyl cats—many of whom bear the names of famous movie stars, from the calico called Audrey Hepburn to a much-photographed black-and-white cat named after classic film star Charlie Chaplin.

◖ The Key West Butterfly & Nature Conservatory

Situated near the southern end of Duval Street, **The Key West Butterfly & Nature Conservatory** (1316 Duval St., 305/296-2988 or 800/839-4647, www.keywestbutterfly.com, 9am-5pm daily, $12 adults, $9 seniors and military personnel, $8.50 children 4-12, free for children under 4) invites visitors to take a stroll through a vibrant glass-enclosed, climate-controlled habitat filled with waterfalls, trees, flowering plants, and hundreds of colorful birds and butterflies. While here, you can also learn about butterfly anatomy, physiology, life cycles, feeding, and migration in the **Learning Center,** which offers a 15-minute orientation film and an up-close view of caterpillars feeding and developing on their host plants. In addition, you can peruse Sam Trophia's kaleidoscopic creations—essentially, a variety of encased butterfly displays—inside the art gallery, **Wings of Imagination** (9am-5:30pm daily). Before leaving the nature center, be sure to browse through the wide assortment of butterfly-related items and other souvenirs in the on-site gift shop (9am-5:30pm daily). As a bonus feature, visitor parking is available in the lot behind the conservatory, but the gate closes at 6pm every day. Although the conservatory is technically open until 5pm each day, the last tickets are sold at 4:30pm.

HEMINGWAY'S KEY WEST

Perhaps Key West's most popular attraction, the **Ernest Hemingway Home and Museum** (907 Whitehead St., 305/294-1136, www.hemingwayhome.com) lures curious sightseers every day. Built in 1851 by marine architect Asa Tift, this two-story mansion became home to Ernest Hemingway and his second wife, Pauline Pfeiffer, in 1931. Today visitors can see descendants of his six-toed felines, plenty of original artwork and family photographs, and the separate writing studio where the Nobel Prize-winning novelist penned several famous short stories and books, including *To Have and Have Not* (1937), the story of a fishing boat captain who runs contraband between Cuba and Florida.

Naturally, this isn't the sole remnant of Hemingway's time in Key West. Not only does every train, trolley, and walking tour mention his name, but you'll also find some of his former belongings in places like **Ripley's Believe It or Not! Key West Odditorium** (108 Duval St.) and the **Custom House Museum** (281 Front St.). In addition, several hotels and watering holes claim ties to Papa Hemingway. The private Mediterranean Revival-style home known as **Casa Antigua** (314 Simonton St.), for instance, was once a residential hotel above a Ford dealership, and it was here that Hemingway and Pauline stayed during their first visit to Key West. He even finished the initial draft of *A Farewell to Arms* (1929) while awaiting the delivery of his new Model A. Supposedly, Hemingway also stayed at **The Southernmost House** (1400 Duval St.), and he frequented **Captain Tony's Saloon** (428 Greene St.) when it was the original location of Sloppy Joe's. Today you'll even catch a glimpse of Hemingway's former bar stool. Meanwhile, the most recent incarnation of **Sloppy Joe's Bar** (201 Duval St.) features the famous Hemingway Look-Alike Contest, part of the annual **Hemingway Days** celebration in July.

Hemingway first came to Key West in 1928.

For the next few years, he and Pauline spent winters in the Florida Keys and summers in Europe and Wyoming. Then in 1931, they acquired the house at 907 Whitehead Street. During this prolific period, his schedule consisted of writing every morning and relaxing every afternoon and evening with his friends. One particularly close pal was Joe Russell, an irascible fisherman and owner of Sloppy Joe's, a speakeasy. Russell introduced Hemingway to deep-sea fishing; Hemingway repaid the favor by immortalizing his friend as Harry Morgan, captain of the *Queen Conch* in *To Have and Have Not*. The backyard drinking fountain that Hemingway built for his cats is actually a refurbished urinal from Sloppy Joe's, which was also where Hemingway met reporter Martha Gellhorn in 1936, who would later become his third wife.

Originally, Hemingway's home was surrounded by a chain-link fence, but in 1935 he erected the perimeter wall that exists today, in the hope of providing his family privacy from gawking tourist hordes. Between 1937 and 1938, while Hemingway was serving as a war correspondent for the Spanish Civil War, Pauline supervised the construction of the first residential swimming pool in Key West. When he returned, he was shocked by the final price tag of $20,000, at which point he removed a penny from his pocket and told her that she might as well take his last cent. Today you can see this penny embedded beside the pool.

Hemingway stayed in Key West for well over a decade before divorcing Pauline in 1940, marrying Martha, and heading to Cuba. Pauline, meanwhile, stayed in the Key West home until her death in 1951. Upon Hemingway's death in 1961, the Key West home was sold to local businesswoman Bernice Dickson, who turned it into a museum in 1964. The home, which was designated a National Historic Landmark in 1968, remains the property of Dickson's family, though Hemingway's spirit is alive and well.

The Key West Butterfly & Nature Conservatory

SOUTHERN SHORE

Along the Atlantic Ocean side of Key West lie several interesting attractions, from military monuments to marine exhibits to fantastic beaches.

◖ Fort Zachary Taylor Historic State Park

Accessible via the western end of Southard Street, **Fort Zachary Taylor Historic State Park** (601 Howard England Way, 305/292-6713 or 305/295-0037, www.floridastateparks.org/forttaylor or www.fortzacharytaylor.com, 8am-sunset daily, $7 vehicles with 2-8 passengers plus $0.50 pp, $4.50 motorcycles and single-occupant vehicles, $2.50 pedestrians, bikers, and extra passengers) is, in fact, the southernmost state park in Florida—and, for that matter, the continental United States. It's also a well-favored destination among history buffs and recreationists alike.

Situated at the convergence of the Gulf of Mexico and the Atlantic Ocean, where the clear, deep waters nurture living coral, yellowtail snapper, tropical fish, lobster, and other marine creatures, the 54-acre park is especially popular with swimmers, snorkelers, scuba divers, sunbathers, and picnickers, not to mention wedding parties. Enhanced by imported sand, the beach here is generally considered the finest in Key West—and an ideal place to watch an incredible Florida Keys sunset. Bikers, hikers, anglers, and bird-watchers also enjoy spending time in this beautiful place. Beyond biking paths and wooded nature trails, other amenities include picnic tables, barbecue grills, public restrooms, outdoor showers, ample parking, as well as beach equipment and water-sports rentals, such as chairs, rafts, and snorkeling gear. In addition, the Cayo Hueso Café offers refreshments from 10am to 5pm daily.

But, of course, it's the 19th-century fort that lures many visitors to this historical state park. Completed in 1866, it was critical during the American Civil War and Spanish-American War and designated a National Historic Landmark in 1973. Although you're free to wander through the fort on your own, you can also opt for one of the narrated 30-minute tours, which are available daily at noon. You'll especially enjoy visiting Fort Zachary Taylor during annual events, such as Civil War Days in February and the Conch Republic Independence Celebration in April, so be sure to plan your visit accordingly.

Florida Keys Eco-Discovery Center

From Southard Street, you can head west toward the Truman Waterfront, where you'll spy the **Florida Keys Eco-Discovery Center** (35 E. Quay Rd., 305/809-4750, www.floridakeys.noaa.gov, 9am-4pm Tues.-Sat., free). The 6,000-square-foot nature center features an array of interactive exhibits, dioramas, and displays about the Keys' varied ecosystems, including upland pinelands, hardwood hammocks, beach dunes, mangrove shores, seagrass flats, and coral reefs. Visitors can take a virtual 1,600-foot dive to the deep shelf; learn why a fort was built in the isolated Dry Tortugas;

Water surrounds Fort Zachary Taylor.

view a 2,500-gallon reef tank, filled with living coral and tropical fish; and walk through a mock-up of Aquarius, the world's only underwater ocean laboratory. Free parking is available on-site, and all net proceeds from the gift shop directly fund educational programs at the Eco-Discovery Center.

USCGC Ingham Maritime Museum

Military-history enthusiasts might enjoy a quick detour to Memorial Park, which holds the **USCGC Ingham Maritime Museum** (Truman Waterfront, Old U.S. Navy Pier, 305/292-5072, www.uscgcingham.org, 10am-4pm daily, $10 adults, $6 children 12-18, free for children under 12 and military personnel), a historical 327-foot U.S. Coast Guard cutter that was built in 1935 and served the nation from 1936 to 1988. Visitors can take a self-guided tour of the ship, which includes authentic artifacts, historical photographs, and interpretive signs outlining the ship's history. While on board, you'll be able to see where the men ate, slept, and played, and for an added fee

($20 pp), you can take a guided tour that includes additional chambers like the boiler room and engine room.

Nearby is the floating **USS Mohawk CGC Memorial Museum** (305/292-5072, www.uscgcmohawk.org, 10am-4pm daily, $6 adults, $3 children 10-18, free for children under 10 and military personnel), a former World War II combat ship that was involved in 14 attacks against Nazi submarines. Built in 1934, this historical U.S. Coast Guard cutter now serves as a memorial to the battles fought in the Atlantic Ocean. Though retired from active duty, the 165-foot-long *Mohawk* is still fully operational, a rarity among decommissioned World War II vessels. Visitors here can watch a brief orientation film, then take a self-guided tour of various chambers, featuring artifacts, photographs, and interpretive signs. The main deck, which is accessible to wheelchairs, also welcomes strollers, making this an ideal stop for families on vacation. Combination adult tickets ($15 pp) are available for those wanting to visit both ships. In addition, parking is one of several intriguing exhibits at the Florida Keys Eco-Discovery Center

available on-site, though you can also walk to the floating maritime museums from Southard Street.

Southernmost Point Monument

Located at the corner of South and Whitehead Streets, right beside the Atlantic Ocean, stands an enormous replica of a marine buoy that marks the southernmost point in the continental United States. Once designated by a mere sign, the spot gained the now-famous monument in 1983, when city officials grew tired of replacing the oft-stolen sign. Colorfully painted in red, yellow, black, and white, the marker simply reads "Southernmost Point Continental U.S.A." Also emblazoned on the monument are the phrases "The Conch Republic," "90 Miles to Cuba," and "Key West, FL, Home of the Sunset." Today it's one of the most photographed attractions in all of Key West, as evidenced by the frequently long line of visitors, waiting for their chance to pose in front of the colorful buoy—smaller versions of which are often seen throughout the city, on

everything from shot glasses to key chains to playing cards.

Beaches

Several public beaches, ranging in size and appeal, stretch along the southern shore of Key West. The good news is that all of them are free and open daily, but the bad news is that they're often crowded, especially on a gorgeous weekend during the peak winter season. Just remember that swimming is at your own risk, given the absence of lifeguards. In addition, just because Key West has several clothing-optional resorts doesn't mean that such a flexible policy extends to the beaches down here; topless and nude sunbathing is actually illegal. Alcohol, drugs, campfires, glass containers, and overnight camping are also not allowed on the public beaches of Key West.

At the terminus of Duval Street, you'll first encounter **South Beach** (7am-11pm daily, free), a cute patch of sand that's a far cry from the similarly named one in Miami. While it offers shallow waters, a pleasant pier, and an incredible view of the ocean, it's much smaller—and calmer—than its counterpart a few hours north. Nevertheless, it's a favorite among locals, despite the lack of restrooms and facilities. East of Simonton, the somewhat rocky **Dog Beach** (7am-11pm daily, free) is obviously popular among pet owners, though it has no restrooms or other facilities. Farther east, alongside Atlantic Boulevard between Reynolds and White Streets, lies another popular Key West beach, the wide sandy **Clarence S. Higgs Memorial Beach** (6am-11pm daily, free), where in addition to swimming and sunbathing, sun worshipers can rent water-sports equipment or stroll amid pelicans and seagulls on the adjacent swimming pier. Other on-site amenities include covered picnic tables, public restrooms, a playground, and chair rentals.

Even farther east, near Atlantic Boulevard and White Street, the wheelchair-accessible **C. B. Harvey Rest Beach** (7am-11pm daily, free) offers sandy dunes, picnic tables, public restrooms, a fishing pier, a yoga deck, and a biking path. Of course, on warm, sunny days, crowds flock to lengthy, artificially made **Smathers Beach** (7am-11pm daily, free) alongside Roosevelt Boulevard, a popular spot for spring breakers and an ideal place to watch the sunrise, have a picnic, or play a volleyball game. Water-sports and chair rentals, biking paths, concession stands, public restrooms, a boat ramp, and ample parking are also available here. **Sunset Watersports Key West** (305/296-2554, www.sunsetwatersportskeywest.com, 9am-6pm daily, $49 pp) even offers parasailing excursions from here.

West Martello Tower

On Higgs Beach, where White Street meets the Atlantic Ocean, stands the **West Martello Tower**, a Civil War-era fort that, as with the Fort East Martello Museum, was inspired by the round, stalwart fortress at Mortella Point in Corsica, an island in the Mediterranean Sea. Constructed during the 1860s by the U.S. Army Corps of Engineers, the West Martello

© DANIEL MARTONE

the swimming pier that extends from Clarence S. Higgs Memorial Beach

Tower was never fully completed, and in the late 1940s, it was nearly leveled for aesthetic reasons. Luckily, demolition plans were thwarted, and it has since been listed on the National Register of Historic Places.

Home to the **Key West Garden Club** (1100 Atlantic Blvd., 305/294-3210, www.keywestgardenclub.com, 9:30am-5pm daily, free) since 1955, this historical locale entices visitors to stroll along brick pathways, amid graceful arches and lush colorful foliage, which features a rare collection of blooming orchids, bromeliads, and other native and exotic flora. Here you can simply sit beside a water lily pond or butterfly garden, enjoy balmy breezes from an oceanfront gazebo, and temporarily trade the hustle and bustle of places like Mallory Square and Duval Street for the tranquil seclusion of a fort by the sea. The facility is closed during the first two weeks of January.

NEW TOWN AND STOCK ISLAND

Although the bulk of Key West's attractions are spread throughout Old Town, you'll find a few worthy stops in New Town, the eastern half of the island, as well as on adjacent Stock Island.

Fort East Martello

South of Key West International Airport stands **Fort East Martello** (3501 S. Roosevelt Blvd., 305/296-3913, www.kwahs.org, 9:30am-4:30pm daily, $7 adults, $5 seniors 62 and over, children, students, and Key West residents, free for children under 6). Modeled after the nearly impenetrable Martello watchtowers of Corsica and other places around the world, Fort East Martello, which was constructed during the Civil War, never actually witnessed hostile action. A testament to military engineering, the fort now serves as the country's best-preserved example of the Martello style of military architecture. Today its citadel, courtyard, and casemates house a vast array of regional artifacts, historical records, and military memorabilia, in addition to the state's largest collection of drawings and painted wood carvings by artist Mario Sanchez, mainly known for his vivid

depictions of life in Key West during the early 1900s. While here, visitors can also tour an 80-year-old playhouse and enjoy panoramic views from atop the central tower.

The Key West Tropical Forest & Botanical Garden

Besides the plethora of flowers, trees, and creatures throughout Key West, nature lovers will find several intriguing attractions—not the least of which is **The Key West Tropical Forest & Botanical Garden** (5210 College Rd., Stock Island, 305/296-1504, www.keywestbotanicalgarden.org, 10am-4pm daily, $7 adults, $5 seniors and military personnel, free for children under 12), the only frost-free botanical garden in the continental United States. Host to various events throughout the year, including Gardenfest Key West, Hot Havana Nights, and the Doo Wop Party, this tropical oasis nurtures rare flora and fauna and serves as a migratory stop for a variety of neotropical birds. After viewing a short orientation film, visitors are welcome to take a self-guided tour of the grounds, featuring a one-acre butterfly habitat, a lush canopy of tropical palms, and two of the last remaining freshwater ponds in the Florida Keys. Parking is free here, and the garden boardwalk is wheelchair-accessible.

ISLAND TOURS

If you're a first-time visitor to Key West, you might benefit from one of the many available sightseeing tours, which will help orient you to the island and its surrounding waters. So before you explore the area on your own, consider choosing from an array of trolley excursions, guided strolls, sunset cruises, or other informative tours.

◖ Train and Trolley Tours

Before exploring the town on foot, consider taking a 90-minute narrated excursion on the **Conch Tour Train** (305/294-5161 or 888/916-8687, www.conchtourtrain.com, 9am-4:30pm daily, $30 adults, $27 seniors and military personnel, free for children under 13 and Key West residents), which offers a look at most of Key

GAY KEY WEST TROLLEY TOUR

Featuring a plethora of gay bars, drag shows, gay and lesbian accommodations, and outrageous events like the annual Fantasy Fest, Key West is indeed a gay-friendly destination. That said, it seems appropriate that the Southernmost City would also be home to the Gay Key West Trolley Tour ($25 pp), a fun, interesting, and often hilarious private charter tour that runs every Saturday at 4pm. This 75-minute narrated excursion, which typically leaves from the corner of Angela and Duval Streets, invites visitors to hop aboard a rainbow-hued trolley and learn about the curious history of this spirited town, from its unique architecture to its wreck-salvaging heritage to its famous residents like Ernest Hemingway.

Of course, given the tour's particular theme, you'll also see gay and lesbian hot spots, hear about previous homosexual visitors such as playwright Tennessee Williams and poet Elizabeth Bishop, and hopefully come to understand the impact that gays and lesbians have had on the culture, politics, and economy of the Florida Keys. For tour tickets as well as information about other gay-friendly establishments, events, and activities, consult the **Key West Business Guild Office & Gay Key West Visitor Center** (513 Truman Ave., 305/294-4603 or 800/535-7797, www.gaykeywestfl.com), incidentally one of the oldest LGBT Chamber of Commerce organizations in the United States.

West's major attractions, including Mallory Square, the Custom House, and the Ernest Hemingway Home. Since 1958, friendly train "engineers" have been guiding visitors around the Southernmost City and along the way sharing snippets of the town's history—real and legendary.

Train tours depart every 30 minutes from the Front Street depot (501 Front St.), where you can purchase tickets beforehand. You can also pick up tickets at three other locations: Mallory Square (303 Front St.), Flagler Station (901 Caroline St.), and 3840 North Roosevelt Boulevard. To save some money, purchase your tickets online or consider buying packages that also include admission to attractions like the Key West Aquarium and the Harry S. Truman Little White House.

As an alternative, you can take the 90-minute **Old Town Trolley Tour** (305/296-6688 or 888/910-8687, www.trolleytours.com, 9am-4:30pm daily, $30 adults, $27 seniors and military personnel, free for children under 13), which offers a comprehensive tour of Old Town, fully narrated by expert conductors. Along the route, you'll get an earful of curious anecdotes and well-researched historical tidbits. At no extra charge, you're welcome to get

on and off the trolley at a dozen convenient stops, including the Bahama Village Market. The ubiquitous orange-and-green trolleys pick up and drop off passengers every 30 minutes at each location. Tickets can be purchased at four different stops: Mallory Square (No. 1) near Wall and Whitehead Streets, Simonton Row (No. 3) at Greene and Simonton Streets, Truval Village (No. 11) at Truman Avenue and Duval Street, and Angela Street (No. 12) between Duval and Whitehead Streets. As with the Conch Tour Train, you can save a little money by purchasing tickets online. Ticket packages and wheelchair-accessible vehicles are also available.

Biking and Walking Tours

For a more active exploration of the city, consider taking **Lloyd's Tropical Bike Tour** (601 Truman Ave., 305/294-1882 or 305/304-4700, www.lloydstropicalbiketour.com, $39 pp with bicycle rental), a leisurely, ecofriendly ride along Key West's quiet streets and secret lanes, amid tropical gardens, historical architecture, and the exotic scents of jasmine and gardenias. Led by a longtime resident of Key West, these one-of-a-kind two-hour tours even enable you to taste a variety of local fruit, such as mangoes, coconuts, and key limes. The bicycles included on this tour are single-speed beach cruisers, equipped with foot brakes, fat tires, wide seats, and convenient baskets—ideal features for novice riders. Children are welcome if accompanied by at least one adult, and reservations are a must. Be sure to wear comfortable clothes and shoes, and bring your own hat, sunglasses, and sunscreen.

If you'd prefer a two-hour walking tour instead, you're in luck. There are several such tours available in Key West, including the **Historic Key West Walking Tour** (305/292-8990, www.trustedtours.com, 10am, 2pm, and 4pm daily Nov.-Apr., 9:30am daily May-Oct., $18 adults, $9 children 4-12, free for children under 4), an entertaining tour of Old Town's lush foliage, unique architecture, varied districts, and diverse culture. Along the tour, guides will share stories about the town's early inhabitants, famous and notorious Key West personalities, historic incidents like the Great Fire of 1886, and the island's varied phases, from its wrecking and cigar-making days to its involvement in both World Wars. Tours depart from the Key West Shipwreck Museum in Mallory Square. Given the limited group size, reservations are recommended. In addition, visitors should wear comfortable shoes, bring bottled water, and check in 15 minutes before departure time.

As an alternative, you can opt for **Trails and Tales of Key West** (305/292-2040, www.trailsandtalesofkeywest.net, 4pm daily, $20 pp, free for children under 12), a zany two-hour walking tour that begins at Captain Tony's Saloon, winds through Old Town and alongside the Historic Seaport, and ends at Jimmy Buffett's Margaritaville. En route, you'll learn about the history of the Conch Republic, including stories about the city's celebrated former residents, from novelist Ernest Hemingway to treasure hunter Mel Fisher to the ever-popular singer-songwriter Jimmy Buffett. Given the limited group size, reservations are required, and comfortable shoes are highly recommended.

If your interests run toward the paranormal, you may appreciate a nighttime stroll with **The Original Ghost Tours of Key West** (423 Fleming St., 305/294-9255, www.hauntedtours.com, 8pm and 9pm nightly, $15 adults, $10 children). Founded in 1996 by David L. Sloan, author of *Ghosts of Key West,* and featured in numerous television programs, this lantern-led walking tour departs nightly from the Crowne Plaza Key West at 430 Duval Street. With a colorful history that includes pirates, smugglers, and wreckers, the town formerly known as Bone Island has its share of curious hauntings, in places as varied as the Banyan Resort, St. Paul's Episcopal Church, the Fort East Martello Museum, and Captain Tony's Saloon—all of which this 90-minute wheelchair-accessible tour encompasses. Reservations are recommended. Many of the same sites are visited through **The Ghosts & Legends of Key West** (305/294-1713, www.keywestghosts.com, 7pm and 9pm nightly, $18 adults, $10 children), a 90-minute narrated tour along the shadowy streets and lanes of Old Town. Along this route, you'll learn about Key West's most intriguing legends and bizarre ghost stories, including tales of island pirate lore, haunted Victorian mansions, and voodoo rituals. The tour departs from the Porter House Mansion at Duval and Caroline Streets, and as with the other walking tours, reservations are recommended.

Boat Tours

Since many of Key West's most memorable attractions actually lie in the waters surrounding the island, you should make some time for one of the many sightseeing cruises available, such as a two-hour glass-bottom boat tour with **Fury Water Adventures** (305/296-6293 or 877/994-8898, www.furycat.com, noon-2pm and 2pm-4pm daily, $40 adults, $20 children 6-12, free for children under 6). From aboard *The Pride of Key West,* a modern smooth-sailing catamaran, you'll be able to gaze at dolphins, sharks, and other marine creatures from the comfort of an upper sun deck or, for an even better experience, observe the colorful coral and tropical fish *below* the boat from the enclosed, air-conditioned viewing area. Other on-board amenities include restrooms and a snack bar. The catamaran leaves twice daily from the marina at 2 Duval Street, between the Ocean Key Resort and the Pier House Resort.

For a more romantic adventure, spend the evening on a sunset cruise. Among those available, Fury offers the two-hour Commotion on the Ocean (305/294-8899 or 877/994-8898, 5:30pm-7:30pm daily late Jan.-mid-Mar., 6:30pm-8:30pm daily mid-Mar.-mid-Sept., 6pm-8pm daily mid-Sept.-Oct., 5pm-7pm daily Nov.-late Jan., $50 adults, $25 children 6-12, free for children under 6), which, in conjunction with the Hog's Breath Saloon, features appetizers, beer, margaritas, and live music amid a famous Key West sunset. As a bonus, Fury donates a percentage of all sales to coral reef conservation.

As an alternative, **Sunset Watersports Key West** (201 William St., 305/296-2554, www.sunsetwatersports.info, times vary seasonally, $59 pp) offers a daily two-hour sunset yacht excursion that features a tropical buffet and a

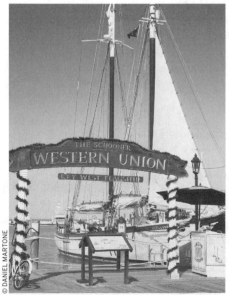

the Schooner *Western Union*, docked in the Historic Seaport at Key West Bight

variety of libations, from soft drinks to champagne. Couples will especially enjoy watching the sunset together and dancing on the lighted dance floor. Reservations are required for the sunset dinner cruise as well as for the basic two-hour sunset cruise ($35 pp without dinner).

Other area possibilities include **Sebago Watersports** (201 William St., 305/292-4768 or 800/507-9955, www.keywestsebago.com, 5pm-7pm daily late Oct.-late Feb., 5:30pm-7:30pm daily late Feb.-early Mar., 6:30pm-8:30pm daily early Mar.-mid-Sept., 5:30pm-7:30pm daily mid-Sept.-late Oct., $39 pp), which includes free champagne, margaritas, and other libations on its catamaran champagne sunset sail.

A truly memorable experience awaits you aboard a classic schooner, such as the 80-foot, square-rigged, Caribbean-style **Schooner *Jolly II Rover*** (800/979-3370, www.schoonerjollyrover.com), which offers two-hour sunset sails (times vary seasonally, $39 pp) and 1.5-hour stargazer sails (8:30pm, $45 pp) every day, all of which depart from the Historic Seaport at Key West Bight. You can also opt for sunset and stargazer sails aboard the **Schooner *Western Union*** (305/292-1766, www.schoonerwesternunion.com, times vary daily, $59 adults, $29 children 5-12, free for children under 5), a historical tall ship and floating maritime museum that also docks at the Historic Seaport. Unlike the *Jolly II Rover,* which invites you to bring your own food and beverages, the *Western Union,* which is listed on the National Register of Historic Places, provides complimentary libations, conch chowder, and live, island style music with each sail.

Among other excursions, **Sebago Watersports** (201 William St., 305/292-4768 or 800/507-9955, www.keywestsebago.com) features two-hour day sails (2pm-4pm daily, $45 pp) and champagne sunset sails (5pm-7pm daily in winter, 6:30pm-8:30pm daily in summer, $49 pp) aboard the **Schooner *Appledore V.*** Other possible adventures include a daily two-hour Wind and Wine Sunset Sail through **Danger Charters** (305/304-7999, www.dangercharters.com, times vary seasonally, $70 adults, $45 children 4-12, free for children under 4), based out of The Westin Hotel Marina at Whitehead and Greene Streets, as well as classic 1.5-hour day sails (1:30pm daily, $45 pp) and two-hour champagne sunset sails (times vary seasonally, $75 pp) aboard the **Schooner America 2.0** (305/293-7245, www. sail-keywest.com), which is based out of the Historic Seaport at Key West Bight and limited to a November-April sailing season. Most of the sails offered in Key West feature online discounts and recommend advance purchases.

Air Tours
If you'd like to experience an aerial tour of Key West and its surrounding waters, consider taking a biplane ride through **Key West Biplanes** (3469 S. Roosevelt Blvd., 305/851-8359 or 305/294-8687, www.keywestbiplanes. com, 10am-sunset daily). Flying out of the Key West International Airport, each narrated tour invites two passengers (besides the pilot) to view coral reefs, shipwrecks, lighthouses, uninhabited islands, and various marine creatures from aboard an original open-air 1942 World War II Waco biplane, at a smooth, 500-foot cruising altitude. You can choose from three different flights: an 18-minute Island Biplane Ride ($160 per ride) that offers a look at nearby shipwrecks; a 35-minute Island and Reef Tour ($285 per ride) that surveys coral reefs as well as Key West attractions; and a romantic 35-minute Sunset Flight ($335 per ride), which is essentially the Island and Reef Tour at sunset. Tour times are flexible, and each quoted price includes two passengers. Cloth helmets, headsets, and goggles are provided with all flights—all of which are wheelchair-accessible—and as a bonus, an on-board camera system can record your flight for posterity. Although walk-ins are welcome, reservations will ensure availability.

Entertainment and Events

NIGHTLIFE
If you like to prowl the streets at night, seeking out spirited bars, live music, and the like, then you've come to the right town. With a slew of late-night watering holes, hotel lounges, piano bars, and other entertainment options at your fingertips, Key West promises the most fun you'll have outside of the New Orleans French Quarter. Of course, Duval Street offers the largest concentration of nightlife selections—hence the term "Duval crawl," a popular activity whereby locals and visitors alike endeavor to stop by every bar along the street, from the Atlantic Ocean to the Gulf of Mexico.

Beyond the late-night chain establishments on Duval, such as the **Hard Rock Cafe Key West** (313 Duval St., 305/293-0230, www. hardrock.com, 11am-close daily) and **Jimmy Buffett's Margaritaville Key West** (500 Duval St., 305/292-1435, www.margaritavillekey-west.com, 11am-midnight daily), you'll spot unique, laid-back establishments like **Willie T's**

Restaurant & Bar (525 Duval St., 305/294-7674, www.williets.com, 11am-2am daily), a popular watering hole that features an enormous selection of mojitos, a daily happy hour (4pm-7pm), and live acoustic music on the patio at 1pm and 7pm every day.

Farther down Duval stands the inimitable **Sloppy Joe's Bar** (201 Duval St., 305/294-5717, www.sloppyjoes.com, 9am-close daily), which has been luring patrons to the corner of Greene and Duval (supposedly even Ernest Hemingway) since 1937 and is now listed on the National Register of Historic Places. Home to the annual Hemingway Look-Alike Contest, Sloppy Joe's offers terrific food, televised sports, plenty of libations, and live rock, country, or funk music all day long, which often entails three different bands or solo artists from noon to 2am.

Across the street from Sloppy Joe's, the **Rick's/Durty Harry's Entertainment Complex** (202-208 Duval St., 305/296-5513, www.ricksanddurtyharrys.com, 11am-close daily) encompasses eight separate late-night options, including a Mardi Gras-style daiquiri bar, and Durty Harry's, which features several televisions and live rock music 8pm-4am daily. At Duval and Caroline Streets, you'll encounter the clothing-optional **Garden of Eden** atop **The Bull and Whistle Bar** (305/296-4545, www.bullkeywest.com, 10am-4am Mon.-Sat., noon-4am Sun.), where body painting is a frequent activity. **Fat Tuesday Key West** (305 Duval St., 305/296-9373, www.fattuesdaykeywest.com, 10am-close daily) claims to have the world's best selection of frozen drinks, including rumrunners, piña coladas, and New Orleans-style hurricanes.

Also on Duval, **Cowboy Bill's Honky Tony Saloon** (610½ Duval St., 305/295-8219, http://cowboybillskw.blogspot.com, 11am-4am daily) invites you to watch televised sporting events, enjoy a specialty tequila, ride the mechanical bull, or boogie on Key West's largest dance floor.

You can also groove the night away at the predominantly gay **Aqua Nightclub** (711 Duval St., 305/294-0555, www.aquakeywest.com, 2:30pm-3am daily), which features a daily happy hour (2:30pm-8pm) in addition to karaoke, live piano and Caribbean-style music, and drag shows ($15 pp). Not far away lie two more gay hot spots: the **Bourbon St. Pub** (724 Duval St., 305/293-9800, www.bourbonstpub.com, 10am-4am daily), which offers three inner bars, a clothing-optional garden bar, and sexy male dancers, and **801 Bourbon Bar & Cabaret** (801 Duval St., 305/294-4737, www.801bourbon.com, 10am-close daily), which features multiple bars, happy-hour specials (10am-6pm daily), karaoke (6pm Thurs. and Sun.), drag queen bingo (5pm Sun.), and a twice-nightly drag show (9pm and 11pm). Both of these lively complexes factor heavily into annual events like Fantasy Fest and New Year's Eve.

For a less rowdy atmosphere, head to the **Pier House Resort** (1 Duval St., 305/296-4600, www.pierhouse.com), where the **Wine Galley Piano Bar** (6pm-close Fri.-Mon.) offers martini specials and live nightly entertainment

on the waterfront. Other enticing hotel options include the weekend cabaret show (9pm Fri.-Sat., $26 pp) at the **La Te Da Hotel** (1125 Duval St., 305/296-6706, www.lateda.com); a full bar inside the **Rambler Lounge** (6:30pm-10pm daily) at the **Casa Marina Resort** (1500 Reynolds St., 305/296-3535, www.casamarinaresort.com); and **Pearl's Patio** (305/293-9805, www.pearlspatio.com, noon-10pm Sun.-Thurs., noon-midnight Fri.-Sat.), the women-only tropical bar at **Pearl's Rainbow** (525 United St., 305/293-9805, www.pearlsrainbow.com) that offers wireless Internet access, a happy hour (5pm-7pm Mon.-Sat.), and special events.

Also off Duval, the **Bottlecap Lounge and Liquor** (1128 Simonton St., 305/296-2807, www.bottlecaplounge.com, noon-4am daily) lures revelers with pool tables, comfortable lounge chairs, oodles of beer, late-night vittles, and live blues and rock music. **Bobby's Monkey Bar** (900 Simonton St., 305/294-2655, noon-4am daily) invites patrons to shoot some pool, play some free Wii games, and try their hand at karaoke (9:30pm Sun.-Mon. and Thurs.-Fri.).

Over on Whitehead, the **Green Parrot Bar** (601 Whitehead St., 305/294-6133, www.greenparrot.com, 10am-4am Mon.-Sat., noon-4am Sun.) has been luring night owls since 1890. Today you'll encounter a daily happy hour (4pm-7pm), an awesome jukebox, and of course, live blues, jazz, rock, and acoustic music almost every night.

Closer to the gulf, you can enjoy live rock and country music, plus a raw bar, at the **Hog's Breath Saloon** (400 Front St., 305/296-4222, www.hogsbreath.com, 10am-2am daily), plus annual events like a bikini contest in October and a Parrot Head tribute party to Jimmy Buffett in November. The **Rum Barrel** (528 Front St., 305/292-7862, www.rumbarrel.com, 11am-1am Mon.-Sat., 11:30am-1am Sun.) provides, as the name implies, a comprehensive rum selection, in addition to live folk, reggae, or classic rock music on an open-air rooftop deck, typically on Thursday, Friday, and Saturday nights.

Captain Tony's Saloon (428 Greene St.,

© DANIEL MARTONE

The popular Green Parrot Bar hosts live music almost every night.

305/294-1838, www.capttonyssaloon.com, 10am-2am Mon.-Sat., noon-2am Sun.), a Key West tradition since 1851 and the original location of Sloppy Joe's from 1933 to 1937, promises, among other things, live contemporary, classic rock, and country music every day, not to mention a glimpse at Ernest Hemingway's former stool. Typically, you can expect solo acoustic performers on weekdays and a house band on the weekend.

Beside the Historic Seaport at Key West Bight, locals flock to the funky **Schooner Wharf Bar** (202 William St., 305/292-3302, www.schoonerwharf.com, 7:30am-4am daily), a weathered, open-air joint that offers excellent seafood, tropical drinks, and live acoustic music three times daily (noon, 7pm, and 9pm). If you haven't had your fill of live entertainment yet, stroll over to the open-air **B.O.'s Fish Wagon** (801 Caroline St., 305/294-9272, www.bosfishwagon.com, 11am-9pm daily) for the Friday night jam session. Closer to Grinnell, **Dante's** (955 Caroline St., 305/953-5123, www.danteskeywest.com, 11am-10pm daily)

features a weekday happy hour (4pm-8pm), daily raw bar specials (4pm-8pm), live entertainment (Thurs.-Sun.), and access to a pool (11am-sunset daily).

You can enjoy some authentic Irish cuisine and live entertainment at **Finnegan's Wake** (320 Grinnell St., 305/293-0222, www.keywestirish.com, 11am-close daily), a lively old-fashioned pub offering an enormous beer, wine, and hot toddies menu. During the peak tourist season, from November to May, you can usually expect Irish music on Friday and Saturday nights, but during the slower summer months, you might encounter local contemporary musicians on a Friday evening. For a more sensual late-night experience, stop by **Better Than Sex** (926 Simonton St., 305/296-8102, www.betterthansexkw.com, 6pm-1am Tues.-Sun. Christmas-Easter, 6pm-1am Wed.-Sun. Apr.-Dec.), an intimate dimly lit bordello-style lounge and restaurant that features live jazz and acoustic music and focuses exclusively on wine and decadent desserts. Even Stock Island has a nightlife option: the casual **Hogfish Bar and**

Captain Tony's Saloon, site of Hemingway's favorite local watering hole

Grill (6810 Front St., 305/293-4041, www.hog-fishbar.com, 11am-11pm Mon.-Sat., 9am-11pm Sun.), which provides waterfront views and live blues, rock, and country music on the weekend (Thurs.-Sat.).

THE ARTS

While the rest of the Florida Keys host their fair share of plays, concerts, and screenings, most cultural enthusiasts head first to Key West—and with good reason. Despite its small size, America's Southernmost City nurtures a number of winning theatrical venues and musical organizations.

Theater and Cinema

Situated on the Florida Keys Community College (FKCC) campus, the **Tennessee Williams Theatre** (5901 College Rd., Stock Island, 305/296-1520 or 305/295-7676, www.tennesseewilliamstheatre.com, show times and ticket prices vary) was saved from permanent closure in 2002 by the newly formed, non-profit Performing Arts Centers for Key West

(PACKW). Since then this fantastic venue has featured a variety of nationally recognized performers and productions, from Lily Tomlin's one-woman show to Patti Lupone's musical reviews. To purchase tickets for events at the Tennessee Williams Theatre and other area venues, contact **KeysTix.com** (305/295-7676, http://keystix.ticketforce.com, 10am-2pm Mon.-Fri.).

Mallory Square features the nonprofit **Waterfront Playhouse** (310 Wall St., 305/294-5015, www.waterfrontplayhouse.org, show times and ticket prices vary), home to the Key West Players. From November to May, theater lovers are treated to a variety of cutting-edge productions, from rowdy musical comedies like *Reefer Madness* to classic dramas such as *Twelve Angry Men*.

The Red Barn Theatre (319 Duval St., 305/296-9911 or 866/870-9911, www.redbarntheatre.com, show times and ticket prices vary) has celebrated live theater for more than three decades. From November to May, the theater showcases a wide array of modern comedies,

© DANIEL MARTONE

KEY WEST

The Red Barn Theatre on Duval Street

dramas, and musicals, plus the springtime Short Attention Span Theatre, a well-favored event featuring an assortment of 10-minute plays.

Occasionally, live dance, musical, and theatrical performances take place at the nonprofit **San Carlos Institute** (516 Duval St., www. institutosancarlos.org, show times and ticket prices vary), a stunning multipurpose facility that was founded by Cuban exiles and now features a museum, a library, an art gallery, a school, and a lovely 360-seat theater. Contact the Institute or **KeysTix.com** (305/295-7676, http://keystix.ticketforce.com) for upcoming events.

Even movie lovers won't be disappointed in Key West. The relatively new **Tropic Cinema** (416 Eaton St., 877/761-3456, www.tropic-cinema.com, show times and ticket prices vary) offers four different screening rooms— the Natella Carper Theater, the Frank Taylor Cinematheque Theater, the George Digital Theater, and the Peggy Dow Theater—and a spacious lobby (dubbed the Sussman Lounge)

that have not only played host to the latest independent, alternative, and foreign films, but also community events, from jazz concerts to literary lectures to songwriting festivals. For information about other cultural events in Key West, consult the **Florida Keys Council of the Arts** (1100 Simonton St., 305/295-4369, www. keysarts.com).

Music

If you appreciate live classical music, then you're in luck. For more than 15 years, the **South Florida Symphony Orchestra** (954/522-8445, www.southfloridasymphony. org, show times and ticket prices vary) has offered remarkable performances to the small community of Key West. Now composed of about 90 orchestral musicians and soloists from around the world, the orchestra splits its time between several venues, including the **Tennessee Williams Theatre** (5901 College Rd., Stock Island, 305/296-1520 or 305/295-7676, www.tennesseewilliamstheatre.com) and the **Broward Center for the Performing Arts** (201 SW 5th Ave., Fort Lauderdale, 954/522-5334, www.browardcenter.org).

Typically from October to March, the nonprofit **Key West Pops Orchestra** (305/296-6059, www.keywestpops.org, show times and ticket prices vary) presents operas, Broadway musicals, and other musical performances at the Tennessee Williams Theatre and other area venues. Past shows have included *My Fair Lady, A Little Night Music,* and *The Pajama Game.* Also featured at the Tennessee Williams Theatre is the **FKCC Keys Chorale** (Florida Keys Community College, www.keyschorale.com, show times and ticket prices vary), Monroe County's only major vocal ensemble, which has been performing everything from pop songs to show tunes for more than 20 years. To purchase tickets for all three of these musical organizations, consult **KeysTix.com** (305/295-7676, http://keystix.ticketforce.com, 10am-2pm Mon.-Fri.).

The **Key West Council on the Arts** has offered **Impromptu Concerts** (www.keywest-impromptu.org, show times and ticket prices vary) for more than 35 years. These concerts, which can range from solo piano performances to brass quintets to world-renowned operas, usually take place at the Tennessee Williams Theatre or at **St. Paul's Episcopal Church** (401 Duval St., 305/296-5142, www.stpaulskeywest.org). For tickets, contact the Tennessee Williams Theatre (305/295-7676).

Another curious option is the **Bahama Village Music Program** (727 Fort St., 305/292-9628, www.bvmpkw.org), a nonprofit group that offers free musical education to the children of Bahama Village, a historical community of multigenerational Bahamian Conchs. The students, who range in age from 6 to 13 and learn various styles of music from piano to percussion, offer free concerts and recitals throughout the year. For more information about musical events in the Key West area, consult the **Florida Keys Council of the Arts** (1100 Simonton St., 305/295-4369, www.keysarts.com).

FESTIVALS AND EVENTS

Key West may have many facets, but above all, it's still a town that knows how to party. Just consider the numerous festivals and events that lure revelers down here, sometimes even during the hottest months. Beyond fishing tournaments and New Year's Eve bashes, you'll find a number of art and heritage festivals, food events, and other exciting celebrations and competitions throughout the year. Perhaps you can even plan your next trip around such unabashed festivities.

Conch Republic Independence Celebration

On April 23, 1982, the U.S. Border Patrol set up a blockade near Florida City to search for illegal aliens and possible drug runners. Following the subsequent traffic jam on U.S. 1, the people of the Florida Keys briefly declared their secession from the United States by forming the "Conch Republic," a mock micronation, and successfully ended the disruptive blockade. Since then, for roughly three decades, the people of Key West have honored the 1982

ceremonial secession with the 10-day **Conch Republic Independence Celebration** (www.conchrepublic.com).

Every spring, in late April, residents and visitors can enjoy a lineup of varied activities around the city, such as the raising of the Conch Republic flag at Fort Zachary Taylor Historic State Park and the Great Conch Republic Drag Race, featuring competing drag queens, on Duval Street. Throughout the celebration, you can enjoy an array of events at area bars and restaurants, from the conch shell-blowing contest at the Schooner Wharf Bar to a fiddler's contest at the Green Parrot Bar. Other events include bed and dinghy races, car and crafts shows, miniature golf challenges, a pirate's ball, and of course, the Conch Republic Naval Parade and Great Battle for the Conch Republic—a mock, on-the-water confrontation between the Conch Republic's "armed forces" and the "U.S. Border Patrol," an homage to the April 1982 protest. Needless to say, the Conch Republic is always victorious in the Great Battle that takes place in Key West Bight.

◖ Hemingway Days

The spirit of Ernest Hemingway, one of Key West's most beloved former residents, endures in the Southernmost City—and not just through the popular Ernest Hemingway Home and Museum or because of the numerous establishments, such as Sloppy Joe's Bar and Captain Tony's Saloon, that claim to have been the famous novelist's favorite watering hole. Every summer, in late July, residents and visitors alike celebrate this fascinating man with the annual **Hemingway Days** (800/352-5397, www.hemingwaydays.org), a six-day event that commemorates Hemingway's lust for life; his passion for activities like writing and fishing; his adoration of Key West, where he spent the better part of the 1930s; and of course, his literary works, several of which he wrote while living on this very island.

Scheduled events typically include a literary competition; a Caribbean-style street fair; dramatic performances about Hemingway's life; a museum exhibit of rare Hemingway memorabilia; a three-day marlin tournament; and perhaps most famous, the Hemingway Look-Alike Contest, for which upwards of 150 stocky, white-bearded old men flock to town to demonstrate their uncanny resemblance to this one-of-a-kind American writer. Another not-to-be-missed event is the wacky "Running of the Bulls," a slow-moving parade that features the "Papa" Hemingway look-alikes, dressed in Pamplona-style apparel, including khaki shorts and red berets, and riding or strolling beside phony bulls-on-wheels—a silly photo opportunity for residents and tourists alike.

Fantasy Fest

Every October, tons of revelers pour into Key West for **Fantasy Fest** (1111 12th St., Ste. 211, 305/296-1817, www.fantasyfest.net), a spirited 10-day event that nearly rivals the Big Easy's annual Mardi Gras celebration. With colorful parades, outrageous costumes, and oodles of drag queens, this is surely Key West's grandest—and gayest—party of the year. Initiated in the late 1970s to help the local economy

during a traditionally slow period, Fantasy Fest has now become such a successful event that it often sustains the hotels, restaurants, and other local establishments until the winter holiday season. Usually held in late October, culminating with Halloween, this hallowed event features everything from a children's costume contest to a two-day goombay street fair in Bahama Village—essentially, a Bahamian celebration that highlights the calypso-style music and dancing associated with goombay drums. In addition, Fantasy Fest revelers will experience fetish and toga parties, headdress balls, pet masquerades, various costume and wet T-shirt contests, body-painting displays, and plenty of other hedonistic activities. Though not for the faint of heart, Fantasy Fest is indeed a bash worth observing—if not participating in.

Heritage Festivals

With a past that includes pirate legends, Bahamian immigrants, Civil War skirmishes, Cuban refugees, and other alluring facets, it's little surprise that Key West plays host to a

Costumed revelers frolic during an annual Fantasy Fest parade.

number of cultural events throughout the year. On multiple weekends from late December to mid-March, for instance, those interested in Key West's unique architecture and gardens can take a **Key West House and Garden Tour** ($25 pp) through the historical Old Town district. Sponsored by the **Old Island Restoration Foundation** (322 Duval St., 305/294-9501, www.oirf.org) for the past five decades, these beloved tours allow both residents and visitors a chance to peer beyond the front porches of some of Key West's most one-of-a-kind homes. Each tour features five private domiciles, all of which reflect the varied tastes of their owners and many of which feature authentic restorations, creative renovations, and impressive art and antiques collections.

Meanwhile, in late February, **The Key West Tropical Forest & Botanical Garden** (5210 College Rd., Stock Island, 305/296-1504, www.keywestbotanicalgarden.org) celebrates the island's bountiful flora with **Gardenfest Key West** (prices vary), a three-day event that typically includes raffles, demonstrations, lectures, nature-oriented artwork, and a plant sale, featuring fruit trees, exotic palms, orchids, bromeliads, and native plants. Also in late February, the city celebrates a three-day event known as **Civil War Days** (fees apply for some activities) with candlelit tours of Fort Zachary Taylor (western end of Southard St., 305/292-6713, www.floridastateparks.org/forttaylor), artillery demonstrations, a military parade down Duval Street, and reenacted engagements between Union soldiers and Confederate blockade runners in authentic 19th-century schooners.

In early March, the Old Island Restoration Foundation (322 Duval St., 305/294-9501, www.oirf.org) hosts a popular, one-day **Conch Shell Blowing Contest** (free), also known as the "Conch Honk," during which children, teenagers, adults, and senior citizens alike demonstrate their shell-blowing skills in order to highlight the significance of the conch in Key West's past. Meanwhile, The Key West Tropical Forest & Botanical Garden (5210 College Rd., Stock Island, 305/296-1504,

www.keywestbotanicalgarden.org) honors the town's Cuban heritage with **Hot Havana Nights** ($25-30 pp), a single-evening in mid-March displaying Cuban music, dancing, and cuisine.

Typically in late April, music lovers will encounter the curious **Key West Songwriters' Festival** (www.kwswf.com, show times and ticket prices vary), a five-day event that presents more than 30 live concerts at popular locales throughout the city, from the Ocean Key Resort to the San Carlos Institute to Jimmy Buffett's Margaritaville. In late May, residents and visitors celebrate the influence of Cuban culture on the development of Key West with the three-day **Cuban American Heritage Festival** (5570 3rd Ave., 305/295-9665, www.cubanfest.com, prices vary), which typically includes activities like a coast-to-coast conga line, a Latin dance party, a Cuban cigar dinner, a domino tournament, and a progressive dinner at various Cuban restaurants.

Besides Hemingway Days, other popular summertime events include the five-day **Key West Pridefest** (305/294-4603, www.pridefestkeywest.com, fees apply for some activities) in mid-June and the four-day **Mel Fisher Days** (Mel Fisher's Treasures, 200 Greene St., 800/434-1399, www.melfisher.com, fees apply for some activities) in mid-July. In a town that possesses a healthy share of gay-friendly bars and hotels—and whose motto is "one human family"—it's no wonder that Pridefest is a much-anticipated event, filled with contests, shows, tours, dance and cocktail parties, a street fair, and a "pride" parade along Duval Street. A month later, Mel Fisher Days honors a different aspect of the city's heritage—its lust for treasure hunting. To honor the anniversary of Mel Fisher's discovery of the *Atocha* mother lode, this event features, among other activities, a parade, a poker tournament, and a bikini contest that offers authentic treasure coins as prizes.

Later in the year, yet another event highlights the laid-back yet zany vibe of this island paradise. In early November, **Parrot Heads in Paradise, Inc.** (www.phip.com), the nonprofit international organization of Parrot Head Clubs—the official fan clubs of singer-songwriter Jimmy Buffett and the carefree tropical lifestyle he exemplifies—hosts a four-day **Meeting of the Minds** for all members in good standing, whether they be members of the virtual club or one of the more than 200 actual clubs that exist around the world.

Food Events

In a city that celebrates so many hedonistic pleasures, it's no wonder that food plays a major role in so many annual events. Some even focus exclusively on the local cuisine. In mid-January, for instance, the one-day family-friendly **Florida Keys Seafood Festival** (www.fkcfa. org, free) highlights the region's commercial fishing industry by offering the freshest local seafood available, from crab to lobster. Later in January, the four-day **Key West Food & Wine Festival** (800/474-4319, www.keywestfoodandwinefestival.com, prices vary) celebrates an assortment of local delicacies, including seafood, Cuban cuisine, tapas dishes, fine wine, and tropical ice cream at various local bars and restaurants. Other activities may include a coconut bowling tournament and a tea dance at La Te Da.

In mid-April, another annual food extravaganza, the one-day **Taste of Key West** ($1 per food/wine ticket), celebrates the cuisine of more than 100 vineyards and 50 local restaurants while benefiting the efforts of **AIDS Help** (1434 Kennedy Dr., 305/296-6196, www. aidshelp.cc/taste.html). A few months later, in early August, residents and visitors celebrate one of their favorite crustaceans with the **Key West Lobsterfest** (www.keywestlobsterfest. com, prices vary), a three-day event, sponsored by Key West Promotions, Inc. (305/744-9804, www.keywestpromotions.com), that features live music, cold drinks, and naturally, fresh lobster.

Art Festivals

Given how influential Key West's landscape has been on local and visiting musicians, writers, and artists, it seems only natural that the Southernmost City would host its share of art related events during the peak tourist season. In late January, the long-standing **Key West Craft Show** (305/294-1243, www.keywestartcenter. com/craft.html, prices vary), a two-day juried outdoor craft festival, attracts over 100 potters, fabric experts, jewelry makers, glass sculptors, wood craftsmen, and other skilled artists to Key West's Old Town. For a more unusual experience, consider visiting during **Sculpture Key West** (305/295-3800, www.sculpturekeywest.com, admission fees may apply), an annual wintertime exhibition of contemporary outdoor sculpture throughout the city, namely at attractions like Fort Zachary Taylor Historic State Park, the West Martello Tower, and The Key West Tropical Forest & Botanical Garden. Typically, you can enjoy this event from mid-January to mid-April.

Usually held in late February, the nationally recognized **Old Island Days Art Festival** (305/294-1243, www.keywestartcenter.com/ festival.html, prices vary), for well over four decades, has celebrated various art forms amid the historical structures of Key West's Old Town. Originally held as a fundraising event for the building that now houses the **Key West Art Center and Gallery (KWAC)** (301 Front St., 305/294-1241, www.keywestartcenter.com, 10am-5pm daily), this two-day juried, outdoor fine art festival features the work of over 100 painters, photographers, sculptors, and other artists, many of whom definitely favor tropical themes.

Fishing and Racing Events

As in other parts of the Florida Keys, outdoor events are popular in Key West, perhaps none more so than the fishing tournaments and racing championships that take place throughout the year. In late January, thousands of sailors from around the world flock to Key West for the **Key West Race Week** (781/639-9545, www.premiere-racing.com, entry fees apply), a five-day international sailing competition in the waters surrounding the Southernmost City. Beginning in mid-March, men, women, juniors, and young children compete to catch and release more than 40 different fish species in the nine-month-long **Key West Fishing Tournament (KWFT)** (www.keywestfishingtournament.com, entry fees apply).

In mid-April, elite anglers also compete in the prestigious, five-day **World Sailfish Championship** (866/550-5580, www.worldsailfish.com, entry fees apply), which typically awards cash prizes that total roughly $125,000. From mid-September to early November, celebrities and ordinary fishing enthusiasts come together for the **Redbone Celebrity Tournament Series** (305/664-2002, www.redbone.org, entry fees apply), a trio of three-day "Catch the Cure" competitions throughout the Keys that seek out permit, tarpon, bonefish, and redfish—ultimately benefiting cystic fibrosis research. Also in early November, a slew of high-speed powerboats race across the waters of Key West to vie for the world championship title in the eight-day **Key West World Championship** (www.keywestpowerboatraces.com, entry fees apply)—a competition that's equally appealing to spectators.

Holiday Celebrations

A year in Key West wouldn't be complete without experiencing the city's annual holiday celebrations. In early December, residents and visitors, often dressed in shorts and sandals, line up along Duval Street for the **Key West Holiday Parade** (free), a family-friendly event that usually occurs on a Saturday evening and features decorated floats, marching bands, and perhaps a few Santas holding fishing poles. On a Saturday evening in mid-December, locals "deck the hulls" for the **Key West Lighted Boat Parade** (free), a maritime tradition that features a procession of vessels in Key West Bight. All the boats, most of which are owned by Florida Keys residents, are enhanced by bright lights, holiday decorations, and live music, from choirs to steel drums. Families especially favor this festive event.

For two enchanted evenings in early or mid-December, the self-guided **Holiday Historic Inn Tour** (www.keywestchristmas.org, $20 pp) highlights some of the city's loveliest properties, all of which are decorated for the holiday season with twinkling lights, poinsettia plants, and festooned palm trees. Often you'll be able to step inside such historical inns as the Cypress House, the Curry Mansion, and The Mermaid & The Alligator B&B. In addition, fine food and beverages are usually available throughout the tour.

Not surprisingly, **New Year's Eve** is a popular holiday in the Southernmost City. Among the various midnight celebrations on December 31st, you'll spy a conch shell dropping from the roof of Sloppy Joe's Bar, a pirate wench descending the mast of a schooner at the Historic Seaport, and a local drag queen being lowered from a Duval Street balcony in an enormous, high-heeled shoe. Many of the bars are open into the wee hours, so the celebrating doesn't typically stop at midnight.

Shopping

With its cornucopia of art galleries, gift and souvenir shops, clothing boutiques, jewelry stores, and food emporiums, Key West promises you the most engrossing treasure hunt in the Florida Keys—at least on land. Here shoppers will find all manner of items for sale, from hammocks to erotic literature to pendants fashioned from sunken Spanish coins. While such diverse shopping opportunities exist throughout the city, certain areas such as Mallory Square and the rest of Old Town offer the lion's share of options, especially for tourists.

Naturally, the suggestions listed here merely scratch the surface of Key West's shopping scene. For even more ideas, consult www.shopkeywest.com—or just take a stroll around the neighborhoods.

BAHAMA VILLAGE

Southwest of Whitehead Street and roughly bordered by Southard, Fort, and Louisa Streets lies a historical neighborhood known as **Bahama Village.** Named for its original inhabitants, many of whom were of Bahamian ancestry, this residential area is a lively place in the daytime and rather quiet at night. Some visitors even find it a little too quiet once the sun goes down. In fact, with the occurrence of criminal activities, such as muggings and drug transactions, local police officers often advise outsiders against venturing into this area after dark.

Nevertheless, the presence of several interesting shops and restaurants, such as the dessert-only eatery Better Than Sex, makes Bahama Village an enticing place for tourists. Shoppers might especially appreciate the **Bahama Village Market,** an open-air flea market near the village entrance on Petronia Street. Here you'll find a collection of colorful stalls, featuring typical souvenirs like straw hats, T-shirts, beads, sponges, and Caribbean crafts.

MALLORY SQUARE

Although technically part of Key West's Old Town, **Mallory Square** (1 Whitehead St., www.mallorysquare.com) operates as its own unique entity. Situated at the northernmost part of Duval and Whitehead Streets, this popular collection of shops, eateries, and attractions is perhaps best known for its daily Sunset Celebration, when hundreds of locals and tourists gather beside the shore to enjoy the antics of musicians, artists, acrobats, jugglers, and other street performers, while paying homage to the sun as it seemingly sinks into the Gulf of Mexico.

If you're in search of souvenirs, you're in luck here. Vendor carts present a variety of goods, from coconut pirates to colorful flip-flops. In Mallory Square, you'll also spot the long-standing **Shell Warehouse** (305/294-5168, 8:30am-9pm daily), which offers an intriguing assortment of shells, jewelry, artwork, and decorations. Another favored tourist stop is the **Sponge Market** (305/294-2555, 8am-9pm daily), which features a variety of local art, model ships, sea sponges, shipwreck treasure jewelry, and other maritime collectibles—not to mention an enormous "sponge man," the subject of many a tourist's photograph, just outside the doorway. Not far away, adjacent to Mallory Square, you'll encounter the **Clinton Square Market** (291 Front St., 305/296-6825, 8:30am-6pm daily), an air-conditioned, two-story mall that contains a variety of shops, featuring everything from jewelry and tropical clothing to toys and pet items.

HISTORIC SEAPORT

From Mallory Square, head northeast to the renovated **Historic Seaport** district at Key West Bight, home to dozens of yachts and tour operators. Generally, people come here to hire charters, board sailboats, stroll along the boardwalk, or dine at lively places like the Schooner Wharf Bar, but shoppers will also find a couple

KEY WEST

© DANIEL MARTONE

Shoppers may appreciate a stroll through Mallory Square.

of curious stores in the vicinity. Difficult to miss is **Mac's Sea Garden** (208 Margaret St., 305/293-7240, 9am-9pm daily), a rustic gift shop, with chimes hanging beneath the porch roof, an old, weathered pickup sitting in the front yard, and the distinct appearance of a Cajun fishing camp. Not far away, at the corner of Elizabeth and Greene Streets, **Kermit's Key West Key Lime Shoppe** (305/296-0806, www.keylimeshop.com, 9am-9pm daily) offers a whole slew of key lime products, from key lime bath soap to key lime barbecue sauce to classic key lime pie, of course.

OLD TOWN

Although Key West's **Old Town** is generally considered the western half of the island, most of the available shopping opportunities are concentrated on or near **Duval Street,** the main drag of this historical district. Here and on surrounding roads, like Greene and Whitehead Streets, you'll find a ton of places to satisfy your cravings for art, souvenirs, fashion, jewelry, food, and so much more.

Art Galleries

If you're an art lover, then you've come to the right place, for Key West boasts well over 30 art galleries—certainly more than any other place in the Florida Keys. Over half of these can be found on Duval Street, in two separate clusters.

On the upscale end of Duval, closer to the Atlantic Ocean, lie nearly a dozen elegant galleries, bunched together amid tropical foliage and historical buildings. At the **Archeo Gallery** (1208 Duval St., 305/294-3771, www.archeogallery.com, 11am-5pm Tues.-Sat.), you'll find hand-chosen primitive art from around the world, such as vibrant Gabbeh rugs from Iran, teak furniture from Indonesia, and masks, sculpture, pottery, and metalwork from Africa. Across the street stands the **Gingerbread Square Gallery** (1207 Duval St., 305/296-8900, www.gingerbreadsquaregallery.com, 10am-6pm daily), which was established in 1974 by Key West's former mayor Richard Heyman, making it one of the oldest art galleries in town. Represented here are the paintings, sculptures, and glassware of several different

© DANIEL MARTONE

Mac's Sea Garden, near the Historic Seaport

artists, from Sal Salinero's lush rainforest land-scapes to Peter Greenwood's whimsical bubble bottles.

The **Key West Light Gallery** (1203 Duval St., 305/294-0566, www.kwlightgallery.com, 10am-5pm daily) features contemporary photography and paintings that highlight Key West's architecture, explore Cuban culture, and exemplify the concept of light in its many forms. A block down the street, the **Alan S. Maltz Gallery** (1210 Duval St., 305/294-0005, www.alanmaltz.com, 10am-6pm daily) displays the stunning images of Florida's official wildlife photographer.

Several blocks down Duval, closer to the rowdier Gulf of Mexico end, lie nearly 10 more winning galleries, including the **Island Style Gallery** (620 Duval St., 305/292-7800, www. islandstylegalleries.com, 10am-8pm Mon.-Sat., 11am-6pm Sun.), which presents artistic jewelry, handcrafted glass, and colorful, tropical-themed home furnishings. On the same side of the street, you'll find the **Guild Hall Gallery** (614 Duval St., 305/296-6076, www.

guildhallgallerykw.com, 10am-8pm daily), which has supported local artists since 1976 and today displays the watercolor and acrylic paintings, contemporary sculpture, and youthful jewelry of more than 20 artists. About a block away, you'll enjoy the dramatically illumined **Peter Lik Fine Art Photography Gallery** (519 Duval St., 305/292-2550, www. peterlik.com, 10am-9pm daily), one of 13 such galleries in the United States.

Perhaps the most famous gallery in town, however, is the flagship store of **Wyland Galleries** (623 Duval St., 305/292-4998 or 888/292-4998, www.wylandkw.com or www. wylandgalleries.com, 9am-10pm daily), the largest Wyland gallery in the world. Inside this spacious store, you'll see an array of impressive glass creations, bronze sculptures, and vibrant paintings by the prolific muralist and environmentalist, whose work typically focuses on photogenic marinelife like dolphins, manatees, orcas, and sea turtles. In addition, this incredible gallery features the work of Wyland's fellow artists, including David Wight's amazing glass

THE WYLAND WALLS

Robert Wyland, better known simply as Wyland, is indeed the most famous marinelife artist in the world. For more than three decades, Wyland—an avid scuba diver, marine conservationist, painter, sculptor, photographer, and world traveler as well as an official artist for the United States Olympic Committee—has used his artwork to spread awareness about the ocean, its inhabitants, and the need to preserve and protect this fragile environment. His oil and watercolor paintings, bronze and Lucite sculptures, and other creations—which typically feature magnificent whales, peaceful manatees, frisky dolphins, giant sea turtles, and kaleidoscopic tropical fish—are on display in galleries throughout the country, most notably in Florida, California, and Hawaii. He even has two **Wyland Galleries** (www.wylandkw.com) in Key West, including the flagship store (623 Duval St., 305/292-4998) and the one near Mallory Square (102 Duval St., 305/294-5240).

Nicknamed the "Marine Michelangelo" by *USA Today*, Wyland has been recognized for his conservation efforts by the United Nations, the Sierra Club, and other public and private institutions throughout the world. In fact, he cares so deeply about the environment that in 1993 he established the **Wyland Foundation** (www.wylandfoundation.org), a nonprofit organization that has supported numerous art, education, and conservation programs, including his most famous endeavor: the monumental "Wyland Wall" mural project. Begun in 1981 in Laguna Beach, California, this impressive series of 100 life-size marinelife murals now spans 13 countries on five continents, from America to Japan to New Zealand, and captures nearly 1 billion viewers per year. Interestingly, you'll even find several of these amazing murals in southern Florida, including *Minke Whales*, which was created in 1990 at Crane Point's Museum of Natural History in Marathon, as well as a more recent offering, which was painted in October 2012 to replace *Florida's Living Reef* (1993) on the exterior wall of the former Waterfront Market in Key West—both are indeed worth a look. For more information about Wyland's art and conservation efforts, visit www.wylandgalleries.com and www.wyland.com.

wave sculptures. Near Mallory Square, you'll spot another Wyland gallery at 102 Duval Street (305/294-5240 or 888/294-5240, 9am-10pm daily), so be sure to stop there, too.

Of course, there are also plenty of worthwhile art galleries off Duval. Near downtown Key West, the **Audubon House & Tropical Gardens** (205 Whitehead St., 305/294-2116 or 877/294-2470, www.audubonhouse.com, 9:30am-5pm daily) includes the **Audubon House Gallery of Natural History,** which offers a number of limited editions of John James Audubon's famous ornithological paintings from the 19th century. Farther inland, the **Haitian Art Company** (605 Simonton St., 305/296-8932, www.haitian-art-co.com, 10am-7pm daily) sells an array of colorful paintings from Haitian artists like Simeon Michel, who focuses on the verdant Haitian countryside, and Soliman Delva, who strives

for social realism. For more information about these and other art galleries, consult the **Florida Keys Council of the Arts** (1100 Simonton St., 305/295-4369, www.keysarts.com).

Gift and Souvenir Shops

Given Key West's supreme popularity among tourists, it surely comes as no surprise that gift and souvenir shops abound in Old Town. For one thing, there's a plethora of strategically placed museum shops in this part of town. In fact, whether they're situated just beyond the front entrance—as with the **Mel Fisher Maritime Museum** (200 Greene St., 305/294-2633, www.melfisher.org, 8:30am-5pm Mon.-Fri., 9:30am-5pm Sat.-Sun.)—or located at the end of the tour, you're usually forced to pass through an eclectic collection of books, DVDs, jewelry, apparel, and the like. If you're interested in less nautically themed items, consider browsing the gift shop at **The Key West Butterfly & Nature Conservatory** (1316 Duval St., 305/296-2988, www.key westbutterfly.com, 9am-5:30pm daily), which features a wide selection of butterfly-themed jewelry, ceramics, books, and other souvenirs.

You'll find several other curious gift shops along Duval. **KW Hammocks** (717 Duval St., Ste. 2, 305/293-0008, www.kwhammocks. com, hours vary daily), for one, has been distributing hammocks and hammock-style porch swings, chairs, and rockers for over a decade, and while it's true that **Jimmy Buffett's Margaritaville** (500 Duval St., 305/292-1435, www.margaritavillekeywest.com, 9am-11pm daily) is part of a famous bar and restaurant chain, that doesn't mean that the attached store isn't worth browsing. Here you'll find all manner of souvenir hats, T-shirts, flip-flops, lawn chairs, dog collars, and of course, Buffett's novels and CDs. Not far away, you can pick up unique aloe-based fragrances, hair products, and skin creams for women and men at **Key West Aloe** (419 Duval St., 305/517-6365, www.keywestaloe.com, 8:30am-5pm daily). Off Duval, another curious locale is the **Pelican Poop Shoppe** (314 Simonton St., 305/292-9955, www.pelicanpoopshoppe.com, 10am-7pm daily), which presents an array of lamps, weathervanes, metal wall art, and other Caribbean-style crafts. Established in 1976, the **Key West Kite Company** (408 Greene St., 305/296-5483, www.keywestkitecompany. com, 9am-8:30pm daily) provides colorful kites, flags, toys, and yard ornaments to residents and visitors alike.

Now, if you've come to Key West with more amorous amusements in mind, consider stopping by **Fairvilla's Sexy Things** (524 Front St., 305/292-0448, www.fairvilla.com, 9am-midnight daily), where you'll find a wide selection of erotic gifts and games, fantasy fashions, and sensual accessories. Just a few blocks away lies a completely different megastore. With a view of Key West Harbor, the 4,000-square-foot **Saltwater Angler** (243 Front St., 305/294-0700 or 800/223-1629, www.saltwaterangler. com, 9am-8:30pm daily) serves as a one-stop shop for anyone interested in saltwater fishing in the Florida Keys. Operated by Captain Tony Murphy and situated within The Westin Key West Resort & Marina, the Angler houses an extensive inventory of travel and fishing apparel for men and women, plus luggage, wind chimes, stained-glass fish art, rare books, and locally made jewelry. While you're here, you can even ask about fishing guide services.

Clothing and Shoe Boutiques

Most of the clothing and footwear stores in Key West focus on carefree island styles. The **Ron Jon Surf Shop** (503 Front St., 305/293-8880, www.ronjons.com, 9am-9pm daily) is no exception. This two-story behemoth offers a wide array of apparel and accessories for the vacationer, from swimsuits to backpacks to sunglasses. In keeping with that laid-back vibe, **Kino Sandals, Inc.** (107 Fitzpatrick St., 305/294-5044, www.kinosandalfactory.com, 8:30am-5:30pm Mon.-Fri., 9am-5:30pm Sat., 10am-3pm Sun.), established in 1966 by Cuban immigrants, invites visitors to watch the sandals being made by hand, before choosing from an array of men's and women's selections. You can also pick up a pair of sandals at the **Port Sandal Shoppe** (218 Whitehead St., Ste. 2, 305/296-0001, www. sandalshoppe.com, 9:30am-7:30pm daily), which houses thousands of different styles from popular brands like Teva, Timberland, and Crocs. For a real island look, consider stopping by **Hair Wraps of Key West** (310 Duval St., 305/293-1133, www.hairwrapsofkeywest.com, 10am-10pm daily) and let the staff adorn your hair with braids, corn rows, and beads. Henna tattoos, charms, and hair accessories are also available.

For fancier duds, visit **Evan & Elle** (725 Duval St., 305/296-4617, www.shopbiton.com, 10am-3pm Mon.-Fri., longer hours Nov.-Apr.), which offers upscale clothing for men and women, ideal for those headed out on a cruise. Off Duval, the stylish **Blue Boutique** (718 Caroline St., 305/292-5172, www.blueislandstore.com, 10am-6pm daily) features high-end, contemporary fashions from today's hottest designers, such as Nicole Miller and James Perse. If you want to match your new outfit with the perfect hat, purse, or necklace, stroll to The Westin Key West Resort & Marina, where the locally owned **Key West Madhatter** (253 Front St., 305/294-1364 or 888/442-4287, www.kw-madhatter.com, 9am-11pm daily) offers, among other accessories, more than 2,000 hats for women, men, and children, from elegant straw hats to goofy holiday fedoras.

Jewelry Stores

You'll certainly find an impressive assortment of shiny, pretty things in Key West, including oodles of gemstones at **Diamonds International** (122 Duval St., 305/293-1111, www.shopdi.com, 11am-9pm daily), the largest duty-free jeweler in the world, as well as emerald, conch pearl, and Australian black opal rings at **Emeralds International** (104 Duval St., 305/294-2060 or 877/689-6647, www.emeraldsinternational.com, 10am-6pm daily). For more precious gemstones—plus Key West's largest supply of Swiss watches—head to **Little Switzerland** (423 Front St., 248/809-5560, ext. 20360, www.littleswitzerland.com, 9am-5pm daily). If your interests run a little less expensive, visit **Local Color** (276 Margaret St., 305/292-3635, www.localcolorkeywest.com, 9am-10pm daily), which since 1988 has offered a wide array of fun jewelry, including locally inspired beads and charms, Happy Hour rings, and silver and gold "KW" hook bracelets. You could also try **Paradise Tattoo** (627 Duval St., 305/292-9110, www.paradisetattoo.com, 10am-10pm daily), which offers basic jewelry in addition to tattoo and body-piercing services.

For valuables that will evoke memories of your trip to the Florida Keys, head to **Mel Fisher's Treasures** (200 Greene St., 305/296-9936 or 800/434-1399, www.melfisher.com, 9:30am-5pm daily), situated at the rear of the Mel Fisher Maritime Museum. Here you can purchase a piece of the famous *Nuestra Señora de Atocha* shipwreck, including pearls, iron spikes, musket balls, pieces of eight, and pendants and earrings crafted from old Spanish coins. In addition, you can speak with the staff

about investing in the site—from which underwater explorers are still recovering hidden coins, artifacts, and other treasures. Just be prepared to spend a bundle. Being an investor isn't cheap, but neither are the goods in the store, where you might spot an encrusted mystery object with a tiny embedded emerald on sale for $19,999.

Food and Beverage Emporiums

Key West residents celebrate all aspects of life, not the least of which is fine food. If you're hoping to take a taste of the Conch Republic home with you, look no farther than the **Key West Key Lime Pie Co.** (511 Greene St., 305/517-6720, www.keywestkeylimepieco.com, 10am-6pm Mon.-Sat., noon-5pm Sun.), which sells award-winning key lime pies in addition to gourmet jellies, marinades, cookies, candies, spices, cookbooks, and other items, including the popular key lime pie bar—a scrumptious treat that features a slice of key lime pie covered in rich chocolate.

Of course, key lime pie isn't all that Key West has to offer. Founded by Cuban immigrant and cigar maker Fausto Castillo, **Fausto's Food Palace** (www.faustos.com) has served the people of Key West with fine wines, gourmet cheeses, and other delicious vittles since 1926. Today Fausto's, which has moved and expanded over the years, offers two locations: 522 Fleming Street (305/296-5663, 8am-8pm Mon.-Sat., 8am-7pm Sun.) and 1105 White Street (305/294-5221, 8am-8pm Mon.-Sat., 8am-7pm Sun.). Wine lovers might also appreciate **The Key West Winery** (103 Simonton St., 305/292-1717 or 866/880-1717, www.thekeywestwinery.com, 10am-6pm Mon.-Sat., noon-6pm Sun.), which features unusual key lime, mango, and other tropical wines, plus a variety of key lime condiments. Another option is the **Cork & Stogie** (1218 Duval St., 305/517-6419, www.corkandstogie.com, 10am-11pm daily), which offers a fine selection of wine and cigars, including those produced by **The Original Key West Cigar Factory** (305/517-7273, www.kw-cigarfactory.com), whose history stretches back to the 1880s.

Sports and Recreation

GOLF

While the Florida Keys archipelago isn't the golf mecca that other parts of the Sunshine State purport to be, that doesn't mean that golfers are without options. Besides private golf courses like those at the Ocean Reef Club in Key Largo and the Sombrero Country Club in Marathon, golfers will find a lovely, palm-studded golf course in the Lower Keys. Encompassing at least a third of Stock Island, the 200-acre **Key West Golf Club** (6450 E. College Rd., 305/294-5232, www.keywestgolf. com, $50-95 with a cart) features an 18-hole, 6,500-yard public golf course, set on the gulf side of U.S. 1, amid dense mangroves, tranquil lakes, varied wildlife, and the ever-present trade winds. This year-round full-service facility—incidentally, the southernmost golf course in the continental United States—also offers a driving range ($8 per bucket), rental clubs ($40 per set), bag storage ($125 yearly), locker rentals ($80 yearly), a pro golf shop and clubhouse, a golf instruction ($410-710 per class), and private parking.

◖ BIKING

Whether you're an experienced or novice rider, Key West is a lovely, welcoming place to traverse by bicycle. Just remember that you'll have to share the streets with cars and other vehicles, so take care while you tour the neighborhoods—and wear a proper helmet at all times. Bicycles can be rented from several different outfitters, including **Eaton Bikes** (830 Eaton St., 305/294-8188, www.eatonbikes.com, 9am-6pm Mon.-Sat., 9am-4pm Sun., $12-45 daily, $40-135 weekly), which offers a range of bicycles, from trikes to mountain bikes to tandems, plus free delivery and pickup service throughout Key West. **The Bike Shop of Key West** (1110 Truman Ave., 305/294-1073, www.thebikeshopkeywest.com, 9am-6pm Mon.-Sat., 10am-4pm Sun., $12 daily, $60 weekly, $180 monthly), the oldest in town, also provides a

wide array of bicycles, plus accessories, bicycle sales, and a service/repair department. All rentals include locks, lights, baskets, and wide soft seats.

Another helpful source for bicycle rentals is **Adventure Rentals** (305/293-8883, www. keywest-scooter.com, 9am-5pm daily, $8 for four hours, $15 daily, $60 weekly), which features multiple locations—at 0 Duval Street, 617 Front Street, 135 Simonton Street, and Cruise Ship Pier B—and also offers scooters ($30 for four hours, $50 daily), Harley motorcycles (starting from $203 for four hours, $268 daily, $935 weekly), and multiple-passenger electric cars ($94-137 per two hours, $159-202 daily). In addition, **A&M Rentals** (305/896-1921, www.amscooterskeywest. com, 8am-8pm daily, $15 daily, $85 weekly) features three spots from which to rent kid-size bicycles, cruisers, and tandems: 523 Truman Avenue, 513 South Street, and 500 Truman Avenue. You can also rent one-seater scooters ($35 daily, $109 weekly), two-seater scooters ($55 daily, $179 weekly), and multi-seater electric cars ($99 daily)—all popular ways to get around town. Free customer pickup and drop-off services are available.

Even Stock Island has a bicycle outfitter. Just north of the Hurricane Hole Marina, **Re-Cycle** (5160 Overseas Hwy., Stock Island, 305/292-3336 or 305/294-7433, www.recyclekw.com, 9am-9pm daily, $18 daily, $65 weekly) offers a full-service shop and free delivery for its wide array of bicycles, so you'll find no shortage of ways to enjoy a ride around this lovely city.

FISHING AND BOATING

Anglers come from all over the world to explore the waters surrounding Key West, a place that boasts year-round fishing opportunities. Every month, several different fish species are in season, and anglers can choose from a variety of fishing locales, including deep harbors, backcountry flats, coral reefs, and offshore waters.

No wonder Ernest Hemingway found fishing down here so appealing.

For a small city, Key West sure does have an impressive number of marinas, from the **Historic Seaport at Key West Bight** (305/295-9225, www.seaportrealtorskeywest.com) near Old Town to the **Hurricane Hole Marina** (5130 Overseas Hwy., 305/294-8025, www.hurricaneholekeywest.com) on adjacent Stock Island. In fact, Stock Island features several marinas, including the deepwater **Old Island Harbor** (7009 Shrimp Rd., 305/294-2288, www.oldislandharbor.com) and the nostalgic **Safe Harbour Marina** (6810 Front St., 305/294-9797, www.safeharbourmarina.com). So if you're planning to bring your own boat in order to fish the abundant backcountry and offshore waters of the Florida Keys, you'll find no shortage of boat slips and marine services in the area.

Most anglers come to Key West with sportfishing charters in mind, and here, too, you'll find no scarcity of options. At the **Key West City Marina at the Garrison Bight** (1801 N. Roosevelt Blvd., 305/809-3981, www.keywestcity.com), for instance, you can hire any number of boats from Charter Boat Row, including offshore fishing services like **Fishcheck Key West Fishing Charters** (Slip #1, 305/295-0484 or 877/434-7459, www.fishcheckcharters.com, $165-750 per half day, $200-900 for six hours, $250-1,100 daily) and **Wild Bill Sportfishing** (305/296-2533 or 305/744-7957, www.wildbillkeywest.com, $150-650 per half day, $185-750 for six hours, $225-900 daily), both of which offer individual seats as well as private charters for up to six passengers. Among the other deep-sea fishing vessels docked at the City Marina, you'll spot the *Ramerezi* (305/294-0803 or 305/745-2789, www.ramerezi.com, $450 per half day, $900 daily) and the **Charter Boats** *Linda D.* (Slips #19 and #20, 305/296-9798 or 800/299-9798, www.charterboatlindad.com, $600-675 per half day, $900-975 daily), all of which are helmed by longtime local fishing captains and can accommodate up to six anglers at a time.

If you're interested in shallow-water flats fishing and saltwater fly-fishing, consider **Almost There! Sportfishing Charters** (5001 5th Ave., Stock Island, 305/295-9444 or 800/795-9448, www.almostthere.net, $450 per half day, $750 daily), Key West's largest charter company, or as an alternative, **Sting Rea Charters** (305/744-0903, www.flyfishingthekeys.com, $400 per half day, $600 daily), which transports its vessel from Sugarloaf Key to various locations and leads anglers to the waters around the Lower Keys and the Marquesas in search of tarpon, barracuda, permit, and bonefish. For reef and wreck fishing, among other fishing styles, consult **Mean Green Charters** (Murray Marina, 5710 Overseas Hwy., Stock Island, 305/304-1922, www.meangreenfishing.com, $600 per half day, $900 daily), **Cheerio Charters** (Hurricane Hole Marina, 5130 Overseas Hwy., Stock Island, 305/797-6446, www.cheeriocharters.com, $600 per half day, $900 daily), or **Boo-Ya Charters** (Charter Boat Row, 1801 N. Roosevelt Blvd., 305/292-6692, www.booyakeywest.com, $600 per half day, $800 daily), through which you'll possibly snag grouper, snapper, amberjack, kingfish, tuna, barracuda, permit, yellowtail, cobia, and sharks. Families may especially appreciate **No Worries Charters** (711 Eisenhower Dr., 305/393-2402, www.noworriescharters.com, $500-600 per half day, $800-900 daily), a company based in the Key West City Marina that allows pets on board; supports catch-and-release fishing, especially for children; and customizes trips to include boating, snorkeling, dolphin-watching, and light-tackle fishing. Rates are often negotiable.

In general, fishing trips are offered daily, and rates, which typically include bait, tackle, ice, and proper fishing licenses, are for the entire trip, not per angler. For most fishing charters, reservations are recommended and deposits are often required. Also, cancellation policies vary between operators, so be sure to check such details well in advance, or else you may lose your deposit.

As an alternative to bringing your own boat or hiring a fishing charter, you can always rent a seaworthy vessel from **Sunset Watersports Key West** (Hurricane Hole Marina, 5130 Overseas Hwy., Stock Island, 305/294-5500, www.sunsetwatersports.info, 9am-6pm daily), which offers a range of vessels, from 17-foot fishing boats ($250 per half day, $325 daily) to 24-foot pontoons ($400 per half day, $500 daily). Boats come equipped with GPS, fish and depth finders, live bait wells, and bimini tops.

If you need to rent a fishing rod or stock up on essentials like live bait and cold beer, head first to the Historic Seaport district, where **Key West Bait & Tackle** (241 Margaret St., 305/292-1961, www.keywestbaitandtackle. com, 7am-7pm daily) features a wide selection of fishing tackle, rods and reels, frozen bait, lures, hooks, sunglasses, towels, and other necessities. Other helpful fishing stores include **The Angling Company** (333 Simonton St., 305/292-6306, www.theanglingcompany.com, 9:30am-7pm daily) and the **Saltwater Angler** (243 Front St., 305/294-3248 or 800/223-1629, www.saltwaterangler.com, 9am-8:30pm daily), a one-stop shop for travel gear, fishing apparel, reels, rods, sunglasses, and other fishing accessories.

As a bonus, all three stores can help you arrange fishing charters. Through Key West Bait & Tackle, you can opt for a backcountry flats fishing charter ($450 per half day, $550 for six hours, $650 daily) in search of redfish, snook, permit, and bonefish; a deep-sea fishing excursion ($800 per half day, $950 for six hours, $1,200 daily) to snag tuna, wahoo, mahimahi, and other game fish; and a light-tackle saltwater fishing charter ($750 per half day, $850 for six hours, $950 daily), which allows you to fish for tarpon in the harbor, marlin and swordfish in the offshore waters, and yellowtail near the reefs. Through The Angling Company and Saltwater Angler, you'll also find a slew of professional guides (rates vary) for flats fishing, offshore fishing, and light-tackle fishing.

KAYAKING

Paddling enthusiasts will find a number of helpful operators in Key West. Based at the Hurricane Hole Marina, **Lazy Dog** (5130 Overseas Hwy., Stock Island, 305/295-9898, www.lazydog.com, 9am-5pm daily) offers two-hour guided kayaking tours ($40 pp) through backcountry waters and winding mangrove creeks. Lazy Dog also features a four-hour kayaking and snorkeling trip ($60 pp) along the Mosquito Coast, plus single and double kayak rentals ($25 per half day, $35 daily), stand-up paddleboard rentals ($30 each), paddleboard tours ($40 pp), and paddleboard yoga ($30 pp). Reservations are required, and complimentary pickups are available. Area maps are provided with all rentals.

Similarly, **Blue Planet Kayak** (305/294-8087 or 800/979-3370, www.blue-planet-kayak.com) offers guided kayaking trips into the fascinating backcountry, such as the 2.5-hour Boca Chica Tour (10am and 12:40pm in winter, 10am and 3pm in summer, $50 pp) and the 2.5-hour Romantic Sunset & Moonlight Tour ($50 pp). Beginners and families are welcome, though advance reservations are required. Since tour guides will only lead a maximum of 10 passengers on each personalized trip, slots can fill up quickly. Complimentary transportation is available for all tour customers. In addition, Blue Planet provides rentals for sit-in single kayaks ($30 per half day, $40 daily), tandem kayaks ($40 per half day, $50 daily), and fishing kayaks ($30 per half day, $40 daily). For the fishing kayaks, only charts, anchors, and advice are included; anglers must bring their own tackle.

For an alternative experience, consider **Key West Eco Tours** (305/290-2047, www.key-westecotours.com), situated in the Historic Seaport at Key West Bight, behind the Turtle Kraals Restaurant and Bar at the end of Margaret Street. As part of a 4.5-hour eco-tour ($99 adults, $79 children under 13) that includes sailing and coral reef snorkeling, Key West Eco Tours offers kayaking trips amid seagrass beds and winding mangrove creeks, where you'll get an up-close look at tropical fish, aquatic birds, sea turtles, spotted eagle rays, dolphins, crabs, sponges, and other marine wonders. Tours occur twice daily

BOATING SAFETY

On especially gorgeous days, you're likely to see a number of powerboats, sailboats, yachts, kayaks, and other vessels in the offshore waters extending from Miami to the Dry Tortugas. With so much action, there's bound to be chaos—unless, of course, boaters obey the following safety guidelines, for the sake of themselves as well as their passengers.

- **Verify Vessel Safety:** Before heading out on the water, make sure that your vessel has been properly maintained, that it meets all local and state regulations, and that your registration numbers are displayed prominently.

- **Equip Yourself:** When planning a boating trip, double-check that you have the following items on board: proper vessel documentation and insurance information, nautical charts, a marine radio, an anchor, a first-aid kit, mounted fire extinguishers, navigation lights, visual distress signals, sound-producing devices, a marine sanitation device, drinking water, extra fuel, and enough personal flotation devices (PFDs) for you and all your passengers.

- **Wear Your Life Jacket:** While it might seem more liberating to ride, fish, or kayak without a PFD, it's imperative that you actually wear one at all times. Not all boating accidents occur in bad weather and rough seas; many happen in shallow water on deceptively calm, clear days, so be sure to wear a life jacket—even a lightweight, inflatable one—whenever you're on the water.

- **Stay Safe and Sober:** Although many boaters will partake of beer and other alcoholic beverages while out on the water, it's simply not advisable to do so. Wind, noise, motion, and sunlight can intensify the effects

of alcohol and prescription medications, making it exceedingly dangerous to operate a vessel while under the influence.

- **Monitor Your Propeller:** Unfortunately, boat propellers are responsible for numerous injuries and fatalities every year. To avoid being yet another statistic, purchase propeller safety devices such as sensors and propeller guards, and don't forget to wear an engine cut-off lanyard at all times—which will ensure that if you and, by extension, your lanyard are thrown from the boat, the engine will immediately power down.

- **Monitor Your Passengers:** To ensure your passengers' safety, never allow them to board or disembark while the engine is running, and insist that they remain seated (in proper seats and not on the bow or transom) while the boat is in motion. In an effort to avoid accidents, assign someone to keep watch around the propeller area whenever other passengers, especially children, are swimming in the surrounding waters. To protect the passengers of other boats, stay alert when operating in congested areas, avoid swimmers altogether, and be aware of boats that are towing skiers or tubers. If someone on your vessel falls overboard, stop immediately, turn the boat around, keep the person in sight as you approach, and shut the engine off before rescuing him or her.

For additional advice or information about boating safety courses, consult the **Boat Owners Association of The United States (BoatU.S.)** (800/395-2628, www.boatus.com) or the **U.S. Coast Guard's Boating Safety Division** (www.uscgboating.org), which aims to prevent fatalities, injuries, and property damage on U.S. waterways by improving the knowledge and skills of recreational boaters.

(9am-1:30pm year-round, 2pm-sunset in winter, 3:30pm-sunset in summer) and allow a maximum of six passengers. Double-seat, sit-on-top kayaks are provided.

Based out of The Westin Key West Resort & Marina at 245 Front Street, **Danger Charters** (305/304-7999 or 305/296-3272, www.

dangercharters.com) operates daily sailing excursions amid pristine coral reefs, deserted mangrove islands, and sponge gardens in the backcountry. These half-day (9:30am, $75 pp) and full-day trips (10:30am, $100 pp) also feature kayaking and snorkeling and include snacks, beverages, and gear.

DIVING AND SNORKELING

Like the rest of the Florida Keys, Key West is surrounded by thriving coral reefs and fascinating shipwrecks. On your own, you can easily dive and snorkel amid the tropical fish and varied coral formations in the bountiful waters near **Fort Zachary Taylor Historic State Park** (western end of Southard St., 305/292-6713 or 305/295-0037, www.floridastateparks.org/forttaylor or www.fortzacharytaylor.com, 8am-sunset daily, $7 vehicles with 2-8 passengers plus $0.50 pp, $4.50 motorcycles and single-occupant vehicles, $2.50 pedestrians, bikers, and extra passengers) and the **Dry Tortugas National Park** (305/242-7700, www.nps.gov/drto/index.htm or www.dry.tortugas.national-park.com, sunrise-sunset daily, $5 weekly), roughly 68 miles to the west. Still, many of the underwater attractions this far south are only accessible through professional diving charters.

Besides offering scuba-diving instruction and equipment rentals, several local companies, such as **Southpoint Divers** (610 Front St., 800/891-3483, www.southpointdivers.com,

8:30am noon and 1·30pm-5pm daily), provide trips to two curious wrecks: the 187-foot *Cayman Salvage Master* ($85-120 pp) and the 522-foot **USNS *General Hoyt S. Vandenberg*** ($115-150 pp), a former troop transport ship during World War II, later the backdrop for the film *Virus,* and now the foundation for an artificial reef. Sunk in May 2009, the ship has since become a habitat for varied fish and offers a unique look at the developing stages of coral growth. Guides are required for all open water dives on the *Vandenberg.* Varied gear—including tanks, weights, regulators, wetsuits, and nitrox bottles—is available through Southpoint Divers, and classes range from a refresher course ($75 pp) to a PADI dive master course ($895 pp).

In addition to leading excursions to the Cayman and *Vandenberg* wrecks, the **Subtropic Dive Center** (1605 N. Roosevelt Blvd., 305/296-9914 or 800/853-3483, www.subtropic.com, 8:30am-12:30pm and 1:30pm-6pm daily, $80-150 pp) and **Dive Key West** (3128 N. Roosevelt Blvd., 305/296-3823 or

Divers explore the USNS *General Hoyt S. Vandenberg,* an artificial reef near Key West.

© HAIG JACOBS/FLORIDA KEYS NEWS BUREAU/HO

800/426-0707, www.divekeywest.com, 9am-1pm and 2pm-6pm daily, $75-164 pp)—one of the oldest and largest full-service diving facilities in the Florida Keys—each offer trips to other wrecks, such as **Joe's Tug**, a storm-battered vessel that sits in 65 feet of water and is now home to assorted coral formations and nosy eels.

Additional diving resources include **Lost Reef Adventures** (261 Margaret St., 305/296-9737 or 800/952-2749, www.lostreefadventures.com, 9am-1pm and 1:30pm-5:30pm daily, $65-180 pp) and the **Captain's Corner Dive Center** (125 Ann St., 305/296-8865 or 305/304-0437, 9:30am-1:15pm and 2pm-5:30pm daily, $65-130 pp), whose 60-foot, aluminum diving vessel was used in the film *Licence to Kill*. Some of these operators even offer night dives as well as trips to reef formations like the deep, spur-and-groove networks of **Sand Key, Rock Key,** the **Eastern Dry Rocks,** and the **Western Sambo Ecological Reserve.** Other curious habitats include the **Kedge Ledge,** a patch reef that contains coral-encrusted anchors from 18th-century schooners, and the **Ten-Fathom Ledge,** a series of coral ledges, caves, and outcroppings that nurture grouper, lobster, sharks, and eagle rays.

Like the rest of the Keys, Key West appeals to snorkelers, too. In fact, all of the aforementioned diving operators also cater to snorkelers, offering at least two trips daily ($40-50 adults, $35-45 children), with rental equipment usually included in the price. In addition, **Sebago Watersports** (201 William St., 305/292-4768 or 800/507-9955, www.keywestsebago.com, 9am-12:30pm and 1pm-4:30pm daily, $49 adults, $25 children), **Sunset Watersports Key West** (201 William St., 305/296-2554, www.sunsetwatersportskeywest.com, times vary daily, $35-40 adults, $25 children 6-11, free for children under 6), and **Fury Water Adventures** (1 Duval St. and 245 Front St., 305/294-8899 or 877/994-8898, www.furycat.com, 9:30am-12:30pm and 1pm-4pm daily, $40 adults, $20 children 6-12) offer snorkeling trips, among other water-related activities. Instruction and necessary equipment are provided with all trips. Based out of the Historic Seaport at Key West Bight, **Sunny Days** (866/878-2223, www.sunnydayskeywest.com), operated by Fury Water Adventures, also features the *Fast Cat* (305/296-5556 or 800/236-7937, 8am-5pm daily, $140 adults, $70 children 6-12, free for children under 6, plus $5 park entrance fee for guests 17 and over), a high-speed catamaran that can whisk you to the waters surrounding Dry Tortugas National Park for some incredible snorkeling opportunities.

Two other noteworthy vessels, the *Echo* catamaran (Historic Seaport at Key West Bight, 305/292-5044, www.dolphinecho.com, 9am-1pm and 1:30pm-5:30pm daily, $74-89 pp) and the smaller *Amazing Grace* (6000 Peninsula Ave., Stock Island, 305/294-5026 or 800/593-6574, www.wildaboutdolphins.com, 8am-noon and 1pm-5pm daily, $95 pp), combine snorkeling trips with wild dolphin encounters. Both offer private charters as well.

You might also want to visit **Snuba of Key West** (Key West City Marina at the Garrison Bight, 1801 N. Roosevelt Blvd., 305/292-4616, www.snubakeywest.com, 9am, 1pm, and 4pm daily, $99 adults, $79 children 8-12, $44 riders or non-Snuba snorkelers), where you can try an unusual form of deepwater snorkeling that requires no dive certification. On these personal guided tours amid the offshore coral reefs, you'll be able to breathe easily underwater without wearing heavy, restrictive diving gear. Just note that children must be at least 8 years old to try Snuba snorkeling.

Though nearly all of the aforementioned diving and snorkeling outfitters should have the equipment and accessories that you need, you can also make a quick stop at **Divers Direct** (535 Greene St., 305/293-5122, www.diversdirect.com, 9am-7pm Mon.-Thurs., 9am-8pm Fri.-Sat., 10am-7pm Sun.), a well-stocked scuba-diving retailer, for any last-minute items.

OTHER OUTDOOR ACTIVITIES

For thrills of a different kind, consider heading to the Sunset Marina, where you can board the year-round **White Knuckle Thrill Boat Ride**

KEY WEST

(5555 College Rd., Stock Island, 305/797-0459, www.whiteknucklethrillboatride.com, $59 pp), an exhilarating, wet-and-wild jet boat experience that features twists, slides, and 360-degree spins in the waters near Key West. If you'd prefer to be in control of your own white-knuckle experience, feel free to rent a Jet Ski, Sea-Doo, or WaveRunner from the following outfitters: **Barefoot Billy's** (The Reach Resort, 1435 Simonton St., 305/849-0815, www.barefootbillys.com, 9am-6pm daily, $70 per half hour, $100 hourly), **Island Water Sports** (The Westin Key West Resort & Marina, 245 Front St., 305/296-1754, www.islandwatersports. us, 9am-sunset daily, $75 per half hour, $100 hourly, $10 per extra passenger), or **Key West Water Tours** (Hurricane Hole Marina, 5106 Overseas Hwy., Stock Island, 305/294-6790, www.keywestwatertours.com, $99 hourly). In addition, all three operators offer guided two-hour tours around the island of Key West every day. Billy's tour times include 10am ($99 pp), 12:30pm ($125 pp), and 3:30pm ($125 pp), while Island Water Sports leaves at 9:30am, 11:30am, 1:30pm, 3:30pm, and 5:30pm ($125 pp, $10 per extra passenger). Key West Water Tours, meanwhile, leads tours at 10am, 12:30pm, 3:30pm, and sunset ($135-155 pp).

Now, if you'd rather be *above* the water, you can always opt for a parasailing adventure. Three such companies operate out of the Historic Seaport at Key West Bight: **ParaWest Parasailing** (700 Front St., 305/292-5199, www.parawestparasailing.com, 9am-6pm daily, $30 pp for morning rides, $45 single riders, $75 double riders, $110 triple riders), **Sebago Watersports** (201 William St., 305/292-4768 or 800/507-9955, www.keywestsebago.com, 9am-4pm daily in winter, 10am-5pm daily in summer, $55 single riders, $85 tandem riders), and **Sunset Watersports Key West** (201 William St., 305/296-2554, www.sunsetwatersportskeywest.com, 9am-6pm daily, $39 pp), which also operates out of Smathers Beach. Another operator, **Fury Water Adventures** (305/294-8899 or 877/994-8898, www.furycat.com, 9am-6pm daily, $40 pp), offers parasailing adventures from two locations:

the Pier House Resort (1 Duval St.) and The Westin Key West Resort & Marina (245 Front St.). All four offer solo and tandem rides, and all promise smooth take-offs, gentle landings, breathtaking aerial views, and safe experiences. No matter which you choose, try to book your trip in advance, especially during the peak winter months.

For a combination of such activities, consider opting for Fury's **Ultimate Adventure** (10am-4pm daily, $139 adults, $70 children 6-12, free for children under 6), an all-inclusive experience that features kayaking, reef snorkeling, Jet Skiing, parasailing, rock climbing, and access to a water trampoline, plus a complimentary meal and unlimited beverages. Sunset Watersports offers a similar package, the **"Do It All!" Party Boat Adventure** (10am-4pm daily, $129 adults, $59 seniors and children under 10), which includes snorkeling, kayaking, rafting, sunfish sailing, knee-boarding, waterskiing, windsurfing, and access to various water sports, plus a grilled lunch. Not to be outdone, Sebago Watersports features its own version of this all-day fun with the **Power Adventure** (10am-4pm daily, $149 adults, $75 children), which encompasses reef snorkeling, a guided kayaking tour, parasailing, and access to personal watercraft, water trampolines, and other water sports—plus free meals, snacks, and beverages. For all three adventures, booking online will typically save you a bit of money.

❰ SPAS AND YOGA

What better way to relax after a hard day of golfing, biking, fishing, kayaking, diving, or parasailing than to experience a soothing massage treatment or beachside yoga lesson. Fortunately, Key West provides an array of such rejuvenating experiences.

Several area resorts, in fact, feature on-site spas. At the **Pier House Resort** (1 Duval St., 305/296-4600, www.pierhouse.com), the full-service **Caribbean Spa** (8:30am-7pm daily) offers manicures ($35 pp), pedicures ($40-70 pp), restorative facials ($65-165 pp), tanning services ($60-140 pp), and moisturizing body treatments ($115 pp), such as the full-body detoxifying mud wrap. Several massages ($70-170 pp) are also available, including the 80-minute hot stone therapy massage and the 80-minute, head-to-toe Caribbean Spa Coma, which proves to be as mind-numbing as it sounds. Guests should reserve appointments in advance and provide at least four hours' notice for any cancellations.

Meanwhile, the adjacent **Ocean Key Resort & Spa** (0 Duval St., 305/296-7701 or 800/328-9815, www.oceankey.com) features the waterfront **SpaTerre** (305/295-7017, 9am-6pm daily), which provides day spa services as well as spa vacation packages. At SpaTerre, men and women alike can experience various massages ($65-175 pp), refreshing body treatments ($70-110 pp), such as the Caribbean Seaweed Body Mask, and incredible Balinese and Thai spa rituals ($165-230 pp), such as the Javanese Royal Spa Treatment, which includes a Balinese spa massage, an herbal exfoliation, a cool yogurt splash, an aromatic shower, and a tub soaking amid rose petals and tropical fragrances. Face and body depilation (rates vary), facials ($60-150 pp), manicures ($20-50 pp), and pedicures ($20-100 pp), including the ultra-special Key Lime Margarita Pedicure, are also available. An adjacent fitness center even offers yoga classes and a stretching patio.

At **Southernmost on the Beach** (508 South St., 305/296-6577, www.southernmostresorts.com), the full-service **Paradise Day Spa** (305/879-7352, www.keywestparadisedayspa.com, 9am-9pm daily) offers an array of salon and spa services. Here hotel guests as well as nonguests can enjoy various manicures ($40-60 pp), pedicures ($50-100 pp), facials ($80-150 pp), massages ($50-130 pp), and body wraps and treatments ($100-150 pp). Other salon services, such as waxing ($20-100 pp) and electrolysis ($30-300 pp), are also available. As with most spas, appointment cancellations must be made 24 hours in advance.

Another top-notch spa can be found at the **Casa Marina Resort** (1500 Reynolds St., 888/303-5717, www.casamarinaresort.com). Only open to hotel guests at the Casa Marina and its sister facility, **The Reach Resort** (1435 Simonton St., 888/318-4316, www.reachresort.com), the **Spa al Mare** presents facials ($100-160 pp), massages ($60-180 pp), aromatherapy treatments ($100-210 pp), and yoga classes ($20-80 pp). Spa packages are also available. Note that all massages are offered either in the studio or on the beach, and bear in mind that guests must notify the spa 24 hours in advance to cancel an appointment.

Beyond luxurious resorts, Key West also contains several stand-alone day spas. The locally owned **Prana Spa** (625 Whitehead St., 305/295-0100, www.pranaspakeywest.com, 11am-7pm Tues.-Sat., 11am-5pm Sun.), for instance, lures both residents and tourists with its clinical skin care ($55-140 pp), exotic spa treatments ($25-300 pp), and massage therapy ($50-160 pp). Specialties include the Thai yoga massage and the Prana Decadence, a complete three-hour experience that includes a body polishing scrub, a 75-minute body massage, an ultimate foot treatment, a 60-minute ultimate rejuvenation facial, and a shirodhara warm oil hair and scalp treatment.

White Street Healing Arts (1217 White St., 305/393-4102, 305/296-5997, or 305/304-5891, www.whitestreethealingarts.com, by appointment) is a holistic professional group that provides massage therapy in addition to acupuncture, chiropractic and Chinese medicine, and intuitive healing. Offerings include Swedish, deep tissue, aromatherapy, and reflexology massage ($90 hourly, $110 per 75 minutes, $130 per 90 minutes), plus hot stone massage ($165 per 90 minutes) and couples massage ($180 hourly, $220 per 75 minutes, $260 per 90 minutes). The licensed massage therapists here are often willing to bring their skills directly to you, but a 24-hour cancellation policy is in effect for all appointments, whether inside or outside the office.

In New Town, on the eastern part of the island, the **All About You Day Spa & Wellness Centre** (1712-1714 N. Roosevelt Blvd., 305/292-0818, www.allaboutyoukw.com, by appointment Mon., 7am-6pm Tues.-Sat.) features an assortment of salon and spa services, including perms, glycolic peels, waxing, and permanent make-up. As at other Key West day spas, you can opt for manicures ($20-35 pp), pedicures ($30-65 pp), facials ($45-100 pp), body wraps ($75-150 pp), and massage treatments ($50-140 pp). Two favorites are the 90-minute hot rock massage and the 60-minute monkeybar massage, during which a licensed massage therapist uses suspended parallel bars to perform a tabletop Shiatsu massage. Farther east, the **Solar Spa of Key West** (2824 N. Roosevelt Blvd., 305/292-6080, www.solarspaofkeywest.com, 10am-7pm Mon.-Sat.), a day spa and tanning salon, offers standard services, such as hair care (rates vary), manicures ($25 pp), pedicures ($35 pp), facials ($75 pp), body treatments ($120 pp), and massages ($80-100 pp).

For relaxation of a more active variety, consider **Yoga on the Beach** (305/296-7352, www.yogaonbeach.com), which offers daily, year-round classes on the beach, either at Fort Zachary Taylor Historic State Park or the Southernmost on the Beach property. Classes at the state park, which can range between the hour-long Yoga Express and the 90-minute Yoga for Every Body, typically cost $15 per person and include the park entrance fee. Meanwhile, classes at Southernmost on the Beach, such as the hour-long Yin Yoga, typically cost $10 for hotel guests and $15 for drop-in clients. Mats, blankets, and props are provided for all classes, and instructors will make every effort to accommodate those with disabilities.

Accommodations

Key West has, by far, the greatest assortment of lodging options in the Florida Keys, from intimate bed-and-breakfasts to sprawling resorts—only some of which are listed here. Organizations like the **Key West Innkeepers Association** (KWIA, 305/295-9500 or 800/492-1911, www.keywestinns.com) or **The Lodging Association of the Florida Keys and Key West** (3152 Northside Dr., Ste. 101, 305/296-4959, www.keyslodging.org) can help you choose the place that's right for you. No matter where you decide to stay, reservations are highly recommended, especially on weekends during the peak season (Dec.-Apr.).

$100-200

Conceived to honor the many literary masters who lived and worked in Key West, the **Authors Key West Guesthouse** (725 White St., 305/294-7381 or 800/898-6909, www.authorskeywest.com, $100-135 d) provides a compound of Conch-style houses, suites, and rooms. Typically named after famous writers or artists, the accommodations range from the John James Audubon room, which contains a queen-size bed and a private bath, to

the Ernest Hemingway cottage, which offers, in addition to a queen-size bed, a trundle bed, a living room, and a full kitchen. Whether you choose to swim in the heated pool or sip an evening cocktail in the garden, the Authors Guesthouse may be the perfect place to start that novel you've always wanted to write.

Nestled amid the varied lodgings on Fleming, the ecofriendly **❰ Eden House** (1015 Fleming St., 305/296-6868 or 800/533-5397, www.edenhouse.com, $125-330 d) offers the ideal setting for a wide variety of visitors, from couples on a romantic getaway to large family reunions. Composed of an art deco-style main building and several renovated Conch-style houses, the Eden House seems a world away from Duval Street, though it lies within walking distance of the busy thoroughfare. While not technically a spa resort, this picturesque place—which once served as the backdrop for *CrissCross,* a film starring Goldie Hawn—certainly has the ambience of one. Surrounded by the lovely buildings, the main focus of the complex is the freshwater pool area, where you'll find shady palm trees, gurgling fountains, numerous tables and chairs, a peaceful gazebo, a sun deck, and a six-person hot tub. Although the rooms and suites vary in size and amenities—from a cozy spot beside the pool to a two-level house with a hot tub of its own—all guests can enjoy the hotel's varied features, including a comfortable library area, relaxing hammocks, wireless Internet access, beach towels that can be used off-site, a daily happy hour beside the pool, a 24-hour staff, and complimentary coffee and tea in the lobby. As a bonus, the Eden House will let you store your luggage even after you check out, so that you can savor a few more hours in Key West.

The motto at the **Garden House Bed & Breakfast** (329 Elizabeth St., 305/296-5368 or 800/695-6453, www.key-west-florida-bed-breakfast.com, $159-219 d) encourages guests to "leave the grumpy attitude at home." That's pretty easy to do when you spot the sumptuous grounds, which include an upper-level sun deck as well as a heated pool with spa jets and a cascading waterfall, all surrounded by lush

Eden House features a palm-shaded oasis, surrounded by several different historic structures.

© LAURA MARTONE

tropical gardens. There are 10 uniquely decorated rooms on-site—ranging from the Gecko Grotto, with its queen-size bed and private bath, to the Writer's King, with its Tiffany-style reading lamps and king-size bed. Not far away, in a quiet area of Old Town, the **Rose Lane Villas** (522-524 Rose Ln., 305/292-2170, www.roselanevillas.com, one-bedroom villas $159-269 d, two-bedroom and three-bedroom villas $402-666) provide a tempting haven for those who want to stay within walking distance of the action. Though the one-bedroom, two-bedroom, and three-bedroom villas vary in size, each has a full kitchen, cable television, free wireless Internet access, and an allotted parking space. Before hitting the town, take an early morning swim in the beautiful pool, accented by a stunning mural of lush gardens. After a long day exploring Key West, finish your evening with a cocktail on one of the peaceful porches or balconies and listen to the murmur of Old Town fading into the night.

Between the grand two-story Victorian mansion and the poolside cabana, the **Pilot House Guest House** (414 Simonton St., 305/293-6600 or 800/648-3780, www.pilothousekeywest.com, $130-210 d) encompasses a variety of accommodations to suit every traveler's needs, ranging from a standard room with a private bathroom, a kitchenette, a queen-size bed, and a balcony to the King Cabana II, which contains a king-size bed, a kitchenette, a Jacuzzi tub, and a private bathroom with a European shower. The grounds also feature a beautiful pool and a semi-private spa, both of which are clothing-optional. The **Mango Tree Inn** (603 Southard St., 305/293-1177, www.mangotree-inn.com, $129-189 d), constructed in 1858, is a gorgeous example of Old Town's historical architecture. Inside, the inn offers comfortable rooms, some with two bedrooms and full kitchens. Relax with a swim in the pool, surrounded by lush gardens and tall palm trees, or chat with the resident celebrities: Jade the parrot and Leilani the cockatoo.

Just two blocks off Duval, **The Paradise Inn** (819 Simonton St., 305/293-8007 or 800/888-9648, www.theparadiseinn.com, $169-199 d)

KEY WEST

provides elegant suites, ranging from a mini suite with two queen-size beds to the Royal Poinciana Suite, featuring two bedrooms, two bathrooms with Jacuzzi tubs, and a wraparound porch. The grounds, teeming with tropical flora, include a Jacuzzi and a fountain-fed pool. What was once, in the 1920s, a bordello and gambling spot has become a simple and affordable place to stay in Key West. At the **Angelina Guest House** (302 Angela St., 305/294-4480 or 888/303-4480, www.angelinaguesthouse.com, $104-149 d), "simple" means having no phones or televisions, allowing you to truly escape your daily existence. Only two blocks from the hustle and bustle of Duval, you'll find infinite tranquility in the verdant garden and heated lagoon-style pool. Here the accommodations vary from having a shared bathroom and full-size beds to having a king-size bed, a private bathroom, and a refrigerator.

The **Truman Hotel** (611 Truman Ave., 305/296-6700 or 866/487-8626, www.trumanhotel.com, $169-199 d), one of the newer boutique hotels in town, prides itself on being "South Beach hip with a Key West flair." With accommodations that range from a standard room to a suite featuring two king-size beds and a living room, each selection contains swanky touches like zebra-striped rugs, leather chairs, and modern lighting. As a bonus, after a long day wandering around Key West, you'll relish a dip in the combination pool and spa.

Among the more reasonable offerings in the Old Town section of Key West is the historical ◖**Chelsea House Pool and Gardens** (709 Truman Ave., 800/845-8859, www.historickeywestinns.com, $170-220 d), which consists of two grand Victorian mansions on an acre of lush tropical gardens. Dating from 1888 and 1906, these two former homes now contain a variety of comfortable guest rooms and suites, with amenities like private bathrooms, cable television, and air-conditioning. Other features include a continental breakfast, a heated pool, on-site parking, free wireless Internet access in the courtyard, and proximity to Key West's most popular restaurants and attractions. With

advance arrangements, you might also be able to bring your pet during your stay. After all, the Chelsea House was named for a cat (a British shorthair named Chelsea) that lived here in the 1970s.

The adults-only **Azul Key West** (907 Truman Ave., 305/296-5152, www.azulhotels. us, $159-219 d) features 11 rooms and suites surrounding a beautiful freshwater pool. Each room includes a king-size bed, a flat-screen television, and wireless Internet access. The suites, meanwhile, range from those possessing shared balconies, with views of the pool or Truman Avenue, to the Aria Suite, situated at treetop level and offering stunning views of the entire area. As an alternative, head toward the quieter end of Duval, where the **La Te Da Hotel** (1125 Duval St., 305/296-6706 or 877/528-3320, www.lateda.com, $100-200 d) features plenty of activities to distract you from the "Duval crawl." Two bars, a restaurant, and a cabaret only add to the charm of this beautiful hotel. The accommodations here range from standard rooms with two queen-size beds, a refrigerator, and cable television to luxury rooms featuring extra touches like British Colonial-style furnishings and 800-thread-count linens.

The **El Patio Motel** (800 Washington St., 305/296-6531 or 866/533-5189, www.elpatiomotel.com, $96-169 d), a 30-room motel designed in the art deco style, features a lush tropical garden, a serene fountain, and a freshwater swimming pool. Accommodations here range from a basic room with a refrigerator to an apartment with a full kitchen. In addition, limited wireless Internet access is available, depending on your location on the property.

OVER $200

Given that it's also a respected museum, **The Curry Mansion Inn** (511 Caroline St., 305/294-5349 or 800/253-3466, www.currymansion. com, $195-240 d) is surprisingly accommodating to its guests. The historical 22-room property contains various types of lodgings, from standard deluxe bedrooms with king-size beds and private bathrooms to magnificent master suites featuring large balconies, comfortable sitting rooms, and cable television. Situated within the bustling heart of Old Town, the Curry still allows you a modicum of peace and quiet, whether you're dining on a full breakfast, enjoying an afternoon cocktail party, swimming in the on-site pool, or simply relaxing on the grounds.

Northeast of the Curry, the **Cypress House** (601 Caroline St., 305/294-5229, www.cypresshousekw.com, $155-325 d) offers comfortable, bed-and-breakfast accommodations in a historical Conch-style building that was erected in 1888. Guests can expect spacious, high-ceilinged rooms with air-conditioning, ceiling fans, cable television, refrigerators, bathrobes, and complimentary, high-speed wireless Internet access. Other amenities on this locked, gated property include lush tropical gardens, a heated swimming pool, bicycle rentals, parking ($10 daily), a continental breakfast buffet (8am-11am daily), and complimentary cocktails (6pm-7pm daily). Note that minimum stay requirements vary seasonally, and guests must be at least 16 years of age.

Two blocks south of the Cypress House, the white, casually elegant, Conch-style **Marquesa Hotel and Marquesa Cottages** (600 Fleming St., 305/292-1919, www.marquesa.com, $190-345 d), originally built in 1884, provide luxuriously furnished hotel rooms and private well-equipped cottages. All chambers are clean, comfortable, and airy, with tropical-style touches like wooden floors, ceiling fans, and vibrant paintings. Despite its proximity to Duval Street, the Marquesa still offers enough of a buffer to make it feel as though you've found a quiet little nook of your own. That's especially true in the well-landscaped pool and garden area, which features a waterfall, two freshwater pools, and numerous chaise lounges and shaded tables. Other property amenities include wireless Internet access and an upscale restaurant, open to hotel guests as well as the public. Farther south, **The Mermaid & The Alligator Bed & Breakfast** (729 Truman Ave., 305/294-1894 or 800/773-1894, www.kwmermaid.com, $148-318 d) truly aspires to be "your home in Key West." This beautiful 1904 Victorian-style home offers eight unique rooms in the main house in addition to a Conch-style cottage on the grounds. Amenities include a full complimentary breakfast, a lush garden, and a heated pool, featuring built-in benches and whirlpool jets.

The stylish **Santa Maria Suites** (1401 Simonton St., 305/296-5678 or 866/726-8259, www.santamariasuites.com, $249-279 d) feature accommodations with private balconies and terraces. Only a block from the Atlantic Ocean and not far from Duval, this lovely hotel provides an escape from the craziness of Key West. The accommodations vary from standard one-bedroom suites to luxury two-bedroom bi-level suites. Other amenities include flat-screen televisions and two heated, garden-enclosed swimming pools.

Closer to the ocean, the magnificent Spanish-style **Casa Marina Resort** (1500 Reynolds St., 305/296-3535 or 888/303-5717, www.casamarinaresort.com, $239-279 d)

KEY WEST

the elegant Marquesa Hotel and Marquesa Cottages

beckons an upscale clientele with its cream colored walls, red roof tiles, and arched entryways. Built in 1920 and now part of the Waldorf Astoria Collection, the largest resort in Key West comprises a wide array of elegantly furnished rooms and suites, from the Island Vista, with two double beds, to the Ocean Vista two-bedroom suite, featuring 900 square feet of space. All accommodations include a mini refrigerator and wireless Internet access. This grand resort also encompasses two enormous pools, a beautiful 1,100-foot beach with hammocks strung between palm trees, the Sun-Sun Beach Bar & Grill, and the Spa al Mare, where you can opt for massages, facials, aromatherapy, or a yoga session. In addition, guests can enjoy live entertainment in the on-site Rambler Lounge and savor a delicious steak at the Strip House, located at the hotel's sister property, The Reach Resort.

Situated on seven waterfront acres on the eastern side of the island, the **Key West Marriott Beachside Hotel** (3841 N. Roosevelt Blvd., 305/296-8100 or 800/546-0885, www.beachsidekeywest.com, $179-349 d) features luxurious accommodations, a lush tropical garden, a waterfront swimming pool, a sandy tanning beach, complete spa services, and immediate access to the on-site Tavern N' Town Restaurant. In addition, all guests can enjoy complimentary high-speed Internet service and flat-panel LCD televisions with cable.

Located on the gulf side of the island, **The Westin Key West Resort & Marina** (245 Front St., 305/294-4000 or 866/837-4250, www.westinkeywestresort.com, $450-575 d) provides splendid accommodations just steps from Mallory Square and the Custom House. This spacious resort features 178 luxurious guest rooms and suites, all of which include specially designed beds and showers, complimentary wireless Internet access, cable television, air-conditioning, and 24-hour room service, among other amenities. Some rooms and suites include flat-screen televisions, vaulted ceilings, Jacuzzi tubs, balconies, patios, and terrific views of the ocean, pool, courtyard, or gardens. Five hundred yards off the coast, the Westin

also boasts the **Sunset Key Guest Cottages** (305/292-5300 or 888/837-4249, www.westinsunsetkeycottages.com, $740-3,010), a sophisticated seven-acre resort on Sunset Key, a 27-acre residential island, where cars are not permitted. Offering seclusion from the hustle and bustle of Key West, the Sunset Key Guest Cottages contain one, two, three, or four bedrooms and can only be reached by ferry. Whether you choose to stay in Key West or on Sunset Key, you'll have access to all the amenities that the Westin resort offers, including the on-site marina, various water sports, a 24-hour fitness room and massage studio, a heated, palm-shaded outdoor pool, and several dining options, such as Bistro 245 and Latitudes. In addition, the Westin's Sunset Deck is an ideal spot from which to watch a famous Key West sunset.

Also within walking distance of Mallory Square, the **Ocean Key Resort & Spa** (0 Duval St., 800/328-9815, www.oceankey.com, $279-550 d) provides fantastic sunset views and easy access to the heart of Key West. The luxurious, tropical-style accommodations range from a 600-square-foot junior suite with a king-size bed, a spacious living room, plasma television, and a private balcony, to a two-bedroom, 1,200-square-foot suite that's purportedly the largest suite on the island. On-site amenities include a heated outdoor pool, water-sports rentals, sailing and fishing trips arranged through the marina, unbelievable body treatments at SpaTerre, and the waterfront Hot Tin Roof restaurant. Situated across the street, the **Pier House Resort and Caribbean Spa** (1 Duval St., 305/296-4600 or 800/723-2791, www.pierhouse.com, $299-575 d) has been serving guests since 1979. Known as the first true resort on the island, Pier House encompasses a private beach, a heated outdoor pool, and a private dock for charter pickups. While here, relax with a massage at the resort's world-class spa, savor a meal at the HarbourView Cafe or the Beach Bar and Grille, or consider deals like the Spa Honeymoon Package, which includes breakfast and a trip to the spa.

You'll be hard-pressed to miss the

Southernmost Hotel Collection (305/296-6577 or 800/354-4455, www.southernmostresorts.com, $300-659 d), set within Duval, United, and Simonton Streets. Each of the four hotels here offers sophisticated accommodations, sometimes with stunning ocean views: the airy 127-room **Southernmost Hotel** (1319 Duval St.), the tropical 123-room **Southernmost on the Beach** (508 South St.), and the elegant side-by-side Victorian-style boutique hotels, the 11-room **La Mer Hotel** and the eight-room **Dewey House** (508 South St.). No matter which property you choose, you'll be able to relax on the private beach, enjoy a dip in one of three pools, work out in the on-site fitness center, relish a delicious meal at the Southernmost Beach Café, sip cocktails at the Southernmost Tiki Bar, or of course, venture onto nearby Duval. Other amenities include free parking, lush gardens, and complimentary wireless Internet access.

Situated near the quieter end of Duval and built as a private residence in 1896, the colorful, Victorian-style ◖ **Southernmost House**

the Victorian-style Southernmost House

(1400 Duval St., 305/296-3141, www.southernmosthouse.com, $280-385 d) has seen its share of dignitaries, from Presidents Truman, Nixon, Kennedy, Eisenhower, and Carter to Key West fixtures like Ernest Hemingway. The accommodations here vary from the Southernmost Point Room, with its private balcony overlooking the Atlantic Ocean, to the Royal Suite, one of Key West's most favored suites, featuring a separate sitting parlor, stunning ocean and island views, and a four-poster king-size bed. While staying at the Southernmost House, refresh with a dip in the oceanside heated pool, then relax with a drink at the poolside bar.

The Reach Resort (1435 Simonton St., 305/296-5000 or 888/318-4316, www.reachresort.com, $319-419 d), part of the Waldorf Astoria Collection, is essentially a tropical playground. This boutique hotel provides the same experience you might receive from a Caribbean resort, with access to a spacious private beach; a variety of sailboats and water-sports gear; and a terrific spa (at its sister property, the Casa Marina Resort) to help renew your focus. Finish your evening with an exquisite meal at the on-site Strip House Steakhouse, before retiring to your luxury room or suite.

On the Atlantic Ocean, the **Coconut Beach Resort** (1500 Alberta St., 305/294-0057 or 800/835-0055, www.coconutbeachresort.com, studios $200-315 d, suites $310-550) contains a variety of accommodations, from studios to two-bedroom suites. In addition, the property features an open-deck pool and Jacuzzi, plus a small sandy beach. Farther inland, the adults-only **Olivia by Duval** (511 Olivia St., 305/296-5169 or 800/413-1978, www.oldtownsuites.com, $129-500 d) offers uniquely decorated rooms and suites, some of which include kitchenettes. Operated by Old Town Suites, this charming inn provides the perfect location for those hoping to experience the action of Duval while still enjoying the serenity of a private guesthouse. Amenities include cable television, air-conditioning, and a clothing-optional pool. For even more solitude, Old Town Suites also operates two lovely cottages on Center and Petronia Streets.

GAY AND LESBIAN LODGING

Key West is definitely a gay-friendly destination, as evidenced by Old Town's numerous gay bars and the city's annual events, from Pridefest to the ultimate bacchanal, Fantasy Fest. There are even several inns and resorts that cater to a gay and/or lesbian clientele.

The 38-room **Island House** (1129 Fleming St., 305/294-6284 or 800/890-6284, www.islandhousekeywest.com, $99-449 d), for instance, is Key West's largest gay male resort—and as some visitors have claimed, the classiest, most outrageous such place in the world. Within this secure, clothing-optional compound, gay men can relax and be themselves in an accepting environment, where a friendly all-male staff is available day and night. Here you'll find a swimming pool, a health club, a poolside bar and café, and a spa that includes a sauna, a five-man shower, and a Jacuzzi. The accommodations, meanwhile, are enclosed within four separate buildings, which were formerly a private residence, a boarding house, a Laundromat, and a cigar factory. The uniquely furnished lodgings range in size, though all have comfortable beds, extra-large bath towels, air-conditioning, and cable television.

In the same block, **Alexander's Guesthouse** (1118 Fleming St., 800/654-9919, www.alexanderskeywest.com, $145-290 d) welcomes a gay and lesbian clientele to a tranquil, comfortable setting, surrounded by lush tropical gardens. While here, you're free to enjoy the relaxing spa and sumptuous pool, which serves as the property's social center. Three levels of sun decks also allow guests a semiprivate setting to catch some rays and forget daily cares. Evenings at Alexander's begin with poolside cocktails, while in the morning, guests are greeted by a continental breakfast. No matter how you spend the time in between, however, you'll be sure to find a room that's right for you, as the inn houses a wide selection of airy accommodations, all individually decorated. In all, you'll find 15 comfortable guest rooms, one well-lit suite ($205-305 d) with

a private patio, and a gorgeous apartment ($275-410) with wooden floors, a full kitchen, a private sun deck, and a front porch with a hammock.

Sixteen elegantly decorated guest rooms and suites make up the men-only **Coconut Grove** (815 Fleming St., 305/296-5107 or 800/262-6055, www.coconutgrovekeywest.com, $139-299 d), set within, as the name indicates, a lovely coconut grove. Featuring a secluded, heated pool and outdoor Jacuzzi, the inn serves wine and hors d'oeuvres nightly and a complimentary continental breakfast every morning. The accommodations range from a standard deluxe room to a presidential suite with two bedrooms, and all guests are welcome to use the free wireless Internet access.

Given that the Big Easy and the Southernmost City share so many common elements, it seems only fitting that you'd find the **New Orleans House** (724 Duval St., 305/293-9800 or 888/293-9893, www.neworleanshousekw.com, rooms and suites $110-220 d, cottages $175-390) in Key West's Old Town. As the only gay, all-male guesthouse on Duval, the New Orleans House puts you just steps away from all the action, including the on-site Bourbon St. Pub. Still, if you're looking to relax, you can do just that on the private sun deck overlooking the pool and hot tub. The accommodations here range from standard rooms with a shared bathroom to an intimate cottage, equipped with a full kitchen and a king-size bed. In all, you'll find eight rooms, one suite, and three cottages here.

Closer to the ocean lies one of the world's largest inns for women, including lesbians and gay-friendly heterosexuals. Just two blocks away from the southernmost point in the continental United States, **◖ Pearl's Rainbow** (525 United St., 305/292-1450 or 800/749-6696, www.pearlsrainbow.com, rooms $89-269 d, suites $199-379 d) offers a wide variety of 38 rooms and suites, ranging from the Skyview Room, with an angled ceiling and a queen-size bed, to the Deluxe Poolside Suite, equipped with a king-size bed, a poolside porch, and a living room with hand-painted furniture, a sofa bed, and two televisions. The property includes five separate structures—the Marrero Building, the Surf Building, the Louisa Cottage, the East Cottage, and the West Cottage—plus a parking lot, two freshwater pools, and two rejuvenating spas. Pearl's also features free wireless Internet access, a restaurant, and Key West's only tropical bar just for women. For more gay-friendly establishments, consult the **Key West Business Guild** (513 Truman Ave., 305/294-4603 or 800/535-7797, www.gaykeywestfl.com).

CAMPING

Although most people visiting Key West choose to stay in one of the city's varied inns, hotels, or resorts, campers will also find a few options on nearby Stock Island. South of the Key West Golf Club, **Boyd's Key West Campground** (6401 Maloney Ave., Stock Island, 305/294-1465, www.boydscampground.com, $55-120 daily) offers tent sites as well as RV spaces, many of which are equipped with water service, 30/50-amp electricity, sewer access, and cable television. Both inland and waterfront spots are available. In addition, the property features a heated swimming pool, a lounging beach, free wireless Internet access, and numerous planned activities, including craft and yoga classes, pot luck dinners, movie nights, line dancing, and casino cruises.

The intimate **El Mar RV Resort** (6700 Maloney Ave., Stock Island, 305/294-0857, www.elmarrvresort.com, $80-115 daily) caters to RV enthusiasts only. No tents, pop-ups, or truck campers are allowed. Situated on the ocean, the property offers 10 spaces in all, half of which have waterfront views. All of the lengthy gravel sites in this park feature patios and full hookups, including 30/50-amp electricity. Closer to the Overseas Highway and not far from the Hurricane Hole Marina, the family-operated **Leo's Campground** (5236 Suncrest Rd., Stock Island, 305/296-5260, www.leoscampground.com, $39-69 daily) welcomes tent and RV campers alike. Pets, however, are only allowed in the RV portion of the park, at a daily fee of $1 per pet. There are also charges for extra people ($8 daily) and trailers ($7 daily). The tent sites, most of which have barbecue grills and picnic tables, are situated along a small, quiet lake, surrounded by mangroves, while the RV spaces feature picnic tables, 70-channel cable television, and full hookups with 30/50-amp electricity. Other on-site amenities include a barbecue area for RV campers, a laundry facility, and a bathhouse with hot showers. Monthly rates ($990-1,550) are also available.

Food

As with lodging options, Key West has the largest selection of restaurants in the Florida Keys, and the cuisine down here runs the gamut from fresh seafood to all-American hamburgers to upscale French and Italian dishes. So whatever your mood, you're sure to find something tasty in the Southernmost City. Of course, only a small percentage of the available eateries are listed here. For more suggestions, consult the **Florida Keys Dining Guide** (www.keysdining. com).

SEAFOOD

Key West, like the rest of the Florida Keys, boasts a plethora of fresh seafood options,

especially near the Historic Seaport at Key West Bight. While meandering around this lively area, be sure to stop by the **Half Shell Raw Bar** (231 Margaret St., 305/294-7496, www.halfshellrawbar.com, 11am-10pm daily, $7-21), a former shrimp-packing facility that has maintained its charm as an authentic fish house. Though offering fried dishes, this laid-back eatery really specializes in raw, steamed, broiled, and grilled seafood. After starting with a bucket of steamed clams, try the stuffed shrimp, prepared with crabmeat and spices and broiled with garlic butter, white wine, and lemon juice.

Along the boardwalk, you can enjoy fresh

seafood on the breezy upper deck of the weathered **(Schooner Wharf Bar** (202 William St., 305/292-3302, www.schoonerwharf.com, 7:30am-4am daily, $8-18). Here you'll find standard Keys fare like the filling seafood sampler, featuring conch fritters, mahimahi, four kinds of shrimp, and fries. In addition, the Schooner Wharf now serves complete breakfasts, such as the shrimp Benedict Florentine. This casual, open-air watering hole also offers live music, starting at noon and continuing late into the night.

Also beside the harbor, the **Conch Republic Seafood Company** (631 Greene St., 305/294-4403, www.conchrepublicseafood.com, 11am-midnight daily, $8-28) provides a casual atmosphere for seafood lovers. Here you'll enjoy raw oysters and clams, traditional dishes like grilled dolphin (mahimahi), 80 different varieties of rum, and daily entertainment, with musicians often playing late into the evening.

Within the **A&B Lobster House** (700 Front St., 305/294-5880, www.aandblobsterhouse.com, 6pm-11pm daily, $24-70), a fancy, white-cloth restaurant that offers signature dishes like grouper Oscar and tuna au poivre, you'll find **Alonzo's Oyster Bar** (www.alonzosoysterbar.com, 11am-10pm Mon.-Sat., noon-10pm Sun., $9-28), a casual eatery that serves key lime garlic oysters, steamed shrimp, roasted mussels, and other tasty treats.

Though not as old or as legendary as some Key West eateries, the family-owned **Two Friends Patio Restaurant** (512 Front St., 305/296-3124, www.twofriendskeywest.com, 8am-close daily, $9-35) is still a lively choice for breakfast, lunch, and dinner. Established in 1967, this open-air eatery prepares filling breakfast dishes like shrimp and crabmeat quiche and crab cake Benedict, as well as terrific "chargrilled" steaks, fresh seafood dishes, and tropical drinks later in the day. As a bonus, you'll find early-bird specials from 4 to 7pm daily, plus live karaoke nightly. Even if you never work up the nerve to take the stage, you'll certainly enjoy the show, and if you're a seafood fan, you can't go wrong at a place that offers everything

Tourists flock to the Two Friends Patio Restaurant.

© DANIEL MARTONE

KEY WEST

Several eateries lie near the Historic Seaport, including the Turtle Kraals Restaurant & Bar.

from conch fritters and raw oysters to a lobster combo platter that includes grilled gulf shrimp, broiled scallops, and a whole Florida lobster tail.

Closer to the ocean, you'll spot **Pisces** (1007 Simonton St., 305/294-7100, www.pisceskeywest.com, 6pm-11pm daily, $23-44), another fine-dining seafood establishment. Here you can enjoy a taste of New Orleans with the grilled shrimp Nola, or try the black grouper bouillabaisse with mussels, clams, and calamari. Other favorites include Lobster Tango Mango and Yellowtail Snapper Atocha. Pisces is the ideal place for a candlelit dinner, which might explain why reservations are recommended year-round. For an alternative experience, head to the **Hurricane Hole Restaurant & Marina** (5130 Overseas Hwy., Stock Island, 305/294-0200, www.hurricaneholekeywest. com, 11am-10pm daily, $11-23), where you can enjoy fresh seafood, steak, and chicken, while overlooking the marina. Bring in some freshly caught fish, and the cooks will grill, blacken, or fry it for you.

AMERICAN AND VEGETARIAN

Seafood isn't the only option for gourmands in Key West. Burgers, steaks, barbecue, even vegetarian dishes are available, too. If you're looking for a well-prepared steak, head first to the **Prime Steakhouse** (951 Caroline St., 305/296-4000, www.primekeywest.com, 6pm-10:30pm daily, $22-48), a fine-dining steakhouse that also offers an excellent selection of complementary wines. Begin with a signature martini before sampling one of the steak specials. Reservations are recommended, especially during the high season. The newly remodeled **Turtle Kraals Restaurant & Bar** (231 Margaret St., 305/294-2640, www.turtlekraals.com, 7am-10pm daily, $8-22) serves typical Keys-style dishes for breakfast, lunch, and dinner, though it definitely specializes in barbecue. Both the quaint indoor dining area and the covered outdoor patio provide the ideal atmosphere for enjoying a barbecue beef brisket platter or one of several other choice selections.

Just a few steps from Duval Street, lies the **Island Dogs Bar** (505 Front St., 305/509-7136, www.islanddogsbar.com, 11am-4am daily, $8-15), one of the few late-night joints in town. So when most restaurants are closed, head directly to this casual bar and eatery, which serves food until 3:30am every night. Here you'll find all-American favorites like chicken wings, hot dogs, burgers, and sandwiches, not to mention an array of alcoholic libations. Both indoor and outdoor seating are available.

❰ Sloppy Joe's Bar (201 Duval St., 305/294-5717, www.sloppyjoes.com, 9am-close daily, $4-13)—a spacious, boxy, white building that's hard to miss with its red-brick columns and the bar's name in giant, black letters—has been a Key West tradition since 1933. Supposedly one of Ernest Hemingway's favorite Key West watering holes, Sloppy Joe's has run an annual Hemingway Look-Alike Contest since 1980. The menu is fairly extensive, with traditional Key West-style cuisine as well as the famous Original Sloppy Joe Sandwich, which features delicious ground beef in a rich tomato sauce with onions, peppers, and spices. The food isn't the only attraction here; various bands keep you entertained day and night.

If you enjoy listening to good music while noshing on good food, then you're in luck. Sloppy Joe's isn't the only game in town. **Willie T's Restaurant & Bar** (525 Duval St., 305/294-7674, www.williets.com, 11am-2am daily, $11-17) also offers live music, excellent food, and terrific libations. In fact, the menu includes 28 different mojitos, from key lime to ginger to espresso. As for the food, Willie T's provides an assortment of tasty dishes, from the goat cheese and avocado salad to the blackened dolphin with avocado butter and red pepper jam.

For an organic, vegetarian meal, stroll over to **Help Yourself** (829 Fleming St., 305/296-7766, www.helpyourselffoods.com, 8am-7pm Mon.-Sat., 8am-3pm Sun., $8-14), which features a fairly extensive menu, including lasagna made with layers of zucchini, brazil nut meat, spinach, pesto, fresh tomatoes, and marinara. If you're just looking for a quick snack, consider ordering a refreshing smoothie, such as

the Chocolate Buzz, made with cacao powder, cacao nibs, and banana.

For a variety of options, stroll toward Key West Bight, where **The Commodore Waterfront Restaurant** (700 Front St., 305/294-9191, www.commodorekeywest.com, 5:30pm-10:30pm daily, $20-38) features traditional Florida Keys-style dishes, including seafood and steaks, in a fine-dining setting along the waterfront. Farther inland, you'll encounter another winning option, **Kelly's Caribbean Bar, Grill & Brewery** (301 Whitehead St., 305/293-8484, www.kellyscaribbean.blogspot.com, 11am-11pm daily, $16-30). Known as the birthplace of Pan American Airlines and now home to the Southernmost Brewery, Kelly's presents a menu of island flavors with such tasty dishes as coconut shrimp and jerked chicken. The food is delicious, but the real draw is the beer, crafted by the on-site brewmaster. Be sure to try Kelly's flagship beer, the Havana Red Ale.

Only a block off Duval, the classy, often noisy, **❰ Café Marquesa** (600 Fleming St., 305/292-1244, www.marquesa.com, 6pm-10pm daily, $20-49) feels as though it could be in Manhattan. The 50-seat restaurant offers contemporary American cuisine like macadamia-crusted yellowtail or pan-roasted duck breast. Whether you're a guest of the adjacent Marquesa Hotel or you're just looking for a fantastic place to start the evening, this small hot spot provides an elegant alternative to Key West's casual waterfront eateries.

The **Blue Heaven Restaurant** (729 Thomas St., 305/296-8666, www.blueheavenkw.com, 8am-close, $7-20) has been serving breakfast, lunch, and dinner since 1992. The full menu features everything from pancakes to Caribbean barbecue shrimp. For dessert, try the Banana Heaven, a banana bread with bananas flambéed in rum, served with vanilla ice cream.

Headed toward the ocean side of Old Town, you'll spot **Camille's Restaurant** (1202 Simonton St., 305/296-4811, www.camilleskeywest.com, 8am-3pm and 6pm-10pm daily, $6-28), a fun, exotic eatery that features

Café Marquesa, an upscale restaurant adjacent to the Marquesa Hotel

fondue to veal saltimbocca, featuring sautéed veal, topped with prosciutto di parma, yellow tomatoes, fresh sage, manchego cheese, and a velvety cream sauce. As a bonus, from 5:30 to 7:30pm, Michaels serves a new light-side menu, featuring smaller versions of all available dishes.

On Duval, you'll spot **⟨ Martin's Restaurant & Lounge** (917 Duval St., 305/295-0111, www.martinskeywest.com, 5:30pm-11pm daily, $23-49), a stylish German fusion restaurant that offers scrumptious dinner options as well as a terrific weekend brunch, featuring specialties like grilled bratwurst, seafood crepes, and eggs Benedict with lobster medallions. Both the menu and the decor illustrate a superb blend of classical and tropical attributes, with a touch of European sophistication. The space is divided into three unique sections: the elegant dining room, the chic lounge, and the sumptuous garden. Unlike many fine restaurants, Martin's welcomes children, which means that busy parents can enjoy delicious food, but couples without kids may find a quiet, romantic meal less than probable.

breakfast, lunch, and dinner. Unique dishes include a three-egg omelet made with fresh lobster, or the tender veal with an Asian panko crust. Despite the delicious food, though, the prevalent sexual innuendos in Camille's might not make it the most family-friendly establishment in town. As an alternative, stroll over to the **Flaming Buoy Filet Co.** (1100 Packer St., 305/295-7970, www.theflamingbuoy.com, 6pm-9:30pm daily, $18-48), where you can savor a New York strip steak with blue cheese butter, or the mojito chicken with fried plantains and brown rice. If you'd prefer to stay in your hotel, take advantage of the Flaming Buoy's delivery option.

EUROPEAN

Situated in a garden oasis, **⟨ Michaels Restaurant** (532 Margaret St., 305/295-1300, www.michaelskeywest.com, 5:30pm-10pm daily, $7-19) provides one of the most romantic dining opportunities in Key West. The menu features a variety of dishes, from

FRENCH

While you won't find too many options for French cuisine in the Southernmost City, there are definitely two standouts. The **Banana Cafe** (1215 Duval St., 305/294-7227, www.bananacafekw.com, 8am-3pm daily, 6pm-10pm Tues.-Sat., $7-30), for instance, is a popular French-style eatery that specializes in delectable crepes for breakfast, including the tasty La Ratatouille, which features cooked eggplant, zucchini, onions, tomatoes, and varied peppers, wrapped in a crepe and topped with a fried egg. The dinner menu is also divine, offering such winners as mussels Brittany or a Parisian-style ribeye. Popular with couples in a romantic mood, **Café Solé** (1029 Southard St., 305/294-0230, www.cafesole.com, 5:30pm-10pm daily, $18-23) combines French sauces with locally caught seafood. Fish dominates the menu, which includes such favorites as grouper Romesco, served with garlic, tomatoes, and a spicy roasted red pepper and hazelnut sauce, scrumptious Peanut Butter Perversion at Better Than Sex

© LAURA MARTONE

and tuna seared in pistachios with wasabi cream and a hoisin garlic sauce.

MEDITERRANEAN

For authentic Italian cuisine, look no farther than **Mangia Mangia Pasta Cafe** (900 Southard St., 305/294-2469, www.mangia-mangia.com, 5:30pm-10pm daily, $10-28). Situated in the heart of Old Town, this corner restaurant channels the ambience of a small Italian village. Here you'll find an array of fresh pastas with delicious homemade sauces, such as the New Zealand mussels with spaghettini, prepared in a garlic-based marinara sauce and topped with shaved parmesan cheese.

If you have a craving for various Mediterranean flavors, visit the well-regarded **Azur Restaurant** (425 Grinnell St., 305/292-2987, www.azurkeywest.com, 8am-2pm and 6pm-10pm Mon.-Fri., 9am-2pm and 6pm-10pm Sat., 10am-2pm Sun., $6-36) beside the Eden House. Serving breakfast, lunch, and dinner on the shaded terrace or in the dining room, Azur features such delicious creations as

Brie and mushroom omelets; charred octopus marinated with garlic, lemon zest, and Italian parsley; and apple and almond tarts with cardamom ice cream.

DESSERT

If you're a dessert connoisseur, you'll definitely find a lot of key lime pie in the eateries of Key West, but that's not the only treat that the Southernmost City has to offer. For something cool on a warm afternoon, head to the **Key West Ice Cream Factory** (201 William St., 305/295-3011, www.keywesticecreamfactory.com, 11am-10pm daily, $7-19). Offering 33 flavors of ice cream, including "Conchy" Cookies 'N Cream or Bermuda Triangle Chocolate, the shop also features 15 flavors of sorbet, including cantaloupe and watermelon. Just be prepared for long waits. Later in the evening, you should skip dinner altogether and head directly to **Better Than Sex** (926 Simonton St., 305/296-8102, www.betterthansexkw.com, 6pm-1am Tues.-Sun. Christmas-Easter, 6pm-1am Wed.-Sun.

Apr.-Dec., $9-13), a bordello-style lounge that prepares unforgettable desserts, such as Peanut Butter Perversion, the Missionary Crisp, and Kinky Key Lime, a creamy mousse concoction

that just might be the best key lime pie in town. Enhance your visit to this exotic, infinitely romantic spot with a glass of dark chocolate-rimmed Merlot.

Information and Services

INFORMATION
Tourism and Government Offices

For brochures, maps, and other information about Key West, plus assistance with hotel and tour reservations, stop by the **Key West Visitors Center** (1601 N. Roosevelt Blvd., 305/296-8881 or 877/296-8881, www.keywest123.com, 8am-10pm daily), the **Key West Chamber of Commerce** (510 Greene St., 1st Fl., 305/294-2587, www.keywestchamber.org, 8am-6:30pm daily), or the **Key West Information Center** (201 Front St., Ste. 108, 888/222-5590, www.keywestinfo.com, 9am-5pm Mon.-Sat.). In addition, you can consult the **Key West Attractions Association (KWAA)** (www.keywestattractions.org), **Key West's Finest** (1107 Key Plaza, Ste. 310, 305/296-0555, www.keywestfinest.com), or the **Monroe County Tourist Development Council** (1201 White St., Ste. 102, 305/296-1552 or 800/352-5397, www.fla-keys.com, 9am-5pm Mon.-Fri.). You can even save money on sightseeing adventures through online companies like **Trusted Tours and Attractions** (800/844-7601, www.trustedtours.com).

For government-related issues, contact the **City of Key West** (525 Angela St., 305/809-3700, www.keywestcity.com, 8am-5pm Mon.-Fri.) or the **Monroe County offices** (1100 Simonton St., 305/294-4641, www.monroecounty-fl.gov, 8am-5pm Mon.-Fri.).

Media

For local news, consult the daily *The Key West Citizen* (www.keysnews.com), the *Key West Keynoter* (www.keysnet.com), or *The Weekly Newspapers* (www.kcysweekly.com). The daily *Miami Herald* (www.miamiherald.com) and the biweekly *Florida Keys Keynoter*

(www.keysnet.com) are also available throughout the Keys.

In Key West, you'll also have access to several radio stations, including the popular **US-1 Radio** (104.1 FM, http://us1radio.com), which offers local news, including up-to-the-minute weather information during hurricane season. In addition, most hotels offer access to the major television stations in the Miami-Fort Lauderdale market.

SERVICES
Money

For banking needs, stop by **Capital Bank** (330 Whitehead St., 305/294-6330 or 800/639-5111, www.capitalbank-us.com, 9am-4pm Mon.-Thurs., 9am-6pm Fri., extended drive-through hours). Another option is the **First State Bank of the Florida Keys** (www.keysbank.com), which offers five locations in the Key West area, from Stock Island (5450 MacDonald Ave., 305/296-8535, 9am-4pm Mon.-Thurs., 9am-6pm Fri., extended drive-through hours) to Old Town (444 Whitehead St., 305/296-8535, 9am-4pm Mon.-Thurs., 9am-6pm Fri.).

Mail

For shipping, faxing, copying, and other business-related services, visit **The UPS Store** (2900 N. Roosevelt Blvd., Ste. 1107, 305/292-4177, www.theupsstore.com, 9am-6pm Mon.-Fri., 10am-3pm Sat.). You can also package and ship items at the two local **post offices** (800/275-8777, www.usps.com). You'll find one on the eastern end of the island (2764 N. Roosevelt Blvd., 305/296-7327, 8:30am-5pm Mon.-Fri., 9am-noon Sat.) and one in Old Town (400

Whitehead St., 305/294-9539, 8:30am-5pm Mon.-Fri., 9:30am-noon Sat.).

Groceries and Supplies

For groceries, baked goods, and other supplies, head to the nearest **Winn-Dixie** (2778 N. Roosevelt Blvd., 305/294-0491, www.winndixie. com, 24 hours daily), which has an on-site pharmacy (305/294-0658, 8am-8pm Mon.-Fri., 9am-7pm Sat.-Sun.). In Key West, you'll also find a **Publix** (3316 N. Roosevelt Blvd., 305/296-2225, www.publix.com, 7am-10pm Mon.-Sat., 7am-9pm Sun.), which includes an on-site pharmacy (305/296-3225, 9am-9pm Mon.-Fri., 9am-7pm Sat., 10am-5pm Sun.). The area also features a **CVS/pharmacy** (530 Truman Ave., 305/294-2576, www.cvs.com, 24 hours daily), which offers limited supplies as well as an on-site pharmacy (9am-9pm Mon.-Sat., 10am-6pm Sun.).

Laundry

If you need to clean some clothes during your trip, you'll find several coin-operated laundries in the area, including two locations of **Key West Laundries** (www.keywestlaundry.com): the **Key West Launderette** (912 Kennedy Dr., 7am-10pm daily) and the **Habana Plaza Coin Laundry** (3124 Flagler Ave., 7am-10pm daily).

Internet Access

Using your own laptop, you can access high-speed wireless Internet service at any number of hotels and resorts in the Key West area. In addition, there are several charming Internet cafés, including the **Coffee Plantation** (713 Caroline St., 305/295-9808, www.coffeeplantationkeywest.com, 7am-6pm daily) and the **Sippin' Internet Cafe** (424 Eaton St., 305/293-0555, www.sippinkeywest.com, 7am-11pm daily). You'll also find useful services, including Internet access, at the **Monroe County May Hill Russell Library** (700 Fleming St., 305/292-3595, www.keyslibraries.org, 9:30am-6pm Tues. and Thurs.-Fri., 9:30am-8pm Wed., 10am-6pm Sat.).

Emergency Services

In case of an emergency that requires police, fire, or ambulance services, dial **911** from any cell or public phone. For nonemergency assistance, contact the **Monroe County Sheriff's Office** (5525 College Rd., 305/292-7000, www.keysso.net, 8am-5pm Mon.-Fri.). For medical assistance, consult the **Lower Keys Medical Center** (5900 College Rd., Stock Island, 305/294-5531, www.lkmc. com). Foreign visitors seeking help with directions, medical concerns, business issues, law enforcement needs, or other problems can receive **multilingual tourist assistance** (800/771-5397) 24 hours daily.

Getting There and Around

GETTING THERE
By Air

Travelers can reach Key West directly by flying into the **Key West International Airport (EYW)** (3491 S. Roosevelt Blvd., 305/809-5200 or 305/296-5439, www.keywestinternationalairport.com). Besides major airlines, such as **US Airways** (800/428-4322, www.usairways. com) and **Delta Air Lines** (800/221-1212, www.delta.com), the Key West airport hosts smaller air carriers, like **Cape Air** (508/771-6944 or 800/352-0714, www.capeair.com, rates vary), which offers daily service between Fort Myers and Key West.

Other area airports include the **Florida Keys Marathon Airport (MTH)** (9400 Overseas Hwy., Marathon, 305/289-6060), the **Fort Lauderdale-Hollywood International Airport (FLL)** (100 Terminal Dr., Fort Lauderdale, 866/435-9355, www.broward.org/airport), and the **Miami International Airport (MIA)** (2100 NW 42nd Ave., Miami, 305/876-7000 or 800/825-5642, www.miami-airport.com). From each airport, you can rent a vehicle from such agencies as **Avis** (800/331-1212, www. avis.com), **Budget** (800/527-0700, www.budget.com), **Enterprise** (800/325-8007, www. enterprise.com), **Hertz** (800/654-3131, www. hertz.com), or **Thrifty** (800/367-2277, www. thrifty.com) in order to reach your hotel or primary destination in Key West.

By Bus or Train

To reach Key West using the regional bus system, you can take the **Miami-Dade County Metrobus** (305/891-3131, www.miamidade. gov/transit), which operates the **301 Dade-Monroe Express** between Florida City and Marathon (5:15am-8:40pm daily). From Marathon, you can then use the **Lower Keys Shuttle,** operated by the **Key West Department of Transportation (KWDoT)** (305/600-1455, www.kwtransit.com, $4 per ride, $25 weekly, $75 monthly), to complete the rest of your journey. The shuttle runs from Marathon to Key West between 5:30am and 11:15pm daily. Other stops include Bahia Honda State Park, Big Pine Key, and several other Lower Keys. Reduced fares may apply for students under 22 years old, senior citizens over 59 years old, military personnel, and disabled individuals.

As for national transportation companies, while **Greyhound** (800/231-2222, www.greyhound.com) offers bus service to the **Key West Greyhound Station** (3535 S. Roosevelt Blvd., 305/296-9072, 7:30am-11am and 3pm-6pm daily) near the Key West International Airport, **Amtrak** (800/872-7245, www.amtrak. com) only provides train service as far south as Miami. Of course, you can always rent a car or hop a shuttle to reach the Florida Keys

Transport from Airports and Stations

If you arrive in the Fort Lauderdale-Miami area by plane, bus, or train—or Key West by plane or bus—you can either rent a car or hire a shuttle service to reach your destination in the Key West area. Some of these companies include **Keys Shuttle** (305/289-9997 or 888/765-9997,

www.keysshuttle.com, $90-100 per shared ride, $400-450 for exclusive service) and **Keys Tropical Transportation** (305/852-3595, www. keystropicaltransportation.com, starting at $130 or $165 per ride, depending on the airport of origin), both of which provide service from the Miami and Fort Lauderdale airports. Another option is **TO'n'FRO** (305/393-0955, www.tonfro.com, $300-400 per luxury sedan ride), a personalized van and car service that offers transportation between the Miami and Fort Lauderdale airports and any destination in the Keys.

By Car

To reach Key West from Miami, simply head south on U.S. 1 (Overseas Hwy.), drive through the Upper, Middle, and Lower Keys—roughly 110 miles from the mainland—and continue toward your destination, likely west of Mile Marker 5. If you're headed from the Everglades via I-75 (Everglades Pkwy.), drive south on U.S. 27, veer right onto SR-997 (Krome Ave.), and follow the signs to U.S. 1. From U.S. 41 (Tamiami Trl.) in the Everglades, head south on SR-997 and continue toward U.S. 1. If you arrive during the peak season (Dec.-Apr.), be sure to call **511** for an up-to-the-minute traffic report.

By Boat

As an alternative to planes, buses, and the like, you can also reach Key West by boat. The **Key West Express** (888/539-2628, www.seakeywestexpress.com, $86-147 adults, $20-40 children under 13, $86-135 seniors 62 and over) offers a fleet of comfortable jet-powered passenger ferries that provide year-round daily service from Fort Myers Beach to Key West—a ride that typically takes 3.5 hours. Passengers can opt for one-way travel, same-day return, or different-day return and, with certain restrictions, may be allowed to bring pets and bicycles on board. All passengers 18 years of age and older must present valid identification in order to ride.

GETTING AROUND
By Car

If you're not on foot or a bicycle, the third best way to travel through Key West is by car or motorcycle—both of which offer easy access to U.S. 1 as well as the residential roads throughout this compact city. The smaller the vehicle, the easier it will be to find street parking when necessary; just remember to watch for parking signs and feed any required meters. Note, too, that Key West offers a few public parking areas in Old Town, including the **Park N' Ride Old Town Garage** (305/809-3910, www.keywestcity.com, $2 hourly, $13 daily) at the corner of Grinnell and Caroline Streets, not far from the Historic Seaport. The garage provides covered overnight parking and convenient access to tourist attractions, and as a bonus, parking here allows you free, same-day access to the city's public transportation.

By Tour or Public Transit

Since Key West is the most populated—and most popular—destination in the Florida Keys, it's not surprising that there are public transit options in addition to taxicabs, pedicabs, and vehicle rentals. Upon arriving in town, you might want to opt for the **Conch Tour Train** (888/916-8687, www.conchtourtrain.com, 9am-4:30pm daily, $30 adults, $27 seniors and military personnel, free for children under 13 and Key West residents) or the **Old Town Trolley Tour** (305/296-6688 or 888/910-8687, www.trolleytours.com, 9am-4:30pm daily, $30 adults, $27 seniors and military personnel, free for children under 13), both of which offer guided excursions through the city—an ideal way to get an overview of all available attractions before exploring them in more depth. In addition, the **Key West Department of Transportation (KWDoT)** (305/600-1455, www.kwtransit.com, $2-3 per ride, $8-16 weekly, $25-50 monthly) provides bus service around Key West and the Lower Keys between 5am and 11pm daily.

By Taxi

Taxicab companies can also help you get around Key West, such as **Perfect Pedicab** (305/292-0077, $1.50 per minute), offering three-wheeled open-air human-operated vehicles, and **Five 6's** (305/296-6666, www.keywesttaxi.com, $2.75 for first 0.2-mile, $0.60 per each additional 0.2-mile), which provides 24-hour service with its pink ecofriendly hybrids that you'll spot seemingly everywhere.

By Bicycle or Boat

Key West is a lovely, welcoming place to traverse by bicycle, whether you're an experienced rider or a novice. Just remember that you'll have to share the streets with cars and other vehicles, so take care while you tour the neighborhoods.

Bicycles can be rented from several different outfitters, including **Eaton Bikes** (830 Eaton St., 305/294-8188, www.eatonbikes.com, 9am-6pm Mon.-Sat., 9am-4pm Sun., $18-45 daily, $40-135 weekly), which offers a range of bicycles, from trikes to mountain bikes to tandems, plus free delivery service throughout Key West. **The Bike Shop of Key West** (1110 Truman Ave., 305/294-1073, www.thebikeshopkeywest.com, 9am-6pm Mon.-Sat., 10am-4pm Sun., $12 daily, $60 weekly, $180 monthly), the oldest in town, also provides a wide array of bicycles, plus accessories, bicycle sales, and a service/repair department. All rentals include locks, lights, baskets, and soft wide seats.

Another helpful source is **Adventure Rentals** (305/293-8883, www.keywest-scooter.com, 9am-5pm daily, $15 daily, $60 weekly), which provides bicycle rentals at multiple locations (0 Duval Street, 617 Front Street, 135 Simonton Street, and Cruise Ship Pier B), plus scooters ($50-70 daily), Harley motorcycles (starting from $268 daily, $935 weekly), and multiple-passenger electric cars ($159-202 daily).

In addition, **A&M Rentals** (305/896-1921, www.amscooterskeywest.com, 8am-8pm daily, $15 daily, $85 weekly) features three spots where you can rent kid-size bicycles, cruisers, and tandems: 523 Truman Avenue, 513 South Street, and 500 Truman Avenue. Here you can also rent one-seater scooters ($35 daily, $109 weekly), two-seater scooters ($55 daily, $179 weekly), and multi-seater electric cars ($99 daily)—all popular ways to get around town. Free customer pickup and drop-off services are available. Take note that such outfitters typically require that all electric car operators possess a valid driver's license and be at least 21 or 22 years old.

You can also experience Key West by boat. Having your own vessel makes navigating these waters even easier, and you'll find no shortage of marinas in the area. If you'd rather rent a boat, stop by **Sunset Watersports Key West** (Hurricane Hole Marina, 5130 Overseas Hwy., Stock Island, 305/294-5500, www.sunsetwatersports.info), which offers a range of vessels, from 17-foot fishing boats ($250 per half day, $325 daily) to 24-foot pontoons ($400 per half day, $500 daily). Also at the Hurricane Hole Marina, you'll find **Lazy Dog** (305/295-9898, www.lazydog.com), which offers two-hour guided kayak tours ($35 pp) in addition to kayak rentals ($20 per half day, $30 daily).

Dry Tortugas National Park

Roughly 68 miles west of Key West lies a cluster of seven islands, composed of coral and sand that are collectively known as the Dry Tortugas. Originally named Las Tortugas (The Turtles) by Spanish explorers, the islands eventually became "Dry Tortugas" on mariners' navigational charts to indicate the lack of fresh water here. Part of the 220-mile-long Florida Keys archipelago, these islands, in addition to the surrounding shoals and waters, comprise the 64,657-acre **Dry Tortugas National Park,** established in 1992 to preserve this unique area and now one of the most remote parks in the National Park System. In addition, Dry Tortugas has been listed on the National Register of Historic Places.

Celebrated for its diverse wildlife, its remarkable coral reefs, its enthralling shipwrecks, and its pirate legends and military past, Dry Tortugas is indeed a must-see destination, the kind of place that really makes you feel as though you're a world away from the Florida mainland. If you have the time, you should definitely board a ferry or come by private boat to this unique destination—popular with sunbathers, swimmers, snorkelers, kayakers, anglers, bird-watchers, photographers, and overnight campers.

SIGHTS

While visiting the Dry Tortugas, you should take a guided or self-guided tour of **Fort Jefferson,** the well-preserved Civil War fort on Garden Key, the centerpiece of these remote islands. Nicknamed the "American Gibraltar," the country's largest 19th-century, coastal fort was initially established in 1846 in order to control navigation in the Gulf of Mexico, though its construction was never quite completed. During and after the war, it served as a remote, Union-affiliated military prison for captured deserters. From 1865 to 1869 it was even home to Dr. Samuel Mudd, who was incarcerated here for setting the broken leg of assassin John Wilkes Booth and thereby participating in the assassination of President Abraham Lincoln. By the 1880s the U.S. Army had abandoned the facility, which became a wildlife refuge in 1908 and a national monument in 1935. An interesting tidbit is that in 1847 seven enslaved African Americans fled Garden Key in a dramatic self-emancipation attempt. Although they were ultimately caught, their daring effort has been officially acknowledged by the National Underground Railroad Network to Freedom Program.

Within the fortified walls of this historical citadel, you'll encounter such sites as the officers' quarters, soldiers' barracks, cistern, magazines, and cannons. The visitor center and park headquarters are also located here. From November to May, parts of Fort Jefferson are closed to the public while mason crews work on much-needed preservation projects. Such temporary closures are not in effect during the hurricane season (June-Nov.), which might only add to the logistical difficulties of this remote marine environment. Note that pets, food, and drinks are not allowed inside the fort. In addition, service and residential areas are closed to the public.

While visiting Fort Jefferson, be sure to take a look at the **Fort Jefferson Harbor Light,** northeast of the boat dock. Established in 1825 and still operational today, the lighthouse, whose present tower was erected in 1876, is a favorite among photographers. In addition, Loggerhead Key, which once housed the Carnegie Institute's Laboratory of Marine Ecology and is only accessible by private boat or charter, features the **Loggerhead Light,** also established in 1825, with an existing tower that was erected in 1858. Just remember that all buildings and structures on Loggerhead Key are closed to visitors, unless accompanied by a park ranger.

Fort Jefferson, part of Dry Tortugas National Park

RECREATION

Although visiting Dry Tortugas National Park is only possible by ferry or private boat, the isolated **Fort Jefferson Beach** is well worth the trip. Besides its proximity to historical Fort Jefferson, it's a terrific locale for swimming, snorkeling, kayaking, fishing, and bird-watching. Certain activities are prohibited, such as spearfishing, lobstering, using personal watercraft, collecting artifacts and marinelife, bartering with commercial fishermen for seafood, or possessing loaded firearms in federal facilities.

Bird-Watching and Wildlife-Viewing

Many people come to Garden Key for the bird-watching opportunities, which are truly excellent out here. More than 200 varieties are spotted annually, especially from March through September, when nearby Bush Key serves as the nesting grounds for migratory birds. During April and May, over 85,000 brown noddies and sooty terns nest on Bush Key. In the spring you might spot herons, raptors, and shorebirds, and in summertime you might observe frigatebirds and mourning doves. The fall and winter months bring such species as hawks, merlins, peregrine falcons, gulls, terns, American kestrels, and belted kingfishers. Other possible sightings include orioles, warbles, cormorants, masked boobies, black noddies, mangrove cuckoos, and white-crowned pigeons. Be sure to pick up an official bird checklist from the visitor center in Fort Jefferson, or consult the **Audubon Society of Florida** (Keys Environmental Restoration Trust, 11399 Overseas Hwy., Ste. 4E, Marathon, 305/289-9988, http://fl.audubon.org) for more information.

While you can spot many of these species during a short visit to Garden or Loggerhead Keys, you might have a better experience on board a bird-watching charter—though admittedly a pricier one as well. **Sea-Clusive Charters** (1107 Key Plaza, Ste. 315, Key West, 305/744-9928, www.seaclusive.com,

$2,600-3,275 per trip) features such tailored excursions, led by professional bird guide Larry Manfredi (www.southfloridabirding.com). While on board, you might also spot other wildlife, such as sharks, dolphins, and if you're lucky, gigantic sea turtles. These cruises can accommodate a minimum of eight passengers and a maximum of 11.

Boating and Kayaking

Since Garden Key and Loggerhead Key are both accessible by private boat, many boaters enjoy this park as well. Unfortunately, the dock on Loggerhead Key is only open to government vessels, but luckily, you're allowed to land south of the boathouse. Docking on Garden Key can also be problematic, as the public dock is often occupied by ferries and supply boats. Given that you can only tie up to the dock for two-hour increments between sunrise and 10am and then again between 3pm and sunset, your best bet is to anchor in the harbor and use a dinghy to reach the island, which offers a dinghy beach for that exact purpose. Overnight anchoring, between sunset and sunrise, is only allowed in the designated anchorage area: the sand and rubble bottom within one nautical mile of the Fort Jefferson Harbor Light.

All boaters should have self-sufficient, fully equipped vessels. Necessary items include life jackets, nautical charts, a tool kit with spare parts, plenty of fuel and drinking water, and a VHF radio to monitor weather forecasts. In addition, all vessels must conform to U.S. Coast Guard regulations.

Kayaking can also be a wonderful way to experience the islands, though you'll need to take care. The currents here can be very strong, making the area suitable for experienced sea kayakers only. If you do choose to tote kayaks along for the ride, make sure to bring a life vest, an anchor, a bailer, extra paddles, drinking water, and waterproof bags for gear. Other necessary safety equipment includes flares, bow and stern lines, a sound producing device, a 360-degree light for operating at night, and the NOAA nautical chart #11438.

Fishing

Anglers are welcome to fish from the public dock on Garden Key, as well as the beach west of the dock. With the recent establishment of the 46-square-mile Research Natural Area (RNA), however, fishing from a boat is only permitted within a one-mile radius of Garden Key. Nevertheless, several local fishing charters operate multiday trips to this area. With proper permits and licenses, these guides are allowed to fish in and around Dry Tortugas National Park. **Andy Griffiths Charters** (40 Key Haven Rd., Key West, 305/296-2639, www.fishandy.com), for instance, offers three-day, two-night excursions ($3,000-3,600) to the Dry Tortugas for up to six anglers. These trips typically last from 10am on Friday to 2pm on Sunday, or from noon on Monday to 2pm on Wednesday.

Dream Catcher Charters (5555 College Rd., Stock Island, 305/292-7702 or 888/362-3474, www.chartersofkeywest.com), meanwhile, offers 10-hour trips ($900-950) for up to six passengers as well as overnight excursions (trip times and rates vary). Another helpful operator is **Lethal Weapon Charters** (1418 Angela St., Key West, 305/296-6999 or 305/744-8225, www.lethalweaponcharters.com, trip times and rates vary). Of course, if you choose instead to fish on your own, remember that Florida state laws, regulations, and licensing requirements apply in these waters. Commercial fishing, spearfishing, taking fish by sling or speargun, dragging a net, casting near sea turtles, collecting shells and artifacts, and possessing lobster, conch, or ornamental tropical fish are not allowed within the boundaries of Dry Tortugas National Park.

Diving and Snorkeling

With numerous patch reefs and shipwrecks, including the 19th-century Bird Key Wreck and early 20th-century Windjammer Wreck, within the boundaries of Dry Tortugas National Park, it's no wonder that snorkelers, scuba divers, and underwater photographers favor this area. Whether you arrive on Garden Key by ferry or private boat, you'll be able to snorkel directly off the beach, near the moat walls and coaling dock ruins, in warm, shallow waters that boast a cornucopia of kaleidoscopic tropical fish, conch shells, lobster and sponges, sea fans and sea anemones, staghorn coral clusters, and occasional sea turtles.

For access to even more snorkeling and scuba-diving sites around the Dry Tortugas—part of Florida Keys National Marine Sanctuary—consult **Sea-Clusive Charters** (1107 Key Plaza, Ste. 315, Key West, 305/744-9928, www.seaclusive.com, $2,600-3,275 per trip), which offers multiday diving excursions for 6-11 passengers. With Sea-Clusive, divers will be able to explore the Windjammer wreck site as well as the overhangs, caves, and swim troughs of these incredible coral reefs, which offer water depths of 45 to 80 feet. Here you'll spot tropical fish, resident jewfish, black grouper, coral formations, and sponges.

If you choose to snorkel or dive on your own, you should be aware of certain offshore protection zones that are closed to the public. In addition, you need to prepare for potentially strong gulf currents. Remember, too, that dive flags are required beyond designated swimming channels at all times.

CAMPING

Since Dry Tortugas National Park has no public lodging, camping is the only option for those who hope to stay overnight on Garden Key. Just a short southwesterly walk from the public dock lies a primitive 10-site campground. Although the group site, which must be reserved in advance, can accommodate 10-40 people, most of the sites are available on a first-come, first-served basis and will suit up to six people and three tents. The campground is a self-service fee area, charging a nightly fee of $3 per person, and the sites offer little more than picnic tables and barbecue grills.

Grocery stores, fresh water, ice, and fuel are unavailable here, so plan accordingly. No trash receptacles are present either, which means that all visitors, boaters, and campers must pack out any and all trash. Unless you plan to anchor a private boat in the harbor near Garden Key, you'll probably be reaching the park by a commercial ferry. If so, be aware that most transportation companies have cargo weight restrictions. On the *Yankee Freedom II,* for instance, campers are limited to 60 pounds of gear plus water, while campers arriving aboard the Sunny Days *Fast Cat* are limited to 40 pounds of gear plus water. Neither ferry allows the transport of fuels like propane or lighter fluid, so campers are encouraged to use self-starting charcoal.

In order to make your camping trip as smooth as possible, there are several items you should be sure to pack, including picture identification, a fishing license, camping regulations, and the current weather forecast. To make your stay more comfortable, bring along a tent, a sleeping bag and pad, rain gear, clothing for warm and cold weather, a wide-brimmed hat, and plenty of food, water, and ice. Cooking equipment should include a portable stove or grill, fuel of some kind, waterproof matches and a lighter, cooking utensils, biodegradable soap, and trash bags. Personal gear, such as medications, a first-aid kit, a knife, a flashlight and spare batteries, sunglasses, sunscreen, and insect repellent, will also prove to be helpful. Although you can bring pets with you, they are only allowed on Garden Key, outside Fort Jefferson, and must be leashed and well-behaved at all times. It probably goes without saying that owners must remove all pet waste from the park. Campers are only allowed to stay for four days and three nights at a time.

INFORMATION

Technically, Dry Tortugas National Park is open all year, though restrictions are in effect on certain islands. Garden Key, which contains Fort Jefferson, is surely the most visited island in the park. Although the island itself is open year-round, Fort Jefferson is only open during daylight hours. Loggerhead is also open year-round during daylight hours. Middle and East Keys, however, are closed from April to mid-October during turtle nesting season, while Bush, Hospital, and Long Keys are closed all year, meaning that visitors should remain 100 feet offshore of these particular islands.

To visit the park, anyone 16 years of age or older must pay an entrance fee of $5. The pass, which is valid for seven days, is typically collected by commercial transportation operators; otherwise, you'll have to remit payment at the Garden Key visitor center. Annual passes, which can be purchased or procured at the **Florida Keys Eco-Discovery Center (FKEDC)** (35 E. Quay Rd., Key West, 305/809-4750, www.floridakeys.noaa.gov, 9am-4pm Tues.-Sat., free) with qualifying documentation, are all honored in Dry Tortugas. These include the National Parks and Federal Recreational Lands Pass ($80) and the lifetime versions for senior citizens 62 years of age and older ($10), disabled visitors (free), and volunteers (free)—plus the now-discontinued Golden Eagle, Golden Age, and Golden Access Passports. All such passes are only eligible to legal U.S. citizens and permanent residents.

The recently designated, 46-square-mile Research Natural Area (RNA)—an ecological preserve that will encompass a little less than half of the park and serves to protect species affected by overfishing and loss of habitat—may eventually limit your fishing access to certain areas and require permits in other areas. For more information about Dry Tortugas National Park, including details about the RNA, contact the **park headquarters** (305/242-7700, www.nps.gov/drto/index.htm, 8am-4.30pm Mon.-Fri.) or the Florida Keys Eco-Discovery Center. You can also consult websites like www.dry.tortugas.national-park.com. In addition, you can download park maps and regulations, plus information about camping, bird-watching, island history, and the RNA, from the official National Park Service website. Books are also helpful resources, such as Thomas Reid's *America's Fortress: A History of Fort Jefferson, Dry Tortugas, Florida* (Gainesville, FL: University Press of Florida, 2006).

GETTING THERE AND AROUND

Dry Tortugas National Park, which lies approximately 68 miles west of Key West, is only accessible by ferry or private boat—all of which can be boarded in Key West. (Incidentally, seaplanes used to be a viable way to reach Garden Key, but the company has indefinitely suspended such trips, pending legal action.) To reach Garden Key by ferry, you can schedule a day trip on the 100-foot catamaran *Yankee Freedom II* (240 Margaret St., 305/294-7009 or 800/322-0013, www.yankeefreedom.com, 8am-5:30pm daily, $165 adults, $155 students, military personnel, and seniors 62 and over, $120 children 4-16, free for children under 4), which is docked in the Historic Seaport at Key West Bight. Reservations are recommended for the ferry, which will charge an additional park entrance fee of $5 per person aged 16 or over. Cancellations must be made the day before your scheduled trip, and all passengers should arrive no later than 7:30am on the day of departure. In addition to day trips, the ferry offers overnight excursions, for which reservations are absolutely required. The *Yankee Freedom II* charges $180 for adult campers and $140 for children; however, such rates do not include the requisite park entrance and camping fees.

For the ferry, which has comfortable air-conditioned cabins, the day trip from Key West begins at 8am. While you journey past the Marquesas, the famous *Atocha* shipwreck, and various marinelife, you'll be treated to a complimentary continental breakfast. Once you arrive on Garden Key, you can opt for a 45-minute narrated tour of Fort Jefferson with one of the ferries' knowledgeable guides, after which you can relax on the pristine beach, go for a swim, have a picnic, or take a bird-watching nature stroll. In addition, you'll have free use of the on-board snorkeling equipment. It's recommended that you bring a swimsuit and towel, sun protection, a camera and batteries, binoculars, sunglasses, water shoes, a jacket, and a hat. A reliable watch is also necessary, as the ferry will leave around 3pm in order to reach Key West by late afternoon.

If you choose to travel to Garden Key by private vessel, bear in mind the docking restrictions, which limit your use of the public dock between the hours of sunrise and 10am, and between 3pm and sunset. On Loggerhead Key, which is only accessible by private boat or charter, you can only land your vessel south of the dock and boathouse. Once on the island, you can explore the developed trails and shoreline, but remember that the dock and all structures are closed to the public.

BACKGROUND

The Land

GEOGRAPHY

Between 25 million and 70 million years ago, dramatic fluctuations in the sea level gradually formed the limestone upon which southern Florida now exists. Beyond the beaches and urban sprawl of Miami lies a fascinating region for nature lovers, most notably in the Everglades and the Florida Keys.

Shaped by water and fire, the Everglades are essentially **subtropical wetlands,** part of a massive watershed in southern Florida. Termed the "river of grass" by writer Marjory Stoneman Douglas in the late 1940s, the Everglades comprise a complex system of interdependent ecosystems, including sawgrass marshes, cypress swamps, mangrove forests, tropical hardwood hammocks, pine rocklands, coastal prairies, tidal mud flats, sloughs and estuaries, and the marine environment of Florida Bay.

The Florida Keys, meanwhile, are essentially a series of low offshore islands composed of sand and coral. While the Upper and Middle Keys are principally made of **Key Largo limestone,** once the peaks of living coral forests, the Lower Keys are basically an enormous shoal, made of sand, compacted oolite, and Key Largo limestone and traversed by

© DANIEL MARTONE

many channels—hence, the reason why the northernmost islands tend to be larger and longer, while the Lower Keys are smaller and more numerous. In the Keys, you'll also find hardwood hammocks, mangrove swamps, and beaches, though many visitors come to experience the ecosystems that can't be seen above the water. Along the Atlantic side of the 220-mile-long Florida Keys archipelago, which technically stretches from Key Biscayne to the Dry Tortugas, lies a series of living **coral reefs,** filled with tropical fish and varied coral formations, constituting the third largest coral reef system in the world—and the only one of its kind in the continental United States. While snorkelers and scuba divers enjoy exploring these offshore coral reefs, anglers appreciate the **patch reefs** closer to the coast, which are usually teeming with worthy game fish.

CLIMATE

Positioned between the Gulf of Mexico, Florida Bay, and the Atlantic Ocean, southern Florida tends toward a **subtropical climate.** Typically, the fall, winter, and spring months, from November to April, are mild and pleasant, with temperatures usually ranging from 61°F to 82°F. On occasion, temperatures can reach over 90°F, and cold fronts, though rare, are indeed possible. Although such cold snaps don't normally last too long, they can create near-freezing conditions, sometimes resulting in the loss of tropical fish, sea turtles, and manatees. Nevertheless, while frost is possible in the Everglades, there is no known record of such an occurrence in Key West.

Summers, meanwhile, are hot and humid, with temperatures usually ranging from 74°F to 90°F and humidity well over 90 percent. Unless you're an avid angler, snorkeler, or scuba diver, in fact, you might want to avoid the unbearable summer months, when mosquitoes are abundant and afternoon thunderstorms are common. Although prevailing easterly trade winds and sea breezes can suppress the summertime heat, Key West has been known, at various times, to reach 100°F.

AVERAGE TEMPERATURES

The table below shows average high/low temperatures in degrees Fahrenheit.

Month	Miami	Key West
January	74/61	74/64
February	75/63	76/66
March	76/65	78/68
April	79/69	81/72
May	83/74	85/76
June	87/77	88/79
July	88/78	89/80
August	89/79	90/80
September	87/78	88/79
October	84/75	85/76
November	79/70	80/72
December	76/64	76/67

Hurricane Season

In southern Florida, the **dry season** usually runs from November through April. During this time, you'll experience abundant sunshine and roughly 25 percent of the annual rainfall. The **wet season,** meanwhile, runs from May through October and usually constitutes about 75 percent of the annual rainfall. Part of this rainfall may include infrequent hurricanes that can occur during the **Atlantic hurricane season,** which typically runs from June through November. Although hurricanes can certainly happen at other times of the year as well, most residents and visitors don't worry about such potentially destructive storms until June 1.

Based on wind speeds, hurricanes are classified on a scale that ranges from a mild Category 1 to a powerful Category 5. While Miami, the Everglades, and the Florida Keys haven't been hit by hurricanes very often, southern Floridians have certainly experienced their share of terrible storms, including the Labor Day Hurricane of 1935, which killed more than 400 people and destroyed the Florida Keys' Overseas Railroad; Hurricane Andrew, which hit the Miami area in 1992 and was considered, until Hurricane Katrina (and, more recently, Superstorm Sandy), the costliest hurricane in U.S. history; and Hurricane Wilma, which caused massive damage in the Everglades and some flooding in the Lower Keys during the 2005 season.

ENVIRONMENTAL ISSUES

In general, southern Florida is heavily dependent upon a healthy environment. The effects of water pollution, overdevelopment, overfishing, and overhunting can easily affect at least two of its major industries—agriculture and tourism—not to mention the fragile ecosystems that compose this fascinating region. Of course, it's these very industries that have, at times, overwhelmed the ecosystems down here, especially in the Everglades, where habitat loss and long-term drainage efforts—to satisfy agricultural needs and a growing population—have had long-term negative effects on native flora and fauna. Oftentimes, the welfare of keystone species, such as the American alligator, has helped to reveal the condition of the entire region.

Researchers and conservationists are equally concerned about the health of the Florida Keys. While visiting the area, you'll find several eco-friendly adventure operators, plus animal facilities—such as the Florida Keys Wild Bird Center near Key Largo and The Turtle Hospital in Marathon—that are doing what they can to save marine birds and animals from detriments caused by humans, such as mercury poisoning, fishing line and net entanglements, boat strikes, intestinal impaction due to the ingestion of floating debris, and oil spills, including the *Deepwater Horizon* catastrophe (also known as the "BP oil spill") of April 2010. Be sure to visit such facilities to learn more about how you can help minimize your impact on the easily susceptible ecosystems of southern Florida.

Flora and Fauna

The varied habitats that extend from the Everglades to the Florida Keys are home to literally thousands of animal, insect, and plant species, more than can possibly be listed here. Nevertheless, consider this section a sampling of what you can expect to encounter while visiting the marshes, forests, beaches, and coral reefs of southern Florida.

TREES

The Everglades, part of a massive watershed and subtropical wilderness north of the Florida Keys, nurture well over 120 different tree species. In Everglades National Park, for instance, you'll spy numerous **wetland tree islands** and **upland hardwood hammocks,** both of which support various mammals and serve as critical rookeries for wading and migratory birds.

The tree islands typically consist of bay, willow, bald cypress, dwarf cypress, or pond apple trees. The **cypress,** perhaps the most recognizable tree in the Everglades, is curious in that it can live either on dry land or in water and, unlike many subtropical trees, tends to shed its leaves every autumn.

The hardwood hammocks, meanwhile, often consist of landlubbing trees, such as slash pine, live oak, royal palm, cabbage palm, saw palmetto, and West Indian mahogany. Another intriguing tree often present in these drier hardwood hammocks, as well as throughout the Florida Keys, is the **gumbo limbo,** a fast-growing, salt-tolerant tropical tree that has featherlike leaves and a shiny red exfoliating bark. Interestingly, it's also called the "tourist tree" due to the bark's resemblance to a peeling sunburn.

Prevalent throughout the marshes and tidal shores of both the Everglades and the Florida Keys is the **mangrove,** a coastal tree noted for its vast interlaced aboveground root system. Mangroves, which constitute many of the smaller keys in this region, are a keystone plant community in southern Florida,

Mangrove forests are prevalent in southern Florida.

PLANTS AND FLOWERS

Oases for nature lovers, the Everglades and the Florida Keys boast a wide array of native plants. In the Everglades, for instance, you'll encounter more than 100 marsh plant species that live in water for most or all of the year. Perhaps the most prevalent of these is **sawgrass,** a hardy sedge named for its serrated leaf blade, which now constitutes thousands of acres of marshland in the Everglades. Here you'll also spy cattails, algae, and a variety of floating aquatic plants like bladderwort, spatterdock, maidencane, and white water lily.

In addition, this warm, often humid region nurtures an assortment of **epiphytes,** plants that grow on the branches, trunks, and leaves of other trees. Deriving their water and nutrients from the air, epiphytes here include beautiful orchids, bromeliads, tropical ferns, and Spanish moss.

Along the beaches of southern Florida, even in the Florida Keys, you're likely to see sandspur plants, the seeds of which resemble little spiked balls, as well as sea grapes and sea oats, both salt-tolerant plants that help to stabilize sand dunes and prevent erosion. While exploring the Florida Keys, you're also bound to see vibrant tropical flowers, whether you're driving along the Overseas Highway or walking amid the lush gardens of a posh resort. Two of the most common flowering plants down here are the **hibiscus** and the **bougainvillea,** both of which are usually ablaze with white, pink, red, orange, purple, or yellow flowers.

MAMMALS

More than 40 mammal species call the Everglades home, including cotton mice, rice rats, skunks, raccoons, opossums, marsh rabbits, river otters, gray foxes, bobcats, and white-tailed deer. Of course, the most well-known and most elusive mammal in the Everglades is the endangered **Florida panther,** the official state animal and the symbol of this vast, fragile ecosystem. Typically, panthers live in the upland areas, where they feed on deer and other mammals.

Raccoons and opossums dwell in the Florida

where they serve as a buffer along the coast. Together, these interlocked trees protect the land from wind and waves, reduce soil erosion, build the soil through growth and decomposition, and provide a border between saline coastal waters and freshwater marshes. Intolerant of cold weather and typically classified as black, white, or red, mangroves are protected by law, so be sure not to damage or deface any while exploring the backcountry waters.

In the Florida Keys, you might also spy small ornamental trees like the buttonwood, the palmlike coontie, and the coral bean, which has spiny magenta-hued leaves and toxic seeds. Flowering trees also abound here, such as the geiger tree, the locust berry, the poisonwood, and the coco plum, the fruit of which is often used in preserves. Other curious native species include the strangler fig, the wild coffee, and the silver palm. In addition, the Keys are well known for several nonnative tree species, such as mango, coconut palm, and key lime.

Keys as well, along with oodles of feral cats. The Lower Keys are also home to the diminutive **Key deer,** an endangered subspecies of the Virginia white-tailed deer. Key deer, which typically weigh 65-80 pounds, tend to stand between 24 and 32 inches high. Researchers believe that the Key deer migrated from the Florida mainland to the Florida Keys thousands of years ago. Found nowhere else in the world, the Key deer were in danger of extinction in the 1940s, until the establishment of the National Key Deer Refuge in 1957.

Naturally, marine mammals are prevalent in the Florida Keys, too. On sightseeing cruises, you're bound to spot an **Atlantic bottlenose dolphin** or an **Atlantic spotted dolphin.** Rare sightings of the endangered **West Indian manatee,** or "sea cow," are also possible in the Florida Keys as well as the Everglades, especially in warmer waters. A giant yet gentle creature, favoring a vegetarian diet, the manatee is actually Florida's state marine mammal.

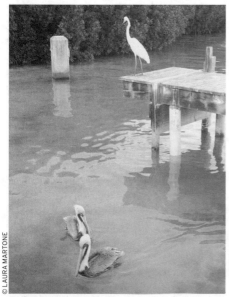

Pelicans and egrets mingle in an Islamorada marina.

© LAURA MARTONE

BIRDS

Boasting over 350 **wading or migratory bird species,** the Everglades and the Florida Keys constitute a bird-watcher's paradise. It's no wonder, then, that the famous ornithologist John James Audubon traveled to southern Florida to paint the region's native birds. Although overhunting and habitat destruction have caused a steep decline in the native bird population since Audubon's time, you'll still encounter plenty of wonderful species during your visit to southern Florida.

In the Everglades, for instance, you'll encounter a variety of wading birds, including the white ibis, glossy ibis, wood stork, green-backed heron, great white heron, great blue heron, great egret, snowy egret, reddish egret, and roseate spoonbill. Other commonly seen birds range from cardinals and meadowlarks to blue jays and red-bellied woodpeckers. If you're looking for raptors, you're likely to spot red-shouldered hawks, barred owls, ospreys, and if you're lucky, a bald eagle or two.

To the south, the Florida Keys nurture many of the same bird species that you'll find in the Everglades. In addition, you might spot common sandpipers, double-crested cormorants, laughing gulls, mangrove cuckoos, mourning doves, turkey vultures, and white-crowned pigeons. Also, no matter where you travel in the Keys, you're bound to encounter the **brown pelican,** which you might see floating in a marina, standing on a beach, or coasting above the water.

REPTILES

While exploring the Everglades, keep a lookout for the more than 50 species of reptiles found here. Whether you're traveling by kayak, canoe, airboat, or foot, you're likely to see at least some of the 27 snake species, 16 turtle species, and various lizards that call the Everglades home. **Snakes** can be found in nearly every habitat, from brown water snakes in freshwater ponds to mangrove salt marsh snakes in the saltwater marshes. Of course, you'll also find several venomous varieties here, including the Florida cottonmouth, the multicolored eastern coral

ALIENS IN THE EVERGLADES

In **Everglades National Park** (40001 SR-9336, Homestead, 305/242-7700, www.nps.gov/ever), several invasive plant species are currently threatening native plant populations. These alien invaders include the following:

• **Australian pine** (Casuarina equisetifolia): Native to Australia, Malaysia, and southern Asia, this tall, fast-growing pine tree was introduced to Florida in the late 1800s. Today dense thickets have displaced native dune and beach vegetation; radically altered the light, temperature, and soil chemistry of beach habitats; inhibited the growth of native plants, upon which native insects and other wildlife depend; and increased beach and dune erosion, which has affected the nesting activities of sea turtles and American crocodiles.

• **Brazilian pepper** (Schinus terebinthifolius): As the name indicates, this bushy, spreading evergreen tree hails from Brazil, Argentina, and Paraguay. Brazilian pepper was imported as an ornamental in the 1840s. Since then, however, the seeds of this fire-resistant, salt-tolerant plant have spread, resulting in the formation of dense monocultures in farm-

lands, pinelands, hardwood hammocks, and mangrove forests. As an unfortunate bonus, chemicals in the lovely leaves, flowers, and berries can irritate human skin and respiratory passages.

• **Latherleaf** (Colubrina asiatica): Found along coastal areas of eastern Africa, India, Southeast Asia, Australia, and the Pacific Islands, this sprawling bush was brought from Asia to Jamaica by immigrants in the 1850s. From there the seeds, which can be dispersed by tides and storms, probably floated to southern Florida on ocean currents. Nowadays, latherleaf has invaded coastal beaches and dunes, pine and hardwood forests, and mangrove estuaries, smothering native vegetation and threatening to form a monoculture.

• **Melaleuca** (Melaleuca quinquenervia): Originally from Australia, New Guinea, and the Solomon Islands, this subtropical tree was introduced to southern Florida in the early 1900s. Today the fast-spreading melaleuca is the greatest threat to the Everglades ecosystem, which faces extreme and perhaps irreversible alteration because of the tree's ability to convert native plant communities

snake, and the pygmy rattler, so be aware at all times. Meanwhile, notable **turtle** species in the Everglades include the striped mud turtle, the peninsula cooter, the Florida red-belly turtle, and the yellow-bellied slider, all of which favor freshwater ponds and marshes. In the pinelands and hardwood hammocks, you may also spy tiny camouflaged **lizards,** such as native green anoles, exotic brown anoles, and Florida reef geckos, the smallest lizards in North America.

Naturally, most visitors come to the Everglades hoping to catch a glimpse of an **American alligator**—incidentally, the state reptile—several of which you might spot drifting in a slough, resting in an alligator hole, or sunbathing alongside the Tamiami Trail. You're also likely to see these prehistoric-looking

creatures in the Florida Keys, especially near places like the Blue Hole on Big Pine Key. In Dagny Johnson Key Largo Hammock Botanical State Park, you might even spy an **American crocodile.** Just be advised that crocodiles can be far more aggressive than alligators. Meanwhile, other commonly seen reptiles in the Keys include brown and green anoles, corn snakes, Mediterranean geckos, and the green iguana, which you'll surely encounter everywhere, from Islamorada's Theater of the Sea to the restful trees of Key West's Old Town.

While exploring the Florida Keys, you might also be lucky enough to spot a **sea turtle,** in either the offshore waters or an onshore facility, such as Theater of the Sea or The Turtle Hospital in Marathon. Some of these species like sawgrass marshes and wet prairies into impenetrable thickets.

- **Old World climbing fern** (*Lygodium microphyllum*): Native to Australia, Africa, and tropical Asia, this vine was introduced to Florida in the 1960s. Since then the climbing fern, which has a dense root system, has blanketed pine forests, cypress swamps, and other Floridian habitats; altered the water flow through streams and wetlands; and provided fuel for fires that would not normally spread through a wetland area.

- **Seaside mahoe** (*Thespesia populnea*): Indigenous to the tropical seashores of Africa and India, this tall flowering tree was brought to Florida as an ornamental in the 1920s. Since that time the seaside mahoe has invaded shoreline habitats where its dense shade has smothered its competitors. Unfortunately, its seeds float in seawater, which means it can also ride the ocean currents to colonize other unsuspecting shores.

You can take action to prevent the introduction or spread of all invasive alien plants into natural areas:

- Not disturbing natural areas, such as clearing native vegetation, planting nonnatives, and dumping yard wastes

- Refraining from the use of exotic species in your landscaping, land restoration, or erosion control projects

- Using ornamentals that are native to your local region

- Consulting a local university, arboretum, nature center, native plant society, or Department of Agriculture office if you have any concerns about a plant that you intend to grow

- Using techniques such as cutting, mowing, pruning, or herbicide to remove or manage any invasive exotics

- Asking local nurseries and garden shops not to sell invasive exotic plants

- Notifying land managers about invasive exotic plant occurrences

- Assisting in exotic plant removal projects

- Working with your local government to encourage the use of native plants in urban and suburban landscapes

include the Kemp's Ridley turtle, hawksbill turtle, leatherback turtle, loggerhead turtle, and green turtle—all of which are either threatened or endangered.

AMPHIBIANS

In addition to numerous birds and reptiles, the Florida Everglades are also home to nearly 20 species of **frogs, toads,** and **salamanders,** including the grass frog, supposedly the tiniest frog in North America, and the Everglades dwarf siren, a salamander that is only found in the Everglades. Of course, most amphibians are nocturnal, well-camouflaged creatures, so you're more likely to hear them than see them. That's certainly the case with pig frogs, whose grunts can be heard in freshwater

marshes, and noisy oak toads, which favor pinelands, hardwood hammocks, and wet sawgrass communities.

FISH AND SEALIFE

Given the prevalence of saltwater, freshwater, and brackish water in and around Miami, the Everglades, and the Florida Keys, it surely comes as no surprise that there are more than 600 species of tropical and game fish in southern Florida, some of which you might spy while snorkeling along an offshore coral reef and some of which you might snag from a fishing boat in the backcountry. Depending on the fishing season, you could encounter redfish (also known as "red drum"), red grouper, bonefish, permit, common snook, amberjack,

ALLIGATORS VS. CROCODILES

Southern Florida is home to a wide variety of reptiles, including snakes, iguanas, and sea turtles. Of course, the most well-known species are the **American alligator** (*Alligator mississippiensis*) and the **American crocodile** (*Crocodylus acutus*). While these two carnivorous crocodilians—which are both members of the Reptilia class and the Crocodylia order—resemble each other greatly, there are a number of differences between them.

Typically, alligators dwell in freshwater habitats throughout the Everglades and the Lower Florida Keys. Their telltale characteristics include black scales; a wide, rounded snout; and a hidden fourth tooth on the lower jaw. Crocodiles, meanwhile, tend to be more elusive—a threatened species within saltwater habitats in the Everglades and places like Dagny Johnson Key Largo Hammock Botanical State Park. Their telltale characteristics include grayish-green scales; a narrow, tapered snout; and a lower fourth tooth that juts out noticeably. As a rule, crocodiles are faster, more active, and more aggressive than alligators, and they tend to spend more time in the water.

Alligators can reach up to 15 feet in length, weigh up to 1,000 pounds, and live for up to 60 years. Normally, they reach maturity after 4-7 years and can lay 10-50 eggs, with hatching occurring after a 65-day incubation period. Crocodiles, conversely, can reach up to 20 feet in length, weigh up to 2,200 pounds, and live for up to 75 years. Unlike alligators, they reach maturity after 10-15 years and can lay 20-60 eggs, with hatching occurring after about 90 days.

Of course, alligators and crocodiles have plenty of common traits. For one thing, the location of their eyes, ears, and nostrils on the top of their heads allows them to conceal much of their bodies underwater, making it easier to sneak up on their prey, which consists of fish, reptiles, rodents, birds, insects, and other mammals—some of which can be half their size. In addition, both alligators and crocodiles are ectothermic, meaning that they rely on external sources of heat to regulate their body temperature—hence, the reason that they often bask in the sun or, depending on the season, move to areas with warmer or cooler water. Moreover, all crocodilians lay their eggs on land, well above the water line, where the females guard them from predators that might try to unearth them. Despite such efforts, though, many crocodilian eggs fall prey to other animals.

Other similar traits include webbed feet, powerful jaws, keen eyesight, acute hearing, an excellent sense of smell, an armored exterior made up of overlapping scales, a broad tail that enables them to swim smoothly and quickly, and short legs that can move surprisingly fast on dry land. In fact, although both species tend to float listlessly in the water like drifting logs, they can actually swim up to 20 miles per hour and run up to 11 miles per hour—a fact that you should well remember the next time you venture into the wilderness.

Spanish mackerel, wahoo, yellowfin tuna, king mackerel (also known as "kingfish"), tarpon, sailfish, blue marlin, and mahimahi, which are also known as "dorado" or "dolphinfish." While snorkeling or diving, you might see some of these very same species, plus colorful Spanish hogfish and yellowtail snapper, torpedo-shaped barracuda, abundant nurse sharks, southern stingrays, spotted moray eels, and kaleidoscopic queen angelfish. In the Everglades, you might also spy freshwater fish like the Florida gar, the mosquitofish, and the official state freshwater fish, the largemouth bass.

Of course, fish aren't the only entities you'll observe while exploring the coral reefs of Florida Keys National Marine Sanctuary. Here you may also notice banded coral shrimp, stone crabs, fire sponges, sea cucumbers, sea anemones, long-spined urchins, jellyfish, sand dollars, sea fans, sea stars, the Portuguese man-of-war, the spiny lobster, the Florida fighting conch, and a variety of coral, including brain coral, fire coral, elkhorn coral, and staghorn coral. Remember, though: As tempting as it might seem, it is illegal to collect any and all coral formations.

WHAT'S IN A CONCH?

While visiting the Florida Keys, you're likely to hear or see the term "conch" (pronounced CONK) virtually everywhere. From menus that feature conch fritters and conch chowder to stores that offer Conch Republic souvenirs, this multipurpose term typically has one of three meanings in the Keys.

First of all, a conch can signify a marine gastropod, such as the large queen conch, the feisty Florida fighting conch, or the imported conch that's often found in Keys cuisine. Since the 20th century, however, the term "conch" has also been used to refer to a resident of Key West. Some residents even go so far as to differentiate between "saltwater conchs," or those residents actually born in Key West, and "freshwater conchs," or those who, though born elsewhere, have lived in Key West for at least seven years. While "conch" is now a widely used term for a Key West resident, regardless of his or her origin, the original meaning of "conch" solely applied to the Bahamian immigrants that arrived in Key West during the 18th and early 19th centuries and made their living by fishing, logging, and salvaging shipwrecks. Many of these so-called Conchs were descendants of European Loyalists who had fled to the Bahamas, the nearest British colony, during the American Revolution. After arriving in Key West, many of these immigrants established a neighborhood in the western part of Old Town that is still known today as Bahama Village.

There are many theories, of course, for why these Bahamian immigrants were called Conchs in the first place. One such theory is that the affluent British Loyalists who settled in the Bahamas looked down upon the native residents, calling them "conchs" because shellfish was an important aspect of their diet. Another theory suggests that Bahamians told British authorities that they'd rather "eat conch" than pay taxes levied by the British Crown. Regardless of the true inspiration, though, the fact is that the term "conch," while considered a derogatory expression for Bahamian immigrants in other parts of Florida, has become a source of pride for those who live in the Florida Keys. Just consider the events of April 23, 1982, when in protest of a U.S. Border Patrol blockade near Florida City, the Florida Keys collectively declared their tongue-in-cheek secession from the United States, forming a micronation called the Conch Republic—an incident that's still celebrated today with such annual events as Key West's Conch Republic Independence Celebration, a zany 10-day festival that typically occurs in late April and features everything from Conch Republic flag raisings to drag queen races to conch shell-blowing contests.

INSECTS AND ARACHNIDS

Between the Everglades and the Florida Keys, there are literally hundreds of insect and arachnid species, ranging in size from the minuscule chigger to the giant diving beetle. In the Everglades, four of the most commonly spotted insects include the large **lubber grasshopper,** which has wings but cannot fly; the **golden orb weaver,** a beautiful spider that weaves intricate webs in the hardwood hammocks; the bloodsucking **mosquito,** which despite being annoying to humans, is a critical part of the food chain in mangrove estuaries; and the gorgeous **dragonfly,** affectionately known as a "mosquito hawk." Other curious creatures in the Everglades include the apple snail and the Liguus tree snail.

Many of these insects, including the pesky mosquito, can be seen—and, in some cases, felt—in the Florida Keys. Besides the mosquito, other bloodthirsty critters include the **no-see-um,** or "punkie," a tiny biting gnat that thrives in coastal areas, especially during the summer months. Down here you may also spy **woodland cicadas,** curious crablike **spiny orb weavers,** and **fire ants,** large, aggressive red ants that are prevalent in tropical areas, capable of building large mounds, and inclined to inflict painful stings.

In both the Everglades and the Florida Keys

© PATRICK M. ROSE/SAVE THE MANATEE CLUB/WWW.SAVETHEMANATEE.ORG

a manatee and her calf

archipelago, some of the most beautiful insects are, of course, **butterflies,** more than 50 species of which can be observed in southern Florida. Some commonly spotted species include the Florida purplewing, the hammock skipper, the mangrove skipper, the sleepy orange, the white peacock, and the zebra longwing, which is actually the official state butterfly.

ENDANGERED SPECIES

More than 20 animal species found in the Everglades and the Florida Keys are federally listed as threatened or endangered, largely due to habitat loss, urban development, water flow alteration, overhunting, and in some cases, highway collisions. Some endangered creatures, such as the Schaus swallowtail butterfly, Key Largo cotton mouse, Key Largo woodrat, and snail kite (a bird that survives exclusively on the apple snail) are perhaps less well known to outsiders. Others, however, such as the Florida panther, West Indian manatee, and Key deer (not to mention the threatened American crocodile),

receive a lot more attention from conservationists, media representatives, and government officials.

The **Florida panther,** a large long-tailed cat of which there are only about 100 left in the wild, is perhaps the most at risk for extinction. Presently, conservation efforts include radio-tracking collared individuals and introducing other panther strains to increase the gene pool.

Meanwhile, the **West Indian manatee,** a gentle creature that feeds on aquatic vegetation and typically inhabits sloughs, shallow estuaries, and saltwater bays, has been systematically diminished by boat collisions, vandal attacks, poachers, habitat destruction, and cold stress. Although it's protected by the Marine Mammal Protection Act of 1972 and the Endangered Species Act of 1973, human actions continue to threaten, harm, or kill the manatee. Luckily, groups like the Save the Manatee Club, which is based in Maitland, Florida, are doing what they can to save these endangered creatures, though individuals can help by obeying speed limits, recording manatee sightings, and reporting criminal activities involving these gentle marine mammals.

Sea turtles, such as the Kemp's Ridley turtle, hawksbill turtle, leatherback turtle, loggerhead turtle, and green turtle, have long been endangered everywhere, though conservation efforts are underway throughout Florida and other parts of the world. Other endangered species in the Everglades include birds: the Arctic peregrine falcon, Cape Sable seaside sparrow, southern bald eagle, and wood stork.

REINTRODUCTION PROGRAMS

Following successful efforts to reintroduce the **eastern bluebird** to the Florida Everglades, the National Park Service is currently overseeing the reintroduction of the **Florida wild turkey** to Everglades National Park. Such reintroduction programs are critical for habitat restoration efforts. In the case of the Florida wild turkey, for example, this reintroduction program has a twofold benefit: to help restore the pine rocklands of the Everglades and to monitor the progress of said restoration.

Perhaps more well known, though, are the reintroduction programs that involve endangered **sea turtles.** In the Florida Keys, for instance, The Turtle Hospital, which opened in 1986, has endeavored to rehabilitate injured sea turtles and return them to the wild. The hospital also educates the public about the plight of sea turtles, conducts and assists with relevant research, and strives for environmental legislation that will make beaches and offshore waters safer and cleaner for these endangered creatures.

History

EARLY CIVILIZATION

Even without written records, it's generally accepted among historians that Native American tribes have inhabited the region now known as southern Florida for thousands of years, perhaps as early as 10,000 BC. As evidenced by archaeological finds and the accounts of Spanish explorers in the early 1500s, the predominant tribes in this region were the **Tequesta Indians** in the Biscayne Bay area near present-day Miami, the **Seminole Indians** in the Everglades, and the **Calusa Indians** in the Florida Keys. The first European explorer to encounter these native tribes was allegedly Juan Ponce de León, who traveled to these waters on behalf of Spain in 1513. Although there's no evidence that he actually interacted with these native peoples, the written accounts of his expedition indicate their presence in southern Florida, even amid the twisted islands that de León named Los Martires (The Martyrs), later known as the Florida Keys.

Once Spain claimed the Florida territory as its own, European interactions with the native peoples increased—interactions that varied from tribe to tribe. While the Tequesta, for instance, welcomed the Spanish explorers that took refuge in Biscayne Bay in 1565, the fierce Calusa subjected others to repeated attacks.

COLONIALISM

After Florida was claimed by Spain, life changed drastically for the native peoples here. Over the ensuing decades, many Native Americans died as a result of European diseases and various battles between the Spanish, French, and British. By the mid-1700s, in fact, most of the Tequesta and Calusa people had either moved elsewhere or been sold into slavery by the British. Those that remained were relocated to Cuba in 1763, when Spain transferred the Florida territory to Britain. Although the Seminole were also adversely affected by the Europeans' presence, they nonetheless managed to survive in the Everglades.

By the 1780s, the United States had been formed, though Florida was once again under Spanish control. Given incidents like the First and Second Seminole Wars during the first half of the 19th century, it took some time for permanent settlements to take root. In fact, by the late 1830s, Miami was little more than a fort beside the sea.

While Europeans were trying to settle this diverse region, pirates were trolling the waters of the Florida Keys, plundering unsuspecting ships and salvaging cargo. By the 1820s, the U.S. Navy had managed to scare away most of the marauding pirates, and permanent settlers, from places like Cuba, the Bahamas, and the northeastern United States, were beginning to populate the Upper, Middle, and Lower Keys. One of the earliest settlements was that of Indian Key, which in 1836 became the first county seat of Dade County and by 1840 was destroyed by invading Seminole during the Second Seminole War, a harrowing invasion that also caused the disbandment of Conch Town, a Bahamian settlement in the Middle Keys. In 1845 while Florida was becoming the 27th U.S. state, four main industries were underway in the Florida Keys: farming, fishing, salt production, and cargo salvaging. By the mid-1800s it was cargo salvaging that had become the most lucrative enterprise, helping to make Key West one of the richest cities in the country by the late 1800s.

CIVIL WAR

By 1860 the island of Key West had become the largest and richest city in the state, and although Florida joined the Confederate States of America during the American Civil War, the isolated Southernmost City remained in Union hands because of the presence of a naval base. **Fort Zachary Taylor,** constructed between 1845 and 1866, became an important outpost during the Civil War, while **Fort Jefferson** in the Dry Tortugas was used as a military prison during and after the conflict. Also in the 1860s and 1870s, many Cuban refugees escaped to Key West, where they initiated a thriving cigar-making industry, which ultimately helped to replace the dwindling salt and salvaging industries in the late 1800s.

Fort Zachary Taylor in Key West

© DANIEL MARTONE

THE FORT TAYLOR TIMELINE

Fort Zachary Taylor was one of the most important fortresses of the mid-19th century.

- **1821:** After the United States acquires the Florida territory, the federal government considers extending the Third System to protect the Gulf Coast.

- **1836:** The U.S. Congress allocates funds to begin construction.

- **1845:** Construction of the fort begins. The foundation is established in offshore waters on the southwestern side of the island. Construction is a challenge. Materials and workers have to be shipped from the mainland, funding problems often interfere, and yellow fever is common among the workers.

- **1846:** A hurricane hits Key West, but construction of the fort continues soon after.

- **1850:** The structure is named for President Zachary Taylor.

- **1859:** Much of the fortress is complete, including cannons, tidal flush latrines, and a drawbridge.

- **1860:** Though unfinished, Fort Taylor is ready for occupancy. Following President Lincoln's election, Florida considers secession. Captain E. B. Hunt, the current commander of the fort, meets with other officers to discuss securing Fort Taylor and nearby Fort Jefferson for the Union. U.S. Artillery Captain John Brannan orders 20 men to move into the fort under the guise of a training mission. Hunt arrives on December 2 with another 60 laborers.

- **1861-1865:** In January 1861, Florida secedes from the Union, and Hunt orders Brannan to assume command of Fort Taylor. Engineers strengthen the cover face and mount additional cannons. During the American Civil War, Fort Taylor serves as the headquarters for the Union Navy East Gulf Coast Blockading Squadron, which captures about 300 Confederate vessels. After the war ends in April 1865, Army engineers continue construction on the cover face. In October 1865, a hurricane passes west of the fort, destroying part of the seawall and the bridge to Key West.

- **1866:** Technically, the fort is complete, though construction continues.

- **1871:** The Secretary of War approves a plan to modify Fort Taylor, with the addition of two barbettes and the fortification of the main magazines.

- **1875:** Another destructive hurricane halts work on the fort.

- **1885:** Secretary of War William Endicott decides to modernize Fort Taylor. Congress approves the plan, but funds are slow to come.

- **1896:** Given the likelihood of a war with Spain, funding becomes available.

- **1897:** Army engineers and civilian contractors begin upgrading the fort.

- **1898:** When the Spanish-American War erupts, soldiers occupy the fort, and construction continues.

- **1903-1945:** The coastal weaponry, operated by the U.S. Army's Coastal Artillery Corps and the Florida National Guard, remains at Fort Taylor until mid-World War II, after which the Army builds new mounts for anti-aircraft guns. At the war's end, the Coastal Artillery Corps is abolished.

- **1947:** After assuming control of the property, the U.S. Navy removes the anti-aircraft guns.

- **1950:** Fort Taylor is listed as government excess property and relegated to a scrap metal yard.

- **1968:** Once the fort is landlocked in the mid-1960s by the Navy, volunteers excavate Civil War guns, cannons, and ammunition from long-abandoned sections.

- **1970:** The Navy transfers the property to the Department of the Interior.

- **1971:** Fort Taylor is listed on the National Register of Historic Places.

- **1973:** The fort becomes a National Historic Landmark.

- **1976:** The Florida Park Service acquires Fort Taylor.

- **1985:** The fort opens as a state park, and soon afterward a moat is dug around the fortress—to prevent easy entry into the structure and to create the illusion of its early days.

THE 20TH CENTURY

By the 1890s, Miami, which was officially in-corporated as a city in 1896, was experiencing a real estate boom and subsequent population growth. Meanwhile, the Florida Keys were thriving because of the sponging and cigar-making industries. By the turn of the 20th century, however, the expansion of this area was due, in large part, to Henry Flagler, who envisioned a 130-mile extension of the Florida East Coast Railway between the mainland and Key West. In 1904 railroad construction began on Key Vaca, now known as Marathon, and by 1908 scheduled daily train service was helping to bring more settlers to Key Largo, the largest and northernmost island in the Florida Keys. By 1912 after the tireless efforts of hundreds of workers, Flagler's costly **Overseas Railroad** had become a reality, and Key West, which became a strategic training base for U.S. Army and Navy forces during World War I, benefited greatly from the new route. Even Prohibition didn't hinder the Southernmost City, which soon wit-nessed a rise in rumrunning and bootlegging.

During the 1920s, Miami also thrived cul-turally and financially, earning its nickname "Magic City." In addition, tourism began to expand in the Everglades, largely because of the Seminole, who made their living from homemade crafts and alligator-wrestling spec-tacles, and the 1928 opening of the Tamiami Trail between Tampa and Miami, the first official road across the Everglades. At the same time, the state completed a highway and ferry service alongside the Overseas Railroad, which continued to bring settlers, tourists, and cargo to the Florida Keys—until, that is, the **Labor Day Hurricane of 1935** brought an end to Flagler's dream. Without mod-ern detection techniques, the people of the Upper and Middle Florida Keys were caught off guard by this powerful storm, eventually considered the first recorded Category 5 hur-ricane to hit the United States. Forming on August 29, 1935, during a relatively quiet sea-son, this legendary hurricane began as a small tropical storm and grew explosively during the Labor Day weekend, eventually making

COURTESY OF THE MONROE COUNTY PUBLIC LIBRARY

a vintage shot of Henry Flagler's Overseas Railroad on the Long Key Viaduct landfall with winds as high as 200 miles per hour. The hurricane was so monstrous that it single-handedly destroyed the Overseas Railroad and claimed at least 400 people in Florida and other Eastern states.

Following the death and destruction caused by the hurricane, the Florida Keys experienced a financial downturn during the 1930s—also as a result of the collapse of trade with Cuba, the decline of the cigar industry, and the closing of the Key West Naval Station. Similarly, Miami experienced an economic decline because of the statewide real estate collapse, an equally devastating hurricane in the 1920s, and of course, the Great Depression. Three factors, however, saved the Florida Keys: the state-funded creation of the Overseas Highway in 1938, the attention of famous residents like Ernest Hemingway and President Harry S. Truman, and the expansion of the U.S. Navy in the Lower Keys. Miami, too, benefited from World War II, and by the 1950s, tourism became the dominant industry throughout southern Florida.

A growing concern for conservation seemed to go hand in hand with this economic upswing. Everglades National Park, for instance, was established in 1947 to conserve this fragile ecosystem and prevent further degradation of its habitats, flora, and fauna. A decade later in 1957, the same year that the Seminole Tribe of Florida officially formed, the federal government designated the National Key Deer Refuge in the Lower Keys.

During the 1960s, while many Cubans were emigrating to Miami and increasing the city's population, the focus in the Florida Keys began to shift to the offshore coral reefs along the eastern side of southern Florida, which together constitute the third largest coral reef system in the world. By 1960 John Pennekamp Coral Reef State Park had become America's first undersea park, and in 1968 Biscayne National Monument was established north of Key Largo, eventually to become Biscayne National Park in 1980. In 1974 Big Cypress National Preserve, which has long been home to the Seminole and Miccosukee Tribes,

became one of the country's first federally protected preserves, and after Key Largo National Marine Sanctuary was established in 1975 and Looe Key National Marine Sanctuary followed in 1981, the Florida Keys archipelago truly began to secure its niche as a world-class underwater diving destination.

Conservation efforts continued into the 1990s, with the establishment of Florida Keys National Marine Sanctuary in 1990 and Dry Tortugas National Park in 1992. Even remnants of "Flagler's Folly" have become part of the tourism landscape, most notably places like the coral rock quarries of Windley Key Fossil Reef Geological State Park, the early 20th-century worker buildings on Pigeon Key, and the old railroad bridge that's now part of Bahia Honda State Park.

Unfortunately, this growing tourism industry experienced a temporary setback in April of 1982, when a U.S. Border Patrol blockade near Florida City caused an enormous traffic jam for those leaving the Florida Keys via U.S. 1. In response to this disruptive search for illegal aliens and potential drug runners, Key West and the rest of the Florida Keys briefly declared their secession from the United States, subsequently forming a micronation called the Conch Republic. Today this incident, which successfully ended the Border Patrol blockade, is celebrated with an annual Conch Republic Independence Celebration in Key West and a similar event in Key Largo. Despite this upset, the Florida Keys continued to thrive, and by 1997 several Upper Keys were incorporated into the town of Islamorada.

Meanwhile, the 1980s and 1990s were not as kind to Miami, which experienced drug wars, hurricanes, and increased crime, among other crises. In fact, Miami is still one of the most dangerous cities in America.

CONTEMPORARY TIMES

In the 21st century, tourism has continued to be the lifeblood of southern Florida. Despite the impact of other industries, such as international trade in Miami, agriculture in the

Everglades, and commercial fishing in the Florida Keys, southern Florida has endured as a popular vacation and recreation destination, making it, in fact, one of the more financially stable regions in a state that was hit hard by a nationwide economic downturn.

Government and Economy

LOCAL GOVERNMENT
In general, the political climate of southern Florida is heavily Democratic. Given the cultural diversity of this region, it might also come as no surprise that, over the years, several of Miami's mayors and commissioners have been Latinos. The local government of Key West, which also serves as the Monroe County seat, has been equally diverse. The mayors down here have included such colorful characters as Carlos Manuel de Céspedes (1875-1876), father of the Cuban Republic, and Richard A. Heyman (1983-1985 and 1987-1989), one of the country's first openly gay public officials.

ECONOMY
Throughout much of Miami's past, seasonal tourism has been the overriding industry. Nowadays, however, the local economy has diversified to include year-round tourism as well as international trade and international banking.

The economy of the Florida Everglades, meanwhile, has long revolved around agriculture, commercial fishing, recreation, and tourism. While some of these industries have become the subject of controversy over the years, due to the detrimental impact on the fragile Everglades ecosystem, perhaps no industry has been as controversial or as devastating as the production of drinking water. Over the years, water suppliers in southern Florida have systematically drained the Everglades, to such a degree that the state is now in the midst of a costly restoration effort. As of 2007, the state of Florida refused to issue new water supply permits for the region and instructed water utilities to develop alternative means of water production, such as desalination techniques, for the growing population of southern Florida, which has, in recent years, depended on an estimated daily supply of 300-600 million gallons of water from the Everglades.

The economic history of the Florida Keys has been just as complicated. During the 19th century, the regional economy evolved from a dependence on cargo salvaging—which, incidentally, helped to make Key West one of the richest cities in America—to a reliance on sponging, cigar-making, and commercial fishing. By the 1930s, the Florida Keys were suffering a financial decline, soon afterward to be remedied by the U.S. Navy, which expanded its presence in the Lower Keys during that time. Following World War II, fishing and tourism became the dominant industries in the Keys, which is still the case today.

Agriculture
Southern Florida is a bountiful place, so it's no surprise that agriculture plays a critical role in the local economy. The Everglades, for instance, have an abundance of plant nurseries, which literally line miles of Krome Avenue north of Homestead. The plethora of farmers' markets in Miami-Dade County is also an indication of the region's agricultural abundance. The subtropical climate allows for a year-round growing season, resulting in a diverse agricultural industry that, according to county statistics, employs more than 20,000 people and amasses more than $2.7 billion annually.

Shipping and Fishing
Given that the Port of Miami is nicknamed the "cruise capital of the world," it makes sense that commercial shipping is a viable industry in southern Florida. In the Florida Keys, meanwhile, commercial fishing is a major part of the

economy. Though plenty of fishing guides and charter services make their living from visiting tourists, several fishing companies actually rely on the wholesale seafood market for their livelihood. Depending on the season, such fisheries sell a variety of fish, shrimp, Florida lobster, and stone crabs.

Tourism

While agriculture and fishing are important facets of the southern Florida economy, it surely comes as no surprise that Miami, the Everglades, and the Florida Keys rely heavily on the tourism industry for survival. The entire area boasts numerous hotels, resorts, fine restaurants, golf courses, sightseeing tours, fishing charters, diving operators, national and state parks, shopping districts, and annual events—all of which help to fund local communities. In the Florida Keys, the peak tourist season—which essentially runs from late December to early January and from mid-February through April—is often so lucrative that it helps to sustain residents through much leaner times, such as the slow, unbearably hot month of September.

People and Culture

NATIVE PEOPLES

Long before Spanish explorers encountered the land now known as southern Florida, various American Indian tribes called this bountiful region home. Although it's difficult to pinpoint all the native peoples that once lived here, archaeological finds have indicated that three specific tribes once dominated the area.

Along the southeastern Atlantic coast of Florida, in the territories now known as Broward and Miami-Dade Counties, lived the **Tequesta Indians.** Also called the Tekesta, Chequesta, and Vizcaynos, the Tequesta inhabited this region from at least the 13th century to the mid-18th century—when they had all but disappeared. During that time, the Tequesta established towns and camps at the mouths of rivers, streams, and inlets, where they fished, hunted, and gathered fruit and roots. In general, their diet consisted of manatees, sharks, sailfish, porpoises, stingrays, sea turtles, snails, lobster, venison, saw palmettos, sea grapes, prickly pear fruit, and other plants. Given the generally mild climate, clothing was minimal, ranging from loincloths made of deer hide to skirts crafted from Spanish moss, and tools consisted of canoes, nets, spears, bows, arrows, and simple pottery. At the height of the mosquito season, the Tequesta would typically relocate to the Florida Keys or to barrier islands in Biscayne Bay.

The Everglades, meanwhile, constituted the home of the **Seminole Indians.** While researchers assert that the Seminole's ancestors lived in the area 12,000 years ago, it was in the early 1500s that Europeans first encountered the tribe that would become known as the Seminole, which at that time, numbered nearly 200,000 people. Unfortunately, thousands of these native people were killed by European diseases, such as measles and smallpox, as well as the resulting wars between the Spanish, English, and French. Unlike the Tequesta, however, the Seminole survived such intrusions and subsequently thrived in the virgin forests and grass flats of the Everglades.

In the early 1800s, the Seminole lived in chickee-style domiciles, essentially palmetto thatch over cypress log frames, and clothing tended to be more complicated and more colorful than that of the Tequesta. Like the Tequesta, however, the Seminole relied on the bountiful flora and fauna of southern Florida for sustenance, including native stone crabs. Although their customs have evolved over the years, some of their traditions still remain, such as an affinity for beadwork, the fashioning of palmetto fiber husk dolls, and the sacred springtime gatherings known as the Green Corn Dance.

Although the Tequesta sometimes inhabited

the Florida Keys, it was the **Calusa Indians** that dominated the region between the southwestern coast of mainland Florida and the Florida Keys. As with the Tequesta, most of the Calusa tribe died out in the mid-1700s, and any remaining native people were sold as slaves or sent to Cuba. Before that time, however, the Calusa thrived in this part of Florida. Known as the "Shell Indians," the Calusa allegedly numbered 50,000 people at one time.

In the early 1500s, when Spanish explorers first discovered them, they were known to be a fierce, warmongering people. Like other native people in southern Florida, the Calusa lived along the coast and inner waterways, relying on fish, eels, turtles, conch, crabs, clams, lobster, oysters, and deer for sustenance. Their homes were typically built on stilts, with palmetto thatch roofs and no walls, and their tools consisted of nets, spears, dugout canoes, and arrowheads made of fish bones. In addition, archaeological finds indicate that the Calusa collected shells, which they used as tools, utensils, jewelry, and shrine ornaments—hence,

St. Paul's Episcopal Church in Key West

the nickname "Shell Indians." They were also known to salvage the wealth from shipwrecks along the coast, much as Key West residents did in later centuries.

THE IMMIGRANTS

Of course, native peoples were not the only inhabitants of southern Florida. Immigrants from Europe, Cuba, Haiti, and the Bahamas helped to establish the communities that exist today. Miami, for instance, is a mosaic of various cultures and cuisines, as evidenced by neighborhoods like Little Havana and Little Haiti. The Florida Keys were also settled, in part, by immigrants. In the early 1800s, for example, Bahamian nationals came to these islands seeking autonomy. Evidence of their presence remains today in the form of specific buildings, such as the Adderley House in Marathon and the Oldest House Museum in Key West, as well as neighborhoods like Bahama Village, adjacent to Key West's Old Town.

MODERN DEMOGRAPHICS

Today the influence of native peoples and varied immigrants is evident in the demographics of southern Florida. In the three-county metropolitan area (Miami-Dade, Broward, and Palm Beach Counties), for instance, Latinos comprise roughly 42 percent of the total population, which numbers around 5.7 million people. The Jewish community makes up around 10 percent of this heavily Democratic population, and other factions include Muslims, Canadians, Europeans, and Caribbean immigrants, plus former snowbirds from the Northeast who tend to be of Jewish, Muslim, Italian, Irish, African, Dominican, or Puerto Rican descent.

Although the population of the Florida Everglades is harder to assess, the people are predominantly Caucasian, Latino, and Native American, most notably Seminole or Miccosukee. The Florida Keys, meanwhile, encompass all of Monroe County; the county seat even lies in Key West. Overall, this archipelago has a population of about 73,900, 71 percent of which is Caucasian and 21 percent of which is Latino, with even smaller percentages of Asian and African American. Curiously, many of the residents here aren't native to the area. You'll find, for instance, that a lot of the locals are actually transplants from other parts of the United States, such as Midwestern snowbirds who decided to stay permanently in this subtropical paradise.

RELIGION

Given the ethnic diversity of southern Florida, it's no surprise that residents tend to practice a variety of religions, or none at all. While you'll find large Jewish and Catholic factions in Miami, for example, you'll also encounter, as with any other multicultural American city, Methodists, Lutherans, Presbyterians, Buddhists, and Muslims. The same can be said for the Florida Keys, where you'll spot everything from the Key Largo Baptist Church to the Southernmost Unitarian Universalist Congregation in Key West to the iconic St. Paul's Episcopal Church on Duval Street in Old Town.

LANGUAGE

While English is the predominant language in most of Miami, the Everglades, and the Florida Keys, Spanish often seems to be a close second, perhaps reflecting the influence of Cuban, Mexican, and other Latino immigrants on the region. In places like Miami's Little Havana, for example, you're likely to hear more Spanish than English—given the prevalence of Cuban exiles and Cuban Americans. Miami's Little Haiti, meanwhile, contains a mixture of English, French, and Spanish speakers, plus a Creole dialect that combines French, African, Arabic, Spanish, and Portuguese. In Miami, you might also hear German, Italian, Russian, and Yiddish. Although many Miami residents are fluent in both English and Spanish—or at least a form of "Spanglish"—the Florida Keys are a different story. Here you'll do more than survive with just a solid command of the English language, even though Spanish, French, Italian, and German can be heard on occasion.

The Arts

LITERATURE

Writers have long favored the inspiring landscapes and diverse communities of southern Florida. Miami, called the Magic City by some and a dangerous metropolis by others, has nurtured several contemporary crime and mystery novelists, including John Katzenbach, a *Miami Herald* crime reporter whose debut novel, *In the Heat of the Summer* (1982), focuses on a dangerous cat-and-mouse game between a clever serial killer and an ambitious Miami journalist. Other popular novelists include Carl Hiaasen, a Florida native and *Miami Herald* columnist whose various madcap novels take place throughout southern Florida, and Charles Willeford, whose well-known crime series about an unorthodox Miami homicide detective began with *Miami Blues* in 1984.

The Florida Everglades—which constitute that vast, mysterious, ever-evolving subtropical wilderness filled with freshwater prairies, cypress swamps, hardwood hammocks, mangrove forests, and coastal lowlands—have also inspired their share of modern literature, from Hiaasen's novel *Nature Girl* (2006) to Susan Orlean's *The Orchid Thief: A True Story of Beauty and Obsession* (1998), a quirky tale of orchid fanatics in the Fakahatchee swamp. But, of course, it's the isolated Florida Keys archipelago that has sparked the creativity of countless writers, including Pulitzer Prize winners like the playwright Tennessee Williams and the poets Robert Frost, Wallace Stevens, and Elizabeth Bishop—all of whom once called Key West home. Naturally, the most famous writer to have been touched by the Southernmost City was Ernest Hemingway, who lived in Key West with his second wife, Pauline, during most of

© LAURA MARTONE

Hemingway's former studio

sculptures, and textiles from the 15th to the 20th centuries.

Farther south, the Florida Keys also present a plethora of enticements for art aficionados, from Key Largo's Bluewater Potters to The Rain Barrel, a working village of artists in Islamorada. Of course, it's Key West that houses the greatest number of art galleries and museum exhibits, including the flagship store of Wyland Galleries, which displays several of the famous muralist's marine sculptures and paintings, and the Custom House Museum, which features Mario Sanchez's colorful wood paintings of life in Key West during the early 1900s. Another curious collection can be seen in the Audubon House, which presents numerous originals and reprints of John James Audubon's famous ornithological paintings, many of which he prepared after observing native birds in the Florida Keys during the 1830s. For information about other art galleries in the Florida Keys, consult the **Florida Keys Council of the Arts** (www.keysarts.com).

Besides offering year-round repositories of fine and contemporary art, southern Florida also features several annual art events, especially during the winter months. In Miami, for instance, you'll find celebrations like the Coconut Grove Arts Festival and Art Basel Miami Beach. Key West, meanwhile, stages events like the Key West Craft Show and the Old Island Days Art Festival, both of which attract numerous artists and artisans to historical Old Town.

the 1930s. It was here, in fact, that the Nobel Prize-winning novelist wrote and published *To Have and Have Not* (1937), the story of a fishing boat captain who runs contraband between Cuba and Florida—no doubt inspired by Hemingway's own fishing experiences in the Florida Keys, not to mention his interactions with the eccentric locals of Key West.

VISUAL ARTS

The varied landscapes and diverse cultures of southern Florida have influenced not only writers but visual artists as well, as evidenced by the variety of art galleries and museums throughout Miami and the Florida Keys. In Miami, home to a thriving community of artists, designers, and collectors, you'll find such engaging sights as the Wynwood Arts District, an entire area devoted to visual arts, boasting well over 70 galleries, studios, stores, bars, and antiques shops all within walking distance. Art lovers might also appreciate the Bass Museum of Art in Miami Beach, which contains a vast accumulation of European paintings,

PERFORMING ARTS

In addition to visual arts, the communities of southern Florida boast a variety of performing arts. The Adrienne Arsht Center for the Performing Arts of Miami-Dade County, for instance, presents everything from opera productions to jazz concerts to contemporary dance performances. You'll find a similar array of entertainment options throughout the Florida Keys, such as theater troupes like The Key Players and music organizations like the Florida Keys Concert Association. As with art galleries, Key West naturally offers the widest array of performance venues, including the Tennessee Williams Theatre on Stock Island, where you can see regular performances of the South Florida Symphony Orchestra, the Key West Pops Orchestra, and the FKCC Keys Chorale. For information about other performance venues in the Florida Keys, consult the **Florida Keys Council of the Arts** (www.key-sarts.com).

CINEMA

For more than seven decades, southern Florida has been a favored spot for filmmakers. Given the diversity of landscapes, architectural styles, and ethnic communities here, it's easy to understand Hollywood's fascination with this unique region. What better place to set a zany gay-friendly film like *The Birdcage* (1996) than in the colorful streets of Miami Beach's Art Deco District, and what would Jerry Lewis's madcap comedy *The Bellboy* (1960) have been without Miami Beach's luxurious Fontainebleau hotel

as its centerpiece? Sultry Miami is also an integral part of high-energy dramas like *Scarface* (1983), *Miami Blues* (1990), *Bad Boys* (1995), *Any Given Sunday* (1999), *Transporter 2* (2005), and *Miami Vice* (2006).

Likewise, the Everglades have served as a key backdrop for crime dramas like *The Mean Season* (1985), inspired by John Katzenbach's debut novel and partially filmed in Everglades National Park, and *Adaptation.* (2002), a bizarre interpretation of Susan Orlean's book *The Orchid Thief,* which wouldn't be the same without the tangled foliage of the Fakahatchee Strand Preserve. Even the small screen has embraced the heat, humidity, and mystery of the Everglades with *The Glades* (2010-present), a TV crime drama in which a former Chicago cop must adjust to his new, murder-solving life in a small Florida town.

Not surprisingly, the Florida Keys have also appeared in various film productions, including classics like *Reap the Wild Wind* (1942), which

© ROB O'NEAL/FLORIDA KEYS NEWS BUREAU

The Southernmost House is a classic example of the gingerbread-style mansions made famous during the Victorian era.

features Key West's ship salvaging industry of the 1840s, and *Key Largo* (1948), in which a former soldier must confront a mob of gangsters during a hurricane. *Flipper* (1963), which also explores the ill effects of a hurricane, was partially filmed on Grassy Key, using several dolphins from the Dolphin Research Center, and the thrilling climax of *True Lies* (1994) took place on the Keys' Seven Mile Bridge. Even in Key West, you may recognize former cinematic backdrops, from the Ernest Hemingway Home, which appears at a pivotal moment in the James Bond flick *Licence to Kill* (1989), to the Eden House, where Goldie Hawn's character and her son live in the movie *CrissCross* (1992). Of course, many real-life people have escaped to Key West over the years, a fact that's embraced in the action comedy *Running Scared* (1986), in which two streetwise Chicago cops plan to retire to Key West, where they hope to open a bar and live a stress-free life away from dangerous criminals.

ARCHITECTURE

Those who appreciate alluring architecture will also enjoy a trip to southern Florida. Indeed, one of the most famous architectural districts in the country lies in Miami Beach. Listed on the National Register of Historic Places, the vibrant Art Deco District comprises several substyles, such as the less decorative Depression Moderne, evident in governmental buildings, and the more whimsical Tropical Deco, which employs relief ornamentation depicting local flora and fauna as well as ocean-liner motifs to reinforce the city's reputation as a seaside resort. Of course, Miami Beach also boasts examples of Mediterranean Revival, an Old World style that features decorative columns, bell towers, arched windows, spindle gates, and picturesque courtyards, and MiMo (Miami Modernism), a post-World War II style that embraces such elements as sun shades, tiled mosaic walls, and open balconies.

With a rich history that stretches back to the early 1800s, the Florida Keys also harbor their share of unique architecture. Down in Key West's Old Town, for instance, you'll find a cornucopia of architectural gems, from Caribbean-style bungalows to Victorian-era gingerbread mansions, such as the colorful Southernmost House, built in 1896 and now a favored inn. Another curious style is the eyebrow house, so named because it has an overhanging porch roof, which conceals the upper front windows. Naturally, while you're free to wander amid Key West's historical buildings on your own, you can also experience the architecture of Old Town on one of several guided excursions, including those that feature the city's most haunted structures.

ESSENTIALS

Getting There

While international tourists will most likely arrive in Miami or the Florida Keys by plane or cruise ship, domestic travelers can reach southern Florida by air, water, rail, or road. Consider your budget, destination, and intended activities before choosing the method that's right for your trip.

BY AIR

With at least five different airports in the region, southern Florida is an easy place to access by airplane. Of course, the two biggest airports are **Fort Lauderdale-Hollywood International Airport (FLL)** (100 Terminal Dr., Fort Lauderdale, 866/435-9355, www.broward.org/airport) and **Miami International Airport (MIA)** (2100 NW 42nd Ave., Miami, 305/876-7000, www.miami-airport.com), both of which accommodate major air carriers, including **American Airlines** (800/433-7300, www.aa.com), **Air Canada** (888/247-2262, www.aircanada.com), **Caribbean Airlines** (800/920-4225, www.caribbean-airlines.com), **Avianca** (800/284-2622, www.avianca.com), and many more. To reach Key West, travelers can fly directly into **Key West International Airport (EYW)** (3491 S. Roosevelt Blvd., Key West, 305/296-5439 or

305/296-7223, www.keywestinternationalairport.com), where you'll find major airlines like **US Airways** (800/428-4322, www.usairways.com) and **Delta Air Lines** (800/221-1212, www.delta.com), as well as smaller air carriers, such as **Cape Air** (508/771-6944 or 800/227-3247, www.flycapeair.com), which offers daily service between Fort Myers and Key West, and **Air Key West** (305/923-4033, www.airkeywest.com), which features quick flights in a five-passenger plane to and from places like Orlando, Miami, Naples, and Nassau in the Bahamas.

Other area airports include **Naples Municipal Airport (APF)** (160 N. Aviation Dr., Naples, 239/643-0733, www.flynaples.com) and **Florida Keys Marathon Airport (MTH)** (9400 Overseas Hwy., Marathon, 305/289-6060), both of which can accommodate commuter flights.

BY TRAIN

If you choose to travel to southern Florida by train, you'll find that **Amtrak** (800/872-7245, www.amtrak.com) offers train service to this region via the Silver Service/Palmetto route. The three southernmost stations include **Fort Lauderdale (FTL)** (200 SW 21st Terr., Fort Lauderdale), **Hollywood (HOL)** (3001 Hollywood Blvd., Hollywood), and **Miami (MIA)** (8303 NW 37th Ave., Miami). Unfortunately, Miami is as far as Amtrak goes, so to reach the Everglades and the Florida Keys, you'll have to rent a car or find alternative transportation.

BY BUS

For those traveling from elsewhere in the country, **Greyhound** (800/231-2222, www.greyhound.com) offers bus service to locations throughout southern Florida. Some of these include the **Miami Greyhound Station** (4111 NW 27th St., Miami, 305/871-1810), the **Central Park Bus Terminal** (2669 Davis Blvd., Naples, 239/774-5660), and the **Key West Greyhound Station** (3535 S. Roosevelt Blvd., Key West, 305/296-9072) near Key West International Airport.

TRANSPORT FROM AIRPORTS AND STATIONS

If you arrive in Naples, Key West, or the Fort Lauderdale-Miami area by plane, train, or bus, you can either rent a car or hire a shuttle service to reach your destination in southern Florida. Some of these shuttle companies include **Keys Shuttle** (305/289-9997 or 888/765-9997, www.keysshuttle.com), **Keys Tropical Transportation** (305/852-3595, www.keystropicaltransportation.com), **SuperShuttle** (305/871-2000 or 954/764-1700, www.supershuttle.com), and **TO'n'FRO** (305/393-0955, www.tonfro.com), a personalized van and car service that offers transportation between the airports in Fort Lauderdale, Miami, and Key West and any destination in the Keys.

BY CAR

If you're driving to southern Florida, Miami is accessible via several major roads, including I-75 from Tampa, Florida's Turnpike from Orlando, and I-95 from Jacksonville. To reach the Everglades from the west, take I-75 through Fort Myers or U.S. 41 through Naples. Alternatively, to reach the Everglades from the east, take I-595 and I-75 from Fort Lauderdale or U.S. 41 from Miami.

If you're headed to the Florida Keys from Miami, simply drive south on U.S. 1 (Overseas Hwy.), pass through Homestead and Florida City, cross Barnes Sound to Key Largo, and keep a lookout for the telltale mile markers (MM)—the little green signs that indicate your position along the 110-mile-long Overseas Highway. Key Largo lies roughly between Mile Marker 110 and Mile Marker 91 while the islands of Islamorada lie between Mile Marker 91 and Mile Marker 72. From Mile Marker 70 to Mile Marker 45, you'll find the Middle Keys, and after crossing the Seven Mile Bridge, you'll encounter the Lower Keys between Mile Marker 40 and Mile Marker 0—an area that includes Key West and adjacent Stock Island, which lie between Mile Marker 5 and Mile Marker 0 and are the most compact areas in the Keys. If you're looking for a particular destination, be advised that heading south on U.S. 1

© LAURA MARTONE

To reach the Florida Keys from the Everglades, you can take I-75 (Everglades Pkwy.), drive south on U.S. 27, veer right onto SR-997 (Krome Ave.), and follow the signs to U.S. 1. From U.S. 41 (Tamiami Trl.) in the Everglades, head south on SR-997 and continue toward U.S. 1.

After arriving in the Keys, be sure to call **511** or visit www.fl511.com for an up-to-the-minute traffic report. This free statewide service is especially helpful during special events, holiday weekends, and the high tourist season (late Dec.-Apr.).

BY BOAT

Given that southern Florida is surrounded by miles and miles of shoreline, plus a variety of marinas, it's no surprise that many visitors arrive by boat—whether by cruise ship, ferry, or private vessel. The **PortMiami** (1015 N. America Way, Miami, 305/347-5515, www. miamidade.gov/portmiami) is, after all, the "cruise capital of the world." In addition, the Florida Keys offer their share of deepwater marinas, including the **Key West Bight Marina** (305/809-3983 or 305/809-3984, www.key-westcity.com) at the northwest end of Grinnell Street in Key West, where the **Key West Express** (888/539-2628, www.seakeywest-express.com) arrives from Fort Myers Beach almost every day and from Marco Island on certain days during December-April.

most people in the Keys use mile markers to denote addresses, and that places are often indicated as lying on the bay side (BS) or ocean side (OS) of the highway. From the western end of Marathon to Key West, where Florida Bay gives way to the Gulf of Mexico, some residents use the term "gulf side" instead of "bay side."

Getting Around

While a private vehicle is probably the most convenient mode of transportation in southern Florida, it's by no means the only way to get around this diverse region.

BY AIR

Several operators invite visitors to tour southern Florida by airplane. **Everglades Area Tours** (239/695-3633 or 800/860-1472, www. evergladesareatours.com, Nov.-May), for instance, offers flights by an Alaskan bush plane from Everglades Airpark and across various destinations, including Everglades National Park, Big Cypress National Preserve, Key West, and the Dry Tortugas. You can also hop aboard sightseeing flights in the Florida Keys—an ideal way to survey the islands, coral reefs, and lighthouses that compose this unique region. One such operator is **Key West Biplanes** (305/851-8359, www.keywest-biplanes.com), which operates out of Key West International Airport.

© DANIEL MARTONE

The Historic Seaport at Key West Bight is home to schooners like the *Jolly II Rover*.

BY CAR

Southern Florida is probably best navigated by vehicle—it's possible to rent cars, RVs, and motorcycles throughout the region. Once you've secured a vehicle, it's a snap to traverse the area's major roads and highways, such as I-75 and U.S. 41, which link the Everglades to Miami, and U.S. 1, which connects Homestead to the Florida Keys.

Rental Cars and Taxis

If you've arrived in southern Florida without a vehicle of your own, you'll easily be able to rent one at the airports in Naples, Fort Lauderdale, Miami, Marathon, and Key West. Depending on the location, the agencies available may include **Advantage** (800/777-5500, www.advantage.com), **Alamo** (888/826-6893, www.alamo.com), **Avis** (800/633-3469, www.avis.com), **Budget** (800/218-7992, www.budget.com), **Dollar** (800/800-4000, www.dollar.com), **Enterprise** (800/261-7331, www.enterprise.com), **Hertz** (800/654-3131, www.hertz.com), **National** (877/222-9058, www.

nationalcar.com), or **Thrifty** (800/847-4389, www.thrifty.com). In addition, you can rely on various taxi services, such as Key West's **Five 6's** (305/296-6666, www.keywesttaxi.com), to help you navigate the region.

RV Rentals

Given the plethora of RV campgrounds in southern Florida, it's no wonder that it's a popular region to traverse by motorhome, travel trailer, or pop-up camper. If you don't have an RV of your own, you can rent one from companies like **Cruise America** (480/464-7300 or 800/671-8042, www.cruiseamerica.com), which offers more than a dozen locations in Florida, including Fort Myers, Fort Lauderdale, and southern Miami. Just remember that, as with rental cars, age restrictions may apply.

Motorcycles and Scooters

Traveling through southern Florida by motorcycle or scooter is also a viable option. In some places, you can even rent them. Key West's **Adventure Rentals** (305/293-8883, www.

MILEAGE BETWEEN KEYS

If you have access to a vehicle, southern Florida is a relatively easy region to navigate, especially given that major highways link the Florida Keys to both Miami and the Everglades. Basic mileage from northern Key Largo and Key West's Old Town to several regional destinations is listed below, though bear in mind that distances between towns in the Florida Keys can vary greatly depending upon your specific origin and destination. For example, the distance between Key Largo and Marathon can range between 30 and 60 miles.

DISTANCE FROM KEY LARGO TO

- Homestead: 24 miles
- Miami: 52 miles
- Fort Lauderdale: 85 miles
- Everglades City: 106 miles
- Naples: 134 miles
- Islamorada: 16 miles
- Marathon: 47 miles
- Big Pine Key: 73 miles
- Key West: 105 miles

DISTANCE FROM KEY WEST TO

- Homestead: 129 miles

- Miami: 157 miles
- Fort Lauderdale: 190 miles
- Everglades City: 211 miles
- Naples: 239 miles
- Big Pine Key: 29 miles
- Marathon: 47 miles
- Islamorada: 72 miles
- Dry Tortugas: 68 miles

ESTIMATED DRIVING TIMES

Assuming that you adhere to posted speed limits and barring any accidents, parades, or popular events (like Hemingway Days or Fantasy Fest), it can normally take 3.5-4 hours to drive from Miami to Key West during the mid- and low seasons (May-mid-Dec.). Below are the estimated driving times that you'll encounter during these slower seasons. Just remember that in the high season (late Dec.-Apr.) you might need to set aside five hours or more to drive from Miami to Key West.

- Miami to Key Largo: 1 hour
- Key Largo to Islamorada: 30 minutes
- Islamorada to Marathon: 45 minutes
- Marathon to Big Pine Key: 30 minutes
- Big Pine Key to Key West: 45 minutes

keywest-scooter.com), for instance, provides Harley-Davidson motorcycle rentals as well as scooters at multiple locations throughout Old Town.

BY TRAIN OR TROLLEY

If you visit Key West without a car, you'll have no problem getting around town. This fairly compact city is easy to navigate on foot. In addition, you can always opt for a train or trolley ride. The **Conch Tour Train** (888/916-8687, www.conchtourtrain.com) offers a look at most of Key West's major attractions, while the **Old Town Trolley Tour** (888/910-8687, www.trolleytours.com), which provides a comprehensive

tour of Old Town, allows you to get on and off the trolley at a dozen convenient stops.

BY BUS OR RAIL

For those who would prefer to travel by bus, southern Florida features a convenient public transit system. In addition to offering routes throughout Miami, the **Miami-Dade County Metrobus** (305/891-3131, www.miamidade.gov/transit) provides service to the Florida Keys with the **301 Dade-Monroe Express** between Florida City, Key Largo, Tavernier, Islamorada, and Marathon. From Marathon, you can then use the **Lower Keys Shuttle** (either the LIME or PINK route), which is operated by

© DANIEL MARTONE

a sightseeing tour in Key West

the **Key West Department of Transportation (KWDoT)** (305/600-1455, www.kwtransit. com), to access Bahia Honda State Park, Big Pine Key, Key West, and other Lower Keys.

As an alternative, you can travel through Miami on the light-rail system. The **Miami-Dade County Metrorail** (305/891-3131, www.miamidade.gov/transit) features 23 stations, offering convenient access to stops such as the Civic Center and Coral Gables.

BY BICYCLE

Miami, the Everglades, and the Florida Keys are all terrific areas for biking enthusiasts to explore. While having your own bicycle might make it more convenient to travel this way, you can easily rent one from several outfitters in the region.

Although the **Florida Keys Overseas Heritage Trail (FKOHT),** a planned 106-mile scenic corridor for bikers, pedestrians, and other recreationists, isn't yet complete, you can certainly travel from Key Largo to Key West using a combination of biking trails, highway

stretches, and bridges. Just remember that you'll have to share the road with motor vehicles, so take care while navigating the highway—and always wear a proper bicycle helmet. For more information about the Heritage Trail, contact the **Florida Department of Environmental Protection's Office of Greenways & Trails (OGT)** (3 La Croix Ct., Key Largo, 305/853-3571, www.dep.state.fl.us/gwt).

BY BOAT

Given that water is so prevalent in southern Florida, it's no surprise that you can easily travel the region by boat. Those with private vessels will find plenty of available marinas, such as the **Key Largo Resorts Marina** (305/453-7171, www.keylargomarina.com), a full-service facility in the Upper Florida Keys. If you don't have a vessel of your own, you can rent one at places like **Robbie's of Islamorada** (305/664-9814 or 877/664-8498, www.robbies.com) or from independent companies such as **Sunset Watersports Key West** (305/296-2554, www.sunsetwatersportskeywest.com) on

Passengers prepare for a Coopertown airboat ride.

Stock Island, which offers a range of vessels, from 15-foot speedboats to 24-foot pontoons, for half-day or full-day rentals.

Of course, tour boat operators are plentiful in these waters, too. In the Everglades, for instance, you'll find about a dozen airboat operators, including **The Original Coopertown Airboats** (305/226-6048, www.coopertownairboats.com), which guides numerous trips through the "river of grass." Down in the Florida Keys, you can even take a glass-bottom boat ride amid the offshore coral reefs with operators like the **Coral Reef Park Company** (305/451-6300, www.pennekamppark.com), based out of John Pennekamp Coral Reef State Park, or Key West's **Fury Water Adventures** (305/296-6293, www.furycat.com). Sunset cruises, such as those offered by **Sebago Watersports** (305/294-5687, www.keywestsebago.com) in Key West, are prevalent here, too.

Sports and Recreation

Although Miami and the Florida Keys boast a number of museums, art galleries, and other cultural attractions, it's the outdoor diversions and athletic endeavors that tantalize most visitors. One thing to keep in mind when making plans is that many activities, such as fishing and snorkeling excursions, are cheaper if you book them online or utilize brochure coupons, which are often available in area visitor centers and chambers of commerce. In addition, you should take safety precautions before embarking on any water-related adventure. If you're a first-timer to activities like kayaking and snorkeling, be sure to ask for instruction before venturing into the water, and no matter what your level of experience, you should always have a personal flotation device (PFD) handy.

SOUTHERNMOST STATE PARKS

While southern Florida's national parks, especially the Everglades, receive the lion's share of media attention, the vibrant region between Miami and Key West also nurtures 14 state parks that are worth a look.

- **The Barnacle Historic State Park:** Located beside Biscayne Bay, this lovely locale preserves the former home and grounds of Ralph Middleton Munroe, a yacht designer and one of Coconut Grove's most influential pioneers.

- **Bill Baggs Cape Florida State Park:** Home to a historical lighthouse—the oldest standing structure in Miami-Dade County—this park is popular among picnickers, bikers, swimmers, kayakers, anglers, and overnight boat campers.

- **Fakahatchee Strand Preserve State Park:** Often called "the Amazon of North America," this linear swamp forest beckons wildlife lovers, who can take guided canoe trips amid bald cypress trees, royal palm groves, and colorful orchids, while it serves as home to alligators, varied birds and snakes, Florida panthers, white-tailed deer, and other engaging creatures.

- **Collier-Seminole State Park:** Situated along the Tamiami Trail in the Everglades, this 7,271-acre park invites visitors to canoe through mangrove swamps, hike or bike amid pine flatwoods, camp beneath majestic royal palm trees, and fish in the Blackwater River.

- **Dagny Johnson Key Largo Hammock Botanical State Park:** Hikers, bikers, bird-watchers, and photographers enjoy the more than six miles of nature trails within this wooded park, situated in northern Key Largo and featuring 84 protected species of plants and animals, from semaphore cactus to American crocodiles.

- **John Pennekamp Coral Reef State Park:** People flock daily to America's first undersea park, where visitors can snorkel amid offshore coral reefs, kayak through mangrove swamps, fish or swim in the warm waters, and view tropical fish and other sea creatures in the on-site aquarium.

- **Windley Key Fossil Reef Geological State Park:** Located near Islamorada, this historical park offers self-guided trails

NATIONAL AND STATE PARKS

Given the diversity of southern Florida's landscapes, which range from marshes to beaches to coral reefs, it's no surprise that you'll find three national parks, one national preserve, and five national wildlife refuges in the region between Naples, Miami, and the Dry Tortugas. If you enjoy escaping into untamed places, consider taking a kayaking trip through **Everglades National Park,** diving amid the coral reefs of **Biscayne National Park,** or exploring the remote islands that compose the 84,351-acre **National Key Deer Refuge**—all of which are accessible to visitors every day. For more information about southern Florida's national parks, contact the **U.S. National Park Service** (Southeast Region, 100 SW Alabama St., 1924 Bldg., Atlanta, GA 30303, 404/507-5600, www.nps.gov), and for more information about the region's wildlife refuges, contact the **U.S. Fish & Wildlife Service** (Southeast Region, 1875 Century Blvd., Ste. 400, Atlanta, GA 30345, 404/679-4000, www.fws.gov/southeast).

Southern Florida also boasts 14 unique state parks, from outdoor oases like **Collier-Seminole State Park** in the Everglades to cultural landmarks like Key West's **Fort Zachary Taylor Historic State Park.** For more information about the incredible state parks in this region, consult the **Florida State Parks Information Center** (3900 Commonwealth Blvd., Tallahassee, 850/245-2157, www.

through the former coral quarry, plus educational exhibits about the connection between the quarry and Henry Flagler's Overseas Railroad in the early 1900s.

- **Lignumvitae Key Botanical State Park:** Not far from Islamorada and only accessible by boat, canoe, or kayak, this wooded offshore island features the kind of virgin tropical hardwood hammock that once thrived in the Upper Keys.

- **Indian Key Historic State Park:** Once the site of a lucrative shipwreck-salvaging business and only accessible by boat, canoe, or kayak, this lovely island near Islamorada lures hikers, swimmers, and anglers alike.

- **San Pedro Underwater Archaeological Preserve State Park:** South of Indian Key Historic State Park is where snorkelers and scuba divers will find this underwater preserve, which features the remains of a Spanish ship that sank in a 1733 hurricane.

- **Long Key State Park:** Between Layton and Marathon, this peaceful park was once the site of a luxurious fishing resort, which was destroyed in a 1935 hurricane, and now is a popular place for canoeists, hikers, anglers, swimmers, snorkelers, and overnight campers.

- **Curry Hammock State Park:** Composed of several islands near Marathon, this park offers a campground, picnic tables and pavilions, playground equipment, and easy access to swimming and kayaking, not to mention a 1.5-mile nature trail through a preserved hardwood hammock.

- **Bahia Honda State Park:** Considered one of southern Florida's finest state parks, this gorgeous, breezy locale features three stunning beaches, a boat ramp, kayak rentals, snorkeling excursions, a small nature center, cabins and campgrounds, and hiking trails, among other diversions.

- **Fort Zachary Taylor Historic State Park:** History buffs and recreationists alike appreciate Florida's southernmost park, which offers access to the finest beach in town, plus guided tours of the 19th-century fort that was designated a National Historic Landmark in 1973.

For more information about these and other state parks, consult the **Florida State Parks Information Center** (850/245-2157, www. floridastateparks.org).

floridastateparks.org), part of the Florida Department of Environmental Protection's Division of Recreation and Parks.

BEACHES AND SWIMMING

Between Miami and the Florida Keys, you'll find plenty of sandy beaches, ideal for sunbathing, picnicking, and general relaxation. Given the typically warm, shallow waters of southern Florida, swimming is also a favored pastime down here.

Where you decide to go, though, will depend on your interests. If people watching is your prime objective, you should head to the beaches of **Miami Beach** or even **Smathers Beach** down in Key West. But, if you're looking for a bit more peace and quiet, consider stopping by **Sombrero Beach** in Marathon, near Mile Marker 50 on the Overseas Highway.

No matter where you choose to go, however, make sure that you understand the rules of that particular beach. For instance, most beaches in this part of Florida have no on-duty lifeguards, which means that you'll be swimming at your own risk, so be aware of undertows, riptides, and other potential dangers. Remember, too, that nude sunbathing, overnight camping, alcohol, drugs, and campfires are illegal on all public beaches.

HIKING AND BIKING

While long-distance hikers might find fewer options in southern Florida than in other parts of the country, this bountiful region certainly

TIPS FOR THE PADDLER

Paddling through the Keys can be a rewarding experience, but it can also be dangerous if you're ill-prepared. High winds and waves can make paddling conditions challenging; in fact, while beginners are welcome to give paddling a try, it's helpful if you've had at least some experience before attempting it here. No matter what your experience level, however, follow these guidelines:

- Ensure that you've had proper instruction for the vessel that you plan to use.
- Check the daily weather forecast, especially predicted wind speeds, beforehand.
- Be aware of tidal conditions, currents, and water levels; under normal circumstances, you should allow for a minimum paddling time of two miles per hour.
- Inform someone on shore of your plans, especially your intended destination and expected return time; leave a float plan with a responsible individual, place a copy of the plan in a visible spot in your vehicle, and contact the onshore person when you do, in fact, return.
- Arrange to have a vehicle (if not yours) and dry clothes waiting at your take-out point.

- Secure a spare paddle to your vessel.
- Place your keys, identification, money, and other valuables in a waterproof bag and secure the bag to the vessel.
- Apply sunscreen and insect repellent, even on cloudy days.
- Wear appropriate clothing for weather and water conditions.
- Have a readily accessible, personal flotation device (PFD) with attached whistle for each occupant; children under six must wear PFDs at all times.
- Bring plenty of food and drinking water (one gallon pp per day) in nonbreakable, watertight containers.
- Bring a cell phone in case of an emergency, but don't rely solely on said phone, as reception can be sporadic in the backcountry and offshore waters.
- Pack up all trash and store it on board until you can dispose of it properly at your trip's end.
- Leave all historical resources, plants, birds, and marine creatures as you find them.
- Respect all wildlife; do not approach, harass, or feed any animals that you see.
- Be considerate of anglers and other pad-

offers a lot of opportunities for hiking enthusiasts to enjoy a range of unique landscapes. In **Big Cypress National Preserve,** for instance, hikers can either use designated trails—part of the **Florida National Scenic Trail (FNST)**—or venture into unmarked territory. Just be advised that, during the dry season (Nov.-Apr.), you'll have to carry all necessary drinking water with you. Conversely, during the wet season (May.-Oct.), you may find yourself tromping through waist-deep water, so be prepared for such problematic conditions. For more information about the Florida National Scenic Trail, contact the **Florida Trail Association** (5415 SW 13th St., Gainesville, 352/378-8823 or 877/445-3352, www.floridatrail.org).

Bikers, too, will enjoy exploring southern Florida. Besides biking through Miami and the Everglades, recreationists can also explore the Florida Keys by bicycle. Even though the planned, 106-mile **Florida Keys Overseas Heritage Trail** isn't yet complete, you can certainly travel from Key Largo to Key West using a combination of biking trails, highway stretches, and bridges. Just remember that you'll have to share the road with motor vehicles, so take care while navigating the highway—and always wear a proper bicycle helmet. For more information about the Heritage Trail, contact the **Florida Department of Environmental Protection's Office of Greenways & Trails (OGT)** (305/853-3571, www.dep.state.fl.us/gwt).

dlers, avoid crossing fishing lines, and stay to the right of motorboats.

- If you're taking an overnight paddling trip and plan to camp somewhere, be sure to camp on durable surfaces away from the water, and minimize the impact from campfires (if they're even allowed where you're staying).

Besides the items already mentioned, you should bring the following essentials with you:

- anchor (if you plan to snorkel or camp) and some rope
- area maps and NOAA nautical charts
- bilge pump and sponge
- binoculars
- camera and extra batteries
- compass or GPS
- duct tape
- extra waterproof bags
- first-aid kit
- insect repellent
- lip balm with SPF
- long-sleeve shirt for extra protection
- pocketknife or multipurpose tool

- repair kit
- signaling devices such as a flashlight, flare, mirror, or air horn
- sunglasses
- sunscreen
- 360-degree light for operating your vessel at night
- towels, extra clothing, and extra shoes in a waterproof bag
- VHF or weather radio to monitor weather forecasts
- wide-brimmed hat

For more information about canoeing and kayaking in the Florida Keys, consult the **Florida Department of Environmental Protection's Office of Greenways & Trails (OGT)** (3 La Croix Ct., Key Largo, 305/853-3571, www.dep.state.fl.us/gwt), the **Florida State Parks Information Center** (850/245-2157, www.floridastateparks.org/thingstodo/activities.cfm), and the **Florida Professional Paddlesports Association (FPPA)** (P.O. Box 1764, Arcadia, 800/268-0083, www.paddleflausa.com), based out of the Canoe Outpost.

BIRD-WATCHING AND WILDLIFE-VIEWING

The varied landscapes and surrounding waters of southern Florida nurture a wide array of bird species, fish, reptiles, mammals, and other wildlife. Between terns in the Dry Tortugas, alligators in the Everglades, sea turtles in the ocean, and Key deer on Big Pine Key, bird-watchers and wildlife lovers will find no shortage of sightings in this part of the state. While you can easily spot such creatures on self-guided excursions through the marshes, in the hammocks, among the mangrove islands, and along the beaches of the Sunshine State, you might see even more on guided adventures, such as airboat rides through the Everglades

with companies like **Billie Swamp Safari** (863/983-6101, www.billieswamp.com), located on the Big Cypress Seminole Indian Reservation. Birding enthusiasts might also enjoy tailored excursions like those offered by professional bird guide Larry Manfredi (www.southfloridabirding.com). Just remember to be respectful of all wildlife that you see. For their safety as well as yours, you should not feed, approach, or disturb them at any time.

HUNTING

Even hunters will find opportunities in southern Florida. In **Big Cypress National Preserve,** which hunters were instrumental in protecting, you'll find various seasons for

FISHING SEASONS AND TOURNAMENTS

Fishing has been well favored in the Keys since the early 20th century, when authors like Zane Grey and Ernest Hemingway explored these very same waters. Today thanks to widely practiced catch-and-release efforts, fishing is still plentiful. While fishing opportunities abound throughout the year, many anglers plan their trips around the region's varied fishing seasons and tournaments.

FISHING SEASONS

Choose from an assortment of fishing styles, including flats, backcountry, light-tackle, deep-sea, wreck, reef, harbor, and bridge. What you catch, of course, will depend on the time of year—and what you keep will be determined by species limits and seasonal restrictions, so be sure to consult local fishing guides beforehand. Although most species are available year-round, some are only prevalent in certain months (and some are better for mounting than for eating). Just be advised that certain marine species, such as bonefish, are catch-and-release only, but others, including sturgeon, goliath grouper, and queen conch, are prohibited at all times. With that in mind, here are some of the more popular seasons (though bear in mind that, when it comes to fishing, nothing is set in stone):

- African pompano: year-round
- amberjack: August-May
- barracuda: year-round
- blackfin tuna: year-round
- black grouper: May-December
- blue marlin: March-October
- bonefish: April-December
- bonito: year-round
- cobia: November-April
- common snook: September-December
- hogfish: year-round
- king mackerel: December-August
- mahimahi: April-September
- permit: August-April
- redfish: year-round
- red grouper: May-December
- red snapper: June-July
- sailfish: October-August
- shark: year-round
- Spanish mackerel: year-round
- swordfish: year-round
- tarpon: year-round

archery, muzzle loading, and general firearms. Although alligator hunting is not allowed within the preserve, hunters can, depending on the time of year, pursue white-tailed deer, turkeys, and hogs. For more information about hunting regulations, including proper licenses, contact the **Florida Fish and Wildlife Conservation Commission (FWC)** (Farris Bryant Bldg., 620 S. Meridian St., Tallahassee, 850/488-3831 or 850/488-4676, www.myfwc. com), and call 888/486-8356 for round-the-clock licensing information.

FISHING AND BOATING

Throughout the year, anglers and boaters flock to southern Florida, most notably the Florida Keys, to explore the offshore and backcountry waters of this abundant region. Considering the variety of game fish in these waters, not to mention the incredible views and gorgeous sunsets, it's easy to see why it's such a well-favored place. From Key Largo to Key West, you'll find more party boats, private fishing charters, boat rentals, sunset cruises, and full-service marinas than you can probably count, especially in

- wahoo: year-round
- yellowfin tuna: year-round
- yellowtail snapper: year-round

ANNUAL FISHING TOURNAMENTS

Every month, at least one highly prized fishing tournament is happening somewhere in the Florida Keys. Here are some suggestions:

- **January:** the **Islamorada Fishing Club Sailfish Tournament** (305/664-4735, www.theislamoradafishingclub.com) and the **Cheeca Lodge Presidential Sailfish Tournament** (800/327-2888, www.cheeca.com/experience/fishing) in Islamorada

- **February:** the **Cuda Bowl Flats Fishing Tournament** (305/294-3618, www.cudabowl.com), an artificial, fly-, and spinfishing competition that usually takes place near Hurricane Hole Marina in late January or early February

- **March:** the **Leon Shell Memorial Sailfish Tournament** (305/289-1310, www.leonshelltournament.com) near the Key Colony Beach Marina and the eight-month-long **Key West Fishing Tournament (KWFT)** (305/295-6601, www.keywestfishingtournament.com), during which anglers compete to catch and release more than 40 different fish species

- **April:** the prestigious **World Sailfish Championship** (866/550-5580, www.worldsailfish.com), which occurs near Key West and typically awards cash prizes totaling about $1 million

- **May:** the **Marathon International Tarpon Tournament** (305/289-2248, tarpontournaments@yahoo.com) and the **Lower Keys Dolphin Tournament** (305/872-2411, www.lowerkeyschamber.com), which usually offers over $40,000 in prizes

- **June:** the **Burdines Waterfront Dolphin & Blackfin Tuna Tournament** (305/743-5317, www.burdineswaterfront.com) near Marathon

- **July:** the **Conch Republic Ladies' Dolphin Tournament** (305/304-7674), which despite being a women-only competition near Key West, does allow male captains and mates

- **September-November:** the **Marathon International Bonefish Tournament** (305/304-8682) in September and the **Redbone Celebrity Tournament Series** (305/664-2002, www.redbone.org), a trio of competitions from September to November that seek out permit, tarpon, bonefish, and redfish

- **December:** the **Islamorada Sailfish Tournament** (305/852-2102, www.islamoradasailfishtournament.com)

For more information about annual fishing tournaments and area fishing guides, consult the following websites: www.fla-keys.com/fishing, www.fishingfloridakeys.com, and www.fishfloridakeys.com.

Islamorada, the self-proclaimed "sportfishing capital of the world." In addition, most of the hotels and resorts along the Overseas Highway (U.S. 1), many of which are situated beside marinas, are more than willing to help arrange fishing and boating excursions for you.

For safety tips and necessary regulations that apply to both anglers and boaters in the Florida Keys as well as up-to-date fishing information, consult the **Florida Fish and Wildlife Conservation Commission (FWC)** (850/487-0554 or 850/488-4676, www.myfwc.com), and call 888/347-4356 for around-the-clock licensing information. In addition, you'll find helpful resources through **The Florida Keys Fishing Directory** (www.fishfloridakeys.com), **Florida Keys Boating** (www.floridakeysboating.com), the **U.S. Coast Guard's Boating Safety Division** (www.uscgboating.org), and *Florida Sportsman* (www.floridasportsman.com).

Also, whether you plan to bring your own properly registered boat to the Florida Keys, rent a vessel, or even charter a fishing trip, you might want to consider joining **Sea Tow** (800/473-2869, www.seatow.com), a nationwide provider of marine assistance for recreational boaters. Membership assures you such services as towing, prop disentanglements, fuel drops, and jump-starts—useful assistance to have when you're stranded in the backcountry.

CANOEING AND KAYAKING

Given its cornucopia of freshwater swamps, mangrove creeks, backcountry waters, and offshore islands, southern Florida is indeed a paddler's dream. Luckily, you don't even have to bring your own canoe or kayak to explore this fascinating region, as you'll find plenty of helpful outfitters between Miami and Key West. In Everglades City, for instance, **Everglades Adventures** (877/567-0679, www.everglade-sadventures.com) provides canoe and kayak rentals from November to April.

You'll find even more outfitters in the Florida Keys, some of which also offer guided tours. **Florida Bay Outfitters** (305/451-3018, www.kayakfloridakeys.com) in Key Largo, for instance, provides an array of canoe and kayak rentals, in addition to three-hour instructional sessions and several guided kayaking trips, from three-hour tours to nine-day excursions. Free pickups and drop-offs at participating resorts are offered for most trips, and reservations are necessary for all of them. No matter where you rent your vessel, however, you should make sure that personal flotation devices (PFDs) are included with each rental or at least available on-site.

DIVING AND SNORKELING

Within the ocean waters east of southern Florida stretches the third largest coral reef system in the world. With **Biscayne National Park** southeast of Miami and the 220-mile-long series of coral reefs that constitute **Florida Keys National Marine Sanctuary,** scuba divers and snorkelers will find no shortage of underwater delights, from brain coral formations to historical shipwrecks to oodles of tropical fish. While you can certainly bring or rent a vessel to dive or snorkel on your own, you'll also have access to a wide array of operators offering snorkeling and diving excursions in addition to equipment rentals and instruction.

In the Miami area, for instance, the **South Beach Dive and Surf Center** (305/531-6110, www.southbeachdivers.com), a PADI 5 Star facility, provides a variety of courses, including an introduction class, a divemaster class, and a digital underwater photography class—plus snorkeling and diving trips in the waters near Key Largo. Of course, you'll also find an assortment of similar operators throughout the Florida Keys, from **Amy Slate's Amoray Dive Resort** (800/426-6729, www.amoray.com) in Key Largo, which provides accommodations in addition to classes and trips, to **Sea-Clusive Charters** (305/744-9928, www.drytortugas-diving.com) in Key West, which offers multiday diving excursions to the Dry Tortugas.

Typically, reservations are required—or at least recommended—for all snorkeling and diving trips in Miami and the Florida Keys, and most of the time, operators include necessary equipment, such as tanks, weights, and snorkels, within their quoted prices. For more information about area wrecks and reefs, consult Florida Keys National Marine Sanctuary (305/852-7717 or 305/809-4700, www.flori-dakeys.noaa.gov), and if you're interested in helping to preserve and protect the living coral reef ecosystems in Florida and elsewhere in the world, contact the **Reef Relief Headquarters & Environmental Center** (631 Greene St., Key West, 305/294-3100, www.reefrelief.org). Lastly, if a diving emergency occurs, such as decompression sickness (i.e., the bends), dial **911** or contact a nearby hospital without delay.

OTHER WATER SPORTS

Some local outfitters, especially in the Florida Keys, make it easy for visitors to embrace a wide array of water sports, from windsurfing to parasailing; some even offer WaveRunner and Jet Ski rentals, plus access to water trampolines and jet boat rides. Not surprisingly, Key West boasts the lion's share of such companies, including Sebago Watersports, Sunset Watersports Key West, and Fury Water

THE SHIPWRECK TRAIL

While many snorkelers and scuba divers primarily come to the Florida Keys to explore the vibrant living coral reefs, others are more interested in the historical shipwrecks that pepper these offshore waters. Several were wrecked by the treacherous coral reefs that lure so many underwater enthusiasts today. Signifying the European Colonial, American, and Modern periods of the Keys' maritime history, nine of these shipwrecks now constitute the official Shipwreck Trail.

- *City of Washington:* Built in Pennsylvania in 1877, accidentally run aground in 1917, and now lying in 25 feet of water near Elbow Reef, this steel hull vessel was the first ship to assist the USS *Maine* following the explosion in Havana Harbor.

- *Benwood:* Constructed in England in 1910, this ship sunk in 1942 after colliding with another vessel; it now lies between French Reef and Dixie Shoals, in water that ranges in depth from 25 to 45 feet.

- *Duane:* Built in Philadelphia in 1936 and now lying in 120 feet of water one mile south of Molasses Reef, this U.S. Coast Guard cutter was formerly used in World War II, eventually decommissioned in 1985, and purposely sunk two years later as an artificial reef.

- *Eagle:* Constructed in Holland in 1962 as *Raila Dan,* this 268-foot freighter went through several incarnations before catching fire in 1985, after which it was renamed *Eagle Tire Company* and sunk as an artificial reef; it now lies on its starboard side (split in two by a 1998 hurricane) in 70-110 feet of water near Lower Matecumbe Key, three miles northeast of the Alligator Reef Light.

- *San Pedro:* This 287-ton, Dutch-built Spanish ship, which wrecked south of Indian Key during a 1733 hurricane, has undergone several salvaging attempts since its discovery in 1960 and now serves as the San Pedro Underwater Archaeological Preserve State Park.

- *Adelaide Baker:* Constructed in Maine in 1863 as the *F. W. Carver,* this three-masted, iron-rigged ship wrecked in 1889 while toting a cargo of milled timber and now lies in 20 feet of water four miles south of Duck Key.

- *Thunderbolt:* Built in West Virginia in 1942 to lay defensive coastal mines, and formerly known as *Randolph,* this 188-foot steel ship was intentionally sunk in 1986 and now lies, encrusted with coral and sponges, in 75-120 feet of water four miles south of Key Colony Beach.

- *North America:* Lying in 14 feet of water in the sand and grass flats north of Delta Shoals, this vessel is believed to be the *North America,* built in 1833 in Bath, Maine, and lost in 1842 while transporting dry goods and furniture.

- *Amesbury:* Originally constructed as a U.S. Naval destroyer escort in 1943 and locally known as "Alexander's Wreck," this vessel was being towed to deep water to be sunk when it grounded and broke up in a storm five miles west of Key West.

A spar buoy identifies each of these historical sites, which are all accessible by private boat or diving charter. Underwater conditions vary from site to site, meaning that you can expect both easy, shallow-water dives as well as deeper dives with swift currents. For more information, contact **Florida Keys National Marine Sanctuary** (305/852-7717 or 305/809-4700, www.floridakeys.noaa.gov) or consult area diving operators, many of whom offer charters or private trips to these sites. To help protect these fragile structures—all of which are artificial reefs that now support tropical fish and other marine creatures—remember to control your buoyancy, avoid anchoring near the sites, and refrain from damaging or removing any and all artifacts that you see.

Adventures. In addition, several outfitters between Key Largo and Key West invite outdoors enthusiasts to try stand up paddleboarding (SUP), an ancient form of surfing used by Hawaiians and now a fast-growing sport that allows paddlers to stand above the water and get a bird's-eye view of the fish and other marine creatures below them.

GOLF

Although southern Florida is a recreationist's paradise, golf is less prevalent here than water-related activities like fishing and diving. Nevertheless, you'll find several golf courses in the region, including the **Biltmore Golf Course** (305/460-5364, www.biltmorehotel. com), a well-landscaped, 18-hole course adjacent to the legendary Biltmore Hotel in the Miami area. Even the Florida Keys have a few options, from the exclusive **Ocean Reef Club** (305/367-5912, www.oceanreef.com), which features two championship 18-hole courses on the northern end of Key Largo, to the 200-acre **Key West Golf Club** (305/294-5232, www.keywestgolf.com), which offers an 18-hole public golf course on the gulf side

of U.S. 1. Many of these courses also provide golf club rentals, so there's usually no need to lug your own equipment with you—which is good news for those traveling by plane, bus, cruise ship, or any method with luggage restrictions.

SPECTATOR SPORTS

If you favor spectator sports, then you can't go wrong in Miami, where you'll find an array of professional teams on display. Typically from September to December, for instance, football fans can watch the **Miami Dolphins** (305/943-8000, www.miamidolphins.com) take on other NFL teams at the Sun Life Stadium, while from April to September, baseball lovers can flock to the brand-new Marlins Park to cheer on the **Miami Marlins** (305/480-1300, http://miami. marlins.mlb.com). Meanwhile, from October to April, basketball fans can catch the **Miami Heat** (786/777-1000, www.nba.com/heat) at the AmericanAirlines Arena, and even hockey fans will be happy in Miami, where the **Florida Panthers** (954/835-7000, http://panthers.nhl. com) normally play between October and April at the BB&T Center.

Festivals and Events

Given the favorable climate, cultural diversity, and carefree vibe of southern Florida, it's no wonder that the region hosts numerous festivals and events throughout the year. In Miami, for instance, you'll learn firsthand about the varied cultures that shaped the city by attending such engaging events as the **Miami Gay and Lesbian Film Festival** (www.mglff.com) in late April; Coconut Grove's **Miami/Bahamas Goombay Festival** in early June; and **Calle Ocho** (www. carnavalmiami.com), which usually occurs in mid-March and serves as one of the largest Latino block parties in the country. The Everglades, meanwhile, have their own curious history, informed by the Native American tribes that have called this mysterious region home. At the **Miccosukee Indian Arts Festival**

(www.miccosukee.com) in late December, for example, visitors can watch Native American dances and browse genuine arts and crafts in the Miccosukee Indian Village.

Naturally, the fun-loving Florida Keys offer their own share of annual festivals and events. In the Upper Keys, for instance, history is honored with zany happenings like the **Key Largo Conch Republic Days** (www. keylargoconchrepublicdays.com), a late April event that honors the 1982 ceremonial secession of the Florida Keys from the United States. The Middle and Lower Keys, meanwhile, celebrate the great outdoors with the **Underwater Music Festival** (www.lowerkeyschamber.com) near Looe Key Reef in early or mid-July and the **Florida Keys Birding & Wildlife Festival**

ANNUAL ART CELEBRATIONS

Southern Florida hosts a number of annual cultural events that appeal to art and architecture aficionados. Every January, the **Art Deco Weekend** lures visitors to Miami Beach's Art Deco District, and the **Key West Craft Show** attracts more than 100 skilled artists to Key West's Old Town. For a more unusual experience, consider visiting during **Sculpture Key West,** an annual wintertime exhibition (Dec.-Mar.) of contemporary outdoor sculpture throughout the city.

In February, art lovers venture south to the **Pigeon Key Art Show,** an annual event featuring live music, art raffles, and the artwork of over 70 fine artists from around the country. Also in February, the **Coconut Grove Arts Festival** lures even more paintings, jewelry, photography, and glass sculptures to the Miami area while the **Old Island Days Art Festival**

celebrates various art forms in Key West's Old Town.

Early December brings two more art festivals to this vibrant region: **Art Basel Miami Beach,** an enormous show featuring an exclusive selection of more than 250 art galleries from North America, Latin America, Europe, Asia, and Africa, and the **Big Pine & the Lower Keys Island Art Festival,** a smaller art and music event ideal for families. Typically from late December to early January, the **Miccosukee Indian Arts Festival** welcomes visitors to the Miccosukee Indian Village, where you can watch Native American dances and browse genuine arts and crafts. At multiple times from late December to mid-March, those interested in Key West's unique architecture can take a **Key West House Tour,** sponsored by the Old Island Restoration Foundation.

(www.keysbirdingfest.org), which typically occurs in September and features field trips throughout the region. As with other cultural offerings, Key West hosts the lion's share of annual celebrations, including the **Conch Republic Independence Celebration** (www.conchrepublic.com) in late April; **Hemingway Days** (www.hemingwaydays.org), which typically happens in late July and celebrates the life of Key West's most famous former resident; and **Fantasy Fest** (www.fantasyfest.com), a rowdy late October event that features colorful parades, outrageous parties, and drag queens galore.

Accommodations and Food

ACCOMMODATIONS

Southern Florida contains a wide array of accommodations, from major hotel and motel chains to luxurious resorts to primitive campgrounds. Naturally, where you plan to stay depends on your interests, budget, and ultimate destination. Though spontaneity can be fun on a vacation, be aware that you might have to make reservations far in advance of your trip. Inns, bed-and-breakfasts, cottages, and campgrounds can fill up quickly, especially during the high winter season, from late December through April.

For more information about southern Florida's accommodations, consult organizations like **Miami Beach 411** (1521 Alton Rd., Ste. 233, Miami Beach, 305/754-2206, www.miamibeach411.com), the **Key West Innkeepers Association (KWIA)** (305/295-9500 or 800/492-1911, www.keywestinns.com), or **The Lodging Association of the Florida Keys and Key West** (818 White St., Ste. 8, Key West, 305/296-4959, www.keyslodging.org). If you're interested in budget-friendly camping options, consult the **Florida Association of RV Parks and Campgrounds**

CLASSIC KEY LIME PIE

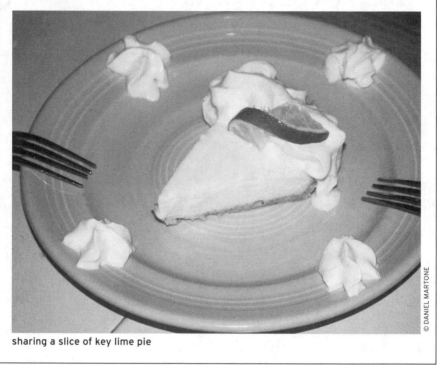

© DANIEL MARTONE

sharing a slice of key lime pie

(FARVC) (1340 Vickers Rd., Tallahassee, 850/562-7151, www.campflorida.com), or contact **ReserveAmerica** (800/326-3521, www.reserveamerica.com) to reserve a spot at one of southern Florida's state park campgrounds.

FOOD AND DRINK

Eating and drinking are popular pastimes in southern Florida, and luckily for visitors, there are a lot of choices available. Given the varied cultural influences in southern Florida, you'll find that the cuisine ranges from Creole dishes in Miami's Little Haiti to *cubanos* (Cuban sandwiches) in Little Havana to seafood galore in the Florida Keys. In fact, depending on the season, you're likely to spot fried catfish, grilled snapper or grouper, Caribbean-style

mahimahi, gulf and rock shrimp, stone crab claws, and Florida lobster in the assorted seafood restaurants between Key Largo and Key West. Throughout the year, you'll be able to sample local delicacies like conch fritters, conch chowder, and key lime pie, and of course, given that it's the South, you'll often see grits and hush puppies on the menu, too. In the region's finer restaurants, you'll also encounter "Floribbean" cuisine, which consists of fresh Florida produce and seafood, with American, European, Caribbean, and Latin American influences. For more information about available eateries between Miami and Key West, consult the **Miami DiningGuide** (www.miami.dining-guide.com) and the **Florida Keys Dining Guide** (www.keysdining.com).

Of all the regional treats favored in the Florida Keys, perhaps none is as widely known—or as universally celebrated—as key lime pie. While you'll encounter a variety of styles down here—from the deep-fried, cinnamon-encrusted version at The Island Fish Co. Tiki Bar & Restaurant in Marathon to the chocolate-covered pie-on-a-stick at the Key West Key Lime Pie Co. in Key West's Old Town—most gourmands seek the classic recipe, a creamy, tangy, sweet concoction on a graham cracker crust, the kind you'll find at Mrs. Mac's Kitchen in Key Largo.

If you simply can't wait to taste this treat on your next trip to the Florida Keys, never fear. With little fuss, you can easily make your own classic key lime pie, using this simple recipe.

CRUST INGREDIENTS

1½ cups crushed graham crackers
3 Tbsp. sugar
6 Tbsp. salted butter, melted

FILLING INGREDIENTS

4 large egg yolks

1 14-oz. can sweetened, condensed milk
½ cup freshly squeezed key lime juice (or bottled, if necessary)

INSTRUCTIONS

· Preheat the oven to 350°F.
· Combine the graham cracker crumbs, sugar, and melted butter in a medium-size bowl.
· Press the mixture evenly into the bottom and sides of a nine-inch pie pan.
· Bake the pie shell at 350°F for 10-15 minutes, or until slightly brown.
· Place the pie shell on a wire rack to cool.
· Beat the egg yolks with an electric mixer until the color turns a pale yellow.
· Add the condensed milk, and mix on low speed.
· Fold in the lime juice.
· Pour the mixture into the pie shell and bake at 350°F for 10-12 minutes.
· Once cooled, refrigerate the pie for at least six hours.
· When you're ready to serve, garnish the pie with whipped cream and lime wedges.

Although you won't find too many microbreweries and wineries in southern Florida, Key West presents a couple of notable options: the **Southernmost Brewery** (305/293-8484, www.kellyscaribbean.blogspot.com), which features such local favorites as Havana Red Ale, Key West Golden Ale, and Southern Clipper Wheat Beer, and **The Key West Winery** (305/292-1717, www.thekeywestwinery.com), which prepares unusual tropical wines, enhanced by flavors like key lime, pineapple, coconut, and jalapeño. In addition, if you choose to stay in self-sufficient lodgings, such as a cottage with a well-equipped kitchen, you'll fortunately find numerous groceries throughout southern Florida, including several branches of **Publix** (800/242-1227, www.publix.com), each of which typically features a pharmacy, a bakery, a deli, fresh sushi and produce, meat and seafood departments, wine and beer, as well as other services, such as automated teller machines (ATMs). Naturally, you'll also find

specialty stores throughout the region.

Tips for Travelers

FOREIGN TRAVELERS

International travelers should understand current American policies before heading here.

Passports and Visas

While international travelers are required to show a valid passport upon entering the United States, most citizens from Canada, Bermuda, and the 37 countries that are part of the **Visa Waiver Program (VWP)**—such as France, Italy, Germany, Australia, New Zealand, Japan, Taiwan, Ireland, and the United Kingdom—are allowed to travel to Florida without a visa. They will, however, still need to apply to the **Electronic System for Travel Authorization (ESTA).** All other temporary international travelers are required to secure a nonimmigrant visa before entering Florida. For more information, consult the **U.S. Department of State's Bureau of Consular Affairs** (202/663-1225, www.travel.state.gov).

Customs

Upon entering Florida, international travelers must declare any dollar amount over $10,000 as well as the value of any articles that will remain in the country, including gifts. A duty will be assessed for all imported goods; visitors are usually granted a $200 exemption for items intended for personal or household use. Illegal drugs, Cuban cigars, toxic substances, and unapproved prescription drugs are generally prohibited. In order to protect American agriculture, customs officials will also confiscate certain produce, plants, seeds, nuts, meats, and other potentially dangerous biological products. For more information, consult the **U.S. Customs and Border Protection** (202/325-8000 or 877/227-5511, www.cbp.gov).

Embassies and Consulates

While the embassies for most countries are located in Washington, DC, some nations have consular offices in Miami. Such helpful European resources include the **Austrian Consulate Miami** (2445 Hollywood Blvd., Hollywood, 954/925-1100, www.austrianconsulatemiami.com, 9am-5pm Mon.-Fri.), the **British Consulate-General Miami** (1001 Brickell Bay Dr., Miami, 305/400-6400, www.ukinusa.fco.gov.uk, 9am-4:30pm Mon.-Fri.), the **Consulate General of the Federal Republic of Germany** (100 N. Biscayne Blvd., Ste. 2200, Miami, 305/358-0290, www.germany.info, 8:30am-4:30pm Mon.-Thurs., 8:30am-1pm Fri.), and the **Consulate General of Italy** (4000 Ponce de León Blvd., Ste. 590, Coral Gables, 305/374-6322, www.consmiami.esteri.it, 9am-noon Mon.-Tues. and Thurs.-Fri., 9am-noon and 3pm-5:30pm Wed.). Other helpful consular offices include the **Consulate General of Canada** (200 S. Biscayne Blvd., Ste. 1600, Miami, 305/579-1600, www.miami.gc.ca or www.canadainternational.gc.ca, 8:30am-4pm Mon.-Fri.), the **Consulate General of Costa Rica** (2730 SW 3rd Ave., Ste. 401, Miami, 305/871-7485, www.costarica-embassy.org, 9am-1pm Mon.-Fri.), the **Consulate General of Mexico** (1399 SW 1st Ave., Miami, 786/268-4900, www.sre.gob.mx/miami, 8am-6pm Mon.-Fri.), and the **Consulate-General of Japan** (80 SW 8th St., Ste. 3200, Miami, 305/530-9090, www.miami.us.emb-japan.go.jp, 9am-12:30pm and 1:30pm-5pm Mon.-Fri.).

OPPORTUNITIES FOR STUDY AND EMPLOYMENT

With several colleges and businesses in southern Florida, there are plenty of educational and work-related opportunities for residents and travelers. If you're interested in such a long-term stay, your best bet would be to research the schools and companies that interest you, consider details like transportation and accommodations, and for foreign travelers, look into U.S. visa policies *before* making travel or relocation plans. Of course, some facilities, such as

© LAURA MARTONE

Typically, pets aren't allowed on public beaches in the Keys.

the **Dolphin Research Center (DRC)** (305/289-0002 or 305/289-1121, www.dolphins.org) on Grassy Key, offer short-term educational opportunities, such as trainer-for-a-day programs ($675 pp), that you might find enriching—without having to uproot your entire life.

VOLUNTEER VACATIONS

Sometimes, being a tourist isn't enough. If you want to explore southern Florida *and* lend a helping hand, then perhaps a volunteer vacation is right up your alley. National and state parks can especially use some extra assistance, and working in such diverse environments can be a truly rewarding experience. For more information about volunteering in Florida's national parks, consult the **National Park Service** (www.nps.gov/volunteer). For more information about volunteer opportunities at southern Florida's state parks, contact the **Florida State Parks Information Center** (3900 Commonwealth Blvd., Tallahassee, 850/245-2157, www.floridastateparks.org/getinvolved).

Of course, parks aren't the only places that need help. **Theater of the Sea** (305/664-2431, www.theaterofthesea.com) in Islamorada, for instance, invites volunteer interns to assist the animal care staff in feeding and attending to the dolphins, sea lions, sea turtles, and other marine creatures on the premises during the spring, summer, and fall months. Curiously, other places, such as the nonprofit **Florida Keys Wild Bird Center** in Tavernier (305/852-4486, www.fkwbc.org), are almost entirely operated by volunteers and interns.

ACCESS FOR TRAVELERS WITH DISABILITIES

Southern Florida offers limited accessibility for those with disabilities. Major store and hotel chains, such as Publix and Holiday Inn, are often wheelchair-accessible, as are attractions like the glass-bottom boat tours of John Pennekamp Coral Reef State Park in Key Largo and the Mel Fisher Maritime Museum in Key West.

As with most federal lands, Everglades

National Park, which is open 24 hours daily, provides wheelchair-accessible visitor centers, featuring designated parking spaces, curb ramps, and automatic doors. In addition, vision-impaired and hearing-impaired visitors can utilize audio recordings, Braille signage, and assistive listening devices (ALDs) for use in the park's interpretive programs. Also, the **National Park Service** (www.nps.gov/fees_passes.htm) offers a special lifetime pass (free) for U.S. citizens and permanent residents with permanent disabilities, allowing them free access to any federal recreation site that charges an entrance fee, including Everglades National Park and Dry Tortugas National Park.

Nevertheless, plenty of establishments, such as independently owned inns and cottages in the Florida Keys, cannot accommodate wheelchairs. So when in doubt about the possibility of access, simply contact the establishment in question.

TRAVELING WITH CHILDREN

With its multitude of beaches, state parks, museums, boat tours, and other amusements, southern Florida is clearly a kid-friendly place. So if you're traveling here with children, you'll surely find something for them to do. Just remember to supervise them at all times, both to keep them safe from harm and to minimize the possibility of disturbing others. Be advised, too, that while plenty of hotels and resorts welcome children, some lodgings, such as the Azul del Mar in Key Largo, are adults-only establishments.

TRAVELING WITH PETS

Although pets aren't allowed on most of southern Florida's beaches and within many hotels, restaurants, and stores, several places do welcome them, including state park campgrounds. In locations where dogs, cats, and other pets are allowed, it's crucial that you understand and follow any relevant rules. Typically, you are asked to keep your pets on a leash at all times, walk them in designated areas, control their behavior so as not to disturb or endanger others, and always pick up after them. Barking or aggressive dogs are usually forbidden everywhere. When in doubt, call ahead to verify the pet policies of a particular park, attraction, or establishment.

WOMEN TRAVELING ALONE

Although southern Florida, especially the Keys, is a relatively safe place for women, things can still go wrong—on the road, in a campground, even in a crowd—so it's important for solo female travelers to take precautions, especially in urban centers like Miami and Key West. If possible, tell someone back home about your intended travel plans, stick to daytime driving, and stay close to busy attractions, streets, and campgrounds. In Miami, for instance, your best bet is to stay in tourist-friendly neighborhoods like Miami Beach, Coconut Grove, and Coral Gables. Just be advised that some resorts in Miami and Key West are clothing-optional, so if public nudity makes you uncomfortable, be sure to choose your accommodations carefully.

No matter where you go, though, try to stow your money, credit cards, and identification close to your person, as big purses make easy targets. If you feel that someone is stalking you, find a public place (such as a store, hotel, or bar), and don't hesitate to alert the police. In addition, you should keep the doors to your lodging and vehicle locked at all times.

Before heading out on your trip, you should also invest in a canister of pepper spray as well as a cell phone, which can be useful in an emergency. Just remember that cellular reception is limited in the region's more remote areas, such as the backcountry of the Everglades and the Florida Keys.

SENIOR TRAVELERS

Southern Florida is an exceptionally helpful place, so senior travelers should have little trouble finding assistance here. For help with directions, there are several visitor centers and tourism bureaus throughout the region, not to mention plenty of locals able to point you in the right direction. In addition, many attractions offer discounts to senior travelers. The **National Park Service** (www.nps.gov/

fees_passes.htm) even offers a special lifetime pass ($10 pp) for U.S. citizens and permanent residents aged 62 or older, allowing them free access to any federal recreation site that charges an entrance fee, including Everglades National Park and Dry Tortugas National Park.

GAY AND LESBIAN TRAVELERS

Parts of southern Florida, namely South Beach and Key West, are openly friendly to gay and lesbian travelers. Besides annual events like Key West Pride and Fantasy Fest, Key West even has exclusively gay and/or lesbian accommodations and a variety of gay bars. For more information about gay-related events and establishments in Key West, contact the **Key West Business Guild** (513 Truman Ave., Key West, 305/294-4603 or 800/535-7797, www.gaykeywestfl.com). Those traveling to Miami, meanwhile, can consult www.miamigaytravel.com.

CONDUCT AND CUSTOMS

Florida is similar to other Southern states in temperament and traditions. While a major city like Miami might not follow the general rule, most areas of southern Florida, especially the Florida Keys, have a laid-back, friendly vibe. Many residents seem to embrace the value of having a good time while treating others with respect, though it's good to remember that a lot of the locals weren't necessarily born here. In fact, plenty of them have escaped colder climates in New England and the Midwest, giving them a sense of appreciation for the benefits of living in a bountiful, comfortable landscape like southern Florida.

Given the region's multiethnic history, reliance on tourism, and proximity to Cuba, foreigners and tourists are generally welcome here. Overall, the residents are helpful, hospitable, and gregarious. So while in Florida, do as the natives do. Be kind and considerate, ask for help when you need it, thank others for their time, and as a courtesy, ask permission before taking a photo.

WHAT TO TAKE

Foreign travelers will need passports, adapter plugs, and current converters. All adults should have **proper identification,** which you'll need to drive a rental car, rent certain equipment, and of course, drink in a Key West bar.

Although you should pack light, be sure to include a swimsuit, a hat, beach shoes, an umbrella, and a lightweight jacket, just in case the weather turns chilly. Attire in the Keys is **casual,** even in upscale restaurants, so there's no need to bring fancy or formal outfits.

Sunscreen and toiletries are available throughout Miami and the Keys, but if your plans include activities like golfing and birdwatching, you might want to bring your **favorite clubs** and **binoculars.** Kayaks, bicycles, boats, and other outdoor gear are easy enough to rent once you get here.

Health and Safety

Despite the best-laid plans, trouble can occur at any time. Before hitting the road or boarding a bus, plane, boat, or train, it's critical that you pack a well-stocked first-aid kit and prepare yourself for the common pitfalls of traveling in southern Florida.

HEALTH RISKS

Given that outdoor diversions reign in Miami, the Everglades, and the Florida Keys, most of the possible health risks that you may face will probably involve the great outdoors.

Contaminated Water

Most of the water you'll encounter in southern Florida will be saltwater in the ocean or brackish water in the backcountry, neither of which you should ever drink, due to the high probability of dehydration. Nevertheless, you may encounter freshwater in the Everglades and a few spots in the Florida Keys. At such times, the water may look inviting, but don't take a chance. Many of Florida's inland bodies of water may be tainted with *Giardia lamblia,* a nasty little parasite that is most commonly transmitted through mammal feces. The resulting illness, **giardiasis,** can result in severe stomach cramps, vomiting, and diarrhea. While Halizone tablets, bleach, and other chemical purifiers may be effective against such organisms, your best bet will be to use an adequate water filter (which filters down to 0.4 micron or less) or boil the water for at least five minutes.

Insects

With the prevalence of marshes and beaches in southern Florida, you'll find a wide array of insects in this region, from harmless ones like dragonflies to more bothersome critters. Perhaps the biggest concerns are **mosquitoes** and **fire ants,** whose stings can cause itchy red welts, or worse.

Mosquitoes are typically more prevalent during the wet season (May.-Oct.), especially during the summer months, when the humidity is at its worst. To protect against these relentless creatures, you should use a combination of defenses, including light-colored clothing, long-sleeved shirts, long pants, closed shoes, scent-free deodorant, and insect repellents containing DEET. In addition, you should avoid grassy areas and shady places. Instead, seek open, breezy locales, especially out on the water, and avoid peak hours for mosquito activity, namely sunrise and sunset. Also, try to open and close your car doors quickly, and keep your car windows rolled up, as it's no fun being stuck in a vehicle with a roving, bloodthirsty mosquito.

Of course, if you are stung by a mosquito, you should be fine—unless you have an unforeseen allergy or the mosquito is a carrier for a disease like the West Nile virus. Beyond cleaning the affected area and treating it with calamine lotion, hydrocortisone cream, or aloe vera gel, all you can do is take some anti-inflammatory or antihistamine medication for the pain and swelling and wait for the skin to heal.

© DANIEL MARTONE

An American alligator keeps a wary eye on tourists.

Fire ants, meanwhile, are large, aggressive red ants prevalent in tropical areas, such as southern Florida. Often nesting in moist soil near riverbanks, ponds, highways, and watered lawns, these ants are capable of building large, dome-shaped mounds. They are also inclined to inflict painful stings, whose aftereffects can be deadly to small animals and sensitive humans. To protect yourself and your pets, try to avoid fire ant colonies. However, if you are stung by an ant—or several—avoid scratching the affected area and instead treat any bumps with a hydrocortisone cream or aloe vera gel. In addition, you can take an antihistamine medication to reduce the itching. Individuals who experience severe reactions, such as chest pain, nausea, sweating, loss of breath, serious swelling, and slurred speech, should consult a doctor or hospital immediately upon contact.

Plants

While hiking amid southern Florida's forests, marshes, and beaches, be careful where you step. It's easier than you think to trip on a root or other obstruction. In addition, unless you're certain that you've found a patch of recognizable fruit, you should refrain from digesting any tempting berries, flowers, plants, and the like without first consulting local residents or expert field guides.

Wild Animals

Since much of southern Florida comprises undeveloped marshes and forests, not to mention the surrounding waters, you're bound to encounter wild animals at times. While many of these, such as the iguanas and roosters that roam the streets of Key West, are fairly harmless, more dangerous creatures, such as alligators and Florida panthers, live here, too. To avoid perilous encounters with such animals, don't venture into places like the Everglades by yourself and try to observe all wildlife from a distance. Although it should go without saying, you should also never taunt, disturb, or feed any of the wildlife that you see.

Heatstroke

Hot, sunny days are common in southern Florida, and it's crucial that you prepare for them. Although sunscreen will help to prevent sunburn (which, if experienced often, can cause long-term problems for your skin), you must apply it frequently and liberally. Prolonged sun exposure, high temperatures, and little water consumption can also cause dehydration, which can lead to heat exhaustion—a harmful condition whereby your internal cooling system begins to shut down. Symptoms may include clammy skin, weakness, vomiting, and abnormal body temperature. In such instances, you must lie down in the shade, remove restrictive clothing, and drink some water.

If you do not treat heat exhaustion promptly, your condition can worsen quickly, leading to heatstroke (or sunstroke)—a dangerous condition whereby your internal body temperature starts to rise to a potentially fatal level. Symptoms can include dizziness, vomiting, diarrhea, abnormal breathing and blood pressure, cessation of sweating, headache, and confusion. If any of these occur, you must be taken to a hospital as soon as possible. In the meantime, your companions should move you into the shade; remove your clothing; lower your body temperature with cool water, damp sheets, or fans; and try to give you some water to drink, if you're able.

Hurricanes

One of the biggest concerns for travelers to southern Florida is, of course, the possibility of facing a hurricane, especially in an isolated place like the Florida Keys. Generally, the Atlantic hurricane season runs from June through November, though hurricanes have certainly occurred beyond this time frame. The best advice is to stock up on extra water, flashlights, batteries, and other supplies during the season, develop a possible exit strategy, and keep apprised of the weather at all times. Although most radio and television stations provide weather updates, it's also possible to contact the **National Weather Service (NWS)** directly; there are offices in Key West (1315

HURRICANE CHECKLIST

Some out-of-towners are apprehensive about visiting the Florida Keys during the Atlantic hurricane season, which usually runs from June 1 to November 30. The truth is, however, that hurricanes are infrequent in this region, and many of the most popular events, such as Hemingway Days and Fantasy Fest, occur during this half of the year. Nevertheless, it's always a good idea to be prepared for the worst. If you do plan to visit the Florida Keys during hurricane season, keep apprised of weather updates and be prepared to evacuate if necessary.

Stock up on certain essentials in advance, as you'll surely face long lines and depleted supplies once the storm threatens. Listed here are some suggested items, which will come in handy whether you're forced to stay through the storm or you find yourself stuck in an evacuation route. Of course, this isn't an exhaustive list, so be sure to set aside whatever else you might need, such as cell phones, identification cards, house keys, photo albums, important documents, and pet supplies.

FOOD SUPPLIES

In general, you should have a two-week supply of nonperishable foods, especially low-salt and low-fat items that will minimize your thirst. Necessary goods, some of which must be purchased just before the storm, include the following:

- bread and cereals
- canned fruit and vegetables
- dried fruit
- dry and canned pet food, if necessary
- ice and drinking water (one gallon pp daily)
- powdered, canned, or other nonrefrigerated beverages (coffee, fruit juice, milk, etc.)
- prepared foods (canned soups, corned beef hash, tuna, etc.)
- raw vegetables
- snacks (crackers, cookies, nuts, etc.)
- snack spreads (peanut butter, fruit preserves, etc.)
- sugar, salt, and pepper

KITCHEN SUPPLIES

The following items will be especially handy if you have to evacuate to a strange place, such as an ill-equipped motel:

- bottle opener and manual can opener
- camp stove and canned cooking fuel
- ice chest or cooler
- paper plates and napkins
- plastic cups and utensils
- pocketknife
- waterproof matches

HARDWARE

Most of the following items will only be necessary if you live in the Florida Keys year-round or stay here for extended periods of time:

- canvas tarps
- hammer and nails
- plastic sheeting to cover furniture
- power screwdriver
- rope and duct tape
- screwdrivers and screws
- sheets of exterior plywood to board up windows

- shovel and pickax
- sturdy working gloves

MEDICAL NEEDS AND TOILETRIES

Given that drugstores will be mobbed just before a storm and closed for days afterward, it's always advisable to collect the following items ahead of time, along with a two-week supply of prescription drugs (which may include items like asthma inhalers):

- aspirin
- bandages, sterile rolls, and adhesive tape
- children's and pet medicine, if necessary
- cotton-tipped swabs
- deodorant
- diarrhea and constipation medication
- disinfectant and antiseptic
- emergency toilet (small, lidded garbage can with disinfectant, deodorizer, and plastic bags as liners)
- feminine hygiene products, if necessary
- first-aid kit and first-aid handbook
- insect bite lotion
- insect repellent sprays and candles
- Medic Alert tags, if necessary
- over-the-counter cold and allergy medicine
- plastic bags and jugs to store extra ice and water
- soap and shampoo
- sunscreen
- tweezers, needles, and a sewing kit
- water filter and purification tablets

BABY NEEDS

Obviously, the following items will only apply to those with children:

- baby cold and pain medication
- baby formula and food
- baby wipes
- diaper-rash ointment or petroleum jelly
- disposable diapers
- medicine dropper

HURRICANE KIT

Typically, it's a good idea to assemble this kit as soon as possible and store it in a cool, dry place. Be sure, too, to refresh the stock when necessary. Important items include the following:

- area maps
- auto supplies and gas can
- battery-operated clocks and lanterns
- battery-operated radio or television
- copies of insurance policies
- emergency and nonemergency phone numbers
- extra bulbs and batteries
- hand-crank flashlights
- operational fire extinguishers
- paper towels
- plastic garbage bags
- television antenna (rabbit ears-style)
- rain gear and extra clothes
- scissors
- swamp boots
- toilet paper

White St., 305/295-1316, www.srh.noaa.gov/key) as well as Miami (11691 SW 17th St., 305/229-4522, www.srh.noaa.gov/mfl).

MEDICAL SERVICES

While southern Florida might feel a bit isolated at times, especially deep in the Everglades and down in the Florida Keys, expert medical services are never too far away. So although you can utilize free services like www.mdtravelhealth.com to learn about infectious diseases and illness prevention in the United States, it's good to know that in-person care is available throughout southern Florida.

Emergency Care

All of Florida is tied into the **911** emergency system. Dial 911 free from any telephone (including pay phones) to reach an operator who can quickly dispatch local police, fire, or ambulance services. While this service also works from cell phones, be aware that you may find it difficult to make calls from the Everglades, Florida Keys backcountry, or offshore waters, where reliable cellular service isn't always guaranteed.

Hospitals and Pharmacies

If you experience an illness or injury while traveling through southern Florida, rest assured that, as with other U.S. states, hospitals abound here, even in the Florida Keys. Some of these area hospitals include **Mercy Hospital** (3663 S. Miami Ave., Miami, 305/854-4400, www.mercymiami.com), **Mariners Hospital** (91500 Overseas Hwy., Tavernier, 305/434-3000, www.baptisthealth.net), **Fishermen's Community Hospital** (3301 Overseas Hwy., Marathon, 305/743-5533, www.fishermenshospital.com), and the **Lower Keys Medical Center** (5900 College Rd., Key West, 305/294-5531, www.lkmc.com). Just be advised that most medical facilities will require you to have insurance or make a partial payment before admitting you for treatment or dispensing medication.

If you need to fill a prescription, you can do so at various pharmacies throughout southern Florida. Besides pharmacies like **Walgreens**

(800/925-4733, www.walgreens.com), you'll find that several area grocery stores, such as **Winn-Dixie** (866/946-6349, www.winndixie.com) and **Publix** (800/242-1227, www.publix.com), have on-site pharmacies, too. If you're a foreign visitor with medical concerns, feel free to take advantage of the region's 24-hour, multilingual tourist assistance by phoning 800/771-5397.

Insurance

Although you might be the sort of traveler who likes to live dangerously, insurance is highly recommended while traveling in southern Florida. Whether you're a U.S. citizen driving your own car or an international traveler in a rented RV, you should invest in medical, travel, and automotive insurance before embarking upon your trip—to protect yourself as well as your assets. Research your insurance options and choose the policies that best suit your needs and budget.

CRIME AND POLICE

Despite the crime-ridden reputation of Miami, most of southern Florida is a relatively safe, laid-back place. People here are, for the most part, friendly and helpful. Still, whether you're visiting Miami's South Beach, Everglades City, Big Pine Key, or Key West, it's important to take precautions.

Never leave valuables in plain view on a car seat; secure them in the trunk, where they're less tempting to thieves. Similarly, in case of an accident on the highway, do not abandon your vehicle, as this might also invite thieves. When sightseeing, keep your money, credit cards, identification, and other important items hidden on your person; purses and backpacks are much easier to steal. Bicycles should be secured properly whenever they're left unattended, and just to be on the safe side, lock your hotel and car doors at all times.

Although the Florida Keys are definitely safer than most urban areas in the United States, it's still prudent to be aware of your surroundings. For instance, you should always stay alert when walking alone at night, especially on poorly lit, residential streets in Key West. As in other tourist hot spots in America, muggings have been known to happen here.

If you're traveling by RV, do not boondock alone in an isolated place. Try to stay in an RV park, a campground, or at the very least, a well-lit parking lot. When venturing into the Everglades, for instance, try to camp with others. If you do find yourself in trouble, don't hesitate to find a phone and dial **911**. Of course, the time it takes police and emergency vehicles to reach you will depend upon your location.

While in the Keys, if you witness a crime of any kind, feel free to contact **Crime Stoppers of the Keys** (800/346-8477, www.crimestoppersofthefloridakeys.com) to offer an anonymous tip. Likewise, you can always consult the **Monroe County Sheriff's Office** (www.keysso.net) in the Upper Keys (305/853-3211), Middle Keys (305/289-2430), or Lower Keys (305/745-3184).

Information and Services

Although southern Florida—especially the Everglades and the Florida Keys—often feels isolated from the rest of the country, you're not as secluded as you might think. In fact, you'll find plenty of necessary resources here, from helpful chambers of commerce to well-stocked post offices.

MAPS AND TOURIST INFORMATION

For general information on traveling in southern Florida, your best source is the state-run **Visit Florida** (850/488-5607 or 866/972-5280, www.visitflorida.com). Your call will be answered by a live person who can send you brochures and field your questions about festivals, activities, lodgings, and more. You may find it even more convenient to surf the website, which offers a comprehensive database of communities, accommodations, activities, golf courses, beaches, parks, attractions, shops, events, restaurants, and other aspects of southern Florida. You'll even find free maps and the latest deals here. Just be aware that some of the information can be out-of-date, so always call ahead when making travel plans.

Suggested Maps

In a state known for its tourism industry, you'll find no shortage of helpful maps, including Florida's official transportation map (www.thefloridamap.com). For more detailed information, you should consider purchasing a map from **AAA** (800/222-1134, www.aaa.com), which offers both a Florida state map ($5.95 nonmembers, members free) and a Miami/Miami Beach map ($4.95 nonmembers, members free) that features smaller maps of Key West, the Everglades, and the Florida Keys. **Rand McNally** (800/678-7263, www.randmcnally.com) also produces several helpful maps, including an EasyFinder Florida map ($7.95), a Miami Metro map ($5.99), and a Key West fabMap ($5.95).

For more detail, **DeLorme** (207/847-1165 or 800/561-5105, www.delorme.com) produces the *Florida Atlas & Gazetteer,* which divides the state into 145 large-scale maps, complete with GPS coordinates. Though the 15-inch-long format is unwieldy for hikers, it's a great resource for planning your trip; it even identifies historical sites, state parks, public beaches, and other points of interest throughout southern Florida. You can find it at many regional bookstores and gas stations for $24.95.

If you'll be exploring the backcountry, you should order an official topographical (topo) map produced by the **U.S. Geological Survey** (888/275-8747, www.usgs.gov). Florida's national parks have topo maps for sale at their visitor centers or ranger stations. Anglers will especially appreciate topo maps as well as nautical charts, such as those produced by **US Chart Services, Inc.** (930 SW 4th St., Fort

Lauderdale, 954/524-6566, www.uschartser-vices.com). These free full-color reproductions of official **National Oceanic and Atmospheric Administration (NOAA)** (800/638-8972, www.noaa.gov) charts of the Florida Keys are available at many local marine businesses.

Tourism Bureaus and Visitor Centers

In addition to **Visit Florida** (850/488-5607 or 866/972-5280, www.visitflorida.com), you'll find several helpful convention and visitors bureaus (CVBs) or chambers of commerce in southern Florida. To reach local tourism offices, consult the **Florida Association of Destination Marketing Organizations** (www.fadmo.org) or simply contact the tourism bureaus directly.

On the Florida mainland, helpful resources include the **Naples, Marco Island, Everglades Convention & Visitors Bureau** (2800 N. Horseshoe Dr., Naples, 239/225-1013 or 800/688-3600, www.paradisecoast.com), the **Everglades Area Chamber of Commerce** (P.O. Box 130, Everglades City, 239/695-3941, www.evergladeschamber.net), which is located at 32016 East Tamiami Trail, and the **Greater Miami Convention & Visitors Bureau (GMCVB)** (701 Brickell Ave., Ste. 2700, Miami, 305/539-3000 or 800/933-8448, www.miami-andbeaches.com).

For information about the Florida Keys, contact the **Monroe County Tourist Development Council** (1201 White St., Ste. 102, Key West, 305/296-1552 or 800/352-5397, www.fla-keys.com). To learn more about the Upper Keys, consult the **Key Largo Chamber of Commerce and Florida Keys Visitor Center** (106000 Overseas Hwy., Key Largo, 305/451-4747 or 800/822-1088, www.keylargo.org or www.key-largochamber.org) or the **Islamorada Chamber of Commerce** (P.O. Box 915, Islamorada, 305/664-4503 or 800/322-5397, www.islam-oradachamber.com) on the bay side of Upper Matecumbe Key, near Mile Marker 83.2. For information about the Middle Keys, contact the **Greater Marathon Chamber of Commerce and Marathon Visitors Center** (12222

Overseas Hwy., Marathon, 305/743-5417 or 800/262-7284, www.floridakeysmarathon.com). To learn more about the Lower Keys and Key West, consult the **Lower Keys Chamber of Commerce** (P.O. Box 430511, Big Pine Key, 305/872-2411 or 800/872-3722, www.lower-keyschamber.com), which is situated near Mile Marker 31 on the Overseas Highway, or the **Key West Chamber of Commerce** (510 Greene St., 1st Fl., Key West, 305/294-2587, www.key-westchamber.org) in Old Town.

COMMUNICATIONS AND MEDIA

Postal and Shipping Services

In southern Florida, a post office is never terribly far away, especially by car, so it's easy to purchase stamps, receive mail (via "General Delivery" for temporary visitors), and send letters and packages all around the world. To locate a post office in Miami, the Everglades, and the Florida Keys, consult the **United States Postal Service** (800/275-8777, www.usps.com). Of course, if you need to send a package quickly (and cost isn't an issue), you'll also find plenty of shipping stores throughout southern Florida, including **The UPS Store** (101425 Overseas Hwy., Key Largo, 305/453-4877, www.theupsstore.com) or **PostNet** (88005 Overseas Hwy., Ste. 10, Islamorada, 305/853-1101, www.postnet.com).

Phones and Internet Access

Public pay phones can be found throughout southern Florida—at airports, gas stations, stores, bars, restaurants, hotels, and so forth. To place a call, listen for a dial tone, deposit the necessary coins, and dial the desired number (including 1 and the area code, if you're making a long-distance call). In the case of an emergency, you can dial 911 at no charge. For international calls, it's probably best to use a prepaid phone card, which you can often purchase in gas stations or convenience stores. To figure out the correct international calling code, visit www.countrycodes.com.

Nowadays, a cell phone is a necessary tool for travelers. It can make it easier to get roadside assistance, call an establishment for directions, and seek help in an emergency situation. Just be advised that cellular reception might be unreliable when you're traveling through the backcountry or in offshore waters.

As for the Internet, it's hard to imagine the days when travel was possible without it. With the help of a computer and a modem, you can research the Everglades' native flora, book a fishing charter, monitor the day's weather, view the menu of a Key West restaurant, and perform a host of other duties. Access to your own laptop can make such tasks even more convenient, especially since several of Florida's hotels, restaurants, and other establishments offer wireless Internet access nowadays. Internet cafés also make it difficult to stay out of touch for long—especially down in Key West. Just remember that not all websites are updated regularly. Consult local residents or contact businesses directly before making any firm travel plans.

Publications and TV/Radio

You'll find publications throughout southern Florida, including daily newspapers like *The Miami Herald* (www.miamiherald.com) and *The Key West Citizen* (www.keysnews.com), the twice-weekly *Florida Keys Keynoter* (www.keysnet.com), plus magazines like *Florida Monthly* (www.floridamagazine.com), the bimonthly *Florida Travel + Life* (www.floridatravellife.com), and the monthly *Time Out Magazine* (www.thekeyshookup.com). Such periodicals are terrific sources of information for festivals, restaurants, sporting events, outdoor activities, and other diversions.

Local television and radio stations, such as Key West's popular **US-1 Radio** (104.1 FM, www.us1radio.com), are also excellent sources for regional information, including up-to-the-minute weather details during hurricane season. Pick up a newspaper in your area for a list of channels.

MONEY
Currency and Credit Cards

Bank debit cards and major credit cards (like Visa and MasterCard) are accepted throughout southern Florida, even in the smallest towns. In addition, automated teller machines (ATMs) have become more prevalent, allowing travelers to withdraw cash whenever they need it. If you're uncomfortable using ATMs, you're sure to find a bank open during regular business hours (9am-4pm daily) and sometimes on the weekend. That said, you'll need cash at self-registration campgrounds, and many independent motels, eateries, and stores will accept only cash or traveler's checks. As any wise traveler knows, you should never rely exclusively on plastic.

Foreign currency can be exchanged at all branches of the **First State Bank of the Florida Keys** (866/298-1858, www.keysbank.com) branches. For up-to-date exchange rates, consult www.xe.com.

Banks and ATMs

Throughout southern Florida, you'll find numerous automated teller machines (ATMs) at restaurants, stores, and other establishments, offering convenient access to your money. In addition, most regional banks provide access to ATMs inside and outside their branches. In Miami, there are several different banks available, including the **First Bank of Miami** (800/831-5763, www.firstbankmiami.com), which offers five branches in the Miami area. **Capital Bank** (800/639-5111, www.capitalbank-us.com), meanwhile, has branches throughout southern Florida, including two in Naples, two in Homestead, a handful in Miami, and several in the Upper, Middle, and Lower Florida Keys. Also in the Florida Keys, you'll encounter several branches of the **First State Bank of the Florida Keys** (866/298-1858, www.keysbank.com), from Key Largo to Key West.

Sales Tax

In southern Florida, most goods and services, save for perhaps movie tickets, often cost more than their listed price. That's due, of course, to state taxes—specifically, the 6 percent sales tax on taxable retail items and services, such as clothing and sightseeing tours.

Tipping

Although the amount of a gratuity depends on the level of service received, general tipping guidelines exist in Florida (and throughout the United States). Typically, restaurant servers should receive 15-20 percent of the entire bill, while pizza delivery drivers should receive at least 10 percent. In addition, taxi and limousine drivers should receive at least 15 percent of the entire fare, while valets, porters, and skycaps should expect around $2 per vehicle or piece of luggage. The housekeeping staff members of your hotel, inn, or resort also deserve a tip; a generally accepted amount is $2 per night.

Remember that tour guides, fishing guides, boat captains, and other excursion operators should be tipped as well. In fact, no matter how much such tours or trips cost, the gratuity is never included in the quoted price. Of course, how much you choose to tip is entirely up to you. While the exact amount of a tip will depend on the cost, length, and nature of the trip in question—not to mention your satisfaction with the services received—it's generally accepted to tip between 10 and 20 percent of the overall cost of the trip. If a guide or operator makes an exceptional effort, such as unexpectedly extending the length of a trip, then it's highly recommended that you increase the size of your tip accordingly. Tipping badly in a close-knit place like the Florida Keys can harm your reputation among other guides and operators, while tipping well could ensure even better service the next time.

Lastly, tourists often overlook the need to tip street performers, such as magicians, dancers, musicians, acrobats, jugglers, caricaturists, fortune tellers, and living statues. On many occasions, spectators have watched an entire performance, only to walk away without even dropping a dollar in the performers' upturned hat, cardboard box, open instrument case, or other tip receptacle. So if you stay long enough to observe a trick, enjoy a song, or take a photograph, be sure to leave a tip behind. After all, many performers depend upon gratuities for part, if not all, of their livelihood.

WEIGHTS AND MEASURES

For the most part, Floridians employ U.S. standard units to measure temperatures, distances, vehicle speeds, cooking volumes, clothing sizes, and everything in between. So if you've come from a foreign country that relies instead on the metric system, visit www.onlineconversion.com to convert almost any measurement.

Electricity

In southern Florida, most standard electrical outlets operate at 120 volts. So if you're traveling from Europe, Asia, or a country that operates at 220-240 volts, you'll need to bring an adapter in order to use your hair dryer, laptop, or other small appliance. Outlets here vary between the two-pronged and three-pronged variety, for which you might also need an adapter—which can easily be purchased in any decent hardware or building supply store. In fact, you'll find several locations of **The Home Depot** (www.homedepot.com) in the Miami area, including one just north of the Florida Keys (33001 S. Dixie Hwy., Florida City, 786/243-9370, 6am-10pm Mon.-Sat., 7am-8pm Sun.).

Time Zone

Miami, the Everglades, and the Florida Keys are all located in the eastern standard time (EST) zone. Florida also observes daylight saving time (DST), so adjust your watches and alarm clocks accordingly.

RESOURCES

Glossary

These regional terms and abbreviations will help you navigate Miami, the Everglades, and the Florida Keys—and perhaps better understand the region's unique people, culture, and ecology:

airboat: a small, open boat driven by a caged rear-mounted airplane propeller and capable of traveling at relatively high speeds through marshes and shallow water; also called a swamp boat

Alligator Alley: a nickname for the stretch of I-75 that runs from Naples, through the Everglades, to Fort Lauderdale; also called Everglades Parkway

backcountry: areas within the Everglades and the Florida Keys that consist of shallow water and islands close to shore, ideal for fishing and kayaking

bight: a body of water bounded by a bend in the shore

bougainvillea: a tropical vine that flourishes throughout the Florida Keys, usually ablaze with colorful white, fuchsia, or vermilion flowers; also known as paper flowers

brackish water: a mixture of freshwater and saltwater

BS: a commonly used abbreviation for addresses on the bay side of U.S. 1 in the Florida Keys

cafecito: Cuban coffee without milk

chum: a foul mixture of fish blood and diced fish parts, usually tossed into open water to lure fish to the area

coastal prairie: a region of vegetation that lies between the tidal mud flats of Florida Bay and dry land

coconut telegraph: the laid-back, word-of-mouth method by which news travels in the Florida Keys

conch: a multipurpose term used to describe a marine gastropod, a Bahamian immigrant, or a native inhabitant of the Florida Keys

conch fritter: a fried ball made with spices and ground conch meat, popular as an appetizer in the Florida Keys

Conch Republic: a micronation declared as a protest secession of the Florida Keys from the United States in April 1982

cortadito: Cuban coffee with steamed milk

CR: a commonly used abbreviation for a county road

cracker: a term that refers to the state's early settlers, who cracked long whips to herd cattle and oxen; now, informally used to designate a native-born Floridian

Creole: a language infused with French, African, Arabic, Spanish, and Portuguese, often heard in Miami's Little Haiti

cubano: a flattened, grilled sandwich made with sliced ham, slow-roasted pork, Swiss cheese, and pickles, popularized by Cuban immigrants who settled in Miami in the early 1900s

cypress dome: a dense cluster of cypress trees in water-filled depressions, found in the Everglades and Big Cypress National Preserve

Duval crawl: the local expression for stopping by each bar along Key West's Duval Street, which stretches from the Atlantic Ocean to the Gulf of Mexico

epiphyte: a plant, such as an orchid, moss, or

fern, that grows on the branches, trunks, and leaves of trees and derives its water and nutrients from the air

estuary: a partially enclosed body of water along the coast, where the freshwater from a river mixes with the saltwater of the ocean

eyebrow house: a type of Key West domicile that has an overhanging porch roof, which conceals the upper front windows

fire ants: large, aggressive red ants, prevalent in tropical and subtropical areas, capable of building large mounds, and inclined to inflict painful stings

fishing guide: a person who is knowledgeable enough to lead a hired charter and teach the passengers how to catch fish in a given region

flats: shallow-water areas that compose most of the backcountry in the Everglades and the Florida Keys, often covered by sand, rocks, or grass

"Floribbean" cuisine: Florida's hybrid cuisine, consisting of fresh Florida produce and seafood, with American, European, Caribbean, and Latin American influences

Florida fighting conch: a feisty mollusk found in the southeastern United States, known for its tendency to fight with potential collectors and predators

Florida lobster: a warm-water crustacean that has no claws, unlike its New England counterpart; also called a rock lobster or spiny lobster

gingerbread architecture: an elaborate Victorian-era style of construction, prevalent throughout Key West

Gold Coast: the area that extends from Fort Lauderdale to Miami, popular among movie stars, musicians, and other wealthy celebrities

goombay: a form of calypso music and dancing popular in the Bahamas; also refers to a type of Bahamian drum, held between the legs and played with the hands or sticks

grass flats: shallow-water areas covered in grass

grits: dried, ground corn kernels, typically boiled and served with a Southern-style breakfast

grouper: a firm white fish, popular in the Florida Keys

Gulf Stream: a swift, warm ocean current that originates off the coast of southern Florida in the Gulf of Mexico and continues along the East Coast toward the North Atlantic Current

gumbo limbo: a fast-growing, salt-tolerant tropical tree, which flourishes in the Everglades and has featherlike leaves and a shiny red exfoliating bark; also called the tourist tree for its resemblance to a sunburn

hardwood hammock: a dense growth of trees on a slightly elevated area above a marshy region, present in the Everglades and the Florida Keys

hush puppy: a crunchy, cornmeal fritter popular in the South and typically served with fried seafood

Intracoastal Waterway (ICW): a 3,000-mile-long waterway, partly natural and partly artificial, along the Atlantic and Gulf Coasts of America, meant to protect small boats from the dangers of the open sea

island time: the perception of a slower, more relaxed way of life on islands like Key West

key: a low, offshore island composed of sand or coral, the name of which is derived from the Spanish word *cayo*, meaning "little island"

mahimahi: a sweet, lean fish also known as a dorado or dolphinfish

manatee: the endangered state marine mammal, a giant yet gentle vegetarian preferring warm waters; also called a sea cow

mangrove swamp: a coastal marine swamp prevalent in southern Florida and dominated by tight thickets of red, black, and white mangrove trees

marsh: a flat, flooded, treeless area in the Everglades, containing plants such as sawgrass and cattails

MM: the abbreviation for "mile marker," how most Floridians designate addresses along U.S. 1 in the Florida Keys

no-see-um: a tiny biting gnat that thrives in coastal areas, especially in the summer; also known as a punkie

Old Florida: a term used to describe Florida prior to theme parks and other commercial developments; now refers to the state parks, sleepy villages, and vast wildlands that still exist

OS: a commonly used abbreviation for addresses on the ocean side of U.S. 1 in the Florida Keys

Overseas Highway: the popular term for the stretch of U.S. 1 that links many of the keys between Key Largo and Key West

patch reef: an isolated coral formation closer to the coast than the main offshore reef and usually filled with fish

pineland: a type of terrain in the Everglades that contains slash pine forest, saw palmettos, and a wide array of tropical plant varieties

red tide: a periodic massive bloom of toxin-producing marine algae, which causes Gulf waters to appear brownish-red, suffocates fish, contaminates shellfish, and affects the respiration of susceptible individuals

riptide: a potentially life-threatening tide that opposes other tides, causing a violent disturbance in the ocean

sandspur: the seed of the sandspur plant, prevalent in grassy or sandy areas and resembling a little spiked ball; also called a sandbur

sawgrass: any of several sedges that have spiny, serrated leaf blades and are prevalent in the Everglades

saw palmetto: a hardy fan palm that has spiny leafstalks and can grow in large clumps, present in places as varied as hammocks and coastal sand dunes

sea grape: a native, salt-tolerant plant that grows on Florida's beaches and helps to stabilize sand dunes

sea oat: a wispy, salt-tolerant plant found along the Atlantic and Gulf Coasts, where it helps to protect the state's beach dunes from erosion

skunked: an unfortunate condition whereby one returns to the dock after a fishing trip, without having caught any fish

slough: a channel of slow-moving water in a marshland

snook: a tropical inshore fish found in the Florida Keys and notoriously difficult to catch

snowbird: anyone who vacations or lives in Florida during the winter months, usually from November to April, to escape the cold and snow in other parts of the country

Snuba: an underwater breathing system, patented by Snuba International, that combines features of snorkeling and scuba diving

Spanglish: a mix of Spanish and English, spoken by many Miami residents

Spanish moss: a specific epiphyte that resembles a grayish, lacy cluster and typically hangs from oak trees

SR: a commonly used abbreviation for a state road

stingray shuffle: the method by which people shift their feet as they venture into Gulf waters to avoid inadvertently stepping on a camouflaged stingray

Tamiami Trail: the alternative name for U.S. 41, which connects Tampa to Miami and traverses the Everglades

trolling: a type of fishing by which baited lines or lures are towed slowly through the water behind the boat

Turtle Walk: a state-organized nighttime event, usually held in June or July, when the public can view sea turtles nesting and hatching on Florida's shores

watershed: a region drained by a river, a river system, or another body of water

wetland: a lowland area saturated by surface or ground water, with vegetation adapted to such conditions, prevalent throughout the Everglades

Suggested Reading

While not an exhaustive list of titles, the following books will shed some light on the singular geography, history, culture, and offerings of Miami, the Everglades, and the Florida Keys. Peruse them before your trip, and bring a few along for the ride.

CUISINE

Whether planning to dine out for every meal or rent a place with a kitchen, you'll find several books dedicated to this region's unique cuisine.

Gassenheimer, Linda. *The Flavors of the Florida Keys*. New York: Atlantic Monthly Press, 2010. From mojitos to conch chowder to key lime pie, this cookbook contains many of the classic recipes popularized in bars, restaurants, and resorts throughout the Florida Keys—some of which would be hard to recreate if not for the author's suggested substitutions for regional ingredients.

Herbenick, Fran. *Appetizing Appetizers from The Florida Keys*. Bloomington, IN: AuthorHouse, 2008. Compiled by a longtime resident of the Florida Keys, this collection features many of the treats found in this flavorful region, from crab fritters to Blackbeard's clam pie.

Raichlen, Steven. *Miami Spice: The New Florida Cuisine*. New York: Workman Publishing Company, Inc., 1993. Penned by a cooking teacher and cookbook author, this collection of lively recipes illustrates the Cuban, Caribbean, and Latin American influences on Miami's culinary arts.

Shearer, Victoria. *The Florida Keys Cookbook: Recipes & Foodways of Paradise*. Guilford, CT: Globe Pequot Press, 2013. Written by an experienced travel and food journalist, this recently updated, multicultural cookbook

presents nearly 200 regional recipes, from lobster ravioli to guava custard pie.

Sloan, David L. *The Ultimate Key Lime Pie Cookbook*. Key West: Phantom Press, 2012. Boasting a slew of tips, tricks, and historical tidbits, not to mention easy-to-follow recipes for an assortment of mix-and-match crusts, fillings, toppings, and sauces, this specialized cookbook enables readers to create more than 150,000 varieties of Key West's signature dessert.

Van Aken, Norman, and Justin Van Aken. *My Key West Kitchen: Recipes and Stories*. London: Kyle Books, 2012. In this unabashed love letter to Key West, two chefs share recipes from their past and present and reveal how Florida's Southernmost City has influenced their multicultural cuisine.

Voltz, Jeanne, and Caroline Stuart. *The Florida Cookbook: From Gulf Coast Gumbo to Key Lime Pie*. New York: Knopf, 1996. Dividing the Sunshine State into six distinct regions, this collection includes southern Florida recipes like frog legs and conch salad.

FICTION AND PROSE

Fictional tales, personal essays, and travel memoirs—though no substitute for practical guidebooks—can definitely give travelers a tantalizing sense of the cultural and natural diversity of Miami, the Everglades, and the Florida Keys.

Breakfield, Jon. *Key West: Tequila, a Pinch of Salt and a Quirky Slice of America*. Key West: Key West Press, 2012. In this true account of a semi-permanent vacation, a U.K. man and his wife impulsively decide to move to Key West, where their once-in-a-lifetime adventure includes wacky locals, a bit of corruption, and unfortunately, a hurricane.

Cerulean, Susan, ed. *The Book of the Everglades.* Minneapolis: Milkweed Editions, 2002. Separating the Everglades into five regions, this lively anthology presents environmental, historical, and human-interest essays from a variety of authors, including Carl Hiaasen and Susan Orlean.

Corcoran, Tom. *The Mango Opera.* New York: St. Martin's Press, 1998. This Key West-based mystery is the first in a series featuring photographer-turned-detective Alex Rutledge. Other titles include *Gumbo Limbo* (1999), *Bone Island Mambo* (2001), *Octopus Alibi* (2003), *Air Dance Iguana* (2005), *Hawk Channel Chase* (2010), and *The Quick Adiós (Times Six)* (2012).

Hemingway, Ernest. *To Have and Have Not.* New York: Scribner Classics, 1999. Originally published in 1937, this novel, which was partially inspired by the eccentric people that Hemingway met in Key West, focuses on a fishing boat captain who runs contraband between Cuba and Florida. Other books written during Hemingway's prolific Key West period include *A Farewell to Arms* (1929), *Death in the Afternoon* (1932), *Winner Take Nothing* (1933), *Green Hills of Africa* (1935), and *For Whom the Bell Tolls* (1940).

Hersey, John. *Key West Tales.* New York: Vintage, 1996. Published posthumously, these short stories offer a snapshot of ordinary Key West residents facing momentous events in their lives.

Hiaasen, Carl. *Tourist Season.* New York: G. P. Putnam's Sons, 1986. This madcap Miami mystery is one of several Florida-based capers written by popular *Miami Herald* columnist Carl Hiaasen, whose extensive bibliography includes *Native Tongue* (1991), which takes place in Key Largo, and *Chomp* (2012), a madcap adventure through the Everglades.

Katzenbach, John. *In the Heat of the Summer.* New York: Ballantine Books, 1982. Adapted for the screen as *The Mean Season,* this debut novel by a *Miami Herald* crime reporter features a dangerous cat-and-mouse game between a clever serial killer who's terrorizing Miami and the journalist who's captured his attention.

Molloy, Johnny. *Hiking the Florida Trail: 1,100 Miles, 78 Days, Two Pairs of Boots, and One Heck of an Adventure.* Gainesville, FL: University Press of Florida, 2008. During this incredible three-month journey, a veteran hiker experiences Big Cypress National Preserve firsthand.

Murphy, George, ed. *The Key West Reader: The Best of Key West's Writers, 1830-1990.* Key West: Tortugas, Ltd., 1989. This impressive collection features the work of some of Key West's most celebrated writers, from Ernest Hemingway to Hunter S. Thompson.

Murrell, Muriel V. *Miami: A Backward Glance.* Sarasota, FL: Pineapple Press, Inc., 2003. In this engrossing memoir, the author shares vignettes about her life in Miami, from the glitzy 1920s through the postwar 1950s.

Orlean, Susan. *The Orchid Thief: A True Story of Beauty and Obsession.* New York: Ballantine Books, 1998. This quirky tale of orchid fanatics in the Fakahatchee swamp inspired the film *Adaptation.*

Reisig, Michael. *The Road to Key West.* Mena, AR: Clear Creek Press, 2010. Set in the 1970s, this novel features two fearless divers on a madcap adventure through the Florida Keys, Cuba, and other Caribbean locales.

Willeford, Charles. *Miami Blues.* New York: Ballantine Books, 1984. In the first of Willeford's well-known crime series, Hoke Moseley, a chronically depressed, unorthodox homicide detective, must pursue an ex-convict who has recently relocated to Miami and stolen Moseley's gun, badge, and dentures.

GEOGRAPHY AND ECOLOGY

Several books aim to familiarize visitors with southern Florida's unique flora, fauna, and topography.

Alden, Peter, Rick Cech, and Gil Nelson. *National Audubon Society Field Guide to Florida*. New York: Knopf, 1998. This comprehensive guide unravels the state's natural history, teaches visitors how to identify varied habitats and organisms, and explores some of Florida's finest parks and preserves.

Alderson, Doug. *Encounters with Florida's Endangered Wildlife*. Gainesville, FL: University Press of Florida, 2010. Blending adventure with cultural and natural history, this book features the state's rare, threatened, and endangered wildlife, from panthers to manatees.

Bartlett, Richard D., and Patricia P. Bartlett. *Florida's Snakes: A Guide to Their Identification and Habits*. Gainesville, FL: University Press of Florida, 2003. A color photograph accompanies the description of each snake in this guide, which covers more than 85 species and subspecies.

Bartlett, Richard D., and Patricia P. Bartlett. *Florida's Turtles, Lizards, and Crocodilians: A Guide to Their Identification and Habits*. Gainesville, FL: University Press of Florida, 2011. This comprehensive guide features helpful range maps, color photographs, and detailed descriptions of roughly 125 different reptiles.

Daniels, Jaret C. *Butterflies of Florida Field Guide*. Cambridge, MN: Adventure Publications, 2003. Containing large color photographs, this easy-to-use field guide helps travelers identify butterflies in the wild.

Hammer, Roger L. *Everglades Wildflowers: A Field Guide to Wildflowers of the Historic Everglades, Including Big Cypress, Corkscrew, and Fakahatchee Swamps*. Guilford, CT: FalconGuides, 2003. This guide offers detailed plant descriptions, drawings, and photographs of roughly 300 common wildflowers in this fertile region.

Hammer, Roger L. *Florida Keys Wildflowers: A Field Guide to the Wildflowers, Trees, Shrubs, and Woody Vines of the Florida Keys*. Guilford, CT: FalconGuides, 2004. Featuring color photographs and detailed descriptions of more than 300 plants, this guide is ideal for botanists and amateurs alike.

Kaplan, Eugene H. *Coral Reefs: Caribbean and Florida*. New York: Peterson Field Guides, 1999. Visitors can use this guide to identify the fishes, sponges, mollusks, corals, and other sea creatures of southern Florida.

Landau, Matthew, and Larry Gates. *Eco-Touring the Florida Keys*. Flagstaff, AZ: Best Publishing Company, 2005. This guide offers travelers an introduction to the ecosystems, plants, and marine mammals that define the Florida Keys.

Levin, Ted. *Liquid Land: A Journey Through the Florida Everglades*. Athens, GA: The University of Georgia Press, 2004. Based on extensive research, this book recounts the negative impacts of draining the Everglades and describes the controversial restoration plan that could revitalize these fragile wetlands.

Lodge, Thomas E. *The Everglades Handbook: Understanding the Ecosystem*. Boca Raton, FL: CRC Press LLC, 2010. This updated third edition provides a comprehensive understanding of the Everglades, including the history of human influence.

Myers, Ronald L., ed., and John J. Ewel, ed. *Ecosystems of Florida*. Gainesville, FL: University Press of Florida, 1990. This book offers a comprehensive examination of Florida's habitats, from pine flatwoods to salt marshes to coral reefs.

Nellis, David W. *Poisonous Plants and Animals of Florida and the Caribbean.* Sarasota, FL: Pineapple Press, Inc., 1997. Filled with illustrated information about poisonous organisms, toxins, symptoms, and treatments, this guide is essential for any outdoor enthusiast.

Renz, Mark. *Fossiling in Florida: A Guide for Diggers and Divers.* Gainesville, FL: University Press of Florida, 1999. This book offers help in finding, identifying, and preserving fossils.

Ripple, Jeff. *The Florida Keys: The Natural Wonders of an Island Paradise.* Stillwater, MN: Voyageur Press, 1995. With this gorgeous book, travelers can learn about the island chain's natural history, from its formation as a living coral reef to the ways in which climate, storms, ocean currents, and other factors have shaped the Keys and their inhabitants.

Taylor, Walter Kingsley. *A Guide to Florida Grasses.* Gainesville, FL: University Press of Florida, 2009. With over 500 color images, this guide will assist hikers, plant enthusiasts, and professional botanists in identifying the varied grasses of the Sunshine State.

Tekiela, Stan. *Birds of Florida Field Guide.* Cambridge, MN: Adventure Publications, 2005. Birding enthusiasts will find this easy-to-use guide helpful for exploring the Sunshine State.

Winsberg, Morton D. *Florida Weather.* Gainesville, FL: University Press of Florida, 2003. This book explains the forces that control the state's climate and offers advice for dealing with seasonal hazards.

Witherington, Blair, and Dawn Witherington. *Florida's Living Beaches: A Guide for the Curious Beachcomber.* Sarasota, FL: Pineapple Press, Inc., 2007. Focusing on the natural history of Florida's beaches, this guide features a variety of animals, plants, minerals, and human-made objects.

Witherington, Blair, and Dawn Witherington. *Florida's Seashells: A Beachcomber's Guide.* Sarasota, FL: Pineapple Press, Inc., 2007. Color photographs and clear descriptions help beachcombers to identify 252 different seashells.

HISTORY AND CULTURE

History buffs, amateur sociologists, and curiosity seekers will find a varied selection of books about southern Florida's intriguing past—and the people that have made Miami, the Everglades, and the Florida Keys what they are today.

Biondi, Joann. *Miami Beach Memories: A Nostalgic Chronicle of Days Gone By.* Guilford, CT: Globe Pequot Press, 2006. Enhanced by hundreds of archival photographs, this oral history features the memories of criminals, taxi drivers, strippers, actors, and others who experienced this colorful area between the 1920s and 1960s.

Bramson, Seth H. *Miami: The Magic City.* Charleston, SC: Arcadia Publishing, 2007. Written by a Miami native and respected historian, this book celebrates the colorful history of southern Florida's megalopolis.

Burke, J. Wills. *The Streets of Key West: A History Through Street Names.* Sarasota, FL: Pineapple Press, Inc., 2004. In this unique take on Key West's history, the author explores the people whose names now grace the city grid, from Truman to Whitehead.

Caemmerer, Alex. *The Houses of Key West.* Sarasota, FL: Pineapple Press, Inc., 1992. This full-color, photographic survey of Key West's architectural treasures celebrates the city's varied building styles, from eyebrow houses to Conch Victorians.

Carter, W. Hodding. *Stolen Water: Saving the Everglades from Its Friends, Foes, and Florida.* New York: Atria Books, 2005. In this exploration of the Everglades and its complicated existence, the author includes encounters with native flora and fauna—plus naturalists, farmers, politicians, and swamp inhabitants.

Cox, Christopher. *A Key West Companion.* New York: St. Martin's Press, 1983. Numerous photographs and several essays illustrate this curious history of the Conch Republic.

Douglas, Marjory Stoneman. *The Everglades: River of Grass.* Sarasota, FL: Pineapple Press, Inc., 2007. Originally published in 1947, this book helped to draw much-needed public attention to the area's rich flora, fauna, and history and to muster support for the creation of Everglades National Park.

Frawley-Holler, Janis. *Key West Gardens and Their Stories.* Sarasota, FL: Pineapple Press, Inc., 2000. Full of color photographs, this book explores the history and features of Key West's lovely gardens.

Fuson, Robert H. *Juan Ponce de León and the Spanish Discovery of Puerto Rico and Florida.* Blacksburg, VA: The McDonald & Woodward Publishing Company, 2000. Filled with critical documents, original maps, and historical illustrations, this extensive biography chronicles the life of the infamous Spanish explorer, who might have been the first Spaniard to set foot on Floridian soil.

Grunwald, Michael. *The Swamp: The Everglades, Florida, and the Politics of Paradise.* New York: Simon & Schuster, Inc., 2006. Written by an award-winning *Washington Post* reporter, this well-researched book explores the modern history of the Everglades, from drainage attempts to restoration.

Gutelius, Scott, Marshall Stone, and Marcus Varner. *True Secrets of Key West Revealed!* Key West: Eden Entertainment Limited, Inc., 2011. Intended for trivia lovers, this reference guide offers bizarre facts about the Southernmost City, such as pirate rules, building oddities, and questions that visitors should never ask.

Hiaasen, Carl, and Diane Stevenson, ed. *Kick Ass.* Gainesville, FL: University Press of Florida, 2009. Originally published in 1999, Hiaasen's first collection of selected *Miami Herald* columns explores development, corruption, and other facets of southern Florida.

Hiaasen, Carl, and Diane Stevenson, ed. *Paradise Screwed.* Gainesville, FL: University Press of Florida, 2009. Originally published in 2001, Hiaasen's second collection of selected *Miami Herald* columns chronicles life in southern Florida over a 15-year period.

Homan, Lynn M., and Thomas Reilly. *Key West and the Florida Keys.* Charleston, SC: Arcadia Publishing, 2006. This collection of historical postcards illuminates the intriguing history of the Florida Keys.

Jinbo, Susan. *Diary of a Key West Innkeeper.* Key West: Phantom Press, 2007. This book chronicles the zany adventures of a Chicago couple who moved to Key West, purchased a guesthouse, and eventually opted for a quieter life.

Kerstein, Robert. *Key West on the Edge: Inventing the Conch Republic.* Gainesville, FL: University Press of Florida, 2012. This engrossing urban history details the evolution of Key West, from its wrecking and cigar-making days through the war years to its tumultuous modern times, during which tourism and development have taken their toll on the city's uniqueness.

King, Gregory. *The Conch That Roared.* Lexington, KY: Weston & Wright Publishing Co., 1997. This spirited book explores the bizarre, true story of Key West's 1982 secession from the United States and the subsequent formation of the Conch Republic.

Linsley, Leslie. *Key West: A Tropical Lifestyle.* New York: The Monacelli Press, 2007. Filled with full-color photographs and anecdotes about homeowners, designers, and architects, this book illustrates the unique character of several Key West residences.

McCally, David. *The Everglades: An Environmental History.* Gainesville, FL: University Press of Florida, 2000. In exploring the formation, development, and history of the Everglades, the author crafts an argument for abandoning agriculture in order to save this fragile ecosystem.

McIver, Stuart B. *Hemingway's Key West.* Sarasota, FL: Pineapple Press, Inc., 2002. For Hemingway fans, this book offers intriguing biographical information about one of Key West's most famous residents, plus a two-hour walking tour of the city.

McKeen, William. *Mile Marker Zero: The Moveable Feast of Key West.* New York: Crown Publishers, 2011. Cultural enthusiasts might appreciate these crazy but true tales of the writers, painters, musicians, pirates, and potheads that have inhabited Key West, an artistic haven and subtropical refuge like no other.

Ogle, Maureen. *Key West: History of an Island of Dreams.* Gainesville, FL: University Press of Florida, 2006. This well-researched book covers the colorful, controversial history of the place formerly known as Bone Key—from its 19th-century days as a pirate haven to its modern incarnation as a tourist hot spot.

Oppel, Frank, ed., and Tony Meisel, ed. *Tales of Old Florida.* Secaucus, NJ: Book Sales, Inc., 1987. This collection of essays from 1870 to 1911 includes stories about boat rides through the Everglades and John James Audubon's birding adventures in the Florida Keys.

Posner, Gerald. *Miami Babylon: Crime, Wealth, and Power—A Dispatch from the Beach.* New York: Simon & Schuster, Inc., 2009. Penned by an investigative journalist, this fresh, forceful narrative shows how Miami Beach evolved from a quiet resort into the convergence of crime, finance, politics, and hedonism.

Raymer, Dorothy, and Tom Corcoran, ed. *Key West Collection.* Lakeland, FL: The Ketch & Yawl Press, 1999. Illustrated with photographs by the mystery writer Tom Corcoran, this colorful collection features three decades' worth of newspaper articles by Raymer, a columnist of *The Key West Citizen* from the late 1940s to the early 1980s.

Reid, Thomas. *America's Fortress: A History of Fort Jefferson, Dry Tortugas, Florida.* Gainesville, FL: University Press of Florida, 2006. A compelling narrative about the history of the "American Gibraltar," once the most heavily armed coastal defense fort in the United States.

Shultz, Christopher, and David L. Sloan. *Key West 101: Discovering Paradise.* Key West: Phantom Press, 2005. This humorous book describes plenty of intriguing facets about Key West, from drag queens to the coconut telegraph.

Shultz, Christopher, and David L. Sloan. *Quit Your Job and Move to Key West: The Complete Guide.* Key West: Phantom Press, 2003. An amusing look at life in Key West, with advice for relocating to this crazy town.

Sloan, David L. *Ghosts of Key West.* Key West: Phantom Press, 1998. Written by the founder of The Original Ghost Tours of Key West, this book contains 13 chilling stories about the spirits that supposedly haunt the Southernmost City.

Standiford, Les. *Last Train to Paradise: Henry Flagler and the Spectacular Rise and Fall of the Railroad That Crossed an Ocean.* New York: Three Rivers Press, 2002. History buffs will appreciate the incredible, ill-fated tale of Flagler's efforts to connect the Florida Keys to the mainland.

Suib, Michael, and Nancy Butler-Ross, ed. *Confessions of a Key West Cabby.* Key West: SeaStory Press, 2003. In this entertaining compilation, a taxi driver shares his quirky columns from *The Key West Citizen* and *The Miami Herald.*

Viele, John. *The Florida Keys: A History of the Pioneers.* Sarasota, FL: Pineapple Press, Inc., 1996. Though slightly outdated, this loving account offers a glimpse into the curious history of these legendary islands.

PARKS AND RECREATION

Outdoor enthusiasts will find several books geared toward exploring and camping amid the beaches, swamps, rivers, and islands of Miami, the Everglades, and the Florida Keys.

Bertelli, Brad. *Snorkeling the Florida Keys.* Gainesville, FL: University Press of Florida, 2013. Offering practical travel advice, GPS coordinates, and historical facts, this guide explores more than 40 coral reefs, shipwrecks, and beaches in the Florida Keys.

Burnham, Bill, and Mary Burnham. *Florida Keys Paddling Atlas.* Guilford, CT: Falcon-Guides, 2007. From Key Largo to Key West, this detailed color atlas provides helpful information for kayakers and other shallow-water explorers.

Clement, Skip, and Andrew Derr. *Fly Fishing the Florida Keys: The Guides' Guide.* Portland, OR: Frank Amato Publications, Inc., 2005. Beyond colorful maps and hundreds of images, this how-to guide offers plenty of helpful information, from fly-fishing techniques to game fish descriptions.

Conway, David. *Fishing Key West and the Lower Keys.* Gainesville, FL: University Press of Florida, 2009. Filled with local knowledge, tips, and techniques, this guide will help even first-time anglers navigate these bountiful waters.

Friend, Sandra. *50 Hikes in South Florida: Walks, Hikes, and Backpacking Trips in the Southern Florida Peninsula.* Woodstock, VT: The Countryman Press, 2003. This guide features hikes throughout southern Florida, including the Everglades and the Florida Keys.

Hammer, Roger L. *A FalconGuide to Everglades National Park and the Surrounding Area.* Guilford, CT: FalconGuides, 2005. Containing historical facts, detailed maps, trail descriptions, and other useful information, this guide helps hikers, bikers, kayakers, canoeists, and wildlife lovers explore this remarkable region.

Harrigan, William. *Lonely Planet Diving & Snorkeling Florida Keys.* Footscray, Victoria, Australia: Lonely Planet Publications, 2006. Filled with maps and color images, this guide offers detailed diving information about 64 underwater sites, including shipwrecks and coral reefs.

Horn, Bill. *Seasons on the Flats: An Angler's Year in the Florida Keys.* Mechanicsburg, PA: Stackpole Books, 2012. Written by a veteran fly-fisherman and Marathon resident, this book details all four fishing seasons in the Keys, offers handy tips and techniques for saltwater anglers, and includes advice from some of the region's top fishing guides.

Jewell, Susan D. *Exploring Wild South Florida: A Guide to Finding the Natural Areas and Wildlife.* Sarasota, FL: Pineapple Press, Inc., 2011. Now in its fourth incarnation, this comprehensive guidebook contains information about southern Florida's habitats, wildlife, parks, and recreational opportunities.

Keogh, Bill. *Florida Keys Paddling Guide: From Key Largo to Key West.* Woodstock, VT: The Countryman Press, 2004. Written by the owner of Big Pine Kayak Adventures, this guide offers route suggestions through this paddler's paradise, plus safety tips and information about regional wildlife and habitats.

Molloy, Johnny. *A Paddler's Guide to Everglades National Park.* Gainesville, FL: University Press of Florida, 2009. Filled with detailed maps and information about campsites, dangerous routes, wind challenges, and packing requirements, this guide reveals the pleasures and pitfalls of canoeing and kayaking through the Everglades.

Moore, Marilyn. *Moon Florida Camping: The Complete Guide to Tent and RV Camping.* Emeryville, CA: Avalon Travel Publishing, 2007. This comprehensive campground directory also contains advice on hiking trails, fishing spots, and other nearby attractions.

O'Keefe, M. Timothy. *Hiking South Florida and the Keys: A Guide to 39 Great Walking and Hiking Adventures.* Guilford, CT: FalconGuides, 2009. Containing detailed information about a wide range of hikes, this user-friendly guide includes excursions through Everglades National Park, John Pennekamp Coral Reef State Park, the National Key Deer Refuge, and other intriguing sanctuaries.

Patton, Kathleen. *Kayaking the Keys: 50 Great Paddling Adventures in Florida's Southernmost Archipelago.* Gainesville, FL: University Press of Florida, 2002. Packed with detailed maps and concise descriptions, this guide features a range of trips, from short paddles to overnight excursions.

Ripple, Jeff. *Day Paddling Florida's 10,000 Islands and Big Cypress Swamp.* Woodstock, VT: The Countryman Press, 2004. In addition to featuring trips for canoeists and kayakers, this guide includes information about equipment, outfitters, low-impact paddling, and the area's history and ecology.

Strutin, Michal. *Florida State Parks: A Complete Recreation Guide.* Seattle: The Mountaineers Books, 2000. Featuring Florida's entire state park system, this illustrated guide

covers a wide array of activities, from canoeing in Fakahatchee Strand State Preserve to snorkeling in John Pennekamp Coral Reef State Park.

Valentine, James, and D. Bruce Means. *Florida Magnificent Wilderness: State Lands, Parks, and Natural Areas.* Sarasota, FL: Pineapple Press, Inc., 2006. Divided into six sections and filled with full-color images, this book provides a stunning journey through Florida's most precious wild areas.

Young, Claiborne S., and Morgan Stinemetz. *Cruising the Florida Keys.* Gretna, LA: Pelican Publishing Company, Inc., 2006. Offering reliable advice about traveling from the Port of Miami to the Dry Tortugas, this second edition includes information about marinas, anchorages, restaurants, attractions, and other facilities.

REGIONAL TRAVEL

Mainstream travel guides typically offer details about southern Florida's towns, attractions, restaurants, and shops.

Goodwin-Nguyen, Sarah. *Key West: A Guide to Florida's Southernmost City.* New York: Channel Lake, Inc., 2011. Part of the Tourist Town Guides series, this revised third edition contains information about the city's beaches, restaurants, hotels, and attractions.

Keith, June. *June Keith's Key West & The Florida Keys.* Key West: Palm Island Press, 2005. Though a bit outdated, this fourth edition offers an insider's look at the subtropical islands that stretch from Key Largo to the Dry Tortugas, including tips about notable events, bars, restaurants, and activities, plus a few hidden gems.

Kinser, Joshua Lawrence. *Moon Florida Gulf Coast.* Berkeley, CA: Avalon Travel, 2011. Among other Gulf Coast destinations, this revised third edition includes information about Everglades City and its environs.

Muirhead, Marsh. *Key West Explained: A Guide for the Traveler.* Bemidji, MN: The Island Journal Press, 2008. This guidebook offers a little of everything, from historical facts to romantic tips to details about transportation, hotels, restaurants, and bars.

Williams, Joy. *The Florida Keys: A History & Guide.* New York: Random House, Inc., 2003. Illustrated by Robert Carawan and written by a part-time resident of Key West, this guide provides details about the Upper, Middle, and Lower Keys, including little-known spots.

Internet Resources

CUISINE AND TRAVEL

Everglades Area Chamber of Commerce
www.evergladeschamber.net
Use this website to find information about airboat tours, fishing guides, campgrounds, attractions, restaurants, and other businesses in the Everglades.

The Florida Keys
www.floridakeys.com
This helpful website offers lodging, dining, and sightseeing advice for those traveling to Key Largo, Islamorada, Marathon, Big Pine Key, and Key West.

Florida Keys Dining Guide
www.keysdining.com
This directory contains a wealth of bar and restaurant information for Key Largo, Islamorada, Marathon, the Lower Keys, and Key West— places that especially favor conch, key lime pie, and seasonal seafood like Florida lobster and stone crab claws.

The Florida Keys & Key West
www.fla-keys.com
Serving as the official website for the Monroe County Tourist Development Council, this portal provides information about the region's accommodations, attractions, events, and recreational opportunities, plus interactive maps and advice about weather, transportation, weddings, and other aspects of traveling in the Keys.

Florida Monthly
www.floridamagazine.com
The official website of *Florida Monthly* magazine contains plenty of information regarding the state's restaurants, festivals, and other facets.

Florida Travel + Life
www.floridatravellife.com
Here you can check out the latest issue of *Florida Travel + Life* and even purchase past issues.

Gay Key West
www.gaykeywestfl.com
Operated by the Key West Business Guild, this website supports gay-friendly accommodations, events, and businesses.

Greater Miami and the Beaches
www.miamiandbeaches.com
The official website of the Greater Miami Convention & Visitors Bureau features a wealth of information about accommodations, attractions, events, dining options, and special offers in the Miami area.

Islamorada Chamber of Commerce
www.islamoradachamber.com
Visitors will find listings of events, shops, restaurants, activities, accommodations, and water sports that pertain to the "sportfishing capital of the world."

The Islands of Marathon
www.floridakeysmarathon.com
Operated by the Greater Marathon Chamber of Commerce, this website features places to stay and things to do on the islands that compose Marathon.

Key Largo Chamber of Commerce
www.keylargo.org
Visitors can check this website for lodging, dining, shopping, and activity suggestions in the Key Largo area.

Key West Chamber of Commerce
www.keywestchamber.org
Here travelers will find information about accommodations, restaurants, activities, events, and festivals in Key West.

Lower Keys Chamber of Commerce
www.lowerkeyschamber.com
This website provides information about activities, events, restaurants, and accommodations on and around Big Pine Key.

Visit Florida
www.visitflorida.com
You'll find a wealth of dining, lodging, and recreational information through this website, the official source for travel planning in the Sunshine State.

ECOLOGY AND RECREATION

Boating Safety Resource Center
www.uscgboating.org
Use the official website of the U.S. Coast Guard's Boating Safety Division to prevent accidents and fatalities while boating in southern Florida.

Florida Department of Environmental Protection
www.dep.state.fl.us
The official DEP website includes information about Florida's state parks, greenways, and trails.

Florida Fish and Wildlife Conservation Commission
www.myfwc.com
Boaters, anglers, and hunters can find a slew of helpful information—from safety tips to wildlife facts to necessary regulations—on this comprehensive website.

Florida Keys Boating
www.floridakeysboating.com
This directory features a wide array of information for those interested in boating, fishing, diving, sailing, and other water sports in the Florida Keys.

The Florida Keys Fishing Directory
www.fishfloridakeys.com
This directory will assist anglers in finding fishing guides, charters, and boat rentals throughout the Florida Keys; included here are articles about specific fish, a fishing calendar, and information regarding weather, tides, lodging, and dining.

Florida Keys National Marine Sanctuary
www.floridakeys.noaa.gov
Snorkelers and scuba divers will find helpful information about the underwater features that compose this sanctuary, from the waters beside Biscayne National Park to the area around the Dry Tortugas.

Florida Sportsman
www.floridasportsman.com
Check this website for gear advice, relevant recipes, boating and diving tips, and local fishing reports in the waters around Miami, the Everglades, and the Florida Keys.

Florida State Parks
www.floridastateparks.org
From this recreational portal, you'll learn everything you need to know about hiking, biking, boating, fishing, snorkeling, camping, horseback riding, and other activities in Florida's state parks and preserves. Also included here are maps, directions, and information regarding lodging, visitor centers, ecology, history, and accessibility.

GORP
www.gorp.com
An in-depth portal for adventure travel and outdoor recreation, this website is an invaluable resource for information about campgrounds, national parks, recreational activities,

and outdoor gear. You'll find plenty of Florida-related content here, including a Key West Weekender Guide.

National Park Service
www.nps.gov
The National Park Service provides detailed maps, brochures, and contact information for each of its roughly 400 parks, monuments, recreation areas, trails, and other natural and cultural sites throughout the United States. Use the state-by-state search function to learn more about southern Florida's protected places, including Biscayne National Park, Big Cypress National Preserve, Everglades National Park, and Dry Tortugas National Park.

Save-A-Turtle
www.save-a-turtle.org
This nonprofit organization educates the public about preserving rare and endangered marine turtles in the Florida Keys.

Save the Manatee Club
www.savethemanatee.org
This nonprofit organization teaches residents and visitors ways to protect the endangered manatee, the state's official marine mammal.

U.S. Fish & Wildlife Service
www.fws.gov
Here you can find useful information about southern Florida's endangered species, such as the Florida panther and West Indian manatee, as well as details regarding national wildlife refuges like Crocodile Lake and Key Deer, both in the Florida Keys.

GENERAL INFORMATION
MyFlorida.com
www.myflorida.com
Through Florida's official website, you can look up state government agencies, research attractions and professional sports, locate highway construction, check campground availability, purchase fishing and hunting licenses, and even learn more about the state's history and landmarks.

Travel.State.Gov
www.travel.state.gov
U.S. citizens can use this website to travel safely, by cruise or flight, to other countries, and international travelers will find guidelines for flying into and out of Florida.

HISTORY AND CULTURE
Florida Department of State's Division of Historical Resources
www.flheritage.com
Here history buffs will find information about the state's archaeological sites, historical markers, and past events.

Miccosukee Seminole Nation
www.miccosukeeseminolenation.com
This website offers historical information about the Miccosukee Seminole Indians, who now dwell in the Florida Everglades and operate one of the area's few casino resorts.

University Press of Florida
www.upf.com
Peruse this website for a wealth of Florida-related books—from biographies to field guides—that shed some light on the state's history and culture.

Index

List of Maps

Acknowledgments

While it seems impossible to thank all of the people who contributed to this guide, I promise to give it a try.

Between family vacations as a child and more recent travels with my husband, Daniel, I've ventured to southern Florida many times over the years. During every stay, Dan and I have encountered plenty of friendly, helpful residents, usually willing to point us in the right direction--for the best key lime pie, the least crowded beach, or whatever else we sought at the time. So, thanks to everyone who's made each of our trips to Miami, the Everglades, and the Florida Keys a rejuvenating experience.

Of course, there are several folks to whom I'm particularly grateful. First, I offer a special thanks to the many hotel and resort owners, restaurant managers, park rangers, adventure outfitters, and tourism officials who made the job of compiling and revising this guide a little easier. Thanks, too, to those who provided a few extra photographs for this book, and to the patient editors of Avalon Travel who offered valuable assistance during the preparation of this guide.

In addition, I'd like to thank my friends and family, all of whom have supported me during each of my frenzied writing projects. Most of all, I'm grateful to my beloved kitty, Ruby Azazel, who encouraged me to take breaks whenever possible, and to my husband, who supported me at each and every turn, even providing many of the images in this guide. As I often say, they're the best traveling companions a girl could ask for.

Lastly, I thank you, the reader. May your next trip to southern Florida, especially the Florida Keys, be as memorable as ours have been.

www.moon.com

DESTINATIONS | ACTIVITIES | BLOGS | MAPS | BOOKS

MOON.COM is ready to help plan your next trip! Filled with fresh trip ideas and strategies, author interviews, informative travel blogs, a detailed map library, and descriptions of all the Moon guidebooks, Moon.com is all you need to get out and explore the world—or even places in your own backyard. While at Moon.com, sign up for our monthly e-newsletter for updates on new releases, travel tips, and expert advice from our on-the-go Moon authors. As always, when you travel with Moon, expect an experience that is uncommon and truly unique.

KEEP UP WITH MOON ON FACEBOOK AND TWITTER
JOIN THE MOON PHOTO GROUP ON FLICKR